FIRE OF MERCY,
HEART OF THE WORD

This fourteenth-century crucifix, in the choir of the Cistercian Abbey of La Maigrauge (Switzerland), is known as the "Smiling Christ". Such a tag is no doubt a popular interpretation. The gesture of the mouth more plausibly expresses the Lord breathing his last breath: Jesus' eyes are shut, and the "smile" is disconcertingly ambiguous. This theme of Jesus' expiration figures prominently in the commentary on Golgotha (pp. 527–62 in this volume).

ERASMO LEIVA-MERIKAKIS

FIRE OF MERCY, HEART OF THE WORD

Meditations on the Gospel according to Saint Matthew

VOLUME FOUR
(Chapters 26–28)

Foreword by Bishop Erik Varden

IGNATIUS PRESS   SAN FRANCISCO

Cover art:
Christ's Last Supper
Codex Rossanensis
Biblioteca Arcivescovile
Rossano, Italy
© Erich Lessing/Art Resource, New York

Cover design by Roxanne Mei Lum

© 2021 Ignatius Press, San Francisco
All rights reserved
ISBN 978-1-62164-122-3 (PB)
ISBN 978-1-64229-151-3 (eBook)
Library of Congress Control Number: 2020951000
Printed in the United States of America ∞

εἰ δὲ ἀπεθάνομεν σὺν Χριστῷ
πιστεύομεν ὅτι καὶ συζήσομεν αὐτῷ.

But if we have died with Christ,
we believe that we shall also live with him.

Romans 6:8

מִכָּל־מִשְׁמָר נְצֹר לִבֶּךָ
כִּי־מִמֶּנּוּ תּוֹצְאוֹת חַיִּים:

Keep your heart with all vigilance;
for from it flow the springs of life.

Proverbs 4:23

Christ is the infinite self-expenditure of God. . . . Excess is God's trademark in his creation; as the Fathers put it, "God does not reckon his gifts by the measure." At the same time excess is also the real foundation and form of salvation history, which in the last analysis is nothing other than the truly breathtaking fact that God, in an incredible outpouring of himself, expends not only a universe but his own self in order to lead man, a speck of dust, to salvation. So excess or superfluity—let us repeat—is the real definition or mark of the history of salvation. The purely calculating mind will always find it absurd that for man God himself should be expended. Only the lover can understand the folly of a love to which prodigality is a law and excess alone is sufficient.

— Joseph Ratzinger

For

Patrick Hoff Carey

sharing in the wine of gladness

CONTENTS

These words, which Rilke puts on our Lady's lips at the end of Jesus' earthly life, are but a bold development of Mary's reproach to the twelve-year-old Messiah, recorded by Luke, when his parents find him teaching in the temple. Exhausted with worry after three days of harrowing search, Mary probes Jesus: " 'Son, why have you treated us so? Behold, your father and I have been looking for you anxiously'. . . . And his mother kept all these things in her heart" (Lk 2:48, 51). This was the very same Immaculate Heart that a mystical sword would pierce now, at the moment of the Passion (cf. Lk 2:35), in tandem with the physical thrust delivered to Jesus' Heart by the soldier's spear (cf. Jn 19:34).

From long experience, Mary came to understand perfectly one thing about her Son: that Christ is indeed by nature "superlative excess", always expecting entirely too much from his Mother, from St. Joseph, and from all those he loves best. To expect the creature willingly to lose its natural life in order to rise to divine life: this is indeed entirely too much, something that can only be wrought by the gracious fire of the Holy Spirit. In Rilke's poem, Mary voices the anguished reaction of tender and vulnerable human nature to the fire the Messiah casts upon all of our lives by ascending the Cross and inviting us to join him there co-redemptively (cf. Rom 8:17; Col 1:24).[3]

We resonate deeply with Mary's trepidation at the approach of so much woe, a yoked suffering from which she could not shield herself precisely because of the intensity of her love for Jesus. Her keen reproach to her Son, far from expressing dissent or disobedience, is rather born from her own excess of love for him. Yes, Jesus plainly inherited his knack for excessive loving from both his divine Father and his human Mother! She exhibits a vigorous humility by emphatically admitting that she understands very little of her Son's ways with her, or of God's ways with man, apart from that central knowledge she possesses of his invitation for the believer to share in his Redeemer's lot. At the same time, we must also ask whether Jesus could have come either to his Mother Mary or to the rest of the world *as*

---

[3] Hans Urs von Balthasar asks whether the fact of the Incarnation, already by itself and prescinding from the Cross as such, does not constitute an extravagant "imposition" or excessive "demand" (*Zumutung*) that God makes upon human nature, which, totally taken aback, exclaims: "How dare God become man? Does he not realize the terrible implications of that move?"

anything but fire, considering humanity's dire need for enlightenment, transforming energy and radical regeneration.

"The God who answers by fire, he is GOD!" This is what Elijah shouts before the false prophets of Baal. The proof for Elijah is in the fire. The identity of the authentic God is for him revealed precisely in the efficaciousness of his work, which is to say, in the Creator's intense activity of illuminating, purifying, and communicating new life. The living and true God is not, after all, in the monotheistic religions, a mythological construct; a static, theoretical entity, fruit of the collective imagination, tucked far away picturesquely in some Olympian heaven; or a convenient political justification for the social status quo. The brisk presence and action of the true God are always detectible by their manner of infusing new life and wisdom and by the change wrought for greater goodness, beauty, and justice in everything the divine Fire touches.

"Let us be grateful for receiving a kingdom that cannot be shaken," the Letter to the Hebrews exhorts us, "and thus let us offer to God acceptable worship, with reverence and awe; for *our God is a consuming fire*" (Heb 12:28–29). In order to be pleasing to God and offer him acceptable worship, we must ourselves become fiery, that is, we must somehow come to share in the nature of the Fire God is. The Blessed Virgin Mary became the Queen of Heaven only by first enduring in her flesh, as the loving and obedient Mother of Sorrows, the all-consuming Mystery that is God. God cannot share the fullness of his life with us—which is to say, cannot perform in us his work of deification—without first communicating to us something of his nature as *the Fire of Mercy*.

In Christ, God is *Fire* because he transforms everything he embraces and will not leave well enough alone; and, equally, in Christ, God is *Mercy* because the only goal he envisions for the often painful process of our transformation is to make us ever more capable of sharing and enjoying the Divine Bliss. This glorious destiny is conferred on us solely by grace since we have no natural claim to it. Our sharing in the life of God is, now and perpetually, an ever-new event of sheer gift and merciful condescension.

Now, we cannot speak of God's presence and activity in Christ as a Fire of Mercy without recalling the context in which the prophet Elijah proclaims that "the God who answers by fire, he is GOD!" For the occasion, Elijah has painstakingly restored a dilapidated altar to the Lord and has laid upon it chunks of wood and the cut pieces of the flesh of a sacrificial bull, finally dousing the whole oblation with generous streams of water. The prophet then pronounces this invocatory prayer to accompany the offering: "Answer me, O LORD, answer me, that this people may know that you, O LORD, are God, and that you have turned their hearts back." Human beings can provide for the offering all that the earth and their own skills can yield, but only God can provide the consuming *fire* that will actually confirm and accomplish the sacrifice: "Then the fire of the LORD fell, and consumed the burnt offering, and the wood, and the stones, and the dust, and licked up the water that was in the trench" (1 Kings 18:37–38).

Note how the text portrays the fire as a sacred element bounding forth from the very Being of God and bridging the terrestrial and divine spheres. All the material elements here listed, which the fire from heaven takes up into itself, are ultimately symbolic of *the hearts of the people of Israel*, which by this process God is converting to himself. This turning back of hearts to the Lord is the ultimate meaning of the transformation involved. Only the divine fire can effect that massive "conversion", which here plays on both the literal and the mystical senses: the combustion of visible substances (even of water, the element most resistant to fire!) and the humble adherence of human hearts to their Creator. A blaze coming from God overpowers and consumes a sacrifice offered by human beings, as an enactment of God's transformative work and of the intense pleasure God takes in uniting his creatures to himself. The fire transforms everything it touches into itself and, thus, communicates its nature not only to the flesh of the bull offered on the altar—a sacrificial victim representing Christ on the Cross—but also to the stones that form the altar, to the water poured abundantly on the offerings, and to the very dust on the ground. This sacrifice shows an unheard-of reconciliation of fire and water, a unification of the two inseparable though contrasting aspects of Christian transformation: on the one hand, the *fire* denotes the painful change and purification involved, and, on the other, the *water* signifies new and joyfully outpoured life.

This unity of the two distinct effects, moreover, derives from the unity of both realities in their Source: the Crucified Christ. On the Cross, Jesus underwent *the fire of suffering* for our sake, exposing every fiber of his and our humanity to its purification, and he then made *the blood and the water of Redemption* to flow out upon the world from his wounded side (cf. Jn 19:34). The indissoluble unity of purifying and atoning *Fire* with eternal, unconditional *Mercy* defines the glorious Heart of the Word. Jesus Christ, crucified and risen, thus reveals himself as the living Image of the "God [who] is love" (1 Jn 4:16) and all of whose works are therefore works of love: "For the Father loves the Son, and shows him all that he himself is doing. . . . For as the Father raises the dead and gives them life, so also the Son gives life to whom he will" (Jn 5:20–21).

א

I FIRST WISHED TO ACQUAINT the reader with the general orientation of my approach. Let us now turn to the structure and layout of the book and to other practical information. This volume is an extended meditation on chapters 26, 27, and 28 of Matthew, the culmination of this Gospel's narrative in the Lord's Passion and Resurrection. These three chapters have been divided into twenty episodes with distinct titles that hint at the commentary's focus in each case. And the episodes themselves have been further subdivided into sections, all to aid the reader in the labor of meditation.

As in the previous volumes, between the individual episodes, and sometimes within them, the reader will find a blank space radiating from א (Aleph), the first letter of the Hebrew alphabet, as we can see above. To explain this graphic arrangement, we now need to retell briefly a parable that appears in the prologue of the *Zohar*, the "Book of Splendor", the chief work of Jewish medieval mysticism.[4] I consider this parable emblematic of my whole approach to reading Scripture in a contemplative mode. Therefore, both the parable and the use of Aleph that it has suggested to me are far more than simply picturesque, a typesetting embellishment, if you will, and so some explanation is here in order.

[4] *The Zohar*, trans. by Harry Sperling and Maurice Simon (London: Soncino Press, 1934), 1:9–13.

The Parable of the Alphabet is set just before the creation of the world. Although created by God, the twenty-two letters of the Hebrew alphabet were thought by the Kabbalists to have existed in God's mind before the creation of the world. Already then, they had their right order, from Aleph to Tau, and for two thousand years God delighted in playing with them. When God decides to proceed with the world's creation, the letters begin presenting themselves to him in reverse order, each asking to be placed first in the work of the divine Poet. Each letter gives a good reason why it should be first. For instance Tau, the last letter, says that it concludes the Hebrew word for "truth" (*emet*). God replies to Tau that it is overlooking something, namely, that it is also the conclusion of the word "death" (*mawet*). The parable proceeds in this fashion with a dialogue between each letter and the Lord, until we arrive at the second letter of the alphabet, Beth. Beth argues that it is the first letter of *berachah* ("blessing"), and this persuades God to grant its request since the whole creation is to be one magnificent expression of God's desire to bless all that shall exist by conferring his divine life upon it. And so Beth becomes the first letter of the creation, which is to say, of the text of Scripture that symbolizes the creation: *B*^e*reshit bara' Elohim* ("In the beginning God created . . .", Gen 1:1).

But one letter, Aleph, still remains unused, although God has already granted to Beth the privilege of being first. Yet Aleph does not come forth on her own to make her request as all the others have; God must explicitly call her to appear:

> "Aleph, Aleph, wherefore comest thou not before Me like the rest of the letters?" She answers: "Because I saw all the other letters leaving Thy presence without any success. What, then, could I achieve there? And further, since Thou hast already bestowed on the letter Beth this great gift, it is not meet for the Supreme King to take away the gift that He has made to His servant and give it to another." The Lord says to her: "Aleph, Aleph, although I will begin the creation of the world with the Beth, thou wilt remain the first of letters. My unity shall not be expressed except through thee, on thee shall be based all calculations and operations of the world, and unity shall not be expressed save by the letter Aleph."[5]

---

[5] In Hebrew, numbers are expressed with letters, and *aleph*, being the first letter in the alphabet, represents the number one.

God is very impressed by Aleph's wisdom in realizing that asking did not do most of the other letters much good. He is also struck by Aleph's humility, since she quietly accepts that God has already given first place to Beth without herself having been taken into consideration. It is this wisdom of humility that makes God seek Aleph out in her silent corner: he has only pretended to be unaware of her existence. Then, too, God admires Aleph's sense of justice when she affirms that it would not be right for God to change his mind and re-assign a gift once conceded. God's answer to Aleph beautifully shows his delight in her attitude. He says that, even though Beth will always be first in the creation of the lower world, this in fact means that it is only *second* in the absolute order of reality. Aleph shall forever be the first of letters, the head of the alphabet that symbolically represents all creation and all its possibilities of combinations and recombinations of elements. Aleph is thus declared to be the most divine of letters.

The attitude of wisdom, humility, and justice that Aleph embodies before God has a very precise equivalent in the realm of linguistics because the letter Aleph has no sound value of its own. Aleph acts, rather, as a "vehicle" for the other sounds, especially the vowels, which, although the loudest of the sounds, do not have letters to represent them and must therefore rely on Aleph in order to exist. Placed before the minuscule dots and lines that represent the vowels, Aleph is the merest breath that makes it possible to pronounce them. And placed after the vowels, Aleph lengthens their value. In the written language, א is like a sturdy, silent tree from which the vowels can hang like fruit.

To the Creator, his humble creature Aleph represents his own un-divided *unity as God*, since it stands for the number One, the smallest of numbers and yet the source of all others. To us creatures, Aleph represents as well the *silence of God*, which makes all speech possible by acting as its receptive horizon, both source and finality of all utter-ances. And Aleph is also the *silence of the creature* perpetually listening to God, to both his silence and his words. For all of these reasons, *Aleph* is first: she is most divine precisely because she is last of all, humblest of all, most silent of all, like the invisible air that supports the flight of birds and makes sound and audible communication pos-sible.

Aleph, in other words, is Christ, who has come, "not to be served, but to serve" (20:28) and who declares in the Book of Revelation:

"I am the Alpha and the Omega, the beginning and the end. To the thirsty I will give water without price from the fountain of the water of life" (Rev 21:6). Aleph is the silence of the servant longing with love to receive her Lord's next command (cf. Ps 122[123]:2). And Aleph shall be an invitation to us, thirsty readers of the Gospel of Matthew, as well, to enter Christ's Reign of glorious humility. Surrounded on the page by the silence of white, vacant space, the noble letter א will mark a restorative pause in our burgeoning thoughts and words and remind us to return periodically to the ineffable Unity and Hiddenness of God by striving to unify our own consciousness. At that point, we will remember that the many words of God in Scripture and in the life and gestures of Christ Jesus point to the one indivisible and eternal Word of God. At the beckoning appearance of א, we should allow silence to invade our soul—silence of the senses and of the understanding and of the affections—in order to facilitate the birth of the Word in our being. Such is the silence celebrated in the Christmas liturgy: "When a profound silence covered all things and night was in the middle of its course, your all-powerful Word, O Lord, bounded from heaven's royal throne."[6]

THE DEFAULT VERSION of the Sacred Scriptures used in this volume is the Revised Standard Version, Second Catholic Edition. As always, however, I have drawn liberally on other highly regarded translations of the Holy Bible whenever euphony or some precise nuance of meaning seemed to recommend it in a given instance. Thus, when no reference to a version is given, the RSV is implied. In all cases, I have freely added italics for emphasis. On occasion, too, I have myself translated certain words or passages directly from the originals,

---

[6] "Dum medium silentium tenerent omnia, et nox in suo cursu medium iter haberet, omnipotens Sermo tuus, Domine, de cælis a regalibus sedibus venit" (Entrance Antiphon, Second Sunday of Christmas [= Wis 18:14–15]).

as will be evident from the context. In the same vein, I am responsible for translating all other material for which a translator's name is not given. And whenever a chapter-and-verse reference does not include the name of any book of the Bible, the Gospel of Matthew is implied.

As with the previous three volumes, I begin volume 4 with a thematic introduction. While the introduction to volume 1 describes my "cordial method" of reading the Gospel, based on what I call "the logic of fire", the introduction to volume 2 is more historical and literary in nature. The introduction to volume 3, in turn, strives to acquaint the reader with the monastic practice of *lectio divina*, that is, with how to enter the interior space of Sacred Scripture as both an ecstatic paradise of delight (*paradisus scripturarum*) and a desert-like battleground of prayer. That essay offers practical pointers concerning the conditions and angles of approach that, in my own experience, make for the most fruitful encounter with the Word of God. In addition, at the end of the present volume, the reader will find a succinct list of "*lectio* tips" that may prove helpful. The introductions to the first three volumes of *Fire of Mercy, Heart of the Word* are still, needless to say, very relevant to volume 4. Taken together, the four introductions amount to a sort of vademecum intended to help the reader plunge into the Gospel as a source of life.

A guide to the transliteration and pronunciation of biblical Greek will likewise be found at the end of the volume, as well as an ancient Cistercian prayer that distills the spirit animating this commentary. I highly recommend the use of this prayer before or after reading a section of these meditations.

THE THEMATIC INTRODUCTION to this fourth and final volume, titled "The Bridegroom's Gesture of Surrender", is more strictly theological in content. It proposes that the whole thrust of revelation—from the creation of the world to the Incarnation of the Word to the death and Resurrection of Jesus—is *Eucharistic* in nature. This means that the essay invites the reader to explore the concept of *parádosis* as central both to Scripture and to the Christian's life with God. The scriptural word *parádosis*, which as we shall see recurs incessantly in different variations during the Passion narrative, refers to God's continual action of *handing himself over* to us in the Person of his Son. Jesus Christ is the Bridegroom who lovingly surrenders all that he is and has to his Bride, the Church, with the understanding that all of mankind is, potentially, the Church.[7] And "all that Jesus is and has", in the end, comprises nothing but the life and love he receives incessantly from the Father who begets him. This gift of the unsurpassable divine extravagance culminates in Jesus' solemn institution of the Mystery of the Eucharist as the very heart of the life of the Church. But the roots of this eternal sacrament of God's merciful condescendence may be seen dramatized on every page of the Gospel of Matthew, particularly in the story of Jesus' Passion that we will contemplate in this final volume.

For Christ to hand himself over to mankind out of love, in all places and at all times, in one unending gesture of passionate *parádosis*, means that the Son of God has no place or time of his own in this world. In order to be available to all he cannot belong anywhere in particular. The Word incarnate is truly the Alien par excellence among us: he cannot be circumscribed by space, and that is the source of both his eternal glory and his utter poverty. Jesus himself revealed his radically marginal status in the world and in society when he assured an enthusiastic scribe that "foxes have dens and birds of the sky have nests, but the Son of Man has nowhere to rest his head" (8:20, NAB). In Marilynne Robinson's novel *Home*, the protagonist Glory's sense of her presence in the world is expressed as follows: "What an embarrassment that was, being somewhere because there was nowhere else for you to be!"[8] This painful discomfiture, this chronic lack of a native place of one's own where one can fully *be*, seems to me to define with chilling accuracy both Jesus' and our existence in this

---

[7] See in the *Catechism of the Catholic Church* the section "The Church—People of God", no. 782, with reference to *Lumen Gentium*, 9, 2: "This people is 'a most sure seed of unity, hope, and salvation for the whole human race.'—Its *destiny*, finally, 'is the Kingdom of God which has been begun by God himself on earth and which must be further extended until it has been brought to perfection by him at the end of time.'"

[8] Marilynne Robinson, *Home* (New York: Farrar, Straus & Giroux, 2008), 37.

world. And yet, as we will see in the course of the Passion narrative, the moment of salvation dawns in our life precisely when our own intimate sense of homelessness meets the homelessness of God in Christ. We are not saved by the *power* of God, at least not as that word is normally understood. Rather, we are saved when we allow the *weakness* of a self-emptying God[9] to inhabit our own alienation. Then God's weakness in us becomes transforming power because it is weakness embraced out of love (cf. 2 Cor 13:4).

Alienation, exclusion, homelessness, abandonment: these are the states of soul that perhaps constitute the very best condition out of which to hear the Word of God. It is the Savior's status as outcast in this world that should attract us to him, not only as a paradoxically sublime theological proposition but, indeed, as we see Jesus' concrete condition of castaway harrowingly embodied in the many thousands of displaced migrants scurrying about for breath in our convulsed and often cruel world. In Shusaku Endo's gripping novel *The Samurai*, it was not, of course, the European missionaries' arrogance that attracted the chaste and honorable protagonist, Hasekura Rokuemon, to Christianity. Rather, ever so slowly and against the warrior's better judgment, the emaciated face and body of the Crucified that he saw everywhere on Christian walls began to speak to his heart even as the samurai's meticulously constructed life began to fall apart and he found himself radically alienated from all social and human relevance. Hasekura's heart responded to a suffering Savior willing to come and share his own misery, and, in the process, the former samurai discovered in himself depths of affectivity and longing he had wholly ignored.

Now, if the Son of Man has no place to lay his head *in this world*, surely it is because his only pillow is the bosom of his heavenly Father (cf. Jn 1:18). By laboring to penetrate the Word of God so that it gradually becomes our only dwelling, we too will become more and more rooted in the bosom of the Father, our only fruitful soil and reliable resting place. In this way radical alienation can become the most valuable of spiritual assets. Only then, sated by the experience of our homelessness, will we be able to cry out with Pascal: "Love

---

[9] "Christ Jesus, . . . though he was in the form of God, did not count equality with God a thing to be grasped, but emptied himself (ἑαυτὸν ἐκένωσεν), taking the form of a servant, being born in the likeness of men" (Phil 2:6–7).

my sufferings, Lord, and may my miseries invite you to visit me.''[10]
We cannot hope to minister to the marginalized of society and bring
them any lasting comfort unless those of us who call ourselves disciples of Christ first become intimately acquainted, in our very flesh
and psyche, with the most absolute alienation of all: that of the Lord
Jesus on the Cross.

Paradoxically, as we see in the plot of *The Samurai*, it is the bitter
experience of my defeat as autonomous agent, together with my own
sense of incurable waywardness, that will give me the heroic strength
needed to cling for sheer life to the Word of God. Extraordinary energy is released from deep in my being when I locate outside myself
the Source of Life that beckons irresistibly. Then suddenly the one
who but a moment ago could barely crawl now soars.

CHRIST'S THROBBING SPLENDOR lurks just beneath the page of the
inspired Word, and I must apply the greatest devotion of heart and
mind to break open the literal surface and so allow the light indwelling
the letter to stream forth freely. Ralph Waldo Emerson wrote in his
journal that, while reading Shakespeare, he actually had to shade his
eyes from the intensity of the splendor emanating from the text. What
would we then have to say about the dazzling *Presence* that infinitely
surpasses in its effects a merely æsthetic radiance and that communicates itself to all ardent seekers willing to toil?

The many words of this commentary are the fragmentary evidence
of my personal toiling along this road, and it is on this pilgrimage to
the Heart of the Word that I invite the reader. Words are like pregnant seeds that once sown, generate countless other words. The words
of the sacred text are already the result of the union between God's
one eternal Logos and the humble receptivity of the inspired biblical

---

[10] "Aimez mes souffrances, Seigneur, et que mes maux vous invitent à me visiter."
Blaise Pascal, *Pensées*, 611.

authors. Their written words are in turn sown in other amenable hearts and bear a harvest of communion in the knowledge of a common love. CHRIST in the eternal Heart of the Father, CHRIST in the chaste womb of his Mother Mary, CHRIST in the inspired text, CHRIST in my own heart: CHRIST—the unifying principle of salvation, the Alpha and Omega of all history, whether universal or personal.

In his commentary on Luke's account of Mary's Visitation to her cousin Elizabeth, St. Ambrose invites his readers to "pay attention to the choice of individual words and to their meanings".[11] And in a polemical treatise, Hippolytus of Rome advises his listeners thus: "Let us strive to arrive at an understanding of the divine realities, not according to our own intelligence, and certainly not by doing violence to the gifts of God, but in the manner he himself has wanted to reveal himself in the Sacred Scriptures."[12] If I follow anything like a "method" in my Gospel meditations, then these statements define it. The listening heart must strive to allow the objective human words of the written text to shed the light and transforming power they contain. The eternal Word has been humble enough to conceal himself within the tattered garments of human words, and it is there that the believer must seek him. The laborious grammatical and etymological soundings that I will frequently undertake in these pages thus assume the status of royal works of love. The lover must seek the Beloved in the exact trysting place where union beckons. I must receive the Spouse precisely as he chooses to give himself. When this vital encounter happens through the medium of human language, the Bridegroom's features take on the form of nouns, verbs, adjectives, and figures of speech, like so many masks he has chosen to wear.

The beginning of Jesus' self-disclosure to me, what I might call his invitation to intimate friendship, is the fact that he has put me on a first-name basis with himself. Because he takes the initiative of calling me by my name, I may reciprocally address him as JESUS (cf. Jn 10:3). In his commentary on the Song of Songs, St. Gregory of Nyssa exclaims to Jesus: "Your name, which expresses your goodness, is the tenderness of my soul for you."[13] And, on a certain day when

---

[11] "Vide distinctionem singulorumque verborum proprietates." *Commentary on Luke*, II, 19 (CCL 14, 39).
[12] *Treatise against Noetus*, c. 9.
[13] *Homiliæ in Cantica*, 2.

St. Francis de Sales was distressed by the thought of predestination, the saint heard these words in reply: "I do not have a name that damns. My name is Jesus."[14] In this connection, I have a confession to make. Throughout the nearly three thousand pages that comprise the totality of this commentary, the continual source of energy, illumination, and unending delight has been for me the opportunity of writing over and over again the single word JESUS on the computer screen. The counter tells me that in volume 4 alone, I have invoked the Holy Name in this way no fewer than 3,466 times!

We know the central importance of the so-called "Jesus Prayer" in the Hesychastic tradition of Eastern Christianity. This school of spirituality teaches that the mindful repetition of the Savior's proper Name, given to him by God himself through the ministry of the Archangel Gabriel (cf. 1:20; Lk 1:31), contains all prayer and therefore is efficacious in fostering full union with God. To say the Name of Jesus with an open and loving heart and a joyful tongue is tantamount to receiving in one's person the whole of God's work of salvation, since the Name evokes the Person and the Person of Jesus contains the plenitude of grace (cf. Col 1:19). However, I must admit that none of these exalted Hesychastic teachings was explicitly on my mind as I experienced a small jab of joy every time I wrote the word JESUS on the page.

Slowly I began to discover that the reason for this quiet, sudden joy lay above all in the simple fact that we all love to take on our lips endlessly the name of one we deeply love. Uttering that name somehow releases a sweet taste in the heart. This realization, in turn, made me more aware of my root intention in writing these books. I saw that I did not so much desire to share with potential readers my thoughts on the Gospel of Matthew as, rather, to choreograph for them an actual encounter with the One who has already encountered me and seduced my heart. And so, every time I wrote down the five letters of the Lord's name, this action amounted to a thrilling presentation of JESUS to the reader, as if I were saying, "Here is my Friend, the enfleshed Word, coming forth in person from these many words

[14] "Je ne m'appelle pas Celui qui damne. Mon nom est Jésus." These words, attributed to St. Francis de Sales, are quoted to François Mauriac by his old friend Père Jean-Augustin Maydieu in a letter of 28 January 1955, in *Nouveaux cahiers François Mauriac* n° 04 (1996).

and offering himself to us in all his beauty, power, and vulnerability. Is he not in every way desirable?"

The heart's loving familiarity with the name and Person of JESUS thus emerges as the outstanding symptom of an affective relationship with the Messiah from Nazareth. In times of great distress, when the terrible knife of affliction or despair or betrayal or personal sin cuts close to the bone, I am convinced that only such an intimate bond of friendship with the Redeemer will see us through. By themselves, neither the certainties of dogma, heroic strength of will, dogged fidelity to vows taken, nor an intellectual understanding of Christian faith—indispensable as all these may be—shall in the end be our salvation. Only the unmistakable, boldly comforting, and ever-faithful presence and gaze of Jesus, alive in my heart's tissues and active in the most recondite spaces of my soul and mind, will enable me to negotiate darkness and desolation. My work serves no other purpose than to add a few twigs to fuel the fire of such a friendship in the reader.

An intrinsic part of Matthew's Passion narrative is Jesus' betrayal by the apostle and future first pope Peter (26:57–58, 69–75). But Peter's was only the outstanding case of betrayal. As Matthew reminds us, at the moment of Jesus' arrest "all the disciples deserted him and fled" (Mt 26:56). For us would-be disciples, too, it is not a question of *whether* we will betray the Lord; the only question is *when* and *to what extent* we will forsake Jesus. And when this terrible event does occur, we shall be saved from the abyss of despair only by our certainty, grounded in previous experience, that his fidelity to us is more enduring than ours to him (2 Tim 2:13; cf. 1 Jn 3:20). Moreover, such certainty can be acquired only by the familiarity with the Person of Jesus that is bestowed by habitual prayer of the heart and the repetition of the Holy Name.

I HAVE GROWN OLD writing this very long work, the first lines of which, on the Lord Jesus' genealogy, go back to the fall of 1983 and my first sabbatical from teaching, which we spent in the South of France. I was then thirty-seven years old and now I am seventy-three—a mere flipping of the digits! It so happens that precisely thirty-seven years also intervene between 1983 and 2020, the time it has taken me to complete the commentary. Perhaps such numerical correspondences have some hidden meaning, at the very least the hint that a vigilant Providence always attends our poor and fractured human efforts to reach the light, working out benevolent symmetries that trump our personal chaos. To have wrestled daily with the Word of God is not a bad way to have spent one's life, laboring under Christ's "sweet and easy yoke" and seeking the face of the Beloved within the interstices of textual difficulties. "Give me the words, Lord", I prayed every day as I set to work. Striving to persevere to the end and reach some sort of lucid understanding—qualities not at all native to my person—I always had the distinct feeling of being a mere scribe. As well, since we human beings are synergistic persons and not mere pipes through which the water of grace flows, this scribe's personal itinerary, with all its joys and sorrows, may be read as in a palimpsest just beneath the surface of my all-too-earnest and objective text. May the heavenly Sophia, who delights in "playing with the children of men" (Prov 8:31), someday teach me how to be more playful!

These thirty-seven years have wrought great changes and, some-times, immense upheavals in my life, which has along the way as-sumed an admittedly most unusual shape: the mature flowering of my children, my unabated delight; the wrenching dissolution of my marriage, five lives' Golgotha moment; my drastic shift from profes-sor to monk; the arrival of eight exuberant grandchildren; the ines-timable gifts of monastic consecration and priesthood; the amusing discovery of myself as author. . . . Such an unpredictable journey can-not take place without ruptures, and so I here beg the forgiveness of all who have been hurt both by the inevitable events of this odyssey and by my culpable failings; and I invite you as well to rejoice with me at finding the pearl of great price. In the end it is always a vast consoling grace that prevails over every manner of turmoil. In the end, only thanksgiving abides.

I was able to complete this volume 4, and thus the whole project, in the late winter and early spring of 2020, due in no small part to the enforced leisure that came with the Covid-19 lockdown in Italy. In such circumstances, the writing of the commentary, the returning day after day to many hours of intense encounter with the Word of God, has been a unique grace, an essential "Logotherapy"[15] (to use Viktor Frankl's brilliant word) that has helped me transform into prayer the deep anxieties and fears that continue to plague us all even as I write these lines. Among many other things, the Word of God should at times be precisely that: a place of refuge, healing, and restoration where our hurting hearts and souls may be nursed back to health. Only by first seeking strength from God's Word can we then hope to make a worthwhile contribution to these grief-stricken times of pandemic catastrophe and global struggle for justice.

I am particularly grateful to Dom Eamon Fitzgerald, Abbot General of the Cistercian Order of the Strict Observance, whose secretary I am, for his generous understanding in allowing me ample time every day for months to devote to this personal endeavor. And I thank Dom Damian Carr, Abbot of St. Joseph's Abbey, Spencer (Mass.), from 1996 to 2020, my former superior, and all my Spencer brothers, for their continual support and encouragement throughout the years. For decades I have relied as well on the unfailing inspiration of Bishop Felipe de Jesús Estévez (Diocese of St. Augustine), and I here wish to express to him my heartfelt gratitude. For their sustained interest in my work, I would also like to thank Fr. Peter John Cameron, O.P., and Fr. Sebastian White, O.P., respectively the past and present editors of the English-language *Magnificat*. And I thank my friend Carolyn Lemon, production editor of Ignatius Press, who for three decades has proven to be the most sweetly relentless and indispensable of motivators.

It would be impossible to list by name all those whose lively enthusiasm for this commentary has proved paramount to its completion, since no one writes in a vacuum. My awareness that many were waiting for the finished product functioned as a powerful stimulus that steadily pushed me forward. I thank in particular all those who, without knowing me personally, took the trouble to send very kind

---

[15] I here adapt a personalized form of the Austrian concentration camp survivor and psychotherapist Viktor Frankl's profound neologism. See in particular part 2 of his *Man's Search for Meaning* (1946).

and generous letters of support. Then, too, many of my brothers and sisters in the Cistercian Order have warmed me with the fire of their charity at crucial moments, and among them I include with appreciation the vibrant brothers of Our Lady of Dallas Abbey (Tex.), who hosted the unforgettable *Carta Caritatis Conference* of July 2019.

But I cannot conclude this preface without inscribing here with pride and gratitude the names of certain persons without whose bright presence my life would surely falter. In the first place, I honor my children, my greatest source of satisfaction and hope: Christiane, for her courageous faith and unwavering devotion as daughter, wife, and mother; Adriana, for her unquenchable thirst for justice and for her faithful heart; and Alexis, forever singing in the water of Life. Unending thanks to Mireya Letayf, most ardent of supporters. Then I thank Carlos and Clariza, Helen and Pedro, for putting up so patiently with their brother the monk. And I treasure the friendships of Monica Lawry, O.S.B.; Zachary Nelson, O.S.B.; Brian C. Palmer; and James Palmigiano, O.C.S.O., who have proven indispensable in connection with the writing of this book.

Finally, I offer the present volume in memory of Dom Isaac Totorika Izaguirre, O.C.S.O. (1961–2020), Brother Francis Mohr, O.C.S.O., (1927–2020), exemplary monks and tremendous brothers, and of Doña Mireya Rentería de Letayf (1923–2020), a great lady.

May the Lord make his face shine upon all of you and give you peace!

Simeon Leiva-Merikakis, O.C.S.O.
Assisi, July 11, 2020
Solemnity of Our Holy Father Saint Benedict

INTRODUCTION: THE BRIDEGROOM'S GESTURE OF SURRENDER

TENDERNESS AND MERCY are the heart of the Gospel. Otherwise one doesn't understand Jesus Christ or the tenderness of the Father who sends him to listen to us, to cure us, to save us."[1] We Christians have been urgently entrusted by God with the mission of allowing the flood of tenderness God has already made to flow into us to flow out farther through us into the whole world. What above all enables Christians both to accept and to carry out such a momentous task of the human heart is, without doubt, their participation in the mystery of the Holy Eucharist. Partaking worthily of the Eucharist gradually works a transformation in the communicant that in brief may be described as growing more and more in the likeness of the Christ who is consumed.

Now, the celebration of Holy Mass consists of two main parts, the Liturgy of the Word and the Liturgy of the Eucharist. This two-part division of the Mass dictates the fundamental rhythm of Christian life, which begins with the faithful being gathered by God's call to listen to his Word and then enters the mystery of the Son's offering of himself to the Father. Like all ritual sacrifices, Christ's self-oblation concludes with our partaking in the Communion of his Body and Blood. This sacramental participation is the driving force of the whole Christian life, precisely what enables Christians to strive *to be* the tenderness and mercy of God in the world.

From the outset, I have envisioned *Fire of Mercy, Heart of the Word* as one extended Liturgy of the Word based on the Gospel of Matthew. As such, it logically constitutes but the first part of the total Christian experience of God's Word and, therefore, calls for completion

---

[1] Pope Francis, interview with Ferruccio de Bortoli, *Corriere della Sera*, March 5, 2014.

in the Liturgy of the Eucharist. Wherever we may begin searching for illumination and life in God's written Word, we will inevitably be led to the celebration of the Holy Eucharist as the unsurpassable fulfillment of every aspect of revelation. *The Word became flesh*, not paper and ink, not ephemeral thought or pious reflection. Therefore the written Word, by its very nature, structure, and rhythms, wants to take us to the intimate participation in the living Person of the Word that only the Eucharist can bestow. And so, before launching into the actual commentary on St. Matthew's text, it is not only appropriate but perhaps even necessary to consider the great Eucharistic Mystery toward which that Gospel text is impelling us with its every verse.

One way of describing what occurs in the Eucharistic Mystery is to say that it effects a nuptial union between God and Man in the Person of Christ, the Word Incarnate, by virtue of his offering himself simultaneously to his Father and to mankind. The main action of the Eucharist, which Christ carries out and we celebrate by our participation, is a mystery of self-surrender. In his person, Christ offers all mankind to the Father, and, in Christ, God offers himself to us, through the power of the Holy Spirit. Communion in the Body and Blood of Christ is a participation in everything that Christ is, at both the human and the divine levels.

And Christ graces us with such intimate participation in his total Person by inviting us to unite our beings to himself as in a bridal union. Christ's act of self-giving to us in the Eucharist is the culmination of a self-surrender that began with his Incarnation. All of Jesus' presence, words and deeds, death and Resurrection, are one continual act of self-surrender to us and to all creation, that we may have life. But nowhere do we see the depths of God's love for us more dazzlingly than in the mystery of the Holy Eucharist, which in a general way we are entitled to call *Christ the Bridegroom's gesture of surrender*, through which he communicates to all mankind God's tenderness and mercy.

All prayer and all meditation on the meaning of Sacred Scripture, including this commentary on the Gospel of Matthew, are but a preparation that enables us to enter the more thoroughly and effectively into the Eucharistic Mystery.

I. CHRIST LOVED US AND HANDED HIMSELF OVER FOR US

The experience of divine tenderness should be for us far more than a private emotion of overwhelming security and consolation. In God, love is not an emotion but the law of his Being, his very identity and substance; and so, too, must such unwavering and substantial love become the law and spontaneous operation of our own being. "Be imitators of God, as beloved children", St. Paul exhorts the Ephesians, "and walk in love, as Christ loved us and [*handed himself over* (παρέδωκεν ἑαυτὸν)] for us as a fragrant offering and sacrifice to God" (Eph 5:1–2).[2] Paul is here describing *how* it was that God's tender love entered the world historically and *how* it continues to operate in our lives today. God's love, he says, is the communication of his person and life to us as the result of a particular free act.

Divine love is not a vague and faceless cosmic "energy", automatically diffused throughout the universe like some ethereal gas. The human heart yearns for far more than the reassurance that the world is somehow pervaded by a friendly, benign "force". If the cosmos is full of the beauty and wonder of stupendous processes, this is because it came into being by the work of a Master Artist whose glory it reflects.

Paul's words convey the double truth that God is a personal being motivated by infinite love and that "our hearts remain restless until they rest in" him, as St. Augustine famously affirms. Christ's "handing over of himself" for our sake reveals the specific act of love we must imitate as God's "beloved children" in order to come to rest in him. God's self-surrender in love was something he decided to do out of his eternal and infinite *freedom*. There is nothing automatic or compulsory about God's gift of himself, because love can never be

---

[2] Usually, though not consistently, the RSV translates the verb παραδίδωμι as "to give up", which is only one possibility for its meaning. For my part, I translate it consistently as "to hand over" as a more literal and precise rendering, particularly in the context of the Lord's Passion, when Jesus was quite literally handed over (παραδίδοται) "into the hands of sinners" (26:45). This physical "handing-over" of the Son of God is the context I continually take for granted in this book. The word παραδίδωμι literally means "to give (δίδωμι) alongside (παρά)", always implying the action of hands, whereas "to give up" has a less graphic meaning. The nuance is crucial for our understanding of Jesus' betrayal by Judas, as we shall see.

the result of constraint or inevitable cycles that recur impersonally. Once God decides to give himself as exhaustively as he does in Christ, he sets the bar of self-giving very high for us.

God came to us in human flesh to make his self-surrender possible and literal. This self-bestowal occurred at a given moment of historical time. To be Christians is to imitate in our own present time an act of total self-surrender that God accomplished in Christ when he was born in Bethlehem. But it was an act of such magnitude that it has vital repercussions in every succeeding age because, in fact, it is an act of unceasing self-surrender in the present. That is how far love made God go: the Uncreated became creaturely; pure Spirit took on flesh; the Infinite accepted limitations; and the Eternal embraced the temporal as his own dwelling place—all for the sake of being with us and sharing our existence fully.

A few verses later in this same chapter 5 of Ephesians, the plot thickens when Paul writes: "Husbands, love your wives, as Christ loved the Church and [*handed himself over* (ἑαυτὸν παρέδωκεν)] for her, that he might sanctify her" (Eph 5:25–26a). God's gift of self, I repeat, is not a floating abstraction; it is the surrender of a lover to his beloved, than which there is nothing more precise and concrete in human experience. Christ's deliberate handing-over of himself is a gesture that reveals that God's love for us is not a generic benevolence but, rather, the specific love driving the Heart of a passionately committed *Bridegroom*.

In the Incarnation, Christ comes to encounter us as the *Bridegroom of redeemed mankind* and of each of our souls. This is his most intimate identity. Think of what being a bridegroom implies by way of desire for union, passionate attachment to the beloved, unceasing labor for her benefit, and fidelity to the point of death. Paul says elsewhere: "The husband does not rule over his own body, but the wife does" (1 Cor 7:4). This principle graphically illustrates how completely wedded spouses should surrender their whole persons to each other. But it also has a strong eucharistic resonance because it shows how unconditionally the Lord Jesus has entrusted his Real Presence into the hands of the Church, for his Spouse to do with him whatever she deems necessary for the salvation of the world. This includes not only the Eucharistic Sacrifice, but also the Blessed Sacrament reserved for adoration and as viaticum for the sick and dying.

This gesture of handing-over of self, moreover, is not only an action

of the incarnate Word himself. It is important to see also that, because
the Son does everything out of loving obedience to his Father, the
Son gives himself to us as total gift only in absolute cooperation with
the Father. Christ makes himself our gift only through the Father's
own action of giving him to us. Christ consents to be given as gift.
"[God] who did not spare his own Son," Paul tells us, "but [*handed
him over* (παρέδωκεν αὐτόν)] for us all, will he not also give us all
things with him?" (Rom 8:32).

The Greek word that I have been translating as "handed over" is
parádosis. It contains a meaningful ambiguity. This one word can be
translated not only as "to hand over" or "surrender" or "give up"
but also, in the figurative sense, as "to betray", because a certain kind
of handing-over can be a betrayal. A father hands his daughter over
to her bridegroom at the altar with love and hope, but Judas hands
Jesus over to his enemies to be rid of him.

2. FOR OUR SAKE GOD MADE HIM TO BE SIN WHO KNEW NO SIN

Such considerations comfort us because they express the more luminous aspects of the Paschal Mystery. But now we must enter the dark
side of the Redemption because this is an unavoidable darkness we
all carry within us. We must glimpse into the abyss of suffering into
which our Lord Jesus was plunged in the hours that led him into the
desolation of his Father's abandonment and, ultimately, to a horrendous death. In the days of his Passion, Jesus, obeying the will of the
Father, willingly and even joyously[3] entered into what Paul calls "the
mystery of iniquity" (2 Thess 2:7, DRA). Fully aware of what was
involved, and with full consent of heart and will, Jesus *handed himself
over into the hands of sinners*, to be treated by them as they pleased.

But who are these "sinners" into whose hands Jesus so willingly
hands himself? Ourselves, of course. Jesus surrenders himself into our
sinful hands just as literally as every day we may receive his Body as
bread in our hands and drink his outpoured Blood as wine. "When
you did not have mercy on one of these, the least of my brothers,
you did not have mercy on me", the all-knowing King will say to us
at the Last Judgment (cf. 25:31–46). How could we forget this stark

[3] "For the joy that was set before him [he] endured the cross, despising the shame"
(Heb 12:2).

truth? Jesus knew who we were; he knew what we would do with him; and still he has surrendered himself totally into our hands. If we are ever tempted to view Jesus' Passion and death as merely the regrettable failure of an otherwise admirable mission, then we should read the Gospels again with greater care. There we would see clearly the dazzling light of an ardent love, a light that blinds our natural logic with the divine truth that the strategy of divine love to redeem the world consisted precisely in Jesus surrendering himself into the hands of sinners he knew would kill him. "For our sake [the Father] *made him to be sin who knew no sin*, so that in him we might become the righteousness of God" (2 Cor 5:21). "While we were [his] enemies we were reconciled to God by the death of his Son" (Rom 5:10).

If we have a sensitive heart open to in-depth understanding, such declarations by St. Paul should make us gasp. Consider the depth of the mystery of divine love: On the one hand, God cannot be God without being from all eternity the Father of his beloved only Son. At the very same time, however, it appears that God did not love the One *by whose sonship he is God* more than us, his creatures! Paul's words above declare this wonderful, terrible truth: *God did not spare his own Son but made him to be sin for our sake.* For us to be liberated from the death of sin, the Father deemed it necessary that his innocent Son should *become sin*, that which is most abhorrent to God! Christ, the All-Holy One, became sin by taking up into his person the full consequence of our sins, namely, death. The very God who would not allow Abraham to kill his beloved son Isaac did not spare his own Son but *handed him over* for us all! The all-powerful King exchanged his dignity for that of the condemned slave. The greatest truths are always unbelievable, and that is precisely why we must believe them. Indeed, we could never append a sufficient number of exclamation marks to revelations of such magnitude.

Now, the supreme power by which Christ is able to destroy death is not human-styled violence raised to an omnipotent degree. No: *God's only power is the power of love*, which means the power of tenderness and mercy, which in turn means that Christ takes upon himself the corporate sin of all ages and allows it to crush him on the Cross. Only the power of God's infinite love is capable of absorbing all evil in this way, like the depths of an ocean into which nuclear waste is sunk. But God's infinite love was housed in no unsinkable super-hero. It made its abode and became flesh within a very human person, Jesus of Nazareth, who bled when wounded and endured horrific anguish when abandoned by those he thought loved him. And so, necessarily, his absorption of the collected sin of the world utterly broke his human frame.

In Christ, God still makes himself vulnerable every day as he entrusts himself into our hands. The mystery of iniquity into which Christ descended in the Passion could only be done away with by the courage of a love that was even greater—the courage of a love that descends into the gaping jaws of hell itself to rescue the beloved. Christ consented to "catching sin" as a dog catches rabies, and he died of it. As the Spanish saying goes, *muerto el perro, muere la rabia*, that is, "once the dog dies, the rabies dies with him." In the Passion, Jesus made himself less than a dog for our sake, as Isaiah prophesies: "He was . . . a man of sorrows, and acquainted with grief; and as one from whom men hide their faces he was despised, and we esteemed him not" (Is 53:3). When Christ came into our midst to redeem us, says a great theologian, he descended so low that after that no one would be able to fall without falling into him. [4]

But what does Christ's handing-over of self out of love look like "on the ground", so to speak, that is, at the level of the concrete events of Christ's life as portrayed in the Gospels toward the end of Jesus' earthly sojourn?

Just before the events of Palm Sunday in Matthew's Gospel, we read Jesus' third prediction of his Passion to his disciples: "As Jesus was going up to Jerusalem, he took the twelve disciples aside, and on the way he said to them, 'Behold, we are going up to Jerusalem; and the Son of man will be [*handed over* (παραδοθήσεται)] to the chief priests and scribes, and they will condemn him to death, and [*hand him over* (παραδώσουσιν)] to the Gentiles to be mocked and scourged and crucified, and he will be raised on the third day'" (20:17–19). And in the Gospel of John, we witness the first station on the Way of the Cross: "Then [Pilate] *handed him over* (παρέδωκεν) to them to be crucified. So they took Jesus, and he went out, bearing his own cross, to the place called the place of a skull, which is called in Hebrew 'Golgotha'" (Jn 19:16–17).

We note at once how the context of the gruesome events of the

[4] Hans Urs von Balthasar, *Heart of the World*, trans. Erasmo S. Leiva (San Francisco: Ignatius Press, 1979), 43.

Passion violently alters our understanding of the expression "to hand oneself over". Until now, it has given us comforting feelings of *gratitude* that Christ would so generously give himself to us. It has also conveyed emotions of a deeply reassuring *intimacy*, of a sweet embracing and being embraced by a cherished beloved, of a human fulfillment beyond all imagining, and all because we now possess the Father's most prized treasure as our very own. These are, indeed, all immensely consoling truths. But suddenly the physical events of the Passion make us feel the full shock of what it means for Jesus to descend into the "mystery of iniquity" that will destroy him. His wedding with mankind is going to be a blood-wedding, the wedding feast of "the Lamb that was slain" from the foundation of the world for the love of his Bride, the Church (Rev 13:8; cf. Rev 19:7).

It has always been an odious injustice to blame the Jews alone for the death of Jesus. In the drama of the Passion, the Jews represented only one portion of guilty mankind. The teachers of the Law, all the non-Jews in Jerusalem, the pagan Roman Pilate himself and his troops, as well as the Jewish high priests and the clamoring multitude outside the prætorium, all taken together, represent *us*, that is, the totality of human beings of all times and places in our collusion with evil. We should honestly confess that, at least initially, we do not very gladly receive the gift of Jesus in our hands and pass it on as something precious. Rather, like that self-serving crowd, we handle Jesus as an object of scorn, as a source of irritation to be done away with, or at best as an object of indifference or mild disdain. From Annas and Caiaphas and Pilate all the way down to the last serving girl, all these representatives of sinful mankind are portrayed as *handing Jesus over* to one another blasphemously as their plaything—for mockery, torture, and, finally, crucifixion.

The players in the Passion reciprocate God's tender gesture of *handing over* his Son to them, not by joyfully embracing him, but by *betraying* him. And the silent Jesus allows it to happen; he allows himself to be made a thing to be maliciously played with and thrown out in the end. And yet he asks: "Do you think that I cannot appeal to my Father, and he will at once send me more than twelve legions of angels? But how then should the Scriptures be fulfilled, that it must be so?" (26:53–54). The Son saves us, not by the visible, super-heroic action of mythological titans, but by quietly obeying the design of his Father. Therein lies all the power of his love.

3. THE LORD JESUS, ON THE NIGHT HE
WAS HANDED OVER, TOOK BREAD

But what does this subject of *parádosis* have to do with the Eucharist? Nothing reveals so emphatically the intimate connection between Christ's historical *handing-over/betrayal* and the *Eucharist* as the clashing *coincidence* in Jesus' life of two antithetical events: one, an event of utter goodness; the other, an event of utter malice, which nevertheless become fused by the power of Jesus' action into the single event of the Redemption.

You may perhaps have wondered now and then why Jesus chose to institute the Holy Eucharist precisely on the very evening of his betrayal, only shortly before Judas kissed him in the garden as he handed him over to the forces of destruction. Quite factually, Judas surrendered Jesus into the hands of his enemies shortly after Jesus handed himself over to him at the Last Supper in sacramental Communion. And, as the betrayer leaves the cenacle to perform his heinous deed, Jesus' words to him are: "'What you are going to do, do quickly.'... And it was night" (Jn 13:27, 30). This is a command by Jesus that seems mysteriously to trigger the drama leading to his own death.

Essential to understanding this mystery of coincidence between Eucharist and betrayal is the paramount text from St. Paul's First Letter to the Corinthians, which memorializes the Last Supper and its permanent centrality to all Christian existence. Let us pay particular attention in this narrative to the *gestures* performed by Jesus to accompany his words:

> For I *received* (παρέλαβον) from the Lord what I also delivered [*handed on* (παρέδωκα)] to you, that the Lord Jesus, on the night when he was [*handed over* (παρεδίδετο)] *took* (ἔλαβεν) bread, and when he had given thanks, broke it, and said, "This is my body which is for you. Do this in remembrance of me." In the same way also the chalice, after supper, saying, "This chalice is the new covenant in my blood. Do this, as often as you drink it, in remembrance of me." For as often as you eat this bread and drink the chalice, you proclaim the Lord's death until he comes.[5]

---

[5]Ἐγὼ γὰρ παρέλαβον ἀπὸ τοῦ κυρίου, ὃ καὶ παρέδωκα ὑμῖν, ὅτι ὁ κύριος Ἰησοῦς ἐν τῇ νυκτὶ ᾗ παρεδίδετο ἔλαβεν ἄρτον [24]καὶ εὐχαριστήσας ἔκλασεν καὶ εἶπεν· Τοῦτό μού ἐστιν

This text portrays marvelously Jesus' intentions and actions on the threshold of the Passion, "on the night he was [handed over]". By recording so objectively the significant words and gestures of Jesus at the end of this momentous meal, Paul is in fact revealing to us—if we know how to "read" the signs—the depth of God's creativity in Christ in the face of the Son's imminent suffering and death. Paul, who was not present at the Last Supper, stresses that he is *handing on* to the Corinthians what was *handed on* to him by the apostles. The solemn care, furthermore, with which Paul frames his account means that he is conscious of the fact that what he is giving us here as his most precious legacy is of supreme importance to the life of the Church, because Christ himself decreed that it should be so. What Paul is here *handing on* is what he himself *received:* namely, the celebration of the Holy Eucharist by the Church as containing and communicating sacramentally the death and Resurrection of Jesus under the material signs of bread, wine, words, and gestures.

In his text, Paul uses, in different verbal forms, the word *parádosis* to refer to his own *handing-over* to believers of the celebration of the Eucharist. Now this is the very same word that we have seen him use to refer to the Son's own *handing-down* to mankind by the Father and that the Gospel also uses to refer to the *betrayal* of the Son by Judas and all sinners. The Latin equivalent of *parádosis* is *traditio*. Thus, we see here that the Eucharist is the core and source of our living tradition as Christians, our most precious heritage. The gesture of surrender contained in the Eucharist, then, communicates, not two, but three interrelated meanings of the utmost theological importance: (1) the eternal action of Father and Son, (2) the temporal action of betrayal at the time of the Passion, and (3) the sacramental action of the Church. All three are *parádosis, traditio, "handing-over"*.

The great act of thanksgiving that is the Mass is, in fact, the obedient execution by the Church of Christ's command: "Do this in memory of me!" The familiar words we daily hear the priest pronounce at the altar as he bends over for the Consecration are really a synthesis

---

τὸ σῶμα τὸ ὑπὲρ ὑμῶν· τοῦτο ποιεῖτε εἰς τὴν ἐμὴν ἀνάμνησιν. ²⁵ὡσαύτως καὶ τὸ ποτήριον μετὰ τὸ δειπνῆσαι λέγων· Τοῦτο τὸ ποτήριον ἡ καινὴ διαθήκη ἐστὶν ἐν τῷ ἐμῷ αἵματι· τοῦτο ποιεῖτε, ὁσάκις ἐὰν πίνητε, εἰς τὴν ἐμὴν ἀνάμνησιν. ²⁶ὁσάκις γὰρ ἐὰν ἐσθίητε τὸν ἄρτον τοῦτον καὶ τὸ ποτήριον πίνητε, τὸν θάνατον τοῦ κυρίου καταγγέλλετε ἄχρι οὗ ἔλθῃ (1 Cor 11:23–26).

of the words of Paul in First Corinthians with the narratives of the institution that we find in the Synoptic Gospels:

> For on the night he was betrayed [and entered willingly into his Passion], he himself took bread, and, giving you thanks, he said the blessing, broke the bread and gave it to his disciples, saying: TAKE THIS, ALL OF YOU, AND EAT OF IT, FOR THIS IS MY BODY, WHICH WILL BE GIVEN UP FOR YOU. In a similar way, when supper was ended, he took the chalice, and, giving you thanks, he said the blessing, and gave the chalice to his disciples, saying: TAKE THIS, ALL OF YOU, AND DRINK FROM IT, FOR THIS IS THE CHALICE OF MY BLOOD, THE BLOOD OF THE NEW AND ETERNAL COVENANT, WHICH WILL BE POURED OUT FOR YOU AND FOR MANY FOR THE FORGIVENESS OF SINS. DO THIS IN MEMORY OF ME.[6]

The most striking aspect of Jesus' actions in this text of the Mass is what can be called Jesus' *creative anticipation* of his death. We begin in the past historical tense, which remembers that Jesus *took* bread and *broke* it. But then we suddenly jump to the present tense, and we see and hear Jesus directly *handing the bread over* to his disciples and commanding them to eat of it right here and now. And the meaning that Jesus himself gives to these gestures and actions is: "for this is my Body, which *will be given up* for you", in the future tense. In other words, here Christ institutes in the past tense (of the Last Supper) a sacramental action that overtakes a destructive historical action (his murder) that has not yet occurred, while at the same time giving to it a startling redemptive meaning for all future time, the whole event made coherent by the memory (*anámnêsis*) of faith. In this way, the actual interior significance and effects of the future action of betrayal are radically changed by divine intervention *before the betrayal occurs*. The malice of man is successfully overtaken by the providential goodness of God. Love swallows up hatred, even though the lover dies of poisoning. A hate-filled enemy—along with his evil intentions and his murderous deed—is embraced as brother and friend.

In the Sacrament, Jesus' death becomes the source of our life because the power of his love anticipates the mangling of his body and the shedding of his blood. The divine creativity of Jesus' love

---

[6] The introductory sentence is from the Roman Rite's Eucharistic Prayer 3, while the clause in brackets is from Eucharistic Prayer 2. Most of the rest of the text is common to all Eucharistic Prayers.

transforms the mangling and the bloodshed from an act of violent hatred into the execution of a sacrifice and the preparation of its victim as vital food. At a moment when one would expect the victim to be overwhelmed with fear, such energetic anticipation is instead a prodigious, transformative action by the One in whom the universe was first created and that he is now re-creating through his Passion.

Jesus *takes* bread, pronounces a thanksgiving that *changes* it substantially into his Body, *breaks it*, and *distributes* it for eating; *takes* wine, *blesses* it, and transforms it into his Blood, and then *pours it out* to be drunk. This is Jesus' way of guaranteeing that the Substance of his being will not fall from the Cross into a bottomless abyss as a result of human violence, but that, rather, that sacred Substance will be made available to all as a source of new life and joy: "This is why the Father loves me, because I lay down my life in order to take it up again. No one takes it from me, but I lay it down on my own. I have power to lay it down, and power to take it up again" (Jn 10:17–18, NAB). This power and choice of Jesus to *lay down his life* contains the whole secret of his love. He was not crucified accidentally or because he, a simple victim of history, could not avoid it.

At the very moment when he is going to allow himself to be handed over to the forces of darkness, Jesus shows himself to be more than ever the sovereign Lord of creation and of history: of creation, because he takes the elements of bread and wine and re-creates them, transforming them into his Body and Blood; of history, because he takes the impending evil deed of his betrayal and transforms it already before it occurs into the best possible occasion for him to surrender his person to us, his betrayers, out of his love as the Bridegroom of the Church, with the total fidelity, dedication, and passionate love that befit a royal bridegroom.

4. DO THIS IN MEMORY OF ME!

Paul's narrative of the institution of the Eucharist has vital implications, and not only at the most obvious level of our liturgical and sacramental life. His account, but above all our eucharistic practice, should also leave a deep mark on our individual life of faith, in which we struggle with doubts and temptations of many kinds, and on our moral life, in which we strive to live by the commandment "Love one another; even as I have loved you" (Jn 13:34). The other command "Do this in memory of me!" that concludes the solemn words of institution refers not only to the *liturgical* celebration of the Eucharist. It also refers to the fact that our everyday life as Christians ought to be the *celebration through our existence* of the Real Presence of Christ in our ordinary interaction with the world.

Love does not forget. Love remembers; and the memory of Jesus in us throbs with the power of his Word and the promise of his Resurrection. How beautiful it is that, when Christ asks us to do to others out of love what he has first done to us, he tells us to do it *in his memory*, as if he were saying: "Just remember me, and love will come easily!" Truly, it is the quality of our interaction with others—at home, in the workplace, in the street where we encounter the homeless—that will confirm or deny the authenticity of the heartfelt devotion we experience when celebrating the liturgical Mystery in church. Or do we simply forget Christ and his gift of self to us when we leave the church? Is the Mass nothing but a sort of ritual fantasy that only establishes me more firmly in my self-complacency? Would not such forgetfulness constitute a sort of "stillbirth" of Christ in us?

When we are overwhelmed by sorrows of any kind or are perhaps suffering the pangs of a devouring guilt that can tempt us to despair; when it seems that our life has reached a dead-end either through the treachery of others or through our own grave errors: then our only salvation is to believe with all our might in the power of Christ's creative anticipation, that is, the sovereign ability Christ demonstrated at the Last Supper and on the Cross to take an evil deed that will lead to his own crucifixion and providentially transform it into an event of Resurrection.

Christ's unconditional handing-over of himself to us in advance of anything we might do ought to give us the certainty that no sin we commit can ever be greater than the mercy of God and that no wound inflicted on us by others is beyond the healing power of the divine Physician. Indeed, Christ has "foresuffered all".[7] We should not stubbornly clutch our sufferings to our chest like greedy paupers; Christ's tender deed of creative anticipation on the Cross has made

---

[7] T. S. Eliot, *The Waste Land*, "The Fire Sermon", with reference to the Greek prophet Tiresias, whom many critics consider a Christ-figure in this poem.

it so that all my sufferings already belong, in advance, more to him than to me.

"Love one another; even as I have loved you", Jesus commands us (Jn 13:34). As Christians, we are not free to love any way we wish, half-heartedly or only when convenient and self-satisfying. We must strive to love as we have been loved, which is with the whole of God's tender Heart. "Mensura amoris sine mensura amare", writes St. Bernard of Clairvaux: "The measure of love is to love without measure."[8] We cause something like a short-circuit in the cosmic circulation of God's love, which is supposed to flow forward through us, if, after receiving Christ from the Father, we do not repeat God's gesture and instead make his outpoured love stop abruptly with ourselves.

In the Sermon on the Mount, Jesus lays down this teaching: "If you are offering your gift at the altar, and there remember that your brother has something against you, leave your gift there before the altar and go; first be reconciled to your brother, and then come and offer your gift" (5:23–24). This means that anger between brothers blocks the free circulation of love, not only between the two persons directly involved in the situation but also within the worshipping community and between each believer and God. And we should note the irksome nuance: the Lord says pointedly *if your brother has something against you*. In other words, the commandment holds whether or not I think my brother is justified in his grudge against me! No, when it comes to loving in Christ, we are never independent operators. The Eucharist cannot be offered by one who hates or even disdains another. Mercy is the power of self-giving; it is meant to flow ever onward; the more of it we give, the more we receive. Whoever receives mercy must give mercy, or else he will choke on it. God gives me his mercy so abundantly that I always will have more than enough for both myself and all I providentially encounter. Like the miraculous loaves, mercy becomes multiplied in the giving. Jesus knows the precise supply of it I will need in order to fulfill what he expects of me, the faithful manner in which I will embody his mercy for others.

The Gospel everywhere urges us to allow the irresistible tenderness of Christ to invade our person and take over our every thought, feeling, and action. Realistically, however, none of us can by nature be as

---

[8] *Treatise on the Love of God*, 1.

selfless as Christ, the Good Samaritan who but glances at a wounded or needy person and at once feels inward tremors of mercy.[9] The problem we face here is not so much that of imposing on ourselves, by an act of the will, a strict and logical consistency between faith and action. Rather, we are called to perform an act of gentle permissiveness, that is, to allow the power of the Christ who has given himself to me with love to have its full effect in my whole person, rather like a pregnant mother-to-be who allows the child to grow in her womb and simply nourishes him by offering him her whole being and doing nothing to harm him.

Similarly, if I allow the Christ life to grow in me according to the intrinsic powers it contains, a healthy birth of the Word from me into the world is all but assured because such was unquestionably God's intention when he planted Christ the Seed in my soul at baptism. This is not our work, but the work of God in us. Christ in us is never a mere static object that we dispose of at will; Christ is always the acting Subject within my person, the risen Lord who strengthens me, and the true Protagonist of my life and history—all in the most intimate, unobtrusive, and tender manner possible.

The act of eating the Body of Christ and drinking the Blood of Christ with faith generates a dynamic process that *forms Christ in us*,[10] and this transformation within us is profoundly linked to the Blessed Virgin's own conception of the Son of God in her womb. We conceive Christ in the womb of our faith by the power of the same Holy Spirit that overshadowed Mary (Lk 1:35). Christ's Presence in the Blessed Sacrament is no inert object for mere distant veneration. Christ wants to pervade my whole person so that I become

---

[9] I am not gratuitously waxing poetic here, but giving a most literal interpretation. Luke uses the word ἐσπλαγχνίσθη ("he was moved with compassion for", Lk 10:33) to refer to the Good Samaritan's spontaneous movement of compassion toward the wounded man. The word derives from σπλάγχνα (*splanchna*) and means literally the "viscera" or inward parts located in the belly that flutter or tremble when affected by a deep emotion. Along with the heart, these viscera were thought by the ancients to be the seat of tender emotions in the whole personality. The verb σπλαγχνίζομαι is the standard New Testament word for "experiencing mercy or compassion", and the physiological involvement of the whole person in the act of Christian compassion has great theological relevance. Christian love, namely, cannot be only a matter of the head, as we see foremost in Christ himself, the archetype of the Good Samaritan.

[10] "My little children, with whom I am again in travail until Christ be formed in you!" (Gal 4:19).

his Real Presence in the world. He wants to be born into the world—he wants to be *handed over* by me to others—through my deeds of love, until his love becomes the vital law and spontaneous impulse of my being, too.

As we now begin to ponder the last three chapters of Matthew's Gospel, then, I propose that you think of this long narrative as the *refraction*—into the myriad colors of Jesus' words, teachings, commands, encounters, gestures, glances, and even silences—*of the pure light* that is Christ our Bridegroom in his incessant action of *parádosis*: his loving surrender of his sacred Self to each member of mankind, to the glory of God the Father. Christ will be satisfied with nothing less than intimate union with our soul, his bride, for "God yearns jealously for the spirit that he has made to dwell in us" (Jas 4:5 alt., NAB).

ABBREVIATIONS

BBE   The Bible in Basic English (1949, 1965)

CJB   Complete Jewish Bible (1998)

DLZ   Delitzsch Hebrew New Testament (1877)

DRA   Douay-Rheims Bible, American Edition (1899)

EIN   Einheitsübersetzung der Heiligen Schrift (1980)

ESV   English Standard Version (2011)

FBJ   Bible de Jérusalem (1973)

JPS   Jewish Publication Society OT (1917)

KJV   King James Version of the English Bible (1611)

LUO   Lutherbibel (1912)

LXX   The Greek Septuagint

MNT   Münchener Neues Testament (1998)

NAB   New American Bible (1991)

NAS   New American Standard Bible (1977)

NET   The NET Bible (2005)

NIB   New International Version (UK)

NIV   The New International Version of the Bible (1984)

NJB   New Jerusalem Bible (1985)

NOV   Nova Vulgata Bibliorum Sacrorum Editio (1979)

NRS   New Revised Standard Version Bible (1989)

PER   La Biblia del Peregrino (L. Alonso Schökel)

R95   Spanish Reina Vatera Update (1995)

RSV   Revised Standard Version of the Bible, 2nd Catholic ed. (2006)

TOB   Traduction Œcuménique de la Bible (1988)

VUL   The Latin Vulgate

Whenever a biblical reference does not give the name of a book of Sacred Scripture, the reference is to the Gospel of Matthew.

The RSV (Revised Standard Version, Second Catholic Edition) is the default translation of the Bible used throughout. Italics used in quotations from Scripture are my own.

ΤΟ ΚΑΤΑ ΜΑΤΘΑΙΟΝ
ΑΓΙΟΝ ΕΥΑΓΓΕΛΙΟΝ
ΤΟΥ ΚΥΡΙΟΥ ΗΜΩΝ
ΙΗΣΟΥ ΧΡΙΣΤΟΥ

THE HOLY GOSPEL OF
OUR LORD JESUS CHRIST
ACCORDING TO MATTHEW

1. THE BRIDEGROOM BEGINS HIS SURRENDER

The Plot to Kill Jesus (26:1–5)

26:1
 ἐγένετο ὅτε ἐτέλεσεν ὁ Ἰησοῦς
 πάντας τοὺς λόγους τούτους

*It happened when Jesus
had finished all these sayings*

*T*O FINISH IS A FIT VERB to launch this last stage of Jesus' earthly journey. A similar formula has been used before by Matthew (7:28, 19:1) to mark the end of a major section in his text; but here the word "all" is added, to signify a definitive break between all that has preceded in the Gospel and what will now follow. The introductory phrase "it happened" adds no real content to the text but does enhance the solemnity of the moment, best evoked in English by the archaic but beautiful "now it came to pass". A reverential hush falls over us as we enter the holy of holies of Matthew's Gospel: the narrative of the Lord's suffering and death, toward which all else has led.

The Greek word *telós* (here in the verbal form for "finish") implies, not only arriving at the conclusion of something, but, more importantly, attaining the *goal* toward which one set out. Jesus' life and person have no other purpose but to accomplish the will of the Father. Matthew here stresses the end of *words*: everything that has gone before in the Gospel has been "words" in the sense that Jesus has been continually teaching *about* the Father and his Kingdom. Arriving now at the threshold of the Passion, a break in kind is indicated between all previous *speaking about* the Kingdom and the *actual arrival* of the Kingdom. It will now arrive, not in word only, but in word and deed, through Jesus' death and glorification.

The word *Pascha* (= "Passover") occurs already in the next verse, 26:2. In his enacting of the Paschal Mystery, Jesus will now demonstrate the all-encompassing extent to which he is Word Incarnate, that is to say, Word-that-is-Act in this world of time, space, and flesh. All of his teaching and all of his pointing to the mystery of God through the use of symbolic human language will now become transformed into one protracted action of self-outpouring, to reveal the full mystery of God's love through the silent act of handing himself over into the hands of sinners—our hands. In this specialized sense, too, we may say that *the Word* who revealed himself in language and gesture during the rest of the Gospel now *becomes the flesh* of his Passion. This theological truth is reflected in the structure of Matthew's text: what now follows—the narrative of Jesus' Passion, death, and Resurrection, which is the very core of the Gospel proclamation—in all likelihood was composed first, and the rest of the Gospel that precedes it only afterward, as a kind of extensive preamble that prepares us for understanding the events that will now occur.

What exactly has Jesus been recently "saying"? What are the words that he has just "finished"? Let us refresh our memory. Immediately preceding chapter 26, we have heard Jesus' account of the Last Judgment (25:31–46). Three things stand out there as most memorable and as highly relevant to the narrative of the Passion that now follows. First, Jesus presents himself as the "Son of man" seated on a glorious throne and coming in glory surrounded by hosts of angels. In this way, Jesus is clearly manifesting his divine identity as King of the universe, Lord of history, and Judge of the living and the dead. At the same time, however, and most paradoxically for our human logic, Jesus identifies himself with the very least of the wretched, the needy, and the suffering of the world. The Lord drives home the crucial point of this self-identification with human misery by listing very specific varieties of suffering, as if from personal acquaintance. And the third thing that we learn from this passage is what we may call the fundamental Christian ethical imperative: that, if we fail to see in practice Jesus' self-identification with human suffering and if we consequently fail to minister to him in his need, then we do not know him at all and will be rejected by him. Our theoretical "faith" has in reality been nonexistent, has been only a matter of thoughts and words with no flesh on them. In practice, we will have denied the Incarnation.

Surely we see at once here the relevance of Jesus' narrative of the Final Judgment to the evangelist's impending narrative of Jesus' Passion, death, and Resurrection. As he speaks persuasively to his disciples, the crowds, and ourselves within time, Jesus of Nazareth *is* the Son of man about to be put to death and *is*, simultaneously, the Son of God who will be raised from the dead as universal Lord and King, to usher us into eternal life in his company. However, in the hinge verse 26:1, the evangelist says, "when Jesus had finished *all* these sayings . . .". Surely he here refers not only to the narrative of the Last Judgment that has just preceded but to everything else that Jesus has uttered in words since the beginning of the Gospel of Matthew. Of course Jesus will continue to speak some human words in what remains of this Gospel; but their number will be much reduced, and we can no longer expect long discourses, since the time for teaching and instruction is now past. The work of redemption will now begin in earnest, consisting, not in words of instruction, but in concrete deeds of love. Be on the lookout, therefore, and observe how the few words that Jesus still speaks will always cast light on the meaning of some accompanying deed by himself or another. These will be acts of flesh and blood revealing God's Heart of Love.

26:2   Οἴδατε ὅτι μετὰ δύο ἡμέρας τὸ πάσχα γίνεται,
        καὶ ὁ υἱὸς τοῦ ἀνθρώπου παραδίδοται εἰς τὸ σταυρωθῆναι

You know that after two days the Passover is coming,
and the Son of man is being handed over to be crucified

TWICE ALREADY (16:21; 20:18) Jesus has forewarned his disciples about his impending destiny of suffering and death; this is why he now introduces this third and final reminder by saying "you know. . . ." However, the fact that he keeps on bringing up the subject at regular intervals hints at Jesus' understanding of weak human nature and his need to strengthen his followers' resolve. In addition, his assuring them with such serenity and conviction that such extreme trials await him initiates his friends ever more deeply into his confidence. No doubt his ultimate pedagogical concern is that they, too, should put on gradually, as their own, his filial understanding of this necessary mission of suffering and dying entrusted to him by the Father.

But now the moment for the Passion to start is no longer in the distant future, and the present verse makes the point alarmingly clear. Whereas the previous two predictions were cast in the future tense, the current assertion practically attacks our complacency. We are *already* in Jerusalem; the Passover is happening in only *two days*; and the crucial verb is in the immediate present tense, as if the action has already begun: "the Son of man *is being handed over* to be crucified." [1] To stress the point that the Passion has already started in anticipation of the Passover, the verb here may also be translated, as I have done above, in the present periphrastic of ongoing action: "the Son of man *is being handed over* [or *betrayed*] to be crucified."

This is not the case of a grammarian being pedantic. Jesus' deliberate anticipation of his betrayal by his use of the present tense in this speech-act signals the freedom of choice with which he is walking into the ordeal of his suffering. As a matter of fact, we may say that

---

[1] Only the Latin Vulgate (*traditur*) and the King James Version follow the Greek (παραδίδοται) precisely in this matter of tense. Every other major version retains the future tense used in the two past predictions, I suppose by force of habit.

Jesus is himself the "choreographer" of his own Passion and death. Only in the following verse, on the heels of Jesus' proclamation, will the high priests and their associates begin to heat up the machinery of power to entrap and kill him, as if by his prediction Jesus has given them permission to do so. Even in his greatest weakness, humiliation, apparent defeat, and obliteration, Jesus will remain to the end the Protagonist, not only of his own life and destiny, but of the life and destiny of Israel and of the whole world.

Of great importance here is the way in which Jesus synchronizes his betrayal and crucifixion with the Passover feast of the Jews. Once again we are astounded by the deliberateness with which he is blithely walking into a situation of certain entrapment and death. Quite clearly, he is choosing the Passover as the moment with which he wants his suffering and death to coincide.

Now, God enjoined the celebration of the Passover on the ancient Israelites in these terms: "The blood [of the Paschal lamb] shall be a sign for you, upon the houses where you are; and when I see the blood, I will pass over you, and no plague shall fall upon you to destroy you. . . . This day shall be for you a memorial day, and you shall keep it as a feast to the LORD" (Ex 12:13–14). In a similar manner, Jesus here is acting as sovereign Lord by choosing the feast of the Passover as the symbolic frame within which to stage his own sacrifice as Lamb of God. His blood, though spilled in scorn, is offered willingly by him to the Father in order to save mankind, not from this or that specific plague, but from all threats of destruction whatsoever, whether interior or exterior, and on behalf not only of the children of Israel but of all God's children of all times and places.

When Jesus refers to himself as "*the Son of man* who is being delivered up to be crucified", this title reveals the universality of his Passion's saving effect. The Son of man will save all his kin, all those who have Eve as mother. Jesus' choice of feast for his death fulfills the truth of Israel's faith in God's saving power. At the same time, however, he universalizes the meaning of the Pasch by extending to all mankind the benefits of his delivering himself up into the hands of sinners.

א

26:3–4   Τότε συνήχθησαν οἱ ἀρχιερεῖς . . .
εἰς τὴν αὐλὴν τοῦ ἀρχιερέως τοῦ λεγομένου Καϊάφα
καὶ συνεβουλεύσαντο ἵνα τὸν Ἰησοῦν δόλῳ
κρατήσωσιν καὶ ἀποκτείνωσιν

Then the chief priests . . . gathered
in the palace of the high priest, who was called Caiaphas,
and took counsel together in order to arrest Jesus
by guile and kill him

J ESUS' REFERENCES in the previous verse have a distinctive cultic-
sacrificial flavor: the Passover feast, the handing-over of a sacrificial victim, crucifixion as means of accomplishing the sacrifice.
This context now naturally evokes the chief priests, that portion of
Israel responsible for its cult, and in particular Caiaphas, whose turn
it was to be high priest that year. We know from other sources that
he was, indeed, in this office from A.D. 18 to 36, and so his name
and dates ground the narrative historically. The word *then*, which
brings the narrative forward, has the theological function of stressing
that Jesus' opponents can start their machinations only after he has
solemnly repeated the prophecy of his Passion to his disciples—as
if the Jewish authorities needed his tacit agreement and permission
to proceed with his sacrifice: "then [*and only then*] the chief priests
gathered". In their own way, though quite unconsciously, the priests
are preparing an unheard-of Passover by conspiring against Jesus.
Despite themselves, they are cooperating with Jesus in infusing this
year's liturgical observance of Passover with most unusual new rituals
and meanings.

The tense atmosphere of a storm gathering against Jesus has been
immediately created in the narrative, particularly by the two verbs
συνήχθησαν and συνεβουλεύσαντο, which quite precisely evoke the
beginning of Psalm 2, on the revolt of the leaders of the nations
"against the LORD and his anointed". The ironical difference Matthew seems to stress between the situation in the psalm and in his
Gospel is that here it is the leaders of Israel, and not pagan kings, who

are battling the Lord of Israel and seeking to "arrest and kill" his beloved Son: "Why do the nations *conspire* (συνήχθησαν) and the peoples *plot* in vain? The kings of the earth *set themselves*, and the rulers *take counsel together* (συνεβουλεύσαντο)." The divine reaction in the psalm to such human revolt squares well with Jesus' own sovereign reaction of serenity to the violence brewing against him: "He who sits in the heavens laughs; the LORD has them in derision" (Ps 2:1– 2, 4). On the one hand, there is manifested the wise plan of the divine Trinity for the world; on the other, the shrill and mutinous response of man to that plan.

For the first time ever, and despite the Jewish abhorrence of human sacrifice, Israel's authorities are, in fact, plotting to substitute a man for the symbolic Paschal lamb whose blood saved the Israelites from destruction in Exodus. As far as they are concerned, of course, the high priests are merely piecing together a legal procedure, hopefully to result in the condemnation and execution of one whom they consider a blasphemer and rabble-rouser. They fail to see what connection there could possibly be between the *legal* process they intend and the *liturgical* feast that is occurring coincidentally. In fact, the trial, as we will see, has to be held in all haste, because, to the leaders of the people, the circumstance is a major inopportune bother that threatens to disturb the smooth ritual celebration of Passover. They have so managed along the way to ritualize, and thus "tame", the drama of the Exodus that they can see no contradiction in a celebration of the Passover during which they themselves, as an apparent side-show, are persecuting an innocent man. Now *they*, the leaders of Israel, have subtly usurped the role of a tyrannical *Pharaoh*, while *Jesus* will endure suffering in place of the innocent *Jews* of old!

However, Matthew clearly shapes his narrative so as to demonstrate Jesus' sovereign role as both Lord of history and liturgical "choreographer", who offers himself as living Victim in the cosmic liturgy of the world's transformation: "But I was like a gentle lamb led to the slaughter" (Jer 11:19). The *kairós*, or divinely "appointed time", for this particular Passover could not, in fact, be more perfect in Jesus' estimation. Only in retrospect would believers later on come to understand fully what Matthew is narrating in the present tense, as in this prayer of Peter and John in the Book of Acts: "For truly in this city there were *gathered together* against your holy servant Jesus, whom you anointed, both Herod and Pontius Pilate, with the Gentiles and the peoples of Israel" (Acts 4:27). Only subsequently, after the events of the Passion and the Resurrection, can the vision of faith comprehend the full extent of this universal conspiracy of all mankind—pagans and Jews together—against God's loving will to come close to us, embrace us, and so redeem us.

There is something ludicrous in all of this running about to connive against the life of one utterly unarmed and poor rabbi of the streets. All of these powerful leaders gather together in the *palace* of the high priest, an eloquent detail that speaks volumes about the tremendous social disparity between Jesus and the authorities persecuting him. This hints at an intended contrast on the narrator's part between political and spiritual power, between someone who naturally exudes moral authority because of the truth dwelling within him and all those others who must resort to endless stratagems and brute force precisely because their pretended moral authority is so hollow. As the story of the Passion unfolds, we will witness so many leaders, so many attendants, so many machinations and painstaking negotiations and ententes behind closed doors in different palaces, all undertaken in order to stifle and do away with one vulnerable human life! Exactly what monumental threat is Jesus posing that could begin to explain such an amassing of forces against him?

The text says that the authorities "took counsel together in order to arrest Jesus [*by guile*] and kill him."[2] This reveals the intrinsic, conscious dishonesty of those plotting against him. Whether they recognize him as Messiah or not, they clearly do know they do not have an honest legal case against this man who irks them, and so they must resort to guile and trickery. The bad conscience of persons who fear losing their standing and power will often escalate the gravity of its stratagems gradually in order to reach its goal: survival at all costs. The authorities realize that, while it is they who officially hold power in Israel, nevertheless Jesus, this nobody who does not come from their elite priestly caste, wields more and more *de facto* moral persuasiveness and popularity. They have the official pedigree, but he has the real spiritual power, as any child can see.

---

[2] RSV has *by stealth* for δόλῳ, but I prefer *by guile*, which adds the nuance of dishonesty and follows other versions that speak of trickery (NJB) and treachery (NAB.) Liddell-Scott defines the term *dolos* thus: "properly, a bait for fish: then, any cunning contrivance for deceiving or catching, as the Trojan horse, the robe of Penelope; generally, any trick or stratagem". The emphasis on entrapment is important here.

They gather in a *palace* (αὐλή) to plot against Jesus; this is ironical because, in fact, the issue of Jesus' *kingship* will come up no less than four times during the Passion (27:11, 29, 37, 42), either as an honest query or in mockery. Jesus has already spoken of himself quite openly as Son of man, King of glory, and universal Judge (25:34, 40), so that at the level of Matthew's narrative the question naturally arises: "Why is the King of Israel a homeless pauper wandering the land, while Israel's priests, his alleged servants, dwell in palaces?" It may well be that, in seeking to overpower (κρατήσωσιν) and liquidate (ἀποκτείνωσιν) Jesus, the leaders of the people are in fact seeking to suppress the mounting urgency of precisely this unbearable question, lurking like an ultimate threat at the edges of their awareness.

26:5

Μὴ ἐν τῇ ἑορτῇ,
ἵνα μὴ θόρυβος γένηται ἐν τῷ λαῷ

Not during the feast,
lest there be a tumult among the people

W E HAVE LONG SINCE WITNESSED the dangerous triangulation that occurs between a powerful person in authority, the people under him, and an individual from among the people who threatens that authority. Of Herod we have read that, "though he wanted to put [John the Baptist] to death, he feared the people, because they held him to be a prophet" (14:5). Even in this John is a forerunner of Jesus. Both John and Jesus embody a social, religious, and human mystery that instills great fear into the powers that be. Unenlightened authority is all about control by force, protection of the *status quo*, and safeguarding acquired privileges and influences at all cost. What underlies most motivations of a self-serving authority is, quite primitively, the *fear* of losing the power that has been acquired by any and all means. Whereas virtuous statesmen look to God or moral philosophy or wise counselors for light and guidance, weak and greedy rulers at bottom believe only in the laws of expediency and force.

The very titles that Matthew uses to refer to those hunting down Jesus—"arch-priests", "elders of the people"—connote persons who, having long worshipped the Lord, studied Torah, and lived faithfully the traditions of Israel, should by now have acquired sufficient internal wisdom and prudence to guide the people along paths of righteousness and peace. Instead of this, we are saddened to see that these leaders' principal motivations are negative in the extreme: on the one hand, an urgent drive to suppress by violence a human existence that they feel opposes their ethos and manner of rule; on the other hand, fear of the people's possible reaction to this intended deed. Also, Jesus strongly embodies a principle of boundless life and freedom that these rulers' world view can neither understand nor control. To them he is, therefore, the great Threatening Unknown.

At the same time, they want to take no chances with the people, who represent another unwieldy force of a very different sort. Strategically, they want to avoid capturing and condemning Jesus during the Passover, with Jerusalem swarming with multitudes of celebrating Jews. These leaders are interested in neither justice nor truth but only in pragmatic results. If the crowds' reaction to their execution of Jesus is negative, the sheer number of protesters would generate a conflict of such magnitude that they would have a new problem on their hands. It is significant that fear of God, fear of desecrating the holiness of the Passover by plotting to murder a just man, nowhere figures in the priests' and elders' considerations. Only hard-nosed and self-serving political motivations seem to drive them. Having the sublime vocation to represent divine authority to the people, they have instead degenerated to nothing but power-grabbing bureaucrats, who fear nothing more than public disorder, not because they love peace, but because they love their power.

In considering the scene, let us not have the hypocrisy of presuming that, had we been there in Jerusalem at that time, we would of course have sided with Jesus and his disciples. As Paul wrote to the Corinthians, "these things happened to them as a warning, but they were written down for our instruction" (1 Cor 10:11). Do we really so readily understand and make Jesus' attitude our own? He desires only to form his followers in the truth, at great risk to himself. Far from seeking his own interests and retaliating in kind, Jesus instead views the gathering darkness with a precision and a serenity that can derive only from profound trust. He contemplates his impending betrayal and crucifixion with an equanimity that must be the fruit of tremendous compassion coupled with a deep knowledge of human nature and the effects of sin upon it. Keenly understanding the roots of sin, Jesus desires nothing more than to forgive its perpetrators. Above all, he quietly assumes, and indeed promotes, his role as redeeming Victim with a simplicity and spontaneity that lack all fear and are the very opposite of the leaders' intricate machinations.

The arrival of this Passover has on Jesus the same effect as would the arrival of his wedding date on a bridegroom who is madly in love. The leaders say, "Not during the feast!" But Jesus insists: "Yes! *During* the feast! For this Passover is my wedding feast with my Bride, mankind, a union to be consummated in my blood."

It is this manner of seeing and feeling and embracing reality that Jesus wants to instill in his disciples when he says: "You *know* that after two days the Passover is coming." Are we prepared and eager to become disciples who know this and want to live by the consequences? Do we really want to move out with Jesus from the confinement of all interior and exterior prisons and pay with our lives the price for such liberation, by leaving behind forever life-as-we-have-known-it? Or are we yet again going to allow fears of all kinds to make us retreat into positions of self-defense, accusation, and violence, hoping to suppress and destroy "out there" what we really most fear "in here", within our own hearts? Surely these anxiety-driven priests and elders so fear the possibility of a "tumult" among the people only because they look at the world and judge it from the midst of the tumult of passions already seething in their own hearts.

Our astonishment should be intense at realizing how well the religious leaders' intent to suppress and kill harmonizes with Jesus' intent to allow himself to be handed over and crucified. In anticipation of all literal violence, Jesus refuses to be drawn into the sphere of his opponents' hatred and recrimination, which aim at maintaining influence and power. Jesus' integrity is such that he will not descend to their level even if it costs him his life! Jesus does not *desire* to die; he does not *desire* to suffer; but he is willing to pay the price of extreme suffering and a most cruel death *if* that deed of self-surrender will somehow drain the venom of the world's hatred—not only the hatred presently directed at himself but the universal hatred of human beings for one another and for God. Where human beings victimize one another, God offers himself as victim in the person of his beloved Son. Jesus wants the absolute purity and indestructibility of his love to count for more, in the sight of his Father, than all the colossal exertions of haters, which will be neutralized at the touch of his precious Blood.

The present passage is the fulfillment, in real time, of the prophecy Jesus entrusted to his disciples in the episode involving Zebedee's wife and their sons, when he said: "Behold, we are going up to Jerusalem; and the Son of man will be delivered to the chief priests and scribes, and they will condemn him to death, and deliver him to the Gentiles to be mocked and scourged and crucified, and he will be raised on the third day" (20:18–19). At that time, Jesus not only proclaimed the prophecy as a warning and instruction for his disciples, but he concluded the occasion by making a comparison between his own kind of rule as King and the manner in which the great of this world exercise their power: "You know that the rulers of the Gentiles lord it over them, and their great men exercise authority over them. It shall not be so among you; but whoever would be great among you must be your servant, and whoever would be first among you must be your slave; even as the Son of man came not to be served but to serve, and to give his life as a ransom for many" (20:25–28). Obviously, these words of Jesus are crucial for understanding the meaning of his whole life, particularly the Passion.

Jesus stands human logic on its head by saying that precisely the one holding greatest authority and power must use these for the benefit of all rather than for self-gain; and he extends universally what God does in his creation and what he, Jesus, will now do in his Passion, so that the divine principle of loving service is proclaimed to be henceforth the moving force and wellspring of *all* human activity as well, beginning with the disciples. While in chapter 20 he said that "the Son of man *will be* delivered . . . to be mocked and scourged and crucified, and he *will be* raised on the third day", he now says that already he "*is being* delivered to be crucified", in the ongoing present tense. And it is ominous that now the reference to the Resurrection is missing, as if, with the reality of the Passion flooding his consciousness, long-range vision is no longer possible.

Above all, the earlier prophecy in chapter 20 not only states the fact of the impending suffering and death, but also gives a precious theological rationale for its deepest meaning: "The Son of man came not to be served but to serve, and to give his life as a ransom for many." The great *parádosis* ("handing-over" or "delivery" or "betrayal") of the Son of man by sinners is possible only because he, on his own volition, "came . . . to give his life as a ransom". No amount of plotting and conniving on the leaders' part would have been of any avail unless Jesus had first walked freely into their midst, consciously and deliberately making himself vulnerable to all their hatred and fear. Perhaps the most succinct possible summary of the Good News of Christianity would be this formula from the lips of Jesus: I HAVE COME TO GIVE MY LIFE. Deliberate vulnerability, which is the opposite of self-defense, is Jesus' chosen means to give himself, as is always the case where love is concerned.

Jesus' passionate ethos of self-giving so runs counter to the reptilian instincts of fallen human nature that—we cannot repeat it often enough—Jesus can be handed over to death as the seemingly *passive* plaything of scorners solely because he has first decided to come into their midst, has first willingly, deliberately, indeed, *actively* made himself available to both men's hatred and their love, has first entered the messy drama of our lives in order to give his life as a ransom for us. Imagine finding one's JOY in such a prospect! Yet so it was with Jesus, "the pioneer and perfecter of our faith, who for the joy that was set before him endured the cross, despising the shame" (Heb 12:2). In planning and executing the entrapment and death of Jesus, the leaders of both Israel and the nations may think they are but carrying out their own hearts' desires, whereas in fact God is using the evil within them as an instrument to redeem the world.

The pivot that allows the pendulum of redemption to swing over fully and transform *betrayal* into *ransom* is nothing other than Jesus' wholly free surrender of himself into our hands, in obedience to his Father. Jesus wants us, too, to be free; he wishes to liberate us so that we come out of the dungeons of our hearts, exactly as prone to fear and hatred and blindness as are the hearts of these priests and elders who conspire to kill Jesus. At the very moment when he is affirming the necessity of his Passion, the Lord drives the spike of his love deep into our hearts, when he says: "Whoever would be great among you must be your servant, and whoever would be first among you must be your slave" (20:26–27). Jesus never asks us to climb to any heights of accomplishment; he asks us only to serve one another as an extension of his service to us. This is the essence of the Passion: Christ's life poured out all at once as a cosmic transfusion of love and grace.

2. A BEAUTIFUL WORK

The Anointing at Bethany (26:6–13)

26:6   Τοῦ δὲ Ἰησοῦ γενομένου ἐν Βηθανίᾳ
ἐν οἰκίᾳ Σίμωνος τοῦ λεπροῦ

Now when Jesus was at Bethany
in the house of Simon the leper

ON THE THRESHOLD OF THE PASSION, it is significant that Jesus takes refuge with his disciples at Bethany, in the house of one "Simon the Leper". We do not know whether or not Simon has been healed of his leprosy by Jesus, but the important thing is Jesus' choice of associating familiarly with someone who is, or has been, ritually unclean. At once this creates a powerful contrast between Jesus' friends of choice—outcasts of all sorts and people of little social account—and Jesus' enemies, who are the powerful, the famous, and the self-styled "pure".

We cannot avoid seeing an emblematic intention in Matthew's reference to leprosy in his introduction to the Passion narrative. From this point on, the story of Jesus' final days as a mortal will be an unrelenting descent by him through every level of human affliction, malfeasance, and disordered passion, as if he were seeking to assume these as his own burden and malady. In fact, he will perish from such deliberate contamination. The story of the Passion cannot be understood without emphatic reference to the perennial ugliness and destructiveness of sin, and the casual-appearing mention of Simon the Leper is the indirect sounding of this central theological motif. The fact that Jesus seeks out Simon at his house, associates freely and publicly with him, and seems quite at home consorting with human corruption further communicates the manner in which Jesus will do battle with sin: namely, solely through the power of compassionate, cohabiting love. Jesus freely makes himself the victim of the disease he has come to cure in others. That is love's way of delivering the beloved from destruction.

The priests and the elders are his enemies, not because Jesus has made them such, but only because, clutching their self-righteousness, they must compulsively view themselves as already clean, pure, and justified before God and man. They are incapable of seeing the leprosy within, and so they must turn outward with violence and persecute those they consider utterly unlike themselves so as to extend indefinitely, by their exercise of forcible control, the kingdom of their imagined justification. What a relief it must be for Jesus to run from the gathering storm of contempt generated against him in the streets of Jerusalem by the religious leaders and take cover for a while in the home of a hospitable man, an openly flawed human being: a leper!

26:7   προσῆλθεν αὐτῷ γυνὴ ἔχουσα
          ἀλάβαστρον μύρου βαρυτίμου
          καὶ κατέχεεν ἐπὶ τῆς κεφαλῆς αὐτοῦ ἀνακειμένου

*a woman came up to him with an
alabaster flask of very expensive ointment
and she poured it on his head as he reclined [at table]*

WE DO NOT KNOW the physical location where Jesus proclaims his impending suffering to his disciples for this third and last time, but it is probably outdoors. He has just finished speaking to the crowds, which always happens in a public setting because of their numbers, and his words to his disciples are spoken as an aside. We have seen how Jesus' prediction mysteriously unleashes the machinations of the leaders of Israel. From this outdoor setting, public places through which threats and dangers begin to whirl ominously, Matthew takes us, with the sure strategy of the wise narrator, to an indoor scene of hospitality. This alternation in mood between exposed vulnerability and sheltered welcome provides a needed balance, both for Jesus the protagonist and for us the readers. The story of the Passion does not crudely present sorrow upon unremitting sorrow, because the evangelist's chief concern is to illuminate the interior meaning of the drama rather than crush us with calamity.

After briefly sketching the climate of intense animosity around Jesus generated by the religious leaders, Matthew now develops a diametrically contrasting reaction to Jesus by introducing this anonymous woman of Bethany. A succinct preamble presents, first, Jesus' superior knowledge and his serene command of the situation and, then, the chief priests' plotting with murderous intent. We may say that, in that brief prelude, Matthew hints at two opposite ways of utilizing the characteristically male drive to prevail over others.

Jesus shows us how wisdom can triumph over adversity and become a light for others by clarity of vision, interior communion with God, and the willingness to be defeated in the body. This is, in fact, how good prevails over evil: by prizing above everything the good of others rather than one's mere personal survival. We must be willing to become victims if this will give others life. This process, rooted in pure love, is the ultimate in sublimating the male determination to succeed and prevail.

The leaders of the people, on the other hand, exemplify how fear and greed can vitiate to the core initial goodwill and godly formation. Under the thinnest veneer of legitimate authority and religious motivation, these priests and elders are in fact indulging the crassest instincts of male human nature for winning at all costs. Neither their holy priesthood nor their venerable stature as elders nor their formation in the truth of Torah can keep them from scheming, like a pack of barking dogs, against one disarmed rabbi. Their only driving force is the raging desire to blot Jesus out from the face of the earth so that their vanity can triumph unchallenged. Under layers of pious observances and correct protocol (we can almost see the wringing of anxious clerical hands), the occasion plainly showcases the apotheosis of the male reptilian brain, unmitigated by the slightest feminine softness or compassion. Jesus, by contrast, shows how equally male willpower, strength, clarity of purpose, and utter determination can yield in self-giving surrender once a man's heart has wedded the beauty of divine Sophia and no longer lives by appearances and the drive of blind passions.

One can hardly avoid thinking, therefore, that Matthew very much intended to paint the present tableau in his text by a technique of glaring juxtaposition. The phrase in v. 5 about the leaders' fear of a tumult among the people is followed at once by the luminous appearance of this marvelous woman bringing a fragrant and precious balsam with which to anoint the head of a reclining Jesus. Fluid, self-effacing, silent, compassionate womanhood suddenly fills the horizon that until a moment ago was occupied by rigid, high-profile, turbulent males seething with hatred and contempt. It is as if Matthew were telling us: "Look: this too happens in the world. Divine goodness is not universally reviled. Who do you want to be, a powerful elder or this faceless woman—or better, this generous woman whose only face is her deed of love?"

Later on, when Judas leads the priests and elders to the Mount of Olives to betray Jesus into their hands, Jesus will exclaim: "Have you come out as against a robber, with swords and clubs to capture me?" (26:55). In anticipation of this moment of betrayal, and as if to redeem it preemptively, the woman comes out to Jesus bearing, not swords and clubs to wound him, but "an alabaster jar of very expensive ointment" with which to anoint him and salve his still invisible wounds. And after his capture, the soldiers would, "plaiting a crown of thorns, . . . put it on his head" in mockery of his alleged kingship (27:29), whereas the woman instead pours all the sweet-smelling oil on his head in worshipful confession of his eternal dominion (cf. 1 Sam 15:1). Thus Matthew shows us that Jesus came into the world to be either violently rejected or lovingly adored, and there seems to be no third possibility.

Jesus receives this outpouring of devotion from the woman as he *reclines* (ἀνακειμένου) at table in Simon's house. Many translations simply see him as *seated* there, in Western style; but in the ancient Middle East, people normally ate in a reclining position, which connotes a relaxed and convivial atmosphere. In our context, it also suggests Jesus' willing availability and receptivity to the actions of others.

He came to mingle with us on our own turf, so to speak, thus making himself susceptible to all manner of treatment. In him, God has delivered himself into our hands through a human body and emotions and needs like our own. By preference, he came to celebrate with us, to eat, speak, and interact with us as friends do. And yet he cannot invite such happy association unless he also leaves himself open to attack and bitter disappointment—open, that is, to the full range of human reactions. His very presence seems to imply: "I am here. I have gladly chosen to come and be with you. I am as vulnerable as you are, indeed, more so since I am incapable of violence. So what will you now do to me and with me?" The full mystery of God's chosen humanity is contained in the gesture of Jesus *reclining* at our table to share whatever food we serve him.

This anointing woman's total anonymity points, perhaps, not so much to any humility on her part as it does to Matthew's desire to make her a universal type of devotion to Jesus. Nor do we know anything about her interior motivation in performing this act. There is no hint that she is a sinner seeking forgiveness or a troubled mother seeking her sick child's cure. What we have is only the unexpectedness of the act itself, which makes it shine all the more brilliantly over the horizon of the Gospel as the bright light of heart-melting, feminine devotion soaring high above the harsh darkness of male aggression and forever enthroning, within our hierarchical awareness, the primacy of love. And her profound and unbroken silence adds yet another level of meaning. She is a human being who possesses so unified a personhood that she can express everything that informs her deepest heart in one great symbolic action, without any need for explanatory words.

Indeed, the woman's action has a double prophetic signification: it points forward both to the *shedding* of Jesus' blood at his death and to the awe-filled *worship* that should spring spontaneously from every creature in the presence of its Creator and Redeemer. The material outpouring of the precious ointment symbolizes both the future flowing of Jesus' blood upon the ground of Golgotha and the woman's own present effusion of adoring love upon his whole person. The occasion, furthermore, is iconoclastic, because only male prophets were sent in Israel to single out and anoint kings on God's behalf, as in the case of Samuel (1 Sam 9:16; 16:3, 12). Here, by contrast, it is an ordinary woman of the people who performs that prophetic function, and not upon just any king of Israel, but upon the person of no less than the eternal King of kings himself!

Considering all of this, we probably do best to see in this mysterious woman at the leper's house, appearing suddenly out of nowhere, the veiled figure of the Church, always waiting upon her Lord from the wings of world history as Jesus advances through time, both confronting the forces of destruction and seeking out those who care to recline at the eucharistic table with him so as to help him usher in the Kingdom. Origen taught us long ago that, wherever in Scripture we recognize an image of the Church, we must by extension also identify there a figure of the individual soul, always seeking out her Beloved single-mindedly in the multitude, so as to attend "without distraction" upon the desires of her Lord and Bridegroom (cf. Song 3:1–4; 1 Cor 7:35).

א

26:8   ἰδόντες δὲ οἱ μαθηταὶ ἠγανάκτησαν λέγοντες·
         Εἰς τί ἡ ἀπώλεια αὕτη;
         ἐδύνατο γὰρ τοῦτο πραθῆναι πολλοῦ
         καὶ δοθῆναι πτωχοῖς

But when the disciples saw it, they were indignant, saying,
"Why this waste?"
for this might have been sold for a large sum,
and given to the poor

NOT JESUS' ENEMIES and not Simon the Leper, but Jesus' own disciples are the ones who object in indignant terms to the "waste" of the balsam. Before their very eyes this reckless woman has, admittedly, squandered a fortune! To what purpose? Perhaps, as far as typical character pairings go, mankind could be divided into the Wasters and the Savers. The "wasters" get a thrill out of squandering, whether money, food, words, affections, or possessions, while the "savers" see intrinsic virtue in the habit of accounting for every penny spent and every compliment given. For these, everything must be used to good purpose, while for the wasters, life is about enjoyment through liberal outpouring. Savers tend to be highly rational types who specialize in measuring and judging, while wasters are careless and fascinated by the boundless.

Character types are not bad or good; they just are. As always, the determining factor is the particular use to which a characteristic tendency is put. If a drunkard of a father squanders his week's earnings at the corner bar while his children go hungry, that is very culpable wastefulness. However, contrast with this the older brother's attitude in the Parable of the Prodigal Son. Out of solid moral reasons, he refuses to "waste" his heart's joy celebrating his younger brother's return because he, the elder, has, after all, been steadily dutiful and responsible while his wastrel of a brother deserves all the woes he has endured. Is this not the sort of economizing that squelches all human feeling and sees human life as one vast accounting ledger?

Seeing only the material loss in the woman's generous deed, Jesus' disciples are blind to its beauty and deeper significance. The pragmatist will often be blind to beauty, since he considers nothing to be worthwhile for its own sake. Everything must have a purposeful use. The great virtue of the romantic "waster", on the other hand, is that, given the right occasion and stimulus, he will be able to leap spontaneously to a more sublime level of existence, while the "saver" will tend to be paralyzed by a whole network of calculations. Quite clearly the prodigal woman of this episode loved Jesus more than did his own disciples, with an intensity of devotion and an abandonment of heart that know no bounds and that are metaphorically expressed in the outpouring of the ointment. The woman was clearly not acting out of a blind, insurmountable impulse to squander; rather, when it came to matters of love, she enjoyed a rationality far superior to that of the accountant since she was able to perform an act of homage that precisely corresponded to the infinite Beauty of the object of her adoration: Jesus, the Son of God. The interior *logos* within her that impelled her to perform this deed was profoundly responding to the eternal Logos incarnate in Jesus. Who more than Jesus deserves being loved and adored for his own sake, without any further considerations?

The apparently *reckless* and unmeasured outpouring of oil resulted quite fittingly from the fact that the woman was clairvoyantly *reckoning* the true nature of the man before her, whom her faith sought out as an ardent bride looks madly for her bridegroom. She intuited that there can be no penny-pinching where God is concerned but only a wholesale outpouring of all the substance of her being, in grateful and just response to how God lavishly poured himself out in creation and was about to do again in the flowing blood of his Son. The woman was at once poet and mystic, managing to pour out her whole life and her very being in one inexhaustibly beautiful act of praise and self-surrender.

The "alabaster jar of very expensive ointment" is a wonderfully apt symbol for these invisible spiritual realities. The fragrant balsam is "very expensive" because such an unguent was work-intensively produced in the ancient world from rare exotic plants that had to be imported with great difficulty from distant countries. Thus, the precious oil signifies a person's capacity for *love*, since love is the greatest treasure one possesses and represents the distillation of one's whole history and personality. And its sudden and total outpouring over the head of Jesus conveys the sweet violence of a love that holds nothing back for itself but bestows the whole being of the adorer all at once upon the beloved.

Love desires nothing less than to overwhelm the beloved suddenly and thoroughly with itself, to drown the beloved in the tide of this impetuous outpouring of self. We saw how Jesus crucially weakened the thrust of his enemies' plotting and even his death's sting (1 Cor 15:55) by himself anticipating with majestic serenity the necessity of his demise. Similarly, the woman's magnificent homage at this strategic moment, too, now infuses the sufferings of the coming Passion with all the fragrant tenderness of love. Her emblematic deed, writ large over the threshold of the Passion, gives us an interpretive key with which to unlock the interior, luminous, life-bringing meaning of events that, viewed only from the outside and judged with strict rationality, would appear to amount to nothing but horror, pain, betrayal, and shameful failure. Moreover, the woman's profuse anointing with healing balm presages the ultimately glorious destiny of Christ's wounds. The horrendous gashes, holes, and lacerations on Jesus' body will eventually be glorious and life-giving because they are willingly received by him out of immortal love, and also because they are in turn willingly embraced out of imperfect love by certain human beings who, like this woman, nonetheless understand and cling with all their might to the Mystery of a Suffering God.

The word Matthew uses that we translate as "waste" is *apôleia*, which in fact means "destruction" or "total loss". Such intensity of meaning is important to convey the totality of the woman's deed: she spares nothing for another occasion, and most likely she will never again have such precious unguent in her possession. She has exhausted all her riches on Jesus, in one shot. This scandalizes the disciples, and their reaction makes us wonder about their worth as disciples at this point in the story. The Greek word for "being indignant" here, ἠγανάκτησαν (*êganáktêsan*), also connotes other strong negative emotions like irritation, anger, vexation, and discontent. It derives from the word ἄγαν (*ágan*), which means "too much". The woman's deed is simply "too much" for the disciples, reflecting the way that Jesus himself is "too much" for most, beginning with his own relatives and townspeople (Mk 3:20–22). The human superabundance of her action corresponds perfectly to the divine Abundance that is Jesus (Col 2:9–10).

The disciples have thus far in this episode been silent, even through Jesus' prediction of his suffering; perhaps they even yawned at that, being used by now to the Master uttering so many weighty and strange-sounding things. But when they actually *see* a valuable commodity being spilled on the ground, then their vexed reaction begins revealing, despite themselves, something of their interior state. The reaction appears so instantaneous and visceral that one is a little suspicious of the high-minded explanation they offer for it: "This ointment might have been sold for a large sum, and given to the poor." The fact is that they have not objected or reacted in any way to Jesus' announcement of the certainty of his impending suffering and crucifixion, and yet they jump up with angry disapproval when they witness a gesture of overwhelming admiration performed in their Master's honor, on his very body. Are they perhaps also shocked by the woman's presumption of intimacy with the Lord? Better by far Peter's reaction to Jesus' first prediction of the Passion: "God forbid, Lord! This shall never happen to you" (16:22), which, though rebellious and lacking in theological depth, is at least rich in human fidelity and empathy. Yes, there is something very wrong with the disciples' irate reaction to the woman, something very ungenerous, close-minded, servile.

Who are they, anyway, to decide how this woman should use what belongs to her, knowing nothing of her heart's predilections? Are they so angry precisely because she is so free and generous with her possessions, in the image of God himself (20:15)? Do they feel at a loss before any form of lavish generosity, since they themselves are so niggardly? Those who are too serious about earthly goods—whether they actually possess them or not—compulsively disdain anyone who appears unaccountably free from material attachments and anxieties and who concretely uses such goods as what they truly are: never ends in themselves, but only means to promote human well-being and communion in love.

The upset disciples complain of the woman's alleged "wastefulness", convinced that an excellent opportunity has been missed for a business transaction that could have benefited the poor. The precious ointment should have been transmuted by sensible planning into social works of "charity" rather than into something as intangible and elusive as a single, fleeting act of praise, adoration, and prophecy. Similar objections are often made in the Church against contemplatives, not only by the uninformed, but also by earnest Christians engaged in an ethos of social service. "Why do monks and nuns waste their lives, dedicated exclusively to prayer in the solitude of their monasteries, when they could both pray *and* minister to the needs of the poor and disadvantaged?" The charitable zeal of such objecting Christians, so sincere and ardent for the most part, is nonetheless theologically imbalanced because it fails to note the uniqueness of the person of Jesus Christ and the hierarchy of values that such uniqueness necessarily stamps on the Christian's manner of arranging his life and prioritizing his activities.

In this connection, let us widen our perspective a little. The Jesus who here so readily accepts the extraordinary homage of this woman and who praises her so extravagantly against his disciples is the same Jesus who just a few verses back preached his apocalyptic vision of the Final Judgment. At this divine reckoning, Jesus affirmed, some would be condemned precisely for failing to identify the poor in their midst with the person of the eternal and universal King: "For I was hungry and you gave me no food, I was thirsty and you gave me no drink. . . . As you did it not to one of the least of these, you did it not to me" (25:42, 45). Eternal separation from God and his life of bliss can result from culpably ignoring the intrinsic relationship between the Son of God and needy human beings. Now, it would appear that the so-called "social gospel" could not be preached in more forcible terms than these. The doctrine comes from the lips of Jesus himself speaking as King and Judge and establishes a truly earth-shaking mystical identification between the Savior and every member of suffering mankind. The astounding intuition of ancient Eastern mysticism, *You are I*, is here recast dynamically by Jesus into a Christian triangulation: the *You* addressed by Christ is referred away from Christ's own person to the *They* of Christ's least ones. *They are I*, Christ is saying, and if *You want to be I*, then *You must serve Them-Me* in their real human flesh.

This being so, we may ask why, in the present scene, Jesus was not motivated by the same objection as his disciples? Should he not have kept the woman from wasting the balsam by grabbing her by the arm as she raised the flask over his head and exclaiming: "Stop, woman! You are well-intentioned but foolishly impulsive! Don't you know you can do far better than perform a merely symbolic gesture for me? I thank you for the thought, but my disciples and I know far better than you to what greater use we can put your precious ointment. We can sell it for much money and with the proceeds relieve at least some of the needs of some of our poor. Let us take over from here, and you go back to your generous prayers. After all, I said I would judge you, not on extravagant symbolic gestures to my person, which produce nothing practical, but rather on your concrete deeds to help the needy."

Could we perhaps here have an instance either of Jesus mysteriously contradicting himself or of the evangelist not realizing in his final redaction that a serious inconsistency has slipped by him in the doctrines presented by his Gospel text?

26:10–11   Τί κόπους παρέχετε τῇ γυναικί;
              ἔργον γὰρ καλὸν ἠργάσατο εἰς ἐμέ·
              πάντοτε γὰρ τοὺς πτωχοὺς ἔχετε μεθ᾽ ἑαυτῶν,
              ἐμὲ δὲ οὐ πάντοτε ἔχετε

Why do you trouble the woman?
For she has done a beautiful work to me:
for you always have the poor with you,
but you will not always have me

MATTHEW INTRODUCES this speech of Jesus to his disciples with the words, "Jesus, aware of [their disapproval], said to them. . . ." The disciples have apparently been muttering their disgruntlement to one another under their breath as they looked on while the woman performed her act of homage. Their duplicity in objecting covertly and her single-mindedness in adoring openly stand in eloquent contrast. What strikes us at once when looking at the structure of this passage is the great amount of text Matthew devotes to Jesus' reaction to his disciples' objection and to the teaching he takes occasion to impart to them by interpreting the woman's deed.

In the RSV, the introduction to the episode and the woman's deed itself take up forty words. The disciples' reaction is told in a mere thirty words, of which only twenty are their own and ten the narrator's. But Jesus' reply to their objection occupies the rest of the text and uses eighty-two words, all in first-person discourse. This means that the passage is highly didactic: Jesus speaks four words for every one the disciples whisper. And yet Jesus' doctrine here is not a typical missionary instruction or sending-forth speech such as we have heard before and will hear again. Rather, Jesus explains the spiritual meaning of a surprising symbolic deed. In doing so, he utters a mystical teaching about the believer's devotion of heart to himself that culminates in a wholly unexpected pronouncement about the place of contemplative devotion in the Gospel of the Kingdom. Jesus puts to excellent use, for our benefit, not only the woman's silent and extravagant deed but also his disciples' grumbling reaction to it.

Jesus' reply to his disciples' objection begins with the question,

"Why do you trouble the woman?", which he directly juxtaposes to their own opening question, "Why this waste?" If his followers are taken aback by the spectacle of the woman's prodigality, which is compounded by Jesus' approving acceptance of the same, Jesus in turn is surprised by that reaction on the part of his chosen friends. Today's impasse is going to teach them something about their Teacher and themselves that they apparently did not know before. While the disciples cannot help criticizing the woman, Jesus will do nothing but heap praise on her. We cannot repeat often enough that the Gospel can never be reduced to Jesus imparting moral teaching, even of the truest and most sublime kind. Rather, conflicts like the present one open the way for the possibility of a deeper relationship between disciple and Teacher.

The heart of Jesus' teaching concerning godly attitudes and behavior is actually *himself*, since his primary function in coming among us is not to act as a moralist but to reveal his Father by revealing himself through word and deed. By revealing the Father through every incident, word, and gesture of his life, Jesus is most fundamentally revealing the fact that God, in himself, is Love Relation and that everything else in Christianity flows from this truth. We cannot know how to interpret and live Jesus' teachings without, first, understanding something about *who Jesus is* and then, crucially, by *coming into a living symbiosis with him*. We can do what Jesus teaches only as a result of entering into an intimate union with his Divine Person, a union so intimate that it transforms its subject into a living member of Christ's very Body.

This reality is already implied toward the beginning of Matthew's Gospel when, in concluding the Sermon on the Mount, Jesus utters the impossible-sounding injunction: "You, therefore, must be perfect, as your heavenly Father is perfect" (5:48). Such perfection, quite earnestly promoted by Jesus, cannot be primarily sought through moral effort, though of course this, too, is essential; rather, it must be received through filiation, by our being adopted in Christ as true children of his heavenly Father. Very flawed creatures though we are, we can embody and live the goodness of the Father only by becoming his sons in the one Son, second Person of the Blessed Trinity and also human Son of Mary. Only if Jesus' divine sonship is extended to us as gift, only if we then willingly participate in it, can we hope to be truly Christians in the strict sense of the Gospel: that is, *other*

Christs possessing through gifted participation all of Jesus' faculties and sharing in his full destiny of both humiliation and glory.

In the light of these uniquely Christian truths, we are now in a better position to unravel the reasons for Jesus' conflict with his own disciples. We may be surprised, on the one hand, that, after three years of intense and constant companionship, the disciples should still be so thoroughly in the dark at the very threshold of the Passion, a mere few days before his death, concerning Jesus' person and deepest mission. On the other hand, the Mystery toward which he has been gently urging them—namely, the eternal God's tangibility in Jesus—is indeed counter-intuitive, iconoclastic, pregnant with disturbing consequences. We ought, therefore, to take our cue from Jesus' own patience with his disciples and realize that the act of faith that is growing within them can only come to full fruition *after* the events of the Passion and the Resurrection. Only Christ's triumph over death can reveal his full glory and the total work of the Father in him.

Let us return, then, to the apparent contradiction between Jesus' reproach to his disciples over the woman's action and his teaching about the nature of the Last Judgment in chapter 25. If Jesus can proclaim his self-identification with the poorest of the poor in the first place, it is only because he is simultaneously the glorious Lord of the universe *and* a God who has chosen the path of humiliation to redeem those he loves. God is so truly Love that in his little ones he suffers more than they do precisely because he alone can suffer the afflictions of all. The needy are "these least of my brothers" because the Son of God has first made himself their brother and chosen to share in their littleness so as to lift them up with himself into his native place of glory in his Father's bosom. Only God can do this. And, consequently, only a vision of faith that first recognizes Jesus' divine identity and then adores with ardent love the Son of God present in Jesus of Nazareth enables a Christian to tend with divine energy, in a dynamic overflow of love, to the needs of Jesus' little ones. Only the relationship with Jesus that faith's recognition and adoration of God in Jesus generate can nourish a person so forcefully that he can abide unflinchingly in works of self-spending practical charity. Any form of social activity, no matter how noble and generous, that is not rooted in the Church's faith in Christ's adorable divinity will eventually peter out. As I have said, Jesus' teaching of self-identification with the poor in Matthew 25:31–46 is not the so-called "social gospel"; it is *The Gospel* pure and simple, of which there is only one, and it is mystical in nature. Its teaching consists of two inseparable aspects: the foundation (Jesus-in-himself) and the application (Jesus-in-others).

"Why do you trouble the woman? For she has done a beautiful [work][1] *to me*": In accepting with spontaneous approval the rightness of the woman's "wasteful" deed done to himself, Jesus is in fact instilling into his followers the necessary hierarchy, or "sacred order", that by nature exists between right worship (*orthodoxy*) and right ministry (*orthopraxis*). Only the person who worships God as God—that is, absolutely, "with all your heart, and with all your soul, and with all your might" (Deut 6:5)—will as a result be able to love his neighbor and minister to him in his need according to the mind of God.

Christ's self-identification with the least of his brethren is not a matter of sentimentality or arbitrary choice on his part; it is one of the weightiest consequences of the Incarnation. Only a God who assumed human flesh and blood can suffer in the afflicted and, hence, be ministered to and comforted in the afflicted. Genuinely Christian works of charity are inseparable from concrete acts of worship of Christ as God, both in the solitude of one's soul and in the mystery of the Eucharist and the liturgy. The Christian must live with the gaze of his heart and the longing of his soul permanently fixed on Christ, and it is this habitual adherence to the Person of Christ in himself that alone will enable him to discover the presence of Christ in all people as well. Christ-in-himself necessarily comes before Christ-in-others in the sacred order of Christian life, because neither the substance nor the message of Christianity can ever be reduced to social activism through works of charity, as if this were the absolute goal and all else (prayer, contemplation, liturgical worship, sacred reading) mere "scaffolding". Of the relationship between the first two commandments, Jesus said to the lawyer: "And a second is like it, You shall love your neighbor as yourself" (22:39). Jesus did not collapse the

---

[1] With the Latin Vulgate (*opus bonum*), NJB, and a number of other versions, I prefer to translate ἔργον literally as "a work" rather than as "a thing" (RSV). This precision could make a difference in explaining the Catholic doctrine of the relationship between faith and works, especially in this mystical context. Jesus is defending a *work* done to him for his own sake as being praiseworthy, even over certain exterior *works* done for the sake of the poor. Far more than a "nice gesture" seems to be involved.

two commandments into one; he said that the second commandment is "like" the first insofar as they both deal with intense devotion of the heart.

The two first commandments are indeed inseparable, since "if any one says, 'I love God,' and hates his brother, he is a liar" (1 Jn 4:20). Nevertheless, in Jewish terms, it would be an act of great idolatry to reduce the first commandment to the second, to make the love of God subservient to the love of man, little more than an "inspiration" for it, as if the only role of God in my life were to spur my conscience to human kindness. The act of loving one's brother may be *proof* of loving God, but the *spiritual capacity and energy* required to love one's brother well can only derive from the primordial act of loving God as God. The order of the soul's acts should reflect the objective order and nature of reality. The Christian doctrine that "God is love" (1 Jn 4:8), and that this God gave his life for us, is not a mere intellectual formula used by the Church as a catalyst to impel people to practice equally heroic love for one another.

The Christian doctrine of God is, in fact, of interest only insofar as it "takes flesh" and becomes actualized and lived through the worship of God in the Sacred Liturgy, and this worship culminates in the reception of Holy Communion, which unites the person of the worshipper to the Person of the Savior. Only subsequently, after Christ has "taken flesh" in me, can my love, now inseparably mine and Christ's, go out to take flesh in another. The classic text in modern times concerning the supremacy of worship over all other activities in Christian life is this passage from the Constitution on the Sacred Liturgy of the Second Vatican Council, which defines the public prayer of the Church as both the source from which all else flows and the goal toward which all else leads:

> The liturgy is the *summit* toward which the activity of the Church is directed; at the same time it is the *font* from which all her power flows. For the aim and object of apostolic works is that all who are made sons of God by faith and baptism should come together to praise God in the midst of His Church, to take part in the sacrifice, and to eat the Lord's supper.[2]

[2] Vatican Council II, Constitution on the Sacred Liturgy *Sacrosanctum Concilium* (December 4, 1963), 10. Italics mine.

The intensely personal relationship Jesus envisions and desires with each of us is very exactly conveyed in his statement, "She has done a beautiful work to me." Compared to the simplicity of this utterance, and the feelings of deep satisfaction and gratitude on Jesus' part that it communicates, all efforts to clarify and justify Jesus' teaching to his disciples appear heavy-handed and plodding. The gratitude and pleasure radiating here from Jesus' Heart, as expressed in his very few words, must have been beaming from his face as he spoke, and this light of grateful acceptance before the whole world, streaming from Jesus' person, must have overwhelmed the woman with an eternal joy.

Jesus calls her deed "a beautiful work". We have seen before that the Greek word *kalón* really means "good" and "beautiful" at the same time. Language sometimes expresses deep ontological intuitions on the part of a people, and this is one such instance: the intuition that only that which is intrinsically "good" can be truly and necessarily "beautiful". According to one's school of philosophy, beauty may be defined as the splendor of either the good or the true. Though some translations have "a good deed" or "a good thing" here, I would insist on both "beautiful" and "work". Beauty's essence is that it can be perceived, and that is why it is conceived as a "splendor" that manifests to the senses a hidden mystery of goodness and truth. The woman's deed is a work, performed in public and at great expense to herself, whereby she bestows on the person of Jesus, with the whole world as witness, the symbolic equivalent of her entire being. This is why I have likened the action to liturgical worship, which invites the believer to join the adoration of God in Christ performed by the Church his Bride. Adoration of God is the most beautiful of human acts precisely because, in language and gesture adequate to the human reality, we acknowledge God's infinite Being and freely return to him our life and our very own being.

This perceivable interplay of elements, in which created realities with total freedom render full justice to the actual order of things divine and human and in which creatures in return receive blessing upon blessing from the Creator: such is the specific *beauty* of the act of worship. I suggest that this attitude is what informed our generous woman's very succinct and profound action and also what elicited Jesus' praise. Jesus calls it a "work", and I think the word is important to guarantee the full weight of what worship entails. "Liturgy", in fact, literally means "public work". Both the disciples and Jesus here compare what the woman has done to a work of charity performed in benefit of the poor. We moderns tend to lend greater importance to "works" that require visible effort and accomplish something quantitative, and we thus radically undervalue (or altogether discount from the category of "work") any deed that is merely symbolic or too spiritual. For the very same reason, we have come to banish transcendental beauty from our midst, since beauty simply *is* and produces nothing. Reacting against this utilitarian tendency, Søren Kierkegaard titled one of his books *Works of Love*, in which he deals with "works" that are realized only within the sanctuary of the soul or as part of a spiritual exchange between persons. The principle is thoroughly biblical, best summarized by Jesus himself. To the question: "What must we do, to be doing the works of God?" he replied without hesitation: "This is the work of God, that you believe in him whom he has sent" (Jn 6:28–29). Is this not precisely what the woman with the jar of ointment is doing?

Indeed, her "work" is to believe in Jesus and in who Jesus is, not only mentally, in the abstract, but enacting her faith through a concrete *work* of adoration as she clings to Jesus with her whole being. Jesus' words thus come as a great corrective because he is here teaching his disciples that there are supreme works of the human spirit that have nothing to do with external or measurable accomplishments. On this particular day, the disciples are learning many essential things about love and beauty and devotion of heart. They are perhaps discovering for the first time the deeper and wondrous identity of someone they thought they already knew well. They are entering at last into the depths of the mystery of the Person of Jesus.

There is yet another reason why the woman's work is "beautiful": through it she brings to fruition the existential human yearning that each of us bears deep in our person to surrender ourselves wholly to another in one great act of exhaustive love. Just as beauty beams forth from an act of worship in which a creature forcefully expresses attunement to the magnificence of the Creator, so too that same beauty dazzles us as it also reveals the interior abyss of love that constitutes our inmost being as living images of God. Ecstatic beauty is a byproduct of human nature attaining its transcendental fullness.

In the face of the splendor emanating from the woman and her beautiful work, how shortsighted and superficial the disciples' calculating objection now appears! It is short-sighted because, as Vatican II teaches, the proper goal of every apostolic work is not simply to enlighten ignorance or relieve human misery but, rather, to bring all God's children to intimate communion with God in Christ through worship. The disciples' choice of a work of practical social assistance *against* an act of worship wholly forgets the perennial goal of Christian life. In fact, it reduces truly Christian charity to mere social activism. If we want to see plainly the difference between the two, we should look to a St. Teresa of Calcutta and her Missionaries of Charity. Although second to none in their ultra-personal service to the poorest of the poor, these sisters spend several hours before dawn every day communing silently with the glorious Christ in their hearts and in the Eucharist before going out into the streets to minister to the suffering Christ, their Bridegroom, in his mystical concealment under layers of rags, infection, and lice. And the disciples' objection is woefully superficial as well because it fails to see *beauty* as a necessary dimension of human and Christian fulfillment, beauty as the transcendental radiance flowing profusely from wherever Christ is present and confessed.

"For you always have the poor with you, but you will not always have me": As Jesus develops his thought, he proceeds from the beauty of the act in itself to its specific beauty and worth in these particular circumstances, that is, as a preamble to the coming Passion. Jesus, in other words, anchors the meaning of the woman's deed in the historical unfolding of his Paschal Mystery. The contrast Jesus makes between the ever-present poor and the uniqueness of his own presence at this moment of history underscores the radical difference in kind between the socio-economic and the mystical planes of existence. The statement clearly hearkens back to an earlier passage in Matthew: "Can the wedding guests mourn as long as the Bridegroom is with them? The days will come, when the bridegroom is taken away from them, and then they will fast" (9:15). He, the Bridegroom, will be taken away from them by the whirlwind of the Passion, and then they will not have him any longer. Both fasting and almsgiving are traditional Jewish devotional practices, and they are beneficial as commanded by God. Jesus never objects to either; in fact, he promotes them both, along with prayer, as continuing validly into faithful Christian lives of devotion. However, his presence on earth as God's Son so radically transforms both the meaning and the practice of Torah and all its precepts that sometimes the traditions must be put in abeyance in order to manifest the more boldly and unequivocally where the source of ultimate life and meaning now lies. The disciples have blindly pitted a deed of social almsgiving against a deed of loving adoration. It is this dichotomized thinking that reveals their obtuseness and lack of understanding concerning their Master's identity.

The unequivocal Source of ultimate life and meaning in the New Testament is, of course, the person of Christ Jesus the Lord, "for in him the whole fulness of deity dwells bodily, and you have come to fulness of life in him" (Col 2:9–10). If what Paul writes here to the Colossians is true, for what other source of life or meaning could we possibly look? Further, Christ is not the transcendental and absolute Source and Meaning in any abstract and disincarnate way but, indeed, as he himself says, as the Bridegroom of the Church (cf. 9:15; Eph 5:23–32). The time of the Passion is precisely the historical moment when Christ's intimate identity as Bridegroom is most clearly revealed, because he "loved the Church and gave himself up for her, that he might sanctify her" (Eph 5:25–26); "in him we have redemption through his blood" (Eph 1:7).

Far from opting for the opposite alternative of the superficial dichotomy set up by his disciples, Jesus in fact suggests how the poor may be better served: precisely by attending to his own person as Bridegroom while he is still visibly present. Note that the Judgment in Matthew 25 is predicated on the visible *absence* of the glorious and powerful King and his visible *presence* in the downtrodden and needy. In the Passion, the historically visible Son of God consummates his total disappearance into human brokenness under the two primary forms of *human anguish* (bodily, mental, social) and *the Eucharist* (broken bread, outpoured wine). Before the Parousia—that is, during the present age of the world—it is in these two manners that Christ is to be sought, served, and adored. We must be nourished in the Eucharist by the Flesh and Blood of the Christ who conquered death in order then to be empowered to minister to the Christ who is still suffering in the wretched of this world.

Jesus teaches his followers that they will never be able to discern the abyss of dignity, beauty, and worth inhabiting every person unless they first enter, through intimate adoration, into the sphere of his own Heart, there to learn the mystery of his deepest identity and redemptive mission. "The poor" are not a socio-economic category of sufferers deserving care and compassion in a stand-offish, condescending way; the poor are the dwelling place of Divinity because Christ chose to make his home in their misery. This is why St. Francis kissed the leper on the lips in an extraordinary act of adoring love. Would that Assisi leper have preferred instead a large sum of spendable money?

א

26:12 βαλοῦσα γὰρ αὕτη τὸ μύρον τοῦτο ἐπὶ τοῦ σώματός μου
πρὸς τὸ ἐνταφιάσαι με ἐποίησεν

In pouring this ointment on my body
she has done it with a view to my burial

WHAT DO THE RESPECTIVE ATTITUDES toward Jesus, on the part of his faithful disciples and on that of the hostile leaders of the people, have in common? They both want to make of Jesus a means to an end rather than acknowledge that he is an end in himself. Judging from the present episode and their objection, the end envisaged by the disciples is to reform society by means of just works on the basis of Jesus' teachings on compassion. The religious and civic leaders, for their part, want to secure their established authority by getting rid of the powerful challenge to it that Jesus embodies. Now, if every human being, already by existing, has such intrinsic worth and dignity that it is immoral to exploit him as an instrument for any ulterior purpose, how much more so is this the case with the incarnate Son of God? Not only the elders but the disciples themselves fail to see the captivating uniqueness of Jesus: they both try to fit him forcibly within their narrow preexisting categories.

91

The first corrective that Jesus' teaching here contains is a powerful warning against turning people into well-meaning projects of any kind. The contrast is glaring between the disciples' appeal to the abstract category of "the poor" and the woman's intensely concrete dealings with the individual person of Jesus of Nazareth. Jesus then meticulously verbalizes her silent intimacy with him by describing her action explicitly as he names one by one the act of pouring, the ointment itself, his own body, and finally his death. Obliquely he thus repeats or extends the prophecy of his impending demise from 26:2, but now infusing the hard fact of death with the loving recognition of the woman's homage. The result is that this verse itself exudes, for those who have the nostrils to scent it, the fragrance of outpoured balm as its language evokes the image of a tender feminine handling of a male corpse that is revered and loved beyond the destruction inflicted by death.

To prepare a beloved corpse for burial implies an act of hope in its resurrection because such preparation implies a "next state" of life. The woman's silent expression of love for Jesus—for this body of his, so soon to be mangled and killed—far outstrips in power and endurance all the cacophonous accusations of the leaders. Thus, she prophesies by her act the ultimate triumph of truth and life over lies and death. In giving his exegesis of the woman's action, Jesus accepts and completes its significance. In their symbiotic vibrancy, it is hard to say where the woman's generous deed ends and Jesus' acceptance and interpretation of it begin. This is precisely what occurs in liturgical worship, in which God is both the object of adoration and the Spirit within the Church energizing such adoration.

In due time, we will see how, when the pious women visit Jesus' burial site, Matthew will give "seeing the tomb" as the reason for their visit (28:1) rather than "anointing the body" (as in Mk 16:1), since in Matthew the anointing has already taken place in the present episode. This anticipated anointing by the woman of Jesus' body before his death, then, fully harmonizes with Jesus' own predictions of his death, which, as we have seen, are a prophetic exercise of his authority and bespeak his sovereign freedom in deliberately handing himself over to the forces of death. We see, therefore, how Jesus' high praise for the woman is wholly bound up with her intuitive understanding of the depths of the Paschal Mystery.

Unlike the disciples, the woman has realized the poignancy of this precise moment in Jesus' life with an accuracy possible only to a woman in love. The noble logic of her love tells her that, if Jesus is about to shed the substance of his being for her, the least she can do is perform this symbolic act of reciprocation. At this moment, Jesus accepts gladly (and in his solitude as one misunderstood is surely consoled by) a lavish act of faith in him that both bows to the painful necessity of his death and yet can also see beyond it. Love does not honor failure as such but has the capacity of detecting, beneath the superficiality of what the world sees as "failure", the enduring substance of the person, that which nothing can destroy.

The self-conscious use by Jesus here of the phrase *my body* is striking in its rarity. It is most instructive to note that this phrase occurs only five times in all four Gospels, and always in the context either of this episode of the balm-bearing woman (26:12; Mk 14:8) or in connection with the institution of the Eucharist (26:26; Mk 14:22; Lk 22:19), which follows shortly after it. On both occasions, Jesus objectifies a part of his person by referring to *my body* in a most unusual way. This is really a very serene way of speaking about his death. He already seems to be bidding his body farewell and expressing his detachment from it, as if he has chosen to make his flesh as incarnate Son common property. Both Jesus' interpretation of this anointing in anticipation of his death and his words of institution of the Eucharist stress the sacrificial culmination of his redemptive mission and the believers' manner of participating in it through worship and sacramental Communion.

Sharing in the life of God through the sacramental ingestion of Jesus' Flesh and Blood thus emerges as the major fruit of Christ's work of redemption, accomplished by him in a sacrifice of reconciliation. We see here that the ultimate goal of the Incarnation of the Logos in God's mind is not solely for him *to assume human nature* in his desire to "experience" it fully and so redeem it from within, as St. Irenæus so boldly states.[3] In addition, the Father intends for

---

[3] "Wherefore [the Spirit] did also descend upon the Son of God, made the Son of man, becoming accustomed in fellowship with Him to dwell in the human race, to rest with human beings, and to dwell in the workmanship of God, working the will of the Father in them, and renewing them from their old habits into the newness of Christ" (*Adversus hæreses*, 3.17.1, in *Ante-Nicene Fathers*, vol. 1, *The Apostolic Fathers, Justin Martyr, Irenaeus*, ed. Alexander Roberts and James Donaldson [1885; Peabody, Mass.: Hendrickson, 1995]), 444.

his Logos *to offer his divine life through his body* as the nourishment of fallen mankind. The Logos uses his enfleshment as the necessary instrument of his self-surrender. From the outset, God has intended both the Passion and the Eucharist that memorializes it.

It is precisely this mystery of redemption that Matthew here dramatizes by showing how Jesus, quite startlingly, *makes his body available* for people to do with it as they wish: either for loving worship in the case of the balm-bearing woman or for murderous contempt in the case of the priests and the elders of the people. But even this contempt-energy is put to good use as God's wisdom preveniently transforms a deed of collective murder, already as it occurs, into a sacrifice of reconciliation and communion. And Jesus very consciously acknowledges and harmonizes both possibilities when he speaks of his body becoming the object of both lavish anointing and mournful burial. The deepest revelation here is Jesus' desire to give all of himself by giving his body. Such is truly the disposition of a bridegroom (Eph 5:23; 1 Cor 7:4).

26:13   ἀμὴν λέγω ὑμῖν, ὅπου ἐὰν
κηρυχθῇ τὸ εὐαγγέλιον τοῦτο ἐν ὅλῳ τῷ κόσμῳ,
λαληθήσεται καὶ ὃ ἐποίησεν αὕτη εἰς μνημόσυνον αὐτῆς

Truly, I say to you, wherever this
gospel is preached in the whole world,
what this woman has done will be told in memory of her

A S IF THIS DENSE EPISODE had not already presented us with enough twists and turns, Jesus has saved his strongest and most surprising affirmation for the end. He cannot seem to say enough to raise ever higher everyone's esteem for this anonymous woman. His teaching to the disciples could have easily concluded with the explanation in v. 12 of the deeper meaning of the woman's action. But no: to conclude, Jesus turns our attention away from himself and back to the woman, exalting her and her deed to the stars in a manner that borders on the scandalous for conventionally pious ears. After he has said his last word, we can practically see the disciples staring at him in slack-jawed unbelief and maybe also a touch of jealous resentment—they who have been known to vie even with one another for first places (20:21).

Jesus introduces his final pronouncement about the woman with the solemn Semitic *amen*, as if the Teacher were trying to assure his disciples of the truth of something that, to them, will be wholly incomprehensible. This emphatic *amen* is far stronger than our "truly" because it is less abstract and refers to something or someone that is completely faithful and trustworthy. Thus, in keeping with its peculiar rhetoric, the Book of Revelation calls the glorified Jesus himself *the Amen*: "The words of the Amen, the faithful and true witness, the beginning of God's creation" (Rev 3:14). These visionary words about Jesus' utterly reliable truthfulness are, in fact, quite relevant to our present passage in Matthew because they stress Jesus' cosmic identity as Lord of creation. This identity, in turn, qualifies Jesus to make the authoritative prophetic announcement that really amounts to a binding royal decree: "Wherever this gospel is preached in the whole world, what she has done will be told in memory of her." In other words, in Jesus' eyes, the woman's deed is no ephemeral act of gushing feminine piety, to be tolerated by more sober male disciples. Indeed, her act and its significance are so monumental that Jesus, in an extraordinary tribute to her, enshrines them as an essential and permanent part of the *evangélion* about him, wherever it is proclaimed. If the core of the Gospel is the coming of God's Kingdom in Jesus the Messiah and the resulting redemption of mankind by our Emmanuel's death and Resurrection, then, in Jesus' view, the woman's action must somehow be intimately related to these mysteries of salvation.

We ought to be alerted, furthermore, to the magnitude of the woman's deed by the simultaneous presence in this one verse of four weighty words: *kêrygma* (proclamation), *evangélion* (gospel), *kósmos* (world) and *mnêmósynon* (remembrance or memory), all key terms in New Testament theology, and they here come prefaced by the solemn *amen*. Referring to the woman, Jesus decrees nothing less than the unheard-of privilege that wherever *he* and his salvation are proclaimed throughout the ages, *she* too will be remembered, along with her role in the story. Her *érgon kalón* ("beautiful work") is thereby added by Jesus to the canon of indispensable New Testament reference points!

We have already considered at some length how, by contrast both to the leaders of the people and to the disciples themselves, the woman represents the dynamic attitude of a faith that is fully attuned to the interior realities of the Christ Mystery. Her act proclaims Jesus in his identity as divine Messiah even as it acknowledges in anticipation the necessity of his sacrificial death. And the specific manner of her worship and confession of faith is the exuberant act of pouring out upon the head and body of Jesus a very precious oil that surely symbolizes the exhaustive totality of her devotion's surrender. Precisely because her faith recognizes the Savior's total gift of himself to mankind, she has invented a unique manner of adequately expressing her own reciprocal gift of herself to him in adoration. The woman's figure thus perfectly encapsulates not only the celebration by man of the Paschal Mystery, but also each person's God-intended participation in it, with the fullness of personal response.

A person can bestow herself on another with such exhaustiveness only because she has first been wholly unified within her being by a transcendental love that is freely received and freely reciprocated. To be truly exhaustive, the act of self-surrender has to be made unanimously by all the human potencies of body, soul, and spirit working in concert. Judging from Jesus' overwhelming testimony to her person and action, the woman does accomplish this all-encompassing unison of surrender to him. If during the Passion the believer will presciently discern in Jesus the fully realized mystery of the Redemption, in this woman, who has now become an essential player in the Gospel story, the believer can already discern a model of the perfect response of faith to Jesus' gift of his own life.

The strict reciprocity that Jesus ascertains between himself and the woman (which is the reciprocity of fulfilled love) clearly emerges when we juxtapose his acknowledgment, "She has done a beautiful [work] to me" (v. 10b) with his present prophecy/decree, "What she has done will be told in memory of her" (v. 13b). The literal Greek makes the point even more emphatically because it uses an identical wording that closely links the two declarations: "She has done a beautiful [work] *unto me (eis emé)*" and "What she has done will be told *unto memory of her (eis mnêmósynon autês)*." The first statement defines the beauty of the work as glorifying Jesus and his death; the second statement returns the glory of that beauty back to the woman with universal validity for all ages to come. The fact that both are statements by Jesus himself and not an interpretation or commentary by the evangelist shows to what degree Jesus wants to make us all partakers of his total mystery. Here, still on the threshold of the Passion, Jesus is speaking as the triumphantly risen Lord of history, making predictions and binding pronouncements and dispensing eternal rewards, even as he sweeps the woman, her act of worship, and everything they represent up into the light of his definitive victory over all forces of destruction. What St. Peter would later say of himself applies fully to this woman already: she is truly "a witness of the sufferings of Christ as well as a partaker in the glory that is to be revealed" (1 Pet 5:1).

"Wherever this gospel is preached in the whole world, what she has done will be told in memory of her": Now, the full extent of the "scandal" that Jesus surely provokes in his disciples by acknowledging and rewarding the woman in this extravagant manner may be measured by the fact that the phrase *in memory* [or *remembrance*] of . . . , which Jesus utters here for the woman's benefit, is used in the whole New Testament only twice: here (and in the parallel text in Mk 14:9) and in connection with the institution of the Eucharist (Lk 22:19; 1 Cor 11:24–25).[4] Both times we hear it as a direct quotation from Jesus' lips. The woman's deed has already been linked to the Eucharist by Jesus' awareness of what she has done to *my body*, and now it is related to the Eucharist a second time by Jesus as he declares the deed most worthy of eternal remembrance. In Luke we read: "And he took bread, and when he had given thanks he broke it and gave it to them, saying, 'This is *my body* which is given for you. *Do this in remembrance of me*' (εἰς τὴν ἐμὴν ἀνάμνησιν)" (Lk 22:19). We may say that the woman has here celebrated with Jesus, by way of prefigurement, a prophetic Eucharist.

---

[4] The phrase μνησθῆναι ἐλέους of Lk 1:54, although translated "in remembrance of his mercy" by the RSV, really only means "mindful of his mercy" or "remembering his mercy" and does not have the solemn sacramental import of the formula *in memory of him*, which uses the weightier noun *mnêmósynon* rather than the more casual verb *mnêsthênai*.

Jesus wants us to remember the deed of this woman to his body in a manner that is closely related to how he wants us to celebrate the Eucharist in memory of him. Indeed, Christian "memory" is not about recalling past events and persons but rather about never losing from sight the paramount truths and events by which we have been saved, all of which truths and events converge on Jesus' death out of love on the Cross and his command that we partake in that sacrifice by celebrating the Eucharist. The balm-bearing woman personifies the believers' essential act of recognition of the Christ Mystery and of their own participation in it through the Eucharist. This totality of the act of faith embodied in the woman in turn merits our everlasting remembrance of her as our model. "Don't forget to love me and worship me as wisely and passionately as she has done", Jesus seems to be telling us.

The Gospel does not set out to promote an ideological program of any kind, even of a religious and doctrinal sort; the Gospel is always promoting patterns of essential *relation between persons* as inspired and ingrained by the Holy Spirit. Foremost among these, of course, is our relationship to God in Christ. But then, necessarily deriving from this relationship, grace creates within us the whole network of interrelationships among people. If the New Testament *kêrygma* culminates in St. Paul's vision of the Church as the Body of Christ, it is precisely because this vision beholds the convergence of all things human and divine in the person of the glorified Savior. And this "convergence" means only one thing: the everlasting communion enjoyed in Christ between the uncreated Trinity, Source of all Relation, and the whole created universe, crowned by God's created image, man.

What Jesus celebrates and enshrines for all time in the icon of the balm-bearing woman, which he holds out persuasively for the conversion and benefit of all his disciples, is the triumph in her of intimate relationship with Jesus over all ideology, whether of the far-right strategies of control of the religious and political establishment (the priests and elders of Israel) or of the far-left dream of rebellious social activism of his own disciples. Abstract ideology with which to fuel social programs is one of the mind's greatest temptations because it identifies God and ultimate meaning with clear, logical ideas. But love knows only relation and soars high above all pragmatic calculation, except insofar as it searches for means to build up and secure authentic and lasting relation.

The very Wisdom of God, Jesus our Lord, chose to reveal and communicate his divine nature, not by founding an ethereal kingdom of crystalline perfections and harmonies, but by descending into the mess of human waywardness and corruption. "For our sake [God] made [Christ] to be sin who knew no sin, so that in him we might become the righteousness of God" (2 Cor 5:21). And St. Paul's resounding reply to the disciples' objection against the woman's "wastefulness" is definitive: "If I give away all I have, and if I deliver my body to be burned, but have not love, I gain nothing" (1 Cor 13:3). In Jesus' eyes, on the contrary, this woman has gained everything because in one stroke she has lavished her entire being on the person of the Savior on his way to crucifixion, as befits the suffering Bridegroom of the Church and of mankind.

3. *PARÁDOSIS:* DEFEAT OR TRIUMPH?

Judas' Agreement to Betray Jesus (26:14–16)

26:14–15a   Τότε πορευθεὶς εἷς τῶν δώδεκα,
ὁ λεγόμενος Ἰούδας Ἰσκαριώτης,
πρὸς τοὺς ἀρχιερεῖς εἶπεν·
Τί θέλετέ μοι δοῦναι, κἀγὼ ὑμῖν παραδώσω αὐτόν;

*Then one of the Twelve,
who was called Judas Iscariot,
went to the chief priests and said,
"What will you give me if I hand him over to you?"*

F OR JUDAS ISCARIOT, the whole unseemly spectacle with this woman is the straw that breaks the camel's back. The loaded phrase *in memory of her*, uttered by Jesus a moment ago and concluding his teaching, propels Judas like a cannonball into the lap of the high priests and all their plotting. Jesus has favored the gratuitous devotion of the heart over pragmatic almsgiving and has rewarded the woman to a scandalous degree by canonizing her deed and its mystical significance. By his decree, she shall henceforth be a requisite part of the Gospel *kêrygma* itself! These two pronouncements by Jesus are more than Judas' hard-nosed realism can bear, and they tilt his will in the direction of brooding betrayal.

Two very negative reactions thus frame the woman's sterling witness. First, we have the disciples' collective grumbling in dismay at the "waste" of such an expensive commodity, spent *merely* on worship, and then Judas' resolute decision that, enough being enough, he must go straightaway to Jesus' enemies in order to silence forever his Teacher's wistful and useless doctrines. For the moment, only the woman is providing the Son of God on earth with an oasis of sympathy; all other active forces around him, whether the leaders of the people or Jesus' own disciples, ominously threaten to engulf his goodness in a black sea of indifference, hatred, and betrayal. It is important, therefore, to see the link between the disciples' more general disapproval of the woman's deed as she performs it and Judas' all too precise action after Jesus' concluding declaration.

We habitually isolate Judas as an "evil traitor" over against the Eleven who, we ponder, might indeed be weak fumblers yet are basically faithful followers of Jesus. Most likely, however, this default reaction is a self-serving strategy on our part to make ourselves feel better. We may admit to wavering at times in our faith like this or that disciple, but we would never admit to communing in the darkness of Judas! And yet Judas does not lack feasible reasons to justify his betrayal of Jesus, the kind of common-sense rationale we ourselves could easily devise. To Judas, Jesus seems oblivious to the dire plight of the Jews, especially the Jewish poor, under Roman oppression. Jesus is simply "too spiritual", not enough of a political activist. Judas thinks he is smarter and more committed than Jesus with respect to the two crucial matters of Jewish emancipation and social utopianism. After all, should not the true Messiah come to establish a Jewish theocracy? Otherwise, what would be the point of bothering about any messiah? The present passage shows that in reality the difference between Judas and the other apostles, in their dissatisfaction with Jesus, is a difference in degree and not in kind. Judas seems, in fact, to possess an admirable boldness and determination for radical action that the rest of them lack. But his decision to betray Jesus in actual deed only concretizes the complaints of the rest. Grumbling is always the first stage of betrayal.

How pathetic to observe that the gateway granting murderous access to the Master's inviolable person did not have to be demolished by his enemies; those doors were, alas, stealthily thrown open from within, by one of Jesus' intimates. Judas is Jesus' personal Trojan horse but gifted by Jesus himself, with all the quirkiness of love, when the Lord freely invited Judas into the inner sanctum of his person. Plenty of evidence tells us that the people's leaders have long been hatching their schemes against Jesus so that their present moves come as no surprise. However, it is an unspeakable shock to witness one of the Master's chosen disciples physically going out from the center of Jesus' intimate circle with the deliberate intent to seek out Jesus' enemies and actually ignite in collusion with them the conflagration of Christ's Passion. How cowardly and devious it is for us Christians to point the finger at the Jews or at the Romans or at whomever, as being responsible for the death of our Lord, when the Gospel shows us clearly that the bridge of betrayal was extended out from the heart of the Lord's chosen band by a proud and disgruntled apostle!

Matthew is careful to construct his successive scenes on the basis of alternating contrasts, aimed at provoking a crisis in the reader by putting him at the crossroads of decision. Everything has impact here, with individual attitude and intentionality expressed not only through spoken words but also through body language. The last episode began with the movement of a woman *coming up to Jesus* (26:7), and the present episode opens with the similar movement of one of the Twelve *going to the chief priests*. What we do with our bodies, and to what purpose we engage them, expresses the deepest commitment of our lives. The anonymous woman uses her soul's discernment and her heart's energy *to go to Jesus* and do him ardent homage, while Judas the chosen apostle engages his whole person *to go to his Lord's enemies* and offer himself as a tool of their hatred. More terrible and devastating than any visceral hatred is the love that turns to bitter contempt. Nor is all ardor necessarily beneficial: the woman's devotion is beautiful because it clings to Jesus with love, while Judas' energy is hideous, indeed Satanic, because it intends the destruction of a trusting friend who also happens to be God Incarnate. This is why monks speak with wise emphasis of the need, before acting, to discern whether a good or a bad zeal is fueling one's motivations.[1]

The woman's deed, furthermore, is so profound, so complete, simple, and transparent that she need not utter a single word to explain it or to pledge her devotion and love. We cannot quote this woman, because she says nothing! We can only point to her single, magnificent *deed*. Along with her oil, she has managed to pour out upon the person of the Savior the whole substance of her being. O blessed woman, capable of such an all-encompassing, visible, yet also mystical

---

[1] See *Rule of Saint Benedict*, chapter 72.

action! You are an epiphany of what our soul ought to be in relation to Jesus! Your whole person has become one meaningful deed, a living sacrament revealing the depths of God's action in you! You represent the pinnacle of fulfillment of the human person in Christ, precisely because you seek nothing for yourself, not even for your name to be remembered. You seek nothing except to honor Jesus, and *therefore* you receive everything!

Judas, on the other hand, expresses the depths of his foul self-interest when he dares to utter the words that transport him to the Satanic realm: "What will you give me if I [hand] him [over] to you?" Contrasting the woman's prodigality, her reckless outpouring of her treasure on Jesus' head to do him honor, Judas is interested only in *what he can get*. Having previously objected to the wasting of a material commodity on Jesus, Judas now, by a grotesque paradox, turns Jesus himself into an appraisable commodity! Judas possesses so scheming and calculating a personality that he dares to haggle over the price of the Savior! He is determined that, by day's end, he is going to get cold cash out of this situation one way or another, and, in the face of the enormity of selling his Master, it is immaterial to our judgment of him whether he intends the money for the poor or for his political cause or for his own purse. He is committing the terrible crime of putting ideology, self-will, and material gain above the dignity and value of another human being, who happens also to be his loving and trusting Friend, his incomparably wise Teacher, and his Lord and Master.

Who can fathom the abyss of frustrated ambition, anguished calculation, crass avarice, and willful refusal of love packed into the single question, "What will you give me if I hand him over to you?" It is very telling that Judas, in referring to Jesus, says only *him* to the priests, obviously not wanting or daring to utter Jesus' name. He thereby reveals the extent of his collusion with them since they all know instantly to whom Judas refers, as if this were not his first exchange with the priests concerning Jesus. A whole chorus of malevolent whispers suddenly can be heard in the background all around Jesus. At the same time, Judas' nameless allusion reveals the fearful *shame* proper to a traitor, a perverted vestige of reverence that, deprived of all repentance, will lead to Judas' final despair. Under the circumstances, he probably fears superstitiously that uttering the holy Name of JESUS at that precise moment would burn his tongue.

The query "What will you give me if I hand him over to you?" manifests as well Judas' inveterate pragmatism: he only truly believes in what *works*. He wants hard results. We will probably never know what the darkening evolution of Judas' interior attitude toward Jesus has been. True, even the first time Matthew mentions Judas Iscariot (when Jesus calls the Twelve to himself in 10:4), the epithet "who betrayed him" is already attached to his name. But that rhetorical tag for Judas became standard in retrospect, after the events of the Passion. It cannot be that Judas was predestined to betray Jesus, as if betrayal were a necessary function of his personality. Nor can it be that Jesus failed to see beauty and potential in the person of Judas; in that case, how could he have chosen him in good conscience? Something must have gone very wrong between his election and his betrayal, and that is a murky psycho-spiritual trajectory that should concern us all.

I can only suggest that Judas must have initially possessed great ideals and a great desire to do good, along with much determination and will power. All these elements are clearly excellent and desirable, but they are merely vehicles. For what? To what end? These are the crucial questions. At the service of what do I put all my talents and natural endowments, including my capacity to seek and do what is good? Do I constantly keep before my eyes the need for humility as I take up my life's endeavors, precisely in order to accomplish great works of the spirit? That is, do I not allow myself ever to forget my nature and condition as a radically limited *creature* who, despite all sterling qualities, am emphatically dependent upon superior guidance and strength? In other words, within my heart and mind, am I very clear about the fact that one who intends to do good must only ever proceed as the servant of Another and according to that Other's will and design, rather than my own? Indeed, only God is inherently good (19:17); creatures are good, not of themselves, but only by participation in God the Primal Good, and if any of them severs this participation and attempts a rebellious autonomy and undertakes to accomplish an independent, self-determined "good", the enterprise shall be doomed by definition.

After receiving God's blessings by the armful, after being initiated even into the secrets of intimate discipleship, we all retain a lethal tendency to hijack our own vocation and throw the God-assigned pilot out of the window in order that we might ourselves henceforth navigate according to whim. We grow restless at having to obey all the time, at being servant all the time: by little creeping increments, our ego aspires to triumph by stealth as sole master of its own realm. We have quoted the dictum before: *Corruptio optimi pessima* ("the corruption of the best is the worst"), and this applies both to the person and to his calling. Precisely because so much creative energy is involved, no one is more cynical and full of hatred than someone who has loved deeply and then been disappointed in that love; and no endeavor becomes more destructive than one that has initially been pursued with great idealism and then fails. Here there is simply more matter to corrupt.

As part of the great Mission Discourse that Judas, too, heard as one of the Twelve, Jesus "[gave] them authority over unclean spirits, to cast them out, and to heal every disease and every infirmity" (10:1), adding: "Take no gold, nor silver, nor copper in your belts" (10:9). And now one of the apostles who embraced this exhortation to become a universal healer and to do so by becoming totally stripped of all possessions—just such a one haggles with the priests for their highest bid on the head of the Master who sent him forth. . . . "What will you give me if I hand him over to you?" Is such demonic pragmatism Judas' way of trying to fill a huge void within himself that threatens to undo him? Does he, midway in his experience of discipleship, suddenly realize that simply too much has been asked of him, that he can frankly not continue to comply with all the personal renunciations that the Mission Discourse enjoined? "Behold, I send you out as sheep in the midst of wolves" (10:16), Jesus has told them. What human being can tolerate such an arrangement—to be sent out on what feels more and more like a suicide mission, bereft of all weapons to fight back in kind? What madness!

And yet, having experienced the joy and fulfillment of intimate companionship with Jesus and the Eleven, Judas now feels not only self-justified in his growing interior alienation from them but also increasingly empty and numb within himself, no doubt because he has already expelled Jesus with violence from his heart. Who could ever fill that particular abyss? What can compensate the abyss of absence left behind by Jesus' expulsion from our heart? Consequently, in centrifugal flight, Judas turns outward with a vengeance, away from his heart, keen to manage manageable realities like money and power and influence. Jesus has proven simply too unruly and uncontrollable for him. The present act of betrayal is but the physical enactment of what has already occurred interiorly, within Judas' soul. To turn with cynicism from the mystical to the pragmatic is, sadly, to exhibit the despair devouring one's heart.

Judas' question incessantly returns to haunt us: "What *will you give* me if I *hand him over* to you?" Judas is here bartering. In the Greek, the second verb is a variation of the first, with a prefix added: "What will you *give* (δοῦναι) me if I *give him over* (παραδώσω) to you?" I have consistently translated this second verb as "to hand over", in order to stress the physicality of the action that soon became literally enacted upon the body of Jesus in the Garden of Gethsemane: "'Behold, the hour is at hand, and the Son of man is *betrayed into the hands of sinners.*' . . . Then they came up and *laid hands on Jesus and seized him*" (26:45, 50).

The word *parádosis* indicates a neutral action, a simple handing-over of something, and is the Greek equivalent of the Latin *traditio*, from which we get the English "traitor". *Parádosis* is like a teeter-totter that can swing either to the good or to the bad. When what is given is a worthy and valuable gift, the giver is by his act enhancing the life of the recipient and honoring him. However, in the case of Judas' present action, we are dealing with something very different: Judas has schemed to sell his Friend and Lord by deception and hand him over to a certain death. This *parádosis* is a handing-over of a person in order to destroy him, and the person in question happens also to be the Son of God. In this case, the *traditio* involved is no longer a communication of honor and life but an attempt at delivering a man to the power of annihilation.

Now, the central question of the different meanings of *parádosis* becomes even more complex when we realize that this is also the New Testament term that indicates the Father's action of handing over his only-begotten Son for the salvation of the world ("He who did not spare his own Son but *gave him up* [παρέδωκεν] for us all, will he not also give us all things with him?", Rom 8:32) and that memorializes Jesus' action of *handing himself over* to us in the Eucharist ("Now as they were eating, Jesus took bread, and blessed, and broke it, and gave [δοὺς] it to the disciples and said, 'Take, eat; this is my body'", 26:26). The one passage in the New Testament that uses the two meanings of *parádosis* simultaneously, with resulting irony, is St. Paul's narrative of the institution of the Eucharist: "For I received [παρέλαβον] from the Lord what I also [handed over (παρέδωκα)] to you, that the Lord Jesus on the night when he was [handed over (παρεδίδετο)] took bread . . ." (1 Cor 11:23).

As we can see, this term *parádosis* holds untold treasure for our meditation because it represents the very crux of our faith in precisely how we were redeemed by Christ. The verb *paradídomi* recurs like a death knell throughout this whole prelude to the Passion (26:2, 15, 16, 21, 23, 24, 25) and will resound again at Gethsemane (26:45, 46, 48) and during the various interrogatories (27:2, 3, 4, 18, 26), a full fifteen times altogether within two chapters. This one dynamic word *parádosis*, when fully grasped, can be a talisman that reveals the wondrous threefold mystery of Christ's Incarnation, crucifixion, and Resurrection: the manner, that is, in which (1) God's act of unfathomable generosity in giving us Christ ("For God so loved the world that he *gave* his only-begotten Son, that whoever believes in him should not perish but have eternal life", Jn 3:16) becomes perverted into (2) an act of unspeakable treason by Judas and all of us sinners ("The Son of man is [*handed over*] into the hands of sinners", 26:45) and (3) ultimately becomes vindicated in the triumph of Christ's Love and Life as the Risen Lord *gives himself* to all in the Holy Eucharist ("The Lord Jesus on the night when he was [*handed over*] took bread, and when he had given thanks, he broke it, and said, 'This is my body which is for you. Do this in remembrance of me' ", 1 Cor 11:23–24).

26:15b–16   οἱ δὲ ἔστησαν αὐτῷ τριάκοντα ἀργύρια.
Καὶ ἀπὸ τότε ἐζήτει εὐκαιρίαν
ἵνα αὐτὸν παραδῷ

And they paid him thirty pieces of silver.
And from that moment he sought
an opportunity to hand him over

THIRTY PIECES OF SILVER: Judas asked for a specific amount as the price of his betrayal, and the high priests are happy to oblige. This precise reward money for the handing-over of Jesus is recorded only by Matthew, ever eager to underpin the events of the New Testament by reference to the Torah and the Prophets. To one immersed in the revealed Word of God, "thirty shekels of silver" is a type of code language that immediately evokes two passages in the Old Testament. The first is in Exodus: "If [an] ox gores a slave, male or female, the owner shall give to their master thirty shekels of silver" (21:32). Thus, the Law considers that thirty pieces of silver is adequate compensation for the life of a *gored slave*. The second passage comes from Zechariah. The prophet, who has been made by the Lord "shepherd of the flock doomed to slaughter", is detested by those who traffic mercilessly with their own sheep because he refuses to treat the sheep only for profitable gain, as they do. Then, in the name of God, Zechariah takes his shepherd's staff, named "Grace", and breaks it symbolically, thus signaling the annulment of the covenant between God and the leaders of the people. The prophet then says to these traffickers: "Give me my wages. . . . And they weighed out as my wages thirty shekels of silver" (11:12). Thus, in addition to being the price for a slave's life, this amount of silver is what greedy traffickers in sheep consider a just wage for a shepherd they have found unsuitable and rejected.

Against this scriptural background, Matthew's text is clearly implying that the religious leaders of Israel at the moment consider Jesus to be no better than a gored slave and a worthless shepherd. Indeed, he who deliberately made himself a slave for our sake (Phil 2:6–7) and would eventually be pierced on the Cross (Jn 19:34) began his ministry with an outpouring of divine pathos at the sight of a humanity adrift in a sea of indifference: "When he saw the crowds, [Jesus] had compassion for them, because they were harassed and helpless, like sheep without a shepherd" (9:36). As of that moment, everything Jesus says and does is predicated on his identity as Good Shepherd sent by the Father to lead, feed, and protect his children in this world and beyond.

Finally, as he is underway with the Twelve to the Mount of Olives after the Last Supper, Jesus says with great sadness to his followers, quoting the very same prophecy of Zechariah: "You will all fall away because of me this night; for it is written, 'I will strike the shepherd, and the sheep of the flock will be scattered'" (26:31; Zech 13:7). Clearly the prophecy of Zechariah provides an essential background to underscore the way in which the events of the Passion have been both foreseen and comprehended by divine providence so that the shame of the thirty shekels may be ironically transformed into the glory of the Redemption.

"And from that moment [Judas] sought an opportunity to [betray Jesus]": The full extent of the terrible irony involved may be measured if we look more closely at the word *eukairía*, the term Matthew here uses for what Judas considers an "opportunity"—a "good chance" for a disciple to hand over his Master, for a wayward friend to deliver his faithful Friend into the hands of murderers. The word consists of the prefix *eu-* ("good") and the stem *kair-*, meaning "season" or "moment", as in *kairós*, which typically refers to the time God has chosen to save his people. *Eukairía*, then, means "favorable opportunity", "convenient moment", "good season", and "right time". More than simply an opportunity to get something done, *eukairía* implies an alternate project, a differing world view for which the time has come. We have already considered how Judas' ideas and motivations differed vastly from Jesus' own, and how Judas saw eliminating the person of Jesus as a necessary step on the way to launching a truly effective design for Jewish salvation. What Judas is really seeking here, then, is quite literally the triumph of the Anti-Gospel of worldly liberation through political and economic strategies, including violence, as opposed to Jesus' Gospel of selfless love unto death that others may live.

In this sense, what Jesus views as good cannot be so viewed by Judas and vice versa. What Judas considers *eukairía*, "a favorable opportunity" for the advancement of his religious cause, is in fact the right moment to do away once and for all with Jesus, this ineffectual day-dreamer who, with his mystical views, thwarts others' reasonable aspirations. Similarly, Joseph's brothers had resentfully plotted their visionary brother's demise even though they knew Joseph's death would irreparably wound their father Jacob's heart: "They saw him afar off, and before he came near to them they conspired against him to kill him. They said to one another, 'Here comes this dreamer. Come now, let us kill him and throw him into one of the pits'" (Gen 37:18–20). The full, universal resonance of Joseph's archetypal story may only be perceived when we see it literally lived out in Jesus' Incarnation and Passion. In turn, Jesus' own story is incomprehensible without seeing the way in which God's Wisdom has already revealed, in coded form, the redemptive meaning of the Passion in the story of Joseph. Once we make this connection, even the slightest detail of the Genesis text blossoms with radiance as it reveals the glory of selfless love:

> And Israel said to Joseph, "Are not your brothers pasturing the flock at Shechem? Come, I will send you to them. . . . Go now, see if it is well with your brothers, and with the flock; and bring me word again." So he sent him from the valley of Hebron, and he came to Shechem. And a man found him wandering in the fields; and the man asked him, "What are you seeking?" "I am seeking my brothers," he said. (Gen 37:13–16)

We see here in dazzling prefiguration the love of the eternal Father in sending his Son to his human brothers, the love of the Son in obeying the Father, and the truth that what motivates both Father and Son is solely the ultimate welfare of the insubordinate brothers they so love, as will be amply shown later on during the great famine.

"What are you seeking, Judas?"—"The favorable moment to be rid of this seductive teacher who is bleeding the vital energies of Israel and thus subjecting us all the more hopelessly to a foreign power. My master plan cannot be enacted as long as this alluring Jesus is around. Don't you see that my motivations are deeply religious and altruistic?

Once I, too, allowed myself to be seduced by him, but no longer. I will show him what's effective in the real world!'' God have mercy on you, Judas! Don't you know that, in betraying Jesus, you are not only betraying the best Friend you have ever had but also the noblest and most God-like part of your own being? In leading him like a sheep to the slaughter, you are disemboweling your own soul.[2]

---

[2] Consider this mysterious and troubling text in the Acts of the Apostles: "Now [Judas] bought a field with the reward of his wickedness; and falling headlong he burst open in the middle and all his bowels gushed out" (1:18).

INTERLUDE I:
THE JOURNEY
TO GOD

T HE PAGES IN WHICH THE GOSPEL relates the critical climax of Jesus' earthly sojourn by their very nature provide us, the followers of Jesus, with a road map of our own spiritual journey following the pattern of Christ's "exodus" to the Father. There is a rich passage in St. Bonaventure's great work *The Mind's Journey to God* that is a good example of how the whole Christian tradition applies to ordinary believers the events of the Passion, as milestones on their own pilgrimage to union with God. The text speaks of our *transitus*, that is, our "going" or "passing over" into the fullness of Christ's Paschal Mystery. This interior "Passover" represents the culmination of the Christian's return to the Father in close identification with Jesus:

In this passage [*transitus*], if it is perfect, all intellectual operations should be abandoned, and the whole height of our affection should be transferred and transformed into God. This, however, is mystical and most secret, which no man knoweth but he that hath received it [Rev 2:17], nor does he receive it unless he desire it; nor does he desire it unless the fire of the Holy Spirit, Whom Christ sent to earth, has inflamed his marrow. And therefore the Apostle says that this mystic wisdom is revealed through the Holy Spirit. [. . .]

If you should ask how these things come about, question grace, not instruction; desire, not intellect; the cry of prayer, not the pursuit of study; the spouse, not the teacher; God, not man; darkness, not clarity; not light, but the wholly flaming fire which will bear you aloft to God with fullest unction and burning affection. This fire is God, and the furnace of this fire leadeth to Jerusalem; and Christ the man kindles it in the fervor of His burning Passion, which he alone truly perceives who says, "My soul rather chooseth hanging and my bones death" (Job 7:15). He who chooses this death can see God because this is indubitably true: "Man shall not see me and live" (Ex 33:20). Let us then die and pass over into darkness; let us impose silence on cares, concupiscence, and phantasms; let us pass over [*transeamus*] with the crucified Christ from this world to the Father (Jn 13:1).[1]

[1] "In hoc autem transitu, si sit perfectus, oportet quod relinquantur omnes intellectuales operationes, et apex affectus totus transferatur et transformetur in Deum. Hoc autem est mysticum et secretissimum, quod nemo novit, nisi qui accipit, nec accipit nisi qui desiderat, nec desiderat nisi quem ignis Spiritus Sancti medullitus inflammat, quem Christus misit in terram. Et ideo dicit Apostolus, hanc mysticam sapientiam esse per Spiritum Sanctum revelatam. [. . .] Si autem quæras quomodo hæc fiant, interroga gratiam, non doctrinam; desiderium, non intellectum; gemitum orationis, non studium lectionis; sponsum, non magistrum; Deum, non hominem; caliginem, non claritatem; non lucem, sed ignem totaliter inflammantem et in Deum excessivis unctionibus et ardentissimis affectionibus transferentem. Qui quidem ignis Deus est, et hic caminus in Jerusalem, et Christus hunc accendit in fervore suæ ardentissimæ passionis, quem solus ille vere percipit, qui dicit: 'Suspendium elegit anima mea, et mortem ossa mea.' Quam mortem qui diligit, videre potest Deum, quia indubitanter verum est: 'Non videbit me homo et vivet.' Moriamur igitur et ingrediamur in caliginem, imponamus silentium sollicitudinibus, conscupiscentiis et phantasmatibus; transeamus cum Christo crucifixo 'ex hoc mundo ad Patrem.' " (St. Bonaventure, *De itinerario mentis ad Deum*, c. 7.4, 6; *Opera omnia*, 5, 312–13). Translation: http://www.catholictreasury.info/books/road_to_God/mind12.php.

4. I SEARCH FOR YOUR HAND IN THE BOWL

The Passover with the Disciples (26:17–25)

26:17 Τῇ δὲ πρώτῃ τῶν ἀζύμων
προσῆλθον οἱ μαθηταὶ τῷ Ἰησοῦ λέγοντες·
Ποῦ θέλεις ἑτοιμάσωμέν σοι φαγεῖν τὸ πάσχα;

Now on the first day of Unleavened Bread
the disciples came to Jesus, saying,
Where will you have us prepare for you to eat the Passover?

*P*ESACH: THE CLIMAX OF JESUS' PERSONAL STORY on earth co-incides with the pinnacle of the Jewish liturgical year in the great feast of *Pesach* (or "Passover"), in Greek known as *Pascha*. Jesus' personal destiny merges at every level with the fate of the Jewish people, both retrospectively with reference to the creation of that people's identity in the Exodus from Egypt, and prospectively, looking forward to the eternal redemption of God's people by Jesus' sacrifice on the Cross. Unleavened bread (*matzos* in Hebrew, *ázyma* in Greek) was so essential a Passover food that it became a synonym for the feast itself. Eating certain symbolic foods is so intimately tied to the celebration of Passover because what is being celebrated is the concrete manner in which God cares for his people as he delivers them from slavery and nourishes them in their desert pilgrimage to the Promised Land.

The repetition of the verb *to eat* in this and the following passage in Matthew points to the inseparability of spiritual from physical acts and processes whereby life is given and sustained. Unleavened bread, in particular, indicates the great haste with which the Jews had to depart from Egypt at God's command to save their lives. They simply did not have the time to allow the leavened dough to rise but had to bake it quickly in thin layers. Instantaneous obedience to God in faith and keen practical measures are the virtues that keynote the enterprise of the Exodus and that account for its success.

"Where will you have us prepare for you *to eat the Passover*?" Though, of course, it is the Paschal lamb that is going to be eaten, this turn of phrase denotes that the eating of the sacrificial lamb is viewed as the central event of the Passover celebration. Throughout the Passion narrative, the counterpoint is continually stressed closely relating the ritual killing and eating of the Paschal lamb with the simultaneous betrayal and crucifixion of Jesus. The Lord has already proclaimed this simultaneity programmatically to the disciples: "You know that after two days the Passover is coming, and the Son of man will be delivered up to be crucified" (26:2). The traditional Passover ritual (generic, typical, prescribed) followed by observant, God-fearing Jews and the simultaneous unfolding of Jesus' own life in terms of human failure (historical, unique, personal) are parallel events that become tightly intertwined in Matthew's narrative. Here the public and the private, the objective and the subjective, the historical and the intimate, the ritual and the existential, become surprisingly interwoven.

Curiously, one of the text's unifying leitmotifs is the recurrence of the verb *to eat*. We will eventually see the full significance of this continual reference. For the time being, we note that the background for the importance of eating in the context of the Passion has already been created by the reference to Jesus "as he sat at table" at the house of Simon the leper (26:7). Later the question is asked about where the disciples should "eat the Passover" with their Master (26:17). And a moment of supreme solemnity eventually arrives toward the end of the festive meal. It is a decisive moment that constitutes the turning point of the story's deepest significance and involves two major and inseparable revelations by Jesus, one destructive and the other constructive, each introduced by the temporal phrase "as they were eating" (26:21, 26). These two revelations are, first, the dramatic unmasking of the betrayer and, second, the institution of the Eucharist. It is noteworthy that the exposure of Judas by Jesus is explicitly linked to the act of eating: "He who has dipped his hand in the dish with me, will betray me" (26:23). Furthermore, immediately after Jesus identifies Judas both to himself and to us as "the one who hands over [= the betrayer]", Jesus proceeds to the institution of the Eucharist, using the language of eating and drinking in the imperative ("Take, eat. . . . Drink", 26:27) and referring it to his Body and Blood. Before us here we have textually the very crux of the negative and positive meanings of *parádosis*.

Quite literally, this is the nexus of salvation, the point of intersection of two antagonistic levels of meaning, or better, the *confluence* of those two previously conflicting levels. It is a merging effected by Wisdom Incarnate as he deliberately couples Judas' *deed of betrayal and destruction* with his own *desire to hand himself over* to the world as its nourishment so as to communicate "salvation". In this context, salvation is understood as eternal life shared with God by consuming the vital substance of the incarnate God. What for Judas, the Jewish priests, and the Romans was the iron-clad *finality* of their sinister plot (namely, to be rid of the troublesome Jesus) is here drastically relativized. Terminal human deviance is transformed by Jesus, with sovereign divine creativity and freedom, into an instrumental *means*, subservient now to his own providential *end*: the salvation of mankind by his redeeming self-bestowal in the Eucharist. The Eucharist thus emerges as the ritual, repetitively accessible, and preemptive distillation of the abomination of the Cross. The malevolent energy of hateful Satanic destructiveness is transmuted by the power of Jesus' sacrificial love into the unbounded energy of eternally shared, indestructible Life.

An aspect of the marvel entailed is that Jesus in no way alters the material externalities of his own demise: he truly *is* betrayed; he truly *does* bleed, suffer, and die; he truly *does* descend into utter humiliation and failure as far as worldly prudence can judge. Indeed, the prospect of a *deus ex machina* solution to the utter finality of the Cross would soon be portrayed by Matthew as the work of a mocking Satanism: "Those who passed by derided him, wagging their heads and saying, '. . . If you are the Son of God, come down from the cross' " (27:39–40), and this challenge echoes the second temptation by the devil at the beginning of the Gospel: "If you are the Son of God, throw yourself down [from the pinnacle of the temple]; for it is written, 'He will give his angels charge of you' " (4:6).

With regard to Matthew's text, we are struck by the way it subtly blends tradition and innovation. On the one hand, we detect a very traditional piety that seeks to observe all the ritual prescriptions of the Law; on the other hand, a new concept of the celebrating community as an all-male group of disciples gathered around himself by a Master for a celebration that radically transforms the traditional Jewish family. After this particular celebration of Passover on the eve of Jesus' Passion, the identity of both the Paschal sacrifice and of the group that celebrates it would be fundamentally and irreversibly transformed. The result of the transformation, brought about by Christ himself, would be a single, unrepeatable,[1] personal, and divine Sacrifice, and a universally united priestly Family, transcending all racial or ethnic origins, which would be called "the Church".

The Passover was always celebrated in the home by the members of one family or tribe. But for Jesus and his disciples, there is no stable "home": the group must look for a make-shift place to eat the Passover because they are the poor, itinerant followers of a rabbi who "has nowhere to lay his head" (8:20). And they are not for the most part related to each other by natural ties of kinship, although there are two sets of blood brothers among them. What binds them into one are the purely divine and interpersonal bonds of vocation, obedience, commitment, and friendship, since they have left everything, including their families of birth, to follow Jesus. A new concept of family has been unobtrusively invented by this Rabbi, one that is not only an alternative to the traditional conception but that actually transcends it as alone having eternal relevance. Just as Jesus' handing-over to death is a radically new, "personalized" version of the Paschal sacrifice, so, too, the traditional Jewish family is transformed by Jesus on this occasion into an all-male group consisting of a rabbi and his students.

The two concepts of *sacrifice* and *community*, essential to Jewish religion, are thus simultaneously transformed by one masterful stroke.

---

[1] While the Sacrifice of Christ is itself unrepeatable, being one and transtemporal, its liturgical celebration may be endlessly repeated. Such ritual repetition is clearly implied in Jesus' words of institution, transmitted by St. Paul: "This chalice is the new covenant in my blood. Do this, *as often as you drink it* [ὁσάκις ἐὰν πίνητε], in remembrance of me" (1 Cor 11:25), which in no way contradicts the affirmation of the Letter to the Hebrews: "By *one offering* [μιᾷ προσφορᾷ] he has made perfect forever those who are being consecrated" (Heb 10:14, NAB).

We may summarize the startling nature of this transformation by noting that the event of the Last Supper, which begins with a practical question about "eating the Passover" symbolically (26:18), shall eventually conclude with Jesus taking some of the matzos and affirming, in a most solemn, existential, and personalist manner surpassing all symbolism: "Take, eat; this is my body" (26:26). In the end, *Jesus declares himself to be the real Passover that is to be eaten!* This declaration is wholly remote from all symbolic ritualism. Jesus is revealed by his own words and actions to be both the Lord that liberates from slavery and the Lamb by the power of whose blood the liberation occurs. And the group of persons he is addressing, though all Jews, do not constitute a traditional family with a divine mandate to generate physical children. Rather, they are men selected by Jesus out of a mysterious freedom and called to beget spiritual children by proclaiming the faith of the Church and baptizing the whole world.

If I seem to be jumping ahead of the "plot" of our story, such a leap is inevitable because this narrative, in a very subtle and tranquil way, presents us with a most dynamic, indeed, explosive, nexus of references, symbols, prefigurements, redefinitions, and realizations, all of which radiate dazzlingly from the central figure of Jesus, the incarnate divine Wisdom who "reacheth . . . from end to end mightily, and ordereth all things sweetly" (Wis 8:1, DRA). We are dealing with a multi-layered text that has a deceptively simple and straightforward surface, and this appearance of being a mere factual narrative without undercurrents is reinforced by our extreme familiarity with the narrative so that very little about it can startle us anymore. In actual fact, however, we have before us here a very dense passage of the Gospel in which God's plan is enacted to "bring everything together under Christ, as head, everything in the heavens and everything on earth" (Eph 1:10, NJB).

As such, the text rehearses the dynamism with which, by express divine design, the whole history of the creation, Israel, and Redemption—in fact, all things are *recapitulated in Christ* (ἀνακεφαλαιώσασθαι τὰ πάντα ἐν τῷ Χριστῷ). Pauline "recapitulation" brings together in convergence (1) the material cosmos, concentrated into the bread and wine that are transformed into living sacraments by Jesus' command; (2) the experience of the Exodus transformed into the liberation from all the slavery of sin; (3) the theology of Passover sacrifice as atonement; (4) the universal expansion of election and redemption to all peoples; (5) the multi-faceted *parádosis*, whereby the Father gives us Jesus, we betray Jesus, and Jesus transforms the destruction wrought by our betrayal into redemptive self-outpouring by surrendering into it out of love. And, finally, (6) Christ's death and Resurrection are partaken of by believers in Holy Communion, out of which partaking the Church is born.

א

26:18b   Ὁ καιρός μου ἐγγύς ἐστιν,
πρὸς σὲ ποιῶ τὸ πάσχα μετὰ τῶν μαθητῶν μου

*My [appointed] time is at hand;
I will keep the Passover at your house with my disciples*

WITHIN THESE NINE VERSES of chapter 26 (17–25), explicit references to the event of *parádosis* occur four times (21, 23, 24, 25), to the point that we could speak of this notion of "handing over" (by another or by oneself) as structuring the whole passage and its meaning. The two contrary meanings of *parádosis* (destructive betrayal by Judas, life-giving self-bestowal by Jesus) are stabilized, and perhaps even in some sense harmonized, by the further presence in Jesus' self-awareness of the *kairós*, or divinely "appointed time". The true backbone of the Passion narrative, the structure and energy determining all its unfolding, is not the plotting of Judas, the high priests, Herod, and Pilate, that is to say, the competing wills of self-serving men as they jostle with one another for supremacy, with Jesus as their plaything. That would be the superficial and wholly worldly reading. The true governing principle of plot and action here, against all appearances, is divine providence, God's sovereign will to save the world through the attitudes and actions of Jesus.

In his message to the owner of the house where he wants to celebrate

Passover, Jesus says, "My time is at hand; I will keep the Passover at your house with my disciples." Jesus here identifies this particular Passover with *ho kairós mou*, "my time", that is, the favorable and appropriate moment appointed by his Father, the author of the plot of salvation, for Jesus to accomplish the task for which he was sent, namely, the task of utter self-outpouring. Inexplicably, the time must be *his* very own favorable moment precisely because it is right now that the powers of darkness have reached their climax and a betrayer has been moved to hand him over from within his shared intimacy with Jesus.

If man's fundamental state as deviant creature is to be thoroughly redeemed, the very worst deviancy possible must become the subject of the healing because that extreme evil would include all lesser evils: a teacher betrayed by his disciple, a lord by his servant, a God by his creature. Heal this, and all is healed. Redeem and forgive this, and all is henceforth redeemed and forgiven. The extreme contains everything intermediate. *My time is at hand*: "The beast is at the door and about to pounce; it is the moment for me to show the depth of my readiness to allow myself to be trampled upon so as to show that my Father is all mercy, compassion, and forgiveness. In my blood, the Father's love will be flowing, like wine from crushed grapes." Jesus declares with an audible thrill in his voice that this moment of betrayal and annihilation is precisely *his kairós of choice* to enter fully into his own as Revealer of the Father.

Such a choice, such exultant obedience in the face of suffering as a man's deepest motivation, demonstrates unsurpassably the prophetic truth that " 'my thoughts are not your thoughts, neither are your ways my ways,' says the Lord. 'For as the heavens are higher than the earth, so are my ways higher than your ways and my thoughts than your thoughts' " (Is 55:8–9). Indeed, it is only by being grounded in the unfathomable depths and radical otherness of the divine Mind that Jesus can take what Judas termed his own personal *eu-kairía* ("good and favorable moment" [to hand Jesus over to death], 26:16), embrace it, and transform it into the solemn declaration: *My kairós is at hand!* Love transforms the offense inflicted upon it into an occasion of highest fulfillment.

Now, Jesus performs this transformation of a massive mortal threat into the desirable climax of his life not only as Son of God but simultaneously as Son of Mary, that is, as a human being like ourselves, subject to every weakness, fear, and vulnerability possible to both body and soul. Jesus rejoices, not because his time of suffering has arrived; he rejoices and readies himself to enter the challenge because the favorable opportunity has come when he can give his all. This is why this Passover is identified by Jesus as *his appointed time*: it is his opportunity to demonstrate before all who care to see and understand how a human being can, with all his faculties, desires, thoughts, and actions, *pass over* totally and visibly from the realm of a tentative search for the good and a more or less mediocre embodiment of virtue to *becoming all burning love.*

Jesus calls this happening quite graphically ποιῶ τὸ πάσχα, that is, "I do the Passover", as a vigorous personal task. And because he intends to undertake the challenge together with his disciples, he obviously hopes that they, too, will, in his company, undergo a like transformation. In his own person and during the course of one evening, Jesus transforms an ancient ritual observance into a world-shattering innovation that changes the course and meaning of history itself. Henceforth, either Love shall rule the world, or all shall be desolation. There is no going back to an era when might made right. Once Christ, by his life and death, has introduced into the world the principle of self-sacrificial love as the ultimate victory over evil, this new dispensation is irreversible and all-engulfing, affecting profoundly even those least aware of the cataclysm that is forever altering the very foundation of things.

26:21b–22   Εἷς ἐξ ὑμῶν παραδώσει με.
Καὶ λυπούμενοι σφόδρα ἤρξαντο λέγειν αὐτῷ
εἷς ἕκαστος· Μήτι ἐγώ εἰμι, κύριε;

"One of you will hand me over."
And they were very sorrowful, and began to say to him
one after another, "Is it I, Lord?"

FROM THE BEGINNING OF THE PASSION NARRATIVE, Jesus proclaimed his impending betrayal: "The Son of man will be handed over (παραδίδοται) to be crucified" (26:2). Then the actual betrayal by Judas was dramatized with the precise term, *parádosis*, that Jesus had used to predict his handing-over (26:15–16). And now, as the small circle of disciples reclines intimately at table to eat the Passover, Jesus returns to the theme, introducing the recurring prophecy with the solemn formula "Amen, I say to you" to call attention to the affirmation, "One of you will hand me over." A situation of intimacy reveals everything about us, both the good and the bad, and this is why most of us fear gazing for too long into another's eyes.

The darkness of the evening has created a space where the only light comes from friendship and mutual trust, and the small circle of twelve vagrants and their Teacher feels unaccountably at home in this strange house, lent for the occasion by a random person. One virtue of material poverty and unsettledness is that these may compel people, perhaps for the first time, to look for meaning and comfort solely in each other as brought together by God. The sharing of a meal, whereby separate organisms ingest the same substance and are together strengthened by it as one, normally signifies preexisting communion and future growth in that communion. Sharing a meal implies a sacred pledge of lasting fidelity exchanged among the eaters, because they have reclined unarmed with others at the same table and have thus exposed communal needs and vulnerabilities. You trust that your fellow banqueters will not poison or harm you in any way and that they desire only your good.

All of this holds in heightened degree for the Passover *seder* since the assembled persons are, communally, the guests of God himself as they celebrate his bountiful intervention for Israel at the Exodus from Egypt and eat the Paschal lamb slaughtered according to God's command. This particular group of twelve men, moreover, doubly qualifies as guests of God because they are, first, Jews and therefore share by rights in the inherited promises to Israel, and, second, they have been personally selected by the Messiah to work with him to extend Israel's salvation to all nations.

"As they were eating, he said, 'Truly, I say to you, one of you will [hand] me [over]' ": The deeply tragic recognition of his fate implied by these words of Jesus has the effect of a knife plunged into the neck of the Paschal lamb. Jesus himself is the only Lamb present at this particular *seder* meal, the human victim inhabited by the Divine Person who willingly takes up his role as sacrificial offering. Is Jesus here being merely denunciatory in proclaiming this message of doom, perhaps hoping secretly that the eleven more faithful disciples will identify the one traitor and pounce on him vengefully in order to prevent the success of his plot? Impossible: this would neither be worthy of the person of Jesus nor harmonize with the new principle of life he is trying to teach them.

To speak of betrayal in the midst of the *seder*—indeed, a betrayal originating from within the group of those celebrating Passover— amounts to nothing less than overturning the whole established social and religious order of mankind and Israel. ONE OF YOU *will betray me*: how infinitely more terrible this pronouncement (in direct second-person address to his friends) is than Jesus' earlier, more impersonal prophecies concerning the handing-over of "the Son of Man"! The plot is indeed thickening. The fleeting phantom of death that has long been roaming around Jesus is now quickly materializing all too visibly. No, Jesus does not make the tragic affirmation in order to denounce Judas and call for action against him, but rather, in an intensely human manner, he does so simply to allow the sorrow of his heart to overflow into the hearts of his beloved friends. How, indeed, could Jesus help having his betrayal foremost in mind? How could he help commenting on the ironical contrast between this scene of friends sharing a sacred meal with friends (in which they symbolically nourish one another by their loving presence as they pass the dishes around) and the betrayal from within that wants to hand the Master over to be devoured by the forces of evil? On the one hand, there can be no question of cowardice on Jesus' part or of his seeking a way out of this terrible impasse by plotting a revenge that would dismember the group of disciples from within. On the other hand, however, we sense the deep wound inflicted on Jesus' Heart at being betrayed in this manner by an intimate friend.

Jesus is an excellent communicator and a thorough realist, and to the end he will be teaching his followers how to live well in the truth in the immediate present. Those around him right now are, after all, the nucleus of the new family he has chosen and created for himself. He wants them to relate to one another, through himself, on the basis of truth and forgiveness; and forgiveness of self or others can occur only if we begin with the sincere recognition of incurred wrongs, leading to sorrow and repentance. The disciples' own reaction to Jesus' heavyhearted affirmation consequently reveals a great deal about themselves and their present state of inchoate spiritual maturity: "They were very sorrowful, and began to say to him one after another, 'Is it I, Lord?'"

On hearing Jesus' firm prediction, the disciples are empathetically receptive to Jesus' sorrow and make it their own. The expected human reaction would have been to point accusing fingers at one another. Instead of this, however, each of them, trembling with humility, instinctively questions himself and then asks the common Lord whether he might be his traitor. This appears a rather odd question for them to ask; you would think the culprit would already know the answer! And yet it seems they have by now sufficiently internalized Jesus' teaching concerning the potential deviousness of the human heart to be less sure of their own presumed innocence in the face of a lurking betrayal: "Out of the heart come evil thoughts, murder, adultery, fornication, theft, false witness, slander", Jesus has proclaimed (15:19). The apostles have learned enough from Jesus at least to be distrustful of their subconscious heart. The twelve now know in their bones not only that no one, not even a disciple, is immune from such wicked afflictions but also that a major aspect of human waywardness is precisely our inability to be constantly aware of the true motivations of our own heart: "The heart is deceitful above all things, and desperately corrupt; who can understand it?" (Jer 17:9). The disciples' question, thus, is quite profound because it implies their wise conviction, as hearts formed by Jesus, that only God can understand our hearts, that only by baring our souls and our fears to him who is the Truth (Jn 14:6) will we ever get to the bottom of our impulses and motivations and identify them as what they truly are.

26:23   Ὁ ἐμβάψας μετ᾽ ἐμοῦ τὴν χεῖρα ἐν τῷ τρυβλίῳ
         οὗτός με παραδώσει

He who dips his hand in the dish with me,
that one will betray me

LURKING BENEATH THE SURFACE of every apparent "coincidence" there lies what is in fact a momentous revelation, for those who have eyes to see. Toward the end of Homer's *Odyssey*, for instance, the old servant Euryclea, who had been Odysseus' wet nurse when he was a child, is given the task of washing the feet of a mysterious stranger who is a guest at Queen Penelope's table. Euryclea suddenly discovers a scar on the man's thigh above the knee that instantly reveals to the astonished old woman that the stranger is, in fact, her beloved master Odysseus come home in disguise. For sheer, slack-jawed joy, she drops his foot into the basin and spills the water on the floor of the dining hall:

> Deep o'er his knee inseam'd remain'd the scar;
> Which noted token of the woodland war
> When Euryclea found, the ablution ceased:
> Down dropp'd the leg, from her slack hand released;
> The mingled fluids from the base redound;
> The vase reclining floats the floor around!

Smiles dew'd with tears the pleasing strife express'd
Of grief and joy, alternate in her breast.
Her fluttering words in melting murmurs died;
At length abrupt—"My son!—my king!"—she cried.[2]

Throughout literature, such peak moments of sudden revelation symbolize the hidden meaning and identity of things and the secret workings of providence underneath a world of flux and apparent randomness. As such, they point to an ultimate "apocalypse", an ultimate cosmic revelation when all that is hidden will be made known and every wrong will be set to rights. Such is also the case here with Jesus' reference to dipping his hand into the dish simultaneously with Judas. It appears to be an odd, superfluous detail, thrown into the narrative almost at random. And yet, like Odysseus' hidden scar, the very graphic gesture carries a world of meaning. As is still the case in the Middle East and much of the non-Western world, persons dining together in the Bible normally eat out of a common dish set in their midst, and they take the food with their hands without the aid of cutlery, usually using bread for scooping. This practice provides a much more intimate and communal eating experience, greatly contrasting our individualistic Western custom of each one eating only out of his own dish with implements that create many degrees of separation among the diners.

To be plotting someone's betrayal in one's mind, while at the same time sharing a meal with him in this Middle Eastern manner, constitutes a most grievous clash between appearance and reality in the life of the traitor. The resulting opposition between external intimacy and internal perfidy produces an unbearable clash. Jesus' saying "You cannot serve God and mammon" (6:24) takes on here a particularly grim and terrible form. By the law of this antinomy, Judas has come to love and serve his rebellious greed, and, consequently, he has come to hate and despise the one with whom he is nonetheless sharing a sacred meal and whom he continues to address as "Master" (26:25). Such cancerous hypocrisy, such a titanic endeavor to affirm simultaneously two things that by nature are mutually exclusive, carves out an abyss of darkness in Judas' soul into which he will soon plunge.

"He who dips his *hand* in the dish with me, will *betray* me": Note

---

[2] *Homer's Odyssey*, trans. Alexander Pope (1942; ExFontibus, 2012), bk. 19, ll. 466–72, p. 289.

the relationship in this declaration of the noun "hand" with the verb "betray", as well as the fact that the statement refers to the meeting of two hands—one that of Judas, the other that of Jesus—in the middle of the act of eating out of a single plate. We further recall that *parádosis* may be rendered both "betrayal" and "handing-over" or "delivery", with an emphasis on the actual physical action that executes outwardly the interior mental disposition of heart and will. The casual-seeming reference, we realize, suddenly becomes tragically luminous, dense with meaning and presentiment. We can indeed identify this as the precise moment when Jesus freely surrenders his life and Heart to Judas' destructive designs.

Jesus allows his own hand, symbol of his divine and human will, to touch and associate with Judas' hand within the serving dish that probably contains the slaughtered Paschal lamb, communal source of sacred nourishment. In this manner, Jesus continues to pledge friendship, communion, and forgiveness to Judas even as he simultaneously *hands himself over into Judas' hand*. Only from our perspective, however, does this involve an antinomy; from Jesus' perspective, there is no contradiction because he has come into the world precisely to put out the finite fires of human hatred with the overwhelming waters of his unquenchable love. *The more he is betrayed, the more will he hand himself over.* By dipping his hand into the dish at the same time as Judas dips his, Jesus, far from denouncing and exposing Judas, is seizing the opportunity to give himself to Judas all the more intensely: Jesus, in fact, longs for contact with the beloved flesh of Judas' hand, albeit the flesh of a betrayer.

The present contact of hands anticipates the kiss at Gethsemane (26:49). Judas' identification as "the one who is handing me over" occurs in a most private manner, between himself and Jesus only. Even this most terrible moment is shot through with intimacy! Each of the other eleven has been asking whether *he* is the traitor; Judas is only the last so to inquire, and we can practically see Jesus discreetly whispering into Judas' ear, eyes brimming with emotion, the two short words Σὺ εἶπας, "you have said so"—"*you*, not I, have said so. I condemn no one" (cf. Jn 8:11) since "God sent the Son into the world, not to condemn the world, but that the world might be saved through him" (Jn 3:17). To Jesus, *Judas is a beloved betrayer* because God's love for us is indefectible, and it can never be conditioned, diminished, or extinguished even by our own worst sins and infidelities.

Jesus' abiding love for Judas, his fidelity to Judas in the very thick of Judas' betrayal, ought to be for us the source of our greatest consolation in our own infidelities. No sin on man's part can ever smother the life-giving Breath of God's love for us. Indeed, God's response to Judas' betrayal is to die on the Cross for him. If anything, Judas' betrayal *intensifies* Jesus' love for him and choice of him as apostle. The sight of Odysseus' scar revealed her master's identity to the faithful Euryclea as she performed a ritual ablution on the apparent vagrant; and in the present scene, the depths of divine mystery are unveiled by two hands that casually dip a bit of bread into a dish. By this action, Jesus reveals himself to be God's Unconditional Love made flesh. But do we, like this faithful servant, possess the eyes and the memory of love, which alone would allow us to perceive Jesus' sublime identity as sole universal Lord underneath his road-dirty, anguish-worn frame?

26:24   ὁ μὲν υἱὸς τοῦ ἀνθρώπου ὑπάγει
               καθὼς γέγραπται περὶ αὐτοῦ,
   οὐαὶ δὲ τῷ ἀνθρώπῳ ἐκείνῳδὶ οὗ ὁ υἱὸς τοῦ ἀνθρώπου παραδίδοται·
           καλὸν ἦν αὐτῷ εἰ οὐκ ἐγεννήθη ὁ ἄνθρωπος ἐκεῖνος

The Son of man goes
as it is written of him,
but woe to that man by whom the Son of man is handed over!
It would have been better for that man if he had not been born

T HE FACT THAT JESUS HAS JUST SAID: "One of you will betray
me" makes it very clear that he is referring to himself in the
third person when he now adds, "The Son of man goes. . . ."
He thus reverts to the oblique prophetic language of the beginning

of the chapter, when he inaugurated the Passion narrative by stating, "the Son of man will be delivered up to be crucified" (26:2). The *me* of his previous sentence, however, now comes within identifying proximity of the phrase *the Son of man* that begins this sentence. He makes it plain that "Son of man" and "Jesus of Nazareth" are fully synonymous. Indeed, we may say it is the rising heat of this narrative of betrayal and redeeming love that is operating the full revelation: namely, that this individual, Yeshua' bar Yosef, son of Mary and of the Nazareth carpenter, whose father and mother are known to all, is simultaneously the "Son of man" of Daniel's visions and the personal, fused embodiment of all mankind before God (Dan 7:13). Only a man can represent mankind; but only a man who also possesses the divine Abyss interiorly can contain all human beings of all times and places within himself and, thus, bring them before the Father: "In him all the fulness of God was pleased to dwell, and through him to reconcile to himself all things, whether on earth or in heaven, making peace by the blood of his cross" (Col 1:19–20).

Throughout the Old Testament, the expression "a son of man" is simply a Semitic turn of phrase that means "a human being". But Jesus' use of it now, with the definite article and referring to himself, lifts that meaning to unheard-of preeminence. In keeping with the traditional meaning, the figure is thoroughly identified with the form and experience of all human beings on earth. And yet, Daniel's precise wording says that "with the clouds of heaven there came *one like a son of man*" who was presented before the Ancient of Days. Daniel is no doubt seeing a man, but this is not an ordinary man like all other men, for his place is above the heavens, and he stands upright in the burning presence of God himself.

And then, marvel of marvels, the prophet witnesses a fantastic event: "And to him was given dominion and glory and kingdom, that all peoples, nations, and languages should serve him; his dominion is an everlasting dominion, which shall not pass away, and his kingdom one that shall not be destroyed." This description of eternal and universal power and authority may rightly be predicated, according to tradition, only of God himself; and yet here Daniel beholds such dominion as being conferred by God himself on "one like a son of man". Such seeing the unheard-of as true, while lacking the ability to understand it, is of the essence of the prophetic charism. But the theological clash of contraries in the prophet's limited mind is so immense that it is no wonder that these nocturnal revelations confound him utterly and exhaust his power of imagination: "As for me, Daniel, my spirit within me was anxious and the visions of my head alarmed me. . . . I fell into a deep sleep with my face to the ground" (Dan 7:14–15; 8:18). The destabilizing effect on Daniel of the complex vision is finally counteracted only by Gabriel's explanation to him that "the vision is for the time of the end" (Dan 8:17).

Now, in the context of Matthew's Gospel, "the time of the end" refers to Jesus' *kairós* of salvation, which, as he himself proclaims, has now arrived in the imminent Passion: "My time is at hand" (26:18). We venture to interpret such coded language on God's part as meaning, "The moment has finally arrived for me to give my life for the good of all, that they may enter with me into fullness of life."

This particular Passover, which coincides with Jesus' betrayal, death, and Resurrection, is his definitive passing over from death to life, both as individual, mortal human being and as the divinely appointed Son of Man, who bears within himself both the archetype and the reality of Man. Because the Savior is inseparably Jesus of Nazareth and the Son of Man, his death and Resurrection sweep up the rest of mankind, too, in their irresistible wake, plunging the whole of creation into the Paschal Mystery of definitive transformation from temporal death into everlasting life.

This act of entering into the Paschal Mystery is what Jesus refers to by his ominous words, "The Son of man goes as it is written of him." How much meaning and power Jesus packs into this little word *goes*! Its resonance here has everything to do with the year's Passover being celebrated at that particular *seder* and also with the ancient Passover when the Jews escaped hastily from Egypt at God's command. Most importantly, this *goes* now uttered by Jesus inaugurates the great unending Pesach or Pascha to which every other ritual and historical Passover points as a herald, that is, the passing over of the Son of Man from this world into eternity in both his humanity and his divinity. He *goes over* through death and great suffering into fullness of Life; and he *goes over* from the earthly realm and all its strife into the tender bosom of the Father, drawing all of us along with him. This is the ultimate "going forth" or "departure" that Luke, using a charged biblical term, explicitly names Jesus' *exodus*, which is the burning topic that wholly occupies the colloquy of the luminous Three on Mount Tabor: "And behold, two men were conversing with him, Moses and Elijah, who appeared in glory and spoke of his *exodus* (τὴν ἔξοδον αὐτοῦ) that he was going to accomplish in Jerusalem" (Lk 9:30–31, NAB).

On this occasion, above all, we should remember Jesus' guiding principle as creator of the New Covenant in his own blood: "Do not think that I have come to abolish the law and the prophets; I have come not to abolish them but to fulfil them" (5:17). Not out of thin air, but out of the very heart of Jewish history and in the context of the yearly celebration of the Exodus does Jesus fulfill both history and ritual through his enactment, in his own body and whole being, of the total Paschal Mystery. In his wake, the whole Body of the Church, which is his own Body, shall evermore partake of it as the heart-blood of her own life, in modes both mystical and existential. "Paschal Mystery", then, is but another way of speaking of the ancient, figurative Passover mystery as fulfilled in the life of Christ. Such is the fuller meaning of Jesus' simple affirmation concerning himself: "The Son of man goes as it is written of him."

26:25   ἀποκριθεὶς δὲ Ἰούδας ὁ παραδιδοὺς αὐτὸν εἶπεν·
         Μήτι ἐγώ εἰμι, ῥαββί;
         λέγει αὐτῷ· Σὺ εἶπας

Judas, who betrayed him, replied,
"Is it I, Master?"
He said to him, "You have said so"

IN ONE SINGLE VERSE (v. 24) Jesus uses the word *ánthrôpos* (man, in the sense of "human being") four times, twice alternating the two phrases "the Son of man" and "that man", which refer respectively to himself and to his betrayer. By such repetitious insistence, he calls attention to the mystery of darkness and light being played out. A mystery of death through betrayal paradoxically produces indestructible life through self-oblation. The historical Exodus was already both of these things for the Jews; but now the pattern and meaning of the historical Jewish Exodus, celebrated ritually in a yearly liturgical feast, is both universalized and absolutized by Jesus' personal experience and express command so that it becomes the mystical vocation of all human beings of all times and places, and it enacts nothing less than the definitive triumph of eternal life over death and of goodness and holiness over sin.

As a result of Jesus' personal Pascha, and by virtue of his radical creative intervention as author of redemption, Christ's Paschal Mystery now becomes a new ontological reality in the order of Being, an unfathomable new pattern of Being that gives mortal, carnal humanity—you and me and all others—free abiding access to Pure Immortal Spirit, without any loss to human carnality or personal individuality. The pattern for all is established by Christ himself as archetype. The risen, immortal, and glorious Jesus still possesses his own recognizable human body, including the palpable marks of his wounds (cf. Jn 20:25–27) as an everlasting memorial of his Passion. From the divine point of view, not only are "wounds" and "glory" not incompatible but, in fact, the latter cannot be had without the former.

This passage, however, and the ominous words of Jesus it conveys, put us squarely before a very difficult and painful question. While answering the disciples' query about who the traitor among them might be, Jesus says: "The Son of man goes as it is written of him, but woe to that man by whom the Son of man is betrayed! It would have been better for that man if he had not been born." More terrible words can hardly be conceived of. The prodigious collision between two verbs—*goes* and *is betrayed*—releases an enormous quantum of both creative and destructive energy. "The Son of man" is the subject of both. The statement "the Son of man goes" imperceptibly becomes "the Son of man is betrayed", so that the first verb perforce yields to the second, and a horrendous betrayal is shown as necessary to a highly desirable exodus. The logical conundrum derives from the fact that, in order to save mankind, Jesus must go forth by his exodus into death; but this going forth, in order to perform its salvific function, requires a betrayal. The exodus through death into life cannot occur without the slaughter of the Paschal lamb, and the betrayal by Judas is precisely the knife required to accomplish the sacrifice. Now, the ultimate source of the difficulty here is the phrase *as it is written of him*, because with this Jesus is simultaneously affirming both the theological necessity and the crass culpability of his betrayal. Jesus seems to be eagerly saluting his own God-appointed destiny as living and ultimate Paschal Lamb and yet, at the same time, ruthlessly dooming the instrument of his oblation.

The word "instrument" falls off-handedly from one's pen. But is this the most adequate term to refer to the function of Judas and his deed? By using it so instinctively, one reveals a penchant for tracing all events, good or bad, to God's will and intervention, as if only divine causality really mattered and as if, consequently, all human motivation and decision making were only really divine instrumentality in disguise. It does so seem the pious thing to do; and yet, much of our instinctual "piety" can often be easily unmasked as concealing less admirable dispositions. Such "instrumental" logic as described above would grievously invalidate human freedom of will and, hence, deprive people of the true capacity either to love or to hate. Not only did God not compel Judas or set him up, however subtly, to betray Jesus; the evidence shows quite the contrary.

Judas Iscariot was chosen especially by Jesus. Through a deed of love, Jesus drew him to himself as intimate disciple and friend, along with the other eleven. He was admitted to the full knowledge of Jesus' Heart and to daily association with the kind and wise Master. Along with the others, Judas has already been sent by Jesus on mission. And now, at this Passover, he basks in the intimacy of Jesus' table. Jesus has withheld nothing from him that he has given to the others and, even in the face of Judas' imminent betrayal, Jesus if anything *intensifies* his marks of affection and love for Judas: he meets his hand in the bowl with his own, and later at Gethsemane he accepts Judas' kiss. In view of all this, a rather monstrous idea of God would be evoked were we to conjecture that, from the outset, divine providence has shrewdly planted Judas among the disciples as a mole, in order to use him at the time of the Passion as the chosen instrument of Jesus' undoing. Such a scenario would construe Jesus himself as mendacious and deceitful, a sanctimonious schemer requiring some poor, doomed subject to help him enact successfully his delusional and suicidal savior complex.

Perhaps most of us would not follow to these unavoidable conclusions the exculpating hunch that Judas was, after all, merely a puppet of providence. God needed a sacrifice, and Judas was "programmed" to carry it out. . . . We would rather stay in a much grayer zone in which we both allow God his choice of a saving project and mentally exonerate Judas of his guilt, without further thought. I suggest that this procedure, in addition to its dishonesty, involves as well an attitude of intolerable condescension toward both Judas in his human dignity and toward God in his utter goodness and innocence. The "solution", if there is a solution, must lie elsewhere. However, I suspect that we are dealing here with one of those dark mysteries that result from the tangle of historical event and human will that can never fully be clarified by rational analysis.

While we must accept as revealed truth Jesus' statement concerning the necessity and inevitability of his own death, we must by no means accept as well what might initially appear to be its corollary: the necessity and inevitability of Judas' betrayal of him. To accept that *someone* must play the traitor does not logically require me to accept that *this particular person*, who goes by the name of Judas Iscariot, must do so! In fact, Jesus' precise words are very instructive in this light: "The Son of man goes as it is written of him, but woe to *that man* by whom the Son of man is betrayed! It would have been better for *that man* if he had not been born." To the very last moment, Jesus keeps open the possibility that Judas may change his mind and repent of his impending betrayal, hence Jesus' anonymous reference to *that man*. He is referring not at all to Judas specifically, but generically to whoever might perform the deed. The guilt and its causality are located solely *in the deed itself*, which obviously is not done until it is done, and not whatsoever *in a particular person's* bent of character, previous history, or putative destiny. Jesus' pronouncement leaves intact Judas' freedom to move in any direction, whether toward deceit and corruption or toward repentance and redemption.

"Is it I, Master?", Judas asks Jesus immediately after the Lord has affirmed the terrible truth that it would have been better for the Son of Man's betrayer if he had never been born. Is Judas' question to Jesus honest or devious? Μήτι ἐγώ εἰμι, ῥαββί; The use of the particle *mêti* in the question means that Judas expects a negative answer, so the more precise rendering would be: "Surely it isn't I?" But Judas has already received the thirty silver shekels from the priests and is waiting for his opportunity to pounce. Is he just playing along, asking of Jesus the same question as do the other disciples, and in precisely the same formulation, while knowing full well that *he* is indeed the betrayer?

This exchange deepens our impression of Judas' guile. Perhaps his arrogance has blinded him enough for him to think that he really does have Jesus fooled. Does he take Jesus, whom he deems a hopeless mystic, for something of a holy simpleton as well? At the same time, we must ponder Jesus' restraint in not denouncing Judas openly, as if he were still leaving room for a conversion to occur. It is strangely moving that, while in John's Gospel the scene of greatest intimacy during the Last Supper is undoubtedly the moment when the beloved disciple leans back on Jesus' chest (Jn 13:23–26), in Matthew's narrative of the same occasion Jesus' attention is wholly focused on Judas. It is as if Jesus were a mother lavishing special tenderness on her most problematic child. What appear to be Jesus' tact and restraint with Judas in this scene may, more deeply, be seen as a delicate balancing act on love's part as it strives both to warn and to persuade the beloved to back off from the edge of an abyss of doom while at the same time leaving his freedom undiminished.

Judas' question to Jesus differs significantly from that posed by the other eleven, not in the formulation of the query itself, but in the title by which it addresses Jesus. Whereas the other disciples ask "Surely it isn't I, *Lord (Kyrie)*?", Judas, coming last of all, says instead, "Surely it isn't I, *Master (rabbi)*?" Is Judas thereby granting Jesus the minimal title of courtesy so as not to stand out as impudent, while at the same time denying him the transcendental title of "Lord", which would acknowledge Jesus' sovereignty and imply willing commitment of heart and soul to this man who is unlike any other man?

In the present context, Judas' alternate title for Jesus certainly sets him apart from the rest of the disciples as a dissenter, and it represents a strategy of language meant to lessen the reproach of his conscience. It may not be an admirable thing to betray one's teacher; nevertheless, a student is by definition on his way to becoming like his teacher, to establishing parity with him, and therefore he may entertain serious differences of opinion and implementation of doctrine from those of his master. One can rationalize the betrayal of one's *teacher* on the grounds that a basically good man has become deluded and is causing great harm among those less perceptive than himself. As a result, an especially "responsible" disciple can feel called—by his conscience or destiny or even God—to a radical action that the less enlightened could consider "betrayal". Socrates, for instance, after Jesus surely the greatest teacher that has ever lived, was legally tried and condemned by Athens for corrupting its youth and for impiety to the gods. But it is well nigh impossible to justify to one's own conscience the betrayal of one's *lord*, especially after considerable experience has revealed that this personal lord has legitimate claims to being *the Lord*. And so, by deftly substituting a lesser term for a greater, Judas engages in an expedient linguistic game of subtle denial and self-exoneration that demotes Jesus from his full rank as Son of Man and Lord of All. Such demotion achieves its intended aim. With impunity it declares open season on the deluded rabbi.

EXTREME, PERILOUS, AND FEAR-INSPIRING though Judas' spiritual situation here may be, we must honestly ask ourselves whether we have never lived this sort of double life. I suggest that Judas' stance with regard to Jesus, though presented by the evangelist as a supremely unique drama, is nevertheless meant to be a universal warning to all of us. We have asked whether Judas was devious or honest in asking Jesus with a straight face whether he, Judas, was the traitor among the apostles, in fact hinting that he was not. Do we not, all of us, grow old cultivating habits of deep compromise with our firmest-held principles and sleeping very well at night after spending the day subtly affirming contraries and incompatibles by our choices and actions if not explicitly by our words? Is treason—yes, deliberate *treason*, not expedient action or inevitable preference or lucky profit—really an experience so foreign to our soul? Which of us, either by a culpable silence or by a sly, ruinous hint, has not sought advantage and promotion for ourselves by covertly disqualifying and leaving behind in the shadows a friend to whom we have ardently pledged our loyalty? Times change, we argue, people change, needs evolve . . .

Nevertheless, betrayal by any other name remains *betrayal*, and this catastrophic mutation in pledged fidelity is indeed the change that leaves the most permanent and deepest imprint on the character of a soul. Betrayal is the suicide of the soul because, for the sake of secondary advantages, it strangles its own ability to love. Jesus knew this as he gazed across the table at his beloved Judas. So little did Jesus, in his unswerving love, want to recriminate against his friend that, with sadness, he let Judas have the last word: *You have said it.* If Judas would be damned, then he would have to damn himself. With his usual perfection, Shakespeare has explored a mental torture similar to Judas' in King Claudius' soul-searching soliloquy sometime after he has murdered Hamlet's father, who was to him brother and king, and married the sister-in-law he had made a widow. By now he has reached a climax of self-disgust and is torn between desiring repentance and despairing of its possibility. As with Judas, we have here a case of the murderous betrayal of one who was lord, brother, and trusting friend:

> O! my offence is rank, it smells to heaven;
> It hath the primal eldest curse upon't;
> A brother's murder! Pray I can not,
> Though inclination be as sharp as will. . . .
>   What then? What rests?
> Try what repentance can: what can it not?
> Yet what can it, when one can not repent?
> O wretched state! O bosom black as death!
> O limed soul, that, struggling to be free,
> Art more engaged![3]

King Claudius is caught in the sticky birdlime of his own conscience, about to be crushed by the contradiction between his unavoidable knowledge of the truth and the obstinacy of his power-hungry will. Both Claudius and Judas despair because their pride hinders them from acknowledging that, horrendous as their sins are, God's mercy is even greater and waiting to be embraced: "By this we shall know that we are of the truth, and reassure our hearts before him whenever our hearts condemn us; for God is greater than our hearts, and he knows everything" (1 Jn 3:19–20). Far from casting any stone, Jesus remains, instead, open to Judas to the very end, even

---

[3] *Hamlet*, III, 3:36–39, 64–69.

welcoming his treacherous kiss (cf. 26:48–50). "When he was insulted, he returned no insult; when he suffered, he did not threaten; instead, he handed himself over (παρεδίδου) to the one who judges justly" (1 Pet 2:23, NAB).

In view of our seemingly insurmountable human penchant for betrayal, perhaps our own wisest reaction to this excruciating scene would be to beg Jesus *not* to allow us to have the last word in the exchange. Having despaired of our capacity to save ourselves or even to construct a decent self, we should implore Jesus to descend to the Hades of our corruption and there whisper tenderly to our shameful and arrogant heart: YOU ARE ALREADY FORGIVEN! YOU HAVE ONLY TO CALL ON ME! I am persuaded that the meaning of Jesus' silence, sadness, and restraint in his encounter with Judas during the Last Supper is, precisely, that the Lord is creating a wide space of welcome between himself and Judas and eagerly waiting for just such a prayer of contrite surrender to reach his ears, both from Judas and from ourselves.

5. "OPEN YOUR MOUTH WIDE AND I WILL FILL IT"

The Institution of the Holy Eucharist
(26:26–30)

26:26a
    Ἐσθιόντων δὲ αὐτῶν
    λαβὼν ὁ Ἰησοῦς ἄρτον . . .

    Now as they were eating,
    Jesus took bread . . .

S OMETHING EXTRAORDINARILY NEW and shocking is about to be born from an ancient and familiar tradition. We Catholic Christians are so familiar with the concept and practice of the Holy Eucharist and its centrality to our life of faith that we tend to detach it from all context and treat it as a dazzling meteor simply fallen in our midst from heaven by a feat of divine generosity and creativity. And yet, as with every birth, the originality of this new creation by Jesus stands in a relationship of organic continuity and fulfillment, and not of opposition, with the Jewish matrix out of which it is being brought forth. Deep-rooted tradition in strict union with radical originality may well define the fundamental characteristic of any family, culture, or religious body that is truly alive, and the dynamic synthesis of astounding originality and organic continuity is surely one of the distinguishing features of the Catholic tradition. Nothing illustrates this better than the full reality of the Holy Eucharist as both Sacrifice and Presence.

The narrative of the Last Supper thus far has presented us with the usual setting: Jews reclining around the *seder* table on this holy first night of Passover. We have noted that the make-up of the group is unusual in that it consists, not of a traditional family, but of an all-male group of friends and companions united around the central figure of their Teacher. Unusual, too, of course, is the subject of conversation among them, which Matthew puts in relief: namely, the imminent betrayal of the Teacher by one of his disciples. But there is nothing extraordinary about the occasion itself and how it is being celebrated. No one passing by and glancing briefly through the window at the group eating together would have given the situation a second thought. However, during this Passover meal, events are occurring that come to life in quiet, subterranean fashion but that are going to change the whole course of society, human relationships, and religion itself. Above all, these events are going to change the fundamental manner in which people come to view and live their relationship to God and God's to them.

"Now as they were eating. . . ." From the outset, this meal among the disciples, with Jesus at the head of the table, already exhibits at least two distinct transformations of the human activity of eating. Man has in common with all living things the absolute necessity to ingest food in order to nourish life. Next to breathing, eating is the most basic activity of a sentient being, the *sine qua non* upon which all else rests. Eating and being alive, eating and life itself, are near synonyms. But since we men are compound beings, consisting of both matter and spirit, there is no physical activity on our part that can be called "purely physical" and no spiritual activity that can be called "purely spiritual". Everything we do, to varying degrees, partakes of both dimensions. And so we may say that, in a real sense, human civilization and culture are born the moment a group of people transforms the activity of physical eating—the individual physiological need to ingest food in order to live and thrive—into a vehicle and a context for nourishing spiritual needs as well. Sharing a meal, whether within the biological family or within society at large, is at the very center of all civilization. Eating the same food at the same time and place is a natural symbol and vehicle for all the other shared experiences and values of a group. This is the first transformation, which imbues a merely physiological process with social and spiritual meaning.

Like all other people, Jews too must eat. But here enters the unique Exodus experience of the Jews as God works through his servant

Moses to save his children from their slavery to Pharaoh. From within the power, anguish, and desperate hope of this experience, the simple human act of eating—not only as physical nourishment but also as celebratory social bonding—is raised to a wholly new and, indeed, sacred dimension. Communal eating is now transformed, by divine institution, into the ritual act of celebrating a people's deliverance from both slavery and the living death that slavery imposes. In the beginning, God created food for man's physical nourishment even before man had come into existence (cf. Gen 1:29); and now God, through this very vehicle of material food, creates a new order of historical, ethnic, and spiritual salvation that bears witness to God's personal care for his beloved creature, man.

The hasty meal of roast lamb and unleavened bread prescribed for Pesach in the Book of Exodus obviously represents not only material food to fortify the Jews physically for their trek across the Red Sea. As well, by divine ordinance, it comes to signify *the reception of life as such* by the active intervention of God's creative mercy and fidelity. God personally ordains the Passover celebration, speaking through Moses as his mouthpiece:

> Tell all the congregation of Israel that on the tenth day of this month they shall take every man a lamb according to their fathers' houses. . . . Your lamb shall be without blemish, a male a year old. . . . The whole assembly of the congregation of Israel shall kill their lambs in the evening. Then they shall take some of the blood, and put it on the two doorposts and the lintel of the houses in which they eat them. They shall eat the flesh that night, roasted; with unleavened bread and bitter herbs they shall eat it. . . . In this manner you shall eat it: your loins girded, your sandals on your feet, and your staff in your hand; and you shall eat it in haste. It is the LORD's Passover. For I will pass through the land of Egypt that night, and I will strike all the first-born in the land of Egypt, both man and beast; and on all the gods of Egypt I will execute judgments: I am the LORD. The blood shall be a sign for you, upon the houses where you are; and when I see the blood, I will pass over you, and no plague shall fall upon you to destroy you, when I strike the land of Egypt. This day shall be for you a memorial day, and you shall keep it as a feast to the LORD; throughout your generations you shall observe it as an ordinance for ever. (Ex 12:3–14)

We Christians hear this foundational passage from the Book of Exodus proclaimed solemnly in the liturgy of Holy Thursday evening, when we commemorate the Lord's Last Supper and his institution of the Blessed Eucharist.

Read with the informed eyes of faith, this passage can be found to contain all of Christian theology. The function of food as sustenance, the social gathering of families, a great and decisive journey, the human yearning for safety and freedom, blood as the essence of life: the Lord God of Israel, at a crucial moment in Israel's history, takes these fundamental elements of universal human experience and transforms them by raising them to a sacramental function. By divine intervention and ordinance, ordinary material and visible realities will henceforth communicate spiritual and invisible meanings. The power of God's intervention on behalf of his people will from now on be contained within the Passover ritual, with its role of memorializing and making present mystically for evermore deeds and effects that once emerged in a particular place and time.

God wills to make the Paschal experience of the Exodus, historically lived by a limited number of Jews, universally accessible to all Jews of all times through the celebration of the Passover ritual. It takes a continuing and believing community, consisting of believing families and the individuals that make them up, to make the Passover a timeless reality shared with all. Furthermore, Israel's joyful obedience to its Lord's Passover ordinances is the specific vehicle that makes the Passover universally accessible. The total salvific meaning of Passover, then, derives not only from God's initiative but from God's deeds and commands in conjunction with his people's obedience to his decrees, both interiorly in their hearts and concretely or "sacramentally" in their rituals. All of this is implied in Jesus' phrase to his disciples *I will make [or keep] the Passover* (ποιῶ τὸ πάσχα) that we have heard (26:18). However, there is no true communion with God without the participation of the heart, and likewise there is no community experience of God's presence and action without the memorializing power of liturgical ritual. Here lies the necessary balance, both Jewish and Catholic, between spiritual life and sacramental practice. Jewish and Catholic faith is profoundly rooted in historical event as revelatory of God's efficacious intervention in human existence.

"Now, as they were eating. . . ." Indeed, God's most sublime actions on our behalf are deeply rooted in our ordinary human existence. Desiring to impart his own divine life to us, and a share in his eternal bliss, God necessarily approaches us as the time-bound earthlings that we are and that he himself has made us to be! This phrase "now as they were eating", defining the particular context of the institution of the Holy Eucharist, is the linguistic shorthand that marks the emergence of an extraordinary and unheard-of event and deed out of the womb of a *fundamental* and, hence, most *ordinary* human activity. In his earthly life, Jesus is the first to obey the whole order established by God: in his incarnate life, he, the divine Word, shares fully, profoundly, and gladly in our total human condition, beginning with the sustenance of the body through eating.

But now Jesus masterfully takes in hand, as a given, certain elements of the biological activity of eating, already transformed into a banquet of cohesive social identity and consecrated as the solemn memorial of the Passover. By his familiar participation in this human meal, Jesus has made his own these three preexistent layers of real signification. Having thus personally assumed them, Jesus now proceeds to mold these given human elements sovereignly into a new creation as he takes up the bread and the cup and makes over them pronouncements that are astonishing, extravagant, to many even scandalous, and in any event totally unheard-of until this particular occasion. By taking up some of the *matzos* bread and a cup of wine at this point, Jesus is highlighting two central ingredients of the Passover meal, as seen in the Exodus narrative. However, his accompanying gestures and the words of eucharistic institution will now fill these elements with a new meaning that, while it does not contradict or exclude their traditional significance, nevertheless utterly fulfills and surpasses any possible previous association and understanding.

26:26b

λαβὼν ὁ Ἰησοῦς ἄρτον
καὶ εὐλογήσας ἔκλασεν
καὶ δοὺς τοῖς μαθηταῖς εἶπεν·
Λάβετε φάγετε, τοῦτό ἐστιν τὸ σῶμά μου

Jesus took bread
and blessing broke [it],
and giving [it] to the disciples, said:
"Take, eat; this is my body"

TREMENDOUS TENSION IS GENERATED here by the extreme contrast between the strange, truly outlandish meaning Jesus is compressing into these words and the very simple, almost casual manner in which he is uttering them, as if they told the most obvious thing in the world. The straightforward simplicity of the pronouncement, however, cannot conceal the solemn, indeed, hieratic tone of this rhythmic succession of syllables or the intense concentration of symbolic action that results from the swift accumulation of verbs: *eating, took, blessed, broke, gave, take, eat*, all of them with *bread* as object. But as the words come forth from Jesus' mouth, their effect is surprisingly natural, the very opposite of studied or artificial. The climaxing revelation toward which it is all leading, however, without abandoning the overarching sobriety of tone, takes a quantum leap far beyond anything that could be expected: THIS IS MY BODY.

Alongside the Exodus narrative of the institution of the Passover, we should here recall the Genesis narrative of the creation of man. Many strands of events and symbols from the Jewish Scriptures coalesce in Matthew 26:26–30, and, again, if we are to go deep into its meaning, it is crucial that we not read this text myopically, as if the Eucharist were an isolated and uniquely Christian phenomenon, with no antecedents. We must not lose from sight what it is that the Eucharist is fulfilling in God's plan, which has existed from the beginning for the salvation and life of the world. The relation between the Passover narrative in Exodus and our Matthew text is obvious; but that between Matthew's account of the institution of the Eucharist and man's creation in Genesis 1–2 is not so evident.

We begin by noting a striking number of parallel motifs between them. Both Genesis (1:27–29; 2:7–8, 15–16) and Matthew present an agent at work creating something new, something that has not existed before: in Genesis, it is man; in Matthew, the Eucharist. The agent in Genesis is God himself, who labors like a potter or a sculptor, taking preexisting material (earth) and shaping it into something that could not ever have been expected. Indeed, the radical transformation of the dust of the earth, as a result of God's creativity that takes it and molds it, results in a living being that resembles his Creator because this Creator has infused something of himself into his creature: his own breath. In Matthew, the agent is Jesus. What is perhaps most striking in this connection could easily be overlooked: namely, that the place of the Creator in Genesis is here assumed by Jesus as he ordains a new order of creation.

Jesus declares something to be which has not previously been, and this solely by the power of his intentionality, gesture, and word. Just as God blessed the Man and the Woman taken from his side after their creation, now Jesus blesses the bread he has taken up. And just as God commanded Adam and Eve, immediately after creating them and blessing them, to "be fruitful and multiply and fill the earth", so Jesus multiplies the bread by breaking it and distributing it to his disciples. He then commands them: "Take, eat." In a similar way God "planted a garden in Eden, . . . and there he put the man whom he had formed, . . . and the Lord God commanded the man, saying, 'You may freely eat of every tree of the garden'" (Gen 2:8, 16).

The specific command that Jesus gives his disciples is: "Take, eat; THIS IS MY BODY." This would appear to be both the wholly disorienting culmination of the narrative and the aspect of it without any possible parallel in Genesis or anywhere else. And so it is. Nevertheless, we may detect an important feature in the Genesis story that, while not being a parallel or a prefiguration of anything in Matthew, still casts abundant light on the institution of the Eucharist. I speak of the manner in which both God and Jesus solemnly proclaim the *identity* of their new creation. God says: "Let us make man in our image, after our likeness" (Gen 1:26). And Jesus takes bread and says: "This is my body." In the first instance, God wills a creature to come into being that will mirror and participate in its Creator's nature and personhood: man as a vehicle and epiphany of Divinity and a sharer of divine bliss. In the second instance, Jesus, likewise as Creator, takes an already existing creature—a sheet of *matzos* bread—and declares it to be his own body, to be broken, distributed, and eaten.

This second creation by Jesus, technically known by the name of "transubstantiation", is far more complex than the first. The Genesis creation involved the bestowal of the divine image, by an act of God himself, on a being simultaneously fashioned by God from material substance and divine breath. We may say that, in this case, earthly matter has been imbued with divine form. But in the transformation involved in the Eucharist, it is the very Person of the Word Incarnate who deliberately assumes the form of an already existing creature— bread—so as to be able to give himself in it, as food both material and spiritual, to the very creature, man, whom he as eternal Word first created in Genesis. In this eucharistic creation, we can come to see the furthest limit of God's humility and love and, in a certain sense, the full blossoming of the Mystery of the Incarnation. Though the theological concepts that try to explain it may sound somewhat convoluted, the reality itself of the Eucharist is luminously simple and astonishing. The Eucharistic Mystery reveals that the ultimate purpose the Word had in mind in becoming flesh was *for him to be able to give himself as food in the form of bread.* By an act of divine institution and re-creation, bread becomes the edible form of the eternal Word. No poetic creativity anywhere can be either more sublime or more real! In this one astonishingly unique yet all-determining case, *the Poet wholly* BECOMES *his Word* and, in turn, recapitulates—brings together within himself harmoniously—the whole hierarchy of the Real: human and divine, material and spiritual, temporal and eternal. Such is the Eucharist, in which are truly present "the body and blood, together with the soul and divinity, of our Lord Jesus Christ".[1] Nothing less would do for God in order to nourish his beloved, man, with divine life; so abyssal did God know man's hunger to be. Christ knew it well for he had himself infused it into man.

It would have been enough for the Word to become incarnate in order to redeem our human nature from within, to acquire the flesh

---

[1] "In the most blessed sacrament of the Eucharist 'the body and blood, together with the soul and divinity, of our Lord Jesus Christ and, therefore, *the whole Christ is truly, really, and substantially contained.*' " Thus teaches the *Catechism of the Catholic Church*, 2nd ed. (Rome: Libreria Editrice Vaticana; Washington, D.C., United States Catholic Conference, 1997), no. 1374, p. 346, quoting the Council of Trent, 1551 (DS 1651); italics mine.

and blood necessary to suffer with us and for us, and to offer them as an atoning oblation to the Father on the altar of the Cross. However here, in the unfathomable mystery of eucharistic *parádosis*, nestled within the equally unfathomable mystery of Judas' betrayal and Jesus' crucifixion, we witness the dynamic depths of the Word's condescension: the destruction of his flesh and the spilling of his blood are transmuted preemptively, by the creativity of the Word's wisdom and love, into the unsurpassable Sacrament that nourishes us unto life everlasting. Here the Word, revisiting the creation of man in his own image and likeness, re-creates his own assumed human form, taken from Mary, and plunges into even greater humiliation, obedient to the Father in his murderous betrayal into the hands of sinners.

In the institution of the Blessed Eucharist at the Last Supper, Jesus accomplishes the unheard-of: HE CREATES FOR HIMSELF A NEW FORM OF EXISTENCE AS FOOD FOR MAN'S LIFE. As supreme culmination of the work of redemption, God the Word Incarnate takes on the created form of greatest possible vulnerability by becoming edible and potable, in an act of creative anticipation and transformation of what would happen to him physically on Good Friday on the Cross. St. Thomas Aquinas has given succinct poetic expression to this mystery of *parádosis* in the hymn *Verbum supernum prodiens* (1264), which he composed for Lauds of the feast of Corpus Christi:

> In mortem a discipulo
> Suis tradendus æmulis,
> Prius in vitæ ferculo
> Se tradidit discipulis.
>
> Se nascens dedit socium,
> Convescens in edulium,
> Se moriens in pretium,
> Se regnans dat in præmium.

"When about to be handed over / To his enemies by a disciple, / To suffer death, he first handed himself / Over to his disciples in the bread of life. // By his birth he gave himself as our companion; / While eating with us he gave himself as our food; / Dying, he gave himself as our ransom; / Reigning in heaven he gives himself as our reward."[2]

---

[2] This Eucharistic hymn is not to be confused with the much earlier Advent hymn

Christ our Companion, Christ our Food, Christ our Ransom, Christ our Reward: in four words, the genius of Aquinas has summed up the whole sweep of our salvation. Truly, Christ became all things for us: "He who did not spare his own Son but gave him up for us all, will he not also give us all things with him?" (Rom 8:32).

Providing nourishment for the increase of life in man seems to be God's abiding purpose throughout the unfolding of his revelation, whether at the beginning of creation in Genesis or in his Passion, death, and Resurrection. Thus in Genesis, God "[plants] a garden in Eden" (2:8, 15–16) and puts man in it that he may have joy and life in abundance. He commands man to eat of all trees save one. And now, in Matthew, Jesus reveals that in the end only his own theandric substance will do to nourish the kind of life God intends for man to enjoy; and so Jesus the Word re-creates himself sacramentally as man's choicest food. And this extraordinary new creation has the result of installing man in the true and unending Eden. It is not surprising, then, that Jesus concludes the episode of the Last Supper with reference to his Father's Kingdom and the communal banqueting that will go on there unendingly (26:29). This merging of the Eden of the beginning with God's eternal Kingdom of the end is the final stunning parallel between the Genesis narrative of the creation of man and Matthew's narrative of the institution of the Eucharist.

THERE IS A PERENNIAL QUESTION that excites the wonderment of every beginning student of fundamental Judæo-Christian theology: "Being wholly without needs, why did God create anything? In particular, why did God create man?" And this question has an astoundingly

---

of the same title. Surely, by choosing the same first line for his hymn in honor of the Eucharist, St. Thomas wanted to link the mystery of Christ's Presence in the Holy Eucharist to the underlying mystery of his Incarnation and birth as a man.

simple and profound answer: God engaged in the act of creation because God, being Love, desired in perfect freedom *to give himself to what was not God.* This desire, as befits every divine desire, was so absolute that from the beginning everything about the first creation was oriented by God toward a second and final creation whereby God would bestow himself as man's food. In the divine institution of the Eucharist, the highest and the lowest coincide: utter majesty and power with utter humility and vulnerability, pure spirit with dense flesh, eternity with time, divinity with humanity, and all in order that God's beloved creature, man, "may have life, and have it abundantly" (Jn 10:10). Yet what can give abundant life everlastingly other than the substantial presence of God himself within us in a manner in which we can assimilate it? "take, eat; this is my body."[3]

We must readily admit that such an affirmation is indeed outrageous, bringing us squarely before the Chestertonian reduction: either this is the affirmation of a madman, or it is literally true. Taken literally, and in isolation from the whole history of revelation, it is likely to provoke natural aversion and elicit repugnance at almost every level of human sensibility, rationality, and mental comfort. Jesus' words would seem to be promoting some form of masochistic cannibalism. And yet we plainly encounter Jesus' unequivocal pronouncements on the matter in the sacred text of all four evangelists, in the affirmations of the apostle Paul, in the earliest patristic documents like the *Didache*, the *Letters* of Ignatius, the *Second Apology* of Justin, and the writings of Irenæus, as well as all along the uninterrupted liturgical and doctrinal tradition of the undivided Church of both East and West: "Take, eat; this is my body. . . . Drink of it, all of you; for this is my blood."

Inevitably endless attempts have been made through the ages by certain naysayers to dilute, reinterpret, accommodate, and spiritualize the Catholic and Orthodox understanding of these words from Jesus' own lips, whose personal authority and express command alone (as attested by the unbroken teaching and practice of the Church) form the foundation for this article of faith. As St. Thomas Aquinas again sings:

---

[3] From this perspective, we can better understand the literal truth of the title of Joseph Ratzinger's book, *God Is Near Us: The Eucharist, the Heart of Life*, trans. Henry Taylor (San Francisco: Ignatius Press, 2003). In the German original, the last part of the title calls the Eucharist "the center of life".

> Credo quidquid dixit Dei Filius;
> Nil hoc verbo Veritatis verius:

> "What God's Son has told me, take for truth I do;
> Truth Himself speaks truly or there's nothing true." [4]

The problem with the literal acceptance of the Lord's Real Presence in the Eucharist does not begin only in the sub-apostolic era, when the Christian Church had to explain her faith to those schooled in Greek ways of thought; nor does it arise only at the emergence of Scholasticism in the early Middle Ages, nor much less at the time of the Reformation, when Protestantism tended to over-spiritualize the concept of "sacrament" to the point of making it vanish from the realm of the real. The scandal of the Eucharist emerges already within the New Testament itself in a most conflictive way, most pointedly in the Gospel of John, during the great discourse on the Bread from Heaven. It is as if revelation itself must anticipate the inevitable conflict between God's eucharistic will and man's very limited capacity to understand it.

Toward the end of his soaring discourse on the Bread of Life in John 6, Jesus declares categorically: "Unless you eat the flesh of the Son of man and drink his blood, you have no life in you", and also "He who eats my flesh and drinks my blood abides in me, and I in him." Then we read poignantly that, in the face of such an offensive teaching, "many of his disciples . . . said, 'This is a hard saying; who can listen to it?'" (Jn 6:53, 56, 60). To this objection, Jesus reacts in a very serene and unapologetic way, replying: "Do you take offense at this? . . . There are some of you that do not believe" (Jn 6:61, 64). Then, seeing that the Master was not about to modify his teaching to accommodate their aversion to it, "many of his disciples drew back and no longer walked with him" (Jn 6:66). And let us not lose from sight that these protestors are not curious bystanders who are casually dropping away after a quick come-see: John stresses the point that they are full-fledged *disciples* who have already followed him for a considerable time. They have been docile and engaged, but this teaching is the limit.

Now, then: What does Jesus do in the face of their defection, when he sees that the uncompromising nature of his teaching is driv-

---

[4] In his hymn *Adoro te devote*, translation by Gerard M. Hopkins.

ing away promising recruits? Does he go running after them with assuaging proposals of accommodation? Does he explain that perhaps he *has* gotten a bit carried away with his metaphors in the heat of inspiration and that, after all, the idea of the Eucharist is still a "work-in-progress" requiring further refinement? Does he try to persuade them that the offending words should be understood at another, more spiritual and symbolic level, because their uncouth rawness has only been meant to capture people's attention?

Absolutely not! None of the above. Rather, just as imperturbably as before, Jesus turns to the Twelve and puts to them a simple question that in fact contains a strong hint: "[Do] *you also* [wish to] go away?" (Jn 6:67). There is something truly stunning in this reaction on Jesus' part. Jesus not only lets the disgruntled go—those who could be perceived as future troublemakers; in addition, he even turns up the heat, so to speak, and excludes no one from the category of the wobbly, those whose faith in him would most likely waver in the face of difficulties, doctrinal and otherwise. In no uncertain terms, Jesus manifests the crucial need for radical faith in his words by proclaiming loud and clear, through this rhetorical question, the utter freedom that the believer must exercise in following him, together with utter trust in his veracity, utter trust in the fact that he knows whereof he speaks: *Truth Himself speaks truly or there is nothing true.*

Do you also wish to go away? This question reveals not only the unbending nature of Jesus' teaching, the fact that he would prefer to have no followers at all rather than dilute the nature of his Father's entrusted truths; the question also shows that Jesus understands the great human difficulty involved and that the act of faith depends on a great *salto mortale*, a massive leap of trust, taken in total freedom, into the abyss of his embrace. The absolute, divine magnificence of what Jesus expects from his disciples is then matched by the humble, human magnificence of the reply of the spokesman for the group of apostles: "Simon Peter answered him, 'Lord, to whom shall we go? You have the words of eternal life'" (Jn 6:68).

In Jesus' unheard-of affirmations in John 6 we see the radical fulfillment of God's invitation to Israel in Psalm 81[80]: "I am the LORD your God, who brought you up out of the land of Egypt. *Open your mouth wide, and I will fill it*" (v. 10). Tragically, however, not only a promise but also a refusal are prefigured and fulfilled in the Scripture. For the reaction of the majority of Jesus' contemporaries to his generous self-bestowal alarmingly "fulfills" the stubborn rejection of God's nourishment recorded in the psalm: "But my people did not listen to my voice; Israel would have none of me" (v. 11).

Peter's humbly wondrous reply exposes the full depth of Peter's faith and trust in Jesus. Very movingly, Peter matches the unyielding nature of Jesus' doctrine. He does not whatsoever voice the complacent claim that he *understands* this doctrine and that, therefore, he has no problem following Jesus with perfect cheer. That would be the height of presumption and conceit! No: What Peter manifests instead—quietly, humbly, yet also with that passionate tenderness so typical of him—is the equally unyielding nature of his trust in Jesus as his friend and his irreversible determination to cling to Jesus' words for sheer life, quite beyond any intellectual question of understanding, acceptance, or rejection of the teaching. What reigns supreme in Peter's heart is his unbounded love for Jesus the Man and, inseparably, his unfaltering faith in Christ the Savior.

Let us also note well that Peter's dogged fidelity to Jesus and his sturdy affection for him, while not based on worldly reasoning, do not derive, either, from a simple disposition of "blind faith". In fact, like the rest of us, Peter has a huge personal stake in the matter. His reply to Jesus' sharp question is: "Lord, to whom shall we go? You have the words of eternal life." His rock-solid predilection for Jesus is a reaction of his whole being that is rooted in his own immense longing for fullness of life, which is exactly what Jesus is holding out to him: "He who eats my flesh and drinks my blood has eternal life, and I will raise him up at the last day. . . . He who eats my flesh and drinks my blood abides in me, and I in him" (Jn 6:54–56). This is not an abstract "eucharistic proposition" in the narrow sense of the term, something to puzzle over and then mentally accept or reject. Rather, Jesus' affirmation shows that the Eucharist at bottom is about nothing other than *life everlasting communicated and enjoyed through the mutual indwelling of lovers.* Jesus' discourse on the Bread of Life has apparently awakened in Peter this burning intuition, and it is by its power that Peter leaps with trust into the most desirable of realities. Peter intuits that the speaker is as good as his word because (outlandish as it sounds) this particular speaker is offering nothing other than himself, his whole self, for consumption by anyone who listens: TAKE, EAT; THIS IS MY BODY. These may well be the most extravagant, astonishing, mysterious, provocative, generous, and true words ever uttered by any human mouth. Their strange uniqueness radiates healing light and peace and, therefore, invites belief. But such wholehearted acceptance can, in turn, be explained only if, together with Peter, we discern that the human mouth that speaks those startling words belongs to a Divine Person.

א

26:27–28   καὶ λαβὼν ποτήριον καὶ εὐχαριστήσας
ἔδωκεν αὐτοῖς λέγων·
Πίετε ἐξ αὐτοῦ πάντες,
τοῦτο γάρ ἐστιν τὸ αἷμά μου τῆς διαθήκης
τὸ περὶ πολλῶν ἐκχυννόμενον εἰς ἄφεσιν ἁμαρτιῶν

And taking a cup and having given thanks,
he gave [it] to them, saying,
"Drink of it, all [of you];
for this is my blood of the covenant,
poured out for many for the forgiveness of sins"

WHAT WOULD BE THE LASTING GOOD of even the most magnificent metaphor if it remained merely a metaphor? While the best poetic and religious symbols available can enlighten the mind on the *manner* of love's communication, only *partaking substantially of Love itself* can nourish the human soul. Are we truly going to base the whole of our lives—all our ethical endeavors, all our actions and exertions, all our loves and renunciations, joys and sacrifices, and our total human quest for fulfillment, including the meaning of our death—on the beauty of a metaphor that never quite blossomed into concrete reality?

During the Bread of Life discourse, Jesus said: "I am the bread of life. Your fathers ate the manna in the wilderness, and they died. This is the bread which comes down from heaven, that a man may eat of it and not die" (Jn 6:48–50). In this contrast between the historical manna of Exodus and Jesus' declared presence as bread, we see very clearly illustrated the crucial difference between metaphor and reality in connection with the Eucharist. Jesus is saying that the manna, though it was a miraculously God-given sign, ultimately proved to be a corruptible food like any other that could not sate man's deepest yearning for fullness of life. In fact, worms began to grow in the manna if it was kept for a second day (Ex 16:20). We see that, within the sweep of revelation, the manna was a very tangible and effective metaphor—but a metaphor nonetheless—of God's care for his people, but not the reality of the gift of life as such. However, as a divinely designed metaphor concretized in a historical happening, the manna already implicitly contains the promise of the Eucharist. In that sense, it is its prefiguration, for it shows that God's benefits for man always must become embodied in realities that adequately correspond to man's total nature and concrete needs.

"I am the bread of life", on the other hand, means that only an incarnate God, by bestowing himself under a material form, can effectively communicate the unending vitality and inexhaustible fullness of incorruptible life. Why? Because only God both *possesses* and *is* Life itself. Therefore, only God can bestow the Life he is, and only a God who is also man can communicate the Life he is in a manner that man can absorb it and make it his own. "Bread from heaven", thus, is the perfect linguistic metaphor to refer to a paradoxical and truly existing reality that derives simultaneously from "below" and from "above", inseparably, a reality that unites the qualities of the divine with the materiality of the earthly and as such is an apt synthesis for the two natures in the one person of the incarnate Word: "I am the bread which came down from heaven" (Jn 6:41). The fact that Jesus here identifies his very person (his "I") with *bread* means that the incarnate Word has come among us explicitly as our food. Only the Word himself in person could make the affirmations Jesus makes in these extraordinary texts. Jesus' astounding self-identification with "bread" reveals his whole existence, as both God and Man, as defined by his boundless availability as *nourishment* for all. For Jesus, *to be* and *to be food* are synonymous.

The metaphor's fulfillment and enfleshed reality (the Eucharist) must, by definition, infinitely surpass the promise and the prefiguration (the manna) that preceded them; otherwise, no progress has been accomplished by God in the course of revelation. There cannot be between promise and fulfillment a difference only of degree; the difference must be of kind; else we still remain within the realm of the purely symbolic, regardless of how sublime and seductive the metaphors become. Even though the manna may *retrospectively* be said to point forward to the Eucharist, the Eucharist itself can by no means be regarded as just another form of manna, that is, as nothing more than an even stronger *reminder* of God's untiring care for man, coming from Jesus himself. When Jesus exclaims in no uncertain terms "This is my body", then we know that the ontological abyss between prefiguration and reality has at long last been bridged by the only One who could do so. Only then has the ultimate and unsurpassable fulfillment of God's every promise been attained: not by man striving "from below", but indeed by God himself reaching down "from above", through his divine designs and institutions.

Only God can fulfill his own promises because this fulfillment, if it is truly *fulfillment*, must be as eternal and boundless and perfect as God himself. Consider carefully that, if the Eucharist did not surpass the manna or any of its other prefigurations by an ontological quantum leap, then the historical manna, though corruptible, would be preferable to the Eucharist because at the very least it offered not only a beautiful metaphor for divine sustenance but actual solid, physical nourishment for one calendar day, while a little piece of merely symbolic *matzos* or a thin Communion wafer hardly amounts to much by way of corporeal nourishment. This is why, in the solemn words that Jesus utters at the Last Supper over the bread and the wine, we should look closely at the single word τοῦτο (*toúto*), which he repeats over each of the two eucharistic elements as he holds it: "*This* is my body. . . . *This* is my blood." In this verbal communication between Jesus and his disciples, three realities are involved: Jesus the speaker, the apostles as addressees, and the bread and wine. We are taken aback in wonderment by how Jesus draws specific attention to the material items he is physically holding while at the same time making a verbal declaration that binds them mysteriously to his own personhood and corporality.

TOÚTO: Let us look more closely at this word, crucial in the present context. "*Toúto* is my body", affirms Jesus. "*Toúto* is my blood". The word *toúto*, which Jesus repeats to solemn effect as he holds the bread and the wine in succession, is a demonstrative pronoun in its neuter form. This grammatical fact ought to interest theologians and ordinary Christians as much as linguists. This little colorless word, in fact, may well be the most concentrated demonstration of how earnestly and literally Jesus means what he is saying. As he speaks these words, Jesus could, for example, point with his hand to his own physical body and say, "This is my body", meaning the utterance in the same way as any of us can say, "This is my nose" or "This is my knee." However, such an understanding would simply belabor the obvious and, hence, lack all interest. In any event, such a meaning is simply impossible given the actual words Jesus pronounces, with their precise lexical significance. As a matter of fact, in context, Jesus is pointing, not to his physical body, as he says, "Take, eat; this is my body," but to the bread he has taken, blessed, broken, and is about to distribute among his disciples.

In the first place, Jesus is not making a general metaphorical statement about his generous availability to his friends as the "food" of their souls in time of need. Rather, he is literally holding in his hand, first, some *matzos* bread and, then, a cup of wine, and it is while referring to these concrete items in his hand that he says, "This is my body" and "This is my blood." It is about these substances in particular that he is concretely making his declarations, and not about his person in general. In fact, it would be quite strange if Jesus were offering his disciples his spatio-physical presence as consolation precisely at the moment when he is about to be wrested away from them forever in this mortal form.

It would seem, rather, that Jesus is mercifully transmuting the manner of his presence to his disciples by inviting them to take with him a wholly unexpected leap into an altogether different dimension of existence. He is offering them an unprecedented manner of presence. In itself, the Eucharist is a most unified and pure mystery of utter simplicity; but, because it is also an absolutely unparalleled mystery, all explanatory analogies must soon capitulate in the face of its incomparability. First and last, we are left with the strange yet also strangely comforting resonance of the incarnate Word's stark affirmations: *This is my body. This is my blood.*

From what the disciples have experienced thus far with him— namely, ordinary human association in the sensory and spatio-temporal realm—Jesus now initiates them to the enjoyment of his real, sacramental presence in the mystery of the blessed Bread and Wine. This sacramental mystery, in fact, despite its stunning novelty, actually corresponds more intimately to the human need to commingle, through Christ's enfleshed mediation, with the life of the Divine Trinity as both nourishing Ground and eternal Home. Again, we cannot call attention often enough to the manner of this staggering deed of divine creativity: the Lord Jesus, precisely at the moment he is entering the hour of his human demise, uses his own violent death, so wantonly inflicted, as a glorious means to transform mere human destructiveness into another and more profoundly nourishing mode of presence. Fire and knives may be used to kill; they may also be used to prepare food for the hungry. In the present and unique instance, the creating Word is using, as tools for transformation, the piercing knives and consuming fire that have been turned against himself by others. Thus, by a providential act of creation elicited by the Father, Jesus, the Paschal Lamb about to be slain (cf. Rev 5:6, 12; 13:8), transmutes in advance his own wanton murder into a sacrifice of efficacious atonement and fruitful communion.

This transmutation of destructive hatred into abundant life by the power of Jesus' creative love is so fruitful a reality that it becomes the dynamic and normative mark of the Christian ethos as such, the very seal of specifically Christian holiness. Recently Pope Francis has expressed this truth explicitly in connection with the seven Trappist monks of Tibhirine in Algeria, murdered in 1996 simply for being a silent and benevolent Christian presence in a place and a time of violent turmoil. With luminous insight, the pontiff points out that *"the murderers did not take [the monks'] life, because they had already given it in advance. . . . They did not flee from violence: they fought violence with the weapons of love, of fraternal hospitality, of communal prayer. . . . There is no other way of combating the evil that is weaving its web in our world".* [5]

Now, looking more closely at the importance of the word *toúto* in the words of institution of the Eucharist: Since it is a neuter pronoun, it has the literal meaning of *this thing here*. It is too concrete a term for it to be understood as referring to a vague "this". The English

---

[5] Philippe Cardinal Barbarin, Marc Trévidic, François Cheng, eds., *Tibhirine, l'héritage*, preface by Pope Francis (Paris: Bayard, 2016). Emphasis mine.

word *this*, lacking any kind of gender ending, is ambiguous and can serve both as a neuter pronoun (as in the present case, meaning "this thing here") or as an adjective in any of the three genders. The precision of the Spanish and French equivalents is much more helpful in this regard. Thus, in Spanish, we have *Esto es mi cuerpo* (with the neuter pronoun *esto* rather than the masculine *este* [R95, PER]), and in French, *Ceci est mon corps* (again with the neuter pronoun *ceci* rather than the masculine *celui* [TOB, FBJ]). Both the Spanish and the French renderings, along with the Greek original, make it perfectly clear that Jesus is saying, *This thing is my body*.

Both the mystery and the power of the eucharistic declarations reside in the linguistic audacity Jesus permits himself. His stunning boldness no doubt mirrors the extraordinary daring of his Father's total design of salvation, admirably summed up in one unthinkable sentence of John's Gospel: "As the living Father sent me, and I live because of the Father, so he who eats me will live because of me" (Jn 6:57). Trinitarian life, mutual indwelling of the Persons, divine mission, *and the human act of eating the Bread of Life* are all shown by Jesus' declaration to be inseparable aspects of the one mystery of salvation in Christ. If, in this cohesive series, the last item—sacramental consumption of the Body of Christ—is degraded to the level of mere "spiritual metaphor", the same fate must befall the first three items. Then the salvation intended by God as participation in the divine Life, simply disintegrates.

If Jesus had pointed to his physical body as he spoke the accompanying words, he would have reverted from the realm of fulfillment to that of mere metaphor. This is so because of the horror and impossibility of anyone actually "taking and eating" his body of mortal flesh cannibalistically or of drinking the actual blood in his veins. Thus, we see that the texts before us, looming hard and clear as a granite mountain, propose one of three mutually exclusive possibilities of interpretation: either repellent cannibalism, mere prefiguration, or sacramental fulfillment. The mistake made in connection with the Eucharist by many persons with a spiritualizing Protestant tendency is, understandably, to flee in disgust from the first possibility and take refuge at the other extreme, opting for some glorified form of the second possibility. But this option surprisingly fails to understand how the third possibility (sacramental fulfillment of the promises) in fact is in greatest harmony with both the sacred texts and the Church's millennial understanding of the Eucharist.

We have observed that at this moment at the end of the Last Supper, by his gestures and the words that accompany them, Jesus is inviting his followers to join him in a staggering leap into a wholly different sphere of existence and presence that we have called "sacramental", meaning something concrete that communicates the mysteries of Christ. Externally, physically, empirically, nothing changes: the disciples see the same borrowed room for the *seder* by flickering candle light, and they present to one another the same haggard and puzzled faces; they bask in the same comforting and challenging presence of the Teacher while smelling the same pungent whiff of rosemary in the balmy evening air. . . . But Jesus' gestures and words on this occasion are even more surprising and fraught with mystery than usual. Human gestures and words, though visible and audible, often act in the realm of the senses as heralds of events and realities not perceivable by the senses. By a kind of divine creative *poiêsis*, the Word Incarnate, consummate cosmic Poet, resorts to certain expressive means to communicate the meaning of a reality that ultimately is beyond both gestures and words: the act of his self-bestowal. Jesus' language becomes formulaic and almost incantatory, both for mnemonic purposes and in order to heighten the sense of the solemnity of what is occurring. All of these means become the perceivable "markers" that trace the trajectory of what I have termed "the leap" ventured by Jesus into the mystical sphere of the sacramental, the sphere where man participates very literally in the life of God, communicated by Christ.

Very significantly, Jesus' words are as elementary, concrete, and succinct as they are fraught with mystery and resonance. Such is always the secret of the greatest poetry, from Homer to Shakespeare to T. S. Eliot. Nothing could be less abstract than these pronouncements of Jesus, fraught with both material references and palpable material referents. As the Paschal meal concludes, the very act of eating and the meaning of food are transformed by Jesus' declarations. An unheard-of kind of food and manner of eating are proclaimed by him to be even now coming into being. The ritual of the *seder*, under his command, almost imperceptibly gives birth to a wholly new ritual, never seen before. The word "rite" is indeed apt here because of the dense accumulation of symbolic elements and actions that occurs in a short compass: the simultaneous progression of word and gesture, the rhythmic and mysterious character of the words, the parallelism of the formulas involved, the officiating presence of a "priest", the presence of a "congregation", the presentation of sacramental "matter", and, finally, a miniature "homily" by Jesus that explains the meaning of his words and gestures and relates the rite vitally to his own impending death. Disparate as these features may sound in their enumeration, in context they constitute a remarkably articulated and unified whole.

If we look more closely at the structure and development of Jesus' words and actions at this moment, we begin to appreciate why the passage is so fundamental and has such impact. In the first place, his eucharistic action is divided into two main parts, that involving the bread and that involving the wine. This separate treatment of the two sacramental "species" or elements has profound theological meaning, for it symbolizes *the nature of the Eucharist as an acceptable sacrifice*, effecting the forgiveness of sins and reconciliation with God. In Exodus and Leviticus, whenever the text prescribes the various aspects of ritual sacrifice, we encounter many passages such as the following two: "The priest shall bring [the bird victim] to the altar and wring off its head, and burn it on the altar; and its blood shall be drained out on the side of the altar" (Lev 1:15). "Then the priest shall take some of the blood of the sin offering with his finger and put it on the horns of the altar of burnt offering, and pour out the rest of its blood at the base of the altar. . . . [A]nd the priest shall make atonement for him for the sin which he has committed, and he shall be forgiven" (Lev 4:34–35). The separation of the victim's blood from its body is the sign of a sacrifice. Thus, when Jesus points separately to the bread as his Body, located in one place, and to the cup as his Blood, at a distance, this ritual separation of the wine/blood from the bread/body in the sacrament anticipates his historical death by crucifixion. At that moment on Golgotha, his literal blood would drain from his literal body and drench the earth as it flowed forth massively from the five great wounds inflicted on him as well as from the thorn-crowned head and sundry other injuries.

Each of the two halves of the eucharistic rite, as instituted by Jesus at the Last Supper, contains a number of elements found in both, thus binding together into unity the one single offering in two species. Of both the bread and the cup the text says twice that Jesus "took" it, repeating the same form of the word (λαβών). This word, in turn, is again repeated at the distribution of the bread, in the imperative plural: "Take (λάβετε), eat; this is my body." The verb is crucial because it signals Jesus' *parádosis* of himself, the moment when he freely takes his life into his own hands, not to clutch and protect it, but only in order to give it away, in anticipation of his physical apprehension in Gethsemane: "For this reason the Father loves me, because I lay down my life, that I may take it again. No one takes it from me, but I lay it down of my own accord" (Jn 10:17–18). The verb "to take", then, here denotes Jesus' sovereignty, the extent to which he is acting as a wholly free agent determining his own destiny and fashioning the triumph of divine love out of impending physical defeat.

Immediately after taking up the bread, but before making any declaration concerning it, Jesus "blessed and broke and gave [it] to his disciples", three weighty and wordless actions that follow the initial "took". "Blessing" here binds the action and its meaning to their ultimate source in the Father, author of the project of redemption through Jesus. "Blessing" is likewise a sign of transformation, in both a general and a restrictive sense. What God blesses he sets apart as holy and as dedicated to his service. That very fact already changes its ordinary, pragmatic functions and converts the blessed item in question into an instrument of salvation. Jesus' act of blessing reflects the approval of the heavenly Father, the profound accord existing between Father and Son, and the good pleasure the Father takes in the new order of things Jesus is instituting. However, in the more restrictive sense, Jesus' *act of blessing the bread* in particular effects its transformation into his Body so that he, the truthful Word, is then justified in declaring it to be such beyond all metaphorical interpretations. This Bread is made holy and set apart by this blessing in the same sense that the person of Jesus is holy and set apart for the exclusive service and glory of the Father.

In the case of the wine cup, rather than "blessing" it, Jesus "gives thanks" (εὐχαριστήσας) over it or for it, and, as we know, it is from this Greek term that we derive our English word *eucharist*. Now, "to bless" and "to give thanks" are nearly synonymous terms in the Hebrew mind because they are both spiritual actions that refer the very existence and goodness of everything that is back to the Creator. No doubt both of these verbs may be understood in this context as applying equally to the bread and to the wine, even though they are each uttered only once, for the sake of simplicity. Both "blessing" and "thanksgiving" are incessantly circulating spiritual activities that go back and forth between the Creator and the creature.

So crucial is the concept of *thanksgiving* to the Judæo-Christian world view that it becomes the central operative term in eucharistic theology. Writing as early as the middle of the second century A.D., Justin Martyr describes the celebration of the Eucharist for a hostile non-Christian audience. He says that at Communion time "the deacons distribute [it] to each one, . . . so that they partake from the 'eucharisticized' (εὐχαριστηθέντος) bread and wine and water."[6] This peculiarly Christian use of the verb *eucharistéô* is clearly a neologism not to be found in Classical Greek and developed in the early Church to refer to the uniqueness of what Justin is describing. The sacramental act of thanksgiving spoken by the priest over the eucharistic species is understood to be so powerful that the bread and wine are seen to become consecrated (in English, we might say "thanktified"!) into Christ's Body and Blood precisely by having had this particular thanksgiving said over them.[7]

As is evident, in this sacramental context, "blessing" and "giving thanks" are far more than simply *notional acts*; at their most profound level, they are *dynamic states of being* that hold sway in a person who relates vitally to God as the universal Source. If we allow their proper dynamism to engage us, habitual blessing and thanksgiving draw us into the torrential flow of the Creator's magnificent energy. And then *undying joy* necessarily springs forth from blessing and thanksgiving for the simple reason that to *bless* something God has created (whether person, thing, event, or the whole cosmos) and to *give thanks* for it are acts tantamount to *completing God's work of creation*. If we sustain such acts with our whole being, we shall certainly enter into the very furnace of divine Love and Joy that first impelled the Primal Goodness to go out of itself in the act of creation. To bless and to give thanks are our royal means of becoming co-creators with God by accepting the summons of his merciful condescension: *He blessed, he gave thanks, and said: Take. . . .* By nourishing us with his own substance, Christ draws us to partake truly in everything he is, both as Creator and as

[6] Justin Martyr, *First Apology*, 65, 5.
[7] Lampe Patristic Lexicon, 579.

Redeemer—that is, to share both in his Joy for creating and in his Passion for redeeming.

Two further verbs now used by Jesus signal specifically sacrificial actions. After taking the bread and blessing it, he *broke* it, and after giving thanks over the cup, he declared the wine it contained to be "my blood of the covenant, which is *poured out*". "Breaking" and "pouring out" are actions that correspond, the one, to the frangibility of bread and, the other, to the liquidity of wine. These two verbs give us the essential key to the theology of sacrifice, for they simultaneously denote a destruction and a plenitude. The nature of bread calls for its being eaten: by being consumed, bread reaches its perfection, its very reason for being. Thus, the breaking of bread is the penultimate step of its perfectioning since only then can it be distributed and eaten. Likewise, the nature of wine calls for its being drunk: by being imbibed, wine reaches its perfection, its greatest potency, and the fulfillment of its existence. In this way, we see that it is only by losing their pristine wholeness to "destruction" that bread and wine paradoxically attain their fullness of purpose, their "plenitude".

Modern Greeks have a curious habit in connection with bread. If for whatever reason (staleness, dirt) you have to throw away a piece of bread, you should first kiss it. This admirable custom, I think, surely contains an allusion to the consecrated bread of the Eucharist, which all bread can be seen to represent. But perhaps at its deepest level, this Greek usage reflects the intuition of faith that all food, created by God, is sacred because it already bears an image of the divine nature as "diffusive of itself". The Eucharist can then be seen to embody the extreme case of this more general truth. The custom instinctively connects the goodness of food as such to the unsurpassable good that is the Bread from Heaven. As such, it harmonizes to perfection with Jesus' seamless transition between, simply, eating with his friends to the institution of the Eucharist. "As they were eating, Jesus took bread. . . ." One unbroken golden thread of revelation leads from the Garden of Eden to the Last Supper. The Lord God "put the man whom he had formed" in Eden, and there, just for him, God "made to grow every tree that is pleasant to the sight and *good for food*" (Gen 2:8–9). And at the Last Supper, Jesus said, "*Take, eat*; this is my body." In all the food that God creates for man's physical nourishment, he is first and foremost revealing, to the retrospective eyes of faith, his own divine desire to give himself away to man so that his beloved creature may have fullness of life.

"Breaking" and "pouring out", then, are the actions by which bread and wine reach their full potential as a sacrifice. By Christ's generous blessing and creating will, they are transformed into something that becomes a means for man to enter into satisfying communion with God. Just as fire transforms wood into fire, light, and heat, so, too, Christ's all-powerful and intentional blessing transforms the substance of bread and wine into his own Body and Blood so that these can be, respectively, *broken and poured out*. These actions appear natural and necessary enough at the dining table and at the altar in the temple of Jerusalem; but they acquire a starkly tragic resonance when the ritual gestures of the Eucharist merge with their existential equivalents in Jesus' lived history. It goes without saying, moreover, that Eucharist and Golgotha *must* merge into one because the ritual sacrifice of the Eucharist is emptied of all meaning apart from its mystical content, which is the redeeming sacrifice on the Cross of wood. Simultaneously, the historical sacrifice of the Cross on that first Good Friday, if it does not become fruitful sacramentally in the Eucharist, remains nothing but just another criminal execution of a particularly unjust and bloody sort.

We should not forget that the ritual of the Eucharist is the real, efficacious, and sacramental representation or "reenactment" of Christ's Sacrifice on the Cross, which took place at a specific moment in time and in a specific geographical location on this earth. Jesus' Passion is the incarnate God's concrete *enactment* or living-out, in space and time, of his eternal nature as Self-Bestower. However, lest we think of God's self-bestowal in terms of worldly grandiosity or aristocratic *noblesse oblige*, let us remember that "though [Christ] was rich, yet for your sake he became poor, so that by his poverty, you might become rich" (2 Cor 8:9). Thus abject humility, poverty, and hiddenness were the mode of God's descent into our realm. This implies in turn that his manner of bestowing his substance has nothing in common with the majestic cosmic flow of a magnificent cataract as it breathtakingly brims over from above upon an arid world. God's self-bestowal, rather, is more nearly like a haggard mother feeding milk, her breast's substance, to her baby with quiet joy in the dark of night while suffering from sleep deprivation, and her only reward for days on end is an intense burning in her flesh. As well, not seldom the bruised mother's own blood may flow into her baby with her milk. *Drink, this is my blood.* Ah, the luminous humility of God hiding in bread and wine and existing, like a nursing mother, only in order to be consumed by her darling child. . . .

Jesus' eucharistic gestures and words at the end of the Last Supper climax in two commands. For the bread, the command is: *Take, eat!* And for the cup: *Drink of it, all of you!* There is very good reason why Jesus' fondest desire is communicated here in the form of imperative commands: without these, who would dare even to contemplate such an action, much less perform it? The entire passage is shot through with and structured by an overpowering sense that, whatever is occurring here and whatever it means, all of it derives solely and mysteriously from the design, will, and execution of Jesus the Lord. What eyes here see and ears hear, only faith can accept and enact. "Odd and forbidding though it all sounds," the disciples must have thought to themselves, "this is the way he wants it, and we must obey whether or not we understand and like what he is ordaining. We must obey because we are convinced that he is both the Truth and the Life, and we trust him." Such a sentiment would be very much in keeping with Peter's reply to the Lord at the end of the Discourse on the Bread of Life in John 6: "Lord, to whom shall we go? You have the words of eternal life" (Jn 6:68).

Implied as well in these eucharistic commands in Matthew is their exemplariness, that is, Jesus' intention that the Church, embodied here in this group of disciples, should in perpetuity do what they now see him do, and intending what he intends. The normative typicality of the ritual instituted by Jesus calls for its sacramental reenactment and is explicitly enjoined by the Lord in Luke's account of the institution (Lk 22:19–22) and in Paul's account of the handing-down of Jesus' words (1 Cor 11:23–25), no doubt already a vital part of the community's liturgical celebration: "I received (παρέλαβον) from the Lord what I also [handed over (παρέδωκα)] to you, that the Lord Jesus on the night when he was [handed over (παρεδίδετο)] took bread (ἔλαβεν ἄρτον). . . ." In a real sense, the apostles are to "impersonate" Jesus when they reenact his words and actions in the Eucharist. They are *not* to say, in indirect discourse, "Jesus said that you should take and eat, because this is his body", but rather they are to repeat his own words verbatim, in the first person, as their own words: *Take, eat; this is my body.* Such sacramental impersonation succeeds in removing all obstacles between the Institutor and the institution, so that the apostles, by obeying Jesus' command, become true transparent servers of the Lord's Presence and Self-Bestowal.

After issuing his command that his disciples should eat of this astonishing Bread and drink from this incomparable Cup,[8] Jesus makes twin declarations about the *identity* of this taken, blessed, broken, and given Bread and of this taken, thanked-for, poured-out, and given Wine. We should note well the crucial difference between what Jesus *could* have said in these declarations of identity and what he actually *does* say. Jesus could have said, for instance: "Take this bread and eat it, because it is *like* my body, or *represents* my body, or should *remind* you of my body." If he had said that, a new and wondrous marvel would still be involved because the statement strongly implies that he, their *Lord*, in some sense should also be their *food*. However, in this case, a comfortable dichotomy would still obtain between the bread Jesus is holding in his hand and Jesus' body itself. Now, let us grant that even the purely symbolic, hypothetical statement would have been an enormity while still remaining within palatable confines.[9] After the initial shock caused by the unusual language, the realization "He meant it only as a symbol!" thankfully sets the queasy mind at ease because all the troubling mystical strangeness has vanished.

As a matter of fact, however, this hypothetical alternate version of the words of institution is not what Jesus says. The three Synoptics, the Gospel of John, and Paul in 1 Corinthians—to say nothing of the unbroken tradition of the undivided Church from the beginning—are all unanimous in affirming the authenticity of the difficult and unadulterated words of Jesus: *This is my body. . . . This is my blood.* These words unequivocally establish an ontological identity between

[8] The First Eucharistic Prayer of the Latin Rite, also called the "Roman Canon", calls the cup of Christ's Blood *hunc præclarum calicem*, "this precious chalice".

[9] I here use the words "comfortable" and "palatable" under the influence of a certain kind of contemporary jargon that speaks of "a religion I'm comfortable with". In this connection, I recall as well the proud (and sensible) declaration by a character in Flannery O'Connor's story "The Displaced Person": "Mrs. Shortley looked at the priest and was reminded that these people [i.e., Catholics] did not have an advanced religion. There was no telling what all they believed since none of the foolishness had been reformed out of it." In *The Complete Stories* (New York: Farrar, Straus and Giroux, 1971), 208. Mrs. Shortley's observation eloquently voices a rather common reaction to Catholic belief in Christ's Real Presence in the Eucharist, a reaction sometimes coming, alas, even from alleged Catholics!

the neuter demonstrative pronoun *this* (referring to the object Jesus is holding in his hand) and the predicate nominative that follows the verb *is*, first, *my body* and, then, *my blood*. Moreover, it is significant that Jesus does not even utter the words "bread" and "wine". He does not say "This bread is my body" or "This wine is my blood." Although these statements do clearly declare that an identity of being exists between the subject of the sentence and the predicate nominative, nevertheless a certain tense polarity is still generated within each statement by the mere presence in it of two different nouns (respectively bread/body and wine/blood).

Thus the precise, canonical form of Jesus' utterance banishes all polarity and immensely simplifies and strengthens the mysterious statement by giving it a deep grounding in the oneness of Jesus' person: *"This [thing I am holding] is my body."* Nothing could surpass such an utterance for both its simplicity and its depth. Linguistically speaking, Jesus has made "bread" disappear altogether, and henceforth it subsists only as *his body*. I believe that this linguistic truth embodies the ontological truth of the Holy Eucharist. What to the eyes of flesh continues to be *mere bread* has become, by Jesus' express declaration, *his Body* to the eyes of the spirit quickened by faith in Jesus' unassailable veracity.

Inevitably, we recall in this context the turns of phrase we read in Genesis describing God's creation of all the individual, primary realities in the world, for instance the light: "And God said, 'Let there be light'; and there was light. And God saw that the light was good" (Gen 1:3–4). Here the word *light*, spoken by God, exists in God's mind before the actual creature *light* comes into being. It is precisely God's uttering the word he has in his mind that brings this desired creature into being. And then on the sixth day, at the end of the process of creation, God sets his seal on his creation by taking joy in contemplating the goodness of all he has created: "And God saw everything that he had made, and behold, it was very good" (Gen 1:31). Three phases are involved, then, in God's act of creation, with God himself as the subject of each stage: these are *conceiving*, *naming*, and *delighting*. This threefold pattern of the divine creating act in Genesis is here recapitulated by Jesus as he institutes the Eucharist.

The taking-up of the bread and the wine, along with the accompanying actions, corresponds to the divine *intentionality*, the conception or desire in God's mind to do something wholly new. To be sure, the

Eucharist is not fashioned *ex nihilo*, from nothing, as are the creatures in Genesis, but from preexisting bread and wine; and yet Jesus the Creator envisions so drastic a transformation for these available entities that we may, indeed, speak of a new creation. There follows the actual uttering of the decisive words that name the new identity of this bread and this wine according to the mind of Jesus. The rhythmic *naming* ("My body", "my blood") efficaciously brings about their transformation into Christ's Body and Blood, just as the threefold repetition of the word "light" in Genesis (a reality first *thought about*, then *spoken*, and finally *seen* by God) brings real light into being. Let us as well keep in mind that Jesus' sole intention in effecting this transformation is *his self-bestowal as nourishment*. Therefore, it goes without saying that he could not have transformed the bread and the wine into anything other than himself! In other words, we are not witnessing here an arbitrary sleight-of-hand by some dazzling wonder-worker; rather, we are witnessing the eternal and all-powerful Word Incarnate choosing to give away his own Being through the instrumentality of his own creation, first at the natural and then, on its basis, on the supernatural level.

Finally, the *delight* that Jesus experiences in crowning the work of redemption by instituting the Eucharist is expressed by his actually distributing his Body and Blood among those he loves in order that he may from now on live in them permanently, in a reciprocal interpenetration of being: "He who eats my flesh and drinks my blood abides in me, and I in him" (Jn 6:56). Nothing could be more sublime, nothing more desirable, nothing more perfectly corresponding to the nature and longing of love. However, such wildly elusive superlatives can become truly subsistent, life-giving Relation only through the self-sacrificial, creative act of the incarnate Word, who always keeps his promises because he both *can* and *wants* to do so. In him, power and love are one, and for this reason his greatest joy and delight is a union of identity whereby everything that he is and has can be enjoyed by his disciples as well. It is not surprising, then, that in the section on Jesus the True Vine in his farewell speech at the Last Supper, the Lord declared: "These things I have spoken to you, that my joy may be in you, and that your joy may be full" (Jn 15:11).

It was for this precisely that Christ came among us. The act of imparting his own eternal life to us by means of his eucharistic self-bestowal is the royal work whereby he glorifies the Father: "As the living Father sent me, and I live because of the Father, so he who eats me will live because of me" (Jn 6:57). Just as self-communication among the Three Persons is the communal joy of the Blessed Trinity, so, too, is it Jesus' own joy to make that life of dynamically circulating love available to as many as accept it. There is nothing, nothing at all, that Jesus possesses from the Father and the Spirit that he does not want us to share with him. Such a statement is saying a great deal, indeed, about a person who is God! And so at the Last Supper, just before his death, Jesus prays to the Father: "Now I am coming to you; and these things I speak in the world, that they may have my joy fulfilled in themselves" (Jn 17:13). Jesus' joy in sharing his life with us in the consecrated Bread and Wine corresponds to the Father's joy in uttering the Word through whom and for whom "all things were created" in the beginning (Col 1:16). And Christ's own joy, divine though it is, is not *fulfilled* until it flows into the bloodstream of our humble human existence. A lover's joy is never perfect as long as it abides only in himself. Only by overflowing into the beloved does it reach perfection.

AS JESUS HANDED THE CUP to his disciples, he said: "Drink of it, all of you; for this is my blood." Let us admit it: at the natural level, there is something extremely repellent, to say the least, in this commandment of the Lord. Ordinary human sensibility recoils viscerally from the idea of drinking any kind of blood, all the more the blood of a familiar person in the very act of speaking to you. If the mere sight of blood makes many people ill, the effect is made even grimmer by someone urging us to ingest it! However, the little conjunction *for* (γάρ) in Jesus' command should radically shift our initial misapprehension. "Drink of it, all of you; *for* this is my blood." It is as if he were saying most soberly and sensibly: "*Because* this is my blood, you *must* drink it!" The explanatory words with which he then follows up do in fact reveal deeper aspects of Jesus' logic, which initially sounds strange and grotesque: ". . . *for* this is my blood of the covenant, which is poured out for many for the forgiveness of sins" (26:28). This specification links Christ's insistence that we consume his Blood to the atoning sacrifices of the Old Testament in which the blood of animals was believed to purify the Jews of their sins in the sight of God.

Beyond the issues raised by squeamish physiological reactions, however, another great problem looms ominously on our horizon: namely, the explicit biblical prohibition against imbibing blood at loggerheads with Jesus' equally explicit command to his disciples that they should drink his Blood. The legal Jewish taboo has nothing to do with the protection of squeamish sentiment but is rooted, rather, in the Jewish symbolic imagination. We have already noted that, in all the prescriptions for animal sacrifice in the Torah, the texts almost never fail to enjoin strictly that, before human consumption of the roasted flesh of a sacrifice, the blood is first to be carefully drained off and allowed to flow onto the altar and the ground. Under no circumstances are Jews to drink blood, whether the blood of animals or, even more inconceivably, human blood.

In its chapter 17, Leviticus spells this prohibition out clearly in a text that also contains both the sanction for violators of the law and the theological reason for the prohibition. It is God himself speaking here:

> If any man of the house of Israel or of the strangers that sojourn among them eats any blood, I will set my face against that person who eats blood, and will cut him off from among his people. *For the life of the flesh is in the blood*; and I have given it for you upon the altar to make atonement for your souls; for it is the blood that makes atonement, by reason of the life. (Lev 17:10–11)

Very succinctly the passage makes three capital points: (1) The prohibition is universal, affecting both Jews and anyone living with Jews; (2) the offender incurs the terrible double sanction of being banished by God from the people of Israel; and (3) the theological explanation for the taboo is that "the life of the flesh is in the blood." Thus, the blood of an animal represents, in a highly distilled form, the source of the life of its flesh. And, since all life comes from God, the life-bearing blood belongs to God exclusively, and the worshipper must return it to God when offering animal sacrifice. To keep the blood for oneself and drink it would be tantamount both to stealing from God and, much worse, to usurping God's privilege as Master of Life.

According to this logic, blood must not be ingested, not because to do so is a disgusting or unsanitary act, but rather because blood is *holy* since it springs from the very source of life itself in God. The outpouring of the blood over the altar is a powerful gesture that plays a fundamental role in the act of sacrifice: it "makes atonement for your souls . . . by reason of the life [contained in the blood]". Sin means to be cut off from God and the life God bestows; offering blood in sacrifice to God atones for sin because the act of returning the life-blood to God acknowledges both the transgression incurred (symbolized in the death of the slain victim) and God's infinite justice as Master of life and Author of the commandments. The atoning sacrifice restores the Jewish sinner to friendship with the God whom he has alienated by his sin. The life God bestows then flows once again in the repentant sinner.

In Exodus 12, we witness the divine institution of the Passover, which perpetually links the Jewish conception of sacrifice to God's act of liberating the Jews from their Egyptian captivity. The Jews' obedience to God's ordinances at one and the same time saves them from death, provides present sustenance for the journey, and guarantees future freedom. In this episode, God speaks to his people through Moses:

> They shall take every man a lamb according to their fathers' houses, a lamb for a household. . . . The whole assembly of the congregation of Israel shall kill their lambs in the evening. Then they shall take some of the blood, and put it on the two doorposts and the lintel of the houses in which they eat them. They shall eat the flesh that night, roasted; with unleavened bread and bitter herbs they shall eat it. . . . The blood shall be a sign for you, upon the houses where you are; and when I see the blood, I will pass over you, and no plague shall fall upon you to destroy you, when I strike the land of Egypt. This day shall be for you a memorial day, and you shall keep it as a feast to the Lord; throughout your generations you shall observe it as an ordinance for ever. (Ex 12:3, 6–8, 13–14)

This passage clearly shows us the interconnection between the capital events of Jewish salvation history and the liturgical memorial of the Passover, a rite that would keep alive forever in the Jewish consciousness the sense of Israel having been redeemed by God's dramatic intervention. Blood plays an extremely dramatic role here since it is the blood of the slain lambs that, by God's command, is to be smeared on Jewish houses as a sign of salvation. Houses not marked with the lambs' blood and their inhabitants would be destroyed by the avenging angel. Two elements are here crucial: first, the power of blood to communicate life and spare from death; and, second, the power of obedience to God when he commands Israel both to slay the lambs and then to smear the doorposts with their blood.

The sense of *sacrament* is also very strong in this text. Obviously, in these events, we are witnessing a dramatic deployment of God's love for his people, an epiphany of his omnipotent will to save them and nourish them and bring them to fullness of freedom. And yet, to have their full effect, God's love and power operate through intermediate elements (lambs, sacrifice, blood) and act in symbiosis with human obedience to divine commands. God provides both the will to save and the means of doing so, but man's obedience must accept and cooperate with God's proposed plan.

We might say that the institution of the Blessed Eucharist by Christ at the Last Supper takes up the sacramental salvation narrative where Exodus left it, with Jesus intending to fulfill that narrative's deepest intentions in paradoxical and utterly unimaginable ways. Both the divine motivation (God's love for his people) and the intrinsic need for sacramental means to realize salvation (sacrifice) remain unaltered in this transition; but Jesus infuses both the *divine motivation* and the *sacramental means* with a wholly new and unheard-of *content*. In particular, the meaning of "blood" is transformed by the Savior from a powerful *symbol* of God's sovereign mastery over all life as its Source to the *reality* of God's Blood under the appearance of wine. Likewise, the divine motivation is unutterably intensified. What has been the unflinching love and commitment shown by God to his people throughout history is now more thoroughly revealed as the unsurpassable mystery of God infusing his people with his own Life, through the handing-over of his Son's Body and Blood as true food and drink.

As part of this stupendous transformation, the Levitical taboo against eating human flesh and drinking any kind of blood undergoes a radical reversal. What has until now been strictly *forbidden* becomes regally *commanded*, but exclusively in connection with the new institution of the Eucharist. What may seem on first impression to be a blatant *contradiction* and a flagrant *violation* may, in the light of Jesus' intention at the Last Supper, be now understood as a true *completion* of the circle of revelation. Within the overarching unity of the divine economy of salvation, the Levitical prohibition may now be seen in its true transitory nature as having been preparatory to God's ultimate intention: the institution of the Eucharist, of which all Old Testament sacrifices were a prefiguration. Who but God himself could have foreseen that it was God's own Son who would one day become the unique and unsurpassable sacrificial Victim for the sins of the world? God spared the life of Isaac on Mount Moriah as Abraham already held the knife on high over his son, about to plunge it into the beloved flesh out of obedience to God's command. But then God's angel suddenly held back Abraham's hand and provided the ram in the thicket as substitute victim. Who could have foreseen that this stray ram, with his horns entangled in the thorns, already pointed to Jesus' Cross on Golgotha as the altar for the all-too-real immolation of the Son of God, whom his Father would not spare, out of love for the world (cf. Gen 22:6-13; Jn 3:16; Rom 8:32)?

In the end, the fullness of revelation shows that the command to sacrifice Isaac that God issued to Abraham eventually ricocheted back to God's own Heart, by his own mysterious intent. God himself, in fact, did what he would not allow Abraham to do precisely because Isaac could not be a universal savior: namely, God sacrificed his own Son for the salvation of the world. When it is God's Son who sheds his blood on the Cross as atoning victim, then *his blood must be drunk!* The prohibition against drinking all other blood thus clearly served as a protection against idolatry: that is, it kept the Jews from looking for fullness of life in a merely material and corruptible element. We can say that, through the prohibitive Levitical legislation, the divine Logos was preparing the way to his act of pouring out his own life's substance. Radical Jewish iconoclasm forbade any pictorial representation of יהוה, I-Am-Who-Am, and forbade as well the pronunciation of this divine Name. Both prohibitions sought to preserve the full awareness of God's unutterable and non-representable reality. "No one has ever seen God" (Jn 1:18), affirms St. John as well. By the same logic, the ingesting of blood was forbidden, not because blood is unclean, but, on the contrary, because it is too fraught with the divine mystery of life. The iconoclasm of the Hebrew Scriptures thus reserved an empty space in the world of images for the eventual emergence within it of the True Face of God in the perceptible physiognomy of Jesus of Nazareth, who declared: "He who has seen me has seen the Father" (Jn 14:9).

In a similar way, the blood prohibition of Leviticus providentially prepared the way for the mystery of the Eucharist, in which the incarnate God decides, in obedience to his Father, to pour out his own humanly divine Blood as the food of eternal life: "He who eats my flesh and drinks my blood has eternal life" (Jn 6:54). One can almost hear Jesus saying, according to the incarnate Word's law of surpassing fulfillment laid down in Matthew 5: "You have heard that it was said, 'You shall not drink blood.' But I say to you", *Unless you eat the flesh of the Son of man and drink his blood, you have no life in you* (Jn 6:53). The ancient prohibition against drinking blood derived both from horror of cannibalism and from God's prerogative as the Creator and Master of all life. But what if this Lord of Life should decide to give his own life away, not only through general acts of goodness and benevolence, but *substantially*, by transforming the murderous outpouring of his blood on the Cross into a wellspring of new life? Cannot the supreme Legislator transcend the letter of his own legislation in order to fulfill its deepest intentions? And so Jesus commands: "Drink of [this cup], all of you; for this is my blood of the covenant, which is poured out for many for the forgiveness of sins."

Any random page of the Gospel at once proclaims loud and clear that anyone who approaches Jesus with faith must not come to him looking for power, success, triumph, control, security, or any kind of invulnerability, at least not in the sense that the world gives to these terms. "You know the grace of our Lord Jesus Christ," writes St. Paul, "that though he was rich, yet for your sake he became poor, so that by his poverty you might become rich" (2 Cor 8:9). In eucharistic terms, this means that the strong and eternal God, the depths of whose Being are inexhaustible, *chose to liquefy himself into temporal carnality* so as to become for us a Fountain of Life. It is for this purpose that he used his omnipotence: to make himself smaller and weaker, not greater and more powerful, by definition an impossibility! To manifest the fullness of his love, God could *only* choose the way of self-reduction, of weakness. Our only path to becoming one with him is to reciprocate his choice. By choice, God made himself "poor" in

Jesus, the incarnate Son, in the sense that he could henceforth hold nothing back for himself. The true God, as opposed to endless idols, may be recognized by his activity of ever flowing out from his center so as to become his creatures' nourishment and joy. God, in a word, finds his most intimate joy in giving himself away.

א

26:29   οὐ μὴ πίω ἀπ᾽ ἄρτι
ἐκ τούτου τοῦ γενήματος τῆς ἀμπέλου
ἕως τῆς ἡμέρας ἐκείνης ὅταν αὐτὸ πίνω μεθ᾽ ὑμῶν καινὸν
ἐν τῇ βασιλείᾳ τοῦ Πατρός μου

I shall not drink again
of this fruit of the vine
until that day when I drink it new with you
in my Father's kingdom

L ISTENING TO JESUS' WORDS at the institution of the Holy Eucharist, the attentive reader is struck by a verbal asymmetry. While in the Greek text, Jesus uses only *seven* words to refer to the bread that he declares to be his Body, he expatiates to fully *nineteen* words in connection with the chalice containing the wine that is his Blood. Why the quantitative imbalance?

We first recall that Jesus' deliberate separation of "blood" from "body" alludes to the Levitical injunctions that prescribe such separation in order for a sacrifice to be performed in a manner that pleases God. Though the separation of blood from body clearly implies the death of the sacrificial victim, the ritual guarantees that the sacrificer has wholly returned the life-giving element to God by pouring out the victim's blood upon the altar and onto the ground. God is the

Author of all life, and the offering of the blood acknowledges God's power and prerogative to bestow that life again wherever and however he should choose to do so. Therefore, Jesus here signifies that the action of the Eucharist, in harmony with the Cross that it anticipates, is not only sacrificial in nature but also pleasing to God, an act of perfect worship.

But why does Jesus, in his verbal formulations, allot so much more explanatory space to the blood than to the body? No doubt because of the specific significance of blood in the Levitical ordinance, as we have seen: "For the life of the flesh is in the blood; and I have given it for you upon the altar to make atonement for your souls; for it is the blood that makes atonement, by reason of the life" (Lev 17:10–11). This passage from Leviticus, crucial for eucharistic theology, suffices to elucidate the formula Jesus utters as he hands out the chalice. His reference to "covenant" alludes to God's rescue operation of the Jews from Egypt at the Passover. God promises to deliver his people if only they obey his ordinances, above all the command to daub the lintels of their doors with the blood of the sacrificed lamb. In the same sentence, Jesus then goes on to make explicit how such liberation applies not only to the believing Jews who participated in the literal Exodus but also to people of all times and places: "My blood", he affirms poignantly, "is poured out for many for the forgiveness of sins."

Though grounded in the historical Exodus, therefore, the covenant Jesus speaks of now has immensely greater reach and connotations, extending universally beyond the frontiers of Israel and Judaism. "The covenant" is precisely what is happening at the very moment Jesus speaks: he is giving himself away to those who believe in him and in the truth and power of what he says. Those who accept his Body and Blood from his hands as their nourishment consequently have all their sins forgiven and receive fullness of life. It is as simple, profound, and earth-shaking as that! This new covenant consists in infinite divine life, outpoured by God in mercy and embraced in faith by the human believer, specifically by receiving and consuming the Eucharistic Gifts with wide-eyed faith and thanksgiving. Out of this covenant, God "gets" only the joy of self-giving while man receives the eternal life of God.

The institution narrative in Matthew is sober, indeed, as befits the moment and the setting. Jesus and Judas both know that the great betrayal is just around the corner and that this is the last night of mortal life Christ will spend on earth. The handing out of the consecrated Bread and Wine anticipates, and infuses meaning into, the shattering of Jesus' Body on the Cross and the spilling of his Blood. The moment is truly transcendental, fraught with meaning and blessing, absolutely unforgettable; but it is also a moment of impending doom and darkness, when the forces of evil will for a while seem to have overpowered the Son of God and his goodness. The celebration of this particular *seder* by Jesus and his disciples combines and reconciles what is normally irreconcilable: death and the promise of life, intimate friendship and the shattering of fidelity, defeat and triumph, grateful joy and sorrowful mourning. All of it is grounded in the divine paradox that it is precisely by allowing himself to be crushed like so many grapes in the winepress that Jesus can become for all a fountain of everlasting life.

Jesus himself sounds the mournful note when he says, in connection with the gift of his Blood: "I shall not drink again of this fruit of the vine until that day when I drink it new with you in my Father's kingdom." This mysterious statement expresses how highly aware Jesus is of the fact that this is his last night on earth and that death awaits him. The trenchant negation made in this statement establishes a mighty cæsura between the present moment of the Last Supper and the future banquet "in my Father's kingdom". In giving his disciples his Body and Blood in sacramental form, Jesus is giving them the essence of who he is, as a permanent, life-conferring possession. But the everyday Jesus, the Jesus of familiar companionship and ordinary presence, must now undertake his dark journey into death. Only a God can accomplish both these things at once, that is, to abide truly with his loved ones through sacramental presence and at the same time to disappear into a death that will shatter his previous historical form.

The heavy pathos of the situation, however, is shot through with bright hope because of the certainty with which Jesus refers to "that day" in his Father's Kingdom when they would all be reunited with unending joy to "drink again of this fruit of the vine". This means that the Eucharist that he has celebrated with his disciples on the evening of Holy Thursday both transforms the meaning of the crucifixion from cruel murder to triumph by love and prefigures the eternal banquet of the Kingdom. Real and nourishing as Christ's presence in the Eucharist is, it also possesses a strong eschatological thrust that makes of its participants radical pilgrims toward the Kingdom. Right after giving them the Eucharist, Jesus must precede them into death in order to bring them all eventually into the undying Kingdom of the Father.

The Eucharist is essentially, and not only coincidentally, a *viaticum*, food for the existential journey, nourishment to sustain believers during their entire journey to the Kingdom. Christ truly gives us his divine life now; but that very possession of God's life within us in the present in fact *hastens* our longing and speed in pursuit of the Fullness, when everything will be subjected to Christ: "Then the Son himself will be subjected to the one who subjected everything to him, so that God may be all in all" (1 Cor 15:28, NAB). Such submission of everything to God in Christ, and the resulting indwelling of God in all things, offers us a reliable and dynamic definition of the glorious state of affairs to which Jesus alludes by his "Father's kingdom".

Though the mood of the institution narrative is thus understandably austere, given the almost immediate unleashing of the Passion, nevertheless, Jesus' sober words convey an explosive promise of joy. This first eucharistic celebration at the Last Supper and the banquet of the Kingdom that Jesus prophesies together bracket the Passion and death of Jesus. The Passion and death, by the power of this bracketing, are thus subsumed prophetically under the sovereignty of Jesus the King: they become but a transitory, middle point of the drama rather than the tragic terminus that worldly logic would have them be. The defeat inflicted by death is thus relativized and so loses its permanent hold and ultimate power.

The narrative of the Last Supper thus includes allusions both to the present celebration and to the everlasting celebration in the Kingdom. The Gospel portrays celebration both before and after the crucifixion! Celebration is the normal mode of divine life, not only in God himself but also whenever God communicates his life to man. The hiatus introduced into the mode of celebration by the temporary triumph of death only makes the permanent triumph of life all the more radical and far-reaching. Jesus himself freely determines when he will drink and not drink of the fruit of the vine. As always, the Suffering Servant retains mastery over his fate because his divine love is stronger than human or demonic hatred. Such mastery does not mean that he can *avoid* or at least *mitigate* death. The Messiah could not do that and also attain his intended goal. But it does mean that he can radically change the *effect* of death from the utter annihilation those inflicting it intended it to be to the ultimate enthronement of the Lord of Life as loving Master of all hearts:

> The four living creatures and the twenty-four elders . . . sang a new song, saying, "Worthy are you to take the scroll and to open its seals, for you were slain and by your blood you ransomed men for God from every tribe and tongue and people and nation, and have made them a kingdom and priests to our God, and they shall reign on earth." (Rev 5:8–10)

This vision of the heavenly liturgy by the seer of Patmos unveils for us the interior reality of the Eucharist celebrated at the Last Supper and described in very muted, almost rubrical, terms by Matthew.

In a moment, the group of apostles will conclude the solemn *seder* celebration by singing hymns and going out to the Mount of Olives (26:30). From the context, we know that the "hymns" in question are in fact the Hallel, that is, Psalms 114[113] through 118[117], those psalms that particularly celebrate God's deliverance of his people from the tyranny of Egypt and from death.[10] The apostles must sing these hymns of thanksgiving with great sorrow and apprehension in their hearts at their knowledge of the impending betrayal. Nevertheless, they, too, like "the four living creatures and the twenty-four elders", sing them in adoration of the Lamb who, in their presence, has anticipated his own slaying and preemptively poured out his blood for them as wine, thus transforming the interior meaning of Calvary beforehand. In so doing, Jesus the Lamb has ransomed all human beings for God and made of them "a kingdom and priests to our God".

The singing of Psalm 118[117] in particular, the psalm par excellence of Paschal jubilation, must make the apostles vividly conscious that Jesus, in bestowing the Eucharist, has just made them living participants in the drama of the Exodus, no longer now only a definitive exit out of tyrannical Egypt, but a radical and permanent liberation

[10] It is misleading to translate "when they had sung a hymn" (RSV). The Greek ὑμνήσαντες (literally, "having hymned") does not specify how many hymns are involved. André Chouraqui (*La Bible* [Paris: Desclée de Brouwer, 1974–1979]) translates interpretively "after singing the Hallel", because these psalms were prescribed as the conclusion of the Passover meal.

out of slavery to sin, an emancipation from mortality itself. The concluding sentence of our passage says in its sober yet very poignant way: "Singing hymns, they went out (ἐξῆλθον) to the Mount of Olives." Why are they going there? Because Jesus is freely and deliberately going out to meet his fate in his favorite place of intimacy with his Father, where he knows his betrayer will find him. This *going out*, this very local *exodus*[11] to the nearby geological formation called "the Mount of Olives", signals, together with the approach of Jesus' sufferings, the approach as well of Jesus' glorification to his Father's Kingdom (which he has just mentioned) through death, Resurrection, and Ascension. His affirmation "I shall not drink again . . . until that day . . ." clearly implies that he is going forth like a new Moses at the head of his people, blazing a trail for them that leads to the Promised Land of the Father's bosom. In the ordinary quiet of this momentous night in Palestine, Jesus *goes out* and plunges into the bottomless Red Sea of his Passion. What is mystically occurring, in fact, within this Pesach celebration, is the deliverance of all mankind through the oblation of the Body and Soul of Jesus—man's ultimate deliverance from the tragic grip of an evil servitude to sin and death through the triumph of Jesus' self-sacrificial love.

The passage quoted above from the Book of Revelation allows the full power and glory, so soberly contained in Matthew's narrative of the Last Supper, to explode with jubilation. The mystery of redemption through Christ's death is always the same, regardless of the key in which it is played—whether in the hush and darkness of Holy Thursday evening or in the resounding splendor of the full-blown Kingdom. The whole Kingdom is already contained in seed form in the hastily borrowed house of an anonymous Jerusalem Jew of goodwill (26:18). In that room, Jesus, faithful friend that he is, has communicated to his disciples both his own substance as nourishment and his most intimate secrets and has asked them to trust him to see them through all the way to the eternal Kingdom of his Father.

Beyond the particular meaning that each of Jesus' actions and words at the Last Supper conveys in itself, we should not overlook the overall atmosphere of sacred solemnity that their rich unfolding creates. Jesus' masterful, many-sided deed above all reveals that infinitely

---

[11] The verb *exierunt* of the Latin Vulgate in this verse underscores this "exodic" character of the move from the room of the Last Supper to the Mount of Olives.

more is happening here than just a memorable final meal with friends before his death. The scene strongly suggests that a momentous, indeed, wholly transcendental, *event* is occurring that Jesus articulates in distinct, incremental stages and that culminates in his stunning declaration concerning the newly imparted identity of This Bread and This Wine, first held forth and then handed out for the taking. It is profoundly moving to see the greatest work of love performed in utter silence:

> Here Eve's shadow, hunt, and red money.
> Clouds, the light breaks through, the evening meal.
> There dwells in bread and wine a gentle silence
> And they are gathered twelve in number.[12]

---

[12] *Hier Evas Schatten, Jagd und rotes Geld. / Gewölk, das Licht durchbricht, das Abendmahl. / Es wohnt in Brot und Wein ein sanftes Schweigen / Und jene sind versammelt zwölf an Zahl.* (Georg Trakl, "Menschheit", in *Gedichte* [Leipzig: Kurt Wolff, 1913], 1:35.)

6. "YOUR ARROWS HAVE SUNK INTO ME"

Peter's Denial Foretold (26:31–35)

26:31a   Πάντες ὑμεῖς σκανδαλισθήσεσθε
          ἐν ἐμοὶ ἐν τῇ νυκτὶ ταύτῃ

You will all stumble
because of me this night

B
Y "THIS NIGHT", JESUS REFERS TO much more than the few
hours of chronological darkness he and his disciples are about
to live through. In John's Gospel, just after Judas leaves the
seder room to go and hand Jesus over to his enemies, the text comments with stark symbolism: "and it was night" (Jn 13:30b). The
present night will fully expose the depth of Jesus' human weakness
and vulnerability and, at the same time, the depth of his freedom and
persevering love. Jesus uses his divine freedom to embrace human
weakness, to abide in it as in his own home, so as to transform it
from within. It is the paradox of immortal love shining through dark
weakness that causes the disciples to stumble and fall. An all-powerful
God, they are convinced along with most of the human race, should
not allow things to reach such a critical point of danger, violence,
and death. But Jesus, for his part, is in love with the night that allows
him to bare his heart to his beloved, a rapturous mystery echoed by
St. John of the Cross:

> Oh night that was my guide!
> Oh darkness dearer than the morning's pride,

> Oh night that joined the lover
> To the beloved bride
> Transfiguring them each into the other.[1]

Matthew has already established a tense juxtaposition between "my Father's kingdom" and "the Mount of Olives" (26:29–30). Jesus leads his followers from the room of the Last Supper to the Mount of Olives as a first step on the definitive journey to the eternal Kingdom; after all, it is on the Mount of Olives that Jesus will fully embrace the will of his Father against all natural repulsion, in the certainty that following the Father's will can only lead to the Kingdom. But the disciples interpret this exodus to the Mount of Olives differently, seeing in it only a deeper descent into defeat and annihilation.

As always, Jesus fortifies his friends by bringing out into the open truths they would rather conceal even from themselves. And so he now proclaims to them the hard prophetic truth: "You will all [stumble and] fall . . . because of me this night." Whereas the disciples are cringing with fear, feeling a massive threat lurking in the night air, Jesus himself, the target of this threat, worries, not about *himself*, but rather about the state of *their* hearts and the crisis of *their* wills. Even in the depths of personal distress, Jesus' thoughts are always concerned with the welfare of others. It is as if Jesus considers the conversion of his disciples' souls a more daunting event than his own falling into the hands of violent men, from whom he expects nothing better. The only night that frightens the Master is the night in his followers' hearts. It is an odd thing, indeed, that, when Christians bewail Jesus' fate in his Passion, they habitually think first of all of the physical sufferings inflicted on their dear Lord by the pagans, all the while forgetting the long, mournful glance that Jesus steadily casts all through the Passion on his disciples' hearts.

In the text Jesus literally says: "You will all be *scandalized* in me this night." Σκανδαλισθήσεσθε (*skandalisthêsesthe*): few biblical terms receive a greater variety of translations—"fall away" (RSV), "have your faith shaken" (NAB), "be offended" (KJV), "be turned away" (BBE), "lose faith" (CJB), "become deserters" (NRS) . . . Every

---

[1] "'¡Oh noche que guiaste!, / ¡oh noche amable más que la alborada!, / ¡oh noche que juntaste / Amado con amada, / amada en el Amado transformada!" St. John of the Cross, *Noche oscura del alma*, stanza 5, trans. Roy Campbell, *The Selected Poems of Roy Campbell* (Oxford and New York: Oxford University Press, 1982), 109.

rendering expresses a different and enriching nuance, some focusing more on the objective difficulty encountered while others concentrate on the responsibility of the subject. All of them, however, point to a radical infidelity inflicted upon one's beloved friend and Master. The root of the verb, *skándalon*, means a "trap" or a "snare", so that a very literal translation would be: "you will all be ensnared by me", or perhaps: "you will all treat me like a trap . . . and be caught in it." The petition of the Our Father "and lead us not into temptation" presents a similar point of view. How can our Father, or Jesus, possibly "tempt" us, or "ensnare" us?

This concept of *skándalon*, when it has God as agent, offers a particularly keen portrayal of the psychology of sin. It exposes the agonizing struggle occasioned in the human soul between the objective challenge presented by a difficult situation and the subjective manner in which a person handles that challenge. In this case, the extreme "objective challenge" consists in this: God has become man; the Omnipotent has assumed dire weakness; God has fallen in love with man and in that sense becomes dependent upon human vagaries; and in Jesus, God has bestowed his own substance on fickle creatures, thus becoming vulnerable unto death . . . Man has had no say in any of this, since God decided this course of action "before the foundation of the world" (cf. Jn 17:24; Eph 1:4; 1 Pet 1:20; Rev 13:8). And it was into the paradoxical logic and harsh consequences of this economy of redemption that Jesus *led* those he called to himself. He then expects them to assume as their own, out of love for him, the harsh mental clashes resulting from his divine course of action. It is not surprising if, under the colossal weight of such contradiction, human nature begins to crack.

No doubt the immense patience Jesus shows his followers in the face of their fearful wavering derives from his clear awareness of their existential quandary and heart-tearing distress. Far from being surprised or angered (though he cannot avoid being saddened), Jesus makes ample allowances for their cowardly, quavering behavior. Indeed, he tells them with clairvoyance that, not one or two, but *all* of them will fall away and abandon him, and he even backs up this assertion with a biblical prophecy. It is almost as if he were telling them: "These terrible things are going to happen, and none of you will be able to remain steadfast in your love for me; but I understand. Take comfort; it is not the end of the world. Can you at least try to retain one little corner of fidelity to me *within* your cowardice and defection? I would consider that little bit enough!'"

However, such depth of empathy on Jesus' part does not mean he absolves the disciples or us of all responsibility when we are guilty of betraying, abandoning, or denying a friend who has been so good to us—*any* friend, but especially the Son of God. Of course, there can always be extenuating circumstances whenever the feebleness of human nature comes up against huge threats to its very existence. This is one reason why human mortality simply cannot do without the constant strength and new life infused into it by forgiveness, compassion, and mercy. It is an immense and indispensable consolation that, within the drama of the Lord's Passion, time and again we find passages making ample provision for human weakness and our chronic tendency to disappoint God and each other. The present verses 26:31–32 are one such passage. Nevertheless, we blaspheme ceaselessly against the mercy God bestows on us when we make such mercy a presumptuous *excuse* for our habitually unfaithful and self-indulgent behavior, which craftily reasons: "*Since* God is merciful, *therefore* I'm not going to worry about any of it!" We can receive mercy only on our knees, with a contrite and bleeding heart full of repentance and ardent to change. Though in our weakness we may be *swept* by tumultuous circumstances into shameful behavior, still we must never *intend* infidelity and betrayal, which are the cancer at the heart of any relationship. An accidental fall is not the same as deliberate desertion.

During their three years of apprenticeship before this night on Gethsemane, Jesus initiated his disciples into the mysteries of his loving Heart and, very concretely, into his plan to save the world by the offering of his life. In the face of such intimate, personal revelation, we may ask: Considering the many weaknesses and limitations of human nature as Jesus found it and as Jesus personally assumed it, was the Son of God in some sense "leading his intimate disciples into temptation" by exposing them to the possibility or even probability of apostasy from so sublime an enterprise? In a real sense, it is a dangerous thing to become an intimate friend of the Savior of the world because then all of one's relatively petty personal concerns and glaring limitations will necessarily be totally subsumed into the one burning interest of Jesus' Heart. Here lies the Christian heart of darkness, the epicenter of the night of the Passion to which Jesus refers when he affirms, "You will all [stumble and] fall away because of me this night." Perhaps here more than anywhere else we should apply to all of us the trenchant words of Jesus in Luke concerning the sinful woman: "I tell you, her sins, which are many, are forgiven, for she loved much; but he who is forgiven little, loves little" (Lk 7:47). Our only hope in the face of the evidence of our many desertions and betrayals lies, not in the indifferentism created by a thoughtless God-is-always-merciful attitude or in the Pharisaism generated by an I-am-not-like-the-rest-of-men outlook: no, our hope then lies solely in the soul-transforming experience of gratitude and reciprocal love resulting from having been unconditionally forgiven.

Only forgiveness, bestowed with love and accepted with thanksgiving, can dissolve guilt. *We can freely live and breathe and act well only as forgiven beings who are loved beyond all conditions and deserts and despite all evidence of our unworthiness.* And here we should note one more Christian paradox: that perhaps the supreme degree of intimacy with Christ was not accessible to his disciples until they had fallen as far as anyone can fall, by abandoning and denying him. Von Balthasar says stunningly that in his Passion and death, Jesus went so low that henceforth no one could ever fall *without falling into Jesus.* This constitutes a most realistic definition of intimacy in love! Perhaps the experience of having been radically, massively forgiven for sins considered unforgivable is essential to establish the closest love union possible between creature and Creator.

In the same line, we should consider that perhaps some element of pride would have continued to lurk in the heart of an otherwise immaculate disciple who had been faithful to the end, through all the bitterness of the Passion. This trace of pride would have proved irredeemable and would forever have continued to taint with self-regard that heroic disciple's relationship with Jesus. Any heroic flexing of virtuous muscles before God, no matter how subtle, does not attract the divine blessing. No one knew this better than Jesus, who made himself the last of all and the servant of all, assuming all the functions of a humble beast of burden mediating between God and man (cf. Ps 73[72]:22; Mk 9:35). In the end, the humility of God in Jesus can turn even the most heinous betrayal into an occasion of grace. His love longs to deliver us above all from the shame of our infidelity to him, if only we turn to him with imploring sorrow. What music to God's ears the muffled cry of the Publican in the temple, who "would not even lift up his eyes to heaven, but beat his breast, saying, 'God, be merciful to me a sinner!'" (Lk 18:13).

א

26:31b   γέγραπται γάρ· Πατάξω τὸν ποιμένα,
           καὶ διασκορπισθήσονται τὰ πρόβατα τῆς ποίμνης

*for it is written, "I will strike the shepherd,
and the sheep of the flock will be scattered"*

JESUS SUPPORTS HIS PREDICTION CONCERNING all his followers' desertion of him with this vivid allusion to the prophecy of Zechariah (13:7). Depending on how one hears the prophet's words from Jesus' lips, as applied to the present occasion, one will be either frightened or consoled by them. Obviously, the Lord sees in Zechariah's words a premonition of his own fate as great Shepherd and the impact this fate would have on the flock of his disciples. Good reason for fright is communicated by the mere fact of the gruesome event: the prophetic image of the "striking of the shepherd" encapsulates the shattering of the tight group of Jesus' followers as a result of violence done to their Head, their Master. And yet, when you consider the foreknowledge of the event by the victim himself and the serene manner in which he is announcing it to his friends, there is in the pronouncement as well a strong element of consolation.

As part of a mystery the disciples cannot begin to understand, not only is Jesus quite aware of all that lies ahead by way of violent opposition but such clairvoyance does not seem to cause him any alarm. On the contrary, his tone is neither accusatory nor troubled but, rather, soothing, reassuring, which is astounding given the circumstances and the magnitude of the impending peril. He has already accepted the certain fact of his abandonment by the only friends he has, and he now goes to the length of confirming the inevitability of this betrayal with a reference to Scripture: "You *will* all fall away because of me . . . *for* it is written . . ." Quite in advance of all our defections, Jesus has already embraced and forgiven our many sins. His announcement of coming catastrophes already contains within it an assurance of his abiding presence and of the tireless creativity of his love. And Jesus does not forgive us generically, superficially, as if someone said to us, "Ah, forget about it! What's past is past!" There is, in fact, no more heinous crime possible to us than the betrayal and abandonment of a friend who has given us all he has to give, even to his very Heart, and who has deposited all of his trust in us unconditionally. *And it is while looking soberly and painfully at this crime of ours that Jesus forgives us for it.*

But this act of his gracious will becomes at once incarnate in his deed of going to Calvary to atone for the sin for which he has already forgiven us. And so Jesus accepts deep within his Heart not only the wound inflicted by our infidelity but also the lethal responsibility of suffering our deserved punishment in our place. This is what it means for us to be nourished eucharistically with the Body and Blood of Jesus. It means that we benefit from his violent abasement and defeat! By the creativity of his love, Jesus has transformed destructive human violence into a divine instrument that crushes Jesus' physical integrity and individuality and "processes" his substance into a universally available nourishment for the many. Jesus gathers us together from the dispersion of sin by scattering himself, and he scatters himself by surrendering willingly to the violence of the Passion. In him, every symbolic victim ever offered to God by man becomes the one true Victim offered to man by God in order thus to communicate God's own life.

If we look closely, we will see at once that Jesus' manner of quoting Zechariah deliberately reinforces this sacrificial core of the events of the Passion. In the Septuagint, the version of the Old Testament normally at Matthew's elbow or in his memory while composing his Gospel, Zechariah's text reads: Πατάξατε τοὺς ποιμένας καὶ ἐκσπάσατε τὰ πρόβατα—"Strike the shepherds and scatter the sheep" (13:7).

God is here speaking through his prophet concerning irresponsible shepherds. Note that the statement is cast as a plural imperative by one voice to a group of individuals for them to perform the stated action on a plural number of shepherds. It is a matter of opinion whether the words are meant in Zechariah as an actual command to perform the action of striking and dispersing or whether it is simply intended as a truism, meaning something like "whenever you strike shepherds, their sheep will be scattered." It is surprising to see, however, that what Jesus himself actually says is quite different, namely: Πατάξω τὸν ποιμένα, καὶ διασκορπισθήσονται τὰ πρόβατα τῆς ποίμνης, that is, "*I* will strike the *shepherd* and the sheep of the flock will be scattered." This is quite a variant from both the Hebrew original and the Septuagint text. Whatever the precise textual history may be, what is clear is that Jesus' idiosyncratic version of Zechariah 13:7, as reported by Matthew, fits his own dramatic context and its theological meaning like a glove. The incarnate Word is obviously free to adapt written prophetic words, which he himself has inspired, in order to reveal new depths of God's design in a present situation involving him centrally.

Jesus' quotation from Zechariah makes two major changes to the original. In the first place, the verb *to strike* is changed from a plural imperative to a future singular in the first person. "Strike, [all of you]!" becomes "I will strike". This transforms a generic observation or an anonymous command into a prophetic statement uttered by God himself. Suddenly God takes responsibility for performing a violent act in the near future, and this future tense has a providential ring. In Matthew's context, this action can only refer to Jesus' imminent betrayal and Passion, culminating in the crucifixion. In fact, at Pilate's palace Jesus will quite literally be "struck . . . on the head" (27:30), yet surely this prophecy "I will strike" refers more globally to the whole drama of the Passion and death. Thus, all the violence that is about to be inflicted on Jesus during the Passion is summed up in the one verb *to strike*, with God as author of the deed by his own admission.

In the second place, in Jesus' own formulation of the passage, *the shepherds* in the plural becomes *the shepherd* in the singular. As a result of these two changes, the pronouncement automatically becomes highly personalized into the interaction between one agent and one object of this agent's action: "I will strike the shepherd." There can be little doubt that the one agent is God and the one Shepherd Jesus himself. Thus, in order to exonerate his disciples of the guilt of forsaking him, Jesus most astoundingly transfers the cause—and, therefore, the responsibility—of their abandonment of him to . . . his Father! "I will strike the shepherd, and the sheep of the flock will be scattered." Moreover, both the move of casting the statement in the first person singular and that of putting the words into God's own mouth are rhetorical decisions that greatly heighten the sense of the action's deliberate intentionality.

What can all this mean except that all the violence and contempt Jesus suffers during the Passion, though inflicted materially by human beings from the free initiative of their perverse wills, nevertheless does not fall outside the purview of God's divine providence and will. This does not entitle us to say, as has often been alleged, that in Jesus' Passion God is therefore manipulating human beings like marionettes in order to accomplish his purpose of making his Son suffer for the good of the world. Such a monstrous conception evokes the image of a sadistic god that is quite in line with any number of pagan deities! Rather, we should understand that God, with Jesus' totally free agreement, takes in hand the violent hatred that man generates against the Messiah and transforms it into an instrument of redemption. Perverse man creates the evil deed and its nefarious finality, and a resourceful God responds by turning this intended end-goal into an intermediary, instrumental cause for his own divine design: the salvation of those very murderers and of all mankind.

The creativity of divine love—its non-retaliatory humility, its capacity to enact the unimaginable, its endless ability and desire to forgive, its longing to retrieve what is lost—can take wanton murder and transform it from within into an atoning sacrifice, with the serene and whole-hearted cooperation of the Victim. It is only in this sense that we should understand the mysterious and humanly unbearable statement by God: "I will strike the Shepherd." How dumbfounding a revelation, that both the heavenly Father and his beloved Son assume joint personal responsibility for the Son's murderers! Yet it is precisely in this that "redemption" consists. It is not mere poetic fancy to say with St. Paul: "You are bought with a great price. Glorify and bear God in your body" (1 Cor 6:20, DRA).

It would appear that Jesus radically adapts the statement of Zechariah's prophecy precisely in order to reveal the Father's direct role in transforming the events of the Passion from mere betrayal and murderous destruction into the enactment of a sacrifice of atonement to the glory of God's Name. Read in this manner, Jesus' Passion, as it unfolds, proclaims simultaneously both the depth of human iniquity and the depth of the Father's love for iniquitous mankind: "He . . . did not spare his own Son but gave him up for us all" (Rom 8:32). For his part, Jesus, the beloved Son, in loving obedience to the Father, thoroughly assumes into his Person the collective guilt and anguish of mankind.

Jesus' willing self-identification with sinners goes so far that in his Passion he can cry out to his Father with perfect truth and out of a breaking heart: "O LORD, rebuke me not in your anger, nor chasten me in your wrath! *For your arrows have sunk into me*, and your hand has come down on me." Only the incarnate God can pray this penitential psalm to his Father through to the end, in such a way that man's absolute dependence on God is manifested in the vehemence of this Innocent's cry on behalf of sinners, a howl of supplication now uttered by a Divine Person within the Blessed Trinity: "Do not forsake me, O LORD! O my God, be not far from me! Make haste to help me, O Lord, my salvation!" (Ps 38[37]:1–2, 21–22). No creature has ever been so desperately in need of God's mercy, and so excruciatingly aware of this fact, than is Jesus Christ, the Son of God, in his Passion and death. With his own precious blood, he is paying for sins he has never committed so that the exonerated criminals can enter into the Kingdom of his Father, which he carries about in his Heart.

Here we see fulfilled the prophecy already contained in the mysterious story of Abraham's near-sacrifice of his son Isaac in the first book of Scripture: "Then Abraham put forth his hand, and took the knife to slay his son. But the angel of the LORD called to him from heaven, and said, 'Abraham, Abraham! . . . Do not lay your hand on the lad or do anything to him; for now I know that you fear God, seeing you have not withheld your son, your only-begotten son, from me'" (Gen 22:10–12). The heart-wrenching deed that the heavenly Father and God of the universe would not allow a mere mortal to perform, that very deed he carries out himself by allowing his Son to be betrayed "into the hands of sinners" (26:45). The Father of Jesus, in his love for mankind, does not withhold his Son from us but "[puts] forth his hand" and sends him into the midst of a sinful world, thus offering him up to our malicious ways, whatever the consequences. And the Lord Jesus, in perfect harmony with his Father and even more obedient to him than was Isaac to Abraham, "loved us and gave himself up for us, a fragrant offering and sacrifice to God" (Eph 5:2).

Thus Jesus, "the Lamb who was slain from the creation of the world" (Rev 13:8, NIV), is prefigured in the story of Isaac's near-sacrifice on Mount Moriah, not by Isaac, who goes off safe and sound from the experience, but by the "ram, caught in a thicket by his horns" which Abraham spots after his son's life is spared. And then "Abraham went and took the ram, and offered it up as a burnt offering instead of his son. So Abraham called the name of that place 'The LORD will provide'" (Gen 22:13–14). By sending us his own beloved Son, "the Lamb of God, who takes away the sin of the world" (Jn 1:29), the Lord does, indeed, provide—superabundantly! How moving this detail, so illustrative of God's exquisite condescension, that our Redeemer should be represented in this foundational story, not by Isaac, the most obvious candidate, who occupies the center of the stage, but by the incidental ram, quietly "crucified" in the thorny bushes, humbly hidden in a corner of the narrative, appearing by surprise almost as an afterthought and only because God suddenly "provides" him out of his mysterious depths! In forbidding the slaying of Isaac, divine providence unobtrusively introduced a long-term hiatus in the history of sacrifices by man so that eventually Christ himself might fill that necessary void with his one, true Sacrifice of himself.

This curious ram here plays the role of a *deus ex machina* in the truest and most positive sense of the term. He is a prefiguration of the true and efficacious Victim that only God himself could provide out of the deepest bowels of his compassion, indeed, out of the benevolent "machinations" of his will to save us by bestowing fullness of life in the slain Lamb of his tender Heart. The Lord does not allow Abraham to slay Isaac because that sacrifice, though proving the patriarch's obedience to God, would have been too local, too limited to only this story. As such, it could not have been an oblation with everlasting meaning and efficacy for all the peoples of the earth, of whom Abraham is predestined to be the father (cf. Gen 22:16–18). Compared to Christ's, all other sacrifices are generic, defective, bound by time and space, and must therefore be endlessly multiplied, their sheer multiplication attempting vainly to compensate for their intrinsic imperfection. Only the one and unique sacrifice of the God-man, foreseen and intended from the beginning by the Father, could have the desired and enduring effect of universal reconciliation: "When Christ had offered for all time a single sacrifice for sins, he sat down at the right hand of God. . . . For by a single offering he has perfected for all time those who are sanctified" (Heb 10:12, 14).

We can now clearly see that the full depth of the mystery of our redemption is not that Christ made himself one of us in the Incarnation, or even that he willingly gave his life for us through great sufferings. The most profound level of the mystery of redemption, simultaneously nadir and apex, is that Christ, by assuming our fallen humanity and by following this assumption through to its bitterest consequences, *identified himself with our sin by the will and action of the Father*. St. Paul describes the event, inconceivable to human ears, in rather shocking language: "For our sake *[God] made him to be sin* who knew no sin, so that in him we might become the righteousness of God" (2 Cor 5:21). Quite literally, the Son of God exchanged his glory and innocence for our shame and decadence and, in the process, saved us from our own self-destruction. Love can accomplish no greater work.

26:32 μετὰ δὲ τὸ ἐγερθῆναί με προάξω ὑμᾶς εἰς τὴν Γαλιλαίαν

But after I am raised up, I will go before you to Galilee

JESUS' TONE OF UNWAVERING SERENITY, maintained throughout his predictions of inevitable catastrophes, is now intensified into an enormously reassuring prophecy, full of consolation: "But after I am raised up, I will go before you to Galilee." This is the promise he will fulfill in due course at the very end of this Gospel (cf. 28:10, 16). The adversative "but" corresponds to the "for" of the previous prediction: "For it is written: 'I will strike the shepherd. . . .'" The import of both statements, taken together, is: "*Even though* Scripture affirms that God will strike me, the shepherd, and my sheep will be scattered, *nevertheless* after I am raised up, I will go before you to Galilee." The destructive divine action of striking now yields, almost "produces", the equally divine but now restorative action of raising up. On leaving the banquet room, Jesus has just spoken of betrayal by Judas, of his abandonment by all his disciples, and of the fact that God's own wrath will strike him, a blow that would disperse all his "sheep". But Jesus at once follows the mention of these approaching terrors with the firm, factual assertion that he will be *raised up*.

It is significant that Jesus does not say "after I rise", in the active voice, but rather "after I am raised up", in the passive. The mere affirmation of a "before" and an "after" establishes an authoritative time frame that radically alters the disciples', and our, perception of the meaning of the coming frightful events. Everything that is going to happen, both good and bad, is the subject of Jesus' prophecies, and so all of it is waiting to happen in the future. However, he now introduces a crucial order of events in their future unfolding so that the death-dealing moments of betrayal, abandonment, and death are followed by a new life-giving era, the era of Resurrection and movement forward, to which he gives the final word. The use of the passive voice, moreover, to refer to his own being raised to life, is essential. This typically Semitic turn of phrase, the "theological passive", suggests that the author of the action is God, whose authorship of the deed is taken for granted. A basic principle of biblical theology teaches that God is the universal Lord of all life and death or, in the words of the Canticle of Hannah: "The LORD kills and brings to life; he brings down to Sheol and raises up" (1 Sam 2:6). This teaching provides the necessary link between God's action of "striking" Jesus the Shepherd in v. 31 and his subsequent action of "raising him up" from the dead in v. 32. Everything that happens to Jesus ultimately flows from the Father's will. Through the unfolding of human events, the Father "strikes" his beloved Son for our benefit because—O supreme paradox!—*the Father apparently does not love us less than he loves his eternal Son.*

And yet, at the same time, *the Father cannot deliver his beloved Son forever to the pit of destruction*: "You will not abandon me to the realm of the dead, nor will you let your faithful one see decay" (Ps 16[15]:10, NIV). The counterweight to the verb πατάξω ("I will strike"), with God as subject, is provided by the verbal phrase τὸ ἐγερθῆναί με ("my being raised up"), with Jesus as subject. Jesus himself has celebrated both his striking and his raising up by the Father in advance a moment ago as he sang Psalm 118[117] with the disciples to conclude the Last Supper (cf. 26:30). Among other things Jesus sang: "The LORD has chastened me sorely, but he has not given me over to death. Open to me the gates of righteousness, that I may enter through them and give thanks to the LORD" (Ps 118[117]:18–19). The Great Hallel had never been sung more truthfully, from the depths of the heart of the second Person of the Trinity, who by his very nature is wholly dependent on the Father. And the Father's action of raising Jesus from the dead is praised by the author of the First Letter of Peter as being the source of all Christian hope and new life: "Blessed be the God and Father of our Lord Jesus Christ! By his great mercy we have been born anew to a living hope through the resurrection of Jesus Christ from the dead" (1 Pet 1:3).

Perhaps most important of all, yet not necessarily obvious, is the fact that our Gospel passage does not present these assertions as abstract "truths of faith"; rather, they are proclaimed by the mouth of Jesus himself in the first person singular, when he is already caught up in the whirlwind of the Passion, and he utters them not only as prophecies for the disciples' instruction and strengthening but, above all, as an ardent dramatic confession of his indestructible fidelity and love for the Father, *de profundis*, out of the depths of his own anguish and torment. Jesus speaks as one experiencing in the present, and simultaneously, both the incandescent suffering of love and the ecstatic rush of new life in God that rewards his surrender.

GALILEE IS HOME to Jesus and his disciples. He is "the prophet Jesus from Nazareth of Galilee" (21:11). It is there that he grew up (Lk 2:39–40), that he was baptized by John (3:13), that he chose his first followers (4:18), and that he performed his first miracles of healing (4:23). Galilee is also the country to which he withdrew for safety in times of danger (2:22; 4:12; 15:29). Finally, Galilee is repeatedly mentioned as the place of Jesus' happy reunion with his disciples after the nightmare of the Passion, the location where they will enjoy the sight and companionship of their Risen Lord and where he will give them their solemn commission for all ages (28:7, 10, 16). And, even though there is no Ascension narrative in Matthew, it is in Galilee that this evangelist shows us Jesus physically for the last time interacting with his disciples. In this sense "Galilee" represents the antechamber to Heaven in the Gospel of Matthew. How fitting that Jesus should choose—at least within Matthew's æsthetic—to end his sojourn on earth in Galilee, where he began it, thus closing the circle of a life lived in perfect harmony with the Father's will. He was conceived in Nazareth, and thus he entered the earthly world in Galilee, and from Galilee he will return to the embrace of the Father, no longer now alone as he came to earth, but taking home with him a rich harvest and exclaiming: "Here am I, and the children God has given me" (Heb 2:13).

"After I am raised up, I will go before you to Galilee": what an oasis of light and peace this one stupendous statement offers in the midst of a desert of arid betrayal and rejection! Just *before* making the simple, factual pronouncement, full of the certainty of one possessing authoritative knowledge of the future, Jesus uttered the prophecy about the stricken shepherd and the scattered sheep; and, immediately *after* evoking this stimulating splendor, Jesus confronts Peter with the certainty of his triple denial. Neither the certitude of a violent death nor the sad knowledge of an intimate friend's betrayal can ruffle in Jesus his sense of the rightness of the road he has taken. There, in the center of his being, abides the immovable and comforting Presence of the Father, like a beacon beaming steadily within the surrounding darkness and like a wellspring slaking Jesus' infinite thirst.

The Father's unshaken fidelity to the Son throughout his ordeals is so profoundly nourishing and so capable of defeating in his heart the most vile storm of violent rejection and ridicule that from that interior Presence Jesus receives the strength and the wisdom to continue in loving dialogue with the very ones who are about to abandon him to a cruel fate. Jesus' factual certainty concerning his being raised from the dead is of a piece with his astoundingly serene equanimity and even benevolence toward the fickle disciples. Rejected, he does not reject; betrayed, he does not betray; abandoned, he does not abandon. One senses, in fact, that even the harsh things he must insist upon— his own demise, their inevitable forsaking of him—are at the service of his deeper will to save them from themselves.

Jesus' absolute fidelity to and reliance on the Father provide him with an interior field of vision that is ineffably vaster than the poor disciples' mental horizon, so compacted by all manner of doubts, fears, and cowardly imaginings. It is Jesus' ability to keep his gaze firmly fixed on the Father's sustaining Presence that allows him to move forward along his path of suffering, certain that it is leading to glory. The benighted disciples for their part, much as they have been taught by Jesus, much as they have grown in real affection for him, nonetheless are still very much works of grace in progress. Jesus knows this, and he fully realizes that they need him now more than ever, right in the midst of their impending abandonment and denial. Therefore, the loving Master continues firmly but tenderly in dialogue with them; it is they who will flee from him in every direction when the blow strikes him. He will never turn his back on them as one disappointed in them and wounded by their inconstancy.

On the contrary, even as he crosses the threshold into a horrifying solitude of heart, he tells his weak friends in the most reassuring terms that, proceeding along this threatening path, *he is but going ahead of them into Galilee*, the home country of splendid freedom, lasting peace, and fraternal jubilation. In fact, the verb Jesus uses when he says that he is "going before them to Galilee" is προάξω, which literally means "to lead forward" or "to bring out". Thus, this is not only a matter of Jesus "going ahead" of his disciples in a temporal or spatial sense; more to the point, he will be performing an intentional deed proper to an epic hero. After his Resurrection, he will be the new and definitive Moses, bringing his people out of the slavery to weakness and tyrannical sin (Egypt) and taking them by the power of his triumphant love into the ultimate Promised Land (Galilee). By framing the events of the Passion in this manner, Jesus is already transforming present darkness into incipient light, and the Way of the Cross is shown to find its final destination, not at Calvary, but in Galilee.

Jesus is already now moving along this road up into Galilee, to the splashing shores and bracing breezes of the cherished lake where it had all begun.

א

GALILEE IS THUS PROPOSED TO US by Matthew's Gospel as the final earthly trysting-place where Jesus may hold open communion with all who love him, and this joy-infused symbolism will be more than validated by Jesus' encounters with the holy women and with the Eleven in Galilee at the end of the Gospel (28:9–10, 16–20). We have already seen that this particular Passover is unlike every other before or since because it is the point of convergence between the Jewish memory of God's great liberation of Israel in the past and God's present deed of delivering all nations of the earth from sin and creating from them all the one People of God: "Now in Christ Jesus you who once were far off have been brought near in the blood of Christ" (Eph 2:13), and this "bringing near" can be effected only through Jesus' willing self-oblation (cf. Heb 9:14).

We see, then, that the reference to Jesus' "exodus" with his disciples (ἐξῆλθον, "they went out", v. 30) from the *seder* room to the Mount of Olives and his own immediate affirmation that he will "lead out" his disciples into Galilee after the Resurrection (προάξω ὑμᾶς, v. 32) together frame this night of the Passion as the concrete historical enactment of Jesus' definitive return to the Father. He returns to the Father, moreover, along with the whole company of all the redeemed, most realistically personified in this small band of cowardly hangers-on who are about to run for the hills. This ultimate exodus is precisely what is ritually symbolized in the procession with the Blessed Sacrament on Holy Thursday evening, following the solemn Mass of the Lord's Supper.

Neither should we lose from sight the communal nature of Jesus' migration to the Father, which we easily could by focusing too exclusively on the details of Jesus' sufferings. We must strive to keep in mind continually the full thrust of revelation. Jesus, indeed, came alone from the Father, but he does not return alone to the paternal embrace. The utter solitude—physical, psychological, spiritual—into which Jesus is cast in the night of Holy Thursday, during the suffering of Good Friday, and in the airless tomb on Holy Saturday is shown, against all material evidence, to be but a *middle phase* within the complete trajectory of his homeward journey. It was in order to engender new children for the Father that Jesus came into the world, and he does not go back to the Father empty-handed. Everything that he did and suffered and became, from the Incarnation to death, was *pro nobis*, for our benefit, specifically that we might be reborn as adopted sons (cf. Rom 8:23, Gal 4:5).

Jesus' overwhelming concern for us informs the very core of his Passion. He says to Pilate: "For this I was born, and for this I have come into the world, to bear witness to the truth" (Jn 18:37). And what is this "truth"? St. John's answer is the quintessence of the New Testament kerygma. The innermost secret of God's Heart is that he "so loved the world that he gave his only-begotten Son, that whoever believes in him should not perish but have eternal life" (Jn 3:16). In other words, and staggeringly, *God the Father has not loved God the Son more than he has loved us!* In the unfathomable logic of the divine Heart, the love of the eternal Son *requires* the love of the sons of earth adopted as such within time. Yes, Jesus' return to the Father is therefore inconceivable without us in tow, since we, who at one time were God's enemies by our sin, are now God's true sons in the one beloved Son (υἱός, Eph 1:5), God's true children in the one holy Child (παῖς):

> O love, O charity beyond all telling,
> To ransom a slave you handed over your Son![2]

---

[2] "O inæstimabilis dilectio caritatis: ut servum redimeres, Filium tradidisti!" Easter Proclamation (Exsultet).

26:33–34   Εἰ πάντες σκανδαλισθήσονται ἐν σοί,
            ἐγὼ οὐδέποτε σκανδαλισθήσομαι—
            Ἀμὴν λέγω σοι ὅτι ἐν ταύτῃ τῇ νυκτὶ
            πρὶν ἀλέκτορα φωνῆσαι τρὶς ἀπαρνήσῃ με

"Though they all stumble and fall because of you,
I will never stumble and fall"—
"Truly, I say to you, this very night,
before the cock crows, you will deny me three times"

TRUE TO FORM, Peter will not take Jesus at his word. The Master has just assured the whole group of his disciples, with great sadness of heart, that "you will *all* fall away because of me this night", and he has gone on to cast light on this prediction with a hard-hitting prophetic text. Jesus has even relativized his followers' abandonment of him by inserting it within God's larger plan of redemption. In this sense, Jesus, even at the very moment of his betrayal, is endeavoring to find a way out for the human frailty of those he loves. But Peter has paid attention to none of this; the only emotion he has registered is wounded pride, the fact that Jesus has unaccountably included *him*, Peter, among those who will forsake him. And so Peter is deaf to all reference by Jesus to God the Father's mysterious role in the events of the Passion, deaf also to the bright promise of Jesus' Resurrection and the group's joyful reunion with their Lord in Galilee. The only thing he has heard is, "You will all fall away this night."

Although this dialogue between Jesus and Peter is brief and understated, to the casual observer, probably a mere whispered aside as they are walking along, the exchange exhibits the stuff of great tragedy. Peter has a loyal and basically good character, long on emotional reactions but short on self-knowledge. Jesus has singled him out for privileged treatment on so many occasions that his position as leader of the group of disciples seems to have gone to Peter's head. And, as every tragic character must, Peter possesses a great flaw: a sense of immunity from the common failings of mankind. He feels such strong attachment to Jesus as friend and avid follower that he actually believes himself incapable of falling from his position of privilege. His personal ardor and his special election by Jesus have, in conjunction, created in Peter a blind sense of entitlement and moral invulnerability. He is certain he could never behave like all the rest. In this respect, Peter looks upon the other disciples very much as the Pharisee in the temple looked upon the wretched Publican. Both Peter and the Pharisee have the audacity to flaunt their spiritual superiority directly to the ears of a long-suffering Lord: "The Pharisee stood and prayed thus with himself, 'God, I thank you that I am not like other men, extortioners, unjust, adulterers, or even like this tax collector'" (Lk 18:11). Both Peter and the Pharisee have so little self-awareness that they dare to cast their pride in the form of a prayer, as if the Lord God were ignorant of their virtue and needed to be reminded of it!

It is a lethal tragic flaw for any one of us to set ourselves apart from the rest of men, as if we did not share in the downward propensities of human nature. Once we do that, we have *de facto*, even if not by intent, put ourselves beyond the reach of God's compassionate mercy, as if we could do without it. Peter has already explicitly denied the redemptive power and necessity of Jesus' sacrificial death when, as Jesus predicted his Passion, Peter abruptly *rebuked* his Master, implying that Jesus did not know what he was saying. Interrupting Jesus' prophecy, Peter insisted brashly: "God forbid, Lord! This shall never happen to you." To this effrontery Jesus replied in the harshest manner, saying: "Get behind me, Satan! You are a hindrance to me; for you are not on the side of God, but of men" (16:22–23).

One of the great paradoxes of the mystery of the Church is the fact that, despite such obtuseness and thoroughly flawed behavior on Peter's part, Jesus never gave up on him, never removed him from his assigned role as spokesman and leader of the chosen group of apostles. No doubt this is because repentance, forgiveness, and conversion of heart are the inevitable center of the Christian experience of redemption and the source of all apostolic ministry. Only a thoroughly flawed yet forgiven person can in turn forgive and extend mercy. Our patience with the follies of others can be profitably nourished only by God's patience with our own. Only the repentant apostle, being an expert in wounds, can heal the wounds of others. Peter's bitter remorse will shortly generate his definitive conversion and become the humble dwelling place of God's compassion in Peter's heart, a transforming energy entrusted to his apostolic care.

To become a Christian is to undergo a harrowing process of transformation and rebirth. When the Lord Jesus enters our human existence, he brings with him the whole dynamism of his Paschal Mystery, which will surely expose the deepest flaws of our person before it can transform them into vehicles of grace. To survive this process takes enormous trust and tight clinging for life to the person of the Savior because it requires that we leave behind the self-centered, presumptuous, and logical selves we have always been.

א

JESUS' REPLY TO HIS SELF-CONFIDENT DISCIPLE is cast in the solemn *Amen* language of crucial pronouncements and prophecies: "Truly, I say to you, this very night, before the cock crows, you will deny me three times." Jesus' highly condensed words evoke a multitude of thoughts and insights. Jesus is confronting Peter with the disciple's utter lack of self-knowledge. The Teacher by no means calls into question the power and generosity of Peter's heroic impulse; but he does point out the collision course on which Peter is bound, the tragic and inevitable clash about to occur between Peter's idealized self-image and his actual moral performance. In other words, Jesus knows this disciple he loves infinitely better than the disciple knows himself.

Jesus harbors no rosy ideas about the strength of Peter's will, and he fully recognizes the gaping disparity between his follower's best intentions and his real capacity to persevere in the face of danger. Peter thinks big and thinks in absolute and contrasting terms, with himself, of course, always on the favorable side of the contrast: "Though *they all* fall away because of you, *I will never* fall away." Jesus, on the other hand, thinks small, thinks intimately and immediately. He retorts to Peter: "I say to you, this very night, before the cock crows, you will deny me three times", apparently implying:

"Only you, Peter, have taken the initiative to reply to my ominous prophecy. I admire your involvement and your enthusiasm. But, my dear friend, you have no idea what you are saying! Fidelity is not an exciting impulse or a satisfying feeling that can be conjured up at will on the spot. You can tell genuine fidelity by how much it costs to achieve, by the self-doubt that it necessarily produces at first in the heart in the face of difficult odds. Aware of his intrinsic weakness, a truly faithful person always enters the path of fidelity, not with bravado, but with a certain interior tremor. I can tell, Peter, that right now you are a very short-distance runner. Your explosive energy cannot last long, cannot propel you all the way to Calvary and the tomb and the bleak, bleak waiting for the Light. You say you will never fall away because of me? Ah, dear one! I can clearly see that this heroic never of your fancy is going to shrink pitifully before you know it into this very night, and before this very night that has already fallen upon us comes to an end—yes, even before tomorrow dawns—you will have denied knowing me not once but three times. That will be the extent of your proud fidelity! But, before you despair and start hitting your head against a wall in sheer self-hatred, consider this: I am saying all this to you calmly because I have known you and your propensities from the beginning. In fact, I knew your weakness before ever choosing you as head disciple. Would I have come this far with you if I intended to abandon you now? Do you think I am so weak as to abandon a friend who has failed, after I have made so many pledges of love and fidelity to him? Or do you think that ultimately the success of my mission depends on the epic strength and integrity of my followers? I rely only on my Father's power and fidelity. As I have already told you, the success of my mission lies on the other side of death. Though I must experience death and its bitter defeat, though I must fail in the eyes of worldly men and even come short in my own natural expectations, my Father shall raise me up from death, and I will go to meet you in the new dawn of Galilee. My Father's fidelity, and not your defection, will have the last word in this drama, a spectacle I share with you. You rely on the fantasy of your own imagined prowess, while I rely only on my Father's proven fidelity. Learn from me to turn away from your self and toward the one and only Source of Life. Learn from me that you cannot rise from the darkness on your own strength; you must trust that Another will raise you, according to his promise. So come: allow your very painful failure, your betrayal of me out of self-reliance, to be taken up into my own earthly failure, and when our Father raises me up out of the gloom of death, he will raise you up with me. I assure you, he won't be able to tell your failure from mine, and he will have great mercy on us both!"

Jesus is even now working tirelessly at Peter's salvation by subjecting him to the therapy of the truth—that is, to the glaring realization of the pitiable truths of the human heart as well as to the balm of the truth of divine compassion. But all these "truths" are not whatsoever concepts that Jesus imparts in the manner of philosophical axioms; they are hard dynamic realities, operating in the sphere of deep personal relationship between the sinful creature and the loving Creator. Jesus reveals these truths to Peter under his breath, as it were, as confidences shared between two friends walking side by side in the night and going from the *seder* meal to the Mount of Olives, where they are going to pray together and keep intimate watch. At the same time that betrayal out of fear is fermenting in the disciples' hearts, Jesus continues to build up a climate of intimacy with his chosen band. And everything that Jesus says, whether hard-hitting or consoling, may be summed up in this one fact of his existence both as God and as man: "I am here with you and for you, and there is absolutely nothing you can do, no matter how heinous, to drive me away from your side." So central is this truth to the Heart of Jesus that it constitutes the final promise and revelation that Jesus makes as he utters the last words of Matthew's Gospel: "Behold, I am with you all days, even to the consummation of the world" (28:20b, DRA).

26:35 Κἂν δέῃ με σὺν σοὶ ἀποθανεῖν,
οὐ μή σε ἀπαρνήσομαι.—
ὁμοίως καὶ πάντες οἱ μαθηταὶ εἶπαν

"Even if I must die with you,
I will not deny you."—
And so said all the disciples

PETER IS THE *CHOREGÓS*, THE LEADER WHO, by Christ's appointment, speaks for the whole chorus of the disciples. This is true even when Peter speaks brashly, unthinkingly, by no means measuring his capacities for endurance against the stark realities presently surrounding the group. Impetuously, he overestimates the strength of his bond with Jesus, blind to all the ways in which both his own character flaws and the terrible threats of the situation make him exceedingly vulnerable. Perhaps, too, he possesses the kind of faith in Jesus as triumphant Messiah that can not conceive that the genuine Son of God could possibly undergo humiliating defeat. Poor Peter! Crushing realities confront him on every side and from within. And precisely for this reason, he is a stand-in for each of us in the narrative of the Lord's Passion.

It is hard to overlook the insistence with which the evangelist Matthew hammers into our conscience the extent of Peter's obduracy. We have only to look at the sequence of statements in this dialogue. Jesus first proclaims, acceptingly, the simple fact that the events of this night will prove a scandal ensnaring *all* of his followers and making them abandon him. To this he adds a glimmering promise of eventual resolution. Peter completely ignores the urgency of both pronouncements as well as the utter reliability of the mouth making them. Instead, he opts for a gut reaction by which he singles himself above the rest as an admirable exception to the rule. But Jesus persists in his original line of thought, now going from the general to the particular by assuring Peter that he will be an exception, all right, but rather in the opposite sense from what Peter imagines: all the rest will simply run away, but Peter the braggart *will deny Jesus explicitly*, not once, but three times, before the night is out.

Peter, however, is still not listening. In Jesus' prophetic character-ization of him, the real Peter simply cannot recognize the Peter he fantasizes about so proudly. And so it is that Peter begins his de-nial of Jesus already now, to Jesus' own face, by rejecting outright the truth his Master is revealing to him with such authoritative pre-science. Peter blurts out with unthinking glibness: "Even if I must die with you, I will not deny you!" These are indeed very heroic words, and Peter no doubt means them with all his heart; but, unfortunately, they voice a high-minded emotion that the stronger passion of fear will trump.

More than a simple conversation is taking place here between Jesus and Peter; indeed, by his contrariness, Peter has transformed the present exchange with Jesus into a verbal *agon* amounting to an out-and-out struggle of convictions with the incarnate Word of God! And Peter refuses to yield any ground to his Teacher. He seems bent on having the last word in this match, and Jesus quietly allows it. Indeed, the passage resembles certain Christians' mode of prayer, whose chief aim appears to be convincing God of their own undying virtues and loyalty. This is the type of prayer that characterizes the self-righteous bigot that was the butt of Léon Bloy's fiercest satires. Such protes-tations, of course, normally manifest an abysmal ignorance of one's true self. However, on behalf of such Christians, we may say that they at least persist in having a dialogue with the Lord, something that in itself opens them to the possibility of growth in self-knowledge by dint of recklessly exposing the grounds of their ailment. In one way or another, Peter abides within the crucial drama being played out, which is more than can be said for Judas Iscariot.

Jesus has just introduced the powerful word "deny" (ἀπαρνήσῃ) into the conversation, and Peter now takes it up in his rebuttal (ἀπαρνήσομαι), intending to nullify Jesus' prediction by robustly deny-ing the possibility of any future denial on his part. What a fall must soon ensue when you climb high on an imaginary stairway, propelled only by delusion! High spirits can enable you to tread air for a bit, but then comes the terrible plunge. Jesus for his part, realizing Peter's self-delusion, is trying to offer him the firm ground of self-knowledge, leading to conversion. Could it be that Peter has by now forgotten that other clashing exchange of viewpoints he sustained with Jesus at Cæsarea Philippi, ironically right after his own investiture as Rock of the Church (16:22–23)?

On that occasion, Peter rejected out of hand as unthinkable the notion of a suffering Messiah, even though Jesus had just proclaimed it as the *only* possibility within the divine plan of salvation. There then boomed out Jesus' fierce cry: "Get behind me, Satan!", terrible words that for once silenced Peter. Immediately after that stinging denunciation, Jesus calmly used the clash of viewpoints to teach all the disciples, including a hangdog Peter, a fundamental lesson in Christian discipleship that prescribes as indispensable for all Jesus' followers the interior motivations of their Lord: "If any man would come after me," Jesus proclaimed, "let him deny himself [ἀπαρνησάσθω ἑαυτόν] and take up his cross and follow me. For whoever would save his life will lose it, and whoever loses his life for my sake will find it" (16:24–25).

The critical crossroads at which every would-be disciple sooner or later arrives is the harrowing decision whether to deny his teacher or to deny himself. Such a decision is indeed "harrowing" because the individual human being does not easily acquiesce to following the way marked by anyone other than himself, even if that other is the Word Incarnate. But no one can read the Gospel attentively and not realize that one cannot at the same time affirm the truth of Jesus' way of discipleship and in the same breath affirm one's own personal and autonomous way, the path one was merrily treading before the encounter with the Master and his unaccountable election for himself of one's very limited person. We cannot have it both ways simultaneously. "To 'deny someone' is to disown him . . . and to 'deny oneself' is to disown oneself as the center of one's existence" (NAB, on 16:24). In such terms, Jesus was teaching his followers at Cæsarea that their existence could not at the same time have two centers.

Could we not say that the present great earthquake in Peter's life results from the collision of opposing forces deep in his being? Is he not pushing his ego-driven will impossibly to affirm *both* the demands of following Jesus genuinely *and* the exigencies of his own separate, autonomous self? Jesus' pronouncement could not be more unequivocal: "If any man would come after me, let him deny himself and take up his cross and follow me." Whoever affirms Jesus as Lord and Center must deny himself, and, conversely, whoever affirms himself as lord and center must deny Jesus. The ego always insists on being first, on blazing idiosyncratic trails that always aim at self-aggrandizement, whereas a true disciple must not lead but *follow—follow a Lord who carried the burden of the cross.* For the apprentice disciple, that is the inescapable crunch.

Peter, however, attempts to elude this narrow gate by indulging in willful, wishful thinking that ultimately cannot carry him through as true disciple. Fear makes it impossible for him to stop being the center of his own existence. If my own desires, worries, and goals are displaced as the focus of all my attention, a mental chasm opens beneath me. I fall into a kind of existential vertigo, fearing I will altogether cease to exist. This fear, of course, is not as substantial or objective as it seems. A death shall be involved, true enough; but it is the death of the old, self-centered, and, hence, false self. And yet, because that is the only self I have thus far known, in this sense I am justified in fearing an absolute demise. Even a groundless or exaggerated fear can, indeed, induce real terror.

Peter claims heroically that he is eager to undergo even physical death together with Jesus, so strongly does he cling to his Lord with his affections; and yet, at the deeper spiritual level of self-renunciation, of self-displacement, he is not able to "lose his life for Jesus' sake" so as to find it in a higher dimension. Peter's loud heroics and brave protestations are but a symptom of how much his ego continues to determine—in fact if not in intention—the course of his life and choices. Even at this critical hour, he has to shine in his own esteem by dint of self-assertion. For the moment, Jesus' Passion merely serves, in Peter's mind, as a stage to display his own heroics. He imagines himself a hero *for* Jesus, and yet he cannot disappear altogether *into* Jesus. Disappearing into Jesus interiorly through mystical death proves, in fact, an infinitely more difficult feat than dying for Jesus exteriorly in the body. We more readily give up our body than our ego.

When Jesus says that "whoever would save his life will lose it, and whoever loses his life for my sake will find it" (16:25), it does not seem that the Lord is speaking specifically about physical martyrdom. The martyr's physical death, admirable and at times inevitable as it is, will always remain the exception and not the rule for Christians. The necessary rule for *all* Christians, regardless of concrete circumstance, is what St. Paul terms the death of the "old self". Paul describes in vibrant, paradoxical language what this mystical death for Jesus' sake entails when he writes to the Galatians shortly before his own beheading: "I have been crucified with Christ; it is no longer I who live, but Christ who lives in me; and the life I now live in the flesh I live by faith in the Son of God, who loved me and gave himself for me" (Gal 2:20). That such extreme identification with Jesus and his fate is still impossible for Peter at the moment of Jesus' betrayal is a fact shown plainly by the jarring contrast in their respective spiritual attitudes as he and Jesus are walking to the Mount of Olives after the Last Supper.

The evangelist concludes this whole passage on a dry, ironical note when, immediately after recording Peter's exalted remonstration, he adds: "And so said all the disciples." This shows that Peter is indeed exceptional, but not for the reason he thinks. He is different from the rest, not because he is more courageous or faithful than they, but because he persists in being their spokesman, in setting a trend. He is foolhardy enough to be the first to voice an idealistic sentiment that all the rest then echo. There is irony, too, in the fact that, while Peter tries to exalt himself by raising himself above his fellow disciples ("though they all fall away . . ."), still they will not concede him that special position but rather drag him back down into the company of the *hoi polloi* by mimicking his heroics. It seems that Peter must lead the group now in their awful self-delusion as the negative part of his training to lead them later on, after the Resurrection, in their authentically heroic effort to build up Christ's Church.

Jesus began this passage with the grim prediction: "You will all [stumble and] fall . . . because of me this night." Perhaps the best commentary on the drama played out between Jesus and his disciples as they go to the Mount of Olives is provided by these words of St. Paul to the Romans: "There is no distinction; since all have sinned and fall short of the glory of God, they are justified by his grace as a gift, through the redemption which is in Christ Jesus" (Rom 3:22–24). We see here clearly that Peter and the other disciples, the nucleus of the Church, are in no way different from the rest of mankind. In the drama of the Passion, it is us they represent, both in our deluded and arrogant sinfulness and in our colossal yearning for the life of God in Christ.

א

7. THE SPACE OF PURE RELATION

Prayer in Gethsemane (26:36–46)

26:36   Τότε ἔρχεται μετ᾽ αὐτῶν ὁ Ἰησοῦς
         εἰς χωρίον λεγόμενον Γεθσημανί
         καὶ λέγει τοῖς μαθηταῖς·
         Καθίσατε αὐτοῦ ἕως οὗ ἀπελθὼν ἐκεῖ προσεύξωμαι

Then Jesus goes with them
into a place called Gethsemane,
and he said to his disciples,
"Sit here, while I go yonder and pray"

THEN JESUS [GOES] WITH THEM [in]to a place. . . ." Into what
kind of a place? Where, precisely, is Jesus now taking his
disciples? ". . . [in]to a place called 'Gethsemane' [the Oil
Press]", explains Matthew. In this darkest of nights, as he plods on
through a murk of delusions, cross-purposes, and impending betrayal,
Jesus does not abandon his disciples or leave them to their own devices, even though he knows they are about to abandon *him*. Rather,
he leads them to a solitary place whose name, *gat-sh^emaním* (oil press),
appropriately evokes a process both of painful crushing and of fruitful
transformation.

Without being mercilessly crushed, ripe olives could never yield
rich oil, a natural substance that offers a wondrous variety of benefits
that sustain and enhance the life of both the body and the soul. As
we know, olive oil flavors food, nourishes the body, relaxes muscles,
protects the skin, heals wounds, anoints athletes, kings, and Christians, and gives light. It would be very difficult to find another single

product of nature that could better signify the full septenary of the riches of God's love poured out on man. It is easy to see why olive oil early on became the sacramental substance symbolizing the Holy Spirit himself. Like this oil, the Holy Spirit, though indivisibly one, has a wide range of effects through his sevenfold gifts, which always meet a particular need with the precise transformative power required.

Gethsemane, then, is a place name that refers geographically to an isolated olive grove on the western slope of the Mount of Olives just outside Jerusalem. As Jesus feels the impending danger closing in upon him from all sides, he chooses to take his disciples into a dark solitude with himself, to a location outside the city, apart from all society and far from the hubbub of Passover celebrations. He takes them into a situation that promises great intimacy with himself and one another, where there is nothing to do except *to be together in the darkness*, waiting and praying together, watching together for the next step in the unfolding of God's plan of salvation. This location at Gethsemane, therefore, is both a geographical reality and a metaphysical space of communion, a profound example in Christ's life with his disciples of what the poet Rilke calls *Weltinnenraum* (world of interior space), an intense experience of "pure relation", that is, a state of being in which nothing but relating occurs. The same ardent love can so permeate disparate beings that it creates existences that interpenetrate as one, as illustrated metaphorically in Rilke's poem "Es winkt . . .":

> *One* single space pervades all beings here:
> an inner world-space. Silently, the birds
> fly through us still. Oh, I who want to grow,
> can gaze outside: a tree will rise *inside* me. [1]

Such "interior space", however, also becomes exteriorly visible drama at Gethsemane, a human and divine narrative that does not *refer* to the mystery of communion occurring but actually *displays* it to the eyes of faith. It is astounding to observe that, the closer death approaches Jesus, and the more he senses the unravelling of his friends'

---

[1] "Durch alle Wesen reicht der *eine* Raum: / Weltinnenraum. Die Vögel fliegen still / durch uns hindurch. O, der ich wachsen will, / ich seh hinaus, und *in* mir wächst der Baum." Poem entitled "Es winkt zu Fühlung fast aus allen Dingen", from Rilke's *Notebooks*, August, 1914, trans. David Young, http://www.cortlandreview.com/features/13/summer/young.php#1.

commitment to him in the face of his death, the greater also grows his desire to commune with them interiorly, with all the intimacy accessible only within the locus of an eternal love. On this occasion in Gethsemane, we are witnessing a supremely transcendental moment in Jesus' earthly life, a moment of divine transcendence into which Jesus refuses to enter alone, without the companionship of his chosen friends. And the locus of divine transcendence is by definition the space of purest Relation and Communion.

Clearly the scene is closely related in structure and meaning to the episode of Jesus' Transfiguration before Peter, James, and John (17:1–13); but here the symbolism is reversed. Whereas the scene on Tabor overflowed with light and, thus, served as a prefiguration of the Resurrection, the present scene at Gethsemane overflows, instead, with darkness and is no prefiguration at all but, rather, the all-too-real threshold of the Passion itself. The Transfiguration occurred in function of the Passion, to enlighten and strengthen the disciples interiorly so that they could bear it. Now, on the Mount of Olives, all symbols have vanished, all references to past or future realities and events have disappeared. There remains only the possibility, for Jesus and his disciples, of *inhabiting a space of pure Relation*, in which twelve human beings, representing all of mankind, have been gathered into his intimacy by the God-man in order for them to appear together with him before the eternal Father.

Jesus intends the creation of a space of pure Relation consisting of different interlocking levels of communion: of the disciples among themselves; of himself with his disciples both individually and as a group; of himself with his Father; and finally, within this primal and eternal communion of Father and Son, the communion with the Father of himself as now truly "enclosing" his disciples in his Heart. The scene at Gethsemane unfolds the ultimate mystery of Jesus as High Priest and Mediator between his Father and mankind, as the One, that is, whose primary mission it is to establish perfect communion between God and man. But Jesus accomplishes this mission in the most humble, hidden, unobtrusive, and intimate of ways.

The great simplicity and poverty of the human scene before us only make more obvious the profoundly and luminously *trinitarian* structure of the experience as narrated by Matthew. For *the* "interior space of pure Relation" is, preeminently, the sphere of God's tri-personal Life. The trinitarian reference and actual *realization* are unmistakable in the manner in which Jesus gives the stage directions, so to speak, as he "choreographs" the moments and levels of communion: "[You] sit *here*, while I go [*yonder*] to pray", he says to the whole group of the Twelve. But from this group he then selects Peter, James, and John and takes them to a farther place, where "he began to be sorrowful and troubled". To these three only he says: "Remain *here*, and watch with me." Then, finally, "going *a little farther* he fell on his face and prayed, 'My Father'. . . ." Jesus thus establishes three "zones" of increasing intimacy and communion. Each of these zones is defined by Jesus' second-person address, either to his disciples or to his Father. Here Martin Buber's seminal category of the bond between the "I" and the "Thou" is being lived in its most intense possible form, precisely because the bond is being enacted within a context of stark darkness, solitude, and agony. The I-Thou relation in this case has nothing satisfyingly worldly to lean upon. It must be generated moment by moment solely out of love's very marrow.

At the center of the three concentric circles just described is the zone of Jesus' utter solitude with the Father. Here Jesus addresses only him, without receiving any apparent answer. Moving outward, the next zone is that inhabited by Jesus with the three chosen disciples, the same ones who witnessed the splendor of the Transfiguration. To these, as he has previously shown them his glory, he now reveals the full agony of his interior state, pleading with them to watch with him. And the third and outermost zone of intimacy contains the other nine, who were asked by Jesus merely to sit and wait. These three interlocking zones of intimate communion are welded into one vast space of pure Relation solely by the person and action of Jesus at the center, who "commutes" between them as Mediator. Beyond this tripartite zone of intimacy, outside the Mount of Olives, there lies the undifferentiated expanse of "Jerusalem", that is, of "the world" Jesus and his disciples have left behind physically and temporarily, but only so as to redeem it later by first having plunged into the Passion's mystery of darkness and death.

This division of the Gethsemane experience into "zones" of deepening communion is not unlike the articulated divisions of intensifying holiness in the structure of the Jerusalem temple, as the priest moves from the outer courtyard of the women through the courtyard of Israel and, then, finally into the Holy of Holies, which the high priest enters alone and only once a year on the Day of Atonement, to plead with God for the sins of his people. Indeed, the structure of Jesus' agony at Gethsemane exhibits him very conspicuously to the eyes of faith as one "designated by God a high priest according to the order of Melchizedek":

> In the days of his flesh, Jesus offered up prayers and supplications, with loud cries and tears, to him who was able to save him from death, and he was heard for his godly fear. Although he was a Son, he learned obedience through what he suffered; and being made perfect he became the source of eternal salvation to all who obey him. (Heb 5:10, 7–9)

Thus, the structure of the Gethsemane narrative in Matthew, with its clear designation of spatial areas of encounter, stresses both Jesus' personal identity as priestly Mediator and the liturgical nature of his suffering and death as single existential Sacrifice that contains and surpasses all previous ritual oblations.

At this moment, Jesus' overpowering love is wielding the terrible anguish in his heart (26:38) as a mighty battering ram, to make a breach in the iron wall of Time and Sin in order to introduce his friends, through that gap, into the joy of the Father's eternal embrace. At this nocturnal moment in Gethsemane, history comes to a standstill because God is suffering on earth, and the very meaning of time and existence are being transformed by God's suffering in solidarity with the anguish of all creation. This night that launches the Sacred Triduum is, at the mystical level, a reversion to the dread and formless chaos of Genesis before the creation (1:2), the primal *tohu wa-bohu* that nonetheless offered itself docilely to the creative power of God's will and wisdom. Everything dissolves in the darkness of the night of God's Passion into a state of amorphousness, but only in order that it may be molded anew by the creating love of the Word in the furnace of his suffering. The disciples' exhaustion and drowsiness, as well as Jesus' agony itself, are vivid signs of this dissolution of the existing order of things under the heat of God's Passion: neither the disciples nor Jesus can retain a firm, controlling grasp on hard "reality" as they have known it.

All things are dissolving, forsaking their previous forms, and thereby descending with Christ into the chaos of death, in order to be re-created together with him in his death and rise with him in his Resurrection. The person of the incarnate Word synthesizes within himself absolutely the total range of Being: divinity, humanity, soul, spirit, bone, cartilage, flesh, both vegetable and mineral substance, and elemental water. Nothing in the cosmos or in the realm of eternity is foreign to Jesus or left unaffected by Jesus' agony unto death on this night.

The extraordinarily sublime purpose of the incarnate Word's mission on earth—the creation of ultimate, enduring communion between God and man, so that man can live the very life of God—now becomes deeply embedded in a most human reality: the harrowing trial by betrayal and abandonment that Jesus is beginning to experience at this moment. Jesus' present state of incandescent agony is producing in his Heart and soul a most understandable result, namely, a dire need for palpable human companionship and support; and this explains why he is simultaneously appealing to his Father in heaven and to his human friends on earth in a tone not far removed from panic. At times, Jesus sounds like a drowning man, and his divine personhood in no way exempts his human nature from undergoing the experience of inwardly exploding grief, as described by Shakespeare:

> Sorrow concealed, like to an oven stopp'd,
> Doth burn the heart to cinders where it is.[2]

How affecting it is to contemplate the humility of God manifested in how the eternal Word, free of all worldly pride, *pleads* with his Father for a reprieve and *pleads* as well with these thoroughly disloyal and untrustworthy men for the alms of their company! Yet they are, after all, the only friends Jesus has, pathetic friends though they might be.

Before the space of pure Relation can also become a sphere of pure joy, it must first host the drama of undiluted sorrow and abandonment. Dreadful, purifying sorrow always seems a required condition to pave the way for unalloyed joy. Jesus' unspeakable experience of abandonment by all—including, humanly speaking, his Father—is precisely what singles him out and anoints him as the great Bridgebuilder (*pontifex*)[3] between God and man: "He had to be made like his brethren in every respect, so that he might become a merciful and

---

[2] *Titus Andronicus*, II, 4, 36–37.

[3] *Pontifex* ("bridge-builder") is the Latin Vulgate's translation of Greek ἀρχιερεύς in Hebrews 2:17 and elsewhere. In English, the Greek term is normally translated "high priest".

faithful [*pontifex*] in the service of God, to make expiation for the sins of the people. For *because he himself has suffered and been tempted, he is able to help those who are tempted*" (Heb 2:17–18). This text makes a stunning correlation between Jesus' capacity and willingness to suffer greatly and his capacity to intercede, to atone, and to help effectively. Jesus' suffering as incarnate Word is the unshakable metaphysical plank that the Savior erects from the side of God to the side of men, over the abyss of sinful rebellion, so that the divine suffering connects and becomes one thing with the human suffering. Jesus can, therefore, cross this bridge of love subsequently in the other direction, laden with the fruits of his Passion as he goes forward triumphantly to present his many brethren to the Father.

The mutuality and communion with human sorrow that Jesus is here establishing through his suffering are punctuated textually throughout our passage by Jesus' use of personal phrases involving the prepositions *with* and *to*. Reiterated in this context, these relational words evoke an almost quivering intensity of feeling: "Jesus went *with them* to a place called Gethsemane, and he said *to his disciples*. . . . And taking *with him* Peter and the two sons of Zebedee. . . . Then he said *to them*, 'My soul is very sorrowful, even to death; remain here, and watch *with me*. . . .' And he came *to his disciples* . . . and he said *to Peter*, 'So, could you not watch *with me* one hour?' . . . Then he came *to the disciples* and said *to them*. . . .'" Such linguistic usage, subtle but relentless, creates an atmosphere in which the human capacities are intensely stretched as they strive for relation. The situation thus created manifests Jesus' overriding desire for soulful communion with his followers. No matter what else is occurring physically or psychologically around Jesus, his one unswerving interior motivation throughout the scene at Gethsemane is *union in love* with those he has chosen as his friends, a union that can be activated and thrive only within Jesus' trinitarian union with the Father in the Holy Spirit.

In a real sense, Jesus is "trapped" between the weakness and fickleness of the disciples and the silence of the invisible Father. The Lord feels left in the lurch by both. And yet Jesus exists exclusively because of and for the Father and to manifest God's plan of saving love to us mortals. Consequently, this moment of supreme abandonment and woeful forsakenness becomes *the* precise moment when the glory of God's love in Jesus can shine in full splendor. In this locus of abandonment, Jesus is reduced to being nothing but self-offering

Gift, seeking nothing for himself but, rather, embracing joyfully the opportunity to show fully who God is. He, the Son, does this by pouring himself out to his disciples: "For the joy that was set before him[, Jesus] endured the cross, despising the shame" (Heb 12:2). The only possible mode of existence that now remains to Jesus is the incessant act of pouring out his being as a joyful oblation to the Father, in the knowledge that this act will bring fullness of life to all mankind. The agony of knowing himself abandoned in an absolute darkness is itself an overwhelming invitation and pre-condition for him to bestow all of himself wholeheartedly to mortals in the name of the Father, that they might become immortal. The death of Jesus the Seed is a prerequisite in order for the Tree of Life to sprout and produce the Church.

Jesus' one overwhelming desire in Gethsemane is to be *with them*, his beloved friends, in the most profound sense these words can convey. Thus, he seeks ardently to fulfill the divine vocation contained in his name *Emmanuel*, "God-with-us". But what kind of "being with them" does Jesus intend? Obviously, he is not going to pour out his life in such a catastrophic manner merely to achieve casual social companionship, the contented coexistence of human beings enjoying life alongside one another. When Jesus expresses his desire to be *with them*, we must understand this in an absolute and transcendental sense. Here everything else—their hopes, accomplishments, power of thought, personal and family history, pedigree, politics, future projects, social connections, and ambitions . . . : in a word, *everything* else has to fall away. This is why we can speak of Gethsemane as a space of "*pure* relation", that is, a place and a moment in time and yet out of time where nothing obtains but the essential presence of Lord and disciples one to the other, whether in fidelity or betrayal, whether in strength or weakness, whether in sorrow or in joy. Such is *the space of pure Relation*, which requires the suspension of all else except the act of being-with itself, the ineffable and yet universally longed-for act of being-as-communion.

Gethsemane represents a mighty hiatus because Jesus has now left everything behind but, nevertheless, is not yet in possession of the Kingdom of the Resurrection. Therefore, he finds himself in a state of radical suspension—between heaven and earth, between darkness and light, between God and men, between life and death. The transparent emptiness of such a state of merciless suspension manifests, in the blaze of the Fire of Mercy, that both Jesus' life and Jesus' sufferings and death are exclusively *for us* because he is the personification of the Father's eternal Love. Gethsemane is the hour of the unquestionable triumph of Jesus' love because it is here that he shows with greatest clarity that he will never stop embracing to his Heart—with all the explosive omnipotence of his divinity—those who are too weak or cowardly or fickle or disloyal to dare to embrace him. When he takes these twelve feeble and shabby men with him to Gethsemane, *to be with him*, he is taking us all there, just as he happens to find us.

א

26:37b–38   παραλαβὼν τὸν Πέτρον
καὶ τοὺς δύο υἱοὺς Ζεβεδαίου
ἤρξατο λυπεῖσθαι καὶ ἀδημονεῖν. . . .
Περίλυπός ἐστιν ἡ ψυχή μου ἕως θανάτου·
μείνατε ὧδε καὶ γρηγορεῖτε μετ' ἐμοῦ

taking with him Peter
and the two sons of Zebedee,
he began to be sorrowful and troubled. . . .
"My soul is very sorrowful, even to death;
remain here, and watch with me"

PRAYER IS THE VERY HEART of the Gethsemane experience, for both Jesus and the disciples. Five times the verb "to pray" is interspersed throughout the passage in four different forms. The evangelist seems to be deliberately making it the structural backbone that unifies the narrative at this point and reveals the deepest intent of Jesus' Heart. The verb "to pray" recurs in these five forms: προσεύξωμαι (v. 36), προσευχόμενος (v. 39), προσεύχεσθε (v. 41), προσηύξατο (v. 42), and again προσηύξατο (v. 44). Such repetition should not surprise us since *prayer* may be said to be the activity par excellence of the state of pure Relation. In the face of the calamity threatening him, Jesus wants nothing more than to commune with his Father from within his sorrow and in the company of his friends. Four of the five instances of the verb's use refer to Jesus himself, to his own act of praying, and the fifth is the imperative command προσεύχεσθε! ("pray!") that Jesus directs to the disciples, as if he were saying: "If you would be my disciples, join me in what I am already doing with all my heart. When you are with me, you must do what I do." To bolster the meaning and intensity of such prayer, Jesus three times associates with it the other verb γρηγορεῖτε (to keep watch, vv. 38, 40, 41), referring in part to his own need for companionship ("Watch with me", vv. 38, 40) and in part to his desire to orient the disciples' whole being to the Father ("Watch and pray that you may not enter into temptation", v. 41, "temptation" being any trial that can potentially separate one from God).

Moreover, Jesus does not start praying straightaway upon arriving in Gethsemane. He does indeed at once express his urgent need and desire to pray as his sole activity of this night, and in this respect Gethsemane is an extension of the *seder* meal. But, after inviting the nine to sit and wait, Jesus selects his three more intimate disciples and goes with them a short distance away from the main group. And now, just before plunging into prayer as into a burning abyss, he reveals to the three with unabashed candor the full turbulence raging in his Heart.

"He began to be sorrowful (λυπεῖσθαι) and troubled (ἀδημονεῖν). Then he said to them, 'My soul is very sorrowful (περίλυπός), even to death; remain here, and watch with me.'" Having earlier this evening given himself—his very Body and Blood—to his disciples in the Eucharist, now Jesus entrusts to these chosen three the deepest secrets of his human heart. He has now created the interior space of pure Relation we have been describing, where nothing has admittance except the naked truths of soul and spirit before God. Within such a space, Jesus "*begins* to be sorrowful and troubled". It is as if, until this moment of intimacy, privacy, and at least exterior tranquility, he has not been free to expose his soul. It is highly significant that he does not turn to his Father in prayer, seeking divine consolation, before confiding to his closest friends the ravaged state of his soul. He must, alone, turn to his Father in the depths of trinitarian communion, in that intimacy of Divine Persons that nothing else can approximate; and yet he does not do so without first opening his soul and heart to these special followers while begging them to keep him watchful company. He wants to conceal nothing from those he most loves, and the reason must be twofold: first, that he badly needs the human support of their presence (yes, astoundingly, even the Father's consolation cannot supplant the comfort of human friends!); and, above all, he wants to initiate them into the mystery of divine compassion. Jesus wants his disciples to become as compassionate as he is precisely by sharing firsthand in the suffering of his Heart.

Matthew sees fit to express the state of Jesus' soul by using two distinct verbs: λυπεῖσθαι (*lypeísthai*) and ἀδημονεῖν (*adêmoneín*). His interior distress is such that no single descriptive verb can do it justice, and the evangelist wants to communicate the condition of Jesus' Heart as precisely as possible, for precision in communicating these interior realities is a major part of love's intimacy. Thus it is worthwhile spending some time to consider the connotations of the two poignant words Matthew chooses to express Jesus' present distress of soul.

First of all, the word *lypeísthai*: This verb, rendered "to be sorrowful" by the RSV, is derived from the noun λύπη (*lýpê*), which means "pain of body" before it also refers to "pain of mind or soul". It may be best to translate the verb as "to be pained, grieved, or distressed", because these passive participles denote a suffering *inflicted upon* the subject in a way that the static adjective "sorrowful" does not. Our first verb, then, communicates an anguish of soul that is the result of violence done to the subject by others. We here envision, in particular, the spiritual violence of betrayal; and the intensity of this sorrow is such that its mental anguish overflows throughout Jesus' body and physical senses as a felt, racking pain. In addition, as Jesus himself now describes the state of his soul, he says, "My soul is περίλυπος (*perílypos*) even to death". This Greek word echoes the root (λύπ-, "pain") of the verb just used by the narrator and adds to it the prefix περί, meaning "around". Thus, when Jesus exclaims "My soul is περίλυπος", he means that it is "afflicted beyond measure", quite literally *surrounded by grief*. Jesus' very graphic feeling of being "besieged by pain on all sides" makes eminent sense as a summary of his own mental state, produced by the almost universal opposition inflicted upon him by the religious rulers of Israel and the people itself, as well as by the incomprehension and impending betrayal of his own disciples. Jesus is like a man drowning in a shark-infested sea of sorrows. In just two verses (26:37–38), Matthew has in this way managed to create an atmosphere of unremitting dread.

"Then [Jesus] said to [Peter, James, and John], 'My soul is [encompassed by grief,] even to death.'" These words of Jesus to the chosen three, describing the storm within his soul, are actually a direct echo of the Septuagint version of Psalm 42[41]:6 (LXX), where the Psalmist queries his own soul: ἵνα τί περίλυπος εἶ ψυχή, that is, literally, "Why are you beset by sorrows, O soul?" The text of the psalm continues with these words so full of trust: "Hope in God; for I shall again praise him, my savior" (Ps 42[41]:5, RSV). However, strikingly, Jesus himself stops short of such an expression of vibrant hope and, instead, adds to the psalm's adjective περίλυπος the terrible phrase ἕως θανάτου, that is, "even to death". In other words, by omitting all reference to consolation and by adding an extreme qualifier to the already dismal περίλυπος, Jesus intensifies rather than lightens the bleakness of the Psalmist's experience of desolation. To do full justice to his Heart's sorrow in communicating it to his intimate disciples, nothing less will do than to reveal to them that "My soul is [surrounded by grief] to [the very point of] death." It seems that Jesus is intent on having his disciples know exactly what it feels like to be Jesus of Nazareth at this moment in the history of salvation.

In Psalm 42[41] the Psalmist addressed his own soul directly as a rhetorical convention, in order to give himself encouragement in the midst of difficulties. By contrast, however, Jesus uses and adapts the same text in order to expose the grief of his soul to his beloved followers, as if wanting to make them a gift of it. Even within the furnace of such mental suffering, Jesus seems far more centered on his friends and their welfare than on the suffering of his own soul. He speaks of his pain only for their benefit, that they might enter the sphere of his prayer and participate in his burning love before the Father. True, he has separately sought their consoling human companionship, but only as a means to involve them in his own drama of love. We can well imagine these disciples later in their lives, after the Ascension, remembering this moment of untold sorrow and disorientation and deriving enormous strength from the knowledge that, that night in Gethsemane, the Lord mingled all their sufferings past and future with his own, beyond separation.

The other verb that the evangelist here yokes to λυπεῖσθαι in order to describe Jesus' mental condition is ἀδημονεῖν, normally rendered "to be sorely troubled". At first glance, this meaning does not seem to add new coloring to its companion verb. A little digging into this word's etymology, however, reveals a rather surprising nuance in Jesus' suffering. The verb's root, δημ- (*dêm-*), also gives us δῆμος (*dêmos*), meaning the "people" of a city, especially "the mass of the people assembled in a public place". From this *dêmos*, in fact, we derive the word "democracy". To form our Gospel verb, there is then prefixed to it the letter ἀ-, which is called the "alpha privative" because it negates what comes after it (as in the word "amoral"). The particular manner of "being troubled" that this verb ἀδημονεῖν communicates, then, appears to involve a person's being deprived of normal social interaction with his own people and community, resulting in psychological and spiritual "homelessness", what the Germans call *Unheimlichkeit* (also connoting "eeriness" and "uncanniness").[4] In Jesus' case, such a state of mental vertigo and disorientation would have been produced by his recent history of misunderstanding, rejection, and betrayal, generating a piercing sense of *radically not belonging*.

This nuance in meaning suddenly opens out new vistas of sorrow and longing in Jesus' request to his disciples that immediately follows: "Remain here, and watch with me." The drowning man, as he thrashes about for life, clings frantically to anything that resembles a human form. *Remain here*, he pleads; in other words: "At least you three, don't go away. After all, I've already shown you my glory, and you have heard the voice of my Father on Tabor bearing testimony to who I am. I don't need mobs of supporters to applaud me. I only need the presence of a couple of intimate friends on whom I can count for simple human warmth. Will you give me that?" *And watch with me*: "Together with me, look to the Father. I must confess to you that I don't feel I have the strength needed to go alone to my Father. I need the energy that our joint watching would provide me. Will you now turn with me to my Father and your Father? Will you, by your mere expectant presence, help me show him that it has not all been in vain, that I do have some fruit to show for all my efforts? You three

---

[4] See ἀδημονέω (entry 88), in: *Thayer's Greek-English Lexicon of the New Testament* (1889, 1995).

can be my fruit, my evidence, if you agree. Please do not let me fall into a vacuum of loneliness! Do I shock you with my pleading? Yes, my Father is the origin and mainstay of my being; but I am not only divine, and my poor human spirit and weak flesh desperately need your living warm human presence at my side."

26:39ab προελθὼν μικρὸν ἔπεσεν ἐπὶ πρόσωπον αὐτοῦ προσευχόμενος καὶ λέγων· Πάτερ μου!

Going a little farther he fell on his face and prayed, saying: "My Father!"

J ESUS NOW ENTERS his "Holy of Holies", that is, the third and most intense zone of relational intimacy he has himself defined, where he is utterly alone with his Father. It is now that he begins to pray in earnest. He first entered the Garden of Gethsemane with all twelve apostles, asking them to stand by for a bit while he went off to pray. John Milton honors such apparently empty waiting as a worthy form of diaconic *waiting on* the Lord:

They also serve who only stand and wait.[5]

To abide still and in silence with nothing specific to do, simply because one's Master has asked one to do so or because in fact there is nothing one *can* do, presents us with a form of contentless obedience that is especially relevant in this situation. Jesus' request to the Twelve within this first zone of intimacy, which he defines when he orders them to "Sit here, while I go [yonder] and pray", quietly

---

[5] This is the concluding line of Sonnet 19 (1655), which begins "When I consider how my light is spent".

underscores the fact that Jesus' exclusive purpose in bringing them to Gethsemane is to forge pure, intimate relation between himself and them: nothing else, with the fire of his suffering as welding force. Besides that, there is no other, more palpable earthly "purpose". The relationship itself is the content of the experience; the relationship between the disciple and Jesus is its own end: it exists *for* nothing else! Moreover, their obedience to his contentless command initiates them to intimacy precisely by inviting them to participate in the vast void that Jesus himself is presently experiencing at the center of his being, an emptiness that will only intensify as his prayer to the Father remains (apparently) unanswered. Jesus seems to be saying: "You are my disciples and I am your Master, and the command I am giving you on this occasion is, *Do nothing! Just be with me*, so that you can feel what I feel! This is the deepest desire of my Heart." Doing always has a *content* that is different from the act of doing, while being does not. The act of being is identical with being itself. Being is because it is; it is its own end, and this is but another formula for love itself. Pure being is being-with because being is essential love.

From the total group of the Twelve, Jesus, in a second moment, chose a more intimate group of three. The mere act of going off with these three into an even more exclusive solitude enables Jesus to bare the sorrow of his soul powerfully to them. We detect a causal relationship between the two events: "[he took] with him Peter and the sons of Zebedee" and "he began to be sorrowful." The first makes the second possible. Indeed, in moments of emotional crisis, we can be most fully ourselves, without putting on cosmetic appearances, only with persons who are closest to our heart and to whom we are attached with bonds of strong trust and affection. The incarnate Word is no exception to this general pattern of human behavior and need. And Jesus' attitude and actions here quite dispel the long-standing prejudice of certain cultural epochs that, under duress, Stoic self-control and lack of emotional expression should be the preferred behavior for Christians, as if faith made us less human. What Jesus asks the three to do only intensifies his command to the nine. The nine were asked to sit and wait while he went to pray; now the three, in the light of Jesus' revelation to them of his mental pain, are additionally asked by him to *remain by* him and to *watch with* him. Clearly Jesus is thus emphasizing his need of and affection for these three. His words are a speech-act of his desiring will that concretizes the sorrow within. Between the initial *wait for me* and the present *watch with me*, a significant intensification has occurred: while "waiting for" still implies a certain distance between the waiter and the awaited, "to watch with" someone obviously implies a greater identification with that person and a sharing in his plight, as if Jesus were saying, "Come and partake of this, too. Let my present experience and emotion become your own."

At this moment, however, Jesus must transcend even this irreducible nucleus of human companionship so as to enter the outermost zone of total solitude, that shared only with God. From the outset, *prayer* has been his motivation and goal, even though, at the same time, he did not see fit to plunge directly into explicit prayer to the Father upon his arrival in Gethsemane. Rather, he chose to approach the zone of pure prayer, of pure intra-divine Relation, gradually, by first setting up interconnecting zones of growing intimacy. In the most authentic Catholic tradition, best expressed in the works of Pseudo-Dionysius the Areopagite, such *hierarchy*, such a sacred order of relationships, has always been regarded as an interconnecting network of communing entities, each of which has its own specific function to perform in the total circulation of grace and love, for the good of the whole. Here Jesus is by no means setting up discriminatory differences within the world's and the apostles' relationship to himself, based on favoritism, as if he were privileging certain groups over others. The model of the cosmic Church that Jesus is here establishing mirrors the reality of the universal dispensation of grace throughout the mutually dependent levels of beings, all of which, despite their extreme variety and differences in function, nonetheless have their common source in the love of God for his cosmos.[6]

---

[6] For a succinct discussion of the Christian notion of "hierarchy", with specific reference to Pseudo-Dionysius, one of the best sources is still Louis Bouyer, *The Spirituality of the New Testament and the Fathers*, trans. Mary P. Ryan (New York: Seabury Press, 1982). A particularly enlightening passage is the following (404–5): "It is in the *Ecclesiastical Hierarchy* that this effective communication of the *agape-eros* is reunited, in all the concrete articulations of its historical realization for us, with the Incarnation and its consequences. The 'hierarchy' of the Church, in fact, is manifested and realized in the communication of the truth by the proclamation of the divine word and in association, in the sacramental mystery, with the life which this truth proclaims, . . . And behind both the one and the other hierarchy ['celestial hierarchy' and 'ecclesiastical hierarchy'], there is Christ—that is, the Logos in which is for ever proclaimed the mystery of unity of the divine thearchy, the mystery into which the angelic hierarchy was initiated by the primary and perpetual communication."

Jesus and his disciples have come to Gethsemane from "Jerusalem" and "the world", that is, from all the people they have been serving in that society for three years. And now, plunged into his Passion, Jesus is taking visibly with him twelve persons from within human society to act as forerunners for the whole of mankind. These Twelve are brought by Jesus, as representatives of all, through the threshold of time and into the presence of the eternal Father. At one end of the spectrum of reality, we have *the World*; at the other end, we have *the Father*, and *Jesus and his disciples* are the bridge between the two poles. This overarching, sacred triad (the World, the Church [Jesus + disciples], and the Father), which identifies all the players in the drama of salvation and hints at the actual means of redemption, then yields to a second, more personal, sacred triad structuring the Apostolic College, naturally with Jesus at the center: the nine, the three, and the one. In our initiation into the deepest meaning of this scene at Gethsemane, it is of paramount importance that we see all these distinctions as *living articulations*, as *interconnecting conduits of life* shaped by God's infinitely imaginative creating Will, and not at all as arbitrarily imposed *separations* or mutually exclusive *zones of privilege*.

As we move up and down such a hierarchic scale, we must acquire a sense of its vitality and see within it what Jesus sees, namely, "the angels of God ascending and descending upon the Son of man" (Jn 1:51). Between these various zones we must recognize *thresholds*, through which the irrepressible and inexhaustible communication of the torrent of Divine Life is mediated to the cosmos, first through the Son, and then, from the Son, through all the members of the Son's simultaneously suffering and glorified body, reaching from the pinnacle of the Holy Trinity down to the most hidden pebble at the bottom of the sea.

"There is one God, and there is one mediator between God and men, the man Christ Jesus" (1 Tim 2:5). Such truly cosmic mediation between the realm of the Divine and the realm of the human, between God and the created order, naturally generates stages in history, a variety of instruments of mediation, the election of mediating individuals who extend the mission of the Son within time and space, and the erection of intervening zones of relationship. Man can perceive and experience only what is mediated, and even within the Trinity there are distinct zones of difference, fully intertwining and reciprocally oriented though they may be. Only the incarnate Word himself, Jesus Christ, the Mediator, provides the overall principle of organization and efficacy in the workings of the divine hierarchy of grace. It is he who is both the Center of the total plan of salvation and the Heart of every stage in history, of every individual member of the Church his Body, and of every zone of particular relationship to himself. "For [God] has made known to us in all wisdom and insight the mystery of his will, according to his purpose which he set forth in Christ as a plan for the fulness of time, to unite all things in him, things in heaven and things on earth" (Eph 1:9–10). Christ the Logos is both the Fulfiller of God's plan and the Plan itself. Christ is the personal Recapitulation of all things created and redeemed, the universal Source of unity and life and harmony. It is important to keep this in mind if we want to plumb the depths of the Gethsemane drama, which launches the Passion that reshapes the world and everything in it.

The Gospel of John proclaims that "the Word became flesh and dwelt among us, full of grace and truth" (Jn 1:14), and Paul writes to the Philippians that "Christ Jesus, . . . though he was in the form of God, . . . emptied himself, taking the form of a servant" (Phil 2:5–7). We cannot begin to measure the full extent of *the eternal Word's precipitous descent into our mortal sphere* apart from these Gospel texts of the Passion, beginning with the Last Supper and Gethsemane. At this point in Matthew, we read that the Father's incarnate Word "fell on his face and prayed". At Tabor, Jesus took the three "up a high mountain apart" and showed them his glory (17:1ff.). There, they heard the voice of the Father declare, "This is my beloved Son, with whom I am well pleased; listen to him"; and when they heard this, the disciples "fell on their faces, and were filled with awe" (17:5–6). At Tabor, Jesus was exalted in dazzling light before the three, and they reacted by falling on their faces, overwhelmed with awe and fear. Now, here at Gethsemane, no light streams from the body of Jesus and no voice is heard from heaven; instead, it is Jesus himself who *falls on his face and prays!*

At the end of the Transfiguration narrative, we read that "when they lifted up their eyes, they saw no one but Jesus only" (αὐτὸν Ἰησοῦν μόνον, 17:8). They see Jesus now no longer caressed by the Father's voice and enveloped in the brilliance of the Holy Spirit, but rather Jesus starkly bereft of all visionary witness, stripped of all signs of the supernatural: *Jesus alone*, Jesus the Solitary in the full poverty of his human nature. Indeed, from as far back as chapter 17, this austere conclusion of the narrative of glory ("they saw no one but Jesus only") stretches forth directly into the present narrative of darkness and dejection. But within it all, glory throbs invisibly. Taken together, the scenes of Tabor and Gethsemane show us that the one purpose of the Son of God in coming among us was, not at all to dazzle us with a garish kind of "glory", but, rather, to enter totally into our own metaphysical desolation and redeem it by infusing it with his own indestructible life, at a great cost to himself. Such an outpouring of Love's substance is synonymous with God's genuine, ever-dynamic glory.

A terrible *admirabile commercium*, or astonishing exchange, is transpiring here: Jesus gives us his life, and we give him our death. Though sinless himself, he accepts contracting our disease of sin so as to take it away from us and heal us from it by taking it upon himself. He who showed us his divine splendor on Tabor as he received the Father's impassioned witness now falls on his face before us in anguish and terror. Tabor's role was to reveal the unfathomable mystery of love's splendor when an Immortal chooses mortality in order to rescue his beloved from death. Jesus' itinerary of salvation leads him from the pinnacle of the Trinity, through the womb of the Blessed Virgin, to the resplendent heights of Tabor, and then to this moment of biting the dust of Gethsemane on the night of the Passover. Ahead of him still awaits his bloody enthronement on the Cross on Good Friday and his descent into the realm of the dead on Holy Saturday. This descent will represent the metaphysical nadir of the Word's ecstatic plunge, out of sheer love, from the paradisal bosom of the glorious Godhead all the way down into the gloom of the shadow of death. But the unfathomable magnitude of that plunge is, in fact, all the while defining the total horizon of creation as the zone of universal redemption, where fullness of Life will at length triumph.

THE LETTER TO THE HEBREWS poignantly affirms: "In the days of his flesh, Jesus offers up prayers and supplications, with loud cries and tears, to him who was able to save him from death, and he was heard for his godly fear" (Heb 5:7). However, for us to hear such an attestation of Jesus' anguished prayer in this calm, meditative style is not at all the same thing as for us to *eavesdrop* on the prayer itself. This is precisely the privilege the evangelist now affords us: to listen in the night to Jesus' raw outcry to his Father. Even the chosen apostles are asleep at this point, although physically present at the scene; but Matthew will not allow *us* not to hear this cry! As we have seen, Matthew creates in this passage an atmosphere of extreme sorrow and distress in the Garden of Gethsemane, using a wide range of linguistic tools, and we are justified by Hebrews to hear Jesus' agony at this moment as accompanied by "loud cries and tears" as he offers up "prayers and supplications". But to appreciate fully the overwhelming sorrow inhabiting Jesus' Heart, we must hear him cry out with disconsolate sobs the two words: *My Father!* How can we begin to comprehend the earthshaking import of such a cry at such a moment, uttered by such a man?

A certain emasculated version of Christian faith has long since accustomed us to a wide range of cuddly sentiments with reference to God as "Father". We imagine God as an indulgent parent who, no matter what we do or do not do, will take care of us, always making our every whim come true for us in the end on the model of bourgeois fatherhood. This is what Dietrich Bonhoeffer calls the longing for "cheap grace", which he considers the blight of Christian faith.[7] When Jesus here, in 26:39b, cries out *My Father!* from the midst of the sea of agony in which he is drowning, he is casting a frantic SOS into the heaving dark waters, hurling a cosmic shriek of torment to pierce the interstellar spaces. Because he receives no audible answer, he will intensify his efforts a second time, and, in 26:42b, he again blares out in agony, *My Father!* It is as if these two words are the only prayer the Son knows. The agony in the garden is for Jesus an experience of most *expensive* grace. At this moment, in the Lucan

---

[7] See Dietrich Bonhoeffer, *The Cost of Discipleship*, trans. R. H. Fuller, rev. ed. (1959; New York et al.: Touchstone, 2018), 43, whose opening sentence reads: "Cheap grace is the deadly enemy of our Church."

parallel, we read: "He was in such agony and he prayed so fervently that his sweat became like drops of blood falling on the ground" (Lk 22:44, NAB).[8] Let us not forget that the literal meaning of the word "agony", taken from the Greek vocabulary of athletics, is "struggle". Jesus is entreating his Father not only with the cries of his voice but even with the blood of his Heart. His divine Personhood in no way makes the ordeal easier for his human nature. In fact, Thomas Aquinas says that his divinity made the intensity of the mental and physical human suffering all the keener because all the more "perfect", so that the pain of Christ's Passion was greater than all other human pain taken together.[9]

Jesus has willingly identified himself with our total human nature and all its weakness and distress, and so he is always very far from praying for himself alone. "We have not a high priest who is unable to sympathize with our weaknesses," we read again in Hebrews, "but one who in every respect has been tempted as we are, yet without sinning" (Heb 4:15). Both in his mental suffering and in his heart-wrenching prayer, Christ is at once himself—the man Jesus of Nazareth, the Son of Mary—*and* our High Priest and Mediator, who bears all of us and all our sorrows in his Heart before the Father. He does so, not theoretically or merely in intention, but quite literally. As *eternal* Word, he contains all of reality: "He who descended is he who also ascended far above all the heavens, that he might fill all

---

[8] This verse is lacking in some Greek manuscripts, and the RSV omits it.

[9] *Summa Theologiæ*, III, q. 46, art. 6 [Whether the pain of Christ's Passion was greater than all other pains?], "Reply to Objection 4. Christ grieved not only over the loss of His own bodily life, but also over the sins of all others. And this grief in Christ surpassed all grief of every contrite heart, both because it flowed from a greater wisdom and charity, by which the pang of contrition is intensified, and because He grieved at the one time for all sins, according to Isaiah 53:4: 'Surely He hath carried our sorrows.' But such was the dignity of Christ's life in the body, *especially on account of the Godhead united with it*, that its loss, even for one hour, would be a matter of greater grief than the loss of another man's life for howsoever long a time. Hence the Philosopher says (*Ethic.* iii) that the man of virtue loves his life all the more in proportion as he knows it to be better; and yet he exposes it for virtue's sake. And in like fashion Christ laid down His most beloved life for the good of charity, according to Jeremiah 12:7: 'I have given My dear soul into the hands of her enemies.' . . . From all these causes weighed together, it follows that Christ's pain was the very greatest." Italics mine. St. Thomas Aquinas, *Summa Theologica*, trans. Fathers of the English Dominican Province, vol. 2 (New York et al.: Benziger Brothers, 1947), 2271.

things" (Eph 4:10); and, as *incarnate* Word, he can suffer the sorrows of all in his own flesh: "Christ redeemed us from the curse of the law, having become a curse for us" (Gal 3:13).

"My Father, if it be possible, let this [cup] pass from me": This is the beginning of the audible portion of Jesus' prayer to the Father. His very being simply *is* intense prayer so that Jesus, by his ontological as well as his deliberate adherence to the Father, fulfills absolutely the cry of the Psalmist: וַאֲנִי תְפִלָּה (*wa'aní t^efilláh*)—"I am [all] prayer" (Ps 108[109]:4, JPS).[10] The psalm is bold in making such an absolute proclamation, for there is a great difference between *praying*, as one activity among many, and *being prayer* as the essential quality and incessant, underlying act of one's very existence. Sometimes, as here, that unceasing, embodied prayer also uses audible words. *My Father!*, Jesus exclaims. The possessive adjective connotes the same emotive pleading for presence and support that he earlier directed to his disciples: *Watch with me!*; and it also echoes the intense degree of awareness of his own interior life when to his three intimates he confided, "*My soul* is [compassed by sorrows]" (26:38). *My* disciples, *my* soul, *my* Father: in his fragile and suffering humanity, the Lord is here struggling to build up relation with both God and men using the very intensity of his isolation as constructive energy.

These energetic leaps of Jesus' Heart into the engulfing void are fueled by an almighty sorrow: they are so many bridges he is erecting between our fundamental human alienation—now residing also in him (who became "a *curse* for us", Gal 3:13)—and the Father, in whom he has his natural home. Even at this moment, perhaps above all at this moment, Jesus is "the only-begotten Son, who is [ineradicably] *in the bosom* of the Father" (Jn 1:18). Only the incarnate Word can bridge such an infinite abyss efficaciously, and the bridge is fashioned out of his agony of love. *My Father!*, he insists all the louder. And this

---

[10] Most literally וַאֲנִי תְפִלָּה should be translated "But I [am] prayer". Only the JPS (as above) and FBJ (*et je ne suis que prière*) render the two Hebrew words, a pronoun and a noun, quite literally. All other versions give softening interpretations by turning the absoluteness of the noun defining the pronoun into a more limited, functional verb: "even as I make prayer for them" (RSV), "even though I prayed for them" (NAB). This robs the assertion of its stunning impact and christological connotations, since only the divine Word, properly speaking, can *be all prayer* in a literal, non-metaphorical sense.

cry, powered in equal parts by trust and by torment, contains all the anguished pleading for compassion and presence that has ever been or shall ever be propelled heavenward from any human heart.

א

26:39bc

Πάτερ μου!
Εἰ δυνατόν ἐστιν,
παρελθάτω ἀπ᾽ ἐμοῦ τὸ ποτήριον τοῦτο·
πλὴν οὐχ ὡς ἐγὼ θέλω ἀλλ᾽ ὡς σύ

My Father!
If it be possible,
let this cup pass from me;
nevertheless, not as I will, but as you will

IT IS REMARKABLE TO SEE HOW, in one and the same breath, Jesus can give voice both to his *difference from* his Father as unique Divine Person and to his absolute trinitarian *unity with* the Father. Moreover, this pointed repetition of a plea that confesses essential relationship even as it begs for mercy also expresses the intolerable sorrow bearing down upon his humanity. It is a prayer that, in a very brief compass, manifests all of Jesus' filial trust, piety, and obedience even as it voices an agony of abandonment. The horrific intensity of his suffering may be measured by the fact that, right in the midst of the work of redemption, to accomplish which he specifically came into the world, he is seeking for some way to escape so much distress. Here we have the Son of God himself very emphatically communicating the full weakness, vulnerability, and near-despair that so often afflict our human nature, which he now owns in common with us.

It is quite possibly here, in this scene at Gethsemane, that the full extent of the divine Word's solidarity with our weak nature is more intensely portrayed than in the rest of Scripture. Nevertheless, where many people channel this experience of apparent abandonment by God in the direction of revolt, self-pity, resentment, or downright suicidal despair, Jesus, instead, chooses the path of loving fidelity, endless trust, and humble obedience, none of which, however, can mask for one instant the intensity of his harrowing trial. Once he has exclaimed "My Father!", he has already said it all, for this outcry from his deepest Heart contains both the most candid confession of distress and the most reliable form of appeal.

"If it be possible," he gently implores. If we take this prayer and its petition seriously, we must admit that excess of sorrow and anxiety seems to some extent to have darkened Jesus' intellectual faculties. His unity of divine nature with the Father by no means guarantees that his human understanding of the mysteries of suffering will always possess crystalline clarity in his created mind. "If it be possible", says the incarnate Word! I do not think this is merely a formula of filial courtesy toward the Father, as if Jesus really does know whether it is possible or not and is only letting the Father decide out of deference. The suffering he is presently undergoing and the imagined horror of the impending Passion during the next twenty-four hours are such that he is hoping there may be another way of achieving redemption, something less formidable than *this*. We must descend with Jesus to precisely this rock-bottom depth of discouragement and fear if we are ever to marvel at the full heroism of his obedience to the Father's will. This prayer of Jesus suggests that only one thing could possibly be more intolerable and inflict greater pain than his present distress, namely, to disobey the will of his Father. Short of that, his own oppressed Heart is madly seeking relief as it can.

Dazed by this depth of Jesus' agony, we might overlook the significance in his prayer of the reference to "this cup". Jesus refers to his present moment of extreme anguish as a "cup" reached out for him to drink. The expression is not unusual in the prophets, and it normally signifies a manifestation of God's will that inflicts purifying punishment. Habakkuk, for example, reminds Israel in the following terms of the consequences of its infidelity: "You will be sated with contempt instead of glory. Drink, yourself, and stagger! The cup in the LORD's right hand will come around to you, and shame will come upon your glory!" (2:16). Thus the children of the promise who have gone astray will not be exempted from the punishment of all the wicked of the world: "For in the hand of the LORD there is a cup, with foaming wine, well mixed; and he will pour a draught from it, and all the wicked of the earth shall drain it down to the dregs" (Ps 75[74]:8). But in Isaiah, by contrast, we read the following: "Rouse yourself, rouse yourself, stand up, O Jerusalem, you who have drunk at the hand of the LORD the cup of his wrath, who have drunk to the dregs the bowl of staggering" (51:17). Here Jerusalem is exhorted to undergo a resurrection after having been punished by the Lord's wrath, which is always purifying, redemptive, and never merely punitive. It is in this context that Jesus' prayer becomes comprehensible.

Jesus fully realizes that it is his beloved Father who is holding out to him the "cup" of his Passion, and he is invited to drink it in loving obedience. At the present moment, the very same hand of the Father who bestows infinite life as absolute source of the Son's being is holding out to him a cup of bitter suffering, which the Son understandably hesitates to drink. The Son is conscious of taking the place of all sinners before his Father, remembering that these, too, are potential *sons*. With this boon of adoptive sonship foremost in mind, Jesus, the sinless one, accepts in his flesh and spirit the punishment that should by rights be inflicted on *sinners*: all he can see in them is *his brothers*. At an excruciating personal cost and enacting a "wondrous exchange", Jesus pours out love and obedience into the place of hatred and revolt. And Jesus' heroic substitution of himself for sinners becomes all the more impressive when we relate this image of the cup of the Lord's wrath, which he must now drink, to the sweet cup of forgiveness and communion that he shortly before handed to his friends at the Last Supper.

We recall that only a few hours before this scene in Gethsemane, Jesus "took a [cup], and when he had given thanks he gave it to them, saying, 'Drink of it, all of you; for this is my blood of the covenant, which is poured out for many for the forgiveness of sins'" (26:27–28). With the cup of his own blood, he nourishes and gives new life to his beloved band of disciples. The sacramental outpouring of his blood leaves an existential void within himself that will now be filled as the Father hands him to drink the cup of divine wrath in which mankind's sins are drowned. Jesus drains to the dregs the cup of pure bitterness in order that others may imbibe the sweetness of God's love and reconciliation. This is the passional aspect of what it means to be the Mediator, the Go-Between who bridges the world of God and the world of man. Like a diligent spider, Jesus throws filaments of suffering over the abyss of man's alienation from God, as a means of establishing lasting communion between the Source and the offspring.

Suffering is never absent from the act of bestowing life, either at the natural level of the mother's birthing pains or at the supernatural level of Jesus' communicating the Father's life to his brothers and sisters. So absolute is Jesus' trust in his Father's way of bestowing life through him that the Son *celebrates* his Father's chosen way even when it requires his own dark passage through agony and death. Whereas we ordinary people instinctively define the furtherance of our physical and psychic life in terms of wholesome habits of eating, thinking, and acting, Jesus defines his own nutritional needs in a uniquely radical way: "My *food* is to do the will of him who sent me, and to accomplish his work" (Jn 4:34). There is something oddly counterintuitive in this declaration because Jesus here defines his only necessary nourishment, not in the usual terms of what he takes in from outside himself, but, rather, in terms of what goes out from him, namely, deeds obeying the will of the One who sent him. Drinking the cup handed him by his Father is a literal illustration of this. We normally eat and drink what nourishes and strengthens us, but Jesus' "cup" is the physical and psychic suffering of his Passion.

The Passion will crush him in every possible way; indeed, it will destroy him insofar as human eyes can tell. And yet his obliteration will be like the crushing of grapes, a destruction that horribly disfigures the fruit's original shape and integrity yet only in order to transform it into an inebriating elixir of life for others to drink and rejoice in ecstatically. God can use men's evil intentions to achieve magnificent ends. If he could not, would he still be the omnipotent, wise, and loving Creator of all? The constant marvel throughout, the unfathomable divine mystery that provides the key to the Passion and the Cross, is this truth of revelation: that, at the threshold of the Passion, *the Father—whose love for his only-begotten Son is the very foundation of both the Godhead and of all creation—does not love us sinners less than he loves the one Son.* This astounding truth is shown in the fact that the Father delivers his tenderly beloved Son, his One and Only, up to death, so that through the lavish squandering of the Son's being we might all have divine life. Even at the cost of his Son's life, the Father does not want to reserve their holy Love for themselves alone! As for the Son himself, he perfectly reciprocates his Father's eternal love, not however in closed binary fashion, but in the triangulation of universal love, by pouring out his Being through the Passion, so that as many as possible can come to enjoy the Father's blissful life that thus becomes available for all:

> God's incessant work is to communicate the good, and he does everything in view of this. Such is the end of everything that already is and of everything that could come into being in the future. "The good", it is said, "diffuses and propagates itself." . . . Such is precisely the work of the economy [of redemption] that has been designed on man's behalf. Here, God was not content to communicate just any good to human nature, while keeping the greater part for himself. Rather, it is "the whole fullness of divinity" (Col 2:9), the whole richness of his own nature, that he infused into man. . . . For, if God has any virtue, any justice, then it consists in communicating his own goods to all, without jealousy, and to share his own blessedness.[11]

---

[11] Nicholas Cabasilas, *The Life in Christ*, trans. Carmino J. de Catanzaro (Crestwood, N.Y.: St. Vladimir's Seminary Press, 1974), 1:27–28.

26:40   καὶ ἔρχεται πρὸς τοὺς μαθητὰς
                καὶ εὑρίσκει αὐτοὺς καθεύδοντας,
                    καὶ λέγει τῷ Πέτρῳ·
       Οὕτως οὐκ ἰσχύσατε μίαν ὥραν γρηγορῆσαι μετ᾽ ἐμοῦ;

And he comes to the disciples
and finds them sleeping;
and he says to Peter,
"So, you were not able to watch with me one hour?"

AFTER HE GOES TO HIS FATHER to appeal to him for help and reprieve, Jesus now "[comes] to the disciples". You can see him in the night of his Passion trudging back and forth, back and forth over the abyss of gloom between his Father and his friends, a void that he can bridge only with the loving distress of his Heart. Only the most intense self-sacrificial love can enable us thus to fly through the vacant air, as it were, and, where nothingness has prevailed, to erect something solid that others may tread upon. His Father and his disciples are the two poles of his interest, and this axis defines Jesus' whole interior world. In the face of the Father's silence, he again turns to his friends for comfort, for human company. But, just as eternity seems locked to him, he also finds the disciples shut down in sleep: they, too, have inadvertently locked him out of their consciousness. The terrible burden of an infinite solitude bears down the more crushingly upon him. The two poles of Relation that fill up his whole affective horizon are to him at this moment two impenetrable fortresses of rejection. Between the two there is only a vast arid wilderness, and it is there that Jesus finds himself. Who can doubt that, plunged in his agony, the incarnate Word remembers these words of Psalm 38[37]: "My heart throbs, my strength fails me; and the light of my eyes—it also has gone from me. My friends and companions stand aloof from my plague, and my kinsmen stand afar off" (vv. 10–11)? And we are certain that he prays the following words from Psalm 22[21], a cry of the heart that expresses the very essence of divine abandonment: "My God, my God, why have you forsaken me? Why are you so far from helping me, from the words of my groaning?" (v. 1).

Jesus has already more than hinted to his disciples concerning the storm of lethal sorrow ravaging his soul, and he has also begged them to stay near him and *watch* with him. We could find elaborate theological and mystical meanings in this weighty word *watch*, so biblical in flavor, and no doubt those meanings would not be false. However, at this moment of extreme existential trial, it seems that Jesus longs with all his Heart for something very basic, some tenuous lifeline to mankind: quite simply, the charity of a shared consciousness, the willingness on his friends' part to help him attain some measure of serenity by peering together with him in silence into the threatening night. Perhaps this frantic longing for wakeful companionship on the part of the incarnate Word does, after all, constitute, not just a pathetic human need, but, indeed, the most paradoxical of theological truths: that the subject of this forlorn longing should be the Son of God! Nevertheless, he is disappointed in that simple expectation and finds his disciples sleeping. Misery, even divine misery, loves company; yet Peter and the other two intimates could offer Jesus only the dubious comfort of their snoring. His reaction, however, shows all the gentleness of his love for them. There are no loud and angry remonstrances, no sharp rebukes, no ironical glances, only the wistful question, "So, you [were not able to] watch with me one hour?" Even as he expresses his sadness, he is also providing *them* with an excuse for their behavior: exhaustion.

Rather than rebuke them or give up on them, Jesus next invites the three to greater closeness to him with a new admonition: "Watch and pray that you may not enter into temptation; the spirit indeed is willing, but the flesh is weak" (v. 41). Previously he has asked them only to watch with him, waiting for his return to them when he was done praying in solitude. Now he suggests they add prayer to their watching. Thus, he wants them to enter more fully into *his* prayer, the central activity that is at present consuming all his energies. Some form of the verb "to pray" is used no less than five times throughout this passage, and thus *intense communion with God* becomes the leitmotif that structures the episode. Both Jesus' mental suffering and the disciples' exhaustion and inability to grasp what is happening become rooted intentionally by Jesus in the life-giving ground of prayer. *Watch and pray*: their vigil is not to be merely an empty, generic waiting for something to happen; it is to be the occasion for directing toward God expressly all the longing of the heart, all the puzzlement of the mind, and all the exhaustion of the body. Watching-and-praying are offered by Jesus as the antidote to yielding to "temptation", that is, the corrective to giving up on God's fidelity, to giving up on the meaning of life in the face of the present excruciating experience.

Sorrow, darkness, persecution, discouragement can all become Satanic threats in the sense that, if we do not encounter these interior adversaries by brandishing the weapons of faith, they will surely imprison us within the dungeon of the present woeful situation and rob us of the inward vision that keeps alive the whole horizon of reality. Sorrow and its entourage will then obliterate in us the vital *memoria Dei* and poison the sources of hope, trust, and godly reason in our heart. Empowered anxieties will make us, quite simply, *forget God and the divine order of things*, as if these did not exist, as if they were but a distant memory from a naïve, mythological dream. Only a visceral faith can keep Jesus himself with his head barely above water.

Jesus witnesses to such faith, to his uncompromising commitment of love, with regard to both his Father and his friends. I do not speak of a symmetrical faith, of course, since his faith in his Father is unconditional while his faith in his friends is necessarily conditioned by his intimate knowledge and experience of the fragility of human nature. Nevertheless, Jesus does not need *only* his Father: in willing the Son to receive a human nature from Mary, the Father himself created in Jesus the need for other human beings. The prayer he does not cease to hurl into his Father's silence from the depths of his soul is surely: "But for you, O LORD, do I wait; it is you, O LORD my God, who will answer. . . . Do not forsake me, O LORD! O my God, be not far from me! Make haste to help me, O Lord, my salvation!" (Ps 38[37]:15, 21–22). At the same time, however, the "prayer" or plea he addresses to the three weary disciples is "Watch and pray [with me]." In other words, Jesus' "faith" in his disciples means that he considers them ripe for being brought into the very same act of watchful self-entrustment to the Father that he is himself endeavoring to complete at present.

Both Jesus and the disciples are struggling during this night in Gethsemane to make the willingness of their spirit prevail over the weakness of their flesh, and Jesus prescribes watchfulness and prayer as the only adequate weapons to win the battle. Throughout this whole drama, Jesus' overriding preoccupation, surpassing even the distress of his own suffering, is that his friends should be with him precisely where he is in his relationship to the Father. Their physical proximity to Jesus in the Garden is only a symbol of Jesus' desire that they should fully identify with him and inhabit his same spiritual space before the Father. In the course of this episode, Jesus has shown once again how he uses a demonstrated failure, infidelity, or weakness on the part of his disciples, never to accuse them or condemn them for it, but rather as an occasion to teach them how to enter more deeply into union with himself and his mission. This is a primary feature of the wise pedagogy of the eternal Word, who is not ethereally static in his eternity as a glorious, disembodied Truth but, rather, perennially engaged on earth as incarnate, familiar Savior.

And now, after this admonition, Jesus goes off a second time to be alone in prayer with the Father, but of course bearing his disciples in his Heart into that situation of ardent prayer. Again he begins, "My Father", as if these two words were the sum total of all his prayer.[12] But this time he repeats the previous prayer in negative mode: "If this cannot pass unless I drink it, your will be done" (v. 42). On both occasions, Jesus begins his prayer to his Father with the restrictive conjunction *if*. What delicacy on the part of the incarnate Word, who, even within the most private intimacy with the Father, does not insist on anything with willfulness and entitlement, even though no one else could be as qualified as he to do so! The previous time he said, "if it be possible", but now he states, "if this cannot pass. . . ." The gradual manner in which Jesus approaches the dawning realization of the Passion's inevitability shows that there is nothing suicidal or masochistic about him and that he is not suffering from a morbid and narcissistic "victim complex". On the contrary, Jesus is here fully witnessing to the instinct for life and happiness that God himself has encoded so deeply in human nature.

Suffering and death may be gladly embraced solely in obedience to

---

[12] The story is told of a very old Carthusian monk who could never manage to pray the whole Rosary because he fell into immoveable contemplation every time he uttered the words *Our Father* . . . He could not advance beyond them because, he discovered, there is no advancing beyond the Father!

the Father's explicit will, in the conviction that, by such harrowing means, a good father can only intend to create greater life for all. Repeated prayer to his Father, and likewise repeated interchanges with his friends, are acts that have strengthened Jesus so that he can now face with total trust the inevitability of his death. From this event's manner of unfolding, we should retain the fact that splendid isolation, self-reliance, and Promethean pride are by no means qualities we can associate with the kind of hero Jesus is. Jesus is no Nietzschean hero. Though he is willing to take upon himself the awful consequences of all the sins of mankind, nevertheless, he does so, not to prove anything about his own capacity to endure suffering, but rather only to manifest the glory of Another—the Father—and what this Other intends to accomplish through his Son's Passion. This is why, at Gethsemane, Jesus constantly returns to the invocation of the Father and reiterates acts of obedience to the Father's will.

It is extraordinary to observe how, even from the purely literary point of view, the character of Jesus of Nazareth in the Gospel narrative can manage at the same time to be both the undisputed protagonist in the foreground of the story and a dramatic human transparency for the presence of a mysterious Other. Never does Jesus allow us to forget that he never stands alone. And this is ever true not only of the way his words and actions are always revealing the Father but also of his relationship with his disciples and friends, whose welfare he always bears foremost in mind and on whom he depends with a most tender human longing. There is no character anywhere in the broad horizon of world literature who embodies so perfectly such a seamless synthesis of immanence and transcendence as does Jesus the Nazarene throughout the four canonical Gospels. And the reason for this æsthetic fact is no doubt to be found in the uniqueness of the theological mystery of the Word's Incarnation.

"My Father . . . your will be done": By attaching the possessive adjective *my* to his threefold invocation of the Father, Jesus is expressing a strong affective nuance. The Father's paternity, and Jesus' emphatic avowal of the Father as the absolute Source of his being, is the unshakable foundation of his person, his history, and all his decisions and actions. Quite literally, Jesus is incessantly spending his life for the Father, from whom he has received and continues to receive it. Jesus apparently takes delight and comfort in frequently repeating the words *Páter mou!* These are his only mantra. No verb or other qualifier need be added. Jesus' voice utters in human language the essential joy of an eternal relationship that happens to be the source and foundation both of the Trinity and of all created reality: the Holy Spirit, we believe in faith, proceeds from the Father and the Son, and all creation proceeds from the Blessed Trinity. Jesus' repeated affirmation—from the midst of his suffering and darkness—of God's fatherhood and his own sonship provides the only key of interpretation needed to understand his Passion and death. The fact of God's being Father and of Jesus' being his Son is the granite Everest on which alone can be shattered the ascendancy of death in the world.

Though Jesus' cry "My Father!" is bursting with deep human sentiment, it is far more than merely a last-ditch sentimental outburst. Rather, it is a profoundly creative word such as only the incarnate Word can utter on earth, a word so powerful that it suddenly brings the Kingdom of God into an earthly landscape devastated by violence and hatred. When Jesus moans the utterance "My Father!" three times over in Gethsemane, even as his soul is crushed with distress and his brow is sweating blood, then and there death has lost its stranglehold over man. For at that moment Jesus has imported from eternity and into our world the Father's omnipotent sovereignty as Generator of life: "You will not abandon me to the realm of the dead, nor will you let your faithful one see decay. You make known to me the path of life; you will fill me with joy in your presence, with eternal pleasures at your right hand" (Ps 16[15]:10f., NIV).

Jesus' cry "My Father!" is an act of visceral and creative faith that extends to all mankind God's unceasing generative activity as Father, through the mediation of the eternal Son's suffering. At Gethsemane, the Father's unique and everlasting generation of the one Son becomes extended in perpetuity to all those who are found in the Son. Now, at the threshold of the Passion, the teaching Jesus conveyed to his disciples in the Lord's Prayer, at the beginning of the Gospel, takes ontological root in our world and in each believer. In the Lord's Prayer, Jesus taught his disciples to pray: "Our Father . . . Thy will be done" (6:9–10). But only now, at Gethsemane, do we witness, and participate in, the historical event that gives dynamic plenitude and efficacy to that prayer. Every day of our lives we can now say "Our Father . . . Thy will be done" without any pretense or hesitation, but fully empowered by the truth of those words, only because Jesus has first said "My Father . . . Thy will be done" from deep within the darkness of his agony. Gifted with the total confidence of *parrhêsía*, now we can whisper or sigh or scream "Our Father!" only because Jesus has first cried "My Father!" out of the labor-pains of the Passion, which gave birth to our coequal filiation with him in the Father's sight.

However, we have now seen the intrinsic connection between Jesus' serene pedagogy when teaching the disciples the Our Father, at the beginning of the Gospel, and this moment of distressed and utterly solitary prayer in Gethsemane. How could we ever forget that all the joyful confidence and thanksgiving contained in the Our Father have their source in Gethsemane, in the anguished prayer of the one Son? "Thy will be done on earth": This "earth" is specifically the soil that drank up the drops of Jesus' blood on that fearsome night, the night when the heaven in which the Father dwells kept impenetrably black and silent. We cannot pray the Our Father with total honesty or efficacy unless we identify interiorly with the Lord Jesus in his night of suffering. And, if such identification must initially draw us into sharing his distress, through that shared distress, it will also draw us out to the dawn of the Resurrection and indestructible life. The choice is simple. Distress abounds in every human life. But will I willfully insist on enduring *my* distress alone, like Prometheus, and so perish utterly along with my pride, or will I wisely allow Jesus to make my distress his, and his mine, so that we can break through it together and thus come to enjoy the life and communion offered us both by *Our Father*, beyond all distress?

26:43   καὶ ἐλθὼν πάλιν εὗρεν αὐτοὺς καθεύδοντας,
           ἦσαν γὰρ αὐτῶν οἱ ὀφθαλμοὶ βεβαρημένοι

And again he came and found them sleeping,
for their eyes were weighed down

GAIN AND AGAIN AND AGAIN . . . Who can conceive the extent
of Jesus' weariness, disappointment, and acedia at this moment? The more he seeks to establish lasting bonds with others, the less response he finds in them and the more things seem
to be falling apart. Whereas his Heart's longing strains outward and
upward with love, toward his friends and above all his Father, everyone else seems to be the victim of an exhausting weight of gravity,
and the Father himself seems immured in silence. The only light still
flickering in the night is Jesus' own. It is Jesus who must go find his
friends, for only he is still actively seeking. And he finds the disciples
passed out, like lumps of humanity brutishly cluttering the earth.

Even though the word "love" does not appear anywhere in this
passage, we see its reality enacted in every detail of the occasion's
drama. For, what else but unconditional and unrelenting love could
account for Jesus' tireless persistence and fidelity and compassionate understanding as he shuttles back and forth between his awful
solitude in the face of the Father's silence and his friends' indolent
half-presence? The three most intimate disciples and friends of Jesus,
whom he has specifically chosen to accompany him on this occasion,
soon allow themselves to be overwhelmed by human weakness and
prove to be of no use at all. They are, quite literally, "useless servants" (Lk 17:10, NJB).

In light of this situation, we must admit to ourselves, humiliating
as it might be, that often enough in our discipleship the very best we
can accomplish in our following of Jesus is to be exactly that: *lumps of
humanity brutishly cluttering the earth*; nor does Jesus for all that forsake us or love us any the less. He hears and takes pity on our twisted
heart's yearning: "I was stupid and could not understand; I was like
a brute beast in your presence. Yet I am always with you; you take
hold of my right hand" (Ps 73[72]:22–23, NAB). And, astoundingly,

he always returns to us to invite us (yes, *us*, the very ones who have failed him so often and preferred so many other loves to his Love)— to invite us once more to keep him company, to abide in his Heart!

"For their eyes were heavy": Is this merely a physiological fact? Does the detail perhaps sound a note of compassion bestowed on the disciples' weakness by Jesus or maybe the evangelist? Or is this, rather, a theological observation, pointing to a divine intervention that deliberately shuts the eyes of the disciples, lest their vision, awareness, and ready empathy with Jesus should in any way curtail the absoluteness of his solitude and forsakenness? The word βεβαρημένοι (*bebarêménoi*), in fact, does not correspond to the simple adjective "heavy"; it is a perfect passive participle that should be translated "having been weighed down" or "made heavy", and thus it implies some deliberate agent.

One is tempted to say that a cosmic conspiracy is afoot, involving sun and moon, enemies and friends, and even God himself. Such a plot would aim to impose on Jesus a dreadful and comprehensive isolation that is all at once physical, mental, affective, and spiritual, quite pitiless in its manner and thoroughly devastating in its effects. Naturally, each of the "conspirators" is acting out of vastly different motivations; but the suffering collectively produced and inflicted on Jesus is one and the same in the end. This crushing solitude suggests itself as the eye of the needle (19:24) through which Jesus must pass in order to enter the Kingdom of Heaven.

26:44

ἀφεὶς αὐτοὺς πάλιν
ἀπελθὼν προσηύξατο ἐκ τρίτου
τὸν αὐτὸν λόγον εἰπὼν πάλιν

leaving them again,
he went away and prayed for the third time,
saying the same word again

S EEING THAT HIS FRIENDS ARE PLUNGED in deep sleep, like a loving mother, Jesus allows them to take their rest a little longer.
He neither joins them in their state of unconsciousness nor
abandons them with exasperation. Rather, he tenderly watches over
them, spreading his prayer over their inert forms like a mother hen's
enfolding wings. Their inability to keep watch with him, their exhaustion and listlessness, only encourage Jesus to triple his own efforts and
renew, all alone, his encounter with the darkness. While his especially
chosen followers sleep, *he* will pray for them and in their stead, *he*
will keep vigil in order to insure that the earth's vital link with its
Creator is not severed. Jesus is here portrayed by the evangelist as the
quintessential Intercessor-Priest, whose every fiber requires of him
that he not abandon his post as God's lifeline to man, regardless of
the cost to himself.

During the Passion, Jesus seems to have no private identity of his
own, no self-definition that would establish him as autonomous operator seeking his own purposes and satisfaction in a life apart from the
common lot of man. Nor does he exercise a separate, self-referential
will of his own that would generate any tension between his Father's
ardent will to save and his disciples' crying need to be saved. We
must conclude from the drama of the Passion, as portrayed by Matthew, that what constitutes the very essence of Jesus' selfhood must
indeed appear paradoxical to the worldly eye, jaundiced by our drive
for "self-fulfillment". The essence of Jesus' selfhood, what defines
the uniqueness of his person as both God and man, is slowly revealed
to be this: *the ability and need to fulfill his person precisely by existing*
for others, by giving himself away piecemeal to others and standing

in the breach for them, like a rampart between mankind and the all-engulfing darkness. In a word, Jesus is the visible, audible, and dramatic human embodiment of the truth that GOD IS LOVE (1 Jn 4:8).

To be with Jesus, to experience Jesus intimately, to perceive the quality of his life, actions, gestures, and even silences, is *to witness God in the very act of being love in a human form*. St. John coined the lapidary phrase "God is love", not as the conclusion of a speculative process or even inspired by a celestial revelation. John's crucial formulation, rather, is a sober and precise record of his own lived experience of intimate companionship with Jesus. In this context, he could imbibe directly the secrets of Jesus' Heart, which are identical with the secrets of God's own Heart but now reliably transcribed into the terms of human communication, verbal and otherwise. John himself, at this point in his life, was still being trained personally by the Word in the ways of God. As such, he was one of the three apostles sunk in deep slumber just a stone's throw away from their Master as Jesus faced the grim darkness in utter aloneness, for the benefit of them all. This intimate experience of bitter, personal failure provides the indispensable background for John then to make his future breakthrough to the ultimate truth that GOD IS LOVE. How could it be otherwise, given the unfolding of this story? GOD IS LOVE is no abstract formula, no philosophical conclusion to a syllogism, no universally self-evident truism, but the private journal entry, so to speak, that John shares with others, proclaiming beyond all doubt that GOD and only GOD IS LOVE. After that night in Gethsemane, John would never forget that only God's love in Jesus is unconditionally and perpetually reliable, as St. Paul asserts: "If we are faithless, he remains faithful—for he cannot deny himself" (2 Tim 2:13). GOD IS LOVE is an ardent, repentant, and joyful proclamation that makes sense only within Christianity, as a discovery made by one who has experienced the mystery of God's redeeming energy in Christ.

Our present verse also forcefully stresses the repetition of actions by Jesus. Such repetition is a sign of Jesus' tenacious fidelity, highlighted by Paul in the passage just quoted: the fact that nothing makes Jesus abandon those he loves—his Father, his friends—or seek an easy way out for himself from the constriction of the Passion. The passage twice uses the word *again*, to refer, first, to Jesus' going once more away to his solitude from the sleeping disciples and, then, to point to the fact that, in his prayer, he is yet again using the very same words he has used before. No amount of suffering, no weight of solitude and melancholy, can sway Jesus away from his purpose. Whereas, in our case, the repetition of necessary but difficult actions normally has the effect of overwhelming us with exhaustion, boredom, and frustration, Jesus seems to make a masterful art out of repeating tough essential actions.

Because he lives from the Source, Jesus continually shuns novelty for its own sake or as an escape and chooses, instead, to dwell consistently with the very few realities that ultimately matter. For instance, prayer. The verse underscores the fact that Jesus is going off to pray *for the third time* as if, whatever else is going on, Jesus is one who ceaselessly returns to prayer as a fish to water. Without praying, Jesus cannot breathe, and who would venture to say that breathing is boring simply because it is repetitious? Surely all this stylistic insistence on circularity in this passage—the repetition of certain fundamental actions—is intended to spotlight Jesus' rocklike and dynamic *faithfulness*, by contrast to the disciples' passive half-presence and utter lack of initiative. In Jesus we see that only the most genuine love can persevere to the end.

Though all Jesus' efforts would appear for the moment to be fruitless because they do not change the fateful plot of the story, nevertheless, the extraordinary power of his steadfast vigilance and the intensity of his unremitting prayer to his Father are fountains of light silently beaming forth their splendor into the night of the world. After healing so many miraculously, after enlightening so many people by his words, Jesus now takes us a decisive step forward as he shows us, out of the depths of his apparent defeat, that he transforms sorrow and suffering more by what he *is* than by what he *does*. This truth may be difficult to assimilate for our achievement-driven culture, but without it, authentic Christianity crumbles. At the moment of what seems his ultimate failure, Jesus deliberately takes into himself, and embraces within his Heart, all the world's sorrow and suffering by making them his own through compassion. There, within his innermost being and interwoven with every fiber of his person, sorrow and suffering become transmuted into energies of joy by the power of what Jesus *is* in his divine nature, namely, THE LIGHT OF THE WORLD (Jn 8:12).

The last phrase of this v. 44, τὸν αὐτὸν λόγον εἰπὼν πάλιν, literally means: *saying the same word again.* Most renderings have either "the same words", in the plural, or "the same thing", changing the noun. Although these versions convey the general narrative meaning, it is important to retain the literal sense in order to delve into the full christological mystery. In this particular manifestation of it, we can sum up the mystery by saying that *the incarnate Word is himself the prayer that he prays*. The very words of Jesus' prayer are repeated without change; the reiteration expresses the fact that the incarnate Word, Jesus Christ, "is the same yesterday and today and for ever" (Heb 13:8). The sameness of the prayer reveals the solid immutability and utter reliability of Jesus the Word, the speaker of the prayer.

God is so blessedly simple and consistent with himself that only in God are essence and existence, word and action, being and doing, one and the same reality. God is perennially trustworthy, unfailing, and dependable because of the utter simplicity of the divine Nature and not as a projection of human sentimentality. All the human words of the incarnate divine Word cannot be anything other than manifestations and extensions of that Word's eternal Being. The rhythmic throbbing of Jesus' human Heart is already the ultimate prayer. We say of a person who is particularly honest and reliable that "he's as good as his word." In the case of Jesus, the Man is his Word, both because of the hypostatic union and because of a deliberate act of the will. Therefore, John can refer to the person of Jesus as "the word of life" (1 Jn 1:1), and Peter can teach: "The grass withers, and the flower falls, but the word of the Lord abides for ever" (1 Pet 1:24–25).

The same truth is expressed dramatically toward the end of the New Testament, in the Apocalypse: "Then I saw heaven opened, and behold, a white horse! He who sat upon it is called Faithful and True. . . . He is [clad] in a robe dipped in blood, and the name by which he is called is The Word of God" (Rev 19:11, 13). In symbolic terms, this vision reveals the triumph, through the Passion, of the incarnate Word, who is utterly reliable both as a manifestation of the Father who dwells in heaven and as a King whose regal robe is empurpled by his own shed blood. In the scene of Jesus' third prayer at Gethsemane, Matthew says that he said "the same word" again because, in praying, Jesus is doing only one thing: surrendering his whole Being over and over again to the Father, and that whole Being is, simply, the Word Incarnate. For Jesus, to be is to pray, and this is why, essentially, there cannot be any plurality or variation or development in that prayer. Its content, both here in Gethsemane at this moment and throughout Jesus' mortal existence on earth, cannot be anything other than total, surrendering obedience to the Father: "For I have come down from heaven, not to do my own will, but the will of him who sent me" (Jn 6:38).

א

26:45b   Καθεύδετε τὸ λοιπὸν καὶ ἀναπαύεσθε;
                ἰδοὺ ἤγγικεν ἡ ὥρα

Are you still sleeping and taking your rest?
Behold, the hour is at hand

TRANSLATORS AND EXEGETES are rather evenly divided as to whether the first sentence here should be understood as an imperative command or, rather, as a question. Should we read, "Are you still sleeping and taking your rest?", or rather, "Sleep on and take your rest!"? Grammatically, either possibility works. Punctuation in the early Greek manuscripts of the Gospel was either very spotty or altogether nonexistent, so we cannot rely on question marks or the absence thereof. Here, in fact, we have a case that illustrates very emphatically the general truth that translation always involves some degree of interpretation. I go with those who construe the statement as a question.

My main reason is that, almost immediately after these words, Jesus says to his disciples, "Rise, let us be going!" (v. 46a), an unequivocally imperative command. Now, if v. 45b is also construed as an imperative, the two commands would contradict each other since one would impose sleep on the disciples and the other, coming on its heels, orders them to rise and depart. The only way of keeping both statements as commands without contradiction would be to introduce a hypothetical lapse of time for snoozing between vv. 45 and 46, a ploy that seems artificial and not really justified by the text. It seems most sensible, then, within the whole context, to hear the question "Are you still sleeping and taking your rest?" as Jesus' wake-up call to his disciples, in both the physical and spiritual senses, a question that he punctuates at once with the emphatic interjection "Behold!" He has already twice allowed them to continue resting; now the time for wakeful action has arrived. As long as Jesus intended to return to prayer he could tolerate slumbering disciples. But now "the hour is at hand", and the time for sleep and rest is past.

Jesus' question could be heard in an ironical vein, though devoid of all sarcasm, as coming from one who is more surprised and saddened than angered or reproachful, as if he were saying: "How could you still be sleeping and resting? Can't you see what is at stake in my life and the life of the world at this very moment? You cannot afford to remain waterlogged in unconscious passivity! The evil that is fast approaching will not go away simply because you bury your heads in the bog of momentary oblivion. You are my beloved friends, who have always been so eager to accept wise words from my mouth and good things from my hands. How can you now lie in a state of escapist inertia while at the same time my enemies, those who hate the Kingdom of my Father, allow their eyes no sleep and are never depleted of energy as they run about hatching plots against me and scouring the land for accomplices in my ruin?"

"Behold, the hour is at hand": Just as Jesus could say to his Mother at Cana, "My hour has not yet come" (Jn 2:4), he can now announce solemnly to his disciples that it has finally arrived. "The hour" and "my hour" refer to the same reality: namely, the precise and awesome moment in the history of the world, appointed by the Father, when his Son is to give his life for the redemption of all. The brief but pregnant statement, "Behold, the hour is at hand", affirms three things of paramount importance: the Son's total clairvoyance concerning the exact will of the Father; his own vibrant readiness to undertake that great and difficult work; and also the fact that everything else that has preceded in his life has been for this. None of his teachings, miracles, or encounters has served any purpose other than to reveal his own identity as Messiah and Savior, and this eternal identity, conferred by the Father, must now achieve its consummation at an appointed time and place and by virtue of his self-sacrificial deed. The serene firmness of Jesus' statement likewise reveals a crucial christological trait we have already contemplated: the fact that, throughout the unfolding of the events of his own Passion and death, Jesus remains mysteriously but sovereignly master of the situation. The catastrophe can fall upon him and crush him only because he exposes himself to it, goes out to encounter it, and embraces it, simply because it is the will of his beloved Father.

From a purely worldly or empirical perspective, it may appear that the shape of history is solely determined by the choices and actions of human beings, particularly those in power, as they wrestle with the arbitrary elements of chance, heredity, and quasi-rational processes, usually with the purpose of imposing their power on the world. If this were so, however, history would amount to little more than a shapeless and chaotic maelstrom, a collective meandering through time and space leading nowhere in particular, exhibiting no comprehensible shape, and yielding no overall meaning. Regarding this Gospel narrative, profane opinion would doubtless conclude that it is really Pilate, the high priests of the Sanhedrin, and, ultimately, Cæsar Augustus in Rome who are shaping history. These individuals and power groups are making the decisions and giving the commands that result in Jesus' condemnation and death. But there is another single Force, another coherent Agency, steadily and wisely at work within the endless multiplicity of these vicissitudes, generated by human volition.

Only the infinite Singular can impose order on the multiple, and only omnipotent Love can give meaningful, lasting shape to the chaos of human initiatives, whether malicious or beneficent, and work the alchemy of grace by extracting the gold of redemption from the variegated dross of human intentions and deeds. The ears of faith hear Christ the Lord exclaim loud and clear from deep within the bowels of history: "I am the Alpha and the Omega, the first and the last, the beginning and the end" (Rev 22:13). This indefectible Presence alone can give history both a shape and a meaning. To the eyes of faith, history is the result of a creative act of God, who offers human beings endless opportunities to give shape to cultural initiatives and traditions that establish a relatively stable context in which people may thrive. However, regardless of whether human beings use such opportunities well or ill, God's own abiding purpose is to move creatively within and around mankind's stages of development in order to bestow ever more life and light on the children of men. And Christ reigns sovereignly as King over the whole process, infusing it with direction, energy, and vital purpose merely by the steady gaze of his love and the constant intervention of his grace.

God's desire to save and bestow life on all will inexorably assert itself independently of man's embracing or rejecting the divine will and purpose. Despite abundant evidence to the contrary, God is the Lord of history. Man is not the lord of his own story, except in a superficial, ape-like fashion. God's plan will not be thwarted by human deviousness and malice. The Holy Spirit endows those receptive to him with the power to peer beyond the often nasty surface of historical appearances, to discover behind them the rich workings of Wisdom that sustain the universe in its path to glorious consummation. The God-appointed hour to which Jesus refers here is a theological determination of time. It signals a supreme moment when God is going to intervene mightily in history in order to reorient its course toward himself. Therefore, when Jesus declares most solemnly "Behold, the hour is at hand", this means that the divine Son on earth, the divine Father in heaven, and the divine Breath of Life pervading all times and places have, in perfect triune harmony, determined that *now* is the moment for the floodgates of grace to burst open and for the world to be inundated by the mercy of God.

If we detect a clear urgency in Jesus' voice at the moment when he is rousing his followers from their torpor, it is because this hour is truly something he has long desired, something toward which he intends to go out actively, something his Heart yearns to embrace even if it means his own suffering and death. The woman giving birth, even though she risks dying of it, feels more joyous than ever at that supreme moment because, through her suffering, new life is coming into the world. Her whole being is focused on the life and destiny of that other. At that moment, it seems to her that all her previous life has been for this and nothing else. In similar fashion, Jesus, as he now prepares to give birth to the Church through the wound on his side, "lift[s] up his eyes to heaven and [says], 'Father, the hour has come; glorify your Son that the Son may glorify you'" (Jn 17:1). Such double glorification constitutes the very substance of the Passion and death of Jesus and the very reason that he came to earth, a mortal man among mortal men.

א

26:45c   ὁ υἱὸς τοῦ ἀνθρώπου παραδίδοται
                    εἰς χεῖρας ἁμαρτωλῶν

the Son of man is betrayed
into the hands of sinners

A T A LATER MOMENT IN THE PASSION, Pilate will exhibit Jesus, bloodied and crowned with thorns, to the crowd and declare, "Here is the man!" (Jn 19:5). But Jesus prophetically anticipates Pilate's gesture now, in Gethsemane, thus taking history into his own hands, so to speak, and he presents himself as Victim-King to the world, declaring: "The Son of man is betrayed into the hands of sinners." Ironically, while Pilate would later attempt to exonerate Jesus, Jesus himself is here leaping in advance into the cauldron of the Passion. Because he is the Lord of history, so constituted by his Father, Jesus is here orchestrating his own demise. Or perhaps it would be more precise to say that Jesus is here shown by Matthew as freely consenting to and embracing what must inevitably come to him as a result of human hatred. In either case, it is of the utmost importance to realize that nothing occurs to Jesus, including (and above all) his death, that Jesus does not personally both foresee and permit. This is not at all to say that Jesus is acting out of a morbidly suicidal impulse in plotting his own murder! It is simply to affirm that Jesus is no accidental savior, no serendipitous hero: what befalls him has been both providentially allowed by the Father and freely embraced by the incarnate Word. The world could never have been redeemed by a tragic fluke of history. If Jesus does efficaciously redeem the world, it is because he is a free and intentional Redeemer, appointed as such by the Father and therefore endowed with all the necessary qualities and powers to effect the universal Redemption.

"The hour at hand", in the immediate physical and historical context, is defined by the act whereby the Son of man, the Flower of humanity, *is handed over* into the hands of sinners. The verb in question (παραδίδοται) is in the "theological passive voice", which means that the implied doer of the action of "handing-over" is God himself. We have already meditated at length in the present volume on the mystery of *parádosis*, with all its rich associations and, above all, the luminous christological paradox at its center.[13] At the literal level, of course, Jesus' affirmation would seem to imply the approach of the mob wielding swords and clubs, with Judas at the head, an event portrayed almost immediately in v. 47. Indeed, at the end of v. 46, Jesus repeats the crucial word in substantive form, when he asserts, "[Behold], my betrayer [ὁ παραδιδούς με, literally, 'the one betraying me' or 'handing me over'] is at hand." We have stressed at length the fact that this same Greek verb means both "to betray" and "to hand over" and that the particular nuance in a given case depends on whether the speaker wants to emphasize malicious intent or describe a morally neutral gesture.

Matthew's text here establishes a strict formal juxtaposition between Jesus' two statements: "Behold, the hour is at hand" (v. 45c), and "[Behold], my betrayer is at hand" (v. 46b):[14]

ἰδοὺ ἤγγικεν ἡ ὥρα—
ἰδοὺ ἤγγικεν ὁ παραδιδούς με.

Does this strict parallelism in formulation serve rhetorically as an intensifying repetition that, therefore, signifies equivalence (namely, that the approach of the hour and the approach of the betrayer are the same thing)? Or, rather, is the juxtaposition adversative (namely, that two realities are indeed approaching simultaneously, but that they are not the same thing)? The two statements, I would argue, are not exactly adversative, because the approach of both the hour and the betrayer result in the same thing, that is, Jesus' arrest and the beginning of the public portion of the Passion. What is more, the enactment of the second statement in Jesus' actual arrest wholly depends for its realization on the power of the first statement, namely, the arrival of the divinely appointed hour of history.

Taken together, the two statements communicate a disturbing "harmony", that between God's purpose to redeem the world by his Son's death and Judas' willingness to hand over his Lord and friend into the hands of sinners. The first expresses God's creative and redemptive will; the second, the manner in which God's powerful love can employ even human wickedness and abject infidelity to ac-

---

[13] See Introduction, 37–52, particularly section 3: "The Lord Jesus, on the Night He Was Handed Over, Took Bread", 43–47.

[14] For some reason, the RSV translates the first ἰδού (v. 45c) as "Behold!", but the second ἰδού (v. 46b) as "See!", thus marring the strict parallelism that the text obviously intends.

complish his redemptive designs. And there are still deeper mysteries here: In each of the statements, behind the primary presence and action of the protagonist, we can also detect the presence and action of the antagonist, as if God the Father and Judas were "shadowing" one another. St. Paul formulates the heart of the mystery thus: "[God] did not spare his own Son but handed him over [παρέδωκεν] for us all" (Rom 8:32, NAB). This declaration points to the specific arrival of the hour, appointed by the Father, when his beloved Son "is handed over into the hands of sinners".

The Pauline formula clearly establishes the fact that Judas can become a hander-over of Jesus only because the Father has first handed Jesus over to Judas and all sinners. The divine action of handing Jesus over to mankind in the Incarnation as supreme Gift anticipates, and thus makes possible, the human action of betraying Jesus to his murderers. In this sense, Judas' betrayal is already foreseen as a "shadow" of the divine act of handing over, since no one could have wrested the Son from the Father by force. The Father gives Jesus to Judas even though the Father knows that Judas will betray him to his death. The Father is doubtless the implied acting subject of the passive verb in the phrase, "The Son of man is handed over. . . ." Contrariwise, even though Judas is plainly the immediate, visible, human agent of the epithet ὁ παραδιδούς με ("the one handing me over" or "betraying me"), nevertheless here Judas is "shadowing" the eternal Father, in the sense that Judas' action was first made possible by the Father's decision to bestow his Son on mankind, regardless of the consequences of such an unequaled and unaccountable action.

It would be quite fitting, therefore, to apply the epithet ὁ παραδιδούς με (*ho paradidoús me*, "the one handing me over") not only to Judas, to indicate his heinous human betrayal of Jesus, but also to the Father himself, who originates the action of handing Jesus over. This paradox is both deeply troubling and magnificently luminous. The tension between its two simultaneously valid and necessary aspects will not be resolved until Christ is revealed in all his glory at the end of time, with celestial light pouring forth from his five resplendent wounds. What an impenetrable paradox and mystery, indeed, that there should occur, at the heart of revelation, this convergence of the highest and the lowest, this identification of opposites, this "conspiracy" between omnipotent divine love and miserable human hatred! And yet, what a source of hope it also reveals to all of us! Yes, God can use even our most abysmal deeds of evil and betrayal instrumentally, to bring about the realization of his plan of universal salvation.

God's love and its strategies infinitely surpass all our static categories and dichotomies. Would it not be repellent, horrifying even, to our pious sensibilities if a student of New Testament Greek carelessly broke the virtuous taboo and, in translating ὁ παραδιδούς με (*ho paradidoús me*, "the one handing me over"), did the unthinkable and applied to the heavenly Father the epithet of "betrayer" of Jesus, conventionally reserved for Judas alone? And yet such a student would not be far off the mark. Inadvertently, he would have alerted all believers to the unfathomable depths of the mystery of our redemption which, far from growing familiar, ought to induce even greater vertigo the more we contemplate it. It was, after all, the Father who first "handed Jesus over into the hands of sinners"—into *our* hands, so much did he love us!—and the believer must live uneasily on the sharp edge of that paradox. If Jesus is so knowledgeable regarding this subject and also the time of his betrayal, it is because he and his Father, with the concurrence of the Holy Spirit, decided on this particular manner of redeeming the world since "before the foundation of the world . . . through his blood" (Eph 1:4, 7).

In the end, Jesus admonishes his disciples, "Rise, let us be going; [behold] my betrayer is at hand." After enduring the darkness, after the struggle with the void, after waiting and yearning for silence itself to yield some light, there comes the vital *action* of faith. Nothing less than a divine energy of determination and hope emanates from these words of Jesus to his friends. The command *Rise!* instills a promise and foretaste of the Resurrection itself. Jesus does not wait for Judas to come to him, to find him cowering in concealment. Jesus goes out deliberately and energetically to meet Judas on his path of betrayal. And yet it is not bravado or superhuman courage that impels Jesus, but rather loving obedience. What we here witness is Jesus enacting his burning desire to hand himself over to Judas and all sinners. Nothing can explain this *passion of self-bestowal* except his eagerness to fulfill the Father's will, which he thoroughly understands as God's plan to communicate life to man by drowning it in the life-substance of the Son, who is Life itself (Jn 14:6). As such, Jesus wishes, in obedience, to give away the Life that he has and is: "The thief comes only to steal and kill and destroy; I came that they may have life, and have it abundantly" (Jn 10:10). "For there is one God, and there is one mediator between God and men, the man Christ Jesus, who gave himself as a ransom for all" (1 Tim 2:5–6).

It is no exaggeration to say that Jesus' energetic determination and eagerness to go forth to encounter his destiny amounts to a sublime *joy*, the joy that can only derive from his perfect union of love with his Father. And it is precisely to this joy that the author of Hebrews invites us all, when he writes: "Let us run with perseverance the race that is set before us, looking to Jesus the pioneer and perfecter of our faith, who for the joy that was set before him endured the cross, despising the shame" (Heb 12:1–2).

INTERLUDE II:
GRACE IS
NOT CHEAP

THE PEACE OF JESUS IS THE CROSS. But the cross is the sword God wields on earth. It creates division. The son against the father, the daughter against the mother, the member of the house against the head—all this will happen in the name of God's kingdom and his peace. That is the work which Christ performs on earth. *It is hardly surprising that the harbinger of God's love has been accused of hatred of the human race.* Who has a right to speak thus of love for father and mother, for son and daughter, but the destroyer of all human life on the one hand, or the Creator of a new life on the other? Who dare lay such an exclusive claim to man's love and devotion, but the enemy of mankind on the one hand, and the Saviour of mankind on the other? Who but the devil, or Christ, the Prince of Peace, will carry the sword into men's houses? God's love for man is altogether different from the love of men for their own flesh and blood. God's love for man means the cross and the way of discipleship. But that cross and that way are both life and resurrection. "He that loseth his life for my sake shall find it."[1]

---

[1] Dietrich Bonhoeffer, *The Cost of Discipleship*, trans. R.H. Fuller, rev. ed. (1959; New York et al.: Touchstone, 2018), 195–96, italics mine.

8. LIKE A PLAYTHING FROM HAND TO HAND

The Handing-Over of Jesus (26:47–56)

26:47ab

ἔτι αὐτοῦ λαλοῦντος
ἰδοὺ Ἰούδας εἷς τῶν δώδεκα ἦλθεν
καὶ μετ᾽ αὐτοῦ ὄχλος πολὺς μετὰ μαχαιρῶν καὶ ξύλων

While he was still speaking,
behold Judas came, one of the Twelve,
and with him a great crowd with swords and clubs

NOTHING TAKES JESUS BY SURPRISE. He is, after all, God's Wisdom incarnate. In fact, at this juncture it is almost as if Jesus needs to give Judas implicit *permission* to approach and betray him. To this encounter Jesus comes from praying to his Father, while Judas comes from plotting with the high priests and elders of the people. To each his own! Jesus announces Judas' imminent arrival to his disciples and reveals precisely what Judas is about to do by referring to him with the terrible epithet "the one-who-is-handing-me-over". The text stresses that Judas' arrival interrupts Jesus' declaration to his disciples almost in mid-sentence: "While he was still speaking, Judas came. . . ." Time and again, the evangelist reminds us that all the horror about to descend upon Jesus' head will occur with the Savior's full knowledge, lucid anticipation, and wholehearted consent of will. In this text, one can almost see a cause-and-effect connection between Jesus' announcement to his friends of Judas' arrival and the launching of the Passion proper by Judas' betrayal. Jesus practically gives the nod for his own Passion to begin.

265

Jesus is, then, like a theatrical director signaling the moment when one of the chief players should enter. Jesus' cue is barely uttered when Judas is already executing it. Humanly speaking, we are indeed witnessing a very strange situation in which the victim so totally embraces his destiny that he is seemingly cast in the role of orchestrator of his own demise. Such foreknowledge and willing consent, nevertheless, in no way attenuate the responsibility of the criminals who eventually do him in. God's acceptance of human evil-doing and his incorporation of it into his plans for redemption by no means destroy man's freedom and accountability. God never collaborates with the forces of darkness, but he does use that darkness to stage the rising of an even brighter sun. In this sense, God may be said to be always creating the world anew, only this time not out of nothingness. His constructive forces are now constrained by the nature of the situation to work in synergy with his creatures' destructive intents. Love always stoops to conquer.

At every step of the plot's unfolding, we can plainly see that the greatness and nobility of soul of this persecuted Man infinitely surpass in depth and power the very worst that men's fears and hatreds can concoct against him. Their worst is to make him suffer physically and mentally and, finally, to drive out the natural life from his body. But he is the first to practice the teaching he gave his disciples in the long Mission Discourse: "Do not fear those who kill the body but cannot kill the soul" (10:28). Through that fearlessness, he triumphs.

"While he was still speaking, Judas came, one of the Twelve." Matthew now highlights two simultaneous facts: that Judas is interrupting Jesus and that the betrayer is doing it as one of the Twelve. An awful dissonance clangors from that conflicting affirmation because Judas does not arrive humbly, with peace in his heart, but rather noisily and aggressively, escorted by a faceless, violent mob. Judas' demeanor, words, and actions readily show that he is in revolt against his own recent identity as disciple, which is to say, in revolt against what only yesterday was still his deepest joy and claim to fame. Matthew cannot wonder enough, and with a very heavy heart, at this one indisputable and scandalous fact: namely, that the betrayer of Jesus, the one who triggers the Lord's suffering in the Passion, is *one of the Twelve*, one of Jesus' intimates, one of those personally selected by the Master to be his friend, confidant, and collaborator in spreading the Gospel.

Judas comes onto the scene in Gethsemane and interrupts Jesus as the Lord is instructing his disciples. A disciple, Judas knows very well, should never interrupt his rabbi when the master is delivering a teaching; a disciple waits until the rabbi is finished speaking and only then asks questions. This is not just a matter of the courtesy that regulates the relationship between persons of different rank. Rather, when a disciple deliberately *interrupts* his master in the middle of a teaching, he is implicitly declaring that he, the disciple, has a private agenda to propose that is more important and urgent than whatever the teacher happens to be discoursing on. Such interruption is therefore insolent and expresses an impatience with being a "mere disciple" who chafes at the bit of discipline. The insolent learner forgets that, whereas in other religions a disciple rightfully aspires to reach the rank of master, in Christianity, because of who Jesus is, the disciple only aspires to become, ever more deeply, *a disciple!* The one who sits at the feet of Wisdom incarnate finds the greatest joy precisely in plunging ever more deeply into the inexhaustible Heart of Wisdom. The disciple of Jesus can never rival Jesus, no matter how long his discipleship may extend. He can only hope to reflect Jesus the Word Incarnate to others ever more accurately.

Judas' breach of courtesy, his trampling of docility, though it may appear almost too subtle to notice, in fact symbolizes the very major fateful shift that has taken place in Judas' identity: he has emancipated himself from his need for Jesus and, therefore, also from his obedience and devotion to Jesus' word. He has violently shaken off Jesus' light and easy yoke and has taken up against Jesus, "gentle and lowly in heart" (11:29–30), the lethal weapons of denunciation and scorn. Now Judas' own agenda reigns supreme in his own imagination, passions, and will. He must take steps to rid himself and the world of the irritation of Jesus' presence, of the seduction of Jesus' mystical absolutes, in order to implement an alternate plan for the salvation of Israel—a carefully hewn design that is more practical and realistic and that, therefore, corresponds more satisfactorily to "real" human desires and needs.

"And with him [came] a great crowd with swords and clubs." Judas does not come alone, and so the ironies mount. Until earlier this very evening, when he shared in the Last Supper and piously communed in the Body and Blood of Jesus, Judas has been a member of a small, select group of only twelve men, known for their docility toward their Master and armed only with the words of truth and light that Jesus offered them. Now Judas arrives at the head of a great, noisy crowd, armed with swords and clubs, seeking vengeance and blood. He has had enough of Jesus' too demanding, too ethereal, and paradoxical teaching. He has lost patience with Jesus' long-suffering, inward manner of redeeming Israel through conversion of heart. Consequently, Judas now shows a true Satanic streak by approaching Jesus and the Eleven aggressively, at the head of a violent rabble, embodying all too well the motivation of Milton's fallen angels: "Better to reign in Hell, than serve in Heaven".[1] Better to be a forceful protagonist, heroically leading a gritty multitude through the darkness, than to be only one of a sorry band of twelve perpetually submissive and disoriented dropouts, who will never rise above the rank of "disciple". "I leave obedience and docility to foolish and insecure children, and to those who don't know any better", Judas' feverish eyes affirm.

But what is it exactly that accounts for so much animosity against Jesus on the part not only of Judas but also of this rabble? Neither Judas nor the crowd advancing at his side to inveigh against Jesus and the Eleven is new to the Gospel landscape. Judas has all along been one of the Twelve, always implicitly included in the group whenever we hear mention of "Jesus and his disciples". As for the anonymous individuals in this mob, they were surely present in the crowds that listened eagerly to Jesus as "he was teaching daily in the temple" (Lk 19:47), and they were surely among those eager and needy ones who sought his miracles and cures. What has happened in the meantime?

The important clue lies in Matthew's phrase to the effect that Judas and the "great crowd with swords and clubs" are coming to Jesus "from the chief priests and the elders of the people." These constitute the religious and scholarly intelligentsia of Israel, and they feel thoroughly threatened by Jesus in their positions of authority and leadership. No doubt many of them are reacting against Jesus in obedience to their moral conscience and for the defense of Israel's sacred laws, rites, and traditions. The mere presence, words, and actions of Jesus have turned the contemporary Jewish scene on its head and made many question the legitimacy and truthfulness of

[1] John Milton, *Paradise Lost* (1667), 1:262–63.

the Jews' established religious leaders. We have seen, for instance, the scandalous impact of certain pronouncements of Jesus, above all the insufferably insistent formula, *You have heard that it was said of old . . .*, *But I say to you . . .* (5:21, 27, 33, 38, 43). To the doctors of the Law, this formula signifies the highest blasphemy imaginable; it connotes that a mere man is elevating himself and his private opinions to the rank of absolute authority above the Law of God himself, and it is utterly irrelevant how virtuous or ardent that man may otherwise appear to be. As far as the Jewish authorities are concerned, Jesus is implicitly and intolerably declaring his own puny, individual "I" to be the equivalent of the omniscient and sublimely autarchic divine "I", with even greater and more definitive authority than the letter of the Mosaic Law, which is the very basis of Jewish ethnic and religious identity.

If Jesus had no followers, if his theological enormities fell on deaf ears, he could perhaps be dismissed as an insane but harmless wretch. However, as it turned out, "large crowds followed him, and he healed them there" (19:2). Jesus' growing popularity with vast multitudes of the people greatly alarm the religious leaders; he might, indeed, succeed in overturning the religious establishment and ousting them from their positions of privilege. And so, as we saw at the beginning of chapter 26, "the chief priests and elders of the people . . . took counsel together in order to arrest Jesus by stealth and kill him. But they said, 'Not during the feast, lest there be a tumult among the people'" (26:3–5).

No doubt the leaders' well-founded theological scandal at Jesus, and their fear of losing their social and religious standing in Israel, are their own motivation to promote Jesus' demise. But what of the people itself, the ordinary folk without any interest in theological nuances and very little concern for their leaders' privileges? The priests and doctors of the Law have to entice the crowds away from Jesus, not with theological abstractions that would never work, but with fare more suited to their plebeian liking and concrete needs. In other words, they have to provide *panem et circenses*—bread and entertainment.

One whole aspect of the tragedy we are here witnessing is that God's chosen people, the Jews, under the stress of their Lord coming among them in the person of the Son, is degenerating before our very eyes into an assemblage of wily demagogues (the religious authorities), on the one hand, and, on the other, the rabble they are rousing for sheer political ends. How can it be that this spiritual disintegration is the immediate effect wrought on Israel by the approach of the Messiah and by his proclamation of God's Word in a manner that fulfills all divine promises extravagantly? Or, to put it in more universal terms, does the approach of the living God *ever* have on people, at least initially, an effect that is other than shocking, disruptive, indeed convulsive? It seems that even—or perhaps especially—the chosen people cannot escape this universal "law", and to an exponential degree, given the unsurpassable perfection of the presence of the divine Fire in Jesus of Nazareth. The first stage of the transformation Christ came to earth to bring about is always *virulent*, in all the many senses of this word: strong, dangerous, powerful, active, infectious, indeed, unsparingly *lethal* in the sense that all our old habits and prejudices must die. The termination of unreality is a good thing. This virulence of God's Word takes hold at the social, familial, and individual levels of experience. It will leave no cell in our bodies, no fiber in our souls, unchanged. And the reaction of these cells and fibers to the invading virus of transforming grace is highly predictable: resistance to the death.

We remember, for instance, that, after the episode of the multiplication of the bread in John, the vast crowds that had eaten their fill at Jesus' hands began pursuing him to make him their king. In the wake of this great miracle, Jesus suddenly appeared to the populace as the answer to all their most pressing problems. Obviously, the one who can single-handedly and effortlessly feed multitudes, as well as heal their diseases, is *the* heaven-sent savior whose kingship would insure a future of plenty, justice, and happiness for the whole people. Jesus, however, had intended his dramatic actions on behalf of the people to be an unequivocal proclamation and demonstration of the coming of God's Kingdom in his person, to the end that hearts should be converted and lives radically changed by his potent, grace-filled presence.

The majority of the people, by contrast, stopped short at the materiality of the deeds themselves and the immediate satisfaction and relief they derived from Jesus' benefactions. They had no interest in holy signification leading to newness of life in their souls. They had no patience for this business of "bread from heaven" that bestows eternal life. Therefore, Jesus and the crowds that had followed him, full of eager yet mercenary expectation, in the end reached an impasse: "Perceiving then that they were about to come and take him by force to make him king, Jesus withdrew again to the hills by himself" (Jn 6:15). Jesus would have no followers and supporters on such terms. He preferred utter solitude and human failure to a success and popularity that he could attain only by selling out the mission entrusted to him by his Father, the mission, that is, to save the world by establishing God's Kingdom on earth through his sacrifice of himself on the Cross. That the crowd wanted to take him *by force* and make him king against his will is an ominous prefiguration of their eager and violent participation in the present scene of the betrayal. It is in keeping with mob psychology to be variable as the wind, one moment exalting a captivating person to the heavens and the next moment crying out for his blood.

So it is that the crowd, now bitterly disappointed by Jesus' cheating them out of their keenest desires, lusts to destroy the very one who would not allow himself to be made king on the mob's grasping terms. And the religious leaders would now basely move to exploit the people's disenchantment with Jesus and thus solidify their allegiance to themselves. They would now provide the rabble with the goriest, most protracted, most titillating show on earth: the capture, trial, torture, and crucifixion of Jesus, this public malefactor and enemy of the pious Jewish establishment and its holiest traditions. The final touch of genius in the whole plan is that the leaders will not so much as lay a finger on Jesus so as not to desecrate their own hands. Instead, they will get those brutal Roman pagans to do all the dirty work for them.

26:48   ὁ δὲ παραδιδοὺς αὐτὸν
ἔδωκεν αὐτοῖς σημεῖον λέγων·
Ὃν ἂν φιλήσω αὐτός ἐστιν, κρατήσατε αὐτόν

*Now the one-handing-him-over
had given them a sign, saying,
"The one I shall kiss is the man; seize him"*

A KISS THE SIGN OF BETRAYAL! Why, Judas, why? Is it just one more ruse, aimed at catching your prey wholly unawares until the very last second when, lightning-like, the cobra strikes? When one considers what Jesus has meant to you until recently, and you to him, your tone of ruthless self-determination fairly chills the blood. Now, finally, it is *you* running the show, running *him* in fact, literally shaping his earthly destiny. You have become wholly depersonalized, rather like a meticulously poised, infinitely accurate nuclear missile hurtling unstoppably toward its target. And yet your language and gestures retain all the outward symbols of reverence and friendship. In advance, and with clever premeditation, you have instructed those who hate your Master: "The one I shall kiss is the man; seize him." But why do you approach him this time surrounded by a mob? Never before were you afraid of the dark, in his company. Is even your own blood chilled by your betrayal?

Moreover, how can tender *kissing* (an action of love) and violent *seizing* (with intent to destroy) become one and the same thing in your heart? How can you affirm such conflictive actions within the same promiscuous sentence? Is this, then, the key to your whole person and tragedy, namely, this intolerable contradiction in your heart, this colossal collision in your breast between the disciple and the betrayer? In that case, how very fittingly you embody us all—all of us, I say, who started off as seekers of the Light, as joyful servants of Highest Truth. But, then, all too often we betray the deepest tenderness and yearning of our heart and must, naturally, set out to destroy the very Source of Love that had so powerfully seduced us, drawing us to his Heart. Are we not often tempted to look upon ourselves as arrant fools for having entertained for even a moment the dream of our souls' betrothal to the divine Bridegroom? And, ah, how well we know that we save for our own heart our cruelest, our all-obliterating violence, in order to punish it for having been so gullible as to be duped by a phantom divine seduction.

Yes, indeed, Judas. Much more than a simple practical ruse must motivate your action of concealing betrayal with a tender kiss. By doing away with Jesus, the object of your erstwhile devotion, you want to wreak vengeance on your own former naïveté and force a poisoned kiss to wipe out every vestige of innocence from your heart, as in an atomic holocaust. For you have now become a political realist and your *Realpolitik* has no toleration for personal feelings of tenderness or the quiet satisfactions of friendship and a shared life of devotion. All that is surely for the weak, for the pansy-souled. Yet are you not the first true victim of your newfangled hatred for both human and divine tenderness and for the mystical universe of joyful communion it represents? Jesus is but the exterior occasion of your self-destruction, the objectification of your own self-hatred. Some people commit murder because they feel unworthy of their victim's love, and to be unconditionally loved with persistence only reminds them of their shameful unworthiness.

But why, Judas, am I intent on holding this distressing dialogue with you? Do you think it is to point my finger accusingly at you? Quite the opposite, my friend! It must be because you are, in turn, the projection of my own flight from the commitment required by intimacy and deep love. How I toil to construct for myself a new, stainless-steel identity based on hard-nosed, this-worldly "realism"! For only such realism is reputed to produce results. And yet this titanic self-determination is such a hollow pretense that, in its wobbly insecurity, it cannot abide anything that reminds it of its sham, and so it must destroy all evidence showing that *truest strength lies in fidelity to the Beloved, even in his weakness, dishonor, and defeat*. True strength of character is to be sought in purity of heart and in steadfast interior devotion to the object of my love.

א

"AND HE CAME UP TO JESUS AT ONCE AND SAID, 'Hail, Master!' And he kissed him" (καὶ εὐθέως προσελθὼν τῷ Ἰησοῦ εἶπεν· Χαῖρε, ῥαββί, καὶ κατεφίλησεν αὐτόν, 26:49). Every human kiss, given within time, in some sense partakes of the meaning of the very first kiss that ever was, which occurred at the beginning of human existence within the very act of God's creation of man: "Then the LORD God formed man of dust from the ground, *and breathed into his nostrils the breath of life;* and man became a living being" (Gen 2:7). It is impossible to breathe air into another's nostrils without kissing that person. By its nature, a kiss cannot be passive or merely symbolic; a kiss is an intimate action of love that bestows life. God bestowed his own divine image on man by means of that primal kiss that was also the very act of man's creation. We owe our existence to a divine kiss! We were created by God's *hands* in our earthly aspect ("dust"), and at the very same time, in our divine aspect, by the life-bestowing kiss of God's *mouth* ("breath" = "spirit"). How could it have been otherwise? Nothing short of the intermingling of God's Being with ours through a momentous kiss could produce the extraordinary creatures that we are! Something of God's personal substance had to pass over into our being so that we would become God-worthy creatures, yes, drawn out of nothingness, indeed, and yet in the end possessing a share in divinity. By God's gracious condescension did we become worthy of sharing the life of God.

What we witness in Judas' present action on the Mount of Olives, then, is a horrendous, sacrilegious *de-creation*, a creation in reverse, man rejecting—if only he could!—the love and very life of God by spewing the breath of creation contemptuously back into the mouth of God. In a very real sense, Judas now remains soulless, emptied out of his specifically human-divine richness, reduced, as we have seen, to impersonal functionalization: Judas the Titanium Missile. Under the mockery of a disciple's pious kiss, his breath still redolent of the eucharistic bread and wine he has received from Jesus' own hands earlier that same evening, Judas now scornfully *spits his soul* back onto the human Face of Christ-God. The present dreadful action by Judas, though bearing the semblance of affection, is actually of a piece with the literal spitting on Jesus' face that would in brief take place at Caiaphas' house (26:67). Both actions aim at the thorough humiliation by man of God the Creator.

This abyssal event of self-decreation, moreover, is the spiritual action that anticipates Judas' physical suicide, which likewise involves two further willful expulsions by him, first of his ambition and then of his very viscera: "Throwing down the pieces of silver in the temple, he departed; and he went and hanged himself" (27:5); shortly thereafter, "falling headlong he burst open in the middle and all his bowels gushed out" (Acts 1:18). No better symbol could be found than this utterly repellent image of Judas' demise to express the catastrophic personal results of his choices. The instantaneous disgust the image instills in us invites to salutary contemplation. Whatever he may or may not eventually do to another in the concrete, a betrayer of Judas' magnitude is always his own first victim as he furiously sets about dismembering his own being. For betrayal by definition means casting into the outer darkness someone who through love has become a part of one's intimate self.

In this context, it is quite suggestive that the Greek verb for "to kiss" used here by Matthew, φιλέω (*philéô*), happens also to be one of two Greek verbs that mean "to love", the other being ἀγαπάω (*agapáô*). Now this last word, *agapáô*, especially in a Christian context, is understood to connote a love or devotion flowing from the will and the intellect, that is, a more purely spiritual kind of love mirroring God's own. *Philéô*, on the other hand, our present verb, connotes a love more grounded in the emotions and thus rich not only in the virtues of will and intellect but especially in strong affection and fondness of heart. Obviously the two concepts are complementary rather than contradictory, and both components are needed for fully human loving.[2]

Now the fact that the one verb *philéô* has these two different though related meanings ("to love with affection" and "to kiss") beautifully enshrines in Greek the human intuition about the inseparability of loving and kissing. Whoever loves, kisses, in order to express his love physically, and whoever kisses is spontaneously showing love. Nor should it surprise us to learn that the Greek word for "friend" is *phílos*, which shares the same root with our present verb. To kiss fraudulently, therefore, to kiss as a premeditated *sign of betrayal* as in Judas' case, presents us with an abhorrent action that betrays not

---

[2] Such necessary complementarity among the different kinds of love is the central subject of Pope Benedict XVI's remarkable encyclical *Deus caritas est* (2005).

only the divine Son of God but human nature itself. It betrays the sacredness of love and utterly vitiates the very center of the betrayer's soul, which consists precisely in his capacity to love.

The kiss of Judas is obviously, then, one of the central events in Matthew's Gospel. It is enshrined as such both by its crucial historical role in launching the Passion and by its symbolic attestation of the human heart's penchant for betraying its dearest love. The importance of this kiss explains why the evangelist now, in v. 49, enhances the root verb for "kissing" syllabically so as to exploit its nuances fully. Whereas in v. 48 Judas had given his henchmen the order to seize whomever he "kissed" (using the simple form φιλήσω), v. 49 records the event itself of the kiss with the word κατεφίλησεν, a compound form of the verb with the prefix κατ- as intensifier. The one-syllable difference between the two verbs could readily be dismissed as mere stylistic variation without any effect on meaning. However, unlike the Hellenistic Luke, the Semitic Matthew rarely strives for mere elegance of style, and so we must look for a weightier reason for the variation. None of the familiar translations, in fact, makes any distinction here. Only three rarely quoted versions of the Bible pay any attention to the nuance. For the act of kissing in v. 49, one has: "And [he] *eagerly kissed* him."[3] Another offers: "And he *kissed* him *demonstrably*."[4] And the third, more suggestively, says: "And [he] *covered* him *with kisses*."[5] This verb *kataphileô* does, indeed, according to the specialized dictionaries, refer to the action of greeting someone with a kiss *fervently and affectionately*, and is sometimes rendered as "to kiss tenderly". In Xenophon it even means "to caress".[6]

We must conclude that, according to this text, there is nothing lukewarm about Judas, whether as friend or as foe. He is an extremist to the bitter end, similar to Peter in this respect. And so, when he kisses Jesus, it is obviously no ordinary peck on the cheek that he bestows. His action of kissing Jesus emphatically, of "covering him with kisses", is, in fact, of a piece with the explicitly violent action to which, by that very means, he is inciting the mob: to lay hands on Jesus and overpower him and, thus, hopefully put an end to his out-

---

[3] *Rotherham Bible* (1999).
[4] *McDonald Idiomatic Translation of the New Testament* (2008).
[5] *English Darby Bible* (1890).
[6] *Liddell-Scott Greek Lexicon*, entry 23416, καταφιλέω.

rageous and unmanageable ways. The passionateness of Judas' kiss, thus, already contains the violent passion of the mob's taking hold of Jesus and, indeed, the fire of Jesus' Passion as well. This chain of events is triggered by overwrought kissing by Judas at this moment of betrayal.

There can be no doubt that the explosive energy contained in Judas' momentous kiss comes straight from his heart; but it is a heart in which something disastrous has occurred. Thanks to Judas in this crucial scene of the Gospel, the demonic alchemy that can fill a sign of love with the venom of betrayal is thus set inescapably before our eyes, to remind us of the dark convolutions and potential calamities of the human heart. Indeed, given the right circumstances of bitter disillusionment, the abiding temptation rises within each of us to destroy what we love best precisely because it will not allow itself to be loved on our own manipulative terms, or because that love has terribly disappointed our most passionate expectations in some way. Oscar Wilde has captured this universal human tendency most poignantly:

> Yet each man kills the thing he loves,
> By each let this be heard.
> Some do it with a bitter look,
> Some with a flattering word.
> The coward does it with a kiss,
> The brave man with a sword![7]

The innocence of an earlier ecstatic love of our heart that has now plummeted to the hell of contempt cannot be more effectively mocked than by casting our new hatred for it precisely in that same love's wonted and most passionate forms.

Following that logic of despair, Judas now covers his Master with kisses that become devouring in a passion of vengeful resentment. The tender energy of love, so pure and ardent at its source, has now become wholly destructive. When Jesus first called Judas to himself by name, the first thing he did was to give him, along with the other Eleven, "authority over unclean spirits, to cast them out" (10:1). Now the disciple finds himself in the terminal stages of the very disease he was commissioned to heal in others. By turning against his Teacher and Savior, Judas becomes par excellence the embodiment of the unclean Spirit.

---

[7] "The Ballad of Reading Gaol" (1898).

When he approaches Jesus to embrace him, the betrayer greets him as his *rabbi* ("teacher"), a word sometimes translated "master". Judas' greeting Χαῖρε, ῥαββί, literally means, "Rejoice, Teacher!" Matthew conveys the intimacy of Judas' greeting by leaving the word for "teacher" in the Aramaic original since that is the very word, the very sequence of sounds, that would have reached Jesus' ears from Judas' mouth. It is interesting to note that, in all of Matthew, this Semitic word is used only twice, and both times it is uttered by Judas: here and, only a while ago, during the Last Supper, when Judas asked Jesus whether it was he who would betray him. "Is it I, Rabbi?" he asked, and Jesus replied: "You have said so" (26:25). It is ironical that both times that Judas addresses Jesus as "rabbi" it is in connection with his betrayal of Jesus, and so it is difficult not to hear a tone of smiling contempt in Judas' voice. Accompanying it we see the leering smile of a student who now thinks of himself as having grown smarter, more relevant, and more efficient than his teacher.

Now *rabbi* means "teacher" only by convention because the literal meaning of the word is "my great one", a meaning that is clearly more generic than "teacher" and does not specifically refer to the didactic art. But, because teaching the divine Torah is the highest human profession conceivable, the person engaging in that activity would be called "great" (*rab*) and his disciple would personalize this recognition of greatness by adding the possessive adjective "my" (*-i*). The honorific title *rabbi*, spoken in greeting to one's master, thus implies something like "you are great because you bring me the truth." At the same time, such sublime public recognition remains as well a highly personal and affectionate expression of love and gratitude.

As for χαῖρε (*cháire*), the first word of Judas' salutation, it is a standard greeting literally meaning "rejoice!" On this occasion, such a greeting adds yet another layer of bitter mockery to the encounter since Judas in fact is wishing Jesus anything but joy. Quite to the contrary, all the conventional forms of love, courtesy, and admiration are here being sabotaged by Judas and converted into instruments of hatred, deceit, and betrayal. It has always been a Satanic skill to mimic perversely the virtues and prerogatives of God. Over and over during the Passion—from the kiss of Judas here to the royal greeting by the Roman soldiers (also inviting Jesus to "rejoice", 27:29) and to the sign affixed to the Cross above his head (27:37)—the honor, glory, and adoration due to God alone will be mocked ironically as leering facsimiles of humble obeisance that are melodramatically served up with the sole purpose of ridiculing Jesus. Judas himself in this passage becomes the embodiment of the Satanic spirit of irony, "the spirit that is always denying",[8] the spirit whose tragic brilliance consists in gnawing away with tiny, hypercritical mandibles through every layer of existence and experience, until only a hollow, worm-eaten universe remains beyond all hope of redemption. When irony rules as the sole mode of intelligence, the only operative force is that of death and nothingness, and contemptuous mockery becomes the choice means of expression. Then language itself, intended by God as a privileged vehicle to reveal the joyous mysteries of being, becomes a parody of truthful communication and an instrument of deceit, and a kiss communicates hatred rather than love.

But precisely such a miserable state of affairs in a human soul can, in the end, showcase in the strongest manner the transformative power of the divine Purpose. With his "Rejoice, Rabbi!" and his ironical kiss, clearly Judas does not *intend* to communicate to Jesus wishes of joy and reverent obedience. Nonetheless, precisely because Judas' worldly logic of power, success, and vengeance have nothing in common with Jesus' own logic of redeeming love, we may say that, in fact, Judas' derisive greeting and kiss *do* bring Jesus joy, for the reason expressed in the Letter to the Hebrews: "For the joy that was set before him, [Jesus] endured the cross, despising the shame, and is seated at the right hand of the throne of God" (Heb 12:2). In other words, *Jesus grieves mightily*, both for himself and for Judas, at this betrayal by his friend and disciple, above all bemoaning the self-destructive course on which Judas is set. However, at the very same time, *Jesus rejoices with all the might of God* because the work of redemption is now starting in earnest and Judas' betrayal at last opens the way for the realization of Jesus' total gift of self to the Father as a sacrifice of atonement for the sins of the world. Only the power of God's love can transform the infamy of jeering betrayal into an instrument of redemption. The human intentions and the material actions they produce remain unchanged, but these are not allowed to be the last words in the awful drama: God's will to save has transmuted betrayal from a shameful *end* into a glorious *means*, even while it remains a culpable betrayal. Now its destructive energy can be rechanneled

---

[8] *Ich bin der Geist der stets verneint*, as Satan defines himself in Goethe's *Faust* (Part I).

constructively. Of course, Jesus will still have to suffer unspeakably and die the death of a criminal; but the joy of ultimately being "seated at the right hand of the throne of God", in the company of all his friends, triumphs over all the intervening pain and shame.

א

26:50   Ἑταῖρε, ἐφ᾽ ὃ πάρει;
τότε προσελθόντες ἐπέβαλον τὰς χεῖρας ἐπὶ τὸν Ἰησοῦν
καὶ ἐκράτησαν αὐτόν

"Friend, why are you here?"
Then they came up and laid hands on Jesus
and seized him

F RIEND!" THIS IS JESUS' FIRST WORD to Judas in reply to his treacherous greeting and kiss. The Greek word used here is *hetáiros*, in the vocative case ("O Friend!"). This grammatical case conveys an affective nuance, and the word itself evokes a whole gamut of intimate associations between two men. The evangelist has gone out of his way not to use the more common, generic term for "friend", *phílos*. When referring to a group of young boys, *hetáiros* can mean "playmate" (11:16). It is the term that men would employ to address one another when they enjoy a mutually binding relationship, for instance, as kinsmen within the same clan or household or as fellow soldiers in the same army. In this case, *hetáiros* would be rendered more precisely as "comrade" or "companion". The disciples of Socrates would be addressed by him, and would address one another, as *hetáiroi*, in recognition of their deep bond as fellow-seekers after wisdom. Those who sat together at a great feast, such as a royal wedding or a victory banquet, would also be *hetáiroi* or "messmates" because in antiquity one shared a meal only with friends.

This last meaning is particularly poignant in our context since Judas and Jesus have just celebrated the Paschal *seder* earlier this same evening as *commensales*, with both dipping their morsel in a bowl at the same time and Judas receiving the Eucharist from the hands of Jesus. Because of the intimacy of Judas' association with Jesus as teacher, friend, and lord, we may say that all these rich meanings of the term *hetáiros* in the Hellenistic world apply to the relationship between them—even that of "comrades-in-arms", since Jesus and Judas are allegedly fighting together with the weapons of love and truth for the triumph of the Kingdom of God.

By addressing Judas with so intimate a term as *hetáiros* at so crucial a moment, Jesus is appealing to his disciple's deepest heart, reminding him of who and what they have been to one another. Indeed, the use of the term in so emphatic and public a manner amounts to a last-ditch effort by Jesus to renew his original invitation to Judas and reestablish him in his friendship. The innocent Jesus seems to take at face value the gestures and words of respect and affection that Judas, for his part, executes with piercing sarcasm and irony. To reciprocate offense with kindness: Has this not always been the naïvely obstinate way of unconditional love? Indeed, the desire for vengeance can never so much as graze the logic of any genuine love. True love never exalts its own wounded feelings and does not give up on the beloved's capacity for transformation.

Love cannot accept—as the last word from the beloved—rejection, offense, or contempt inflicted on itself. Love is above all conscious of its mission to instill in the beloved a noble mind and renewed generosity, even and especially when the human prospects for such renewal appear tragically dim. This is why, properly speaking, unconditional love is a divine prerogative, which may be practiced by human beings only by way of participation and not as an autonomous, innate natural capacity. No human being, severed from love's source in God, is capable of loving unconditionally. Unconditional love unto death is at root trinitarian, that is, it has its origin, not in some static divine state of being or attribute, but in the dynamic circulation of the torrent of Love among the three Divine Persons. The love of Jesus can never be exhausted because it is ceaselessly being replenished from the infinite fount of his eternal Father, who unendingly begets him. To its last pulsation this side of death, the Heart of Jesus longs to win his friend and companion Judas back to its affection.

It is possible to render Jesus' phrase to Judas, ἐφ᾽ ὃ πάρει, in rather different ways. The NAB ("Do what you have come for") and the New Latin Vulgate (*Ad quod venisti!*) translate it as a command by Jesus, whereas the RSV interprets it as a question: "Why are you here?" This last translation seems best to convey the persistence of Jesus' love for Judas just mentioned. To the end, it is Judas who must choose what to do with Jesus—whether to serve him or betray him—while Jesus' own choice of unconditional love was already made long ago when he first called Judas to discipleship. To the end, the questioning mode leaves open the door to conversion. But Jesus' tender and hopeful question to Judas, inviting him to reconsider his evil designs, is cut short brutally by the onslaught of the mob: "*Then* they came up and laid hands on Jesus and seized him." Judas, for his part, perseveres in his betrayal, which at this moment reaches a climax. He does not repent and give a counter signal, which would have abrogated his earlier instructions to his co-conspirators.

The only answer Judas gives to Jesus' earnest question is simply to stand back in supercilious silence and allow the fury-driven rabble to pour disastrously onto the scene and overpower Jesus. The mob then does the only thing mobs can do: rage and destroy. One wonders how many members of this thuggish gang have also been present in the crowds that followed Jesus around Palestine for three years, seeking to be entertained by his words and healed or sated by his miracles? But this nocturnal rabble can *lay hands on Jesus* solely because the Betrayer par excellence, the *Paradidoús*, has first *handed him over* to them. And, if Judas in the first place has the power to hand Jesus over to the rabble, it is solely because the Redeemer, at his own initiative, has first handed his sacramental Body to Judas at the Last Supper, thus allowing himself to become the plaything of men. Now begins in earnest the drama of Jesus being handed over at will, back and forth from hand to murderous hand, similar to the way we handle the eucharistic Body of Jesus at Communion, a risky privilege and blessing that also makes us all into potential Judases. At this moment, Jesus' prophecy in 26:45 is literally fulfilled, which says: "Behold, the hour is at hand, and the Son of man is betrayed into the hands of sinners." Nothing escapes the knowledge and wisdom of the incarnate Word; and, if these tragic events now descend upon him, it is solely because he has first chosen to hand himself over into our merciless grasp—fickle, greedy, vengeful beings that we are, so easily swayed by our latest yens and lusts.

א

26:51   εἶς τῶν μετὰ Ἰησοῦ ἐκτείνας τὴν χεῖρα
        ἀπέσπασεν τὴν μάχαιραν αὐτοῦ
        καὶ πατάξας τὸν δοῦλον τοῦ ἀρχιερέως
        ἀφεῖλεν αὐτοῦ τὸ ὠτίον

one of those [who were] with Jesus stretched out his hand
and drew his sword
and, striking the slave of the high priest,
cut off his ear

VIOLENCE ELICITS VIOLENCE, blow corresponds to blow: this appears to be, alas, one of those unpitying cosmic laws inscribed in nature. What is disconcerting here is that this violence originates in one of Jesus' own disciples, no doubt reacting viscerally to the aggression he sees advancing upon his Friend and Master. But the evangelist behaves admirably as a narrator at this crucial turning point in Jesus' story. Precisely at the very moment of the betrayal, at the time of greatest vulnerability for Jesus when, humanly speaking, everything is about to be lost, Matthew refuses to look at the world in black-and-white absolutes, with all the guilty ones shown to be colluding with the religious authorities and all the innocent ones portrayed as already thoroughly formed disciples, meekly bending the head to the Father's redemptive will. The evangelist, rather, uses the moment of betrayal to continue revealing essential aspects of the Heart of the Savior and of the specifically Christian meaning of

283

salvation. Matthew the Evangelist is the finished Christian, not the man who draws the sword to defend Jesus on earthly terms.

We are surprised, in the first place, to see any of Jesus' followers having a sword ready to hand. In fact, we must admit, albeit with dismay, that in this scene it is actually a follower of Jesus who sheds blood. It is clear that for many of the disciples, at least at this point, following Jesus is analogous to joining a political party or radical power-group, a conventicle whose identity is defined extrinsically over against their enemies rather than by any intrinsic, transcendental truth. Therefore, the method of self-defense for these neophytes is going to mirror the strategies of Jesus' enemies, not excluding resort to preemptive attacks. The physical well-being of the Master must be protected by all available means. They probably muse along these lines: "Is this not what it means to be a loyal follower? He provides the spiritual doctrine, and we back it up with brawn: an invincible formula God must surely bless. Together these two weapons—Jesus' wisdom and our courage, one divine and one human, acting in unison—will conquer the world!" Is it possible that Jesus allows persons with a desire for violent insurrection to join his group, in the hope of slowly introducing them to the divine battlefield of the spirit? In any event, the word translated "sword" here (*máchaira*) cannot be construed as a mere kitchen knife haphazardly picked up: it always refers to a curved, small weapon for close combat. This particular follower of Jesus is definitely armed, at least for purposes of self-defense if not aggression.

Even after its all-too-efficient, violent use, Jesus does not confiscate the weapon and throw it away. Rather, he limits himself to saying to his brutally impulsive follower: "Put your sword back into its place; for all who take the sword will perish by the sword" (v. 52). The focus of the evangelist's narrative is not material or political but spiritual. He desires to use the occasion to impart a mystical doctrine and reveal more of Jesus' divine character. The word for "sword" used here (*máchaira*) inevitably recalls an earlier usage by Jesus of the same Greek word in Matthew, when the Lord affirms quite alarmingly: "Do not think that I have come to bring peace on earth; I have not come to bring peace, but a [*máchaira*]" (10:34). Perhaps the present cutter of ears himself welcomed that statement with dull, literal ears of his own, recording its stunning image in his memory in isolation from all context, and then of course failing to remember anything else Jesus taught that day on the subject.

In that passage, Jesus in fact was speaking most emphatically of the "sword of separation" that would radically discern between all relative natural loves (even the love of relatives) and the absolute love owed to himself alone: "He who loves father or mother more than me is not worthy of me; and he who loves son or daughter more than me is not worthy of me; and he who does not take his cross and follow me is not worthy of me" (10:37–38). This application by Jesus of the meaning of the "sword" he brought on earth makes it clear that the primordial battle he instigates in an individual is the struggle with his own ego. Jesus thus urges him to restructure within himself a new hierarchy of loves based on the fact that only God may be said *to be Love*. It is a battle that prominently features as adversary nothing other than the raw natural instinct for survival and self-assertion at all costs, what can be called the urges of the "reptilian brain", seemingly the calamitous default setting in fallen human nature.

Therefore, Jesus concludes the whole passage by proclaiming the great mystical paradox that is the only effective antidote to our reptilian impulses: "He who finds his life will lose it, and he who loses his life for my sake will find it" (10:39). Instead of seeking to lose his own life along with Jesus and for the love of Jesus, the sword-bearing disciple at Gethsemane pitifully caricatures Jesus' earlier doctrine by acquiring an enemy's ear as that night's battle trophy! St. Paul would later enshrine the correct understanding of the sword Christ brought when he admonishes the Ephesians to put on "the helmet of salvation, and the sword [*máchaira*] of the Spirit, which is the word of God" (Eph 6:17).

As a reaction to his disciple's violent act, Jesus teaches: "Put your sword back into its place; for all who take the sword will perish by the sword." Violence can beget only more violence, Jesus is saying, since raw violence is an ignorant, blind force whose lone skill is instinctual self-propagation and that, therefore, cannot help continuing to secrete its own toxic ooze into the atmosphere shared by all. The one who ruthlessly inflicts violence, if he had any foresight, would realize that by his deeds he is really but writing his own equally ruthless death sentence. Violence to others is always suicidal in the end! By this pithy admonition to his violent disciple, in the form of a command followed by a wisdom saying, Jesus is teaching all of us how to avoid both physical and spiritual death and to move along the path to fullness of life.

We note, however, that Jesus, consummate pedagogue that he is, employs a manner of correction that is transformative and creative rather than repressive and condemnatory. He does not confiscate the culprit sword and put out a political call for dogmatic pacifism. Rather, in commanding that the sword be "put back in its place", it seems that Jesus is proposing the *rechanneling of aggressive energies*, that is, the hard personal and collective work of transforming the blind, passional drive in us into a potent, upbuilding principle pledged to serve, not individualistic lusts, but the enhanced life-energy of all. What a miracle of the divine alchemy it is that the very same blind energy that, like a wild river in spate, can ruin whole stretches of the soul should, under the transforming synergy of love, become a life-giving source of fertility, growth, and fraternal communion!

26:53 ἢ δοκεῖς ὅτι οὐ δύναμαι παρακαλέσαι τὸν Πατέρα μου,
καὶ παραστήσει μοι ἄρτι
πλείω δώδεκα λεγιῶνας ἀγγέλων;

*Or do you think that I cannot appeal to my Father,
and he will at once send me
more than twelve legions of angels?*

T WELVE LEGIONS OF ANGELS are a great many angels—sixty thousand, to be precise, since in the time of Jesus a Roman legion consisted of five thousand soldiers. Imagine the dramatic effect of sixty thousand dazzling beings of light suddenly swooping down from the skies upon the gloom of that terrible night in Gethsemane, the radiant messengers of God's glory suddenly paying obeisance to the persecuted and betrayed Jesus of Nazareth as to their own Emperor and Commander! It would be too facile to dismiss Jesus' language here as nothing but overwrought, apocalyptic imagery with a touch of the psychedelic, used for a cowing rhetorical effect. Perhaps building on the martial symbolism of the prominent *sword*, Jesus tallies up the minimum number of angelic choirs at his disposal using the terminology of the Roman army. Expressions like "hosts of angels" or "heavenly armies", however, are also familiar from the Old Testament. The Latin-Hebrew phrase *Dominus Deus Sabaoth*, repeated in the Sanctus of every Mass, means "Lord God of armies".

Now, Jesus does not choose the number *twelve* fortuitously. This number, in fact, connects his angelic reference to the present scene in a most enlightening way. Any grouping of twelve in Scripture evokes both the twelve patriarchs of Israel and their descendant tribes as well as Jesus' twelve apostles, the latter group no doubt mirroring the former microcosmically. Moreover, although Matthew does not name the aggressive, sword-bearing disciple, he is surely one of the apostles. (John's Gospel says it was Simon Peter, 18:10.) Also, this speech of Jesus about the angels is directed to the culprit apostle in the second-person singular. When Jesus asks ἢ δοκεῖς; ("Or don't you think . . . ?"), he is looking at only one person. Thus Jesus' words on this occasion bear the same personal stamp of intimacy that we remember from Jesus' individual calls to discipleship early in the Gospel when he engages individuals in an intense encounter. And let us not forget that all twelve disciples are still present around Jesus at Gethsemane at this moment, although they will soon desert him. We conclude that, by implication, Jesus is here setting up a dramatic contrast between his ragged band of weak, hesitant, and benighted human followers who are twelve in number, on the one hand, and the numberless heavenly hosts, attendant upon God's eternal Glory and reflecting it over all creation.

These resplendent armies of angels are, no less than the apostles, Jesus' "followers", officially dispatched to him by his Father, and they always stand ready to serve him instantly with a vigorous, utterly reliable, lightning-like obedience that only puts in bolder relief the pitiful shabbiness of the earthly apostles. Jesus' present reference to the hosts of heaven as his own personal attendants is far from unique in Matthew's Gospel. We remember that, at the conclusion of the episode of the temptations early in the Gospel, the text says: "Behold, *angels came and ministered* to him" (4:11). And the parable of the sheep and the goats was introduced with this apocalyptic image: "When the Son of man comes in his glory, *and all the angels with him*, then he will sit on his glorious throne" (25:31). In fact, Jesus' *parousia*, his cosmic arrival escorted by armies of heavenly attendants, is a recurrent theme of the New Testament, as when St. Paul writes to the Thessalonians referring to the end-time as that decisive moment "when the Lord Jesus is revealed from heaven *with his mighty angels* in flaming fire" (2 Thess 1:7).

The two crucial questions, therefore, that the text asks of us at this junction are, first: Why, having permanently at his disposal a numberless and, by definition, undefeatable army of God-appointed, heavenly beings, does Jesus in fact *not* call upon his Father to dispatch them to him at this moment of extreme human need, when the whole tragedy of his Passion and all its tortures is about to be launched? And, then, there is the corollary question: Why, in the light of infinitely better options, does Jesus choose instead to abide in the company of pathetically unreliable, feeble, and treacherous followers and companions who, he is quite certain, are about to abandon him to a man (26:31, 56)?

In the next verse, Jesus himself answers both these questions but in a very succinct and cryptic form, namely: "But how then should the scriptures be fulfilled, that it must be so?" (26:54). Such a sober statement at this point, uttered for the instruction of the erring disciple, refers him and all his wavering fellow-disciples not only to every prediction of the Passion Jesus has made throughout the Gospel but to the mystery of the Cross itself and, most all-inclusively, to the mystery presupposed by the Cross: God's plan to redeem the world by the Incarnation. Because the Father is nothing but Mercy and Love, it is his will to save the world, not by "defeating evil" in any purely mechanical and extrinsic manner, but by infusing it with the divine life of his Heart. This can be accomplished only by God radically sharing with mankind the dear Son of his Heart, even if this means that this Beloved, wearing human flesh, will be torn to pieces by perverse Satanic and human violence. Only this can demonstrate that God's love is, ontologically, the only invincible force in the universe, stronger than the power of hatred and of death itself. If intimate contact between the life-giving Word and fallen, carnal man can happen only in this way, then the Father is willing to pay the price, and Christ accepts to take up the yoke necessary to accomplish that task: the Cross. Having another's blood on one's hands is a dreadful yet very effective way of achieving intimate contact with him.

The main objective of the Word, as he obeys his Father in the project of his Incarnation, is not to defeat the forces of evil in the cosmos. Many fewer than twelve legions of angels would suffice for that! But no: the Word's goal, the ardent desire of his Heart is, rather, to coexist with man intimately, in fact TO INDWELL MAN, so as thus to communicate to man the divine life the Word contains, the divine life the Word IS. This is as well the reason why Jesus chooses to abide by his disgraceful band of hangers-on after all, soberly foregoing the cosmic light-and-sound spectacle of glory and triumph that could have been provided by sixty thousand angels. Jesus loves his disciples tenderly, abidingly, unconditionally, whether or not they are faithful to him. In their weakness and penchant for infidelity, his tender love for them can discern only a more intense need for his presence and support.

Nor is Jesus a "superman". As a true and complete human being, Jesus has affective needs, severe doubts, haunting fears, since the only thing he is incapable of is sin itself. In every other respect, he shares our mortal condition. One of the Trinity cannot live an isolated, aseptic existence on earth as incarnate Word, true man, and true God. By definition, Christ has to manifest the Trinity's Being as essential community precisely by clinging to his friends even when they are unworthy of him and reciprocate his love with betrayal. He both enjoys and needs his friends' company as we have amply seen at the Last Supper and during the Agony in the Garden. In choosing, at the moment of his betrayal by Judas, the company of his twelve scruffy apostles over that of twelve legions of resplendent angels, Jesus is both revealing his origin within the realm of God's eternal glory *and* affirming the way of the Passion (including betrayal by his disciples) as the most efficacious manner of accomplishing his Heart's desire.

We can never ponder sufficiently the truth that Jesus is not out to "save himself"; if that were the case, he would never have come to earth in the form he did. He is God, which means that the deepest laws of his Divine Person impel him to pour out his vital being for others without reckoning the price, to the end that all might have fullness of life and enjoy eternally the very joy of God.

א

26:55   Ἐν ἐκείνῃ τῇ ὥρᾳ εἶπεν ὁ Ἰησοῦς τοῖς ὄχλοις·
Ὡς ἐπὶ λῃστὴν ἐξήλθατε
μετὰ μαχαιρῶν καὶ ξύλων συλλαβεῖν με;
καθ᾽ ἡμέραν ἐν τῷ ἱερῷ ἐκαθεζόμην διδάσκων
καὶ οὐκ ἐκρατήσατέ με

At that hour Jesus said to the crowds:
"Have you come out as against a robber
with swords and clubs to capture me?
Day after day I sat in the temple teaching,
and you did not seize me"

H UMAN TREACHERY AND VIOLENCE will indeed win out in the Garden of Gethsemane. Jesus will inevitably be captured, manhandled, tortured, and delivered over for execution. And yet at the level of serene, rational thought, it is Jesus who has the last word. Though weapons driven by brawn and hatred will mangle his precious body, throughout the ordeal his word will emerge from the depths of his soul as a diaphanous witness to God's truth. We must constantly keep in mind these two levels of the plot of the Passion. The sheer horror of the Lord's manifest physical and moral suffering will reach such a pitch and be so realistically portrayed that we are likely simply to sink into mournful despondency and fail to discern the internal divine activity governing scene after scene from the depths.

Right now, at the moment of his capture, Jesus utters significant words that truly light up the scene from within and reveal the mind of God at work. At this point, after teaching his disciples about his own divine origin and resultant manner of exercising power, he addresses the armed mob. Matthew introduces Jesus' speech with the solemn phrase *at that hour*. This cannot of course refer to the time of day, for this would be a silly tautology. Rather, Matthew is here referring to the "hour" of which Jesus himself spoke at the conclusion of his prayer in the Garden when he asked the disciples: "Are you still sleeping and taking your rest? Behold, *the hour is at hand*, and the Son of man is betrayed into the hands of sinners" (26:45). The fateful "hour" announced by the evangelist now appears wholly immersed in scriptural prophecies concerning the necessity of the Passion, which Jesus repeatedly stresses. In the previous verse (v. 54) Jesus has affirmed that angels cannot come to defend him now because the divinely inspired prophecies of the Passion must be fulfilled. And in the following verse (v. 56), Jesus will refer to his betrayal and impending capture as a done thing, so bent is he on fulfilling the prophets' declarations concerning the earthly fate of the Messiah and his manner of establishing divine order in the world by the power of his own suffering and death.

To say that Jesus' chief role as Messiah is to fulfill the Scriptures is simply to affirm that the essential motor-force driving Jesus as Savior to accomplish redemption is not personal power or wisdom or virtue of any kind, or even his will-to-save or his desire for self-sacrifice, but solely and uniquely obedience unto death to the Father's will, the all-consuming passion to do nothing apart from the Father (cf. Phil 2:8; Jn 5:30). The majestic serenity and self-assurance with which Jesus utters these pronouncements before a dangerously armed and vicious mob also display, for our own personal instruction, the effect that total submission to God's will has on human nature: namely, it fosters the dynamic integration of the whole person and all his faculties into the single purpose of serving the truth. Obedience given to God unto death paradoxically produces a person who is free of paralyzing fears, intellectually lucid, and triumphant over this world's paltry categories of judgment. Such is Jesus at this moment, when *his hour* has arrived. Out of mercy does he allow himself to be swept out mercilessly to death's ocean by a torrent of violence.

For the evangelist, it is paramount that we know how very freely and majestically Jesus is embracing the moment of his demise, just before he is overwhelmed by wave upon wave of destruction. Because this is the hour the Father has chosen, and because this is the means the Father has likewise prescribed for the redemption of the world, Jesus goes to his annihilation impelled by God-rooted self-assurance and joyful singleness of purpose and, yes, above all by the *loving desire* that makes a bridegroom tread into his bridal chamber with lilting step. Indeed, Jesus is running interiorly toward the divine vision of a human Beloved that the Father is holding out to him, that is, mankind transformed in the bath of his blood and reborn as Christ's resplendent Bride, the Church (cf. 1 Pet 1:18–19; Eph 5:25–27; Col 1:20; Heb 10:19; Rev 7:14, 21:9). Not for nothing, therefore, do we call this drama of dramas, about to start unfolding, Jesus' *Passion*, hearing the word with its full resonance connoting the human and divine energy of *eros*, and not just as a hackneyed formula of piety. All of the ebullient passion of Jesus' soul and heart, always quietly the source of his every word and deed, is now about to burst forth for all to see, with all the force of an aortal gush.

Jesus is no Stoic; he does not meet his fate with either jaw-clenching resignation or mere philosophical quietude of mind, based on "true rational principles". Here we witness Jesus hastening, more eagerly than ever, if that were possible, to fulfill his Father's design of salvation. The Father's love for him is his very life-blood, and to please his Father his quintessential joy. Welded together by the one fiery breath of the Holy Spirit, Father and Son have conspired to redeem mankind and transform the universe into the Kingdom of God by the vivifying power of the Lamb's outpoured Blood: "You know that you were ransomed . . . with the precious blood of Christ, like that of a lamb without blemish or spot" (1 Pet 1:18–19). *This* trinitarian relationship, *this* reciprocal desire to please, *this* paternal plan of salvation, is what together defines Jesus' unique identity. And it is for this reason that throughout the events of the Passion the evangelist presents Jesus to the world both as the utterly vulnerable sacrificial *Victim*, in the drawn-out process of being immolated, and, simultaneously, as the utterly free and sovereign *Kyrios* of all history, the *Lord* whose obedient will-to-save is at this very instant directing the course of events toward the Father's glorification, even as his own crushing human drama unfolds.

OUT OF THE ABYSS OF PATHOS into which his destiny has plunged him, Jesus asks his persecutors: "Have you come out as against a robber, with swords and clubs to capture me?" How do we hear him uttering this rhetorical question, whose positive answer is all too obvious? Jesus stresses the extreme contrast between how he has habitually treated them for a long while now and how they are treating him at present, the scandalous disparity between what he has been for them and what they are choosing to be for him in return. There must at least be shock and hurt and sorrow in his voice. His chosen words, however, seem to preclude anger or recrimination, and yet the question form itself invites reflection. Could he still be hoping for a change of heart by making them see the wild incongruence in behavior between them and himself? Jesus implies that he does not deserve what he is getting as he strives to awaken their collective memory to their recent, everyday experience of his manner of presence among them—who are his people Israel.

"Have you come out as against a robber, with swords and clubs to capture me?" The word for "robber" used here, λῃστής (*lêstês*), possesses a wide gamut of meanings. The one thing it does *not* mean is an ordinary "thief". It is, in fact, the term used by Luke for the highwaymen who attack the traveler in the parable of the Good Samaritan (Lk 10:30). *Lêstês* evokes any man who engages in public violence, from a common brigand or outlaw all the way to a more politically minded insurrectionist or guerrilla. It implies someone operating violently outside the law for the sake of personal gain. Every item in this definition is symmetrically opposed to everything Jesus stands for in both word and action. Jesus is "gentle and lowly in heart" (11:29). His only "violence" is the chastisement of a hardened and sinful heart. Just moments ago he severely lectured the disciple who had drawn his sword and wounded a fellow human being. Jesus sees himself as someone who does not abolish the Law but only takes it to ultimate fulfillment (5:17). And, far from doing anything for the sake of personal gain, Jesus almost seems to address our present scene when he declares quite explicitly in John's Gospel: "The thief comes only to steal and kill and destroy; I came that [my sheep] may have life, and have it abundantly" (Jn 10:10).

The deep pathos of this scene at Gethsemane, furthermore, derives first of all from the sad tone of Jesus' reproach to the mob, which reminds us of the *improperia* of the Good Friday liturgy. But this pathos also results from the violent discrepancy revealed in the clash between two figures: *Jesus the Benefactor* of mankind, as Matthew's Gospel has consistently portrayed him, and *Jesus the Brigand*, a nonexistent figment of the vengeful human imagination, maliciously constructed as scapegoat by the religious leaders and now being vilified as such by their pawns, the vicious mob. In the face of who Jesus really is, coming to capture him with swords and clubs is like trying to kill a canary with a bazooka. In the end, however, and in all honesty, we have to allow that Jesus is indeed an "insurrectionist" and a "revolutionary", though not of the sort imagined by the priests, this mob, and even some of his disciples.

What would a casual Jewish or Roman passerby have concluded if he had happened to overhear Jesus' clearly incendiary statement the day he proclaimed to his followers: "Do not think that I have come to bring peace on earth; I have not come to bring peace, but a sword" (10:34). Why, even after twenty centuries of exegesis on the text, even we, who consider ourselves faithful followers of Jesus and privy to his Heart's intentions, still have difficulty interpreting such a passage! In addition, most people are literalists by instinct and do not hang about waiting for the spiritual explanation of such bold statements. Politics is based on hearsay and appearances, not on substance and real meaning. And so the religious leaders of the people and the holders of political power feel massively threatened by Jesus' very presence and the mysteriousness of all his words and deeds. They feel in their bones that *something* monumental, earth-shaking, life-transforming is being introduced by this rabbi, something that threatens to upset the world and society as they knew it drastically, and foremost the traditional notion of God, from which all other religious ideas and social conventions are derived.

Jesus is every inch a revolutionary in their eyes, even if they can conceive of "revolution" only as a massive threat to material, social, and institutional power. Consequently, they react to the threat Jesus poses in the only way they know how: namely, with political strategies (such as rabble-rousing and quickly assembled cliques) and material weapons of subjugation (such as swords and clubs, steel-pointed whips, and the queen of weapons: the cross).

In the face of such aggressiveness, of this manifest public will to annihilate Jesus at all costs, we are entranced by the quality of his continuing dialogue with his dear creature, man, even when humanity takes the form of a violent mob. At no point is it Jesus' intention to defend himself by clever rhetoric so as to somehow wiggle away from the tsunami of violence about to crush him. Moment by moment, he seems more concerned about the state of his aggressors' souls than by the prospect of his own bloody demise, and this attitude will endure throughout the Passion. When he asks the crowd if they come to capture him as they would a robber, Jesus is holding up to them a mirror of their actions and stoking in them at least a minimal instant of lucid self-awareness in which both to realize the ludicrous incongruity of the present scene and, blushing for shame, hopefully to undergo a change of heart that would allow a sense of greater justice to dawn in their hearts. We may add that, in this sense, Jesus' objective in engaging in dialogue all around him—even those most hostile to himself—has always been "Socratic", that is, its goal has always been to shepherd others toward the truth by any linguistic means available. However, in the end Jesus offers *himself* to others as, precisely, the incarnate, personified Truth, something Socrates had the wisdom and nobility never to venture.

א

H AVE YOU COME OUT *as against a robber, with swords and clubs to capture me?"* With this hard-hitting rhetorical question, Jesus holds up to the crowd the improbable image of himself as would-be robber, an image constructed by their own attitude and actions. Immediately afterward, he appeals to their memory of his lived recent association with them. First, he offers for their consideration two wildly different versions of himself so that they can decide which the true one might be: "Which will it be for you, Jesus the nasty brigand or Jesus the unarmed, reasonable man now speaking calmly to you?" Next, he urges them to retrieve from their own memories the image of themselves as peaceable, God-seeking folk hungrily searching for the truth as they daily came to the temple to imbibe the teaching of this highly unusual and ever so attractive rabbi: "Day after day I sat in the temple teaching, and you did not seize me." This last affirmation, "and you did not seize me", has the function of effectively connecting the image of Jesus the Robber with the drastically incompatible image of Jesus the Teacher so as to cause a logical short-circuit in their awareness and thus hopefully awaken his hearers to the whimsical confusion reigning in their own minds.

How profoundly moving, and how crucially instructive for us, for the way *we* live our daily lives, that, even in the face of a violent death, Jesus does not allow the passions of fear or anger to interfere with his role as Savior! Rather, he uses the energy of precisely those passions to create poignant verbal images and to formulate incisive questions wielded as instruments of salvation. What we are witnessing here is Jesus transmuting within his own person the destructive human energies of fear and anger into the sovereign energy of saving love. He does not look out before him and see an irredeemable conglomeration of the lost. In this ferociously threatening and irrational mob, Jesus sees, rather, persons clamoring for the catalyst that will make them see the Light and embrace the Life that he is; and he enacts this exalted vision of the human heart by his steadily piercing words and deeds that aim at opening up hardened hearts. This is always a labor of love.

Yet Jesus is no divinely programmed teaching device, no remote dispenser of grace. For him to remain immoveable in the fulfillment of his mission by no means implies impassibility. Jesus finds himself concretely in a situation of massive threat and harassment; he feels the anguish of the tragically misunderstood lover; he experiences the deep hurt of the betrayed friend. All of these sorrows now converge on his infinitely sensitive Heart like cruel projectiles. For all our admiration of Jesus' equanimity and abiding altruism under such circumstances, we should not fail to hear the plaintive note of sadness in his voice as conveyed, for instance, by his use of the imperfect tense: "Day by day *I used to sit* (ἐκαθεζόμην) in the temple teaching. . . ." This imperfect tense describes an action that was repeated habitually over a considerable period of time, signaling the patient Jesus' perseverance at the work of salvation.

But the imperfect here also points to the fact that that period of Jesus' life and that daily, peaceful activity are now over definitively, having been brutally ended by his betrayal by Judas and the onset of the Passion. During the three years of his public life, Jesus has shown forth the goodness of his Father by continually radiating it in the form of words, gestures, and abiding presence. Even if he had done nothing more, the loftiness of his teaching and the incomparable nature of his presence would still compel us to consider him the unrivaled master of universal wisdom. However, Jesus is far more than a mere master of true wisdom, more than merely a certified spokesman for the Unseen God. Jesus *is the Unseen God* become visible and palpable under the veil of human flesh.

The simple fact that the one and only sublime Lord, the Creator of all matter and all spirit, enters the visibility of the human world already reveals God's nature as substantial, indefectible Love. Only immortal Love can condescend to enter our world and become subject to time, space, and conflict. In Jesus, God becomes vulnerable, exposing himself to the whims of his creatures. When the moment arrives for God to reveal the full depth of his Being as immortal Love (and this moment is *now!*), Jesus ceases to utter comprehensible *words*. In their stead, he begins to discharge eloquent *drops of humanly divine blood*. Even the best and most affecting words must still travel a certain distance between the speaker and the listener. Words cannot of themselves effect a work of redemption that aims at the ultimate union of speaker and listener. Only divine Blood, which has ever only flowed through the veins of Jesus Christ, being in itself a principle of life, can finally bridge that gap and create abiding communion between the loving Speaker and his beloved listener, between Jesus the Bridegroom and humanity his bride. The Passion of Christ dramatizes a blood wedding. If Jesus had been only the greatest of teachers or the greatest of prophets or the greatest of friends, mankind would have been greatly enlightened, inspired, and reassured, but it would not have been *redeemed*. Beyond all other forms of relationship between Jesus and mankind, the only one that ultimately matters is his identity and deeds as *Jesus our Bridegroom*. "Let us rejoice and exult and give him the glory, for the marriage of the Lamb has come, and his Bride has made herself ready" (Rev 19:7). "In Christ Jesus you who once were far off have been brought near in the blood of Christ" (Eph 2:13). "You know that you were ransomed . . . with the precious blood of Christ, like that of a Lamb without blemish or spot" (1 Pet 1:18–19).

26:56b   Τότε οἱ μαθηταὶ πάντες ἀφέντες αὐτὸν ἔφυγον

Then all the disciples forsook him and fled

THE STRATEGIC "THEN" inserted by the evangelist here has powerful implications. It is not merely a rhetorical connector in the narrative. It means that human malice and cowardice and violence cannot erupt with full force into Jesus' life *until* God allows them to. Only *then* can they break loose. Jesus sovereignly disposes of the time and rhythms of his Passion, which unfolds according to the divine will. He must first speak all the words he has intended and declare that the whole course of his story has run and shall continue to run in keeping with the Father's design of salvation, clearly foretold throughout previous revelation: "All this has taken place, that the scriptures of the prophets might be fulfilled" (v. 56a).

Jesus enters his Passion as a master diver ventures his leap at the right moment, jumping up forcefully into the heights and then plunging vertiginously through the air into the water far below, all according to his own interior freedom and in obedience to the Father's wisdom. The Word's decision to take on the flesh of man has already trained him to plummet from the heights of glory to the depths of mortality. That "then" of the historical Incarnation is now renewed in this "then" of the incarnate Word's leap into his Passion. The third "then" that will complete the triad will be the hidden moment of his Resurrection.

The existential *shape* of Jesus' whole earthly life—the actual events that fashion it—is a far greater revelation of the Heart of God than any accumulation of *words* could ever be, whether spoken by the prophets or even by Jesus himself. Existence itself is greater than speech because existence contains and conditions speech. After conveying the truth *about* God in words throughout the Gospel, Jesus now shows, exclusively by the shape of his life, *who God is. Pointing to God* is different from *showing forth God*. And in the shape of his Passion, Jesus shows God to be a Lover betrayed and rejected by those to whom he has shown his love most intimately. Jesus' almost total vocal silence from now until his death will now show God to be a forsaken Lover, abandoned by all his creatures and cast by them into a terrible solitude of suffering. Only the Passion of Jesus could reveal, in flesh and within time, this ultimate depth of the Divine Being— God's capacity and willingness for self-sacrifice, enacting his deepest nature as Love.

"Then all the disciples [forsook] him and fled": This unimaginably wrenching moment signifies the silencing of Jesus the Teacher and the emergence of Jesus the Victim. Words of wisdom now become transmuted, first, into the unheeded gasps and sighs of Jesus' absolute solitude and, a little later, into the generous flowing of Christ's blood. Divine Wisdom incarnate is ever inventing new ways to continue pouring out his life-substance, according to the circumstances. We glimpse the prodigious extent of our Lord's unabated tenderness, patience, and benevolence toward his disciples when we remember that he has known all along that this moment of cowardly abandonment by all of them would arrive. Indeed, he has already said to them with prophetic sadness: "You will all fall away because of me this night" (26:31), and "The hour is coming, indeed it has come, when you will be scattered, every man to his home, and will leave me alone" (Jn 16:32).

This advance knowledge of their desertion, however, neither deflects Jesus from his purpose as Savior nor embitters him against his friends. To the objections of the Pharisees, who were scandalized at his consorting with all the tainted of this world, Jesus has replied: "Those who are well do not need a physician, but the sick do. Go and learn the meaning of the words, 'I desire mercy, not sacrifice.' I did not come to call the righteous but sinners" (9:12–13, NAB). And at this moment of such gravity for himself, the heavenly Physician must drink some of his own medicine, so to speak, by having to persevere in his mission of healing sick sinners even if it means plunging all alone into a fiery abyss of suffering. He has not "desired [any extraneous ritual] sacrifice", it turns out, because he himself is the appointed sacrifice the Father will provide, in astounding fulfillment of Abraham's gesture of obedience (cf. Gen 22:1–14).

Does it not make us tremble a bit to see Matthew record the blunt fact that *all* Jesus' disciples abandon him and flee? All along the Gospel narrative, we have always read the standard phrase "Jesus *and* his disciples" as we saw them doing this or that in unbroken unity. But now, by a tragic reversal, we must read about "Jesus [*forsaken by*] his disciples". What is a master without disciples, and what are disciples without a master, indeed, *against* their master? At this point in his life, they can no longer follow him. The shape of Jesus' life has now become too threatening, too forbidding and terrible. As long as Jesus' comforting words still negotiated the distance between themselves and the all-consuming Fire of Mercy, the disciples basked gladly in the remote warmth. But now that Jesus is himself entering that Fire, becoming one with that Fire, and straining mightily not to allow the roots of his humanity to be torn out of the ground of his divinity, *now* his poor disciples panic out of woeful cowardice and fear and swiftly run away as far as they can from the conflagration. Even Peter, who in one of his most splendid moments refused to leave Jesus, exclaiming "Lord, to whom shall we go?" (Jn 6:68)—yes, even dog-faithful Peter now abandons him. And even John, who laid his head on Jesus' breast (cf. Jn 13:23, 25; 21:20) in order to "listen to the thoughts of God's Heart", as Origen magnificently says—even John the Beloved now abandons him. Indeed, it seems that the only aid Jesus' disciples can at this moment provide him, the sole contribution they can make to the work of the world's redemption, is to help their Lord, *by their collective fleeing*, to construct a perfectly forsaken solitude.

It would seem that, for the incarnate Word's suffering to be unblemished, it must forego any smallest touch of human consolation. Jesus did indeed insistently seek such support when he declared, "My soul is very sorrowful, even to death; remain here, and watch with me" (26:38); but in Gethsemane he also had to learn to renounce it. Only an incarnate God can be alone to such an unfathomable degree. Jesus' perfectly unalloyed solitude in his Passion, through all the throes of human desolation, thus dramatically *represents* to us (in the literal sense) the resplendent and majestic solitude in eternity of the One Lord God who exists both before all creatures and also wholly independently of all creatures.

The truth of Jesus' difficult teaching in John 12:24 holds not only for man but for God as well: "Unless a grain of wheat falls into the earth and dies, it remains alone; but if it dies, it bears much fruit." God, too, must die in utter aloneness if his death is to produce an abundance of fruit, which in turn will yield many new grains to be sown, also alone, into the earth. While all his friends flee from him like drops of water in a centrifuge, Jesus abides. He perseveres, even in his disciples' absence, as the steadfast center of their sacred circle that he himself created. Jesus is at this moment the sturdy stem of a forlorn rose all of whose petals have been ravished by a storm.

9. INTO THE DEEPENING DARKNESS

Jesus before the Sanhedrin (26:57–68)

26:57   Οἱ δὲ κρατήσαντες τὸν Ἰησοῦν
         ἀπήγαγον πρὸς Καϊάφαν τὸν ἀρχιερέα,
         ὅπου οἱ γραμματεῖς καὶ οἱ πρεσβύτεροι συνήχθησαν

Then those who had seized Jesus
led him to Caiaphas the high priest
where the scribes and the elders had gathered

AND WHAT A DEVASTATING STORM it is, sufficiently vicious to make the incarnate God bend physically to its will! How ironical to see God's embodied Wisdom on earth, him in whom and through whom the galaxies and all cosmic energies were created, now being bounced about at the whim of men! Deserted by his disciples, the Master now has no one to lead and is therefore constrained to follow the spurious leadership of the malevolent! This night of the first Holy Thursday will, indeed, be a very long and agonizing one for the Savior as he is bandied about as an object of sarcasm and contempt. The drama of this night could well be summed up in the Psalmist's cry of the heart: "I am for peace; but when I speak, they are for war!" (Ps 120[119]:7).

No one in that immense mob or among the Jewish leadership can ascertain how so much radiant peace and serenity can emanate from someone who, to them, has suddenly become so utterly contemptible and obnoxious. As they seek to seize him, to overpower him (ἐκρατήσατε, v. 55; κρατήσαντες, v. 57) in order to contain him and then banish him from this world, they must marvel at the source of this palpable light that uncontainably escapes through their own fingers in their attempt to manhandle him: the irrepressibly oozing light that infiltrates the surrounding darkness. The more they tug and squeeze, the more liquid splendor pours out from Jesus' body.

Just a couple of verses ago, the Lord mused out loud to the crowd: "Day after day I sat in the temple teaching, *and you did not seize me*" (26:55). But now the evangelist narrates that "those *who had seized Jesus* led him to Caiaphas the high priest." Obviously, no earthly force could overpower the Son until he decided to allow himself to be overpowered. However, this overpowering of God by man is no historical accident, no failure in the divine strategy. The overpowering of God by man in Jesus, scandalous as it appears to mere human logic, is but the visible, human aspect of the self-surrender out of love accomplished by the second Person of the Holy Trinity in the fullness of time, in keeping with God's eternal design of salvation and by precisely this means.

The gift of God's fullness of Life and Wisdom that inhabits Jesus of Nazareth[1] cannot be forcibly wrenched from God; it can only be graciously bestowed by him in his own time and manner through an unfathomable act of Mercy's self-surrender to us. At this point in Matthew's Gospel, we have finally arrived at that appointed time, and in this violent act of Jesus' capture, we are witnessing the manner of divine self-bestowal decreed by eternal Wisdom. If Jesus is truly the Lover of mankind, and if every lover is always longing for his beloved's embraces, we can then well understand why Jesus would yield to the violence of the crowd: in them, his loving Heart sees, not God's enemies, but his own bride-in-the-making.

Matthew now reminds us that, while the events surrounding Jesus' person were being narrated in the foreground throughout the very long chapter 26 (anointing in Bethany, betrayal by Judas, institution of the Eucharist, agony in Gethsemane), the priests and elders of Israel have been holding an intense session behind closed doors in the background, to find the final solution to their central problem: Jesus.

---

[1] "For in [Christ] the whole fullness of deity (τὸ πλήρωμα τῆς θεότητος) dwells bodily, and you have come to fullness of life in him (ἐστὲ ἐν αὐτῷ πεπληρωμένοι), who is the head of all rule and authority" (Col 2:9–10).

In v. 3 we read: "Then the chief priests and the elders of the people *gathered* in the palace of the high priest, who was called Caiaphas." This forms an inclusion with the present v. 57: "Then those who had seized Jesus led him to Caiaphas the high priest, where the scribes and the elders *had gathered*." Foreground and background now merge. These two verses, side by side, convey how dense an atmosphere of threats and impending doom fills the present moment in Jerusalem and, in particular, the life of Jesus and his disciples.

We should not be so shocked at what appears to be this sudden and radical change in Jesus' status in the sight of Israel. He appears to have fallen overnight from a great height of popularity to the depths of public rejection and scorn. But we should not forget, on the one hand, the animosity shown to Jesus from the beginning by the leaders of the people (the priests, scribes, and elders) and, on the other hand, the fickleness of the crowds' response to him: happy when being fed but otherwise indifferent or hostile. True sympathy and at least partial understanding he found only in the intimate circle of his followers, and now even they have abandoned him. Jesus' present situation is defined by both abandonment and persecution, to the point that he has been totally unmoored from all human grounding. He has become everyone's contemptible plaything, delivered into the hands of human fear, resentment, and discontent. Quite literally *all* may dispose of him as they will, the disciples to cast off and forsake him, the persecutors to jostle and shove him about.

But this flaming-out of men's destructive passions onto Jesus' person is but the extreme dramatic unfolding of the interior law that has from the outset governed the life on earth of the incarnate Word. This "law" he himself formulated with unforgettable precision early on in Matthew, in his answer to the scribe who swore he would follow Jesus wherever he went. To this man he replied sternly: "Foxes have holes, and birds of the air have nests; but the Son of man has nowhere to lay his head" (8:20). In other words, what is the natural, normal, and expected entitlement of even the least creatures on earth—namely, a place of safety and refuge of their own—precisely *that* is denied the enfleshed God! Imagine a person's condition in this world that is fashioned solely by the experience of vagrant rootlessness, dangerous exposure, anxious vulnerability, restless instability, humiliating disenfranchisement, and painful ostracism, all of it resulting in chronic

exhaustion and alienation . . . Such precisely is the existential condition of the Son of God in this world at the moment of his Passion.

In our era, we are daily becoming more aware of the rising number
of people who have been made homeless migrants and exiles, sometimes within their own country of birth. But Christians should not
forget that the most homeless of all migrants was and is Jesus Christ
himself, who willingly exiled himself from eternity into time that he
might share in our own universal denudation and exposure. Could we
not, then, affirm that "not having anywhere to lay his head" in this
world is *necessarily* the earthly condition of the incarnate God? We
may even venture to say that human desolation and utter material
and social homelessness is the perceptible earthly form that divine
Omnipotence and Omnipresence must assume if we human beings
are to perceive the foundation of God's essence as being love and
self-surrender. Jesus has no place to lay his head on earth because
the mind and will and Heart of the Word can only truly rest εἰς τὸν
κόλπον τοῦ Πατρός, "in the bosom of the Father" (Jn 1:18). This is
the deepest reason for Jesus' radical poverty: to manifest unequivocally where his sole mainstay lies. Jesus has no earthly dwelling of his
own so that he can exercise his divine omnipresence efficiently: he
must make his home in *every* home. This is also the reason why, in the
Gospel, Jesus is always passing through, *passing through*, never settling
down. Jesus cannot belong definitively in any one place because the
Word by nature belongs in *all* places.

But God's healing and nourishing Omnipresence, when it inhabits
one man of flesh and blood, the son of Mary from Nazareth, will also
necessarily *crack that being open* like a pod so that the divinity he contains can be scattered throughout creation. As Jesus sees it, to deliver
himself as a plaything into the hands of violent men as he now does is
but a providential means for the seeds of light and goodness that he,
the living Word of God, contains to be sown abroad with the greatest possible fruitfulness. The following words of the Jewish-German
visionary poet Nelly Sachs convey precisely the tenor of Jesus' soul
at this terrible juncture:

> But as for you,
> but as for you,
> how shall I nourish you?

. . .
With my downfall
shall I nourish you—[2]

The more his lonely suffering intensifies, the more his Heart becomes wholly centered on the welfare of the weak, fleeing beloved. Such is the unfathomable logic of divine omnipotence, admirably formulated in the liturgy: "O God, who manifest your almighty power above all by pardoning and showing mercy."[3]

א

26:58   ὁ δὲ Πέτρος ἠκολούθει αὐτῷ ἀπὸ μακρόθεν
        . . . ἰδεῖν τὸ τέλος

But Peter followed him at a distance
. . . to see the end

H OW VERY DIFFERENTLY Peter now follows Jesus from the way he did during the previous three years of leisurely disciple-ship! He has apparently managed to quiet his wild fears and confusion sufficiently to come out of hiding and expose himself to danger. Stealthily he gravitates back to his beloved Master, whose very life now hangs in the balance of human whim. This move of Peter's eloquently expresses, without need for words, the tragic con-flict raging in the hearts of all the disciples. Even with regard to such a

---

[2] "Aber du, / aber du, / wie nähre ich dich? / . . . / Mit meinem Untergang / nähre ich dich—". Nelly Sachs, "Mit Wildhonig", in *Fahrt ins Staublose: Gedichte* (Frankfurt am Main: Suhrkamp Verlag, 1988), 225.

[3] "Deus, qui omnipotentiam tuam parcendo maxime et miserando manifestas. . . ." Collect, 26th Sunday in Ordinary Time.

highly personal dilemma, Peter is representative of the chosen band's interior plight. It is indeed a major stroke of genius on Matthew's part as a writer that he inserts precisely at this point in his narrative this revealing episode of Peter's change of mind. He thus juxtaposes, in almost unbearable tension, the grim determination of the authorities who hold all the earthly power alongside the fearful disciples' authentic devotion to Jesus, which is like a tender shoot battered in a storm.

Such edgy apposition lends vitality to the plot of the Gospel and introduces a moving subjective dimension that strongly involves the reader. The Gospel text never imparts mere information but always intends to prompt its reader to grow in faith. And so we see Matthew here very deftly weaving bonds of empathy between the disciples' personal quandary and the reader's heart. The evangelist wants to raise the level of his readers' stakes in the drama to the same intensity as is now weighing down mightily upon Jesus and his followers. Speaking of the drama of Jesus' life as portrayed in Scripture, Hans Urs von Balthasar observes that the sacred text is intractable: it allows no one to remain an innocent bystander, merely an anonymous member of the audience. Rather, through his text, the evangelist creates a critical situation in which everyone must climb the stage and join in the action of the main players. The Gospel writer brings about in his reader a vital change of status from casual observer to deeply implicated participant, and this crucial change, which really amounts to a change of identity, imposes on the reader-participant all the anguish and constraint of existential choice already demanded of the *dramatis personæ*.

Only two verses back, Matthew recorded that all the disciples had abandoned Jesus and fled. Shockingly, no friend of Jesus was excluded from this desertion. However, now Peter's special apostolic role emerges in light of the fact that only he came back to hover near the embattled Lord. Jesus' power of attraction proves stronger for the moment than Peter's fear. We can picture Peter in mid-flight immediately after his desertion at Gethsemane, stopping suddenly to tremble and weep in the shadow of an olive tree, his soul convulsed by the vying forces of fear and love. But his burning shame at having deserted his faithful friend soon wins out over his terror for his own life—soon enough for him still to be able to catch up with the malevolent procession made up of those dragging Jesus to Caiaphas' house, the willing accessories to the crime who more or less consciously are leading the Lamb of God to the slaughter (cf. Is 53:7).

The Greek text says that Peter is indeed following Jesus but ἀπὸ μακρόθεν (*apó makróthen*), that is, "from afar", a rendering that is more incisive than "at a distance". This turn of phrase suggests that Peter is attempting to negotiate a middle course between loving ardor and piercing dread. He keeps as far away as he can from the focus of action in order to avoid being seen and identified as a disciple, while yet remaining close enough not to lose Jesus from sight. What a balancing act, revealing a soul that is simultaneously devoted and cowardly! But what Christian cannot identify often enough with precisely that predicament in the life of discipleship? Moreover, we must admire Peter for his inability to allow grievous circumstances to tear him away utterly from the love of his heart. In his own way and as best as he can within the fragility of his human nature, Peter continues to follow Jesus despite all the looming threats.

The apostle realizes clearly that the life-giving romance of following Jesus must continue at all costs, under whatever conditions— whether triumphant or devastating—in which Jesus may happen to find himself. Peter is well aware of the fact that the declared disciple is likely to share in the eventual fate of his Master. Paul, for instance, was later to confide to his disciple Timothy how Jesus' abandonment by his followers at Gethsemane was being literally replayed in his own apostolic experience. On this occasion, Paul's reaction to those betraying him is precisely that of Jesus: "At my first defense no one took my part; all deserted me. May it not be charged against them! But the Lord stood by me and gave me strength to proclaim the [message] fully, that all the Gentiles might hear it. So I was rescued from the lion's mouth" (2 Tim 4:16–17). This is how the Messiah's Paschal Mystery plays itself out in the concrete history of his disciple Paul. Other players and different geographical locations are involved, but the painful pattern remains the same: proclamation of the Gospel, painful abandonment by one's trusted intimates, followed at last by rescue from death by the powerful God who alone remains faithful. Association with Jesus plunges a person inevitably into the full pattern of Jesus' own life.

Are not the precariousness and ambiguity of Jesus' earthly fate one of the most demanding aspects of the Christian vocation as such? What will become of Jesus? And what will *therefore* become of me if I should choose to follow him? In this sense, Peter is literally living out at the moment, through a night of overwhelming fear, the generous desire we have already heard the anonymous scribe proclaim to Jesus in happier, risk-free circumstances: "Teacher, I will follow you *wherever* you go!" (8:19). Somewhere along the way, Peter must have felt an upsurge of courage. On arriving at the high priest's residence, he no longer observes things "from afar" but actually ventures inside the courtyard and even sits down with Caiaphas' "household servants". Some versions (RSV, NET, R95) here translate ὑπηρέτης as "guard", no doubt because of the context; but the word more generically means "servant". Caiaphas' courtyard was probably full of all kinds of attendants, among whom guards would also have been found, loafing about during Jesus' interrogation by the Sanhedrin. These guards, no doubt rough and ruthless mercenaries, most likely were the very men under the chief priests' hire who had gone to Gethsemane with Judas to arrest Jesus.

In any event, as he chooses to mingle with the rabble in the courtyard, Peter knows he will have to chat with them and thus risk giving away his dissenter's identity. He is a sort of spy who has infiltrated behind enemy lines. We also glimpse here the thorough ordinariness and plebeian status of Peter as we see him blend into a crowd of servants. Outwardly, nothing sets him apart from other common, working-class Jews. Only the interior stress, the gravitational pull of Jesus tugging at his heart, makes Peter different. Only the love of Jesus—the Lord's for him, his for the Lord—smoldering within his chest fills Peter with great urgency, keen desire, and a sense of purpose. However, only God can see these things bubbling up within him. Even in his own eyes, his impetuous risk-taking remains a mystery. He is clearly acting thoughtlessly, out of barely acknowledged motivations. Well might Peter now have whispered under his breath into the surrounding darkness the bride's avowal from the *Dark Night of the Soul*:

> Upon that lucky night
> In secrecy, inscrutable to sight,
> I went without discerning

And with no other light
Except for that which in my heart was burning.[4]

The only motivation Matthew's text explicitly attributes to Peter in his present endeavor is that he follows Jesus at a good distance "in order to see the end" (*télos*). Surely we can identify with Peter's state of mind at this moment, recognizing all too well the welter of questions seething in his soul. How could it all have come to this—all the enthralling words and promises and shared visions? How can Jesus be what Peter knows him to be—Truth Incarnate, God's Anointed— and still be swatted like a fly by the machinations of petty tyrants, the envy of disputatious priests?

Peter has always found repellent in the extreme any talk from Jesus concerning the necessity of the Messiah's suffering and death. We recall Peter's reaction the first time Jesus foretold the certainty of his Passion and death to the disciples: "God forbid, Lord!", he blurted out with endearing insolence. "This shall never happen to you." This astonishingly cheeky remonstrance from a disciple was routed at once by the Master's terrible rebuke: "Get behind me, Satan! You are a hindrance to me; for you are not on the side of God, but of men" (16:22–23). After that confrontation, and fruitfully schooled by such severity, Peter apparently began to "put on the mind of Christ Jesus" (cf. Phil 2:5). For, when the Lord announced a second and a third time the certainty and necessity of his impending death (17:22–23; 20:17–19), Peter at least kept silent.

Naturally, we sympathize with Peter. His instinctual reactions in the face of such dire predictions are rather typical of the human attitude toward the prospect of personal failure and demise. Peter represents all of us, at least in sharing and voicing our unspoken thoughts regarding the frequent dubiousness of God's wisdom in our eyes. How often, at unguarded moments, we viscerally start rebuking God and his ways! How quick we are to find God's judgments and designs at fault when they do not square with the expectations of our own logic and desires! However, even within this commonality with us,

---

[4] "En la noche dichosa, / En secreto, que nadie me veía, / Ni yo miraba cosa, / Sin otra luz y guía, / Sino la que en el corazón ardía." St. John of the Cross, *Noche oscura del alma*, stanza 3, trans. Roy Campbell, *The Selected Poems of Roy Campbell* (Oxford and New York: Oxford University Press, 1982), 114.

Peter is quite unlike most of us in that he does not censor himself and put on a falsely compliant countenance but, rather, has the courage to blurt out before the Lord his genuine feelings of repulsion and fear. Only such an act of honest avowal can provide the basis in our subjective truth that opens the door for grace to intervene and transform a purely human rationale by infusing into us God's vision of things.

And so Peter, "going inside [the courtyard], sat with the guards to see the end." This affirmation of the evangelist's is full of a challenging ambiguity. It communicates both a certain muted *eagerness* on Peter's part not to be altogether absent from his Master's side as Jesus' fate plays out, and, at the same time, it reveals a marked *passivity* on Peter's part. The desire "to see the end" conveys an attitude of resigned fatalism. Yes, Peter wants to share in Jesus' fate sufficiently for him not to be able to stay away from the scene of the judgment; and yet it does not seem that at this point Peter can detect any divine purpose or life-giving fruit at all in Jesus' demise in this world. Again, we must admire in Peter the abiding love of a friend who wants to remain near his teacher to the bitter end.

To defend Jesus, Peter (the most likely candidate for this action) has already tried the method of physical violence earlier in the evening, when he cut off the ear of the high-priest's servant, only to be yet again severely scolded by Jesus (26:52–54; cf. Jn 18:11). Peter now feels bereft of all sense of direction, purpose, or guiding ideology. The grim events of the evening thus far—the rebuke by the Lord, the plainly downward turn in the fate of the Twelve, the capture of Jesus—all of this has contributed to Peter's dejection. Perhaps at this point he is reduced to a groping kind of dark, interior prayer, striving to unite his heart to that of Jesus and under his breath repeating for and with Jesus the words of the Psalmist: "Give me not up to the will of my adversaries; for false witnesses have risen against me, and they breathe out violence" (Ps 27[26]:12). If such is indeed the case, perhaps then his apparent passivity is not so inert after all. Perhaps this is the moment when, caught in dire straits, Peter for the first time in his life begins to turn inward, to seek for meaning in another dimension, at a depth greater than mere socio-religious success, an attainment even of an enlightened, messianic sort.

In any event, he intends *to see the end*. "The end" in what sense? The Greek word *télos* is famously fraught with meaning. It seldom means "end" in our sense of an abrupt stop to a process or function. More richly, *télos* connotes the result of what has come before, whether in connection with a battle, a career, an endeavor, or the whole of a human life. Thus we could translate that Peter wishes to see the "fulfillment" or the "completion" or even the "consummation" of Jesus' arrest and, by implication, of Jesus' life, since by now even Peter is beginning to understand that this affair will not end well. When a human life is at stake, *télos* can be a euphemism for the culmination of that life, that is, the person's *death*. The Greeks, however, always searching for hidden causes, never looked on human death as simply a biological fact—the cessation of existence—but, rather, saw it as the sublime or wretched culmination of a whole lifetime on the stage of the world. Solon's quip to King Crœsus, reported by Herodotus, sums up the Greek outlook nicely: "Call no man happy until he is dead."[5]

It seems, then, that Peter is vitally interested in witnessing what will happen to Jesus, what will be the final word on his life and person. The twin driving forces behind his dogged desire "to see" are, on the one hand, his deep affection for his Master and, on the other, his exasperating inability to harmonize the ignominy of Jesus' looming "end" with his intimate knowledge of him as Teacher of the Truth and as "the Christ, the Son of the living God" (16:16), which he himself has proclaimed him to be. How can the Truth embodied in God's Anointed be crushed and banished from the earth, along with his Person, by the indecent plots of self-righteous bigots and measly, power-grabbing functionaries? Much later, after the Resurrection, when the time of Peter's own arrest and persecution for the sake of Jesus has arrived, Peter will at last be able to refer to the events of Jesus' Passion as a necessary part of the pattern of God's saving design. Only then, in retrospect, and strengthened by the power and wisdom communicated to him by Christ's Resurrection, will Peter be able to pray with John, saying:

> Sovereign Lord. . . . "The kings of the earth set themselves in array, and the rulers were gathered together, against the Lord and against his Anointed"—for truly in this city [of Jerusalem] there were gathered together against your holy servant Jesus, whom you anointed,

[5] Herodotus, *The Histories*, I, 32.

both Herod and Pontius Pilate, with the Gentiles and the peoples of Israel, to do whatever your hand and your plan had predestined to take place. And now, Lord, look upon their threats, and grant to your servants to speak your word with all boldness. (Acts 4:24, 26–29)

But Peter could only reach this broad and deep perspective of faith by going first in his flesh through the tormenting experience of the absolute night of his Lord's Passion, when his only certainty is "the flame which in my heart was burning". It is this night of fearful confusion and disorientation that begins to void him of his vanity and to meld his soul to Christ's in the fire of suffering.

א

26:59–60a   Οἱ δὲ ἀρχιερεῖς καὶ τὸ συνέδριον ὅλον
ἐζήτουν ψευδομαρτυρίαν κατὰ τοῦ Ἰησοῦ
ὅπως αὐτὸν θανατώσωσιν
καὶ οὐχ εὗρον
πολλῶν προσελθόντων ψευδομαρτύρων

Now the chief priests and the whole council
sought false testimony against Jesus
that they might put him to death
but they found none,
though many false witnesses came forward

C AIAPHAS MUST BE hosting quite a large gathering because we are told that "the whole council" is gathered together at his residence. In its totality this "council", or *Sanhedrin*, the ruling tribunal of Jewish authorities, consisted of seventy-one members according to the Talmud: scribes, elders, prominent members of high-priestly families, and the high priest of the year, who acted as president of the council. The Roman rulers of Judæa granted this body the authority to try the more important cases within the people of Israel. However, in the event that a death sentence is imposed, it has to be validated by the Roman procurator for it to be executed.

Sanhedrin is a curious word, not really Semitic at all. It is, in fact, an Aramaization of the Greek word *synédrion*, meaning "a place where people sit together". In the Hellenistic context, *synédrion* referred to a body of men assembled in council, especially the Roman senate. The word invites us to visualize the present scene at Caiaphas' house. See the dense group of seventy-one religious worthies *sitting* in a circle, with Jesus *standing* alone in the middle. This dramatic visual contrast between the collectively sitting authorities and the solitary, standing Jesus may be the most important symbolic element in the scene: the collectivity amassed against the individual. The self-satisfied and entitled take their ease, while the accused is harassed, deprived of the barest courtesy, in a choreography intended to push him physically and psychologically to the limits of human endurance. Authority is made to weigh down ruthlessly upon the one who has struck a mighty note of dissonance in an already destabilized society. The ritual positioning of bodies at the trial already has a built-in element of humiliation and ostracism.

Not only his judges but everyone on the scene, except Jesus, is sitting. Matthew repeatedly drives home the symbolic point. In v. 58 we have just read that Peter entered the courtyard of the high-priest and "sat with the guards". That is Peter's way of blending in with the crowd. He joins the crowd of hirelings who are whiling away the boring hours of the night, kept from their beds by this nocturnal trial. We recall as well that, at the scene of his capture at Gethsemane, Jesus reminded his assailants that "day after day *I sat in the temple teaching*, and you did not seize me" (26:55). Indeed, a sitting position has often been used in the Gospel to underscore a particularly solemn moment in the life of the Messiah as Teacher and Lord. At the beginning of the Sermon on the Mount, for instance, we read: "Seeing the crowds, [Jesus] went up on the mountain, and *when he sat down* his disciples came to him. And he opened his mouth and taught them" (5:1–2); then at once he proclaims the Beatitudes. We remember as well that, as he entered Jerusalem triumphantly on Palm Sunday, Jesus *was sitting on* a colt (21:7). He received the adoration of the woman at Bethany as he *sat at table* (26:7). And, in his parable of the Last Judgment, Jesus portrays himself as *sitting on* a throne of glory (25:31). There are many other examples of the symbolism of sitting in the Gospel.

Thus, Jesus' present *standing position* before the sitting members of the Sanhedrin represents his drastic loss of status at the beginning of his Passion. In the public eye, he has fallen from the figure of a revered teacher, in whose words many delight, to the contemptible category of dangerous insurrectionist and blasphemer who is scorned and feared by all. Jesus has fallen below even the social status of the mob of servants out in the courtyard: they are all sitting, after all, with Peter among them. The Master has now fallen below the rank of the disciple precisely as at the Last Supper, when Jesus girt himself like a slave and fell to the floor to wash his sitting disciples' feet, as if *they* were his masters (cf. Jn 13:3–17). While the whole world sits, the Creator stands. While the whole world rests and judges, or merely slouches in bored irritation, the Savior labors strenuously at redemption. "Foxes have holes, but the Son of man. . . ."

Jesus' judges make him stand, intending thus to humiliate and subjugate him. But is it not objectively fitting that a person who never ceases laboring should remain tirelessly erect? In fact, except for the times when, spent, he falls to the ground on his way to Golgotha, Jesus will observe an upright position until at length he slumps into death. Only then will he take his rest, his labor accomplished. And, with a deep irony, Jesus standing there in the courtyard in degrading isolation, in the midst of the elders of Israel, also makes him to be the very center of the scene, the one on whom all eyes are focused, the one whom all seek with a vital ardor, whether with good or malicious intent.

This magnetic pull that the tormented Jesus nonetheless exerts on everyone around him on this fateful night is but the negative, earthly image of what the divine Word already is in his eternal glory: namely, the One in whom and for whom "all things were created, in heaven and on earth", the One who "is before all things, and in [whom] all things hold together" (Col 1:16–17). The obsessive fixation on the person of Jesus by the members of the Sanhedrin is the perverted version of the angels' continual attendance upon him in the heavens (cf. Jn 1:51). Jesus' beauty and power of enthrallment are such that it is impossible not to gaze on him, out of either love or hatred. Even the Devil cannot ignore God; his very rebellion against the divine order is an act of thwarted love.

Our scene at Caiaphas' house represents the humiliation of the incarnate Word at the hands of men, the attempt by poor sinners to silence his wisdom once and for all, and the beginning of the fulfillment of his own prophecy that he would triumph over death as such only by means of his own death. It is as if the Sanhedrin were, despite themselves, working very hard at constructing the very setting of Jesus' eventual apotheosis as seen by the seer of Patmos: "Between the throne and the four living creatures and among the elders, *I saw a Lamb standing, as though it had been slain*, . . . and the four living creatures and the twenty-four elders fell down before the Lamb" (Rev 5:6, 8). Whether seen through the eyes of detestation or of adoring love, it is the same Jesus in both instances, both humiliated and glorified. The divine creativity is infinite.

Now, the religious leaders of Israel want to observe the letter of their Law and the prescribed form for a trial. And so they must find witnesses against Jesus. As religious authorities, they must guarantee at least the appearance, if not the substance, of justice. The so-called trial, however, is obviously a farce because the judges have already settled on a death sentence as the best thing for the nation in its present situation of oppression under Roman rule. The text paints the priests and elders as thoroughly corrupt politicians who could care less about the objective guilt or innocence of their prisoner than about the continuance of their religious, juridical, and political power. The *first* item on the priests' agenda is to decide on the verdict they wish to impose on Jesus. This has clearly been the subject of all the behind-the-scenes strategizing we have perceived since the beginning of chapter 26: "Then the chief priests and the elders of the people gathered . . . and took counsel together in order to arrest Jesus by stealth and kill him" (26:3–4).

The conspiracy of hate has been seething all along in the background while Jesus was anointed in Bethany, while he was giving his body and blood for the life of all, while he was suffering his agony of forsakenness at Gethsemane. At the very same time that the religious experts (that is, those vowed to divine truth and justice) were insidiously crafting Jesus' demise, he was laboring for their enlightenment and salvation. Only once they have settled on their strategy of destruction do the members of the Sanhedrin go about finding the witnesses necessary to make it happen. Therefore, they must perforce search for false testimony against Jesus that they might put him to death. Is this not typical of our human skill for indulging our basest passions while at the same time concealing our real motivations and projecting a benign public image of uprightness?

Truth himself, obviously, can be found guilty and condemned only by means of lies and fabrications. For Wisdom to have made himself so vulnerable was a necessary consequence of the Incarnation. The members of the Sanhedrin are used to judging, not to being judged, even in the event that God should appear before them in person. But, at a deeper level, Jesus' mere presence judges all around him despite all their strategizing, judges them silently by the moral power of his sheer goodness, truthfulness, and utter lack of prejudice. Jesus will not be coopted by any human self-interest group, even that of the rulers of Israel. Therefore, he must be destroyed, and no human weapon is more destructive of justice than legal lies.

The Gospel phrase describing this state of affairs is a little awkward. It says that they "sought false testimony (ψευδομαρτυρία) against Jesus . . . but they found none, though many false witnesses (ψευδομαρτύρων) came forward". Matthew emphasizes the atmosphere of mendacity permeating the Sanhedrin's proceedings by repeating the prefix *pseudo-*: here it not only means "false" in the generic sense of "inauthentic" but also refers to acts of deliberate lying, as in "lying testimony", "lying witnesses". We are speaking of the shameless promotion of perjury by the very guardians of Israel's sacred, God-given Torah. We note as well the simultaneous abundance of lying witnesses coming forward alongside the scarcity of contrived testimony that could be publicly dressed up as the truth about Jesus' guilt. What must the quality and credibility of those scrounged-up witnesses have been when even the eager elders of the people, highly skilled in machinations, found their testimony frustratingly unusable? If the Pharisees insisted on anything, surely it was on correctness of form! They wanted the death sentence at all costs, but a death sentence that would readily receive the required approbation of the Roman procurator. Therefore, the capital charge had to be presented to him through testimony and evidence that were at least theoretically tenable and consistent in their argumentation.

Wordlings will always prefer pleasing smoothness of form over a disturbing, substantial content. The intensely critical scene and the

Sanhedrin's scandalously pragmatic choices mirror back to us as well a judgment on our own mode of presence before the accused Christ. How easily we, too, can move on impulse to kill an emerging truth that threatens the stability of our fastidious life! How swiftly we can abandon a friend or an ally who has fallen on hard social or financial times because of his unswerving moral convictions and his commitment to justice! How automatically, in other words, we can fall into a shameless survival mode and throw to the wind all honorable pledges made in sunny moments of ease . . . With what consummate skill our tongue-darting, reptilian brain pounces to devour the Holy Spirit of God in midflight within us!

26:60b–61   ὕστερον δὲ προσελθόντες δύο εἶπαν·
οὗτος ἔφη·
Δύναμαι καταλῦσαι τὸν ναὸν τοῦ Θεοῦ
καὶ διὰ τριῶν ἡμερῶν οἰκοδομῆσαι

*At last two came forward and said,
"This fellow said,
'I am able to destroy the temple of God,
and to build it in three days' "*

TWO WITNESSES AGREEING ON a serious charge against Jesus are all that are needed to make the guilty verdict stick. Deuteronomy legislates: "A single witness shall not prevail against a man for any crime or for any wrong in connection with any offense that he has committed; only on the evidence of two witnesses, or of three witnesses, shall a charge be sustained" (Deut 19:15). With these two witnesses coming forward to testify against Jesus, the Sanhedrin can just barely fulfill the letter of the Law even though obviously *three* witnesses would have added more substance to the charge. Significantly, the text stresses the time and effort it took to concoct a serious charge credibly: "[They] sought false testimony against Jesus, . . . but they found none. . . . *At last* two came forward." The truth is diaphanous and surfaces with ease; it is the imposition of a *credible lie* that requires a great labor of fabrication and persuasion.

And the charge the two witnesses bring is a curious one: "This fellow said, 'I am able to destroy the temple of God, and to build it in three days.'" Nothing here concerning the forgiveness of sins or the breaking of the Sabbath, which are the two standard charges repeatedly brought against Jesus. The accusation, rather, involves two enormities: first, the blasphemy that would be incurred by anyone even *thinking* of destroying the holy temple, God's dwelling place on earth and the center of Jewish worship, much less claiming to be able to do it; and, secondly, the titanic claim to possessing superpowers, that is, the ability to reconstruct single-handedly in *three days* something that took more than *forty years* and countless laborers to build. It is interesting that the only other reference to the destruction of the temple in Matthew occurs at the Cross, when passersby jeer at Jesus in connection with this very charge (27:40).

However, the charge must have its source in a real saying of Jesus, although in its present form as a trumped-up accusation it is plainly preposterous. Rumored sayings, especially mysterious ones, have a way of becoming automatically adjusted to the mental capacity and world view of the rumormonger. What Jesus actually said on this topic, as reported only by John, is: "Destroy this temple, and in three days I will raise it up." The context for this statement by Jesus was his expulsion of the merchants from the temple, and it was uttered as a response to the question by the authorities: "What sign have you to show us for doing this?" After Jesus' mystifying reply, they asked him a second question: "It has taken forty-six years to build this temple, and will you raise it up in three days?" Jesus did not answer this question; the evangelist instead inserts this crucial exegetical comment: "But he spoke of the temple of his body. When therefore he was raised from the dead, his disciples remembered that he had said this; and they believed the Scripture and the word which Jesus had spoken" (Jn 2:18–22). We can clearly see, then, that Jesus' original meaning in speaking about the destruction of the temple must now be twisted to mean the opposite of what he intended; only thus could it be turned into a charge of blasphemy against him. We see plainly, however, that the Word knowingly and necessarily exposed himself to such lethal misunderstanding and venomous garbling of meaning when speaking human words into prejudiced human ears. He knew that by so doing he was putting his life at risk, hoping that in this way he might win at least some listeners over to the truth.

The first disfigurement of Jesus' meaning is changing the expression "Destroy this temple" (obviously meaning "If you or someone were to destroy this temple") to "This fellow said, 'I am able to destroy the temple of God.'" Jesus had been asked for a sign by the Jews to justify his authoritative action of driving out the merchants from the temple, and he replied with a vivid conjecture referring to the temple. The rumor feeding the false witnesses' testimony, moreover, has now transformed Jesus himself into the boastful wrecker of the temple, and the possessor of superhuman powers to boot: "I am able to destroy the temple of God, and to build it in three days." Now this is no longer a conjecture, or even a statement taken out of context, but rather an emphatic, arrogant, and barely veiled *threat*. This formulation would make Jesus boast of being practically more powerful than God since it says he can destroy at will the very heart of Judaism, God's abode of choice among his people.

Such a perception of Jesus and his teaching could, in fact, be seen to symbolize rather accurately the manner in which the leading members of the Sanhedrin understood him: as a wrecker of the heart of Israel and its faith. But here lies precisely the tragic essence of the double confrontation between Jesus-Messiah and the contemporary rulers of Israel: whereas Jesus was always speaking at the spiritual and eternal level of reality, they were always fixated on the material and socio-political aspects of religious practice; and, whereas they were searching for a Messiah who would be a God-sent savior in the militaristic and this-worldly image of Old Testament heroes like Joshua, Saul, and David, Jesus came as a Victim-Messiah, ready to lay down his own life for the ransom of many.

Hence the importance of the evangelist's annotation: "But he spoke of the temple of his body", and of the interpretation of Jesus' statement "Destroy this temple" as practically an invitation by Jesus for his adversaries to come and take hold of him for their purposes, since his Father had decreed that he should deliver himself into the hands of men. This is why in Jesus' words in John, which we can consider the "original" form of the temple statement in question, there is no talk at all of a humanly self-willed and boastful "building" or "constructing" (οἰκοδομῆσαι) of the temple, but rather of "raising up" (ἐγερῶ) or "being raised up" (ἠγέρθη) by the power of God in the promised Resurrection.

Hidden in terribly disfigured form, then, deep within the maliciously concocted accusation of the lying witnesses against Jesus, we may indeed find the truth of the Paschal Mystery. Such intentional or unintentional disfigurement (by the vagaries of gossip or the malice of hatred) of the message of salvation embodied in Jesus' messiahship may be seen to be the social, juridical, and literary equivalent of the physical and personal disfigurement of the Suffering Servant in Isaiah (53:2) and of the face and whole body of Jesus in the Passion, a drama that fulfills and exceeds Isaiah's prophecies concerning the brutal humiliation and mangling of the Messiah in both body and soul. We begin by cagily disfiguring a person's *words*, and we end by literally mangling the entire *person*—face, hands, feet, and heart.

26:62–63a   καὶ ἀναστὰς ὁ ἀρχιερεὺς εἶπεν αὐτῷ·
                    Οὐδὲν ἀποκρίνῃ;
                    τί οὗτοί σου καταμαρτυροῦσιν;
                    ὁ δὲ Ἰησοῦς ἐσιώπα

And the high priest stood up and said to him,
"Have you no answer to make?
What is it that these men testify against you?"
But Jesus was silent.

T HE HIGH PRIEST STANDS UP TO express his outrage at Jesus' alleged declaration about his ability to destroy and rebuild the temple. The testimony of the lying witnesses is made more striking by the fact that the words they attribute to Jesus are relayed by them in direct quotation rather than in the third person. This clever technique adds vividness to their evidence because it is as if the whole Sanhedrin had now heard Jesus make his blasphemous boast with their own ears. Direct quotation heightens the drama; it adds body to the accusation and heats up the atmosphere. It is not difficult to imagine certain members of the priestly caste rehearsing these witnesses in private ahead of time on how to present their testimony in public most efficaciously. They seem to be reciting a speech learned by heart. And the high priest's split-second reaction, too, appears mechanical, canned.

From the outset, in fact, the trial unfolds as a performance that has been carefully choreographed and scripted. Such detailed planning must have been an important aspect of the *symboulê*, the long sessions of deliberation during which the priests and elders have labored so conscientiously at Caiaphas' palace as they brainstormed to determine how best "to arrest Jesus by stealth and kill him" (26:4). The resulting plan is shrewd and effective, but any alert observer would note that it proceeds too much like clockwork, exhibiting all the stiffness of a minutely orchestrated plot.

Right on cue, without missing a beat after the two witnesses' one-sentence accusation, the irate Caiaphas rises and, without giving Jesus any time even to consider the charge, hurls at him the question: "Have you no answer to make?" The presider of the Sanhedrin moves so fast with his interrogation that it is obvious he does not really *want* an answer! Clearly Caiaphas is well-acquainted with the accusation, since he probably fabricated it himself. Strategically, however, he ought to have paused a little, with a shocked expression of pious incomprehension on his face, rather than lunging at once into the accused. And he insists without any pause, at once firing a second question that is a rewording the first: "What is it that these men testify against you?" The self-righteous anger in his voice, together with his jumpy impatience and manifest loathing for Jesus, are mounting to a pitch of hysteria that will soon reach its paroxysm. The rapid-fire drilling is meant to destabilize Jesus, perhaps even to lure him into engaging in an argument or self-justifying dispute.

"But Jesus was silent", the evangelist notes. What a contrast between the anxious Caiaphas' jitteriness and bullying and this silence of the incarnate Word, which seems to create a luminous zone of transparency at the heart of discord and dissimulation! A non-engaging silence in fact may well be the only worthy manner of responding to conspiracies, lies, and threats. Jesus does not take the bait either to refute his adversaries or to defend himself, for he has nothing to prove or disprove. Jesus simply continues to do at this moment what he came into the world to do: offer himself as he is and as what he is. While the elders make much noise endlessly arguing and strategizing, Jesus effortlessly assumes in their midst the mode of unassailable Sovereign Presence, the silent mode of I AM WHO AM, the unfathomable Creator and Redeemer of Israel who reveals the undying Fire of his Mercy only through the consuming fire of his Passion. At this moment, Jesus embodies more than ever the Lamb of God, "that before its shearers is silent, so he opened not his mouth" (Is 53:7). Such transcendental silence, wholly unexpected by men at this juncture, is both sublime (as befits the ineffable God) and sorrowful (as befits a sacrificial victim).

We have already noted how, after the agony at Gethsemane, Jesus utters fewer and fewer words, and we saw how this progressive muteness on the part of the Eternal Word coincides with his more fully *embodying*—as opposed to *signifying*—God's long-suffering love. He no longer discourses on God's mercy; rather, he visibly *becomes* God's Mercy by delivering himself into the hands of men; and his physical silence becomes the strongest possible pointer to his status as expiatory Victim, the enfleshed God now living in this world the experience of the Psalmist: "Malicious witnesses rise up; they ask me of things that I do not know" (Ps 35[34]:11). God is innocent of all lies, and therefore he is incapable of responding to lies with human words.

As for Peter, sitting with the rabble out in the courtyard at this very moment: perhaps he has caught enough of a glimpse of the proceedings against Jesus before the Sanhedrin to be able to recall vividly later on, in his First Letter, his Lord's total equanimity in the face of Caiaphas' rage: "When he was reviled, he did not revile in return; when he suffered, he did not threaten; but he trusted to him who judges justly" (1 Pet 2:23). Jesus' silence before Caiaphas has nothing to do with indifference, defiance, haughtiness, or trembling fear. Jesus' silence, on the contrary, most eloquently proclaims the truth that he obeys only God his Father and that the treasure of God's love he has come to lavish on the world cannot be obstructed by even the most dire human threats.

26:63bc–64a   καὶ ὁ ἀρχιερεὺς εἶπεν αὐτῷ·
Ἐξορκίζω σε κατὰ τοῦ Θεοῦ τοῦ ζῶντος
ἵνα ἡμῖν εἴπῃς εἰ σὺ εἶ ὁ Χριστὸς ὁ υἱὸς τοῦ Θεοῦ.
λέγει αὐτῷ ὁ Ἰησοῦς· Σὺ εἶπας

And the high priest said to him,
"I adjure you by the living God,
tell us if you are the Christ, the Son of God."
Jesus said to him, "You have said [so]"

FULMINATION IS A MODE OF EXPRESSION that comes easily to Caiaphas, as is frequent with self-important people unused to being opposed. After riddling Jesus with questions and pausing for breath only in the face of Jesus' silence, the high priest now unleashes power of a higher order. From his exalted status as high priest, Caiaphas solemnly invokes the Name of God to "adjure" Jesus to reveal his innermost identity. "To adjure" someone is to order the person authoritatively to disclose information he is supposed to possess. The setting before the Sanhedrin, the person of the high priest doing the adjuring, and the invocation of the Name of "the living God" all combine to invest supreme rhetorical transcendence on this moment. Caiaphas leans on the vagrant rabbi Jesus with all the crushing moral might a high priest can summon, in order finally to entrap Jesus in a corner from which he cannot escape while being true to himself.

As is always the case with heroes of the spirit, Jesus' very virtue—his simple truthfulness, his loyalty to his Father and to his mission, his inability to "strategize", that is, to pretend to be other than who he is—is going to prove his undoing. "I adjure you by the living God, tell us if you are the Christ, the Son of God": This wording of Caiaphas' question strongly evokes the critical dialogue between Jesus and Peter at Cæsarea Philippi: "[Jesus] said to them, 'But who do you say that I am?' Simon Peter replied, 'You are the Christ, *the Son of the living God*.' And Jesus answered him, 'Blessed are you, Simon Bar Jona! For flesh and blood has not revealed this to you, but my Father who is in heaven'" (16:15–17). Moreover, the alluring jeer in the high priest's tone also evokes another terrible exchange early in Jesus' public life: "And the tempter came and said to him, 'If you are *the Son of God*, command these stones to become loaves of bread'" (4:3).

How vastly different the phrase *You are the Son of God* sounds in the mouth of St. Peter, on the one hand, and in the mouths of Caiaphas and of the Tempter, on the other, who introduce it with the leering particle *if*! And how quickly the beatitude that Jesus uttered over Peter, in recognition of the truthfulness of his confession of faith, would turn to the severest of rebukes when Peter rejected the necessity of the Passion! Issues of the greatest magnitude seem to hinge for everyone involved upon the factual truth of Jesus' innermost identity. At the time of his confession, Peter, no more than Caiaphas or Satan himself, could comprehend, much less accept, the compatibility and mysterious kinship intimately binding Jesus' divine identity as Son of God to his Passion and death. This context puts us in a better position to appreciate the dramatic centrality of Caiaphas' question as he viciously demands an unequivocal answer from Jesus. The question, in fact, resumes at this point the whole spiritual landscape of the Gospel. The whole meaning of the Gospel may be opened with the key of the expression "Son of God" and the different ways in which it is used.

Already at the very beginning of the Gospel, the evangelist quotes Isaiah's prophecy (Is 7:14) to proclaim the fact that the Son of the Virgin Mary shall be "Emmanuel", *God-with-us*. At the baptism and the Transfiguration, the very voice of God the Father in person resounds from the heavens, declaring Jesus—both times in identical language—to be "*my beloved Son, with whom I am well pleased*" (3:17; 17:5). By extreme contrast, we next hear the two Gadarene demoniacs crying out to Jesus in anguish: "What have you to do with us, *O Son of God*? Have you come here to torment us before the time?" (8:29). Finally, after Jesus saves Peter from drowning and calms the storm, "those in the boat worshiped him, saying, 'Truly *you are the Son of God*'" (14:33).

Jesus' dynamic presence and deepest identity is a sort of radioactive power galvanizing all spirits, whether to declarations of salvation and love and to acts of pleading and adoration or to anguished, cowering, and spiteful rejection. The resplendent presence of Jesus of Nazareth at the Jordan and on Tabor even opens the heavens and calls forth the Father's testimony. Thus we clearly see that both the gloomy valleys of the denial of Jesus' identity as Son of God and the sun-drenched peaks of its proclamation, together, determine the spiritual geography of the Gospel. According to Matthew, the search for salvation and its finding are quite evidently tantamount to the quest for Jesus' divine sonship, followed by either embracing or rejecting it. In either case, a transcendental, life-changing event occurs.

Now the fulminating Caiaphas does not appear the least bit interested in the objective truth of whether or not Jesus is the Son of God. In fact, he does not at all ask a proper question of Jesus but, rather, shoots a wrathful command at him, seeking in Satanic fashion to entrap him. It is clear that he *wants* Jesus to affirm that he is the Son of God. Similarly Herod sought out the Messiah and commanded the Magi to "go and search diligently for the child, and when you have found him bring me word, that I too may come and worship him" (2:8). Worship was obviously the last thing on either Herod's or Caiaphas' mind when assiduously seeking out Jesus' identity! What they both sought, rather, was Jesus' destruction, and they sought it with such vehemence and careful strategy *precisely because he was the*

Son of God and not despite the fact. No one but the authentic Son of God can occasion so much difficulty, so much upheaval, in the life of one who refuses to become integrated into God's plan of salvation for the world. Rejected or ignored, the presence of Christ in human life necessarily becomes the most unbearable thorn in the flesh, to be gotten rid of at any price.

When Caiaphas then screams at Jesus, demanding an answer and putting the desired words of the answer into Jesus' mouth, by a supreme poetic reversal Jesus replies ever so quietly, uttering, in the Greek, three simple syllables: Σὺ εἶπας (*Sy eípas*)—"You've said it", or better, "It is you who have said it." While Caiaphas wants definitions and avowals (no doubt because he has a trial to win), Jesus prefers simply being, quietly doing, enacting his identity rather than boastfully proclaiming or defining it (no doubt because he, for his part, has a world to save). However, once Caiaphas has uttered the true words, the human words that factually refer to Jesus' ontological reality, Jesus has no choice but to break his silence and affirm the correctness of the title Caiaphas has attributed to him. Caiaphas, then, has successfully caught Jesus in his trap.

The incarnate Word is innocent, incapable of returning deceit and manipulation in kind. Jesus can only agree with a truth that has been stated even though he knows that that truth is the most lethal weapon that can be used against him. Jesus' identity as Son of God, which means salvation and life for everyone else, elicits abhorrence, vengeance, and destruction for Jesus himself. Upon Jesus people can freely discharge their hatred for God and God's ways. But Jesus has made himself so much one of us—so common, so ordinary, so near us—that those who unload their detestation for God on this Poor Man while also entertaining visions of a majestic God high in the heavens can do so with apparent impunity and continue to consider themselves devout, God-fearing believers. The Sanhedrin consisted, after all, of Israel's highest religious authorities. This makes it a mirror of the clerical vices of all ages, of the crimes of the ministers of any religion who pervert their priestly grace into a tyranny of self-indulgence and transmute select shepherds into smiling wolves.

א

26:64bc
πλὴν λέγω ὑμῖν·
ἀπ' ἄρτι ὄψεσθε τὸν υἱὸν τοῦ ἀνθρώπου
καθήμενον ἐκ δεξιῶν τῆς Δυνάμεως
καὶ ἐρχόμενον ἐπὶ τῶν νεφελῶν τοῦ οὐρανοῦ

But I tell you,
hereafter you will see the Son of man
seated at the right hand of the Power,
and coming on the clouds of heaven

TO CAIAPHAS, JESUS REPLIED VERY BRIEFLY, after a long silence, in the singular form (*Thou [su], hast said it*), indicating a certain degree of one-on-one intensity and probably staring sharply into the high priest's eyes. At once, however, Jesus turns to the whole Sanhedrin, addressing its members in the plural ("But I tell you [all, ὑμῖν], hereafter you [all] will see [ὄψεσθε] . . ."). Significantly, Jesus in no way rebukes or even scolds Caiaphas. He breaks his silence only in order to confirm the truth of what Caiaphas himself has just stated.

But Jesus' accompanying glance into Caiaphas' eyes, made all the more penetrating precisely for emerging out of a deep silence, must have conveyed to Caiaphas something like the following queries: "How can you mouth even hypothetically the possibility of my being the Son of God and at the same time allow yourself to be swept away by such a torrent of anger and loathing toward me? How can you not stop and seriously reflect? How can you skate all over this question with such political deftness, using it and me merely as a jumping board to your own ulterior motives? Do you not value your own soul at all or spare even a passing glance to the weight of God's designs?" In Caiaphas, this supreme aggressor, the Son of God can see nothing but one more soul to be saved.

The manner in which Caiaphas wields the phrase *the Son of God* against Jesus so contemptuously, as an accusing weapon, shows the vast difference between a theology based on abstract definitions and a lived theology that is identical with communing in the Being of God with one's total human reality, a theology that labors "on its knees". This is why Jesus never says explicitly "I am the Son of God." Even in his reply to Caiaphas, he avoids repeating the phrase. He simply affirms, "You have said so." Again, Jesus does not want to *point to God*; all the saints before him have done that. He does not even want to *speak for God*; all the prophets before him have done it. Jesus wants *to show God, to embody God* in his person and history. And he wants to show and embody God in his person and history in such a way that the witnesses of that showing and embodying will not be able to avoid entering into the dynamics of the divine drama being played out on earth, invitingly, right before their eyes.

Therefore, Jesus never uses the definitional language of abstract theology, which can be both alienating and arrogant; its user, riding the gleeful wave of smug hyper-definition, could then presume possession of the whole truth. Such language is often perceived as defiant, as a weapon begging to be hurled back at its source. This is why Jesus' accusers at the trial have to reduce the whole rich import of his multi-faceted ministry, preaching, and miracles to the one damning formulation, "Tell us if you are the Christ, the Son of God." Jesus' widely attested goodness, wisdom, and patiently abiding presence among the people amount to nothing now, in the face of the razor-sharp theological reduction by the doctors of the Law. They know you must first demonize what you intend to damn and destroy, and the most efficient method of demonizing is the theological reduction because it carries the supreme penalty of blasphemy. The objective content of the theological reduction in this case, "Tell us if you are the Christ, the Son of God", is of course perfectly true from the evangelist Matthew's viewpoint; but, in the absence of all context and when used as a means to corner the accused and expose his guilt, objective theological truth is here transformed into an efficient subjective weapon for juridical assault.

The self-proclaimed intimate of the gods usually turns out to be either a madman or a deceptive charlatan. Jesus, by contrast, rather than present himself blatantly as "the Son of God", quite naturally chooses to live the life of the Son of God unassumingly among men and let that existence and praxis speak for themselves. This means that the revelation of his divine sonship occurs gradually and indirectly throughout the Gospel, as when partial beams of light from a hidden source are deflected obliquely around objects. In linguistic terms, the insistent leitmotif in the Gospel of Matthew that is a vehicle for the revelation of Jesus as true Son of God is Jesus' striking use of the expression *my Father* in every imaginable context.

The phrase *my Father* occurs in Matthew no fewer than fourteen times, distributed rather evenly from the beginning to the conclusion of his Gospel. It flares up when least expected and casts a transforming light on the rest of the text around it. The most important feature of the two-word phrase, both as a speech-act and as a theological datum, is the fact that Jesus always utters it in relation to *communion with God*—either as a dynamic revealer of his own ongoing communion with his Father or as a gauge of human dysfunctionality in our own relationship with God. Because it is Jesus speaking the words *my Father*, an immediate triangulation is created by that utterance, with Jesus as mediator between God and the people who hear him utter the phrase.

Let us recall some of the passages where our phrase occurs, paying particular attention to the concrete existential setting surrounding Jesus' use of it. In chapter 10, as part of his instruction that his disciples should "not fear those who kill the body but cannot kill the soul", Jesus declares: "Whoever denies me before men, I also will deny before *my Father* who is in heaven" (10:28, 33). Then in chapter 11, we eavesdrop as Jesus addresses his Father in a sublime prayer, which a great exegete[6] has called "Matthew's most precious pearl". Here Jesus affirms God's paternity of himself, Jesus of Nazareth, human Son of Mary, no fewer than five times in one crucial passage, once with the possessive adjective and four times without it:

> I thank you, *Father*, Lord of heaven and earth, that you have hidden these things from the wise and understanding and revealed them to infants; yes, *Father*, for such was your gracious will. All things have been delivered to me by *my Father*; and no one knows the Son except *the Father*, and no one knows *the Father* except the Son. (11:25–27)

This extraordinary prayer reveals a great deal of inner-trinitarian life and proclaims the fact that only those who are as childlike as the eternal Son will have access to the communion of reciprocal knowledge and love that constitutes the divine life. This passage is the most explicit and substantial portrayal of the triangulation we spoke of: the Son, the Father, and the "infants".

---

[6] Père Marie-Joseph Lagrange, O.P. (1855–1938), founder of the École Biblique of Jerusalem.

But the rhythm of Jesus' references to God as his Father does not cease here. In chapter 12, we hear: "Whoever does the will of *my Father* in heaven is my brother, and sister, and mother" (12:50). Then, when Peter proclaims him to be "the Son of the living God" in chapter 16, Jesus replies: "Flesh and blood has not revealed this to you, but *my Father* who is in heaven" (16:17). Referring to little children, Jesus affirms in chapter 18: "In heaven their angels always behold the face of *my Father* who is in heaven" (18:10). In the parable of the Last Judgment in chapter 25, Jesus portrays himself as the King who says, "to those at his right hand, 'Come, O blessed of *my Father*, inherit the kingdom prepared for you from the foundation of the world'" (25:34). Finally, we recall the three times Jesus refers to his Father during his agony at Gethsemane in chapter 26, twice in direct prayer and once speaking to the rabble: "Going a little farther he fell on his face and prayed, '*My Father*, if it be possible, let this chalice pass from me; nevertheless, not as I will, but as you will'" (26:39). "Again, for the second time, he went away and prayed, '*My Father*, if this cannot pass unless I drink it, your will be done'" (26:42). And: "Do you think that I cannot appeal to *my Father*, and he will at once send me more than twelve legions of angels?" (26:53).

From all of these texts taken together, it should be clear that Jesus' intent always and everywhere is not by any means to call attention to himself by a shrill proclamation of his privileges and titles, as a special being set apart by God and offering himself for worldly idolization. This is precisely what one would gather he has done, judging only from Caiaphas' accusation. Ironically enough, the high priest seems incapable of conceiving the divine identity in any but the crassest worldly terms. Rather, throughout the Gospel, *Jesus enacts the dynamic meaning of his divine sonship* by linking confession of faith on earth to heavenly recognition of kinship with him; by inviting sinful disciples to enter into his intimate dialogue with his Father as sole source of truth and life, whether in the joy of thanksgiving or in an agony of suffering; and by prophetically anticipating his return as King and Judge in divine glory.

Now at the trial, Caiaphas and the Sanhedrin are wholly concentrating on achieving a definitive victory over this dangerous insurrectionist, Jesus of Nazareth, and their strategy has been to attack him with a truth that is the abstract, diabolical reduction of

Jesus' true identity as Son of God. There is great poetic irony in the contrast between the lengthy convolutions to which the priests have resorted—all the huffing and puffing of an irate Caiaphas—and, on the other hand, the perfect, almost casual ease with which Jesus accepts the charge of making himself God's equal, when he says: "You have said so." Rather than marring the obvious moment of his legal defeat with any sign of anger, dejection, or even Stoic equanimity, Jesus instead proceeds unperturbed to paint a dazzling prophetic vision of the only victory that will ever have mattered in the history of the world: the Second Coming of the Son of Man. Spurred by that glorious vision, Jesus grows positively prolix as he evokes a dramatic end-of-world scenario. Caiaphas had commanded him in the strongest terms, "Tell us if you are the Christ"; yet, after briefly admitting the truth of the statement as self-evident, Jesus launches all those present onto a transcendental dimension no one could have foreseen: "*But I tell you*, hereafter you will see the Son of man seated at the right hand of [the] Power, and coming on the clouds of heaven."

Here again, rather than get into a battle of words with the theologians of the day, the incarnate Word makes a statement that totally overshoots all their categories and capacities and draws back the veil on a reality to which only he could existentially be privy as Son of God. Rather than *define*, Jesus *acts out*. With authority he can promise everyone present what "you will see" simply because he is himself the protagonist of the future scene he portrays. At the present moment, he is physically subject to an earthly authority; but this unjustly humiliated and downtrodden Jesus is the very Jesus who will return as "the Son of Man" to judge the world, including the "you" addressed, that is, the members of the Sanhedrin now judging and condemning him. And, inverting the present arrangement symbolically, at that future time of the *Parousia*, Jesus declares it is *he* rather than his current judges who will be "seated at the right hand of [the] Power" while the high priests and elders will be standing in the dock being judged, along with the rest of mankind, just as Jesus now stands being unjustly judged and condemned by them. "Even though princes sit plotting against me, your servant will meditate on your statutes" (Ps 119[118]:23). This psalm verse expresses rather precisely Jesus' exclusive concentration at this moment, as he stands before the Sanhedrin, on his mission from his Father to come as Judge and Redeemer, to "put down the mighty from their thrones, and exalt those of low degree" (cf. Lk 1:52).

א

26:65 τότε ὁ ἀρχιερεὺς διέρρηξεν τὰ ἱμάτια αὐτοῦ λέγων·
Ἐβλασφήμησεν· τί ἔτι χρείαν ἔχομεν μαρτύρων;
ἴδε νῦν ἠκούσατε τὴν βλασφημίαν

Then the high priest tore his robes, and said,
"He has uttered blasphemy. Why do we still need witnesses?
Behold, you have now heard the blasphemy"

W E CAN READILY SEE why the dramatic tearing of one's own garments in public could be felt by the tearer and perceived by others as a physical gesture expressing extreme horror, sorrow, or outrage. At a moment of high drama in Genesis, we read that "when Reuben returned to the pit and saw that Joseph was not in the pit, he tore his clothes" (Gen 37:29). Here Reuben expresses horrified guilt at the disappearance of his younger brother. The tearing of clothes may be seen to signify the breaking of the subject's heart. When Elijah was taken up into heaven and disappeared from the sight of Elisha, the disciple "took hold of his own clothes and rent them in two pieces" (2 Kings 2:12). In this case, Elisha is expressing sheer sorrow at the loss of his beloved mentor and also mourning the end of the most significant period in his life.

But for pious Jews, the greatest horror of all is, of course, blasphemy, the crime against God himself. The blaspheming of the Holy Name is tantamount to an outrage committed against the God of Israel personally. It is a crime with dire consequences, according to Leviticus: "He who blasphemes the name of the LORD shall be put to death; all the congregation shall stone him; the sojourner as well as the native, when he blasphemes the Name, shall be put to death" (Lev 24:16). Whoever attacks the Source of life forfeits his own life, bestowed on him by that very Source. Therefore Caiaphas, as devout upholder of the Holiness of God and of the Law of Israel, manifests publicly, by tearing his garments, the alleged wound inflicted upon his own believing heart by Jesus' admission that he is the Son of God. No greater offense upon the divine Holiness can be imagined than some mortal making himself out to be the Son of God while not being so by nature (cf. Jn 19:7). For Jewish theology, naturally, such an enormity was the greatest of impossibilities: "I am the LORD, and there is no other, besides me there is no God" (Is 45:5). The one and only true God of Israel can have no "son", in the strict sense of the word, according to a literalist monotheism. Not only would such a proposition introduce multiplicity into God's absolute unicity, thereby shattering it, but the word "son" specifically projects onto the Deity a very anthropomorphic concept of temporal generation.

The idea of God as trinitarian community of persons was simply inconceivable in official Jewish theology, despite certain mysterious passages in the Jewish Scriptures, later put to good use by Christian apologists for the Trinity. Indeed, even we Christians, despite our firm trinitarian creed, know full well that the Holy Trinity is a mystery that had to be specifically revealed by Christ not only in his teaching but above all by his manner of life among us. Who better than Christians should be able to appreciate the tremendousness and irreducible mystery of Jesus' identity as incarnate Son of God? Not even the most profound philosopher could have foreseen this truth as self-evidently inevitable or as a demonstrable proposition of reason. Quite frankly, if all that was involved on the Jewish Sanhedrin's part were honest and righteous indignation against a blasphemer, even a misunderstood one, we Christian believers should, in all justice, be willing to exonerate Caiaphas and the others of guilt in their violent reaction against Jesus.

However, this passage in Matthew narrating the trial and condemnation of Jesus by the Sanhedrin bristles from beginning to end with patent ironies and dishonest machinations. Both the planting of instructed witnesses and the harassing of the accused, to whom lines are fed, clearly reveal the prejudices and hidden agenda of the tribunal. It is difficult to read Caiaphas' words and actions as anything but a duplicitous and well-rehearsed spectacle that from the outset intends to arrive with the force of a juggernaut at only one conclusion: the death sentence for Jesus. Against Jesus' better wisdom and preferred silence, Caiaphas force-feeds to Jesus the phrase "the Son of God" in such a manner that Jesus cannot avoid assenting to its truth without denying his own deepest identity and mission and thereby incurring the truest kind of blasphemy against his Father, their unity in the Holy Spirit, and the divine plan of salvation. "Who is the liar but he who denies that Jesus is the Christ? This is the antichrist, he who denies the Father and the Son" (1 Jn 2:22).

But Jesus' assent to Caiaphas' declaration is far from triumphalistic. It does not convey the attitude of one defeating an enemy. A lesser man, indeed, *any other man* but the one who was also the Son of God would in this situation surely have invoked the authority of the majestic Psalm 110[109]: "The LORD says to my lord: 'Sit at my right hand, till I make your enemies your footstool'" (v. 1). But Jesus does not do this. He is out to redeem the world, not to crush his enemies, those who do him injustice. On the contrary, Jesus' response to Caiaphas is understated, even humble, a mere acknowledgment of the truth of what his accuser has himself first stated. And the irony intensifies when, as he continues speaking, Jesus refers to himself not at all as "the Son of God", which is what would have been expected at that point now that his true identity has been exposed and acknowledged. Rather, he refers to himself as "the Son of man", his favorite title for himself. Yet Caiaphas, maniacally bent on pursuing his one purpose, seems wholly to miss the further irony involved when Jesus affirms it is this "Son of man" and not "the Son of God" who shall in the end be seen by all, "seated at the right hand of [the] Power, and coming on the clouds of heaven". Now, *this* is a theological affirmation that ought to have raised every hackle in the house, and how profusely Jesus paints the picture, in great contrast to his previous taciturnity!

Horror of horrors, Jesus is here envisioning a mere man as co-sharer of the glorious majesty of the *Dýnamis*, the "Power", which is a late-Jewish euphemism for God himself. Jesus' prophetic statement strongly suggests that it is he himself, the accused Galilean rabbi standing before them, who as a matter of fact *is* that very Son of Man who will come riding on the clouds of heaven, something that is clearly a divine prerogative (cf. Is 19:1; Ps 104[103]:3). What appears most innovative and, therefore, most shocking in this speech by Jesus is the way in which, with just a few words, he manages to overturn all Jewish theological categories, seeming to mix up humanity with divinity, the present *chrónos* with the future *kairós*, and, worst of all, identifying himself—despite his glaring and weaponless weakness and status as underdog—with that very Judge and King of glory whom no one shall be able to avoid seeing and adoring in the end. And yet here, too, irony enfolds within irony as Jesus proclaims in pious and reverential language a daring vision of himself as co-equal with God. In his mouth not only has the transcendental title "Son of God" suggested by Caiaphas become the far lowlier "Son of man", but Jesus refers to his Father with humble veneration as the "Power", thus avoiding the utterance of God's Holy Name. Jesus' piety in referring to his Father, however, is neither strategic (for the sake of outwitting Caiaphas) nor merely rhetorical (a routine echo of popular usage). Jesus' piety reveals his profound nature as suffering Savior, an aspect of his identity that is just as authentically a part of his person as is his prerogative as King and Judge of the universe. Hence the ultimate vision of the Apocalypse, which melds these two aspects into one: "Behold, he is coming with the clouds, and every eye will see him, every one who pierced him" (Rev 1:7). Among these piercers, of course, the members of this very Sanhedrin occupy the first seats.

It is remarkable to observe how slapdash Caiaphas now becomes, drunk with the glee of finally having entrapped Jesus. His mind has reached such a pitch of excitement that you can practically hear his interior voice muttering ecstatically, "Got him! Got him!" After tearing his robes melodramatically and exultantly charging Jesus with blasphemy, he blurts out: "Why do we still need witnesses?" Throwing protocol to the winds, Caiaphas cannot help baring his fangs for all to see, and the laborious orchestration of evidence he has worked at so diligently now yields to an explosion of sheer sadistic vengeance.

In great contrast to Caiaphas, Jesus now again lapses into silence, thereby impugning Caiaphas' hot irrationality. Having admitted his title of divine sonship and revealed his vision of the end, Jesus now speaks no more. He reverts to being a passive object, the plaything who willingly delivered himself into the hands of men at Gethsemane, for them to abuse him to their hearts' desire. Without further ado, Caiaphas extracts from the Sanhedrin the sentence of death. At this point in Christ's Passion, the bigoted and self-serving judgment of men triumphantly obliterates the glimpse of the divine Final Judgment that Jesus' words portrayed just a few moments before. But passionate human iniquity can triumph only in the short term, flaring up briefly like a bonfire in the star-studded night of providence. Christ, on the other hand, triumphs by embracing his suffering with love. In this way, he embraces the very ones who are running at him with weapons and hatred, and, in this embrace of his aggressors, he reveals the true splendor of God's power and glory, which permanently illumines the long night of history: "[Christ] reflects the glory of God and bears the very stamp of his nature, upholding the universe by his word of power. *When he had made purification for sins*, he sat down at the right hand of the Majesty on high" (Heb 1:3).

26:67–68   Τότε ἐνέπτυσαν εἰς τὸ πρόσωπον αὐτοῦ
καὶ ἐκολάφισαν αὐτόν,
οἱ δὲ ἐράπισαν λέγοντες·
Προφήτευσον ἡμῖν, Χριστε,
τίς ἐστιν ὁ παίσας σε;

Then they spat in his face,
and hit him with the fist;
and some slapped him, saying,
"Prophesy to us, [you] Christ!
Who is it that struck you?"

*T*HEN: THE VERY INSTANT the Sanhedrin, prompted by the high priest, has as a body shouted out Jesus' death sentence by acclamation, these priests, scribes, and elders of the people fall upon him like a pack of dogs on a helpless prey. The passions against Jesus are running so high that for the moment there is no question of delegating punishment to some official torturer, thus making the vengeance inflicted more genteel and juridically correct. The bitter animus the Jewish leaders have been nurturing against Jesus for three long years must explode without delay in acts of violent contempt— namely, spitting, hitting, and slapping. These religious leaders cannot postpone the titillating satisfaction of administering pain and humiliation to this alleged wise man who has so effectively challenged their authority and lured people away.

There is no rabble here; the *hoi polloi* were left out in the courtyard or the surrounding countryside. Here at the trial, there are present only the sitting members of the Sanhedrin and Jesus standing in front of them like a loathsome exhibit. The spectacle we now witness has the effect of a surprising disgrace to the much-vaunted dignity of the highest religious authorities in Israel. They do not hesitate to get "down-and-dirty" on this rare occasion because their irrational hatred and contempt for Jesus as upstart and pretender-Messiah are stronger than their sense of the dignity of their office. And yet no amount of pragmatic argumentation, in defense of the need to uphold the establishment of any religion, shall ever justify in the eyes of God what we are here witnessing: powerful men visiting flagrant injustice and brutality on a weak and vulnerable fellow-human—and all in the name of God. The Sanhedrin's dishonorable, lurid, and purely vindictive behavior at this moment brings out into the open at last the mostly hidden motivations against Jesus that we have observed throughout this Gospel on the part of the religious authorities.

The physical abuse here described by Matthew readily evokes the ordeal of that other mysterious figure, the Suffering Servant of the Lord in Isaiah: "I gave my back to those who struck me, and my cheeks to those who pulled out the beard; I hid not my face from shame and spitting" (Is 50:6). Furthermore: "He was oppressed, and he was afflicted, yet he opened not his mouth" (Is 53:7). In an episode already rich in ironies, here lurks the further irony that these very texts, sacred to the Jewish tradition, may have been solemnly read that same morning in the synagogue by those now jeering at Jesus and gratuitously inflicting pain on him! And so the question emerges: If Jesus is not fulfilling the crucial Isaian prophecy to the letter right here and now, and at the very hands of God's hierarchical servants, then who could ever fulfill it?

Let us not miss the utterly precise correspondence between the free handing-over of self by the protagonist in Isaiah's vision (*I gave my back, my cheeks, my face* . . .) and Jesus' incessant gesture of spontaneous *parádosis* throughout his Passion. This is Jesus' life-form and the very heart of his mission. The most recent shape taken by this *parádosis* is, precisely, his silent reverting to the status of inert plaything and object of derision, first of all in the hands of the Sanhedrin. It seems that in this scene, Jesus is embodying, for all time, the great and painful paradox to which Georges Bernanos alludes when he quotes Père Clérissac, a young Dominican killed at Verdun in 1916, who exclaimed: "It is nothing to suffer *for* the Church. The keenest suffering is *at Her hands.*"[7]

We should not be so naïve as to think that Jesus' suffering occurs exclusively at the hands of Jews and Romans or that it is limited to the historical duration of his Passion. All the world's unjustly oppressed of all times and places are mystically present in Jesus at this moment, and therefore he is likewise present in them whenever and wherever they are enduring their suffering. A very special share in Christ's sufferings is reserved for those lovers of Christ who labor unjustly under the temporal authority of Christ's Church. One must participate intensely in Christ's redemptive virtue in order to kiss obediently the very hand that slaps and rejects you.

"Prophesy to us, you Christ! Who is it that struck you?" This mocking challenge to prophesy is no doubt prompted by Jesus' audacious prediction to the Sanhedrin of his future glorification in union with the Father, as we have recently seen: "Hereafter you will see the Son of man seated at the right hand of [the] Power" (v. 64). It simply could not enter anyone's head that a mortal human being, who can so blatantly be subjugated by a few slaps and blows and whose face retains the mucous smear of saliva as any other human face would, could with any credibility pretend to a future glorification! The slaps and blows may be a great release of long-pent-up anger and frustration. But this sarcastic question "Who is it that struck you?" that scoffingly demands a "prophecy" is nothing but mockery for sport,

---

[7] Italics mine. "J'ai déjà cité bien des fois la phrase, pour moi inoubliable, d'un jeune dominicain tué à Verdun, le Père Clérissac: 'Cela n'est rien de souffrir pour l'Eglise, il faut avoir souffert par Elle.'" Georges Bernanos, *La Vocation spirituelle de la France* (Paris: Plon, 1975), 226.

an expression of the victorious relief experienced at getting this dangerous insurrectionist finally under control.

The sadistic merriment in which these worthies are engaging at Jesus' expense really reduces them, exalted hierarchs that they are, to the status of spiteful bullies in a playground. This begs the question as to who exactly it is that becomes most risible in this scene. The scoffers' intended tone is conveyed by the jingly sound of the taunt in the original Greek:

> Prophéteuson hêmín Christé,
> Tís estin ho paísas sé?

By their meter (three strong accents per line), their acute rhyme in –é and their general sing-song effect, these two verses amount to a mocking refrain intended to be funny and that one can imagine being repeated over and over in derisive humiliation by a chorus of voices. In English, the impact of the mocking words could take this form, which preserves the crucial rhythm and rhyme:

> Próphesy to ús, you Chríst,
> Whó just now your fáce has slíced!

That the sham "prophecy" demanded has to do with Jesus' immediate experience of being struck reduces the procedure to mere slapstick entertainment at Jesus' expense. Jesus is thereby further degraded to the status of a buffoon.

Furthermore, the mocking refrain addresses Jesus as *Christ* only in order to ridicule his alleged claim to messiahship and divine filiation. The full title that Caiaphas "fed" him was "the Christ, the Son of God". Caiaphas' question, obviously, was uttered, not as an ardent query from the heart of a religious seeker, but, rather, as a destructive weapon fueled by religious outrage and fear of losing an authority on the wane. The very presence of Jesus threatens all self-serving human constructs. Grim purposes can masquerade behind apparently "fun"-loving antics, especially when another person is made the butt of one's hate-fueled mirth and this quantum of loathing is exponentially powered by mob dynamics. One thinks of the drunken camaraderie, the jovial "fellow feeling", that fueled many a heartless lynching in the American South.

What is perhaps the darkest, most Satanic side of the human psyche revels in inflicting humiliation on another person. I say "Satanic" in the strict theological sense of a mind-set seeking to supplant God. This whole process of sitting in judgment on another member of one's race, using careful manipulation of the evidence and planting rehearsed witnesses so as to secure a blatantly unjust death penalty: What else is this but a more or less conscious attempt at taking the place of God as supreme Judge, precisely in order to justify an iniquitous judgment that God himself would never condone? Furthermore, once this victim of the official but unjust legal system has been "legally" condemned by all manner of deception, then the hidden poison secretly feeding the whole process from the outset cannot but burst forth and, now feeling juridically secured, manifest itself in its true colors. The true face of Satanic injustice and manipulation is the wanton humiliation of the innocent scapegoat, which always has a whiff of the libidinous about it. While true justice is always sober, restrained, and grave, especially on the occasions when it must condemn, triumphant iniquity gives itself away by the obscene glee with which it tramples its victim and celebrates its victory. The noble pagan soul, on the other hand, reacts quite differently even when justice is authentically carried out, as is shown by Odysseus' reproach to his nanny Eurykleia after the suitors have finally been avenged: "I'll have no jubilation here. It is an impious thing to exult over the slain."[8]

At the end of Jesus' trial, such obscene glee, oozing from the Sanhedrin's every pore, in itself reveals the true nature of the religious authorities' motivations. Hatred for Jesus the Truth here takes four forms of violence: Caiaphas' tearing of his own garments, the spitting on Jesus' face, the striking him in sundry places, and the taunting him for prophecy. Here we see both the bodies and the creative imagination of his persecutors at work, the latter driving the former. It is impossible to recreate the scene to any degree in one's mind without conjuring up an orgy of pleasure derived from humiliating a fellow human being both physically and psychologically. Such reckless self-indulgence on the part of the official guardians of the divine Law would be highly depraved even if the prisoner were truly guilty, as Homer reminds us. What must we then say in this case, in which the prisoner Jesus has been condemned to death solely on the basis of trumped-up evidence and a devious manipulation of words?

[8] Homer, *The Odyssey*, XXII, 411, as quoted by H. W. Clarke, *The Art of the Odyssey* (Englewood Cliffs, N.J.: Prentice Hall, 1967), 77.

"Then they spat in his face": This is only the first time that Jesus would be bathed in human spittle during his Passion. It will happen again this very night at Pontius Pilate's house, when the soldiers will spit on him as, kneeling before him, they hit him on the head (now wearing a crown of thorns!) during their little Satanic skit titled "Jesus, King of the Jews" (27:29–30). Men here use their drool to show utter contempt for the One who used his saliva, instead, to anoint and heal the blind and the deaf-and-dumb (Mk 7:33, 8:23). And, being but one more human, I myself must wonder: How many times have I, too, struck Jesus over the head with the reed of my contempt or indifference for his little ones, all the while kneeling before him piously in alleged prayer? How many times have I pitched the phlegm of my disdain at Jesus' face by judging the innocent as retrograde and daft? The disdainer of the innocent disdains him who affirmed: "Let the children come to me, and do not hinder them; for to such belongs the kingdom of heaven. . . . For I am gentle and lowly in heart" (19:14; 11:29). This is but one more poignant example of how the sacred text is always holding up a mirror of recognition not only to people in general but to believers in particular. The Gospel text is continually revealing to us not only something important about God but also, simultaneously, something crucial about ourselves, something we are not likely to see on our own because of our dire lack of critical self-awareness. Before it can heal and save us, the Word of God must indict us by shining the light of truth in our hearts.

Along with every other aspect of his Passion, Jesus has already foreseen the eventuality of his receiving the slaver of men upon his face and has announced it to his disciples: "For [the Son of man] will be delivered to the Gentiles, and will be mocked and shamefully treated and spit upon" (Lk 18:32). Spitting on another person is universally viewed as a way of expressing visceral contempt for that person. The action intends to distance the spitter utterly from the spat-upon. In the Old Testament, the action picks up the meaning of covering someone with shame (Num 12:14; Deut 25:9). Beyond this, as we see in the case of Job, who exhibits certain prophetic aspects as a Christ-figure, spitting can be a sign for the thorough loathing one wants to express for someone who has been ostracized from respectable society. Thus we hear this startling self-definition by Job: "[The Lord] has made me a byword of the peoples, and I am one before whom men spit. . . . They abhor me, they keep aloof from me; they do not hesitate to spit at the sight of me" (Job 17:6; 30:10). Spitting, then, is the ultimate symbolic expression of contempt for another. No act, short of invasive violence, could be more humiliating than hurling onto the face of one's victim, personal locus of sacredness and individuality, the slimy waste coughed up for the occasion from one's bodily recesses.

In this context, it is enlightening to see, as striking testimony to the nature of God, something we have just mentioned in passing: the clearly *sacramental use* that Jesus himself made of his own saliva on at least two occasions, as one element of his ministry of healing. First, we have the encounter with a mute man: "And they brought to [Jesus] a man who was deaf and had an impediment in his speech; and they begged him to lay his hand upon him. And taking him aside from the multitude privately, [Jesus] put his fingers into his ears, *and he spat and touched his tongue*" (Mk 7:32-33). Then we also have the case of the man born blind, recorded in both Mark and John in slightly different versions: "[Jesus] spat on the ground and made clay of the spittle and anointed the man's eyes with the clay" (Jn 9:6). Mark's version adds an element of force to the action: "And he took the blind man by the hand, and led him out of the village; and *when he had spit on his eyes* and laid his hands upon him, he asked him, 'Do you see anything?'" (Mk 8:23). While John clearly alludes to Jesus' divine artisanship in re-creating the blind man by the work of his hands, recalling the creating Lord in Genesis, Mark emphasizes the forceful invasive gesture of a holy violence that communicates something of Jesus' physical substance to the being of the man who has never seen the light: *when he had spit on his eyes.*

In the cases of both the mute and the blind man, Jesus, the eternal Word and Light of the Father, chooses to restore a fallen creature to his pristine splendor as created by God by means of an astoundingly intimate action. Jesus not only has the will and the power to heal by word of command and gesture of touching; above all, he has the *love* to heal by bestowing himself—*all* of himself, humanity and divinity—on his beloved creature—*all* of his beloved creature, body and soul. This is the deepest meaning of Jesus' act of healing by word, touch, *and anointing with spittle.* Jesus' healing use of his sputum to restore hearing and sight on grieving, fallen man could be considered a particular extension of the creating God's act of blowing the breath of life from his mouth into the face of Adam in the beginning: "The LORD God formed man of dust from the ground, and breathed into his nostrils the breath of life; and man became a living soul" (Gen 2:7).

During the Liturgy of the Adoration of the Cross on Good Friday afternoon, the Church puts into the mouth of the suffering Jesus a moving litany of *Improperia*, or "Reproaches", addressed to the people of Israel and inspired by God's many works on their behalf throughout their long history. One of these "Reproaches" is the following:

> My people, what have I done to you?
> Or how have I grieved you? Answer me!
> I opened up the sea before you,
> And you opened my side with a lance.

In this same vein, and inspired by the vengeful events at the conclusion of Jesus' trial, we could fittingly add one more strophe to the Reproaches:

> My people, what have I done to you?
> Or how have I grieved you? Answer me!
> With my spittle I enlightened the eyes of the blind,
> And you smeared my face with your slime.

Through all of the words, symbols, gestures, and dramatic exchanges of Matthew's narrative of Jesus' trial before the Sanhedrin, we arrive at this grim but inevitable conclusion: that, while God consistently works to bestow on man *fullness of life* in and through Jesus' humanity, man, on the contrary, when cut off from God as selfserving and autonomous operator, seeks frenetically to inflict nothing but *disgrace and death* on God through the human vulnerability of his Christ.

The Satanic motivation of this drive on man's part is all too evident. Not being able to withstand the fiery, transforming presence of Goodness, Purity, and Holiness in the person of the Word Incarnate, man must strive to exclude God, indeed, to supplant God ("Satan" means "the plotting Adversary") by wreaking vengeance *for his goodness* on the person of Jesus, as the Psalmist lamented: "Those who are my foes without cause are mighty, and many are those who hate me wrongfully. Those who render me evil for good are my adversaries because I follow after good" (Ps 38[37]:19–20). This deicidal project to stomp out all graciousness from the world has a dismally Promethean goal: to manufacture an alternative world to the one God created and sustains, a wholly efficient world more in keeping with man's voracious lust to banish all mystery and paradox from his habitat, to reduce all knowledge to mathematics and science, and thus achieve total mental and technical domination over society and the cosmos.

Such a "utopia" must be undergirded by abstract ideologies, which are always tyrannical because they exalt some favorite idea of humanity above concrete human beings with unique personhoods. To become socially enforceable, any ideology must first attempt to banish all transcendental mystery and paradoxical wisdom from the world, in order to make way for the absolute triumph of the human will. This would be a world that strangles love, faith, and beauty, and, therefore, man himself as well, in the specific humanness that distinguishes him from both animals and machines. Yet we know that "in fact man does not live on the bread of practicability alone; he lives as *man* and, precisely in the intrinsically human part of his being, on the word, on love, on meaning."[9]

But who exactly shall be in charge of the glorious utopia, and who will select the trail-blazers for such an enterprise? History, in all its tragic details, has amply taught us a cruel lesson: neither National Socialism with its death camps, nor Communist totalitarianism with its gulags, nor Capitalist imperialism with its sweatshops, nor militaristic theocracies of whatever stripe have had any other driving force than the compulsion ultimately to displace God as sovereign Creator and King from the controllable aspects of society, education, and government. Even church hierarchs, under billowing clouds of incense, have been known to scheme most piously to banish God's Majesty from religion itself! Such an abomination, however, is not wrought only at the collective, global level. The politico-military juggernaut of titanic ideologies derives its all-demolishing strength and its efficiency in lying and abusing from the very same minuscule source in the unredeemed human heart that largely motivates you and me at the individual level and that motivated Caiaphas and the Sanhedrin at Jesus' trial on Holy Thursday night. They, too, felt a mighty inflow of power in their veins as just reward for their actions of humiliating, hitting, and spitting upon the innocent and helpless Jesus.

[9] Joseph Cardinal Ratzinger, *Introduction to Christianity*, trans. J. R. Foster, 2nd ed. (San Francisco: Ignatius Press, 2004), 72–73.

And yet, no matter how devastating our ultimate vision into the darkness ruling the human heart, we should never forget, if we are honest, that we are here peering only into our own heart. Though capable of immense iniquity, the human heart is also capable of repentance and conversion, and therefore St. John encourages us to "reassure our hearts before [the Lord] whenever our hearts condemn us; for God is greater than our hearts, and he knows everything" (1 Jn 3:19–20). St. Paul for his part declares to the Romans that his only hope rests, not on anything like the "innate goodness of man", but rather on faith's conviction, against all human logic and shame, that in fact, in the economy of Christian salvation, an infinitely exponential inverted ratio between sin and grace is powerfully at work with us. This paradoxical reality of how God operates is captured in the lapidary formulation of the Latin Vulgate, *Ubi autem abundavit delictum superabundavit gratia*: "Where sin abounded, grace did much more abound: That as sin hath reigned unto death, even so might grace reign through righteousness unto eternal life by Jesus Christ our Lord" (Rom 5:20–21, KJV).

Holy and Immortal One, have mercy on us!

10. IN YOUR BITTERNESS, REMEMBER LOVE!

Peter's Denial of Jesus (26:69–75)

26:69

Ὁ δὲ Πέτρος ἐκάθητο ἔξω ἐν τῇ αὐλῇ·
καὶ προσῆλθεν αὐτῷ μία παιδίσκη λέγουσα·
Καὶ σὺ ἦσθα μετὰ Ἰησοῦ τοῦ Γαλιλαίου

Now Peter was sitting outside in the courtyard.
And a maid came up to him, and said,
"You also were with Jesus the Galilean"

LIKE AN EXPERT CINEMATOGRAPHER, Matthew suddenly shifts the focus of his camera from the scene of the trial to the courtyard of Caiaphas' house. This æsthetic technique freezes the pathetic face of the battered and spit-smeared Jesus in our mind as the fraught background image presiding over the ensuing action that will now play itself out in the courtyard. By this sudden shift of focus, Matthew leaves the trial's conclusion suspended, without closure, and thus he makes Jesus' dreadful humiliation permeate his reader's consciousness most vividly. The utter humiliation of the Son of God has not been make-believe. No: incomprehensibly, legions of angels have, in fact, *not* swept down from the heavens to avenge their Lord. The irony abides that, at the very moment when the divine Master *stands* and endures endless scorn, having no place to take refuge, his disciple Peter cowers in anonymity, *sitting* only a few yards away.

As a man of deep faith, the evangelist Matthew views the trial of Jesus before the Sanhedrin as nothing less than the unspeakable indictment, by mortal men, of the only God's eternal Word. Despite Jesus' utterly unassuming and pitifully humiliated exterior, the

349

condemnation to death by the Jewish authorities of him who is *Torah Incarnate* must necessarily have cosmic consequences, and Matthew at once sets out to explore them. The first creature to feel the tremor is Peter.

The rhythm of Matthew's Gospel narrative now begins to move in ever-widening circles, expanding outward from the person of the suffering Messiah at the center. The evangelist thus seeks to record the reactions of different kinds of people—and, indeed, even of nature itself (cf. 27:50–53)—to man's assault upon God. Matthew first takes us to Caiaphas' courtyard, and there we find Peter where we left him, sitting as unobtrusively as he can in the milling crowd of sundry guards and servants. His real *love* for Jesus impels him to be as close to his friend as possible in this dark time, but his equally real *fear* dictates supreme caution. Striving to pass incognito is his compromise between the two conflicting emotions battling in his heart.

But God loves Peter too much to allow him to get away with this halfhearted arrangement; and so divine grace comes to chivvy Peter out of his mole-hole, in the form of two servant girls and some bystanders. When both love and fear coexist in our hearts, the fear must somehow be exorcised so that we may come to love with the full energy of our whole heart. For this were we created, and therefore it is to this that grace is always impelling us.

Out of nowhere, and without apparent motivation, the first maid approaches Peter (but why precisely Peter?) with intuitive certainty and says to him with a leer, for all to hear: "You also were with Jesus the Galilean!" The girl's taunt to Peter is a weaker echo of the taunt to Jesus we have just heard from members of the Sanhedrin: "Prophesy to us, you Christ! Who is it that struck you?" (v. 68). Both accusations concern true identity. Both jabs imply: "We don't really believe you truly are who you say you are!" A sharp suspicion is troubling the depths of the accusers' consciences: they sense that their world cannot go on being what they want it to be *if* Jesus is who he says he is and *if* Peter turns out to be his faithful disciple in mufti.

The power and viewpoint of the ruling masters is naturally transfused into the outlook of the servants, who thus somehow also come to share vicariously in that power. And the believer who tries to witness to God's truth, which surpasses this world, will always be subject to taunts because of the clash of two radically opposing visions of reality. The servant is accusing Peter of guilt by association. In her mind, instinctively, she must help her masters rid the world of the contagion Jesus has brought into the world and of which Peter is a carrier. By this procedure, the girl seeks both to secure for herself the credibility of the world she inhabits and to rise higher in her masters' estimation for work well done: she wants to show she is two steps ahead of their orders.

The precise wording of the girl's accusation is significant. "You also *were with Jesus* the Galilean", she says to Peter. In Mark's Gospel, we read that the chief finality for which Jesus chose his apostles was that they might *be with him*: "And he appointed twelve, *to be with him*, and to be sent out to preach" (Mk 3:14). Note that here apostolic "mission" comes only after, and as a result of, an intimately shared *existence* as ongoing life condition. This paramount fact is, of course, implied in all the accounts of the apostles' call to discipleship, but Mark makes it explicit. The maid's charge does not, at first, seem to amount to much; Peter is guilty, she hints, simply of keeping company with Jesus. However, when we give such association the full weight it deserves in light of Jesus' deepest intentions, then we do grasp the seriousness of the accusation. "Abide in me, and I in you", says Jesus to the disciples in John. "As the branch cannot bear fruit by itself, unless it abides in the vine, neither can you, unless you abide in me" (Jn 15:4). Who, indeed, can determine where the vine ends and the branch begins?

Jesus' explicit desire that the disciple should *be with him* reveals a vocation to such an intensity of friendship, loyalty, and interiorized imitation that it practically amounts to self-identification between Master and disciple. The theologically unambiguous formulation of this mysticism of union and identification with Christ comes, as is to be expected, from the pen of Paul; but it is already present in the Gospel and is certainly not a theological "invention" of Paul's. One of Paul's formulations in this connection appears in Galatians and stresses the ontological union between Jesus and his disciples. There we read: "I [Paul] have been crucified with Christ; it is no longer I who live, but Christ who lives in me; and the life I now live in the flesh I live by faith in the Son of God, who loved me and gave himself for me" (Gal 2:20). In other words, in all his thoughts, words, and deeds, the true disciple ought to be as guilty or as innocent as his Master, depending on the observer's point of view. For the true disciple is simply another Christ. It is striking to see how the servant girl, despite all her contempt for Jesus the underdog and her reward-seeking ambition, nevertheless goes realistically to the heart of the matter. In her accusation of Peter, she instinctively "sniffs out" the essence of the Christian vocation, which she quite profoundly, albeit unwittingly, describes as *being with Jesus* and assuming everything that simply being-with-Jesus implies, even when such intimate association can prove to be one's undoing in this world.

א

26:70   ὁ δὲ ἠρνήσατο ἔμπροσθεν πάντων λέγων·
         Οὐκ οἶδα τί λέγεις

But he denied it before them all, saying,
"I do not know what you are saying"

THE SECOND PURPOSE, according to Mark, for which Jesus chose his apostles was that they might "be sent out to preach". Peter's presence in Caiaphas' courtyard already witnesses to the fact that Peter knew that his place was with Jesus, as physically close to Jesus as possible in these dire circumstances. Peter is willing to enter enemy territory, but only up to a certain point; he does not really want to risk his wellbeing for the sake of Jesus. And so he does everything he can to avoid being discovered and exposed as a follower of Jesus. The girl's aggressive question, however, now presses the matter to the extreme. Feeling cornered and threatened with exposure, Peter utterly fails to be faithful to the second imperative of his calling: bearing public witness to the wonder of Jesus Christ.

We know that, in the Gospels, "being sent to preach" is code language for proclaiming Jesus of Nazareth to the world as Messiah and Redeemer and as the priceless treasure and Beloved of one's own soul. The verbal accusation by a mere serving girl that Peter is the condemned prisoner's intimate friend instantly knocks Peter to the ground of shameful denial. Not only does he not acknowledge Jesus openly for who Jesus truly is, but Peter actually *rejects* any association whatsoever with Jesus. The fear of sharing the abused Jesus' fate overwhelms his senses, his reason, and his will, and he categorically distances himself from his Master. "I do not know what you [are saying]", is Peter's mock-offended reply.

The text incisively affirms that Peter performs this action of denial, not discreetly and quietly, but openly and loudly, "before them all". The Gospel is supposed to be proclaimed openly, before the whole world, as the good news of salvation; but ironically what Peter proclaims openly and loudly, for all to hear, is instead his *denial* of Jesus, thus hoping to avert further interrogation. Matthew wants to underscore the sad fact that Peter is putting all the energy and intelligence of his soul, at this moment, at the service of the rejection rather than the proclamation of Jesus. He thus embodies tragically the diametrical opposite of his identity as apostle. Indeed, his overreaction to the girl's charge can be seen as a glaring instance of "the gentleman protesting too much".

No doubt fear, atrocious fear, has made Peter forget Jesus' explicit warning: "Whoever denies me before men, I also will deny before my Father who is in heaven" (10:33). Fear of man for the moment has far greater sway in Peter's heart than fear of God. Which of us cannot sympathize with him? Nevertheless, seen very objectively, we must affirm that through his action of denial, Peter is attempting to save his hide, at the very high cost of assuming the heinous role of *antichrist*, according to St. John's definition: "Who is the liar but he who denies that Jesus is the Christ? This is the antichrist, he who denies the Father and the Son" (1 Jn 2:22). In the Christian vocation, faith in Christ and intimate identity, faith in Christ and concrete life, are so inextricably linked that, in denying his human association with Jesus, Peter is also denying the reality of the Christ as Savior and his mission from the Father.

At this terrible moment in his life, Peter is in fact toying with self-destruction. We cannot call by any other name than this the consequences of his denial of Jesus. Peter is very literally and actively preaching an anti-gospel of rejection that aligns him fully with the Sanhedrin and its condemnation of Jesus, rather than the authentic

gospel of proclamation of Jesus as Savior; and yet this latter proclamation was the very purpose for which Jesus chose him and set him
at the head of the apostolic college in the first place. We clearly see
here what a risk a person assumes at any time by entering into an
intimate relationship with Jesus and affirming the Christian faith.

Nor need we belabor the point that the office of apostle is no merely
external function, quite distinct from the core of one's personality.
In denying Jesus so blatantly and viscerally, Peter is denying his very
own reason-for-being, his own precious and unique identity as man
now living the life of God, since intimate association with Jesus implies nothing less than the full blossoming of human existence and
potential through union with the creating Word.

26:71–72 ἐξελθόντα δὲ εἰς τὸν πυλῶνα
εἶδεν αὐτὸν ἄλλη καὶ λέγει τοῖς ἐκεῖ·
Οὗτος ἦν μετὰ Ἰησοῦ τοῦ Ναζωραίου
καὶ πάλιν ἠρνήσατο μετὰ ὅρκου
ὅτι Οὐκ οἶδα τὸν ἄνθρωπον

And when he went out to the porch,
another [maid] saw him, and she said to the bystanders,
"This man was with Jesus of Nazareth."
And again he denied it with an oath,
"I do not know the man"

PROPERLY SPEAKING, THE GREEK WORD *pylôn*, rendered "porch"
above, means a "gateway" or "main entrance". Therefore, to
see Peter moving out toward the *pylôn* of Caiaphas' house implies that he is a man on the run, trying frantically to make a quick
escape. The heat has been turned up on him in that courtyard, and

his fear is rising to the boiling point. But there is for him no getting away from this danger zone, where circumstances have precipitated the determining crisis of his life.

A priest, once validly ordained, will always remain a priest no matter what his subjective moral state or canonical standing. The grace of priestly ordination has wrought a permanent change in his being, a so-called ontological transformation, which cannot be reversed by anything or anybody, not even by any amount of sinning or blaspheming on the priest's part. Peter's case here is similar. The power of his inalienable identity as an apostle is still very much active within his person at a level deeper than his fear and blatant infidelity. To put it differently, the divine grace Peter has received through intimate association with Jesus is not going to allow him to hide his true identity forever. And so this grace now acts through various human instruments that happen to be present in Caiaphas' courtyard, all in order to expose Peter's abject lie and betrayal. Only along this painful path can Peter be healed.

This second denial by Peter introduces several new elements that make it distinct from the first. The person making the accusation this time is still one of the serving girls, but she addresses the charge to the bystanders rather than directly to Peter. It appears also that this girl is not merely echoing the revelation of the first maid but is acting on her own. The joint effect of their accusations is stereophonic: even as he is trying his best to slip out, Peter is accosted from all sides by the truth of his identity, as if a conspiracy against him were afoot. Now the unmasking accusation lies not only behind him but before him as well and is resounding all about as the truth of the matter spreads.

It appears astounding that the evangelist would choose to devote so much space in his Passion narrative to this episode of Peter's denial of Jesus. While the narrative of the trial takes up eleven verses, the story of Peter's denial occupies a full eight (if we include v. 58, noting Peter's presence in the courtyard). Such attention to Peter's personal drama in the context of Jesus' Passion surely underscores the permanent paradigmatic importance of the theme of the *struggle for fidelity* in the concrete life of the Christian believer, in the face of the dire opposition and mockery that faith always attracts.

"This man was with Jesus of Nazareth": Jesus is now identified as "the Nazorean", a tag that makes the earlier label of "Galilean" even more precise. The connection has now been made between Peter and this condemned rabbi from a specific region and city. Even as the consequences of Jesus' inmost identity are unleashing an ocean of suffering upon him, Peter's intimate identity and history are being brought out into the open as well. This servant girl, too, like the first, words her accusation in the same poignant expression of unitive coexistence: "This man *was with Jesus.*" The very same declaration that, under happier circumstances, would have been heard by Peter with exultant ears and a grateful heart as his highest claim to glory instead, on this occasion, becomes a shameful denunciation. Peter has not yet made his own the truth of the proverb: "The fear of man lays a snare, but he who trusts in the LORD is safe" (Prov 29:25).

Even after we have gladly and openheartedly accepted the love of another, even after we have pledged our love in return to that person, how great a part of our being remains in its former darkness, still unable to shake its knee-jerk selfishness, still untouched at the core by the transforming fire of love! We can understand why many of us choose never to love or be loved, precisely because the admission of love into our soul lays us wide-open to all manner of unforeseen and undesired vicissitudes. Chief among these is the way in which Peter's present situation exposes him before the whole world in all his inglorious cowardice and disgraceful incoherence of life. Quite bluntly stated, his reptilian instinct for survival at all costs is for the moment strangling his deepest desire to proclaim the defeated Jesus as being nonetheless his heart's singular Beloved. This future universal shepherd of souls still has no serene spiritual vision of his own as ballast for his own soul in the midst of the storm.

The intensification of the accusation and the accumulation of specifying details make us, as attentive readers of the Gospel, actually *feel* Peter's growing distress at seeing himself ever more tightly cornered. This second time, his denial of Jesus becomes angrier and more categorical. The first time, he pretended not even to understand the charge, as he replied to his accuser quite coolly: "I do not know what you mean." This reaction is still not so much a denial as a dismissal of the whole subject, as if Peter were nothing but a curious, uninformed bystander. But now naïve dismissal escalates to angry swearing. Reacting like one insulted, Peter shouts back with an oath: "I do not know the man!"

We are not told the precise nature of the oath, but clearly Peter is perjuring himself before God and man. And his denial of Jesus is not generic, as before. Not only does he deny having any association at all with Jesus; he actually affirms in the most absolute way that *he doesn't even know the man*. This formulation of his denial is not only a personal affront to Jesus and a betrayal of their relationship as Master and disciple. At an even graver level, Peter's reference to Jesus as "the man" (with the definite article) also repudiates "the Son of man", the messianic title Jesus himself used when speaking to the disciples at his arrest in Gethsemane (26:45) and just now at the trial, when identifying himself to Caiaphas (26:64). To disown Jesus as Messiah is to reject salvation itself.

26:73   μετὰ μικρὸν δὲ προσελθόντες οἱ ἑστῶτες
           εἶπον τῷ Πέτρῳ·
           Ἀληθῶς καὶ σὺ ἐξ αὐτῶν εἶ
           καὶ γὰρ ἡ λαλιά σου δῆλόν σε ποιεῖ

*After a little while the bystanders came up
and said to Peter,
"Truly you are also one of them,
for your accent betrays you"*

G RACE'S STRATEGY of love's repossession closes in around Peter in a tightening circle of pressure. We should not forget that, in Luke's version of this drama, just before predicting Peter's denial, Jesus says to him: "Simon, Simon, behold, Satan demanded to have you, that he might sift you like wheat, but *I have prayed for you that your faith may not fail*; and when you have turned again, strengthen your brethren" (Lk 22:31–32). Here we see that the Lord has, in anticipation of the coming betrayal, provided not only the warning but also the cure. His hounding grace will never stop tracking Peter, and at this moment it moves into open action through certain persons who happen to be, along with Peter, in Caiaphas' courtyard.

Now on this third occasion, it is no longer a single individual who levels the damning charge of discipleship at Peter but an indeterminate number of bystanders who point the accusing finger. The fire of mean human denunciation, a searing instrument of the Fire of Mercy, has spread, and Peter now has nowhere to escape to and hide. His guilt is deepening hand in hand with his fear, for now he has denied his friend and Lord not once but *three times*. Not only does the repetition of the denial compound his responsibility, but so does the passage of time. Matthew stresses this aspect of the drama when he says that these latest accusers came up to Peter *after a little while*, that is, after he has had additional time to reconsider his options.

This "little while" is giving him the equal opportunity either to reject Jesus yet again or to retract his previous two denials and finally confess his Lord. Tragically, Peter goes the way of all flesh and continues sliding down the slippery slope of instinctual self-protection, which, according to the Gospel's paradoxical logic, means the slope of self-destruction. With what scorching precision Jesus' words apply to him: "For whoever would save his life will lose it, and whoever loses his life for my sake will find it" (16:25). Peter has still to embrace the profound saving truth of this Paschal paradox. Genuine disciple though he might be, made such by Jesus' election and by no merit of his own, for the moment his emotions and his will are still ruled by the reptilian logic of the world. In his panic, he is quite prepared to throw Jesus under the proverbial bus. The precarious nature of the devotion we often pledge to God is quirkily illustrated by this admission of Madeleine Delbrêl: "Lord, I love you above all things . . . , generally speaking; but, in this passing minute, how I'd love an English cigarette so much more than you—or even a Gauloise."[1]

These latest accusers are hurling new evidence at Peter: "[Truly] you are also one of them, *for your accent betrays you*", they say. This remark adds solidity to the previous references to Jesus as "Galilean" and "Nazorean". The charge also reminds us of how truly and thoroughly *incarnate* the eternal Word became in Jesus of Nazareth: Galilee and Nazareth, the scenes of his childhood and much of his

---

[1] *La joie de croire* (Paris: Éditions du Seuil, 1968), 69.

ministry, are topographical and cultural extensions of the sacrament of his human flesh. Both Jesus' identity as Messiah and Peter's momentary denial of that identity are inseparable from the history and topography of revelation. The efficacy of the divine Word, present in the world, will not at any time or in any place ever be disembodied or abstract because the incarnate Word is not a fleeting ghost but a true man of flesh and blood, deeply and inextricably rooted in the human family of all times and places. On this truth both Jesus' capacity to suffer and, therefore, the redemption of the world depend.

Peter's denial of Jesus—of their association, their shared history, their common roots as Galileans—is not merely a notional and verbal social act whereby he distances himself publicly from a condemned prisoner. At the ontological level, Peter's disavowal of Jesus is nothing less than a perverse act of attempted *dis-incarnation* of his person from the living "habitat" that is Jesus the Word Incarnate. Consequently, it is an act that, probably unaware of what he is doing, denies the Incarnation as such and strives to "undo" God's act of redemption both subjectively and objectively. Peter's threefold denial of Jesus is a case of obstinate blasphemy against God and God's plan of salvation, a sacrilege infinitely compounded by the degree of intimacy to which Jesus has invited Peter. We should understand this not only in the generic sense of the grace bestowed on all the apostles but specifically in the uniquely privileged sense that applies to Peter alone as head of the apostolic college.

"[Truly] you are also one of them, *for your accent betrays you.*" In Greek, the final part of this sentence literally reads: "For your speech makes you evident." However, the majority of translators in various languages prefer to render it more idiomatically, along the lines of *your accent betrays you* or *your speech gives you away.* Very rarely does a freer translation improve the original, but in this case, the verbs "to betray" or "to give away" bring out a powerful irony inherent in the situation, and it is this: No matter how many efforts Peter makes to disown Jesus, no matter how radical his flight might be from his real persona into the concealment of an invented abstraction, Peter can no more undo his vital association with Jesus than he can get rid of his native Galilean accent. Both things—the association and the accent—are now an essential and inalienable aspect of his very being, as truly defining his human and spiritual identity as the ingredients of his DNA.

Therefore, in the very same speech-act in which Peter is *betraying Jesus by denial*, Peter's own speech patterns and intonation are *betraying Peter by affirmation* or, in police lingo, by "positive identification". The truth will out. Peter might be able mentally to control what comes out of his mouth in the form of lying words, but he cannot alter the peculiarities of his speech, slowly ingrained over decades in his memory and linguistic organs from the day he was born. Our speech is an intrinsic part of who we are, a second nature. Despite Peter's efforts at artificially abstracting himself from the reality of his experience of Jesus, the very texture of the sounds that come out of his mouth betrays his origins and as well his association with the infamous rabbi from Galilee. Peter's speech habits prove themselves here wiser and sturdier and more reliable as indicators of his deeper faith than the fear that has driven him to betrayal. Despite himself, Peter belongs to Jesus, and this is why divine grace cannot stop its pursuit of him.

26:74
τότε ἤρξατο καταθεματίζειν
καὶ ὀμνύειν ὅτι Οὐκ οἶδα τὸν ἄνθρωπον
καὶ εὐθέως ἀλέκτωρ ἐφώνησεν

*Then he began to invoke a curse on himself
and to swear, "I do not know the man."
And immediately the cock crowed*

WE HAVE SEEN HOW EACH OF Peter's three denials increases his culpability, not only because he obstinately reiterates his rejection of Jesus, but also because each occasion adds new evidence to his association with Jesus as disciple, so that he is given ever more sacred substance to disown. And Peter's reaction escalates in frantic intensity precisely as the evidence against him mounts. He becomes more verbally violent and outrageous. This process reaches its paroxysm in the present verse, which conveys Peter's entrapped state of mind with one unusual Greek verb reinforced by a second more common one: "He began *to invoke a curse on himself* and *to swear*."

The first of these verbs is *katathematízein*, related to our more familiar word *anathema*. Already in v. 72, we saw Peter backing up his denial "with an oath" (μετὰ ὅρκου). The depth of both Peter's guilt and his despair can be measured by his repeated recourse to swearing and oath-taking, particularly when no one is demanding it of him. It is bad enough simply to lie on a matter of this gravity; but spontaneously to spout off oaths, not once but twice, using the strongest language possible, is an insistent act of the most dire perjury in connection with the most sacred realities. The very sound and length of the word *katathematízein* conveys powerfully the ominous embroilment in which Peter is involving himself. This verb implies that its subject is calling down great evils on himself, cursing himself vehemently, if what he is asserting to be true is in fact false. Who can measure at this point the extent of Peter's actual freedom of will and clarity of understanding when invoking such a curse upon himself, given the enormous pressure generated in him by visceral fear? The fact remains, however, that he does not have to allow himself to escalate his denial to such terrible heights of cursing and swearing. He could stick to simple, stubborn denial. Instead, he is in fact calamitously appealing to the divine tribunal itself as witness to the veracity of his unconditional declaration that he does not "know the man" Jesus. But we are well acquainted, alas, with Peter's impulsive extremism, his tendency always to pursue any course of action to the utmost. Such passion, which could be the greatest asset in the practice of love, is at the moment proving to be his greatest self-inflicted scourge.

This whole time—while Peter is venting his fear through impassioned cursing and swearing, and madly struggling to be rid of the contamination of Jesus as if his Lord were a pestilence—Jesus himself has been right next door, still before the Sanhedrin where we left him, suffering in silence, no doubt painfully aware of his dear Peter's betrayal of his person. How could Jesus at this moment *not* call to mind Peter's brave words to him earlier that very evening, uttered in the same impassioned tone with which Peter is at present disowning him? "Even if I must die with you," Peter had blurted out, "I will not deny you" (26:35). And, even if these courageous words of Peter could be construed as tinged with hollow bravado, how could Jesus forget Peter's extraordinary confession of faith in him at Cæsarea Philippi, when the future pope proclaimed for all to hear the true identity of Jesus of Nazareth? At Cæsarea he had affirmed: "You are the Christ, the Son of the living God" (16:16). Indeed, Jesus' immediate promise to Peter in reply had famously been: "Blessed are you, Simon Bar Jona! . . . I tell you, you are Peter, and on this rock I will build my Church" (16:17–18).

Now Jesus never goes back on his promises because "if we are faithless, he remains faithful—for he cannot deny himself" (2 Tim 2:13). While Peter can deny his discipleship with Jesus, Jesus himself cannot deny himself, that is, he cannot negate his identity as Love Incarnate. Fortunately for Peter and the rest of us, it is love rather than strict human justice that sets the pace of Jesus' Heart. We may rightly say that grace's unremitting pursuit of Peter intends not only the salvation of Peter as an individual but also envisages the Lord's commitment to fulfill his promise to Peter, and, through Peter, to the Church and mankind. It will forever be a central element of Peter's eventual humility and sanctity that his glorious confession of Jesus' divine messianic identity came *before* his denial of Jesus in Caiaphas' courtyard. Peter will never be able to forget the chasm separating an ardent and true *faith* proclaimed with words that the wind blows away and a lived *fidelity* upheld at a high cost to oneself.

Even the paramount confession of faith at Cæsarea Philippi was, as Jesus stresses, not a product of Peter's own mystical insight or intelligence ("flesh and blood"), but rather a gracious revelation of "my Father who is in heaven" (16:17), for the sake of the Church. When left to ourselves—that is, when either a hostile intention or the force of adverse circumstances barricades us self-defensively within our ego and we disconnect ourselves from the expansive dimension of God's Kingdom—then we will know and enact only wretchedness, no matter how sterling and admirable our behavior might have been earlier on. Grace—sheer, unmerited, and overwhelming goodness inexplicably pouring down upon us from God—must have the last word, must have its way with us. We must experience what it means for our sinful selves to drown in God's love. There is no other path to sanctity. It is, after all, the *divine life* and nothing else that is our destiny and deepest desire.

None of us is saved on the basis of entitlement or merit. Our good deeds and all our protestations of genuine faith and love, real as they may be, are always overshadowed by all the murkiness lurking in our lives, are always predicated on our nature as weak, fickle, and at times treacherous creatures. In this Gospel episode, the evangelist certainly intends Peter to be a stand-in for each of us, ardent but terribly flawed disciples of Christ. Therefore, we must here apply to Peter, as exemplar, Paul's masterful words to the Romans:

> Since all have sinned and fall short of the glory of God, they are justified by his grace as a gift, through the redemption which is in Christ Jesus, whom God put forward as an expiation by his blood, to be received by faith. This was to show God's righteousness, because in his divine forbearance he had passed over former sins. (Rom 3:23–25)

Jesus never denies, never condemns. His silence is the silence of saddened fidelity, of the heavy-heartedness of someone who sees his beloved friend inflicting great harm on himself. Peter's invocation of a curse on himself reveals with awful starkness the fact that we can be our own worst enemies by yielding to our lethal impulses. It is only we who condemn ourselves, only we who are capable of taking the dreadful leap into the abyss. For his part, God, whose most beautiful name is Faithful Mercy, condemns no one, abandons no one, is ever on the watch for the slightest flicker of repentance on our part to come rejoicing to our aid yet never violating our freedom.

At that fatal moment, precisely as Peter teeters on the edge of perdition, *immediately* after he has invoked a dire curse upon himself, *the cock crowed*. That very earthy, homey, and piercing sound that out of the darkness presciently announces the beginning of a new day in Jerusalem, signals the crucial turning point of Peter's life. The abyss of perdition can yet perhaps become an abyss of hope. The bottomlessness of free-fall despair is revealed, despite the emotional overcharge, *not* to be a necessary creature created by God, but, rather, a construct fashioned by human fear and guilt and then projected onto the world of God's creation, whether in our psyche or in the objective world outside ourselves. Despair is a human creation, predicated on human limitation, blindness, and our penchant for nothingness. God did not create despair, just as he did not create death (Wis 1:13). Not only does it pain the Lord of Israel to witness the suffering of his creatures, but he intervenes forcefully to do something about it even when no one appeals to him for help (Ex 2:23–25; 3:7–9).

The text says incisively that "*immediately* the cock crowed" at the very moment when Peter utters the last syllable of his third "I do not know the man." This adverb *immediately* surely plays an important theological role, since otherwise it would dangle there idly at the beginning of the assertion. Surely its first purpose is to confirm as quickly as possible the veracity of Jesus' prophecy recalled in the next verse (v. 75). But I believe its more important function is to reveal the fact that God does not allow us to suffer one instant longer than strictly necessary. The moment Peter has hit the utmost bound of his treachery and shown us all what we become when abandoned to our own worst phantoms, a faithful little signal, slender as a rooster's throat but piercing as its shrill crowing, mercifully invades the horizon of our sealed consciousness. And its message is: beyond this despairing horror, there still exists the possibility of a renewed life, a new dawn of grace.

An ancient biblical dynamic of love is at work in this scene, which embodies in Peter the experience of Israel with God at the time of her infidelity and promiscuous dalliance with the idolatrous *goyim*. In a first movement of wrath against Israel, God declares through the prophet Hosea: "Now I will uncover her lewdness in the sight of her lovers, and no one shall rescue her out of my hand" (2:10). This gesture on God's part adequately describes the threefold exposure of Peter's wanton infidelity as fear makes him fawn on the powerful of this world. But only four verses later, God reveals what his ultimate purpose has been in turning to his faithless but beloved Israel full of a jilted lover's anger: "Therefore, behold, I will allure her, and bring her into the wilderness, and speak tenderly to her" (2:14). Exposure followed by tender embrace: every move on God's part, no matter how apparently violent or irate, is eventually revealed to have been nothing but a strategy of love.

And then finally, addressing Israel/Peter directly, God the Bridegroom promises: "And I will espouse you for ever; I will espouse you in righteousness and in justice, in steadfast love, and in mercy" (2:19). In the end, we see that all of love's merit has clearly been on God's part, and all the rejoicing in love's utter gratuity, in love's eagerness to forgive, belongs to the one whom God has embraced and made his own despite his most glaring infidelities.[2]

[2] The primacy of repentance and conversion in the Christian dispensation has recently received vivid contemporary expression in an open letter of Archbishop Carlo Viganò to the former cardinal Theodore McCarrick, dated January 13, 2019: "You, paradoxically, have at your disposal an immense offer of great hope for you from the Lord Jesus; you are in a position to do great good for the Church. In fact, you are now in a position to do something that has become more important for the Church than all of the good things you did for her throughout your entire life. . . . A public repentance on your part would bring a significant measure of healing to a gravely wounded and suffering Church. Are you willing to offer her that gift? 'Christ died for us all when we were still sinners' (Rom 5:8). He only asks that we respond by repenting and doing the good that we are given to do." Though McCarrick was never pope, his previous exalted position in the American hierarchy and in the universal Church closely parallels that of Peter in the apostolic college. Viganò is correct in pointing out the great fruit that public repentance could still harvest from an otherwise dismal situation. Only the alchemy of Christ's indefectible love can distill durable joy from lurid tragedy.

26:75 καὶ ἐμνήσθη ὁ Πέτρος τοῦ ῥήματος Ἰησοῦ εἰρηκότος
ὅτι Πρὶν ἀλέκτορα φωνῆσαι
τρὶς ἀπαρνήσῃ με·
καὶ ἐξελθὼν ἔξω ἔκλαυσεν πικρῶς

And Peter remembered the saying of Jesus,
"Before the cock crows
you will deny me three times."
And he went out and wept bitterly

T HE FULFILLMENT OF JESUS' PROPHECY in the sudden crowing
of the cock signals twin realities, not to be dissociated. First,
it confirms the dense gravity of Peter's terrible offense, which
must have struck the anvil of Jesus' Heart in anticipation of the hammer of Golgotha. Earlier this same night, we recall, Jesus had in fact
said to Peter with astounding serenity: "Truly, I say to you, this very
night, before the cock crows, you will deny me three times" (26:34).
However, we must be careful not to attribute this foreknowledge on
Jesus' part merely to his objective omniscience as incarnate Word;
above all, we should appreciate in this dispirited revelation the intuitive clairvoyance that intimate friendship bestows. Jesus knows Peter
and all his wayward heart thoroughly simply because he loves Peter
beyond all regret.

Consequently, Jesus' prophecy to Peter also bears, enfolded within
the wounded friend's sorrow, the glad tidings that Jesus has foreseen
it all and yet has not disowned Peter in return. Our gravest sins, our
most savage onslaught against the innocent trust of this true Friend,
reveal themselves as already drowned in a tide of Mercy the very instant we recognize them as sins and allow sorrow for them to pervade
our hearts. "For God has consigned all men to disobedience, that he
may have mercy upon all" (Rom 11:32).

The astounding truth bears repeating: not only does Jesus not reveal any slightest trace of recrimination, anger, or disappointment in
his premonitory words to Peter concerning the latter's impending
betrayal; on the contrary, on sustained reflection, we are dazzled by
Jesus' deepest motivation in making his revelation to Peter as the

Passion begins. This motivation, amazingly, is that Jesus surely wants to comfort Peter, to infuse a reserve of hope into Peter, to protect Peter from his own approaching mischief so as to keep him from despairing. This fundamental desire on Christ's part always to safeguard those he loves is no doubt reflected in St. Paul's famous encomium on charity, when he writes: "Love does not insist on its own way; it is not irritable or resentful. . . . Love bears all things, believes all things, hopes all things, endures all things. Love never ends" (1 Cor 13:5, 7–8a). We could hardly find a more literal and concrete illustration of these attributes of divine Love than in Jesus' attitude toward Peter in the light of the great betrayal.

Matthew's text tells us that, the moment the cock crowed from within the deep darkness of that fateful dawn on the first Good Friday, "Peter *remembered* the saying of Jesus." As a direct and immediate result of this remembering, like a stunt man shot out of a cannon, Peter "went out and wept bitterly". Memory clearly plays an essential role in the repentance and salvation of Peter. I am reminded of the terrible confession that the beautiful Estella makes to the undyingly hopeful Pip toward the end of Charles Dickens' *Great Expectations*: "You must know, Pip, . . . that I have no heart,—if that has anything to do with my [having no] memory" (chap. 29). Not only does Estella manifest by this admission a growing self-awareness that signals the first crack in her fortifications against Pip's love for her, but she also points out the paramount link between memory and the loving heart.

Peter's instantaneous reaction to the crowing of the cock—that is, his remembering the Lord's words to him earlier that night—likewise reveals that his love for Jesus runs much deeper than the fear that pushed him into his betrayal. Otherwise, Jesus' premonition to him would have already been drowned by the tide of the cruel events. His triumphant fear would have imposed forgetfulness. But the loving heart remembers because, like a lifeline, it is *memory* that connects the heart, caught in the midst of overwhelming circumstances, to the heart's sources of hope and strength, grounded in previous experience. One of memory's primordial functions is to rescue us from the shipwreck of the present moment, when all seems lost and we are drowning, by transporting our mind and heart miraculously to a vision of our total lives, to the undying reality of love's experienced fidelity and power.

At this moment, as the cock instinctively repeats his daily activity of crowing merely to announce the rising of the sun, his wholly natural action, by God's grace, has a supernatural effect on Peter, triggering in him remembrance of the foundation of his being. Peter now remembers Jesus' words to him with reference to the cock's activity. If he remembers them despite his present distraught and shameful state, it is only because Peter at bottom loves Jesus beyond return, with a love that ultimately proves mightier than all fear, and this love of Peter's for Jesus, in turn, is consciously nourished by the memory of everything Jesus has been to him and has done for him.

Peter can now remember and repent because his remembering is no mere neutral recalling of a past fact. His remembering plunges him again, with love's unique violence, into a still ongoing and all-determining relationship that nothing can abolish or confine to a tragically shut-out past. This is an intense friendship that cannot be unilaterally destroyed but *can* be unilaterally upheld, grounded as it is on who Jesus is and on Peter's clarion knowledge that Jesus' love for him is everlasting and utterly undefeatable. Peter's memory of his association with Jesus over the past three years, from the moment of his mysterious election as disciple to this very night of betrayal, is all of a piece: its substance is quite simply the unshakeable knowledge that he, Peter, could never be so unfaithful, so weak, so cowardly and treacherous toward Jesus that the combined power of his most extravagant misdeeds could ever surpass and leave behind the enduringness of Jesus' love for him.

Peter now knows in his bones that even the full mass of collective evil fabricated by man, no matter how heinous, can never overwhelm, defeat, or divert uncreated Divine Love. Furthermore, Peter owes the dawning of this rocklike conviction in his consciousness to the sudden crowing of this particular neighborhood cock behind Caiaphas' house, which awakens him out of the nightmare of sin, fear, and betrayal. How astounding that a daily recurring feature of irrational nature should spark a momentous conversion toward the light in a human heart, with the memory of Jesus' words catalyzing the event. What an extraordinary instance of nature and grace working in tandem! As a consequence of this shrill sound piercing his ears from outside the mental prison of his shameful little drama, Peter is capable of entertaining only one thought, which now throbs within him like newborn life: "Jesus knows all, and Jesus has known it all along, and still Jesus will never reject me. Jesus and only Jesus can enfold all into his embrace!''

Such is the effective intercessory power of God-given *memory*. Our memory can save us almost despite ourselves by performing, just when it is most desperately needed, a great moral miracle: it can instantaneously banish the tormenting nightmare of guilt from our souls and make to dawn upon them the radiant awareness of God's love for us, which is as trustworthy as the rising sun and can be touched in the presence of ''Jesus Christ, [who] is the same yesterday and today and for ever'' (Heb 13:8). When our conscience oppresses and condemns us, our memory acts like an infiltrating guerrilla warrior, blessedly sent by God to detonate within our barricaded heart the bomb of God's ever-greater Mercy, which shatters all resistance.

''And he went out and wept bitterly.'' No matter how intense and well-founded our awareness of the Lord's undying love for us, however, massive betrayal cannot be magically transmuted into joy without traversing the intervening phases of shame, regret, and contrition. The sturdiest promises planted within us can only grow when watered by the bitterest tears. After committing betrayal, we have to learn how to love with sturdy fidelity, and such learning takes time. God never wishes to humiliate us merely to watch us squirm. This would be unworthy of his love. A tender Father, God takes no pleasure in shaming us; but he will allow the salutary shame oozing spontaneously from our conscience to perform its medicinal function. God does want us to learn humility so that we can once again live in the truth, that is, in a relationship of generous reciprocity both with him and with the world. Moreover, nothing can teach us humility like experiencing the scorching shame of measuring with lucidity how abysmally low we can at times fall beneath our highest dignity as creatures called to practice faithful love like God's own.

Therefore, before Peter can rejoin Jesus to share in the mystery of his Lord's Passion, the apostle must undergo the bitter experience of dwelling for a while in a stark solitude in which he can plainly consider what he has done and allow that sorrow thoroughly to pierce his heart. Only such piercing will finally provide the permanently open entryway by which Jesus' love for him can access his deepest being, there to abide forever. There is no way around it: *God enters by the wound.* No matter how ''religious'' our more external habits and language may appear, we shall remain hermetically sealed off to the eager approach of the Bridegroom until our hearts are perforated by the golden arrow of repentant sorrow. Such piercing is the initial grace of conversion.

"And he went out and wept bitterly." The original Greek entails a marvelously expressive formulation:

ἐξελθὼν ἔξω ἔκλαυσεν πικρῶς
[exelthón éxô éklausen pikrós].

These insistent gutturals (*ex, ex, ek, kr*), combined with the stresses, are like hard hammer blows upon an anvil or like strangled sobs. The stabbing memory of Jesus' faithful love for him impels Peter, first, to *go out*, that is, to forsake his shameful association of convenience with the power-holders of the establishment before whom he has groveled, in order to go apart by himself and set his heart in order anew in a wrenching solitude. He must leave behind the courtyard of Caiaphas' house, which symbolizes the security and sham identity offered him by mingling in the ordinary crowd of profiteers who gravitate around this center of Jewish religious and political power. He must purge his soul of the fear that has made him prefer the secure anonymity of a mob to the risky solidarity with his Jesus, a condemned man. And in that solitude apart, Peter must now dedicate himself to *weeping bitterly*: that is, he must allow the fire of Jesus' love overtaking his heart to melt down the ice of a frozen will and let the torrents of new life being infused into him irrigate his whole person. The poisonous sweetness of betrayal must slowly yield to the medicinal bitterness of healing contrition. The outpouring of endless tears is but the visible sign of the subterranean upheaval reshaping his deepest soul into a treasure-house of enduring fidelity. Legend has it that Peter wept so long and so intensely that for the rest of his life deep furrows ran beneath his eyes. Well might Peter in his tearful solitude have exclaimed with Thomas à Kempis: "I want no consolation that takes from me my sorrow for sin. . . . If a grace makes me more humble, more prudent, more ready to renounce my own desires, then I bid it welcome with all my heart."[3]

---

[3] Thomas à Kempis, *The Imitation of Christ*, trans. Ronald Knox and Michael Oakley (New York: Sheed & Ward, 1959), II, 10, 3, pp. 86–87.

PETER'S *THREEFOLD* DENIAL of Jesus is a deed that not only fulfills Jesus' own prophecy but also reveals the depth of Peter's fear and the thoroughness of his rejection of his Master. However, the very negative symbolism of the number 3 on this occasion naturally evokes the other threefold affirmation of Peter's love for Jesus that we witness at the end of John's Gospel: "When they had finished breakfast, Jesus said to Simon Peter, 'Simon, son of John, do you love me more than these?' He said to him, 'Yes, Lord; you know that I love you.' He said to him, 'Feed my lambs.'" This exchange repeats itself twice more with slight variations (Jn 21:15–17). It is as if, by this means, Jesus is giving Peter ample opportunity, as part of the grace of the Resurrection, to redeem himself before all, just as Peter had denied him before all. This lakeside scene shows that at the *root* of contrition there is faithful love, reciprocally given and embraced by both parties. This being so, it also shows that the *fruit* of contrition has to be universal love demonstrated through service, since the generativity of love always bears fruit beyond the two principal players.

When all is said and done, finally, we must not forget that, if Peter had at all been in a position of denying Jesus, it was only because he had first chosen to follow him right into the lion's mouth! We may draw a contrast here with the other apostles, who, except for Judas, did not deny Jesus formally and explicitly simply because they fled into hiding and thus were not engaged enough in Jesus' fate for them to be questioned or accused by anyone as Peter was. Thus, even in his denial of Jesus, Peter is in an altogether separate category from the other apostles. His relationship to Jesus shows the unique aspects of his role as head of what came to be known as the "apostolic college". Peter may have been a coward, but his conscience is neither dead nor even dormant. The very moment he hears the cock crow, he *remembers* Jesus' prophecy, and that memory immediately transfixes his heart into contrition.

In contrast to the members of the Sanhedrin with their hopelessly entrenched stances, Peter, equally a Jew with them, showcases the very complex character of the human heart by displaying for all to ponder the whole range of the heart's capacities: initial enthusiasm and positive response; for a while loyalty, tenacity, and passion; then fearfulness, cowardice, and betrayal; and in the end, sorrowful repentance and regeneration. The multifaceted portrayal of Peter in the Gospels may well make him the richest and most complex personality in the New Testament, second only to Jesus himself.

This episode in the Gospel of Matthew, with its parallels in the other three Gospels, is of such central importance to Christian faith and piety that it has inspired many musical and artistic creations. By far the most sublime and well-known of the musical compositions is the cycle of madrigals called the *Lagrime di San Pietro* ("The Tears of St. Peter") of Orlando de Lassus (1532–1594), the crowning achievement of this Renaissance composer, who produced it in the last weeks of his life. This masterpiece features a complex polyphony for seven voices, set to poems by Luigi Tansillo that explore every aspect of St. Peter's process of sorrowful repentance and return to Christ's friendship. The composition has been said to contain some of the most expressive religious music ever written. Here is a sample of Tansillo's poetry:

> The anguish and the shame but greater grew
>   In Peter's heart as morning slowly came;
>
> No eye was there to see him, well he knew,
>   Yet he himself was to himself a shame;
>
> Exposed to all men's gaze, or screened from view,
>   A noble heart will feel the pang the same;
>
> A prey to shame the sinning soul will be,
>   Though none but heaven and earth its shame can see.

For the medium of painting we must mention El Greco (1541–1614) first and foremost. He was so fascinated by the topic that he produced no fewer than four or five different renderings of Peter's contrition. The most famous of these portrays Peter frontally with hollow gray cheeks, a downturned mouth, and glistening eyes brimming with imploration as they look upward with hope. Georges de la Tour (1593–1652), for his part, was a painter known for his "tenebrist" style, and he gives us a profile view of Peter's gaunt face, bathed in a splendid light coming from a single candle burning before him, while all around is darkness.

A third example of the genre is *St. Peter the Penitent* by Jusepe de Ribera (nicknamed "Lo Spagnoletto", 1591–1662), a Spaniard who worked and died in Italy. This is a composition that moves us deeply by the manner in which it portrays the anguish of Peter's soul not only by the distraught expression on his furrowed face but also by the deformation of his whole body into a brown, shapeless heap upon the ground, with hands joined tightly in supplication and the face wrenched upward at an extreme angle that deforms it as well. The only light comes from above, shining palely on Peter's face and somewhat relieving the gloom of his brown garment, from beneath which the existence of a bright green undergarment is briefly revealed at his left sleeve and right knee, no doubt to signify the hope growing deep in his heart. Peter's mouth gapes in prayer as he repeats for the millionth time the words "Forgive me, my Jesus!" One will scarcely find a representation of the human form that expresses more emphatically and stirringly, from the person's every pore, a faith that has learned to expect *everything* from God's sheer grace.

11. OF BLOOD MONEY AND DESPAIR

Jesus' Condemnation and Judas' Suicide
(27:1–10)

27:1   Πρωΐας δὲ γενομένης συμβούλιον ἔλαβον
πάντες οἱ ἀρχιερεῖς καὶ οἱ πρεσβύτεροι τοῦ λαοῦ
κατὰ τοῦ Ἰησοῦ
ὥστε θανατῶσαι αὐτόν

When morning came,
all the chief priests and the elders of the people
took counsel against Jesus
to put him to death

MUCH EARLIER DURING THIS FATEFUL NIGHT, we have already heard the high priest Caiaphas roar with rage as he addressed his fellow members of the Sanhedrin, exclaiming: "'You have now heard his blasphemy. What is your judgment?' They answered, 'He deserves death'" (26:65b–66). Then came the spitting, the hitting, and the mocking as visceral confirmations of the rightness of the death sentence, and the crucial episode of Peter's denial followed at once. Matthew has portrayed a most dismal panorama unfurling before Jesus, in which we encounter not only the fury and outrage of the religious authorities against Jesus but also the abandonment and treachery of even his most intimate disciples. Jesus' unimaginable solitude gapes bottomless beneath him. The Emmanuel who

375

bears closeness to man etched into his very name and nature has in the end been forsaken by both friend and foe.

The cock's crow, however, has also ushered in the dawn and, with it, Peter's colossal repentance. Peter's bitter tears now fall like a balm of consolation on the Heart of Jesus and glow like a light of grateful remembrance that gladden Jesus' sorrowful eyes with the knowledge that all his redeeming labor has not been for naught. But the new morning—the morning of the first Good Friday—at the same time acts like a ruthless stimulus for the Sanhedrin to tidy up its business, to reiterate by orderly deliberation the visceral death sentence they have already imposed raucously and angrily on Jesus in the course of the night: "All the chief priests and the elders of the people took counsel against Jesus to put him to death." Whether their one consuming desire has been expressed more viscerally or more officiously, Jesus' *death* is what they have sought from the beginning. The threat Jesus poses to their world view, power, and way of life is so extreme that only death can remove him from their midst effectively. The very same light of morning that signals Peter's repentance also witnesses the hardening of the Jewish authorities in their evil purpose.

Despite the mildness of Jesus' words and demeanor before them throughout the night, the Sanhedrin sees fit to bind Jesus' wrists as they send him off to Pontius Pilate, the Roman governor, as they seek the latter's required secular ratification of their own religious death sentence. The discrepancy between Jesus' consistently peaceful behavior and this measure of tying him up, normally applied to common criminals, only reveals the depth of the authorities' haunting fear of him. These men are merely attempting to shackle their own overweening phantoms, generated by ambition and guilt. "And they bound him and led him away and delivered him to Pilate the governor" (27:2). Matthew now again enriches his narrative by portraying two simultaneously occurring events. As the Sanhedrin dispatches a group of guards to escort its condemned prisoner Jesus off to the Roman governor's residence for the secular trial, Matthew introduces the subplot of Judas' fate. This parallel narrative performs at least three functions, at once theological and literary.

First, it deepens and expands the dynamic centrality of Jesus' influence at all levels of the people of Israel, an influence that paradoxically only seems to grow in strength precisely as the Lord becomes more silent and apparently passive and is humanly losing all ground.

Secondly, it is obvious that Matthew wishes to demonstrate with vivid starkness the ultimate contrast between the fates of two great sinners, Peter and Judas, both of whom have betrayed Jesus. Indeed, it seems that, of all the apostles, only Peter and Judas "hung around" the trial at Caiaphas' house. We know this explicitly concerning Peter and may deduce as much from the fact that Judas is said to have found out immediately about Jesus' condemnation (27:3). Thirdly, by Jesus' present transfer from Jewish to Roman hands, Matthew underscores the universal responsibility of all mankind—both Jews and pagans— for the rejection and demise of the Messiah. Thus, Matthew is painting a vast canvas that portrays the drama of redemption both within the microcosm of Jesus' intimate friends throughout the ages and at the macrocosmic level of world history.

27:2–3a   καὶ δήσαντες αὐτὸν ἀπήγαγον
καὶ παρέδωκαν Πιλάτῳ τῷ ἡγεμόνι.
Τότε ἰδὼν Ἰούδας ὁ παραδιδοὺς αὐτὸν
ὅτι κατεκρίθη, μεταμεληθεὶς

And they bound him and led him away
and delivered him to Pilate the governor.
When Judas, his betrayer, saw
that he was condemned, he regretted

I N THE GREEK TEXT, JUDAS' EPITHET ὁ παραδιδοὺς (*ho paradidoús*), translated above as "the betrayer", is the participial substantive form of the verb rendered above as "they delivered" (παρέδωκαν). The original insists on using the same term twice to refer to the action of both the Jewish authorities and the wayward disciple. We have often before referred to this particular play of words and its significance. The passage could be translated more literally though less elegantly: "and they *handed him over* to Pilate the governor. When Judas, his *hander-over*, saw. . . ." Matthew repeats the same word, not because he is at a loss for varied vocabulary, but rather because he deems it essential for us to keep before our eyes both the concrete, physical action of "handing-over" and the strict connection between the unjust deed of the Sanhedrin and its source in Judas' betrayal of his Lord. If only external forces imperiled the welfare of the Church in this world, Christ's community would be sure to preserve its integrity. Most destructive is the assault of infidelity from within. No one expects the world as such to be faithful.

"To deliver" and "to betray" are too neat and too genteel a pair of words to express what is actually occurring in this episode. These words do not convey the physical onslaught and violent manhandling Jesus has to endure. We should never forget that the Creator of all things, who holds the world continually in his hands, thus sustaining it in existence, at the same time chose to become little and vulnerable so that he could be encompassed and disposed of by human hands. " 'Non coerceri maximo, contineri tamen a minimo, divinum est' (Not to be [surrounded] by the greatest, but to let oneself be encompassed by the smallest—that is divine)." [1]

Jesus experiences both excruciating corporal suffering and mental torture as he becomes a universal plaything in men's *hands*. The present plaything status of the Creator of the Universe, whose *hands* formed Adam from the clay of the earth (Gen 2:7), is set in relief very forcibly here by three rapidly fired verbs of subjugation that make him the triple *object* of man's action and execute the will of men over their captive God: "They bound him and led him away and [handed] him [over]." We should marvel at the nobility of God's Omnipotence as it consents to become powerless in the grip of our hands, so graciously created by its hands! The all-powerful God with full deliberation gave us hands that could one day tear him apart! Who can fathom this mystery of both grandeur and iniquity?

---

[1] This dense Latin epigram, heavy with paradox, is known as "Ignatius of Loyola's epitaph". It is quoted in Joseph Cardinal Ratzinger, *Introduction to Christianity*, trans. J. R. Foster, 2nd ed. (San Francisco: Ignatius Press, 2004), 146. See footnote 18 in that chapter, where Ratzinger traces the origins of the epigram and shows how it entered German literature through its use by Hölderlin at the beginning of his lyrical novel *Hyperion*.

The "reduction of divinity" is a constant theme in the Gospel, showing how the God who is unbounded and illimitable by nature sought nonetheless to make himself containable. The theme reveals the incarnate Word's innermost motivation when coming among us, and we may trace it from the Infant in Mary's arms at the Nativity and in the arms of Simeon at the Temple all the way to the institution of the Eucharist and the arrest at Gethsemane and, finally, to the crucifixion, the deposition, and the entombment. In all these cases, the Divine Person of God's Son, through the mediation of his sacred body, is held and manipulated, for a variety of purposes, by human hands. The Son of God's generous impulse to rest in our arms—he the *Maximum* contained within us the *Minimum*—is in the end most fully reciprocated by Mary Magdalen's passionate cry to the unknown Gardener: "Sir, if you have carried him away, tell me where you have laid him, *and I will take him away!*" (Jn 20:15). Her wholly irrational human longing has in advance overcome all material obstacles (the weight of the corpse of a full-grown male) and alone does justice to Jesus' divine madness in wanting to be contained within our puny lives.

Matthew wants us to see the tainted *hands* of these ruffians at their pitiless work. The process triggered in Gethsemane and sealed at Caiaphas' house ends, after all, not in a jail term for the accused, but in his drawn-out and agonizing death. And Jesus' public execution, eventually sanctioned by both the religious and the military authorities working in concert, is made possible by the *handing-over* of Jesus by an intimate friend into whose hands the trusting Jesus has first *handed himself over* both figuratively, in his unreserved friendship, and also quite literally, in the Eucharist, at the Last Supper: "Jesus took bread, and blessed, and broke it, and gave it to the disciples and said, 'Take, eat; this is my body'" (26:26). Jesus can be handed over in betrayal by Judas, or by any of us, solely because he has first handed himself over to us in love. In this is the full omnipotence of the incarnate Word revealed: in his divesting himself of his omnipotence for the sake of his beloved.

The dawn of the first Good Friday has a powerful but impressively contrary effect on all the main players in the drama of Jesus' Passion. In Peter what we witness is the awakening of his heart out of its long night of fear to the luminous memory of Jesus' abiding love for him despite everything. This sudden remembering has the effect of a lightning bolt that ignites in Peter's whole being a fire of fathomless sorrow for his abject betrayal of his friend and Lord. On the high priest and his cohorts, on the other hand, the material light of the rising sun pours down instead a murky fog of spiritual darkness. This interior gloom confirms them with grim calmness in the evil intent of murderous injustice against Jesus that they have long since been incubating within themselves like the eggs of poisonous serpents. The moment has arrived for the hatching of all their malevolent plots.

As for Judas, who unbeknownst to us has all along been lurking about Caiaphas' house: the condemnation of Jesus, as the text poignantly records, brings for him, as it did for Peter, a moment of massive conversion. However, Judas' "conversion" represents an option diametrically opposed to that of Peter. As we have amply seen, Peter's change of heart represents its true awakening to a new life of trust and loving fidelity under the transforming fire of penetrating sorrow. But there are changes and there are changes. Judas' change of heart only plunges him headlong from the simmering guilt of treacherous ambition and ambiguous political ideals into the deepest depths of despair.

The contrast between the respective "conversions" of Peter and Judas is mirrored with precision by the verbs the text uses to describe them. In the case of the former, Matthew says that Peter "remembered" (ἐμνήσθη, *emnêsthê*) the words of Jesus about the crowing of the cock. Though with great sorrow, Peter instinctually turns to Jesus as the source of forgiveness and new life, taking refuge and comfort in the thought of Jesus' unswerving love for him. By contrast, Matthew records that the news of Jesus' condemnation does indeed trigger in the traitor Judas a violent regret; yet it is one, not lifting him up to a hope for regeneration, but rather plunging him down into a perilous despondency. The text here uses the word μεταμεληθείς (*metamelêtheís*) to express the nature of Judas' change of heart. Though it can be generally rendered as "repenting" or "regretting", which could of course have positive connotations, it should be pointed out that, quite literally, this verb *metamélomai* means "[to bear] a care afterward". It definitely does not convey the same sense of a new start in life after a conversion of mind and heart as is communicated by the classic Christian term *metánoia*. In other words, the news of Jesus' condemnation by the Sanhedrin becomes an impossible burden for Judas to bear. It becomes a gnawing remorse eating away at his soul, as when a dog writhes in a twist biting himself full of wounds.

Perhaps Judas speculated that a little roughing-up at the hands of the authorities would instill some practical wisdom into Jesus and bring him around to Judas' own political way of seeing his messiahship. But now that Jesus' death by public execution is hourly drawing nearer, Judas can no longer live with this concrete result of his treacherous actions. Nevertheless, the crucial point illustrating the extreme contrast between Judas and Peter lies in the fact that Judas remains enmeshed within the net of his own thought patterns: mentally he is a prisoner entrapped by his own habit of nauseous self-concern and self-reliance. He is incapable of breaking out of this confinement within the walls of his own ego in order to fall, like Peter, at the feet of Jesus, ever-present in his heart, and tearfully beg for forgiveness. It seems that, tragically, Judas commits the unpardonable sin of considering himself beyond pardon. Obstinate sin always is rooted in insurmountable pride. At certain moments, we would rather destroy ourselves than appeal for mercy and be saved.

Objectively speaking, Peter's betrayal of Jesus is far worse than Judas', for the simple reason that Peter's relationship with the Lord is far more intimate and his privileges in the apostolic college outstrip those of all the others. Peter has been present at all the paramount moments of Jesus' public life, either singly or together with James and John, and Peter has also been the continual spokesman for the group, for better and for worse. The gravity of a betrayal must always be measured by the depth of the fall from the heights of a previously existing love. What is the decisive quality in Peter, then, that finally saves him, whereas Judas in the end falls prey to black despair? The answer lies, precisely, in Peter's *bitter tears*. Despair never weeps; despair rages and lashes out and at length becomes silent as the grave with contempt because the despairing soul will forever seek the source of its evil actions outside itself, incapable as it is of turning within and humbly and quietly acknowledging its guilt.

Guilt humbly acknowledged is guilt forgiven, but unacknowledged and unrepentant guilt can only fester. Despair is the fruit of a haughtiness that cannot avow the gangrene within and that therefore closes itself off to all surgical intervention. Or, conversely, despair can result from an affliction that is only too vividly and pathologically acknowledged, but to the exclusion of all possibility of a cure. "My disease is too terrible for even God to heal." By contrast, Peter deliberately goes out into his bitter solitude and thus wisely surrenders, full of trust, into the surgical hands of grace.

Peter repents and starts off on a new life because he is capable of *humility*. At the very same time, moreover, he activates within himself a *faith* in the steadfastness of Jesus' love for him. These two very concrete activities, the practice of ready humility and the lively exercise of faith, are but two aspects of the same reality. Together they make up the one reciprocal interplay of faithful love that can only be lived by two persons conjointly. Peter is not proud enough to think that the evil he has committed is so great that even God himself cannot handle it. Judas, on the other hand, is arrogant and conceited even in the midst of his self-destructive rampage; his "faith" is a warped and narcissistic vice because he believes more in his own capacity for evil-doing than in the healing power of God's love for him. To the bleak end, Judas must always be at the center of his own concerns and worries, and so he feels compelled to push Jesus out to the distant periphery of his life. His guilt over what he has done to Jesus in the end carries more weight than the living person of Jesus.

The only thing that separates life-giving repentance from lethal despair is the firm awareness and acceptance of the loving God's readiness to forgive. But what an abyss such separation carves out! Mankind should not be divided into so-called "saints and sinners" predestined to be such by God. The determining gulf, rather, is man-made. On the one side, we see assembled those who, experiencing themselves as evil-doers and traitors, are nevertheless urgently aware of their need for help and, therefore, seek and embrace forgiveness. And on the other side of the chasm, we see those who, enamored of a grim and uncompromising self-sufficiency, persist in rejecting the very possibility of being forgiven. "For godly grief produces a repentance that leads to salvation and brings no regret, but worldly grief produces death" (2 Cor 7:10).

27:3b–4   ἔστρεψεν τὰ τριάκοντα ἀργύρια
τοῖς ἀρχιερεῦσιν καὶ πρεσβυτέροις λέγων·
Ἥμαρτον παραδοὺς αἷμα ἀθῷον.
οἱ δὲ εἶπαν· Τί πρὸς ἡμᾶς; σὺ ὄψῃ

He brought back the thirty pieces of silver
to the chief priests and the elders, saying,
"I have sinned in betraying innocent blood."
They said, "What is that to us? See to it yourself!"

MATTHEW APPARENTLY FINDS it difficult to take his attention away from the person of Judas, his actions, words, and motivations. Therefore, we, too, must sustain our gaze yet awhile upon this deeply troubled and troubling figure. Indeed, Judas offers all ages a painfully eloquent archetype for one possible major stance in our relationship with God and the world. No doubt the evangelist sees in Judas' choices and destiny a distinct possibility for every person, not only in our dealings with God and Jesus but also with one another. Which of us has never betrayed a friend, driven by considerations that at the time seemed unimpeachable? Let us never forget that, at bottom, what the writers of the Gospel are always intending is our own conversion of heart and surrender into the arms of God's forgiveness and mercy. After announcing that Jesus has been officially condemned to death and led off to the Roman governor, Matthew therefore opens a parenthesis to bring Judas to the foreground and prompt us to ponder, while in the back of our mind he has simultaneously planted the image of Jesus being dragged off to Pilate. Matthew wants us to feel keenly the terrible tension generated between Judas and Jesus by the obduracy of the one and the pliancy of the other.

Of the four evangelists, only Matthew records the precise sum given by the high priests to Judas as the reward for his betrayal: thirty silver pieces. The exact amount, first mentioned at the time of the transaction at 26:15, is now recorded again. Indirectly, this meticulousness on Matthew's part intends to characterize Judas as a calculator, someone in whose heart the addiction to managerial accuracy and successful results has won out over the messy untidiness of love. We remember that this price of thirty silver pieces occurs in Zechariah as the negligible amount owed a rejected shepherd (11:12–13). In Exodus, furthermore, it is the compensation to be paid to a person whose slave has been gored by one's ox (21:32). These associations of such a sum with a slave and an undesirable employee stress Jesus' worthless social status in the eyes of both the high priests and Judas.

It is also highly significant that, on sorely regretting the catastrophic effect his betrayal is now having on Jesus, Judas turns at once, for relief, not to Jesus or to God, but rather *to his co-conspirators*. His gnawing remorse makes him go backward rather than forward (cf. the verb ἔστρεψεν = "he brought back"). Even his repentance takes the form of a new transaction as he seeks to undo what he has done by returning the money. But the Sanhedrin now has safely in hand what it has sought for so long and obtained with Judas' ready help, and its members no longer have any time or patience to be bothered with Judas or the tortures that his conscience might be inflicting on him. The contrast with Peter's actions at this point is glaring: Matthew tells us that Peter *went out* from those among whom he was hiding to a place where he had never been before, *out*, that is, to a painful but purifying solitude (26:75), while Judas in his distress *goes back* to the very hotbed of his betrayal.

To grasp fully the grim implications of Judas' instinct to run to the high priests seeking solace rather than to God, let us consider for a moment the reactions of a sampling of great sinners in Scripture when awakening to the gravity of their sin. When Pharaoh, for instance, repents of having persecuted the Jews, he says to Moses and Aaron: "I have sinned this time; the LORD is in the right, and I and my people are in the wrong" (Ex 9:27). Even this arch-pagan, the supreme ruler of the world he oppresses, recognizes the sovereignty of God's judgment against him and appeals to God's mercy through his representatives. Again, after Saul on winning a battle disobeys an explicit command of the Lord out of self-serving avarice, the king goes to Samuel and confesses: "I have sinned; for I have transgressed the commandment of the LORD and your words, because I feared the people and obeyed their voice" (1 Sam 15:24). Sinner though he is, Saul here does have his religious categories in good order and knows to whom to appeal for forgiveness. And when the Tarshish-bound sailors in Jonah's ship regret having thrown him overboard in the middle of a storm, they appeal earnestly to the God of Israel, pagan though they are, and cry "to the LORD: 'We beg you, O LORD, let us not perish for this man's life, and lay not on us innocent blood'" (Jon 1:14). Finally, after his ruthless double sin of murder and adultery, the great King David himself does not hesitate to confess to the Lord: "Against you, you only, have I sinned, and done that which is evil in your sight, so that you are justified in your sentence and blameless in your judgment" (Ps 51[50]:4). David here clearly understands that, just as God is ultimately the chief offended party in every sin, so, too, are we to appeal to God himself as the sole source of pardon and redemption.

It is against this biblical background of genuine repentance and conversion that we must evaluate Judas' manner of reacting to his feelings of devouring guilt. Read within the context of the repentance of Pharaoh, Saul, the pagan mariners, and David, Judas' words and actions are chilling and ominous. He does not spare the merest thought to the divine omnipresence and judgment in the way even the pagan sinners did, nor does he show the slightest inclination to ask for forgiveness: "When Judas, his betrayer, saw that [Jesus] was condemned, he repented and brought back the thirty pieces of silver to the chief priests and the elders, saying, 'I have sinned in betraying innocent blood.'" These words chill us to the bone because, for all their soberness, they nonetheless reveal the interior hell of a man who is locked up with his own guilty conscience as with a famished hyena. He is incapable or unwilling to appeal or even refer to the God he has offended. Judas rather seems to expect some kind of redemption to come to him *from his fellow conspirators against Jesus*, hoping they can somehow turn back the clock for him and undo their shared, murderous intrigues.

True redemption, however, can be obtained only from God himself or from a representative of God acting in his name, such as Moses, Aaron, or Samuel in our examples. Judas, instead, tragically embodies the proverb, "Like a dog that returns to his vomit is a fool who repeats his folly" (Prov 26:11). How could we ever expect salvation to come from the source of our sin or from our accomplices in sin? Forgiveness and redemption cannot be merited or wrested by us, whether cleverly or despairingly. They have to come to us gratuitously from Another, on condition that we hold out an open and sorrowful heart to receive them like a parched earth longing for the rain. And only sincere humility and bitter contrition can break open a human heart to the plentiful waters of redemption God wants to pour over us.

"I HAVE SINNED IN BETRAYING [παραδούς, *paradoús*] innocent blood": This confession of sin on the part of Judas certainly grips us. It is eerily poignant to hear Judas on this one occasion apply to himself and fully own the fraught term that Matthew has already applied to him many times: παραδούς. His confession may be more literally translated as "I, the hander-over of innocent blood, have sinned." In his mouth, the action of betrayal is no abstract concept; it takes on an extreme physical density, as if we could *see* the great efforts of mind and body required over time for Judas to achieve his purpose. And now he is expending equally great energies trying to undo what he has done, trying to redeem himself by the titanic effort of erasing the past. If before he has sold Jesus for thirty pieces of silver, the same logic makes him think that he can now buy his own ransom by giving back that silver! In either case, he remains entrenched as the master of all transactions. Even as one consumed with guilt, he cannot let go of the reins of power.

It is also curious, indeed, that he is making his confession of guilt to the very persons with whom he plotted against Jesus and who he knows despise Jesus and fear his mysterious power. Though Judas admits the fact that he has greatly sinned and assumes as well the horrible guilt for such a sin, nevertheless, his confession is completely invalid in the theological sense. It amounts to an emotional outburst. It has no life-giving efficacy because of the persons to whom he has chosen to make it. These can recognize no sin in his betrayal of Jesus; on the contrary. Above all, there is no genuine change of heart: *Judas is all regret but no contrition*, the very definition of despair.

Judas' total lack of humble, human repentance is conveyed by the language of his confession. He depersonalizes and objectifies Jesus by referring to him, a suffering innocent *person* and close *friend*, in the purely legal language of Torah: "I have sinned in betraying innocent blood." If he were feeling genuine, heart-shattering contrition, Judas would say something like "I have betrayed my Lord" or "my friend" or at least "my teacher who so trusted me and who was so good to me". Instead, he refers to Jesus as "innocent blood", thereby reducing Jesus to a legal concept. He may perhaps be attempting to obliterate even the memory of the living, subjective bond of his heart with that of Jesus, a bond he has destroyed and that could again give him life only if it were restored by Jesus himself in gracious response to Judas' pleading for forgiveness.

Moreover, Judas' horrific guilt, the real depth of his sin, lies, not in the fact that Jesus is admittedly innocent, but rather in the fact that this Jesus whom he has betrayed was his faithful friend, master, and Lord. By refusing to acknowledge these intimate bonds between his person and the person of Jesus, Judas willingly manifests only the fact that he, the great calculator, has committed a terrible error of judgment and an objective injustice, but not that he has broken personal fidelity with someone who loves him. It is appalling to witness thus the legalism of Judas' mind. Such legalism is a kind of armor of the heart that precludes the piercing of grace. This is corroborated by the fact that Judas' "conversion", or, rather, change of outlook, takes place only "when Judas . . . saw that [Jesus] was condemned" (27:3). Up until that point, apparently, Judas' conscience did not bother him in the least, but now the Sanhedrin has gone too far, farther than Judas thinks was justified. Only the imposition of capital punishment by the Sanhedrin finally shakes him because such a final solution is more than he calculated as the desirable result of his betrayal.

Again, by extreme contrast to Judas' sanctimonious confession of a legal violation, we recall that Peter's instantaneous thought upon hearing the cock crow was *the person and words of Jesus*, together with the shattered state of his personal bond with the Lord: "And Peter remembered the saying of *Jesus*" (26:75). Judas' loud exclamation to the elders, "I have sinned in betraying innocent blood" may be self-excoriating, but it still remains theatrically centered on himself as the subject of greatest interest. We know from Dante's *Inferno* that, far from being incompatible, colossal pride and self-consuming hatred feed on one another most efficiently. We think of the mythical being called the *ouoróboros*, the serpent perennially devouring its own tail, on this occasion as a symbol of arrogant self-sufficiency. Peter's shame, on the other hand, makes him remember Another, impels him to escape from the stinking dungeon of his ego-bound betrayal as he gasps for air and light. Like a doomed, shipwrecked man suddenly grasping a plank, Peter instinctively redirects all his thoughts and emotions to his Lord and Friend. He valiantly breaks out of the vicious cycle of fear and betrayal and slinks off quietly to weep in the solitude of love's surrender.

Sin, obsessively clutched in arrogance, can lead only to despair because that obsessive clutching enthrones it as the supreme idol of the guilty soul. Deified sin then mutates into an insatiable god like Moloch and requires human sacrifice (Lev 18:21). If a sinner is to be reborn to new life, he must first find God to be more engaging and fascinating than his sin. He must use his piercing guilt, not as a suicidal weapon, but as an instrument to lay his sin open to the healing balm of mercy and forgiveness. He must vigorously abandon his lair of sin—the familiar and cozy hideout of his habitual self-indulgence—in order to enter the bracing dimension of unconditional love where much will be given but much will also be demanded by an unpredictable and exacting Lover.

"WHAT IS THAT TO US? See to it yourself!" This apathetic reply of the Sanhedrin delivers to Judas' face a slap of ruthless unconcern. If he has gone to the religious leaders of Israel expecting any kind of understanding or commiseration, how very humiliating and inhumane their rebuff must feel! Judas used Jesus as a pawn in his political game with the powers that be; now it is Judas' turn to feel like a thrown-away and useless thing. The repentant Peter voluntarily separated himself from the throng and entered a bitter solitude, a harsh isolation that was nonetheless fruitful because it favored a new encounter with God in atoning gratitude. But, instead of returning with quiet contrition to the solitude of his own heart like Peter, Judas in his torment ran to his co-conspirators, appealing to their camaraderie and hoping they could help him undo his crime. No one but God, however, can lift the unbearable guilt crushing our conscience, least of all those who have incited us to sin in the first place. The most terrible aspect of the elders' reaction is its very detached and casual coolness. What to Judas is a burning matter of conscience is to them, quite simply, business as usual. They are old men whose religious self-sufficiency and entitlement have hardened their hearts with age. They seem to imply: "You fell into our trap as a groveling collaborator against your friend? Too bad . . . We don't know you. Fend for yourself!"

By its very nature, sin is Satanic because in all its operations it bears the family resemblance of the Father of Lies. Sin lies when it tempts us by making glamorous and chummy promises it can never fulfill. Then, in the aftermath, sin not only disappoints bitterly but, in fact, betrays the one whom it has lured to betray God. The gruesome state of Judas' soul at this point has to be gauged not only by the fact that he has turned his back on Jesus and his fellow apostles but also by the further fact that his co-conspirators, to whom he is appealing, have cruelly turned their backs *on him.* His sense of utter isolation and abandonment by all must be absolute. The occasions and the partners of our sin not only cast us off afterward like tiresome wretches; in addition, they spitefully push us down with their heel deeper into the quicksand of sadness and perdition that is already sucking us down.

27:5   καὶ ῥίψας τὰ ἀργύρια εἰς τὸν ναὸν
ἀνεχώρησεν,
καὶ ἀπελθὼν ἀπήγξατο

And throwing down the pieces of silver in the temple,
he withdrew;
and he went and hanged himself

V IOLENCE EXPLODES FROM THIS VERSE with double force. The
torment of Judas' soul now expresses itself in the two dramatic acts of throwing down the money in the temple and
of putting an end to his own physical life. By a strange solidarity,
Judas experiences in advance, in his own flesh and by his own hands,
some of the violence Jesus will soon have to endure. Both Judas and
Jesus die on the same day, and both deaths result from Judas' act of
treachery. A dark synchronicity is at work here. From a human and
purely psychological point of view, we can see nothing on this bleak
horizon but failed love, ambition, despair, and annihilation. But it is
also possible to see the events from the perspective of divine creativity, as wholly subsumed and transformed by the abiding efficacy of
Jesus' faithful love, which not even death can destroy. Good Friday
is a day of unsurpassable awe, silence, fear, and hope precisely because it contains all the tremendous mysteries of both man and God
in unrelenting conflict and ultimate resolution. The struggles of that
Day of Passion irreversibly and fundamentally changed the meaning
of both life and death for all mankind.

Judas acts as if the thirty pieces of silver, shameful symbol of his
betrayal of Jesus, are burning holes in his hands. He hoped that, by
giving them back to the elders, he could atone for his guilt. With
obstinacy and a bizarre naïveté Judas remains fixated on the money,
as if returning it would undo the crime he committed by accepting
it, as if the money were the all-consuming protagonist of this story
rather than Jesus. Such behavior can occur in persons who go mad
after committing a great crime, a wide-eyed mother smiling eerily
as she pets the doll of her daughter whom she has just killed. An

390

external object, related to the gruesome events, can become a momentary fetish, saving one from entering one's own heart and facing the unfaceable horror.

Judas thus *throws down* the pieces of silver the elders have not accepted, throws them down forcefully on the stone floor of the temple. The clinking-clanking sound they make is an echo of his despairing conscience. He realizes that it was to gain this material element, silver, which can do nothing but make a passing noise when hurled at stones, that he sold the friendship, wisdom, and affection of his loving Master. The elders withdraw from Judas. Their disdainful rejection of him creates a large, empty space in the temple. He finds himself in "the courts of the house of the Lord", in "the treasuries of the house of God, and the treasuries for dedicated gifts" (1 Chron 28:12), where the priests store the offerings large and small that the faithful have made to enhance the beauty and dignity of the temple and the worship of God that takes place within it. Since this treasury is a place that symbolizes generosity and self-consecration to God, it is an ironical location for Judas' despair to be consummated. This is the moment and the place of his decision to kill himself and descend into nothingness rather than give himself over into God's compassionate hands. The torture of his own conscience and the elders' callous refusal of his appeal in the end prove stronger than any glimmering memory of Jesus' trustworthiness as loving and forgiving friend.

What idea of a faithful friend do I actually entertain when I allow my overwhelming guilt for offending him to defeat my certain knowledge of his abiding love for me? To give ultimate primacy to my own guilt over the capacity of another to love and forgive me is a most efficacious formula for suicide of the soul, if not necessarily of the body. When someone loves me unconditionally and intensely desires to forgive me because I myself mean more to him than my sin, then there is nothing admirable or virtuous in the pseudo-humility of my refusal to forgive myself and surrender to that forgiving other. Humility distributes new life all around, but arrogance deals death.

And so Judas *withdraws* (ἀνεχώρησεν, *anechôrêsen*) from the temple, the place of divine worship and of sacrifices of praise and atonement, the place, too, of his association with the religious leaders of the people, the sacred place he has doubly desecrated, first by here agreeing to hand over Jesus and now by here deciding to kill himself. One by one, Judas has shut down all avenues of escape from guilt precisely because he refuses to walk down the one way of humble repentance leading straight to Christ's welcoming Heart. The clinking of the silver coins he has just hurled, emphasizing the emptiness of the temple's corridors, pushes Judas over the edge. *He departed*, and *he went*: these two verbs signal his withdrawal *from* all earthly hope and his determination now to proceed *toward* self-destruction. Judas seems not to allow a third possibility: that of divine hope, founded on his intimate knowledge of Jesus' person.

"He went and hanged himself": Our heart cannot help but register a tremor of horror as it reads this sentence. The human act of *going*, the capacity for purposeful locomotion, is twisted by Judas into an act of self-annihilation, the act that necessarily excludes all possible future *goings*. We can say that someone *goes* to meet a friend, *goes* to admire a landscape, *goes* to sow a field, *goes* to play an instrument, *goes* to write a poem. . . . In each of these instances, we smile with satisfaction because these actions imply communication and enhancement of life. But when we hear that Judas *goes to hang himself*, a deep instinct within us revolts, and we want to run and stop him. Human beings should not play God by undertaking absolute deeds, and suicide is an absolute deed. It attempts to determine the future absolutely, and it deliberately destroys the possibility of any further life or deeds on this earth. It violently excludes all friends, landscapes, fields, instruments, and poems. Above all, at least objectively, it attempts to exclude the possibility of experiencing love.

The Greek verb ἀπάγχομαι (*apánchomai*, "to hang oneself") derives from the root verb ἄγχω (*anchô*), which means "to press tight" or "to compress". When having the throat as object, it means "to choke", "to throttle", or "to strangle". These Greek verbs have a common root with the Latin words *angustus* or *anxius*, meaning "tight" or "narrow", giving us words like the English "anxiety" and "anguish". All these meanings stress the deliberate or accidental exclusion of air from the lungs by the forcible constriction of the throat. Thus Judas' chosen manner for ending his life by hanging himself with a rope is a true Dantean *contrapasso*, a so-called "punishment fitting the crime". Judas' final physical action of hanging himself is but the exterior metaphor for a spiritual choice that has already been made interiorly by Judas' soul. Just as the tight rope from which he now dangles blocks the passage of air through his trachea to his lungs, so Judas has already cut off the supply of life-giving oxygen to his soul and whole person by squeezing out from his life the presence of Jesus. Judas has accomplished such a feat not only by his original betrayal and revolt, regretted yet unatoned, but most especially now by his refusal to "remember" Jesus and thus admit Jesus' regenerative forgiveness into his soul. As prized trophy Judas takes with him into his self-inflicted death only his revolt against the primacy of Jesus as Lord. Judas will be second to none, not even God, even if this entails his extinction.

27:6   Οἱ δὲ ἀρχιερεῖς λαβόντες τὰ ἀργύρια εἶπαν·
         Οὐκ ἔξεστιν βαλεῖν αὐτὰ εἰς τὸν κορβανᾶν.
         ἐπεὶ τιμὴ αἵματός ἐστιν

The chief priests, taking the pieces of silver, said,
"It is not lawful to put them into the treasury,
since they are the price of blood"

T HIS SUBSTANTIAL JUDAS EPISODE in the middle of the Passion narrative (27:3–10) is one of the rare passages in the Gospel of Matthew when we are given to experience the *absence* of Jesus and its implications. The evangelist focuses his attention on two players in the Gospel story—the treacherous disciple and the San-hedrin—who have turned their backs on God's Messiah and have violently excluded Jesus from their lives. Matthew wants to give us a glimpse into the state of soul that characterizes those who reject the Jesus whom the Father has sent as Savior. Both *evangélion* and "Gospel" mean "good news", and so we wonder how being made to peer with such prolonged attention into the heart of darkness can be an aspect of accepting the good news about Jesus. Quite simply, how could we grow to appreciate and yearn for the light of pure love that will be fully manifested in the Resurrection unless we first recognize and taste the primal gloom of an existence without Jesus—a life, that is, in which we prefer to be left wholly to ourselves to bask in glorious self-sufficiency?

The thirty pieces of silver Judas has violently scattered on the temple floor continue at the center of the action even after Judas' tumultuous departure. How masterfully the evangelist here uses symbolism, substituting for the absent Jesus, as center of attention, the wages paid for his head! The priests have disdained to move any little finger to help Judas out of his predicament, yet the money does retain their attention. They are not about to leave it lying about for others to pick up. Whereas Judas saw in its return a possibility of atonement, the priests consider it as presenting a procedural problem. But for both Judas and the high priests, it is not persons that retain their interest, but rather this material sign of social power and influence. This intense concern with the money itself reveals the mental level at which the priests habitually live. To keep the tradition (and their jobs) going smoothly, the letter of the law must be observed. A gaping irony strikes us between the ease with which they plot to take a human life unlawfully and the meticulous care they apply to dispose of the money according to the law.

The callousness of the priests' conscience is stressed by the fact that τιμὴ αἵματος (*timê háimatos*) does not literally mean "blood money" (RSV) but, rather, "the price of blood" (NAB). The priests and elders have agreed to put a monetary price on a human life (symbolized by the concept of "blood"), thus reducing blasphemously the image of God by making it the object of a business transaction, beneficial to themselves. And the "blood" in question happens also to be that of the Messiah, the incarnate Son of God. Nevertheless, with Jesus on his way to Pilate for a confirmation of the death sentence, the priests who condemned him by deceitful plotting are chiefly interested in what to do with the returned money. They are professionally absorbed with the practical issue of how to dispose lawfully of tainted money.

At the same time, they wholly neglect to ask themselves *whose blood* did the tainting (whether animal or human? whether merely human or human *and* divine?) and *by whose hand* that blood is about to be shed. How precisely the Lord's ironical condemnation of the Pharisees applies here: "You blind guides, straining out a gnat and swallowing a camel!" (23:24). This cold, managerial *modus operandi*, for which transactions and neat results are more important than persons, even at the religious level, is the inevitable symptom for the state of the devout soul that seeks to apply the letter of the law but has wholly forgotten the Heart of the living Author of the law and his intentions. For the priests at this moment, the man of flesh and blood Jesus of Nazareth has been reduced, incredibly, to these thirty pieces of silver. The question of what to do with this monetary Jesus-substitute poses for them a far more engaging problem than the issue of crucifying the body of the living Jesus, a necessary climax to the story that the priests take in their stride. The inestimable value of the Lord of the universe is reduced by the priests to the price of a worthless slave.

"So they took counsel, and bought with [the thirty pieces of silver] the potter's field, to bury strangers in. Therefore, that field has been called the Field of Blood to this day" (27:7–8). "Potter's field" is a mysterious designation, perhaps referring to a place outside the Jerusalem city walls that served as dumping ground for useless fragments of pottery. Such areas exist in many ancient cities such as the Testaccio neighborhood in Rome that grew around a veritable hill of potsherds. In any event, the minimal information Matthew gives us illustrates what was an acceptable use for the "blood money" paid for Jesus' head. The priests attempt to transform their own and Judas' heinous deed into a work of piety by providing a burial place for pagan strangers, who could not be buried alongside Jews in holy ground since a goy's corpse would pollute the earth of a Jewish cemetery.

These priests use money from blood they are plotting to shed to perform a pious deed. Is this procedure not quite in keeping with a certain self-righteous penchant on the part of religious people for whitewashing crimes committed in the name of God? "Woe to you, scribes and Pharisees, hypocrites!" exclaims Jesus at one point, "for you are like whitewashed tombs, which outwardly appear beautiful, but within they are full of dead men's bones and all uncleanness" (23:27). This new-bought burial ground represents the priests' conscience, full of the rot of spiritual death. But by making the name

"Field of Blood" stick to what was formerly known as "Potter's Field", the popular imagination keeps alive the true memory of the crime committed. The blood of Jesus cries out from the earth of this field (cf. 4 Ezra 15:8).

A further association of this Field of Blood, moreover, is the horror of Judas' despairing death. Judas' suicide by hanging and the priests' purchase of the field occur simultaneously in the narrative. The two events are causally related, since Judas' despair led to his return of the money, which in turn led to the purchase of the Potter's Field. Judas' betrayal of Jesus, his regret for this deed, his subsequent despair and suicide, and Jesus' eventual death later in the day are all elements that coalesce in the symbolic meaning of this plot of land. Deuteronomy dictates that "a hanged man is accursed by God" and that he shall therefore not be buried in consecrated ground (Deut 21:23), all the more so in the case of a suicide, since he incurs a double curse. The Potter's Field/Field of Blood thus brings together in one place the death of all outcasts from official religious society: the death of the innocent but pagan stranger, the death of the innocent but condemned Jew, Jesus, and the ignominious death by suicide of the traitor Judas. In the eyes of polite society, this is a suspect locus of shame and pollution; but its association with Jesus' death transforms it for the evangelist into a locus of sure hope and redemption for all the outcasts of the world.

27:9–10   Καὶ ἔλαβον τὰ τριάκοντα ἀργύρια,
            τὴν τιμὴν τοῦ τετιμημένου ὃν ἐτιμήσαντο
            ἀπὸ υἱῶν Ἰσραήλ,
            καὶ ἔδωκαν αὐτὰ εἰς τὸν ἀγρὸν τοῦ κεραμέως
            καθὰ συνέταξέν μοι Κύριος

And they took the thirty pieces of silver,
the price of him on whom a price had been set
by some of the sons of Israel,
and they gave them for the potter's field,
as the Lord directed me

MATTHEW INTRODUCES THIS PROPHECY with the sentence: "Then was fulfilled what had been spoken by the prophet Jeremiah, saying, 'And they took . . .'" The experts are puzzled as to why Matthew would attribute this quotation to Jeremiah, since it cannot be found in his book as extant. It appears to be a conflation of Zechariah 11:12–13 with aspects of three different texts from Jeremiah that deal with: a potter (18:2–3), the purchase of a field (32:6–9), and a new burial place (19:1–13). Evangelists are not meticulous scholars and do not use footnotes, nor was it unusual in antiquity to quote texts from memory, sometimes combining them with other texts and then giving, if any, only one general attribution.

Obviously, the mere name of the prophet Jeremiah carries authoritative weight, and the fulfillment of a prophecy can be seen to occur by the convergence into one event of different strands of prefiguration. What is important for our purposes is to see what the evangelist thus achieves by way of throwing prophetic light on the present situation in his Gospel. To throw prophetic light, furthermore, always means to show how a present happening has already been assumed from of old into God's providential design.

No amount of speculation is going to clarify the present passage completely, although its meaning appears to have been perfectly clear to Matthew. We have already seen that the priests' attempt to whitewash a criminal deed of betrayal and injustice into a work of charity is fraught with hypocrisy and sanctimoniousness. However,

Matthew makes too much of the potter's field as a place of burial, at the conclusion of his tragic Judas narrative, for this field merely to symbolize the fruit of perennial Pharisaical attitudes. By introducing this lengthy prophecy that Matthew now considers fulfilled, his narrative has admitted a powerful ray of divine light into the dismal scene. This light of providence reminds us of God's continual presence even amidst the worst horrors and crimes, and letting in such light suddenly floods our minds with an interval of peace between Judas' suicide and Jesus' trial before Pilate. Neither Judas' betrayal and despair nor the priests' inveterate hypocrisy and hatred can possibly thwart the course of providence as embodied in Jesus' Passion.

The center of interest in Matthew's quotation from "Jeremiah" surely is "the price of him on whom a price had been set by some of the sons of Israel". The Greek original drives home the concept of "price" by the consecutive repetition of three different forms of the same word, *timê*. He writes: τὴν **τιμὴν** τοῦ **τετιμημένου** ὃν **ἐτιμήσαντο** ἀπὸ υἱῶν Ἰσραήλ, which literally rendered gives us "the price of the priced one whom some of the sons of Israel priced". Clearly, by this device Matthew wants to record in lapidary fashion the enormity of human beings daring to put a price on God's head. "They, mere mortals, had the effrontery to estimate the Holy One's worth!", he seems to imply. Now, the phrase "some of the sons of Israel" obviously refers to the members of the Sanhedrin who offered that price and to Judas, who accepted it. And we know that putting a price on a person's head is but a prelude to shedding that person's blood.

But the point of the prophecy and the reason for its inclusion at this juncture by Matthew seems to be that all the criminals in the world, even joining forces, shall never have the last word; God's providence shall; and the evil misdeeds that intended the downfall of righteousness shall in the end, by an ironical reversal, contribute to its ultimate glorification. The present interlude at the Potter's Field shows how the blood money wrung from Jesus' betrayal has unexpectedly been converted, "as the Lord directed me", into a source of peaceful benefit for many anonymous others. The field will now serve as a resting ground for strangers who happen to die in Israel. This is "currency conversion" of a mystical and prophetic kind.

The prophetic intervention of providence extracts a beneficial result out of dark and treacherous hatred, and this result—the creation of a plot of earth waiting to embrace the bodies of the dead—will long outlast both Judas and the conniving priests. Thus, what is true about this microcosmic event—the purchase of a modest cemetery with blood money—also applies macrocosmically to the whole drama of the Passion and to the power of the Blood of Jesus, which "tainted" these thirty pieces of silver *with his holiness* to begin with and which will redeem (*buy back*) the whole world from the power of the Devil. Because of the shedding of Jesus' Blood upon the world, everyone, even foreign non-Jews who have no covenant with God and no financial means of their own, may henceforth die in peace.

This peace-bearing conclusion of the drama of Judas' betrayal is more than just the fitting fulfillment of a prophecy. It may also be seen as an anticipation of the burial of Jesus himself in the new tomb that his disciple Joseph of Arimathea will soon provide (27:57–60). Matthew's narrative infuses both the Potter's Field and the place of Jesus' new tomb with the silent hum of an intense hope in the impending fulfillment of even greater promises. God's benevolent and all-powerful providence is the enveloping and sustaining horizon of the Passion, especially at its most despairing moments, and all events played out in the foreground are continually being assumed and transformed, by the power of God's all-embracing Wisdom, into the boundless background of ever-watchful Love.

א

INTERLUDE III:
LOVE'S INFINITE
EXPANSION

A NYONE WHO HAS STRETCHED his existence so wide that he is simultaneously immersed in God and in the depths of the God-forsaken creature is bound to be torn asunder, as it were; such a one is truly 'crucified'. But this process of being torn apart is identical with love: it is its realization to the extreme (Jn 13:1) and the concrete expression of the breadth it creates. . . . It is not pain as such that counts but the breadth of the love that spans existence so completely that it unites the distant and the near, bringing God-forsaken man into relation with God. It alone gives the pain an aim and a meaning. . . . It is the story of the God who is himself the act of love, the pure 'for', and who therefore necessarily puts on the disguise of the smallest worm (Ps 22:6[21:7])."[1]

---

[1] Joseph Cardinal Ratzinger, *Introduction to Christianity*, trans. J. R. Foster, 2nd ed. (San Francisco: Ignatius Press, 2004), 290–92.

12. "WHAT SHALL I DO WITH JESUS?"

Jesus' Trial before Pilate (27:11–26)

27:11 Ὁ δὲ Ἰησοῦς ἐστάθη ἔμπροσθεν τοῦ ἡγεμόνος·
καὶ ἐπηρώτησεν αὐτὸν ὁ ἡγεμὼν λέγων·
Σὺ εἶ ὁ βασιλεὺς τῶν Ἰουδαίων;
ὁ δὲ Ἰησοῦς ἔφη· Σὺ λέγεις

Now Jesus stood before the governor;
and the governor asked him,
"Are you the King of the Jews?"
And Jesus said, "You have said so"

PILATE'S STRAIGHTFORWARD QUESTIONING of Jesus stands in stark contrast to the tendentious interrogatory at Caiaphas' house. This is another instance of the New Testament theme of the ironical disparity between the natural predisposition to virtue on the part of many pagans and the religiously conditioned scorn of many Jews. Pilate's tone is that of a person honestly looking for correct information, perhaps even inwardly searching for the truth, while the members of the Sanhedrin simply sought to condemn Jesus by any and all means available, without an honest investigation.

Pilate's question to Jesus "Are you the King of the Jews?" is remarkable in itself because at this time Herod Antipas, a son of Herod the Great, still holds considerable power locally and is recognized by the Romans as one of four legitimate rulers of Palestine. Though he does not formally hold the title of king, this man nevertheless is popularly known as "King Herod" by association with his father. Pilate's question to Jesus, therefore, honestly seeks important political clarification.

Pontius Pilate, as Roman governor or "prefect" of Judea at the time of Jesus' death, was the embodied presence of the power and jurisdiction of the emperor in far-off Rome. His power extended even to the naming of the high priest. Well might Pilate, therefore, have sought clarification on the question of who was king of the Jews, so that the right hierarchy of local power might be established in his mind. Kingship interested the Romans and pagans in general far more than priesthood, as we recall from the Nativity scene. The wise men had come from the East to Jerusalem seeking, not a religious authority or a philosopher, but rather asking, "Where is he who has been born *king of the Jews? For we have seen his star in the East, and have come *to worship him*" (2:1–2).

Now the Greek word we normally translate as "governor" in connection with Pilate is *hêgemón*, literally meaning a "leader, commander or chief" who has authority over others, from the verb *hêgéomai*, meaning "to go before" or "lead the way" for others to follow. In the Roman context, it became a technical administrative term designating a "provincial governor" responsible directly to the emperor. In our passage, it appears that Pilate is initially interested in the prisoner Jesus simply as part of his official capacity as provincial governor. By interrogating Jesus, Pilate is simply doing his job. However, the manner of Jesus' presence, his cryptic reply and his emphatic silences soon begin to have an interior effect on the man Pilate. Slowly it begins to dawn on the administrative governor that the silent, bound man before him might himself be a *hêgemón*, but in an altogether different sense: one who mysteriously *leads the way*, not politically, but spiritually, and not only in Judea and among the Jews, but everywhere and for everyone. The two senses of the word, therefore, the technical-political and the religious-spiritual, may be seen as contending for primacy in Pilate's mind and heart.

Pilate's line of inquiry, furthermore, also reveals the sharp contrast between the Jewish and Roman outlook and ruling passions. Caiaphas' question to Jesus was whether or not he was "the Christ, the Son of God" (26:63). The fact that the question is devious, meant to entrap Jesus, does not change its theological slant, whereas Pilate now asks

Jesus whether or not he is "the King of the Jews", a query of the political order. Jews are congenitally consumed with an interest in salvation and thus are always searching for a divine Savior; Romans, on the other hand, have a passion for power and its orderly administration, and so they want to identify clearly this world's legitimate rulers. Both lines of questioning, nevertheless, converge on the one person, Jesus of Nazareth.

Why does Jesus reply curtly to Pilate "You have said so", rather than affirm somewhat less ambiguously, "Yes, I *am* the King of the Jews"? Does Jesus perhaps not consider himself the King of the Jews after all? Or is being king an unimportant matter to him?

Interestingly, Jesus' unemphatic, three-syllable (in the Greek) answer to Pilate is almost identical to the one he gave Caiaphas. To Pilate, he now affirms Σὺ λέγεις (*sy légeis*, "you are saying [so]", 27:11), whereas to Caiaphas he replied Σὺ εἶπας (*sy eípas*, "you have said [it]", 26:64). In both cases, the muted reply by Jesus surely points to the vast difference in outlook between Jesus' understanding of divine sonship and kingly identity, on the one hand, and that of Caiaphas and Pilate respectively, on the other. In so answering, Jesus reveals himself as the masterful teacher who perfectly intuits the actual mentality of his "pupils" and can anticipate their real mode of perception. He will masquerade neither as a *usurper of divinity* nor as a *temporal monarch*, the only two modes in which Caiaphas and Pilate could understand the divine and the regal titles. Jesus' reply also shifts the burden of further search back onto the shoulders of the questioners because a simple yes or no answer would be more misleading than enlightening. Jesus' mode of reply tests the authenticity of his questioners' actual desire to discover the truth.

The rest of the answer Jesus gave Caiaphas establishes him, the Son of man, not only as a human king but as a super-celestial and universal Ruler, albeit more by image than outright declaration: "Hereafter you will see the Son of man", Jesus declared to Caiaphas, "seated at the right hand of Power, and coming on the clouds of heaven" (26:64). Such visionary language, particularly the sitting imagery, means that the glorified Jesus, coequally as Son of man and Son of God, shall one day appear for all (and not just Caiaphas) to see, sharing the sovereignty of God and revealed for all time as the Lord of all creation. The Book of Revelation proclaims Jesus' supreme and universal royal status most unequivocally while at the same time linking his kingly task with the shedding of his blood: "Jesus Christ [is] the faithful witness, the first-born of the dead, and the ruler of kings on earth. [He] loves us and has freed us from our sins by his blood" (Rev 1:5). Part of Jesus' hesitation to reply to Pilate without qualification stems from the fact that Pilate is both too worldly and too restricted in his conception of kingship. Jesus is not only *a* king but *The King* surpassing all kings, and not only the King *of the Jews* but the King of all mankind in all places and times. How could Jesus at this point communicate such a magnificent and universal vision of his true identity? Therefore he opts for near-silence while not denying the kernel of truth the question contains.

Another great irony of the present scene at the prætorium is that, as at Caiaphas' house, the King of Kings who shall come in glory "*seated* at the right hand of Power" is said by Matthew to be *standing* (ἐστάθη) "before the governor". The standing Greater, hands bound like a slave's, waits in attendance upon the sitting Lesser. Truth is interrogated by doubt, the teacher serves the whim of the disciple, the power of love bows low before the power of arms. God condescends to man. Heaven comes to earth. Jesus waits upon Pilate. The Incarnation!

27:12–13   ἐν τῷ κατηγορεῖσθαι αὐτὸν
ὑπὸ τῶν ἀρχιερέων καὶ πρεσβυτέρων
οὐδὲν ἀπεκρίνατο.
τότε λέγει αὐτῷ ὁ Πιλᾶτος·
Οὐκ ἀκούεις πόσα σου καταμαρτυροῦσιν;

When he was accused
by the chief priests and elders,
he answered nothing.
Then Pilate said to him,
"Do you not hear how many things they testify against you?"

T WO GREEK VERBS IN THIS PASSAGE act like heavy hammer
blows twice striking the anvil. They thereby enhance our
perception of the cacophonous atmosphere at this trial as
endless violence and vitriol descend upon the body and psyche
of Jesus from all sides. The verbs are κατηγορέω (*katêgoréô*) and
καταμαρτυρέω (*katamartyréô*), both beginning with the aggressive prefix *katá* ("against") and meaning, respectively, "to speak publicly
against" (and thus "to accuse"), and "to testify against". The first
verb, *katêgoréô*, carries a political connotation since it specifically
means to accuse someone publicly, that is, in the open assembly of
citizens (the *agorá*, hence also the "marketplace"). The reference implies a formal and grave accusation, made before the whole community, which could ruin a person utterly. Such a public denunciation
suggests that the accused poses a serious threat to the common welfare. The other verb, *katamartyréô*, implies presenting evidence against
the accused in support of the accusation. By these means, Matthew
here succeeds in creating an ambience of massive opposition and es-
calating menace against Jesus. He does so not only by his choice of
verbs but also by using mounting plurals concerning *priests* and *elders*
and the *many things* said against Jesus. The whole world, it seems,
has come out to hurl invectives against this one central target who,
ironically, until very recently, has rather been the object of almost
universal admiration. Such is the fickleness of human nature and of

407

mobs in particular. The person of Jesus always exerts a mysterious power of attraction, eliciting either awestruck surrender of the heart or visceral loathing. But no one can simply ignore him.

Oddly enough, it is the Roman governor, supreme civil authority in Palestine, who shows Jesus any trace of sympathy. Pilate seems to have no vested interest in the case one way or the other. He seems to be fair-minded and, if anything, he reveals a certain personal fascination for the accused man he sees before him.

Jesus' total silence in the face of so many accusations, moreover, astounds Pilate, and he actually encourages his prisoner to defend himself. "Do you not hear?" he asks emphatically, sounding very much like the Psalmist as he stirs a seemingly indifferent God into action: "He who planted the ear, does he not hear? He who formed the eye, does he not see?" (Ps 94[93]:9). But, as is often the case with God, Jesus answers only with his silence. He refuses either to reply in kind, accusation for accusation, or to defend himself, knowing that he faces an iron wall of insurmountable prejudice and disdain. Jesus does of course "hear" every one of the charges and is consequently busy the whole time in his Heart forgiving his ill-intentioned accusers. But why speak if he knows he will not be listened to? He will not enter the arena of mutual human recrimination and contempt since his one objective is *to save* and not *to win*. He will not yield to an adversarial logic of aggression and hatred even though his life may be compromised by his refusal.

Pilate is utterly fascinated by Jesus' silence as his sole reply, under conditions of ruthless attack against his name and very existence. Despite his broad political experience, the Roman governor has never witnessed such puzzling behavior. Jesus' unfathomable attitude, which no set of reasonable or frantic human criteria can account for, draws Pilate at least momentarily to peer beyond the barriers of the everyday world and into a beckoning zone of dazzling spiritual light, a world full of fresh possibilities of how to be human *differently*. Here standing before him Pilate sees a humiliated man headed for a most wretched sort of annihilation, yet someone who nonetheless refuses to raise a finger or utter a single syllable in self-defense! What motivates him? Is he perhaps nothing but a pathetic holy fool? Does this prisoner not know that the governor has almost unlimited power to sway the case in either direction? And, furthermore, does this brooding Jew not perceive that the impartial Roman prefect is showing him humane signs of interest and sympathy?

"But [Jesus] gave [Pilate] no answer, not even to a single charge, so that the governor wondered greatly" (27:14). For the second time, Matthew highlights Jesus' silence before Pilate. Neither the wanton accusations against him nor Pilate's plea for engagement can stir Jesus to provide the expected reaction. The text, rather, records Pilate's reaction of utter amazement to Jesus' silence, saying that Pilate θαυμάζειν λίαν (*thaumázein lían*), using the Greek verb that connotes wonderment before an event or a fact that cannot be explained in any of the usual ways. Sometimes the word *tháuma* means a "miracle". The great source of wonderment here is the question of how anyone could so value anything above his physical life that he abides in an obstinate silence before those who hold his destiny in their hands.

Jesus makes not the slightest attempt to defend himself or find fault with his accusers or appeal to any sympathy from his very powerful Roman judge. There is something "miraculous", indeed, about such behavior from the Roman perspective, what we might call a "moral miracle" that transcends all the ordinary categories of human motivation. Standing as a bound prisoner before the Roman governor, Jesus *stands out* amazingly by the abyss of inward mystery his glowing silence reveals to even a pagan observer; and a great aspect of this mystery is the way in which Jesus' chosen stance of silence eloquently manifests the vast interior freedom enjoyed by this physically bound man.

Pilate, however, can penetrate no farther than this general sense of Jesus' magnetic differentness from all others, his sovereign independence in the face of human coercion, an attitude that, from a superficial perspective, could appear to be nothing but grim Stoic resolve. Pilate can obviously not identify the precise mystery housed in Jesus' Heart, the vocation that makes of Jesus the literal, historical fulfiller of Isaiah's prophecy concerning the prefigurative Suffering Servant of the Lord: "He was oppressed, and he was afflicted, yet he opened not his mouth; like a lamb that is led to the slaughter, and like a sheep that before its shearers is silent, so he opened not his mouth" (Is 53:7).

Moreover, how could Pilate or anyone else at the scene intuit that the particular reason for Jesus' "not opening his mouth" is that the Son ardently realizes that his only salvation can come from his Father and that therefore his only appeal, his only plea for rescue, will be wordlessly shouted from the depths of his being to the Father, for no mortal to hear? What is more, because of his love for his Father and his obedience to his Father's plan of redemption, Jesus can invoke no source of justice or relief or strength or hope or liberation from suffering other than his Father, as we hear in the hymn-like prose of the First Letter of Peter:

> When he was reviled,
>   he did not revile in return;
> when he suffered,
>   he did not threaten;
> but he trusted to him who judges justly. (1 Pet 2:23)

Jesus' profound and unremitting silence in the face of impending annihilation is the externally perceivable form of his eternal union and communion with his Father in the Holy Spirit.

To those unschooled in the logic of the Fire of Mercy burning within Christ, the choices motivated by the most divine wisdom can understandably appear to be nothing but pitiful human madness or plain obnoxious stubbornness, even though neither of these possibilities can stand up to close scrutiny in the present context. Pilate cannot perceive the fact that, at this very moment and in the depths of his silence, Jesus is intensely active. The prospect of defending himself before his accusers shrinks to insignificance compared to Jesus' present engagement in the titanic feat of *creating human nature anew* by absorbing all the hatred of all time into the all-transforming furnace of his magnanimous Heart. Neither Pilate nor any other Roman or Jew in Jerusalem that day, no matter how genuinely virtuous or pious, not even Jesus' disciples, could possibly comprehend that there is no moment of his life when *the man Jesus of Nazareth* can cease to be *the Christ, the redeeming Messiah*. There is no single instant when Jesus can put his innermost identity as Savior temporarily on hold and withdraw to a merely private sphere of self-involved personal concerns and strategies of self-defense in the face of colossal threats. As Karl Barth has declared memorably: "[In Jesus] we cannot detect a personality with its characteristic concerns and inclinations and affections independently of its works, [that is, his mission of redemption]. . . . Where necessary, these features accompany the description of His work, and it is always in the latter and never in the former . . . that He Himself is recognizable and is really this man for the Evangelists. . . . He is only as He lives for the many, for the world. . . . We cannot separate His person from His work."[1]

This is, then, the secret of Jesus' unyielding silence before Pilate: he cannot pause his work of Redemption, he cannot cease momentarily being Redeemer, in order to defend himself of these myriad charges. That would be tantamount to his allowing himself to flow along with the self-interested logic of the world. Either in eternity or in time, God has no leisure to be interested in himself, to take time out for himself, to defend himself. God has no "privacy"! God cannot take a break from being God, which by definition means *being-for-others*. God is too busy *being love* and performing the works of love to retreat into the safe sanctuary of his omnipotence, to use his sovereignty as a shelter from sorrow and suffering. To be falsely accused and to suffer the dire consequences of such accusations is, for Jesus, part and parcel of the Father's plan for the salvation of the world through his Son. The world's capacity for hatred first has to be spent, with Jesus as target-victim. For the Son to offer himself obediently to play such a role is the unsurpassable expression of the outlandish Heart of God—equally all-powerful, all-wise, and all-loving, and *therefore* open to every form of humiliation and violence, for the sake of his aggressors. To Pilate's immense credit, such an unheard-of and bizarre spectacle of total non-violence and silent non-engagement on the part of Jesus the prisoner has the effect of putting the Roman governor in a state of "great wonderment".

---

[1] Karl Barth, *Church Dogmatics*, III, 2, trans. H. Knight et al. (Edinburgh: T&T Clark, 1960), 57–61. See also Hans Urs von Balthasar, "Two Modes of Faith", in *Creator Spirit*, trans. Brian McNeil, C.R.V., Explorations in Theology, vol. 3 (San Francisco: Ignatius Press, 1993), 99–100.

27:15–16   Κατὰ δὲ ἑορτὴν εἰώθει ὁ ἡγεμὼν
ἀπολύειν ἕνα τῷ ὄχλῳ δέσμιον ὃν ἤθελον.
εἶχον δὲ τότε δέσμιον ἐπίσημον
λεγόμενον Ἰησοῦν Βαραββᾶν

*Now at the feast the governor was accustomed
to release for the crowd any one prisoner whom they wanted.
And they had then a notorious prisoner,
called Jesus Barabbas*

THE PLOT NOW THICKENS AS MATTHEW unexpectedly introduces a new element into the Passion narrative: the custom of giving liberty to a prisoner of the crowd's choice at the Feast of the Passover. At once we are struck by the fittingness of such a tradition. We remember the gist of the message that God sent to the King of Egypt through his prophets early in the Book of Exodus: "Moses and Aaron went to Pharaoh and said, 'Thus says the LORD, the God of Israel, 'Let my people go, that they may hold a feast to me in the wilderness'" (Ex 5:1). Such formulaic language would be repeated at least ten times throughout this book, underscoring its central importance. The essence of the historical Exodus was indeed God's liberation of his people from Egyptian slavery, and the Feast of Passover celebrated precisely this event and its meaning.

To release a prisoner every year at Passover time would be seen by the people as a most concrete reenactment of the Paschal event within each Jew's own immediate historical experience. Apparently the Roman authorities went along with the custom at the time of Jesus, in order to satisfy the people who would see in the event a reaffirmation of itself as "the People of God". Furthermore, the element of free popular choice ("any one prisoner *whom they wanted*") added a pleasing dimension of autonomy to the experience, bolstering both Jewish pride in the face of the Roman invader and the people's sense of sharing magnanimously in their God's penchant for forgiveness as liberator from oppression. Such a mixture of nationalistic pride and mystical religious sentiment is not surprising in the lived practice of any religion, which has to accommodate both the transcendental and the time-conditioned aspects of human experience.

In this particular instance, however, we sense that the evangelist is investing the custom with a specifically Christian theological meaning. After portraying in great detail the involvement of the Jewish authorities, of the cowardly apostles, and, now, of the pagan Roman governor in determining the fate of Jesus, Matthew turns his spotlight on the Jewish people at large. The evangelist steadily intensifies the high electric tension, already crackling in the atmosphere, generated by the contrast between Jesus' manifest innocence and the scorn and ill-will assailing him from all sides. By such means, Matthew wants to dramatize the divine irony that Jesus embodies as imprisoned Liberator, perishing Savior, condemned Innocent, murdered God—and all this through the collusion of all human beings without exception. As Pascal famously declared: "Jesus will be in agony until the end of the world."[2]

This truth implies that daily we can all participate both in the annihilation of Jesus the Word and in the experience of his gracious redemption. The Passion of Christ is not whatsoever an exclusively historical, earthbound event trapped in the amber of time. The drama of Christ's Passion and crucifixion is shot through with eternal, trinitarian implications. As a dramatic happening in the human life of a Divine Person, as an event originating in the Heart of the Father and carried forward to realization by the Holy Spirit, the Passion exists simultaneously both within and outside chronological time. It is thus universally present and accessible to us, particularly in the suffering of the innocent and abandoned of every age, as Jesus himself forcefully insisted in his prophecy of the Last Judgment in Matthew 25. In this visionary anticipation of the eschaton, Jesus reveals his own expectant presence, through all time, in the persons of his suffering little ones. Yes, his *expectant* presence: in these his least ones he, the Lord and King of Glory, lies hidden, waiting for us daily to come to his assistance in them. And in this crucial passage of the Gospel, Jesus stresses, astoundingly, how our attitudes, actions, or indeed our indifferent non-actions, will be a matter of life and death *for both ourselves and him.*

---

[2] Blaise Pascal, *Pensées*, trans. A. J. Krailsheimer (New York: Penguin Books, 1966), 313.

The crowd (or, better, *mob*) of the people has been left for last by Matthew for inclusion in his mural of the Passion narrative, with all mankind portrayed in one or another guise. He has proceeded expansively from the depiction of individuals (Peter, Judas, Caiaphas, Pilate, the servant girls) to that of distinct groups (all the disciples, the whole Sanhedrin, the servants in Caiaphas' courtyard), finally to arrive at the portrayal of an anonymous throng that symbolically and cumulatively includes all of us. The evangelist's theological concern, quite obviously, is to reveal the universal guilt and collusion of all human sinners who, united as a race, are together responsible for the condemnation and execution of God's Word made flesh, as St. Paul comments: "Since *all have sinned* and fall short of the glory of God, they are justified by his grace as a gift, through the redemption which is in Christ Jesus, whom God put forward as an expiation by his blood, to be received by faith" (Rom 3:23–25).

The condemnation and murder of the Son of God, the savaging of God's eternal Word, Jesus Christ, formally constitutes the *non plus ultra* of all possible human sins. God could never be offended in a more thorough and savage and thankless manner. The collective sin of our human race against our innocent Savior includes, by definition, all other possible sinfulness, both in kind and in degree. We may say, therefore, that mankind first existed as a foul and corrupt "mystical body", bound together in perverse communion only by its sinfulness, before it was transformed by the power of Jesus' blood into the Mystical Body of Christ, dazzlingly holy and immaculate (cf. Eph 5:27).

Now, nothing of what has been here said about the alleged Jewish custom of releasing a prisoner at Passover is invalidated by the fact that no historical proof has yet been found outside the Gospels that argues for or against this having indeed been a tradition practiced every year in the Jerusalem of Jesus' day. However, its symbolic and theological significance remains strong on its own merit, particularly with regard to the two aspects of the *universal human communion in sin* and of the consequent need for each one of us *to make a personal decision* in the face of the innocent Jesus' condemnation. Will we join in with the obstreperous majority, thus losing ourselves in an orgiastic frenzy of contempt, or will we stand fast by his innocence, regardless of the cost to ourselves?

What I here call the *universal human communion in sin* is simply a given of salvation history, amply attested throughout the Old Testament, especially in the books of the prophets. By way of example, let us recall the following typical denunciation, in Jeremiah, of the whole people of Israel and a fortiori of all mankind. God speaks through the mouth of his prophet:

> They did not obey or incline their ear, but walked in their own counsels and the stubbornness of their evil hearts, and went backward and not forward. From the day that your fathers came out of the land of Egypt to this day, I have persistently sent all my servants the prophets to them, day after day; yet they did not listen to me, or incline their ear, but stiffened their neck. They did worse than their fathers. (Jer 7:24–26)

Naturally, such a passage and many others like it do not constitute the basis for anything like a doctrine of "original sin" as such. However, such forceful prophetic declarations certainly do establish beyond a doubt the unremitting and universal human penchant for revolting against the Creator and his will, an almost innate tendency from the beginning that Scripture identifies as God's explicit motivation for sending the purifying Flood at the time of Noah: "The LORD saw that the wickedness of man was great in the earth, and that *every imagination of the thoughts of his heart was only evil continually*" (Gen 6:5). Thus, along with our mother's milk, we seem to imbibe both the capacity and the inclination to think, desire, and do evil, and it does not appear we have much choice in the matter. However, neither the *capacity* nor the *inclination* to evil yet constitutes an actual sinful *deed*. Hence we see the crucial importance of the question of *choice* in the perpetration of evil deeds, both great and small, whether individual or collective. And so Matthew's text continues as follows, highlighting the role of the mob in the plot of the Passion by its exercise of free choice: "They had then a notorious prisoner, called [Jesus] Barabbas. So when they had gathered, Pilate said to them, *'Whom do you want me to release for you, [Jesus] Barabbas or Jesus who is called Christ?'* For he knew that it was out of envy that they had delivered him up" (27:16–18).

The version of Matthew's Gospel just quoted for this passage will be surprising to many. We are not accustomed to hearing the name of "Jesus" linked to that of the criminal "Barabbas" in this way, as part of the felon's proper name. Historically, the holy Name of JESUS has come to designate one person and that person only. However, we must remember that, in its Aramaic form of *Yôshúʿa*, the name "Jesus" was a rather common Jewish name, meaning "savior". It is true that only a few manuscripts of the Gospel of Matthew give the double name "Jesus Barabbas" for the notorious malefactor whom Pilate paired with Jesus the Nazarene before the hostile mob. Yet such a full name for Barabbas is entirely feasible as perhaps having been the original (though not the received) text of Matthew. Scholars speculate that, given the presence of this double name for Barabbas in some "witnesses" (that is, manuscripts) of this Gospel, we are in fact dealing, not with a scribal insertion or doctrinal aberration, but rather with a pious *omission*. In other words, it is probable that most of the extant manuscripts deliberately excluded "Jesus" as part of Barabbas' name out of respect for the Savior's uniqueness and the sacredness with which his Name became invested by believers very early in the history of Christianity.

Twice in the present episode, then, the full name of the "notorious" Barabbas is given by some manuscripts of the Gospel as *Jesus Barabbas*. The stark Greek phrasing of this version of v. 17b has a solemn resonance to it, with its emphatic accents on four final syllables:

$$\text{Ἰησοῦν τὸν Βαραββᾶν}$$
$$\text{ἢ}$$
$$\text{Ἰησοῦν τὸν λεγόμενον Χριστόν;}$$

[Iêsoún ton Barabbán ê Iêsoún ton legómenon Christón?]

Indeed, in the Greek, the use of the definite article between the two names (*Jesus* the *Barabbas or Jesus who is called* the *Christ?*) hints that the choice Pilate is offering the crowd is between two different kinds of savior. Matthew stresses the fact that Barabbas was *epísêmos* as a felon, that is, "notable", "remarkable", well-known for his criminality, in the same way that, symmetrically, Jesus the Nazarene was called "the Christ", that is, "the Anointed One", by definition equally *epísêmos*, but famed for his wisdom, holiness, and benevolence rather than infamous transgressions of the Law. The circumstance that both prisoners, in this reading, have an identical "first name" gives Matthew the renewed opportunity to heighten the irony of the choice Pilate sets before the people. By the tenor of his narrative, Matthew now fully extends the application of the doctrine of universal guilt in mankind's collusion against Jesus of Nazareth. The evangelist would thus seem to suggest that the mob's eventual choice of *Jesus Barabbas* over *Jesus Christ* signifies its obstinacy, its persistence in the human revolt against God's will and his plan to save them through his Anointed Son whom he has sent to them.

Christ's sharing his first name with the criminal Barabbas symbolizes poignantly the manner in which the incarnate Word has wholly entered into our common human nature, allowing himself to be put on a par and confounded with this notorious outlaw and, hence, with all lawlessness. The play on names here is a particularly striking way of conveying Jesus' self-identification, by the will of the Father, with universal human sinfulness. The doctrine is starkly formulated by St. Paul: "For our sake [God] *made him to be sin* who knew no sin, so that in him we might become the righteousness of God" (2 Cor 5:21). In Jewish tradition, a name reveals the intimate identity of a person; and so "Jesus", applied to Barabbas, connotes that God's Anointed has come to save him by taking his place as condemned man, thus assuming his guilt; and the same name of "Jesus", borne by the Father's incarnate Son, connotes his power and willingness to enact salvation for Barabbas, who here stands in for Everyone. We are dealing here with yet another instance of the *admirabile commercium*, the "wondrous exchange" that took place when the all-holy second Person of the Blessed Trinity assumed human nature in Jesus of Nazareth. Two who share the same name are called to commune in the fullness of each other's nature and all that comes with it.

On the other hand, however, the crowd's impassioned choice of a certified outlaw and criminal *as their kind of "Jesus"*, as their personal "savior", loudly proclaims its members' refusal to change any of the criminality in their own hearts. Jesus the Barabbas clearly represents a flagrant collective projection of the interior dispositions of a mob seeking to be, not *redeemed from* its depravity, but merely *reaffirmed in* it by its freedom of choice, ratified by the highest official authority on earth, that is, the Roman governor and, through him, the emperor himself. The mob chooses, not the Savior it needs, yet fears and despises, but the savior it deserves and admires: one wholly like themselves but with the difference that he has carried the latent iniquity of their own hearts to full fruition in the public forum, and has written INIQUITY large on the screen of heroic excess and acclamation. Jesus the Christ can offer no boastful glamor of this social sort, which can prove so smashing for a day's vulgar entertainment.

In this decadent, psycho-social process, we see "salvation" implicitly defined as the alleviating validation of our most nefarious self-indulgence, which paradoxically comes to be regarded as a kind of admirable "virtue" because it promises a certain societal success. But the Jesus who truly saves us *from ourselves*, corrupted as we are by both our inherited nature and our oppressive nurture, does not flatteringly validate us outright just as he finds us. Jesus can only *save* us—that is, heal us from our afflictions of the will and the heart and make us spiritually healthy and whole—by leading us resolutely *out of the space of self-indulgent license* we have long inhabited, toward a conversion of heart and the quiet pursuit and service of the truth that has always been proclaimed by the prophets as the way of righteousness. Such salvation has no glamorous appeal and generates no useful social currency; it will exercise a magnetic pull only for those who hunger and thirst for justice and holiness. Jesus Barabbas, by contrast, is a dark icon of triumphant egotism, and the soul of anyone who gazes on it with gleeful fascination will be stultified as by the lethal glance of Medusa. His heart will be turned to stone, made incapable of practicing the freedom to seek and please God. Such is the choice Pilate sets before the people. Quite obviously it involves far more than simply picking a favorite prisoner to release on a high holy day.

A final irony that clenches Matthew's symbolic play on the name *Jesus* in this passage derives from the fact that, in Aramaic, the name "Barabbas" means "son of the father". Thus, translated in full, the name *Jesus Barabbas* means "savior, son of the father"—a truly extraordinary title representing a climax of irony when we see it applied to a notorious criminal. The Aramaic-speaking members of Matthew's early Judæo-Christian community would have been struck by this irony at once. The type of "savior" people would see in Barabbas naturally depends on who his "father" might be, that is, his source and generating origin. In the case of a boastful criminal, we can hardly avoid seeking insight for his lineage in the passage in John's Gospel where Jesus denounces this same crowd of the people for proving by their actions that they have been begotten by the most vile father possible: "You are of your father the devil, and your will is to do your father's desires. He was a murderer from the beginning, and has nothing to do with the truth, because there is no truth in him. When he lies, he speaks according to his own nature, for he is a liar and the father of lies" (Jn 8:44). For elucidating our context, nothing can surpass this passage in John as characterizing both the desire for wanton gratification that drives the heart of the mob in clamoring for the release of Barabbas ("your will is to do your father's desire") and Barabbas' own role as an icon of triumphantly rewarded iniquity ("he was a murderer from the beginning").

This exegesis of the name *Jesus Barabbas* now enables us to understand better the implications of Matthew's observation: "For [Pilate] knew that it was out of envy that they had delivered him up (παρέδωκαν)" (27:18). The statement subtly implies that Pilate was neither foolish nor lacking in insight into human motivations, specifically those of the mob crowding his prætorium. This affirmation suggests that there lurks in the Roman governor a winsome streak of pagan innocence. It implies his clear sense that, despite the envy of the people toward Jesus as the driving force behind their outrageous behavior, surely, if given the choice of releasing either someone they merely *envied* and a full-blown, certified *criminal*, they would in the end have the humanity to release the innocent Jesus, who had done them so much good in both word and deed!

And here, in connection with Pilate's insight into the crowd's motivation, that fraught word παρέδωκαν (*parédôkan*, v. 18) yet again resounds, replete with theological and dramatic undertones. For the substantive form of the idea, we recall that *parádosis* means the "delivering up", the "handing over", the "betrayal", or even the "tradition". This word and the crucial theme it evokes are like a deep-sounding gong tolling the death of Jesus at regular intervals in sympathetic anticipation, measuring his swiftly diminishing distance from Golgotha. "He knew that it was out of envy that they had [handed] him [over]", says the text: Pilate's insight into the motivation of the Great Betrayal seems here to refer to more than just the immediate attitude of the mob but probably extends as well to the machinations of the leaders of the people. The envious "they" of Pilate's reflection appears to have been left deliberately indefinite so that its reference can be extended almost universally. The situation playing out before Pilate unveils, in fact, the existence of a sick symbiosis at work between the religious leaders and this local lynching mob. Throughout the Gospel, we have seen how fear of the people's favorable opinion regarding Jesus has constantly been one of the Pharisees' and elders' strongest concerns. At the same time, the people, left to themselves, could not possibly have produced this day's terrible debacle. The priests and scholars rely on the people for their popularity and approval, and the people rely on the religious authorities for legitimation of all their desires and petitions. Pilate understands all of this as a skillful governor familiar with the political terrain in Palestine.

The great irony of Pilate's own attitude, however, will emerge in due course. However insightful concerning dark human motivations and however sympathetic toward Jesus though Pilate might be, at the end of this episode Matthew will predicate of the Roman governor as subject the same fateful verb of betrayal and cowardice that he has just applied to the religious authorities and the crowds, and before that to Judas: "Then he released for them Barabbas, and having scourged Jesus, *[handed] him [over]* (παρέδωκεν, *parédôken*) to be crucified" (27:26).

We should be clear, however, that the symbiosis between official power and visceral contempt thus revealed really includes anyone of any time urgently wanting Jesus out of the way of their lives and behavior. The mere presence of Jesus, dynamically alive in our midst, is an irritant and a stumbling block to anyone wishing to lead a wholly autonomous existence ruled only by the criteria of power, pleasure, and gain. If the person of Jesus stands for anything, then surely it is this: that the only use of human freedom pleasing to God is the freedom to love unreservedly by dying to oneself as an autonomous entity and rising to a new life of belonging to others. The two main theological words that adhere to the person of Jesus as parts of his very name are "Word" and "Son", and both of these are intensely relational and dynamic terms. A *word* is spoken by one person to another, connecting the one with the other. And a *son* is begotten by his father and is given to others, to the world. Ratzinger comments brilliantly on what makes the personhood of Jesus so different from that of all other men: "The peculiarity of Jesus' I", he writes, "of his person [who is both Word and Son], . . . lies in the fact that this 'I' is not at all something exclusive and independent but rather is Being completely derived from the 'Thou' of the Father and lived for the You of men." [3]

From this understanding of Jesus' inward motivations, we may draw certain conclusions with regard to the *envy* Pilate attributes to the

[3] Joseph Cardinal Ratzinger, *Introduction to Christianity*, trans. J. R. Foster, 2nd ed. (San Francisco: Ignatius Press, 2004), 208.

shouting crowd. We can be quite certain that no one who approaches Jesus that day at the prætorium has any inkling of the finer points of Christology. Nevertheless, we can readily believe that Jesus' person is so diaphanous a reality, and God's intervention in our world through him so efficacious a deed, that the extraordinary goodness, wisdom, and power emanating from Jesus surely communicate themselves in some way to all who encounter him, whether more consciously or more subliminally. This efficacious communication to the world by the Father of the mystery of his Word, through the power of their Holy Spirit, suffice to elicit extreme reactions from the recipients of such communication. They may not be able to express in articulate language the content of their reaction to Jesus, but neither can they ignore the mystery and effect of this vibrant and enticing Personality in their midst.

Jesus' mere presence changes everything in a person's interior world. The disciples were seduced. Of these, one committed suicide in despair and another plunged into an ocean of tears out of repentance. The elders and priests seethe with ire and contempt, while Pontius Pilate feels a certain magnetic attraction and sympathy. The hearts of Mary his Mother and of Mary Magdalen melt with sorrow as they hold their breath for his return to them in splendor. In the meantime, the mob rages against Jesus out of envy, says Pilate, and wallows vicariously with orgiastic lust in the brutal carnality of Barabbas. In this context, we should meditate carefully on the following extraordinary prophetic passage in the Book of Wisdom that reveals with the accuracy of a scalpel the mental and visceral processes motivating so many unquiet souls when they find themselves simply and dangerously threatened by the presence of pure Goodness. Mysteriously, the passage strikes one as a most precise meditation on the historical fate of Jesus:

> Let us lie in wait for the righteous man, because he is inconvenient to us and opposes our actions; he reproaches us for sins against the law, and accuses us of sins against our training. He professes to have knowledge of God, and calls himself a child of the Lord. He became to us a reproof of our thoughts; the very sight of him is a burden to us, because his manner of life is unlike that of others, and his ways are strange. We are considered by him as something base, and he avoids our ways as unclean; he calls the last end of the righteous happy, and boasts that God is his father. (Wis 2:12-16)

Envy, says Pilate, naming the chief adverse passion elicited by the reality of Jesus. It is easy to imagine the envy of Jesus that the Pharisees, the priests, and the scholars of the Law nourish in their hearts. After all, they work so hard at exact observance, burn the midnight oil in the study of Torah, so carefully cultivate the support of the people, and so valiantly protect the nation of Israel from the Roman invaders. . . . In a fleeting three years, the Jewish authorities have seen this upstart rabbi from Nazareth turn their carefully constructed world upside-down. This Jesus has become a powerfully influential public figure who seems to demean sacred traditions, who claims to have the authority to correct the Scripture all by himself, who declares himself to have a unique relationship of direct sonship to God, who appears indifferent to the political plight of his fellow Jews and, instead, proclaims too ethereal a Kingdom.

Now, the fact that precisely *this* dubious and dangerous personage should significantly revolutionize religious attitudes and move hearts to a degree of faithful adherence to his person unimaginable at least since the time of the prophets or of King David or of the patriarchs themselves: all of this is more than the religious leaders can countenance! Pilate is right on target: simple, undiluted *envy* can indeed often be the hidden cause of what becomes expressed in self-righteous language as "God-fearing outrage", "holy zeal for tradition", "brave defense of national and family values", and so forth.

It seems, however, that this sort of envy, based on professional rivalry and the challenge that a brilliant outsider always poses to the establishment, cannot be the case of the mob clamoring for Jesus' blood. Some other, more intricate mechanism of the passions is at work here that is more difficult to unravel. We must seek for a key of interpretation in the fact that these very same crowds, as recently as five days ago on Palm Sunday, were hailing Jesus triumphantly in the streets of Jerusalem. On that joyful occasion, those who "went before him and that followed him shouted, 'Hosanna to the Son of David! Blessed is he who comes in the name of the Lord! Hosanna in the highest!'" (21:9). The mechanism in question has to do with a pendulum swing from extreme, gleeful admiration and, indeed, adulation to an equally extreme contempt and recrimination. How can envy, jealousy, ill-will—all meanings of the Greek word φθόνος (*phthónos*) that Matthew uses—explain the radical shift in the crowd's relationship to Jesus?

Could it be that a passion of murderous jealousy can be ignited in us at the sight of a person who embodies all the qualities we secretly want to possess and yet, for whatever reason, we are certain we never shall possess? The reasons for this negative certainty can be various: perhaps we do not feel capable of doing the work necessary to reach such accomplishments; perhaps we despair of being given the opportunity even to try; or perhaps we feel ridiculous in entertaining such dreams, even though a deep instinct within us skyrockets the desire of our heart to the stars. Envy, or jealousy, is always the result of a battle being waged within our soul between an aspiring higher self and a self-deprecating lower self, and the violent contest is engaged when we behold in the flesh a real human being outside ourselves, very starkly and objectively *there*, who already *is* what we vaguely and sometimes despairingly dream of *becoming*.

"You refuse to come to me that you may have life", Jesus declared to the Jews at one point (Jn 5:40). What a poignant and extraordinary declaration this is, emerging from the depths of the incarnate Word's penetration into the dark labyrinth of the human heart. What a dark and terrible mystery, this deliberate refusal of life, simply because it is *bestowed* by Another and must therefore be *received*! Fullness of life, possession of divine life, is by definition something we can neither fabricate nor seize by our own power and wisdom. The Father, who bestows fullness of divine life on his Son by unceasingly begetting him, has sent him among us so that he, the Son, can in turn bestow this same divine life on us. All men are thus destined by providence to come to Christ in order to acquire life. However, if we do not want to go to Christ *to* have *life*, we will nevertheless unavoidably go to Christ, but *in order to inflict death on him*, who is the Life we do not want. We must destroy all evidence of what we refuse because otherwise it will always be *there*, judging our mediocrity and failure of desire.

We are, then, left by Pilate to ponder this strange mystery of the explicit declaration of lust to kill the Just One who is plainly recognized to be such. Why do we want to get rid of him, other than because we cannot bear the sight of the One whose example and word relentlessly challenge us to change our mind-set and manner of life? The greater the obvious moral perfection of this Innocent One, the more unforgiving the need to be rid of him. And Jesus appears before us as the manifest and undisputed peak of all human perfection, witnessed to as such by no less an authority than the Father and the Holy Spirit themselves. Initial frenzied admiration will in time turn to murderous contempt once we despair of possessing on our own what we so admire. A lethal *phthónos* (*invidia*: envy, jealousy, grudge) will then impel us to destroy the person we dream of becoming but imagine we can never become. By so destroying that person, however, we are also destroying what is best in ourselves, what attracted us to that person to begin with. Nevertheless, in the case of Jesus' trial before Pilate, the envious priests and mob do not realize that Jesus has come precisely in order to *give them freely* what they think can only be *wrested by covetous violence*.

But let us not be too quick to condemn the many in the crowd clamoring for Jesus' death. For, what sentient creature does not fear the approach of fire, even if it be the Fire of Mercy, an endlessly creating and re-creating love that bestows mercy precisely by a work of transformation? And no transformation occurs without pain. The life of God cannot be bestowed upon limited and sinful creatures in any way other than by a process of painful transformation, ignited by the advent of Jesus into our lives. Our initial reaction to this advent is very likely to be that of the denouncers of the Just One, as we have seen: "The very sight of him is a burden to us, because his manner of life is unlike that of others, and his ways are strange" (Wis 2:15).

27:19   Καθημένου δὲ αὐτοῦ ἐπὶ τοῦ βήματος
         ἀπέστειλεν πρὸς αὐτὸν ἡ γυνὴ αὐτοῦ λέγουσα·
         Μηδὲν σοὶ καὶ τῷ δικαίῳ ἐκείνῳ·
         πολλὰ γὰρ ἔπαθον σήμερον κατ' ὄναρ δι' αὐτόν

While he was sitting on the judgment seat,
his wife sent [word] to him, saying
"Have nothing to do with that righteous man,
for I have suffered much over him today in a dream"

A SHAFT OF PIERCING LIGHT unexpectedly enters this dark and tense scene in the form of a message to Pilate from his wife. We note that the question Pilate asks the people (about whom they wish to see released) remains suspended in v. 17b; the answer will come only in v. 21, after Pilate has asked the question a second time. This technique of narrative interruption and suspension allows Matthew to create a space of reflective deliberation in his listeners. We his readers are thus urged by the text to examine our own consciences and decide for or against Jesus, in this case after pondering the mysterious witness of Pilate's wife, who represents the solitary dissenting voice pleading for Jesus to be spared. Clearly, from the evangelist's viewpoint, this woman introduces the voice of wisdom into the pathos and frenzy of the scene. From the turn that Pilate's negotiations with the people will soon take, we will know that the governor is strongly affected by his wife's plea. While the two trials have been going on during the night and in the early dawn, she has had a deeply troubling dream concerning Jesus. She is obviously a woman touched by grace. In her interior life, Jesus has suddenly emerged as protagonist of an important drama affecting her conscience, just as for God he is the protagonist of the divine plan of redemption. For everyone else, he appears to be nothing but a condemned criminal and a troublesome disturber of the status quo. This woman senses strongly that Jesus' person and mission originate in the depths of the mystery of God.

To gauge to what extent Pilate's wife represents a prophetic mouthpiece of divine wisdom, we should place her dream in the context of the four dreams Matthew includes in Jesus' infancy narrative, namely, the three dreams of Joseph and the shared dream of the Magi (1:20; 2:12, 13, 19, 22). The present dream affecting this aristocratic pagan woman has in common with those other premonitory dreams the fact that they all occur in extreme circumstances of distress and danger and have the character of a divine intervention intended to guide persons involved in the drama of salvation in a moment of dire need. All of these dreams originate in the realm where God dwells and are meant to cast the light of revelation upon the entanglements of human history and the perversity of human choices.

Two allusions on the woman's part confirm the divine origin of her vivid oneiric communication. First, she calls Jesus "that righteous man", and, second, she testifies that what she saw in her dream has made her "suffer much". Alone against an irrationally raging multitude, ranging from the high priest and the elders and scribes all the way to the least member of that street rabble, Pilate's wife proclaims to her powerful husband that Jesus is *ho Díkaios*, "the Just (or Righteous) One". This is the designation par excellence of the Messiah, particularly in the figure of Isaiah's Suffering Servant: "By his knowledge shall the righteous one, my servant, make many to be accounted righteous; and he shall bear their iniquities" (Is 53:11b). Isaiah also takes for granted the fact that in this sublunary world the Righteous One will be persecuted, and he envisions this persecution in a way that quite mirrors the present drama at the prætorium: "The righteous man perishes, and no one lays it to heart", laments Isaiah; "devout men are taken away, while no one understands" (Is 57:1).

We have already seen, furthermore, how the Book of Wisdom dramatizes the fate of the Righteous One at the hands of the mob as it gives free rein to its own worst human instincts. There we hear the thoughts of the scoundrels: "Let us oppress the righteous poor man. . . . Let us lie in wait for the righteous man, because he is inconvenient to us and opposes our actions" (Wis 2:10, 12). In the face of this universal show of disdain and hatred toward God's appointed Messiah, Pilate's wife raises a lone voice of opposition. We perceive in her inflections a tremor that surely expresses her fear of God, her trepidation at the horror afoot in the world as God's Righteous One is being violently banished from the midst of men. What is occurring here amounts to nothing less than an attack upon the holiness and justice of God himself, localized in the concrete person of the Righteous One he has sent. Jesus, we must conclude for our part with fear and trembling, is the vulnerability of God.

Pilate's wife also moves us by her expression of great personal suffering as a result of her dream, which sounds more like a nightmare. Quite literally she says πολλὰ ἔπαθον ("I have suffered much", or "many things"), which is exactly the same language Jesus uses in his first prediction of the Passion, just before the Transfiguration, to refer to his own necessary fate: "From that time Jesus began to show his disciples that he must go to Jerusalem and *suffer many things* (πολλὰ παθεῖν) from the elders and chief priests and scribes, and be killed, and on the third day be raised" (16:21). The woman's experience of a harrowing dream in connection with Jesus' suffering, her clairvoyance in seeing in him the Righteous One of God, and her courage in proclaiming him as such to her husband, the Roman governor, and, most importantly, her communion with Jesus in his Passion by way of her own interior torment, described in terms that echo precisely Jesus' own suffering: all of this surely makes of this pagan woman, whom early Christian tradition names Procula, a prophetic vessel of revelation.

Like all the prophets who communicate God's authentic word, Procula must suffer from the Fire of the Word coursing through her being so that it can shine brightly in the night of blindness engulfing the world. As so often in the Gospel, the truest light of revelation and the most spontaneous act of faith are here embodied by someone standing outside the Jewish tradition, without the benefit of belonging to God's chosen people. It is one of the great ironies of the Gospel that frequently Jesus is recognized in his true identity by persons standing outside the realm of Old Testament revelation. Often enough, in-depth objective possession of a knowledge of the Scriptures and the practice of Jewish religious traditions are shown to be the greatest obstacle to the act of faith in Jesus, while honest pagans and sinners are more likely to be moved by his goodness and wisdom. Thus, though we know her from only one verse in Scripture, Procula belongs squarely in the company of the Magi (2:1–12), the Roman centurion (8:5–13), and the Canaanite woman (15:21–28), among others, and the importance of her heartfelt testimony is all the greater as she bears it at such a crucial moment in Jesus' life. One dream sufficed to reveal to her both Jesus' identity as God's Righteous One and the horror of the injustice being inflicted upon him.

It is quite in keeping, moreover, with her role as a woman of the ancient world and her status as Pilate's wife that her concern is not at all political but, rather, personal. She represents the tenderer, more private aspect of the Roman governor's life, and her manner of intervention humanizes him in our eyes. What impels her to act as she does is simply her love for her husband as she attempts to save him from the evil consequences of condemning most grievously the Righteous One of God. Her clairvoyance and capacity for compassion attempt to offset her husband's purely political considerations and his desire to placate his Jewish subjects at all costs. "Have nothing to do with that righteous man", she urges him, "for I have suffered much over him today in a dream." Indeed, how much dynamic content, how much awestruck piety and human affection, Matthew has packed into this single half-verse! And we can be sure that Procula's trembling, instinctual empathy with Jesus' sufferings, though she can hardly understand the depth of her experience, cannot go unrewarded.

Now, we are told that her urgent admonition was sent by Procula to Pilate "while he was sitting on the *bêma* (or judgment seat)". It is important for us to visualize the scene so as to appreciate fully the dramatically clashing intersection occurring here between the official, public sphere of human life and the personal, private domain. Procula normally stays in the inner recesses of her home, tending the flames of the family's hearth like a good Roman wife. She must therefore send a servant girl bearing the anxious communication to her husband, who is in the midst of exercising a public function as governor, out in the public forum. The fact that Procula cannot wait until she has a moment of privacy with Pilate later in the day is a measure of the urgency of her message. The maid arrives with a message from the house's interior, probably from the bedroom where Procula has just awakened from her dream in the early morning. We can surmise that the dream itself came to the lady of the house as an emissary from the realm of God. Therefore, the maid's sudden appearance at the prætorium, her interruption of the prefect in the middle of his deliberations as he sits upon the judgment seat, clearly represents the incursion—into the realm of purely horizontal human activity and concerns—of a vertical prophetic word from the realm of the divine.

We here witness how a divine word in anguished, feminine disguise arrives forcefully onto the human scene in a most ironic manner: it comes to judge with infallible divine justice the human judge who is pretending to judge with feeble human justice the Judge of the Ages! It is as if a divine tribunal were now giving its own verdict and, thus, succinctly but most radically invalidating the human verdict that the Sanhedrin has already reached. And the divine verdict is emphatic: *This Jesus is the Righteous One of God par excellence, though human envy, arrogance, and hunger for power may condemn him.* Divine light, truth, and justice are here being dazzlingly beamed into the blind world of arrogant male power-play by the intermediary of Procula and her maid, two women who are wholly deprived of any official status in society and can therefore represent the freedom and sovereignty of God's judgment all the more efficiently and in a surprising manner that bears the seal of divine authenticity.

The light of revelation, conveying the truth about this prisoner Jesus, has come in the form of a prophetic dream into Procula's intimate alcove, an interior realm of existence quite out of the sight of the populace and the power-brokers of society, as hidden as the divine realm itself, totally removed from the transactions and conflicts of all those struggling for favor and preeminence in court, marketplace, and temple. We cannot help but associate the alcove where Procula had her dream with the secluded room where the Mother of God received Gabriel's visitation and conceived the Word (cf. Lk 1:26–38).

When his wife's maid interrupts him with her message, we are invited to see Pilate *sitting on his official judgment seat,* a symbol of his power as governor. This indication reminds us, by contrast, that *Jesus himself has been standing* throughout the night during his two trials, first at Caiaphas' house and now at the prætorium. Through these physical details, the present judgment scene ironically calls to mind the manner in which Matthew introduced his great parable of the Final Judgment in chapter 25: "When the Son of man comes in his glory, and all the angels with him, *then he will sit on his glorious throne"* (25:31). Two trials, two judges, two seats of judgment stand in glaring contrast here. Jesus' present condition as condemned criminal, now undergoing a second trial in one night, is but an intensification of his general condition throughout the Gospel as servant, indeed, as slave, of all, always ready to assume any and every role imposed upon him by man's wickedness if only that willing assumption will contribute to that same wicked man's redemption.

The New Testament continually recalls how this present age of the world is strongly subject to the power of the Prince of Darkness, "the spirit that is now at work in the sons of disobedience" (Eph 2:2). Under such malevolent influence, all the righteous will suffer at the hands of the unrighteous and disobedient ones. Jesus, being divine Righteousness incarnate, will by definition have to suffer more than anyone else and be humiliated the most horribly. Judged by the standards of the present world and by the self-serving motivations of the vast majority of its inhabitants, Jesus and all like Jesus can only experience violent rejection. Matthew's present portrayal of the silent Jesus' humiliation before Pilate should be contemplated alongside the evangelist's vision of the Last Judgment, when Jesus will no longer be standing before a human judge. At that moment, rather, he will be sitting majestically on his throne of glory, revealed for all to behold in his true nature as his Father has always seen him, namely, as the appointed King and Judge of all ages.

Pilate's *bêma*, or judgment seat, is a material and temporary object that this particular Roman governor happened to occupy for ten short years between A.D. 26 and 36, preceded in his office by Valerius Gratus and succeeded by Marcellus. But Jesus' Throne of Glory, an intrinsic attribute of his person, belongs to him forever by his nature as Son of the eternal Father, and his judgment is not confined by time. Only the truly Divine can conceal itself in such utter anonymity without fear of losing itself! The *kénosis* (or "self-emptying") of the second Person of the Blessed Trinity, which began at the Incarnation (cf. Phil 2:7), is now in the process of being consummated during the Passion and death of Jesus of Nazareth, through the Savior's unending *parádosis* ("handing-over") of himself into the hands of sinners.

Those who cling to power and all its manifestations are precisely those who are most painfully aware of its fleetingness. But the divine Son, "though he was in the form of God, did not count equality with God a thing to be grasped" (Phil 2:6), as if he feared losing his divine sonship. Rather, it was this very divine sonship, grounded in his Father's inexhaustible love, that urged the Son to empty himself of the glory of divinity for the sake of identifying himself with sinners in their condition of wretchedness. At this very moment before Pilate, at a level deeper than what eyes can see, Jesus' humility, silence, and meekness are sitting in judgment of Pilate's spinelessness and the mob's bloodthirsty envy. The Son's throne of glory, though at present invisible to human eyes, nevertheless belongs to Jesus by right and inalienably, in a way that Pilate's *bêma* could never belong to him. While Pilate merely *represents* the Roman emperor's political authority, itself unstable and subject to all manner of vicissitudes, Jesus, though distinct from the Father, does not "represent" the Father in the same sense. Rather, Jesus *is* the very presence of the Father and the embodiment of God, "for in him all the fulness of God was pleased to dwell" (Col 1:19). To Philip, he made the remarkable affirmation: "He who has seen me has seen the Father" (Jn 14:9). In the person of Jesus, who is the visibility of the Father, therefore, it is truly the God of Israel who this night is being humiliated, bound, judged, struck, spat-upon, and condemned by both Jews and Romans.

No physical or material distance or metaphysical separation, then, can exist between Jesus and the Father such as necessarily exists between Pilate and the Emperor Tiberius, for "I and the Father are one" (Jn 10:30). Though under the hidden form of humiliation, all the glory of Divinity is truly present that day at the prætorium as Jesus bows his head before the Roman governor. While Pilate is surrounded by a host of soldiers, guardians, attendants, and servants, Jesus himself, the condemned King of the ages, is no less surrounded by all his angels, though these hosts of the heavenly powers defer to the Savior's will to save the world through patient love and, therefore, observe a reverential stillness. The glory of the true God is never manifested by what the worldly mind-set imagines to be the distinctive signs of majestic power. In the present age of the world, while the struggle between light and darkness, compassion and hatred, continues, the Glory of God makes no noise but reveals itself through sublimely unobtrusive acts of steadfast presence, quiet admonition, refusal of vengeance, will to forgive, in a word, all the gestures of self-surrendering love, behind which stands hidden the omnipotent and omniscient Creator of the universe. Jesus stands before Pilate compelled only by his will to serve, because servants do not sit while there is work to be done, and the work of salvation is the most strenuous of all. However, Jesus, in his unwavering resolution *to stand in the service* of mankind, at the same time *sits in judgment* of the blindness and hardheartedness of the recalcitrant and disobedient who will not yield to God's love.

"Now the chief priests and the elders persuaded the people to ask for Barabbas and destroy Jesus" (27:20). Those bent upon clinging to power in society so as to perpetuate the way things have been, those refusing to admit a dazzling light and a transforming fire into their hearts, those unwilling to share the abundance of God's blessings universally, will always prefer to liberate the Barabbas-principle into the world and so enthrone self-will, greed, and the basest human instincts and prejudices. But Jesus, who is the divine principle of generosity and truth, they will seek not only in order to marginalize him, not only in order to disable him, not only in order to punish him, but, to use Matthew's term, *in order to destroy* (ἵνα ἀπολέσωσιν) him.

Certain translations of this passage tend to gloss over the flagrant brutality and guilt that Matthew explicitly attributes to the religious authorities and the people. For example, the NJB renders v. 20 thus: "The chief priests and the elders had persuaded the crowd to demand *the release of Barabbas and the execution of Jesus*" (27:20). Of course this persuasion and this demand are already bad enough. But the Greek text goes beyond this neat rendition and literally says: "The chief priests and the elders persuaded the people that they should ask for Barabbas and *that they should destroy Jesus* (ἵνα αἰτήσωνται τὸν Βαραββᾶν, τὸν δὲ Ἰησοῦν ἀπολέσωσιν)" (27:20). Matthew thus allows the full responsibility for Jesus' murder to descend upon the heads of the authorities and of the clamoring crowds, exposing the former as the brains and the latter as the brawn of the crime. That the Roman soldiery will be the physical agent actually to crucify Jesus seems for the moment a technical detail in the eyes of Matthew.

The eventual killing of Jesus this very afternoon is here attributed to a collusion between the priests and the rabble as true subjects of the verbs and, therefore, of the actions. Likewise, Matthew makes a radical choice of verbs to convey the idea of killing. He does not here use ἀποκτείνω (*apokteínô*), the ordinary verb for killing a human being, but rather ἀπόλλυμι (*apóllymi*), a verb with devastating implications. It means "to destroy utterly", "to demolish", "to waste", "to annihilate", and is more properly applied to the destruction of a whole army, city, or kingdom (as in the Homeric epic poems) than to a single individual. This verb therefore is a measure of the extraordinary visceral hatred and violence for Jesus that Matthew wishes to attribute to the frenzy of the chief priests and the screaming multitude. The verb implies that they wish to see Jesus wiped off the face of the earth and will be satisfied with nothing less than his total annihilation.

Theologically, as well as affectively, the verb is an important lexical choice: it portrays the gathered sum of the world's scorn for God hurtling like an apocalyptic mountain down upon the head of Jesus, while Jesus for his part is steeling himself to drown the world's evil in the flood of his precious Blood.

We should never lose from sight the incredible and all-determining fact that this preparation for self-surrendering oblation takes place, not by blind historical accident or by an inevitable fatality, but purely as an act of deliberate and sovereign freedom, the transcendental freedom of divine love, conditioned by nothing but the divine Nature itself. Jesus became the vulnerability of God on earth because he first chose to become the visibility of God when he became man and consequently took on every attribute of human nature, including the capacity to die. Some would even argue that the chief motivating force that urged the eternal Word to become man was his intention to acquire a mortal body that would enable him to give away his divine life by enduring a human death.

27:21b–23 Τίνα θέλετε ἀπὸ τῶν δύο ἀπολύσω ὑμῖν;
οἱ δὲ εἶπαν· Τὸν Βαραββᾶν.
Τί οὖν ποιήσω Ἰησοῦν τὸν λεγόμενον Χριστόν;
λέγουσιν πάντες· Σταυρωθήτω.
ὁ δὲ ἔφη· Τί γὰρ κακὸν ἐποίησεν;
οἱ δὲ περισσῶς ἔκραζον λέγοντες· Σταυρωθήτω.

"Which of the two do you want me to release for you?"
And they said, "Barabbas."
"Then what shall I do [with] Jesus who is called Christ?"
They all said, "Let him be crucified."
And he said, "What evil has he done?"
But they shouted all the more, "Let him be crucified."

THE RAPID-FIRE DIALOGUE between Pilate and the mob has to be reproduced with some fullness if we are to receive an adequate impression of its high drama. Before us we see the two principal representatives of mankind in the Gospel—the Romans and the Jews—conducting a tug of war to determine the fate of the Son of God. Matthew does not cease driving home the intensity of the rabble's bloodthirstiness, stressing the repeated occasions the people of Israel were given to change their mind and spare Jesus. Over and over, the populace makes a heinous choice, in the same way that Peter, first among the apostles, did earlier that day. Pilate here acts as the people's conscience, confronting it with its true, macabre desires. Because Pilate provides the non-involved, pagan point of view on Jesus, the passage makes patent the extent to which the animosity against Jesus and his eventual death were the result of specifically religious prejudice and fear.

Those who ritually enshrined the *Books* of Moses and of the prophets as the ultimate in revealed wisdom now, at the same time, refuse to hear any new *living word* from God that might shake their codified and minutely explicated traditions—even if that "new living word" happens to be the one and only divine Word in person, in whom the world was created. According to Charles Péguy's famous rhyme, the *mystique* of God's burning interventions in early Israel has over the centuries been cooled down to the *politique* of Pharisaical logic and rigid observance. Such hardening of the communal heart results in the most tragic paradox history has ever known: Jesus, the living and embodied *Word of God*, who has come to the Jews in person by being born of a Jewish woman, has to be destroyed in order to preserve the petrified legitimacy of the many prophetic *words* that, ironically, originated in him (cf. Heb 1:1). The precious Tree of Life is hacked at the roots in order to protect the fruit hanging from the branches! Here more than ever Jesus' terrible words denouncing religious hypocrisy apply:

> You are like whitewashed tombs, which outwardly appear beautiful, but within they are full of dead men's bones and all uncleanness. . . . You build the tombs of the prophets and adorn the monuments of the righteous. . . . Thus you witness against yourselves, that you are sons of those who murdered the prophets. (23:27, 29b, 31)

The death principle clearly inhabits and motivates, not Jesus, but those who are clamoring for his demise. They seek his death because they are possessed by the rampant spirit of death.

We have noted that, when Pilate first put the question to the crowds in v. 17b, asking them whom they wished him to release to them, "Jesus Barabbas or Jesus the Christ", the question remained suspended. At that moment the arrival of the servant girl with Procula's message interrupted the proceedings of the trial. It is as if, by that momentary suspension of the dialogue, Matthew wanted to highlight one of the climaxes of the Passion's drama when three points of view on Jesus suddenly collided: that of the envious elders and crowd (*visceral condemnation*), that of the questioning Pilate (*aloof neutrality*), and that of his visionary wife (*incipient faith*). These three points of view, coexisting in the same place at the same time and catalyzed by the presence of the humiliated Jesus, obviously present us with three possible stances we ourselves could assume. This is the evangelist's way of engaging us, the readers, in the drama, by allowing our hearts to be tugged in different directions by different aspects of our own persons. Reading the Gospel attentively always launches an arduous interior battle in the reader with an open heart.

And so the prefect now repeats the question that remained unanswered in v. 17: "Which of the two do you want me to release for you?" It is fascinating to note that the Greek word here for "to release", ἀπολύσω (*apolýsô*), is very close in form and sound to ἀπολέσωσιν (*apolésôsin*), the word Matthew used in v. 20 to indicate the priests' and mob's ardent desire that Jesus should be *destroyed*. We recall the ironical similarity of name within an opposition of meaning between the Savior and the preferred criminal: "Jesus Barabbas" and "Jesus the Christ". So, too, now Matthew plays on the similarity of sound of two words that clash in the diametrically opposed meanings of the destiny each evokes. Humanity as a whole, represented by the mob, chooses to *release* the guilty one and *destroy* the Righteous. Here we have the whole drama of salvation summed up in the mnemonic nutshell of these two verbs. The theological clash of contraries involved has been best described by St. Paul: "God shows his love for us in that while we were yet *sinners* Christ died for us. . . . For if while we were *enemies* we were reconciled to God by the death of his Son, much more, now that we are reconciled, shall we be saved by his life" (Rom 5:8, 10).

God responds to the outrage and destruction we inflict on him with a death out of love that reconciles us to him *while we were enemies!* This fact exemplifies how the Word is the first to live and die by his own teaching, which, when first heard homiletically at the beginning of the Gospel, could perhaps still have passed for a lovely theory: "But I say to you, Love your enemies and pray for those who persecute you" (5:44). At this moment before Pilate, the teaching first proclaimed in words of instruction is becoming fully embodied in the silent Word's suffering and imminent death. Only in Jesus is there no gap but only total identity between word and life. This is one aspect of what it means for him to be *the Word, God's Truth and Love, Incarnate*.

The depth of our corporate iniquity and perversity, out of which we could not save ourselves, is measured by the fact that as a race we sought to destroy the very One who came to give us life, while simultaneously preferring to release from guilt and applaud a common criminal, that is, someone very much like ourselves. The mob's choice of Barabbas over Jesus confirms and glorifies with sordid exultation our own persistent choice of ourselves over God. RELEASE (*apolýsô*) or DESTROY (*apolésôsin*): Nothing could illustrate better than this poignant play of words by Matthew the fact that we are saved exclusively by the grace of God's love for us, *despite our fiercest efforts to the contrary*. Nothing could be more perverse than man's wicked zeal to destroy his own Redeemer. Not only is deicide the most heinous of sins; it is also by nature a contortedly *suicidal* choice. Hatred of the divine order and its Author will always in the end reveal itself as rooted in hatred of the self.

After the multitude has chosen to spare Barabbas rather than Jesus, the criminal rather than the Savior, Pilate asks them: "Then what shall I do with Jesus who is called Christ?" Each moment of this dialectical exchange adds a new element that intensifies the mob's responsibility and makes more blatant the evil nature of its choice. In this present question, Pilate is reminding the crowd of the true identity of the prisoner they are condemning: he is "the Christ", the Anointed One of God sent to Israel to perform the work of God's redemption. However, Pilate casts the proclamation of Jesus as Messiah in a noncommittal manner that aims at a pose of neutrality ("Jesus *who is called* Christ", he says), as if the whole matter of salvation concerned only the Jews. Nevertheless, by her anxious and fervent intervention, Pilate's wife has already shown that it is not only the Jews who are looking for salvation but the Romans, too, as well as all men. In addition, the tenor of this dialogue demonstrates that the governor himself has been more affected by Procula's anguished dream than he cares to manifest.

"What shall I do with Jesus?" Pilate asks the mob, revealing that he has a big problem on his hands and that this trial has brought him, too, to an interior crisis. This crisis, this urgent quandary of "What shall I do with Jesus?" has been inscribed in the very fabric of the human condition from the moment "the Word became flesh and dwelt among us" (Jn 1:14). Nothing can henceforth remove Jesus from our lives as the unquestionable, converging Center of All Reality, both personal and cosmic, both eternal and temporal.[4] Jesus the

---

[4] This truth was confirmed for me unexpectedly at a recent (May, 2019) encounter at the Gare de Lyon in Paris. A young and very affable Arab Muslim who was helping us with our bags, seeing we were monks traveling together, could not refrain from looking us straight in the eye on parting and asking the question: "Who is Jesus for you?" The three of us responded almost simultaneously: "The Son of God!" Then, with an almost worried look, Waheed asked: "How can that be if God is only *one*?" (This attribute of God means a great deal to him because his own name, *Waheed*, is one of the 99 Divine Names and refers to Allah's absolute Oneness.) For this young man, too, "What shall I do with Jesus?" is obviously a burning question, although naturally he perceives the issue as an irritating puzzlement at the faith of Christians.

Christ, the Heart of the World, is just as surely present and active at the center of our lives, both conscious and subconscious, as the Sun, which we also normally take for granted, majestically reigns from the center of our solar system, beaming out its rays of life-giving energy and leading the planets around itself in their joyful dance (cf. Job 38:5; Bar 3:32).

To the Colossians Paul writes that in Christ "all things were created, in heaven and on earth, visible and invisible, whether thrones or dominions or principalities or authorities—all things were created through him and for him. He is before all things, and in him all things hold together; . . . he is the beginning" (Col 1:16–18). To the Ephesians, furthermore, Paul proclaims God's plan to "bring everything together under Christ as Head (ἀνακεφαλαιώσασθαι), everything in the heavens and everything on earth" (Eph 1:10, NJB). And these transcendental Christ-events are taking place before our eyes as Jesus stands being judged by Pilate. *This* is how his meek dominance is being established; *this* is how the whole of creation is being recapitulated under him as Head.

Jesus' current manner of presence before a wavering judge and a hostile public may appear to be all silence and passivity, weakness and shameful defeat. In actual fact, however, this is the visible mode whereby the incarnate Word of the Father is exercising his role as Still Center of the universe. Round about him we see orbiting the tumultuous passions, resentments, and treacherous ambiguities of men. Jesus' silence and apparent "passivity" are performing a redemptive function: they are his manner of taking into himself the violence and recalcitrance of rebellious sinners so as to transmute them by the alchemy of love into the peace of his Heart. This very same and sole absolute Principle of Life is present and at work in Jesus of Nazareth as he stands in humiliation today before Pilate in the prætorium. His nature as self-outpouring Love is revealed only the more efficaciously under his present form of humiliation, which enables him to "bring all things together" in his Heart from the inside out and from the bottom up, so to speak, since in him God himself is suffering as one of our sinful race, ontologically identified, we might say, with our fallen and suffering race.

Jesus is not one among many possible saviors; Jesus is the one and only Savior because there is only one God who has only one Son whom he has sent. We could say that Pilate's question "What shall

I do with Jesus?", which can appear casual and merely pragmatic, is henceforth *the central question of every human life,* for it takes for granted that Jesus has already been given to us, has already given himself to us, a fact that cannot be undone regardless of how we choose to react to it. That a Savior has already been given, and who that Savior is, are no longer open questions; they are settled facts of the history of salvation. But the crucially open question does remain, *What shall I* do with Jesus? . . . now that I have him, now that I have received him in his suffering flesh?

So there we find ourselves, left suddenly in the middle of life's marketplace, in the middle of our lives, and without having been previously consulted, but nonetheless *holding Jesus in our hands.* Should it not fill us with bone-rattling awe that the Word, the Beginning, the Head of all things, the *Sine Qua Non* of all reality and experience, has so made himself available to us, has so thoroughly handed himself over to us, that he has created a situation in our lives that compels us to ask, "What shall I do with Jesus?" What an unheard-of privilege is ours, and how dreadful our responsibility. We can and must *do something with Jesus!* Only ardent lovers hand themselves over with such radical eagerness.

As for Pilate himself, he masks his personal responsibility behind a cool façade of apparent impartiality. Even though he realizes that the final decision either to condemn or to exonerate Jesus lies in his own hands, still he seeks to reroute the onus of decision by way of the mob since it is they that he now consults. He fastidiously avoids asking his own conscience the crucial question "What shall I do with Jesus?" and refers it to the populace instead. And their immediate response, full of cruel delectation, is the horrendous Σταυρωθήτω (*staurothêtô*), *crucifigatur: Let him be crucified!* They answer at once as with one voice because they have been thoroughly rehearsed by the elders and priests. They reply like a screeching demonic choir. Jesus' enemies have agreed on death by crucifixion, which, because of its excruciating slowness and the unbearable pain inflicted by the piercing nails, was the most horrible form of Roman capital punishment, far worse than death by stoning, hanging, or beheading. Crucifixion also offered the ultimate in public humiliation.

Mark's version of the mob's damning verdict shouted at Pilate is in the direct imperative, "Crucify him" (Mk 15:13). This form of the request makes Pilate himself the subject of the verb and thus subtly shifts onto him the responsibility for the heinous deed. Matthew's passive form, "Let him be crucified", underscores, rather, the active desire and guilt of the people, an emphasis that this evangelist has steadily sustained. By every means available to him, Matthew wants to keep his readers from disengaging too easily from the burden of collective guilt for Jesus' murder by the hypocritical old trick of attributing "the deplorable event" to the blind processes of history and the robotic mind-set of official decision makers.

Now Pilate, clearly convinced of his prisoner's innocence, appeals to the crowd once more, replying to their demand for crucifixion by asking, "Why, what evil has he done?" At this point in the so-called dialogue, we are impressed by two things that stand in radical contrast. The first is the ease with which a rabble's fury can whip up to the peak of irrationality and inject with a lust for blood at all cost persons who otherwise are very ordinary shopkeepers, butchers, and housewives. The other thing is Pilate's nonchalant attitude of detachment, as if the drama unrolling before him were merely a part of that day's official duties and had nothing to do with his private person and moral conscience. Neither the mob nor Pilate seems particularly concerned with the fact that the life-or-death destiny of a man is here being played out, and this is considering the drama only at the level of ordinary human decency and a minimal regard for justice, quite apart from specifically theological issues.

When Pilate then asks the crowd what evil crime Jesus has committed in order for them to want him crucified, "they shouted all the more, 'Let him be crucified.'" Obviously, Pilate is playing the role of the naïve foreigner while the mob is giving proof of its irrational animus against Jesus by its collective shouting. Shouting can be a substitute for reasoned thought and internal conviction, an efficient way to drown out one's conscience, which instinctually leans toward justice. The crowd's vociferous reply amounts quite simply to "We want him crucified because we want him crucified!", nothing more reasoned than that. Sheer destructive lust has possessed their collective will. Matthew's psychological acumen is impressive in this scene as he peels back layer after layer of complex human motivations and interactions that in the end produce unthinkable crimes. Fundamentally, the true justifying cause for Jesus' condemnation is the concerted will of the hysterical majority. For how could all the elders and priests of Israel, together with all the people of Israel, be wrong in their corporate judgment of the deleterious nature of Jesus' presence and influence? So they proceed to kill the Son of God in the holy name of God! The real subtext informing the desire and action of this hyper-religious people is: "It is a bad thing to take God too seriously! It is a dangerous thing to allow God to come too close! We can be happy only with a god we can control and manipulate, a god after our own hearts."

27:24   ἰδὼν δὲ ὁ Πιλᾶτος ὅτι οὐδὲν ὠφελεῖ
ἀλλὰ μᾶλλον θόρυβος γίνεται,
λαβὼν ὕδωρ ἀπενίψατο τὰς χεῖρας ἀπέναντι τοῦ ὄχλου
λέγων· Ἀθῷός εἰμι ἀπὸ τοῦ αἵματος τούτου·
ὑμεῖς ὄψεσθε

So when Pilate saw that he was gaining nothing,
but rather that a riot was beginning,
he took water and washed his hands before the crowd,
saying, "I am innocent of this blood;
see [to it] yourselves"

DEPENDING ON WHICH PART of our heart is most active at the moment, the wavering Pilate's vacillation as he feels caught between Jesus and the crowd will strike us as either cowardly or understandable. We certainly recognize in him our own hesitation, when the odds are too high, to embrace the cause of justice regardless of the consequences to ourselves. Pilate clearly believes Jesus to be innocent, and his better heart inclines him toward Jesus in the desire to protect and exonerate him. And yet, though this inclination reveals in Pilate a real clarity of thought and a nobility of soul worthy of a Stoic philosopher, nonetheless, his right judgment is severely compromised by the pragmatic administrator in him with his high regard for efficiency and status above all else. He can now safely say to himself, "I tried to save the man, but all to no avail. After all, this trial affects the fate of only *one* man, and the possible riot emerging here, if unchecked, could result in harm to dozens of people and a nasty stain on my administrative record in the eyes of Rome."

In the end, Pilate gives priority to pragmatic results and the upholding of the status quo of civic peace and harmony over the intrinsic truth of one person's innocence. He speculates that the importance of "the truth" can, as we all know, be overrated, since it is, after all, an abstract and relative concept that depends on different individuals' points of view. He concludes his meditation by deciding that what is needed are concrete results for the benefit of the many *and* of course also of his political career. The philosopher in Pilate thus capitulates to the pragmatism and narrow-mindedness of the civil servant and administrator. "What would Emperor Tiberius want in this case?" seems to be the question looming in Pilate's mind, and this servile query gags the voice of his sovereign conscience. The naked threat of the mob's riotous mood tramples down the tender grass of wisdom and righteousness growing in Pilate's heart. At this point, he constrains himself to dismiss his initial misgivings as an unmasculine manifestation of sentimentality in the style of his lady wife, Procula, so prey to feminine anguish and hysteria. He loves and needs her very much, but he also considers her ignorant and ineffective in political matters, quite literally "a dreamer".

In order to salvage some self-respect in his own eyes, however, Pilate attempts to take his distance from the whole affair by "triangulating", that is, by refusing to take too drastic a position for or against Jesus, thinking he can thus construct a third, middle option of neutral non-involvement. But it could be argued that this attempt at fabricating for oneself a theoretical exemption from all involvement is the greatest chimæra of all. We may also say that a person like Pilate, who sees the truth and yet chooses not to defend it, is guiltier than perpetrators of injustice who are purely driven by blind instincts of vengeance and have little capacity for reflection, particularly when acting as members of a raving mob.

Both Pilate's exalted public office and his basically noble and ruminative personality naturally set him apart from any cabal. He stands alone as free agent before both Jesus and the Jewish agitators. And aggravating Pilate's responsibility on this occasion is the fact that he happens to be the Roman governor, someone possessing the effectual juridical power either to condemn or to absolve Jesus. The choice is truly his, although he next acts craftily in an attempt to convince both himself and the world at large that things stand otherwise.

As a diversionary strategy to mask his guilt, Pilate has recourse to the ritual gesture of handwashing, which only Matthew records. This ritual, with the specific meaning of declaring oneself free of guilt, is attested by only one passage in the Hebrew Scriptures (Deut 21:1–8), but the passage in question is significant because it, too, involves murder and the shedding of innocent blood. In the case that a person is found murdered and the killer is unknown, the elders of the city closest to where the victim was found are to go out to the corpse and offer a heifer as sacrifice of expiation. Then these same elders "shall wash their hands over the heifer whose neck was broken in the valley; and they shall testify, 'Our hands did not shed this blood, neither did our eyes see it shed.'" To conclude the ritual of purification they are to recite this prayer: "'Forgive, O LORD, your people Israel, whom you have redeemed, and set not the guilt of innocent blood in the midst of your people Israel; but let the guilt of blood be forgiven them.' So you shall purge the guilt of innocent blood from your midst, when you do what is right in the sight of the LORD" (Deut 21:7–9).

Obvious as the relevance of this passage is to the present situation in the prætorium, we must nonetheless ask why Pilate, a Roman official, would perform such a Jewish ritual. Could it be that the Roman bureaucracy in Judæa has by now taken on some of the symbolic gestures of the Jewish people diplomatically, for the sake of fostering a favorable social harmony? Or, rather, could it be that Matthew attributes to Pilate an action that would have been very eloquent to his Judæo-Christian readers in broadcasting the innocence of Jesus, the present victim about to be murdered, even though Pilate himself intends it as a distancing manoeuver? Either way, Pilate's dramatic gesture of washing his hands in the sight of all has always conveyed the profound and culpable ambiguity of his elected position.

As he performs the ritual, Pilate solemnly and loudly utters these words: "I am innocent of this . . . man's blood; see to it yourselves." In this way, the governor wants to win everyone present over as witnesses, but I suspect he also wants to mute his uneasy conscience. By this public and solemn affirmation in word and in deed, Pilate attempts to legitimize his impartiality and safeguard his pristine reputation as Roman official. However, in actual fact, the affirmation reveals the internal contradiction of his position. His own words expose him as a moral fraud, for one cannot logically affirm all three items of his proposition simultaneously: the innocence of the accused, the innocence of the judge, and the judge's action of turning the accused over to his accusers for crucifixion. A gesture originally intended by Deuteronomy to proclaim the hand-washers' innocence and purify them from every suspicion of guilt in the present case rather proclaims this hand-washer's cowardice and compromising stance. Perhaps Pilate is so eager to wash his hands for another, less conscious reason: namely, because he feels on them in a premonitory way the stickiness of the blood about to be shed that very afternoon on Golgotha. We can sin just as gravely by omission as we can by commission, and it could well be that Pilate's behavior on this Good Friday morning in the prætorium was the gravest sin of omission ever committed by a human being.

The original ritual prescribed by Torah contains the declaration: "Our hands did not shed this blood, neither did our eyes see it shed." And now, as he performs the ritual, Pilate thinks he will remain guiltless because Jesus' blood will not literally besmear *his* own hands and because *his* eyes will not directly see Jesus' blood being shed. With good reason, then, does he say to the Jewish mob, "See to it yourselves", thus tossing back to them the political and moral hot potato. Can he not see that he is, without any doubt, signing Jesus' death sentence by the very act by which he seeks to extricate himself from all responsibility? How contemptible, this option to safeguard one's public and official image above all other priorities! How fallacious, this maneuver to purchase a short span of soul's ease at the price of perpetual restlessness! How hollow and insubstantial, this inability (or refusal) to take a firm stand and risk detriment to oneself for the sake of justice! At least the vigorous sinner can be forgiven once he confesses his burden of weighty sin, whereas it is obvious that Pilate will never think he has anything to repent of as he floats off weightlessly—but with *thoroughly washed* hands [5]—into galaxies of moral suspension, a mere specter of the man God intended him to become.

א

27:25–26   ἀποκριθεὶς πᾶς ὁ λαὸς εἶπεν·
Τὸ αἷμα αὐτοῦ ἐφ᾽ ἡμᾶς καὶ ἐπὶ τὰ τέκνα ἡμῶν.
τότε ἀπέλυσεν αὐτοῖς τὸν Βαραββᾶν,
τὸν δὲ Ἰησοῦν φραγελλώσας παρέδωκεν ἵνα σταυρωθῇ

All the people answered,
"His blood be on us and on our children!"
Then he released for them Barabbas,
and having scourged Jesus, handed him over to be crucified

A SIGNIFICANT CHANGE in vocabulary now occurs, which greatly enhances the solemnity and fraught quality of the moment. Throughout his narrative and until now, Matthew has referred to the "crowd" or "mob" agitating against Jesus with the word *óchlos*, either in the singular or the plural. It means "throng" or "mass" or "multitude", normally with a pejorative nuance, as in the English word "populace". By definition, an *óchlos* is faceless, undisciplined, and potentially violent, like cattle waiting to stampede at any sudden

---

[5] Pilate's fastidiousness and anxious search for self-justification through public ritual are reminiscent of the following "commandments" for wise living found in W. H. Auden's poem "A Reactionary Tract for the Times", from the collection *Under Which Lyre*: "Thou shalt not be on friendly terms / With guys in advertising firms, / Nor speak with such / As read the Bible for its prose, / Nor, above all, make love to those / Who wash too much."

noise. Matthew has just used this word in v. 24, when he says that Pilate "took water and washed his hands *before the crowd* (ἀπέναντι τοῦ ὄχλου)". But immediately, on reaching the climax of this passage, the evangelist records the crowd's reply to Pilate's question of what he should do with Jesus in these terms: "And all the people answered, 'His blood be on us and on our children!'" To introduce this momentous imprecation, pivotal both to the plot and to the theological significance of the passage, Matthew now no longer uses the word *óchlos* to refer to the Jewish throng but shifts to the very different word *laós*. Now *laós*, from which we get our English words "lay" and "laity", is the term of choice in the Septuagint to refer formally to "the People of God", that is, the nation of Israel, elected and formed personally by God starting at the Exodus from Egypt.

When Matthew now says that "all the people" (πᾶς ὁ λαὸς) replied to Pilate, he is specifically viewing the throng before Pilate no longer now as a faceless mob but, rather, as the symbolic totality of all Israelites, the whole of the people especially chosen by God as his own. In Exodus, we read of God saying to Israel: "Now therefore, if you will obey my voice and keep my covenant, you shall be *my own possession among all peoples* (λαὸς περιούσιος ἀπὸ πάντων τῶν ἐθνῶν, LXX); for all the earth is mine" (Ex 19:5). Even though the whole world and all its myriad peoples already belong to God by rights, nevertheless, Israel is God's favorite, the one people God chose as his very own from among all other nations.

A little later in the same passage, and as a result of this declaration by God that Israel is his uniquely treasured possession, we read that "Moses brought the people (ἐξήγαγεν Μωϋσῆς τὸν λαὸν) out of the camp to meet God; and they took their stand at the foot of the mountain" (Ex 19:17). No other people on earth have ever yet been initiated into such face-to-face intimacy with God. And the following passage from the prophet Hosea may be the most explicit declaration by God of the way he and Israel belong to one another with all the mutuality of husband and wife: "I will say to Not my people, 'You are my people' (ἐρῶ τῷ Οὐ λαῷ μου λαός μου εἶ σύ); and he shall say 'You are my God'" (Hos 2:23). It is, then, against this background of reciprocal trust and mutual belonging between God and Israel that we should read the present passage in Matthew, for Matthew's dramatic choice of the word *laós* clearly establishes such a context.

And so the evangelist records with sad astonishment the loud declaration "His blood be on us and on our children!" as uttered by the lips of the uniquely favored people to whom God has sent his Son Jesus as priceless gift—the very best he has to give them. Matthew's lexical change from *óchlos* to *laós* at this point expresses the will of the people as an active, unified subject and signals a crucial event in the history of salvation and of Israel's relationship with its God. It marks, in fact, the moment of Israel's greatest infidelity and most heinous refusal of love. We are now witnessing, no longer a faceless, riotous mob here clamoring for Jesus' death, but, rather, God's beloved bride, the chosen People of Israel, to whom the Father has sent his only-begotten, beloved Son as Bridegroom-Messiah. The sin that Israel is committing at this moment inverts with symmetrical spite the meaning of the prayer cited above in connection with the washing of hands prescribed in Deuteronomy (21:7-9). Rather than humbly asking God to "set not the guilt of innocent blood in the midst of your people Israel", as the ritual enjoins, God's people are, in fact, ferociously demanding of God that he let Jesus' "blood be on us and on our children!" While Pilate washed his hands symbolically to drive all suspicion of blood-stain far away from his person, the people of Israel, on the contrary, are calling for the blood of God's Righteous Man par excellence to shower down upon their heads for generations to come.

This turn of events only thickens the plot, for "the stone which the builders rejected has become the cornerstone. This is the LORD's doing; it is marvelous in our eyes" (Ps 118[117]:22-23). Man's most heinous deeds can be the compost for God's most beautiful growths. Two interlocking events, in fact, are occurring here simultaneously as a result of Israel's violent rejection of God's Messiah. The first of them is profoundly tragic when viewed in all the stark isolation of its culpability. On this Good Friday morning, Israel forfeits the unheard-of privilege it has enjoyed since the days of the Exodus from Egypt: it ceases, namely, to be God's one and only chosen people, the *laós perioúsios* especially set apart by God as his intimate pride and joy. This unimaginable loss on the part of Israel, however, is not the end of the story but, rather, as we have said, its pivotal point. Many New Testament texts seek to understand Israel's massive infidelity in its assault upon Jesus in terms of its ignorance of God's hidden ways. St. Paul, for instance, writes to the Corinthians: "We impart a secret and hidden wisdom of God, which God decreed before the ages for our glorification. None of the rulers of this age understood this; for *if they had, they would not have crucified the Lord of glory*" (1 Cor 2:7–8).

In other words, God's plan for the redemption of the world through the suffering love of his Son is so profound a conception, and so wildly jarring with the ordinary thoughts and ambitions of men, that, of all the human race, it takes nothing less than the Immaculate Heart of God's own Mother to give that plan her *fiat* in the perfect darkness of faith. No one else rises to the occasion. And so, in his speech to the Jews at the synagogue of Antioch, Paul returns to the same theme that he, as former persecutor of Christians, understands all too well: "Those who live in Jerusalem and their rulers," he explains, "because they did not recognize [the Christ] nor understand the utterances of the prophets which are read every sabbath, fulfilled these by condemning him. Though they could charge him with nothing deserving death, yet they asked Pilate to have him killed" (Acts 13:27–28).

Such statements neither damn nor exonerate the Jews as a people for their collective guilt, incurred by their treatment of *Y^ehoshua' ha-Mashiach*. Rather, they open up the way for the realization of the second of the two interlocking events mentioned above. Yes, Israel's willful and shameful capitulation as uniquely beloved people bears a precious fruit no one could have foreseen, namely, the universal election of all those who make their act of faith in Jesus as Messiah. These will now become the new People of God, that is, the Church of Christ, in which a tiny group of believing Jews will form the nucleus as the necessary leaven for the whole dough. This is why Mary of Nazareth and the Apostolic College, all of them Jews, gathered at Pentecost, will forever represent the birth of the Church as ever-ancient, ever-new Bride of God. Israel has proved fecund indeed, even in its infidelity, yielding a thousandfold and fulfilling all the promises to Abraham.

But the transformation from racial Israel to universal Church does not happen automatically; the shedding of the Blood of the sacrificial Lamb must intervene. Jesus' wholly Jewish blood must be poured out so that its very squandering can then make way for him to be filled with the power of God's Spirit, who raises him from the dead through an outpouring of infinite, inexhaustible Life. Christ dies as "only a Jew" in order to rise as the New Universal Man. His risen human nature, of course, does not lose its rootedness in particular time and place, in a particular mother and family of Nazarenes; but the divine life so permeates it after the Resurrection that all people of all times and places now find within the Mystical Body of Christ the place that belongs to them specifically.

Christ's being humanly a Jew in the end is not a narrowing limitation but, rather, a universal liberation for all peoples: his inalienable Jewish identity is itself rooted in divine election as its deepest cause, and it is this plan of universal election, hidden from the beginning within the Jewish people, that now emerges for all to see. This reality elicits eternal praise in the hymn that the twenty-four elders of the Apocalypse sing to the Lamb: "By your blood you ransomed men for God from every tribe and tongue and people and nation, and have made them a kingdom and priests to our God, and they shall reign on earth" (Rev 5:9-10). Thus, Israel's betrayal, Christ's crucifixion and blood-shedding, and the birth of the universal Church are three simultaneous events that cannot be dissociated from one another because they each play an essential role in the work of redemption. The divine blood shed by sinful betrayal has greater power than the betrayal itself.

The Jewish people's savage demand to Pilate "His blood be on us and on our children!" should at once trigger in our memory the action and words of Jesus during the Last Supper on the previous evening: "And he took a chalice, and when he had given thanks he gave it to them, saying, 'Drink of it, all of you; for this is my blood of the covenant, which is poured out (ἐκχυννόμενον) for many for the forgiveness of sins'" (26:27-28). By anticipating in this way the event of the shedding of his blood demanded by the mob, Jesus transforms in advance the curse of a crime into the blessing of a sacrifice. The culpable intent to destroy him is re-channeled by the power of his Heart's love into a eucharistic self-outpouring, and the horror and ignominy of the Cross, embraced by omnipotent love, are metamorphosed into the glory of an altar of sacrifice at which the very sin that spills the divine blood is forgiven. Those clamoring with rage are transformed into chaste acolytes dutifully holding the cruets for the Consecration. The gruesomely invoked shower of literal blood, marking the victim's horrendous death, is transmuted beforehand at the Last Supper into wine-blood that Jesus himself pours out (ἐκχυννόμενον) into the cup and from there into his disciples' mouths.

Great sin, then and now, embraced and forgiven by powerful love, becomes Eucharist, thanksgiving, new divine Life in human hearts, souls, and bodies. In a real sense, the people clamoring for the outpouring of Jesus' blood are only fulfilling his own prophetic and sacramental anticipation of his death in the mystery of the Last Supper. The attempt by sinners to destroy Jesus only succeeds, by shattering him to smithereens, in scattering the seeds of his flesh and the wine of his blood universally throughout the cosmos and all the choirs of angels. No human hand can thwart the mighty urgency and extravagant fulfillment of God's designs of self-bestowing love.

Therefore, not only does the blood of the loving Lamb drown the betrayal in mercy and forgiveness, but, in that very act, that same blood extends universally to all peoples the grace of election previously enjoyed only by the Jewish betrayers. The very act of attempted destruction, once embraced by the targeted Victim out of obedience to his Father, transforms the intended annihilation into a eucharistic broadcasting of seeds and an irreversible diffusion of Life. Unbeknownst to themselves, the Jewish people, as they clamor for the shedding of Jesus' blood on Good Friday before Pilate, are mysteriously collaborating with God's plan of universal redemption and, indeed, extending their own privilege of election to all nations. Such powerfully transfused blood cannot be restricted in its transformative effects:

> The gifts and the call of God are irrevocable. Just as you [Gentiles] were once disobedient to God but now have received mercy because of [the Jews'] disobedience, so they have now been disobedient in order that by the mercy shown to you they also may receive mercy. For God has consigned all men to disobedience, that he may have mercy upon all. O the depth of the riches and wisdom and knowledge of God! How unsearchable are his judgments and how inscrutable his ways! (Rom 11:29–33)

"THEN HE RELEASED for them Barabbas, and having scourged Jesus, delivered him to be crucified:" The Roman authority gives in to the will of the Jewish people. The lust of blind vengeance prevails over the individual light of conscience. In a mutually beneficial collusion, the Jews and the Romans set the criminal Barabbas free, and Jesus they thrust forward to an ignominious and painful end. There is real truth in this manner of viewing the conclusion of today's events in the prætorium; but this is also a relatively superficial summary. There exists as well another and deeper level of the truth involved.

If we viewed the events from the standpoint of dynamic human existence, we would have to say that such a conclusion to Jesus' trial before Pilate merely confirms all the principals, except Jesus and Pilate's wife, Procula, in their miserable prejudices and self-serving passions and ambitions. What has the bloodthirsty mob/People of Israel ultimately gained but the nauseous surfeit and exhaustion that come from sated lusts? They will go home to sleep off this day's spectacle as they would a drunken orgy, but obviously without any lingering aftertaste of true joy. It is always more curse than blessing to experience the fulfillment of iniquitous and ungodly desires. Further, Pilate himself will that evening have to confront the sad gaze of his visionary wife, Procula, in quiet privacy, when he can no longer hide behind the tumult of the crowd and his pliant soldiery. Her mere presence from now on will be a continual reminder of the cowardly defeat of his conscience, of the sad end of his instinctive search for the light of truth. The specter of mediocre self-interest and pragmatic calculation will pursue him all his waking hours and probably haunt his dreams with piercing intimations of mauled virtues. Following the line of Judas and of the priests and elders, Pilate himself now becomes a chief agent of *parádosis* as he *hands Jesus over* (παρέδωκεν) *to be crucified*. Does Pilate realize that, in flogging Jesus and handing him over to death, he is really betraying and mangling the better part of himself, his very soul? No doubt without intending it directly, Pilate nonetheless becomes part of the conspiracy to extinguish the Light of the World.

Procula will no doubt suffer, particularly as news of that evening's execution reaches her. She will feel great pain at her husband's gross miscarriage of justice and at hearing the details of the excruciating torments that Pilate's lack of nerve have visited upon the righteous man from Nazareth whose innocent face she saw in her dream; but her suffering will be truly *clean*, far cleaner than her husband's hands, because she followed the prompting of her conscience and intervened on the prisoner's behalf. She will suffer, too, from the unavoidable rift this unforgettable event must now hollow out between her and Pilate. But she will remain a soul oriented toward the light, moving forward toward the realm of greater and purer freedom to which all the righteous aspire, and righteous she must herself no doubt be in order to have recognized righteousness in another.

As for Jesus himself, through his silent and unflinching stance before his accusers, he shows himself to be ever faithful and obedient to the will of his Father: namely, that he should work out the world's redemption by not fleeing from his persecutors but by accepting the worst the world to be redeemed can inflict upon him. It is extraordinary to see the rapt attention Jesus commands by his mere presence in this passage of high drama, even though he has spoken only two words (σὺ λέγεις, "you say [so]", v. 11) in sixteen verses (27:11–26). He is now the Word become pure radiant Presence, pure throbbing Heart and Center, in no need of spoken words to make the truth of his Father's love felt and seen in the world.

But there is more. By moving ever forward serenely into a fate of gaping horror, into situations of calamitous pain and humiliation from which there is no escape, Jesus exhibits the unprecedented dynamism and courage of *a person who fulfills himself only by spending himself utterly for the sake of others*. Jesus' only comfort, pleasure, and joy lie in heroic love, in living to the hilt an existence for others that perpetually keeps him from retreating to take refuge in a place of tested and sure repose. Jesus fully embraces his vocation to live as one continually exposed to the needs of the world, which makes him at the same time the most vulnerable of men and the most magnificent and powerful of Kings:

> The willing subject thus appears as the true ruler; he who humbled himself to the utter abasement of emptying himself of his own being is for that very reason the ruler of the world. . . . He who does not cling to himself but is pure relatedness coincides in this with the absolute and thus becomes Lord. . . . As king he is a servant, and as the servant of God he is king.[6]

[6] Ratzinger, *Introduction to Christianity*, 221, 220.

13. A THORN-CROWNED KING

The Soldiers Mock Jesus (27:27–31)

27:27

Τότε οἱ στρατιῶται τοῦ ἡγεμόνος
παραλαβόντες τὸν Ἰησοῦν εἰς τὸ πραιτώριον
συνήγαγον ἐπ' αὐτὸν ὅλην τὴν σπεῖραν

Then the soldiers of the governor
took Jesus into the prætorium,
and they gathered the whole battalion before him

THE ATTITUDES AND ACTIONS of the priests and scribes, of the
people of Israel, and of Pilate himself amply illustrate our human penchant for always blaming someone else when things
go wrong. Somehow we manage, with a good conscience, to see ourselves as wholly untainted by wrongdoing. In certain dire situations
involving human suffering, we all want to be titillated, but only as
innocent bystanders. The religious authorities and, under their manipulation, the Jewish nation attribute all civil unrest and danger to
Jesus, that mystical maverick. The Romans, of course, are seen by
the Jews as perennial aggressors from whom nothing better can be
expected. And, as he washes his hands clean of the responsibility for
Jesus' blood, Governor Pilate, for his part, shifts the onus onto the
persistent mob, when he decrees: "See to it yourselves!"

Of course, the next moment those very same thoroughly scrubbed
hands of Pilate *hand Jesus over* (παρέδωκεν) to scourging and crucifixion! In the end, only Jesus himself, guilty solely of speaking the truth
and doing good, breaks this tiresome pattern of everyone "passing
the buck" by taking on himself the hideous guilt of all through his
obedient silence and his serene refusal to defend himself in any way.
Yet, does it truly take a cannon ball to kill a hummingbird?

That is precisely the impression we get when we read that "then the soldiers of the governor took Jesus into the prætorium, and they gathered the whole battalion before him." The *whole* battalion? In order to secure a single unarmed and famously nonviolent prisoner? The whole scene reeks of overkill, a phenomenon that is no doubt a compensatory, subconscious mechanism to obliterate from the face of the earth all evidence of manifest collective criminality. The Greek word here translated "battalion" is σπεῖρα, whose Latin equivalent is *cohors*. The military "cohort" was a unit of soldiers in the Roman army that normally consisted of some six hundred armed men! By his use of this technical military term, Matthew here means to emphasize the laughable contrast of this confrontation between the amassed military power of the Romans and the bruised, defenseless Jesus as he now stands alone surrounded by the brute, sneering soldiery. Now is the appointed hour when the heathen, taking over from the Jews, will not be cheated of their turn at humiliating the One sent to them also as Savior. The opening of Psalm 2 spontaneously comes to mind as the divine commentary on this scene: "Why do the nations rage and the peoples plot in vain? The kings of the earth set themselves, and the rulers take counsel together, against the Lord and against his Anointed" (Ps 2:1–2, ESV).

The conspiracy against Jesus, then, is universal as befits his true status as Lord of all. *All* must rage against him, both Jews and pagans, because they all sense the cosmic sway of his scepter and rebel against it. And each player in the drama acts out his deepest motivations true to character, according to his nature. Thus, while the soldiers obey the commands of their rulers with the brutal glee of programmed robots, Jesus obeys with all the powerful assent of his love his Father's commandment to give his life for the world. In itself, "obedience" is not a virtue. Some obedience is holy and life-giving, and some is criminal and accursed by God.

The text says that the soldiers now "took Jesus into the *prætorium*". This ambiguous use of the Latin word must refer specifically to some vast courtyard belonging to the Roman military garrison in Jerusalem. The broader meaning of *prætorium* is the governor's palace as such, where the events in connection with this trial have been unfolding since v. 11. This particular palace, which Pilate and his family use as their residence at special times like the Passover, was built by Herod the Great for himself and is reported to have been magnificent. It therefore forms a fitting location for royal events, and this fact now adds dramatic irony to the scene with Jesus being played out. Such a splendid palace, scene of the ritual humiliation now being enacted there by the soldiery, may be seen as symbolizing a solemn entryway into the final events of the Passion. It represents the immediate prelude to the *Via Crucis* that will bring Jesus step by step to Golgotha and to the Cross—the Altar and Throne from which he will reign as Savior King: *Regnavit a ligno Deus.* [1]

The present passage offers a unique interlude in the Passion narrative because it consists wholly of symbolic actions and contains no dialogue at all. The only words uttered during the events it portrays is the jeering acclamation by the soldiers, "Hail, King of the Jews!" And yet the passage is dense with meaning because it is playing out simultaneously at two levels that are in conflict with one another. These levels are determined by two diametrically opposed points of view, God's and man's. The raw human intention motivating the symbolic events is simply to humiliate the prisoner. Such an orgy of contempt, enacting the public humiliation of a condemned man, fulfills both a political and a managerial purpose. Pilate's action of turning Jesus over to his soldiers for them "to have a little fun with him" is a political recognition of the status and respectability of the Jewish authorities whose side Pilate has taken by implication if not explicitly. At the same time, the occasion offers the soldiery some welcome entertainment and the opportunity to release pent-up frustrations and hostilities, which will now fall with impunity on the head of the worthless culprit from Nazareth, already as good as dead.

True, this diabolically fun-filled and politically fraught public humiliation of Jesus was probably nothing but exactly that in the eyes of most witnesses that day. Nevertheless, Matthew is using the cruel scene of naked human malice to portray, for the eyes of faith, a vastly different dimension of meaning contained within the very same physical events. The happenings that Pilate's handwashing and judgment have just set in motion are clearly meant by the evangelist to be read as a very odd and particular sort of royal ceremonial that will culminate, despite the venomous intentions of its perpetrators, in the enthronement and crowning of the one true King from which all other kingship derives its name.

This enthronement of Jesus in the prætorium and on the Cross

---

[1] "God has reigned from a tree", from the Lenten hymn *Vexilla Regis* by Venantius Fortunatus (530–609).

today is the eternal and universal fulfillment of the proclamation God makes in Psalm 2 referring historically to David, Jesus' ancestor: "I have set my king on Zion [Jerusalem], my holy mountain", and the Son then responds to the Father by declaring: "I will tell of the decree of the LORD: He said to me, 'You are my son, today I have begotten you'" (Ps 2:6–7). Indeed, in the theology of the Fourth Gospel, Jesus' crucifixion and death coincide with the glorification of the Son of God on earth. *Jesus' obedient exposure of himself to today's orgy of humiliation is his glorification and enthronement as King*, because such a consummation of his life is the fulfillment of the will of the Father: "The hour has come for the Son of man to be glorified. Truly, truly, I say to you, unless a grain of wheat falls into the earth and dies, it remains alone; but if it dies, it bears much fruit. . . . I glorified you on earth, having accomplished the work which you gave me to do" (Jn 12:23–24; 17:4).

Though at this moment, human eyes can see only the fearsome Roman troops in their hundreds amassed against Jesus, nonetheless, we know that he who can never cease being the King of Glory is here and now also surrounded by myriads upon myriads of angels and heavenly powers. These sublime and resplendent spirits are presently serving their downtrodden Lord by their pure incandescent compassion for his humiliation as well as by their praise and thanksgiving to the Father for the work of redemption thus being accomplished. Did not Jesus say to Peter at Gethsemane just hours before: "Do you think that I cannot appeal to my Father, and he will at once send me more than twelve legions of angels?" (26:53). Now, while a cohort contains some six hundred troops, it numbers but a tenth of *one* legion. Twelve legions of angels would then consist of no less than seventy-two thousand dazzling heavenly beings! Such numerical symbolism speaks for itself, including the hint that for every wavering apostle Jesus has a whole legion of angels at his disposal. Such symbolism underscores the contrast between brute, earthly force and weak, human faith, on the one hand, and the spiritual might of angels and of the King they serve, on the other. And Jesus' angelic troops are not invisible and silent out of weakness or cowardice but only as their mode of cooperating with their King in accomplishing, in God's way, his victory over the powers of darkness.

It is crucial here to stress very emphatically the fact that the ceremony of Jesus' elaborate abasement by the soldiers in Pilate's prætorium is not the only factual reality involved, one that pious Christians, if they so wish, can *then* choose to interpret very imaginatively by transposing it to the realm of spiritual kingship. The evangelist, clearly, has not *first* fashioned a text describing degrading physical events that later, as an afterthought, *can perhaps* be interpreted "spiritually" by pious believers. Rather, by its attention to exhaustive detail and its continual use of irony, Matthew's text is so constructed that the soldiers' acclamation "Hail, King of the Jews!", meant by them intentionally as mockery, must at the same time be understood at a higher yet equally literal level as referring to the interior, transcendental meaning of the event taking place. The scene derives its magnificent pathos precisely from the ambiguity throbbing at its center, whereby Jesus is truly being enthroned as King of the Jews and of the universe yet *under the form of willing self-abasement out of love.*

The worst intentions of Jesus' harassers are powerless to change this fact or to conceal the power of God to reveal his might and glory through Jesus' obedient silence and the vulnerability of his flesh. In the case of these soldiers, too, we could say that "they know not what they do" (Lk 23:34). When love is the operating principle in the heart of a victim, fatally terminal humiliation becomes fecund glorification and invincible power:

> What "almightiness" and "lordship of all" mean only becomes clear from a Christian point of view in the crib and the Cross. It is only here, where the God who is recognized as Lord of all has voluntarily chosen the final degree of powerlessness by delivering himself up to his weakest creature, that the Christian concept of the almightiness of God can be truly formulated. At this point simultaneously a new concept of power and a new concept of lordship and dominion are born. The highest power is demonstrated as the calm willingness completely to renounce all power; and we are shown that it is powerful, not through farce, but only through the freedom of love, which, even when it is rejected, is stronger than the exultant powers of earthly violence.[2]

[2] Joseph Cardinal Ratzinger, *Introduction to Christianity*, trans. J. R. Foster, 2nd ed. (San Francisco: Ignatius Press, 2004), 149–50.

27:28–29

ἐκδύσαντες αὐτὸν
χλαμύδα κοκκίνην περιέθηκαν αὐτῷ
καὶ πλέξαντες στέφανον ἐξ ἀκανθῶν
ἐπέθηκαν ἐπὶ τῆς κεφαλῆς αὐτοῦ καὶ κάλαμον ἐν τῇ δεξιᾷ αὐτοῦ
καὶ γονυπετήσαντες ἔμπροσθεν αὐτοῦ ἐνέπαιξαν αὐτῷ λέγοντες·
Χαῖρε, βασιλεῦ τῶν Ἰουδαίων!

they stripped him
and put a scarlet robe upon him
and plaiting a crown of thorns
they put [it] on his head, and [put] a reed in his right hand
and kneeling before him they mocked him saying,
"Hail, King of the Jews!"

JESUS' PERFECT PASSIVITY during these shameful proceedings stuns us. While the soldiers' feverish activity around and upon Jesus is described with multiple rapid-fire verbs, Jesus himself is not the subject of any verb at all but, rather, the direct receptor-object of all the soldiers' actions. The soldiers take Jesus into their courtyard, gather the battalion against him, strip him, clothe him again, crown him with thorns, scepter him, kneel to him, mock him, spit upon him, hit him on his thorn-crowned head, strip him again, clothe him again, and at length lead him away to crucifixion: a total of twelve transitive verbs in the brief space of five action-packed verses, involving acts that directly impact their seemingly inert object both physically and morally and that violently impose the will of many others upon the porous and universally compliant volition of the prisoner. Indeed, he appears to have no will of his own at all.

During this episode, Jesus behaves, to all appearances, very much like an impassive rag doll, wholly at the whim of the children torturing it. Stylistically, vv. 27–31 form one very long run-on sentence, interconnected eight times by the conjunction *and*, which returns ruthlessly like hammer-blows to add injury upon injury. The overall effect is that of a breathless reportage that very quickly sketches a scene brimming with swift movement, vulgar jocularity, and manic fantasy, all at the service of the pleasures afforded by officially sanctioned cruelty and lewd contempt. There is an orgiastic thrill, almost sexual in nature, released by the license to wallow collectively in acts of unbounded graphic hatred for a helpless victim. Matthew's panting polysyndeton allows us to hear the loud guffaws and jeering catcalls of the soldiers egging each other on as they perform their backstage ritual of mock-enthronement.

And yet, despite this riotous atmosphere defining the scene's aspect of cruel and deliberate humiliation, there is also present in the details of the text another starkly contrasting aspect. We detect a solemn rhythm of literary expression and a thoroughness in the execution of the ceremony that jointly hint at the serious theological substance of the event in the eyes of the narrator-evangelist. This latter aspect aims at nothing less than portraying the exaltation and glorification of Jesus as true King. The fact of Jesus' kingship, not only over the Jews but over mankind and the cosmos itself, is, for the narrator, so dynamic and incontestable a truth that it bursts through mankind's greatest efforts to suppress and deny it. Matthew sets out to dramatize precisely this conflict.

Knowing this to be the evangelist's intention, we are invited to read his narrative with an eye for the positive background import of the negative foreground details of Jesus' ritual humiliation.[3] Every gesture and object is thus symbolically charged. The gathering of the whole battalion before Jesus is intended as an aggressive show of frightening power against the fragile captive; at the same time, however, we read it as a gathering of troops coming to pledge fealty to their king. The stripping of the poor man's clothes and the donning of the scarlet robe are meant to show Jesus' "true" origin as contemptible plebeian who only in jest can pretend to be royal; instead, the denudation and re-clothing reveal his underlying glory, always present as his truest form though hidden under layers of rags. The overflowing richness of Jesus' divine poverty would, indeed, be wholly obscured by any trappings of worldly glory. As for the crown of thorns: scholars tell us that in the Hellenistic world, kings typically

---

[3] For the fundamental interplay in biblical narrative between "foreground" and "background", *Vordergründigkeit* and *Hintergründigkeit*, see the first chapter ("Odysseus' Scar") of Erich Auerbach's seminal work *Mimesis: The Representation of Reality in Western Literature* (Princeton, N.J.: Princeton University Press, 1953).

wore what was called a "radiant crown" or diadem consisting of a round base with golden spikes projecting upward. Here, long thorns ironically replace the expected golden beams. Instead of shining outward with proud vainglory, the thorn-spikes pierce the head of the prisoner inwardly when struck with the reed. This detail, elaborately described by Matthew, is a truly memorable symbol for the specific manner in which Jesus is King: rather than dazzling the people with the ruddy splendor of a triumphant athlete's face, Jesus' soft flesh admits into his head and whole being the collective pain inflicted by all people's vices in their revolt against God and his Anointed. By absorbing universal iniquity through his flesh into the furnace of his love, Jesus intends to exhaust and destroy the sinfulness of mankind. And let us not overlook the implied fact that at some point the soldiers' blood must have mingled with Jesus' since one cannot pleat a crown of long thorns without injury to one's own hands.

Finally, to make the "sacrament" of enthronement valid, the inventory of requisite royal paraphernalia is completed when an ordinary reed, stand-in for a precious scepter, is duly placed in Jesus' *right hand*, symbolizing the king's power as he dispenses judgment. Matthew has overlooked no symbolic detail in this paradoxical public act of glorification-through-humiliation. Because the Son of God has set out to redeem the world by self-emptying suffering, according to his Father's express design and decree, therefore even the smallest attempt by corrupt mortals to thwart the divine purpose *must necessarily contribute to the fulfillment of Jesus' obedient will*. God's love will not be thwarted. Jesus shows divine omnipotence through readily embraced humiliation. He will do whatever it takes to reconcile sinners to his Father. The Son of God has come to earth as the servant and lover of sinners. Consequently, this miserable, back-room, mock coronation and enthronement are the only ritual of royal glorification and recognition Christ Jesus is ever going to get on earth, and at the hands of the very sinners he has come to save. This is, after all, the famous Rabbi whose central teaching to his disciples was: "Whoever would be first among you must be your slave; even as the Son of man came not to be served but to serve, and to give his life as a ransom for many" (20:27–28). And so the soldiers now treat the King of Glory as the most worthless of slaves. How could Jesus complain when he is only acting out his own teaching? He proves he is the King of Love by his very submissiveness to their brutal manhandling and rejection.

For their part, the soldiers prove his identity as King by their inability to let go of the question already formulated by their boss Pilate during the trial: "The governor asked him, 'Are you the King of the Jews?' Jesus said to him, 'You have said so'" (27:11). In the same way that a curse carries most weight when it is made by invoking something unquestionably sacred, so too here: the soldiers' enacting in a mocking mode the ritual of Jesus' enthronement as King reveals the inevitability of the very thing they are attempting to deny. It reveals as well the fact that they are acting, despite themselves, as agents of a powerful providence whom they can serve only as rebels, but whom they *must* serve, nevertheless. Already the first verses of Matthew's Gospel declare Jesus Christ to be the son of *David the king* (cf. 1:1, 6). Then at Jesus' birth, the Magi come from the East asking everyone in Israel the burning question: "Where is he who has been born *king of the Jews?*" (2:2). On Palm Sunday morning, Jesus gives two of his disciples instructions to go find an ass and a colt for him to ride on, and the evangelist comments that this transaction "took place to fulfil what was spoken by the prophet [Zechariah], saying, 'Tell the daughter of Zion, Behold, *your king is coming to you, humble, and mounted on a donkey*, and on a colt, the foal of a donkey'" (21:4–5; Zech 9:9). Later that same morning, the crowds acclaim Jesus with the royal title: "Hosanna to *the Son of David!* Blessed is he who comes in the name of the Lord!" (21:9).

We remember as well with what expansive majesty Jesus himself sets the scene for the Final Judgment: "When the Son of man comes in his glory, and all the angels with him, then he will sit *on his glorious throne*. . . . Then *the King will say* to those at his right hand, 'Come, O blessed of my Father'" (25:31, 34). Finally, on the afternoon of this first Good Friday at Golgotha, the soldiers will conclude the ritual they have initiated that morning by putting "over his head . . . the charge against him, which read, '*This is Jesus the King of the Jews*'" (27:37). And with exquisite irony, it is "the chief priests, with the scribes and elders" who proclaim the royal Messianic title of Jesus for the last time in the Gospel as they "mocked him, saying, 'He saved others; he cannot save himself. *He is the King of Israel*; let him come down now from the cross, and we will believe in him'" (27:41–42). How profoundly and confoundingly prophetic, the fact that it is the priests of Israel who declare Jesus unequivocally to be their own king in a statement that they intend to be ironical but that, despite themselves, escapes their mouths in the indicative mood that can only affirm an objective fact: ΒΑΣΙΛΕΥΣ ΙΣΡΑΗΛ ΕΣΤΙΝ, they declare, that is: HE IS THE KING OF ISRAEL. This is not the first time that a prophetic word from God is uttered against the speaker's will and understanding. The essence of prophecy is that it manifests a truth that men could not have discovered on their own but that God alone can communicate. In this sense, the prophetic word must always burn its way through the prophet's natural resistance.

The soldiers' *mock homage to the true King* by means of cloak, crown, and scepter therefore results in a most effective proclamation of Jesus' hidden identity and in his glorification in his Father's eyes. Glorification through humiliation: what have always been polar opposites in the history of the world and of human logic now, through the love of God outpoured, become a *coincidence of opposites*, and this reversal, wrought in Jesus' Heart, will henceforth change our whole manner of perceiving the true nature of success and failure, weakness and strength, life and death. Once the soldiers kneel to the cloaked and crowned Jesus and shout out the acclamation of HAIL, KING OF THE JEWS!, that very local cry—screeched out in mockery in a remote courtyard in Palestine on a Friday morning in the springtime around the year A.D. 33—will resound forevermore among the stars as the most sublime of angelic hymns.

Clearly the proclamation of Jesus as eternal King of the Jews and of all mankind is a central structural theme of the Gospel of Matthew, resounding as it does from one end of the book to the other. The attempt by the religious authorities and others to deny this truth, together with the doubts of Pilate and the mockery of his soldiery concerning Jesus' divine kingship, paradoxically have the joint effect of keeping that theme only the more strikingly visible before our eyes. Only in the Book of Revelation will the veil of humiliation be torn back as Jesus' royal identity is proclaimed triumphantly without any shadow of irony or denial: "[Ten kings] will make war on the Lamb, and the Lamb will conquer them, for he is Lord of lords and King of kings, and those with him are called and chosen and faithful" (Rev 17:14). Jesus' twin inseparable titles as both "the Lamb who was slain" (Rev 5:12) and the conquering "King of kings" together summarize the whole mystery of his ultimate triumph through freely embraced humiliation and death.

"And they spat upon him, and took the reed and struck him on the head. And when they had mocked him, they stripped him of the robe, and put his own clothes on him, and led him away to crucify him" (27:30–31). Immediately after the apostles' experience of Jesus' splendor at his Transfiguration, "when they lifted up their eyes, they saw no one but Jesus only" (17:8). In a similar manner here, after Jesus' moment of royal notoriety on the stage of his enthronement by the soldiery, *the Lord is now stripped even of his mock glory* and he returns to being "Jesus only". This is the ultimate in humiliation, which coincides with the ultimate in magnificence: we are granted the immense grace of encountering nothing but *the unembellished Jesus*, who thus reaches his peak of intensity as "the image of the invisible God" (Col 1:15). This dramatic scene of extreme humiliation manifests the infinite abyss of God's love because it shows us Christ preferring to embrace human suffering over any other possibility and to make it his own so as to relieve the pain of others and help them transform it into joy.

Henceforth, no one will ever again have to suffer alone, and this fracturing of the sufferer's adamantine solitude by the advent of Jesus *within my sorrow* is by definition the beginning of joy. Jesus' moment of greatest humiliation and defeat is also his most divine moment because "God *is* as he *shows* himself; God does not show himself in a way in which he is not," as Ratzinger insists, "and the Christian experience of God rests on this affirmation."[4] There now remains nothing in Jesus to strip back, to purify, or to remove so that "the God in him" can appear all the more clearly! In his spat-upon Face and pierced Brow we behold the trampled core of our own humanity, so dear to the Heart of God that God has made it his own dwelling place. If we do not recognize Jesus *here*, in this form of utter humiliation, we will not recognize him anywhere. God prefers the depths to the heights because that is where he finds us, his dearly beloved. "We see Jesus, who for a little while was made lower than the angels, crowned with glory and honor because of the suffering of death, so that by the grace of God he might taste death for every one" (Heb 2:9).

The proclamation of Jesus' kingship in this ritual we have just witnessed, far from altering the fate of the prisoner, has in fact only confirmed it the more definitively. At the very end of the trial, we heard

---

[4] Ratzinger, *Introduction to Christianity*, 165.

Pilate's decision: "Then he released for them Barabbas, and having scourged Jesus, delivered him *to be crucified*" (27:26). And now we read: "When they had mocked him, they . . . led him away *to crucify him.*" Both passages end with that forbidding word *crucify*. From the beginning of his life, all of Jesus' attitudes, words, deeds, gestures, and silences have paved the way to crucifixion. Jesus' whole life has been a Way of the Cross, and the first sign of it was Herod's persecution of the Infant Jesus and the Holy Family's flight into Egypt (2:13-23). The more gloriously the goodness and humility of God are revealed in Jesus, the more surely is crucifixion ratified as his inexorable destiny. The prætorium has today been the scene where the ancient prophecy of Isaiah concerning the Lord's mysterious Suffering Servant has been historically fulfilled in Jesus, who through his eloquent silence is saying:

> I gave my back to those who struck me, and my cheeks to those who pulled out the beard; I hid not my face from shame and spitting. For the Lord GOD helps me; therefore I have not been confounded; therefore I have set my face like a flint, and I know that I shall not be put to shame; he who vindicates me is near. Who will contend with me? Let us stand up together. Who is my adversary? Let him come near to me. (Is 50:6-8)

14. "THIS JESUS WHOM YOU CRUCIFIED"

Jesus Is Nailed to the Cross (27:32–44)

27:32
Ἐξερχόμενοι δὲ εὗρον
ἄνθρωπον Κυρηναῖον ὀνόματι Σίμωνα·
τοῦτον ἠγγάρευσαν ἵνα ἄρῃ τὸν σταυρὸν αὐτοῦ

*As they went out, they found
a man of Cyrene, Simon by name;
this man they compelled to carry [Jesus'] cross*

AS WE FOLLOW MATTHEW's narrative of the Passion, we often hear the pronoun *they* used to refer to those performing actions directly affecting Jesus. However, the exact antecedent of the pronoun, making clear who precisely is performing those actions, is normally uncertain. In the present case, we have to backtrack a bit to remind ourselves that the *they* going out with Jesus from the prætorium and compelling Simon of Cyrene to carry Jesus' Cross very likely refers to Pilate's soldiery, the very ones who have just performed the mock ceremony of enthronement; but this identity is not crystal-clear. Is such uncertainty a clumsy oversight on Matthew's part, or is it rather a deliberate ambiguity, a part of a spiritual-literary strategy? I lean toward the latter possibility.

We have amply seen that the Gospel often focuses on the interior drama of specific players in the Passion, for instance Caiaphas, Peter, Judas, Pilate, Pilate's wife . . . Nevertheless, a constant underlying element of the Passion narrative is the *collective guilt of all mankind* in the humiliation and execution of the Son of God. Almost always, whenever we encounter an ambiguous *they* in the story, we are invited to fill in the blank, so to speak, and read, instead, "all mankind", or "all of us sinners", or, indeed, "myself". In the present passage, we encounter a new individual, Simon of Cyrene, on whom the collective *we* driving Jesus to crucifixion unloads the heavy burden of Jesus' Cross, which we in our present role as Jesus' accusers refuse to carry. Continually, the Gospel holds up the mirror of recognition to our eyes, flashing back and forth between Jesus' accusers and his defenders, to compel us to seek in that mirror our own truest countenance. The ambiguous use of the pronoun *they* will continue throughout this episode of the crucifixion, and it is clear that Matthew deliberately leaves the reference open-ended, since he could not expect his readers to have "the Roman soldiers" as the sole, specific antecedent over such a long haul. Matthew sees the whole sea of mankind as deeply involved in the proceedings that are shoving the incarnate God toward his death. But as for ourselves: when we read *they* referring to persons who inflict some suffering on Jesus, who exactly is it that first comes to mind?

Verse 31, concluding our previous section, ended with the word *crucify*, and v. 32, beginning this new passage, at once takes up this leitmotif by referring to the *cross of Jesus*. Explicit reference to the cross will recur no fewer than *six* times in these thirteen verses, with the words *crucify* or *cross* hammering the reality of the event into our memory as surely as the material hammers drove the nails into Jesus' flesh.

The passage begins with the word ἐξερχόμενοι ("going out"). This word not only marks the soldiery's change of physical location (they are leading Jesus out of the prætorium), but it especially designates the banishment of the prisoner—and of the curse he represents—away from the sanctity of God's holy city, Jerusalem. Jewish laws are largely about the separation of clean from unclean, at both the material and the spiritual levels, and the condemned prisoner Jesus of Nazareth definitely ranks as unclean. He has been publicly declared a blasphemer by the Sanhedrin, the highest religious authority, and as such he is an unclean, corrupting presence, seen as polluting the vital spiritual space between Israel and God. His execution, furthermore, with its associations of criminality, guilt, sin, and death, can only take place outside the city walls. Jesus is considered a ritual pollution as long as he remains in the midst of the holy nation of Israel and, specifically, within the walls of the Holy City wherein there rises the Temple of God's Presence.

Like Jesus' humiliation through his mock enthronement by the troops, so too his expulsion from Jerusalem carries a hidden nucleus of glory at the center of his condemnation as a criminal and blasphemer. This fact is most evident in the Gospel of Luke. In his passage on the Transfiguration, we read that Moses and Elijah appeared alongside Jesus "in glory and spoke of his exodus (τὴν ἔξοδον αὐτοῦ) that he was going to accomplish in Jerusalem" (Lk 9:31, NAB). Although this term ἔξοδος is sometimes rendered generically as "departure" in this passage (RSV, NET), Luke's use of the technical word *exodus* seems deliberate, theologically charged, intending to refer explicitly to the Jews' great liberation from Egyptian slavery after much suffering. The choice of term, therefore, places Jesus' own humiliation and suffering in an entirely new light as the necessary, God-willed baptism by fire that blazed the path to Jesus' Resurrection and glorification.

Once again what men intend to achieve as Jesus' definitive rejection and destruction is not the end but, in fact, only the *middle* movement of the Redeemer's ultimate triumph over sin and death. The machinations of mortals are, at best, intermediary and, thus, temporary, while both the source of the story in the Incarnation and its culmination in the Resurrection remain firmly within God's grasp. The same divine pattern of steadfast power and fidelity that saved Israel from Pharaoh will now rescue Jesus from the ultimate human enslavement to death.

Furthermore, Jesus is not rescued by God as an isolated individual. Along with Jesus, all people are also rescued because Jesus' shedding of blood is the universal atonement for the sins of all, as we read in Hebrews: "Jesus . . . suffered *outside the gate* in order to sanctify the people through his own blood" (13:12). In this sense, Jesus is the true and efficacious "scapegoat" who bears upon his head, along with the crown of thorns, the sins of Israel and all mankind, as prefigured vividly in a ritual first performed by the high priest Aaron:

Aaron shall lay both his hands upon the head of the live goat, and confess over him all the iniquities of the sons of Israel, and all their transgressions, all their sins; and he shall put them upon the head of the goat, and send him away into the wilderness by the hand of a man who is in readiness. The goat shall bear all their iniquities upon him to a solitary land; and he shall let the goat go in the wilderness. (Lev 16:21–22)

467

The Jews have found Jesus guilty of blasphemy because he "made himself", as they see it, the Son of God, and so they must get rid of this pollution by destroying the offending blasphemer outside the city gates. In actuality, however, they have gotten the meaning of the material story the wrong way around. Jesus' forced march under the bullying of the soldiery, this violent exodus that expels him to Golgotha from the sacred precinct of Jerusalem, is in fact the unsurpassable fulfillment of the merely symbolic meaning of Aaron's ritual. If Jesus has *become one with every sin of mankind*, including blasphemy, it is not because he has committed such sins but only because his Father has loaded on his person the iniquities of all people of all times and places. Jesus' Jewish accusers and Roman executioners are merely playing the role of the ritual "men in readiness" leading the scapegoat into the wilderness to leave him there to die in utter solitude. Along with Jesus, and by virtue of the death of Jesus, the sins of all—which have now become one thing with him—will be extinguished and be no more. The Spanish proverb bears repeating: *Muerto el perro se acabó la rabia*, "Once the dog dies the rabies dies with him."

This aspect of the atonement is both horrible and necessary for us to contemplate because it constitutes an essential aspect of God's plan for our salvation. Only Jesus' voluntary self-identification with our sin gives us the full measure of his love for us, as St. Paul clearly affirms: "For our sake [God] *made him to be sin* who knew no sin, so that in him we might become the righteousness of God" (2 Cor 5:21). What an unfathomable mystery of horror and glory is contained in this unimaginable statement: *God made him to be sin!* No, there is nothing neat and tidy about the final hours of Jesus' mortal life. All of the horrors of his protracted torture, agony, and physical disfigurement are the raw and intractable revelation of the nature of sin and of its effect upon both the human and the divine natures of the Son of God. A perfectly good and loving Being is perfectly offended by sin, which is the wounding denial of that very goodness and love. In Jesus, God made himself vulnerable to man out of an ardent desire for intimate union with man. The true lover will spare himself no lengths of woe for the sake of the beloved.

א

"THIS MAN THEY COMPELLED to carry the cross of Jesus": We know nothing about this man Simon except that he comes from Cyrene, then an important city in Northeastern Africa, on the coast of what is today Libya. The name Simon is typically Jewish, and so it is likely that this man has come from his home city to Jerusalem to celebrate the Passover. However, the more meaningful feature of his permanent identity is that, for some reason, *they* pick him out from a passing crowd of pilgrims and force him to become, for all time, *The One Who Carried the Cross of Jesus* on the Savior's way to Calvary. Perhaps he is brawny in appearance, and perhaps as well he seems to be the obliging sort, qualities that invite the soldiers' choice of him for the repellent task.

By this time of the day, Jesus must be thoroughly exhausted, drained of all energy both physical and mental after spending a sleepless night subject to non-stop interrogation, betrayal, torture, and humiliation. In Matthew's version of the story, Jesus is so weak that he cannot carry his own Cross. The text does not say that Simon *helped* Jesus carry his Cross but that he was forcibly compelled to carry it all by himself. *Angaréuô*, the technical term here used for Simon's recruitment, means "to requisition" or "to press into service" and refers to the right of Roman garrisons occupying Palestine to compel Jews to perform any military or civil service needed. The event is portrayed by Matthew in an extremely matter-of-fact way. We know nothing of Simon's interior response to this coercion, nothing of whether he even knows who this condemned prisoner is whose instrument of death he is now tasked with carrying, beyond all refusal.

How did Simon look on his life that Good Friday morning on rising? What were his plans for the day? Perhaps to go up to the Temple to pray? Or to visit the house of relatives or friends in Jerusalem in order to join them in a seder meal? Assuming he is a pious Jew, we can well imagine the massive disruption that this unwelcome compulsion, enjoined upon him by the Roman authorities, must introduce into his plans to celebrate a quiet and joyful Passover in a familiar setting, in obedience to the Law of Israel. How can he possibly know that, by no conscious choice of his own, he is in fact carrying a burden that by rights belong to the Lord of the Passover himself, the very Lord whose might delivered the Hebrews from Egyptian bondage?

And this burden Simon is carrying signifies the whole world's liberation from slavery to sin and death . . . By a mysterious fluke of history, of human whim, of sheer vicissitude, Simon of Cyrene, in the twinkling of an eye and propelled by a hidden providence, soars over the abyss separating the figurative, merely ritual representation of the Exodus and lands squarely in its unsurpassable fulfillment in the Passion drama of the incarnate Savior.

What sudden glances of dawning recognition must be exchanged between Simon and Jesus at the moment when the Cyrenean, no doubt muttering under his breath, begins to take the cross from the shoulders of the stumbling Nazarean—at the moment when, despite himself, he thus helps Jesus redeem the world? Could Simon come into such intimate, objective contact with the Son of God in the very flesh of Jesus' suffering, to the point that he himself tastes the Savior's atoning pain *in his own flesh*, without the course of Simon's life and outlook undergoing a major conversion? And what can we learn from Simon, against every rebelling instinct of our smugness? How can we learn from him to embrace, with a generous heart, a sudden adversity that targets our indifference while at the same time a wiser, more cordial instinct whispers to the ear of our faith that this disruptive hardship might well conceal the very Cross of Jesus-Messiah, source of universal salvation? Are we prepared to reject such a royal invitation only because it comes formatted in the humble Redeemer's scandalous anonymity?

27:33-34 Καὶ ἐλθόντες εἰς τόπον λεγόμενον Γολγοθᾶ,
ὅ ἐστιν Κρανίου Τόπος λεγόμενος,
ἔδωκαν αὐτῷ πιεῖν οἶνον μετὰ χολῆς μεμιγμένον·
καὶ γευσάμενος οὐκ ἠθέλησεν πιεῖν

And when they came to a place called Golgotha
(which means "the place of a skull"),
they offered him wine to drink, mingled with gall;
but when he tasted it, he did not want to drink it

G OLGOTHA, A NAME THAT HAS become a synonym for a place
of ultimate torture and suffering, is an Aramaic word meaning "the skull place". Matthew himself translates the foreign
term in this verse for the benefit of his Greek readers. The place of
Jesus' crucifixion, the precise geographical spot on earth where the redemption of the world is enacted for all time, deserves memorializing
in two languages as *Golgotha* and *Kraníou Tópos*. Soon the equivalent
Latin word *calvaria* will become its third name. From it we derive the
English word *Calvary*, a term with broad metaphorical connotations.
Because Christ suffered and died there, a very unremarkable hill north
of Jerusalem with a shape thought to resemble a skull is thus exalted
in human memory and cultural tradition as a space where suffering
becomes atonement and so opens the way to new life. And the first
thing that occurs in this place, before the crucifixion, is that Pilate's
soldiers offer their prisoner a drink, a peculiar beverage consisting of
"wine mingled with gall".

It is possible that the soldiers' action is presented by Matthew as a
fulfillment in Jesus' Passion of the words of Psalm 69[68]:21, "They
gave me gall for food, and for my thirst they gave me vinegar to
drink." This view would have us think that the soldiers are unrelenting in their search for new ways to increase Jesus' suffering. When
they see how dehydrated and strung out their prisoner is after dragging himself along the Way of the Cross, instead of offering him
cool water, they add insult to injury by plying him rather with acidic
"wine" laced with bitter gall.

471

However, a very different and, in my opinion, preferable interpretation is possible. The view just given would simply reinforce yet again the bestial cruelty of the soldiers, with little else gained. The other possibility, which disputes the very negative reference to the psalm, adds theological depth to the narrative and a touch of humanity to Jesus' wardens. Both of these features are more in keeping with Matthew's general thrust, which consistently explores the ambiguity and evolution of human behavior rather than prematurely depicting dead-end moral failures. Wine of whatever quality is clearly an alcoholic drink with a dulling effect on the senses, and the "gall" (*cholé*) referred to here most likely was "a bitter substance made from wormwood, [which is] a plant yielding a bitter-tasting dark-green oil that is alcoholic in its effect". [1] In other words, the intention of those dispensing this tart and bitter concoction to Jesus on arrival at Golgotha could well be to *drug* him mercifully in some measure against his sufferings, particularly in view of the harrowing pain about to be inflicted during the crucifixion. Even ruthless Roman soldiers cannot altogether renounce their humanity. Matthew's inclusion of this detail could signify that no one—not even those crucifying Jesus—is a priori excluded from the possibility of conversion and, hence, of salvation, provided a glimmer of compassion remains in his heart.

This impression is further substantiated by Jesus' refusal to drink the potion after barely tasting it. If the drink was in fact an added punishment and humiliation, surely Jesus would have accepted it in the same way that he accepted every other form of violence and contempt during the whole Passion narrative. We can hardly conceive of Jesus turning up his nose at the brew because it is too bitter to his palate! On the other hand, for Jesus to imbibe a mercifully tranquilizing drink would have meant for him to embrace a consolation coming from men, thereby deviating from his total reliance on the presence and support of his heavenly Father.

Jesus' refusal of all earthly comfort in the face of torture may appear strange to us, and the suspicion of masochism may not be far from our post-Freudian mind-set. However, as the Letter to the Hebrews insists, Jesus, "for the joy that was set before him endured the cross, despising the shame" (Heb 12:2). For him, there can be no deviation

---

[1] Friberg's *Analytical Greek Lexicon*.

from the acknowledged will of the Father, and Jesus knows full well that Golgotha, the place where he has now arrived, despite the horrible pain and suffering it brings, represents the dramatic culmination of the whole thrust of his life, hence the symbolic importance of the elevation of both Golgotha Hill and the Cross itself: "And I, when I am lifted up from the earth, will draw all men to myself" (Jn 12:32).

Matthew's narrative has already referred to drinking on two significant occasions during the previous night of Holy Thursday; the present reference to the potion offered by the soldiers on Golgotha on Good Friday is the third instance. We remember that, during the Last Supper, Jesus "took a chalice, and when he had given thanks he gave it to them, saying, 'Drink of it, all of you; for this is my blood of the covenant . . .' ", and at once he added: " 'I tell you I shall not drink again of this fruit of the vine until that day when I drink it new with you in my Father's kingdom' " (26:27–29). Jesus' refusal now to drink of the wine and "gall" mixture, then, is in keeping with this promise to his disciples.

Once he has invited his followers to the communion in his blood in the form of wine, there can be no more earthly feasting with ordinary wine: partaking of Christ's blood is an immediate anticipation of eternal life in the Kingdom. Heart-gladdening nourishment and lasting joy can henceforth derive for the Christian only from sharing in Christ's life-blood. Jesus refrains from drinking what is offered him on Golgotha to proclaim that, even in the face of death, he can only *be gift* of the Father to mankind. As such he can derive consolation, life, and sustenance only from the Father whose love he embodies.

The second reference to drinking occurs in the narrative only a couple of hours later, during Jesus' agonizing prayer in Gethsemane: "And going a little farther he fell on his face and prayed, 'My Father, if it be possible, let this chalice pass from me; nevertheless, not as I will, but as you will' " (26:39). This most difficult of all prayers reveals to us two things about Jesus' interior state at this moment. First, it exposes quite blatantly Jesus' human fragility and fear of suffering, the fact that he naturally shares with the rest of our race a healthy, life-affirming instinct that makes him rear back in the face of pain. This is the very opposite of masochism. At the same time, his anguished request that, if possible, the "chalice" of suffering and death might pass from him undrunk also reveals that he is no self-made hero on a self-defined mission, no seeker after glory by recklessly jumping into the fires of martyrdom. The statement is extremely sober. It lucidly weighs his personal desire *not* to undergo such suffering against his overriding purpose to fulfill at all cost his Father's will. Jesus is ready to surrender his life absolutely, but only in response to the will of the Father that he should do so, only as an act of divine and human obedience that is the very opposite of an ambitious feat of bravado.

The third reference to drinking occurs now on Golgotha and involves Jesus' *refusal* to drink the wine mingled with "gall" held out to him. This refusal confirms the fact that he has already made his definitive choice between human and divine consolation. Consequently, his only food and drink are going to be the will of his Father that he, the beloved Son, should redeem mankind by pouring out all of his blood and exhaling his very last breath of life on the Cross on Golgotha, because "my food is to do the will of him who sent me, and to accomplish his work" (Jn 4:34). The bond of love between Father and Son, and their shared love for their creature man, is so absolute, so unnegotiable, that *Jesus can receive life from his Father only by giving his life to us.*

Indeed, in a certain awe-inspiring sense, we must say that the temporal economy of redemption has introduced a significant and permanent alteration into the stability of eternal trinitarian relationships. *Ever since the moment of the Incarnation, the eternal relationship between Father and Son becomes inconceivable without the incontrovertible presence of that needy creature, man, between them: so extravagantly fruitful and engendering of new life is God's nature as Love.* This is a bold affirmation, and yet it seems to me that no tamer explanation can adequately account for the enormity of the Father's decision that his beloved and only-begotten Son should shed his blood on the Cross for the salvation of mankind.

By an unthinkable paradox capable of displacing mountains of rational theological axioms (cf. 17:20), we may say that, in a real sense, the Father has made the salvation of mankind by the Son's oblation of himself a "condition" for the love between the Father and his beloved Son, the incarnate Word. *The Son cannot love the Father without loving us in the bargain, and the Father cannot love the Son without requiring of him our redemption.* Jesus is nothing but the Father's love for us, now made visible person, embraceable brother, tender spouse. "You[, Father,] have given [your Son] power over all flesh, to give eternal life to all whom you have given him" (Jn 17:2).

א

27:35-36   Σταυρώσαντες δὲ αὐτὸν
διεμερίσαντο τὰ ἱμάτια αὐτοῦ βάλλοντες κλῆρον,
καὶ καθήμενοι ἐτήρουν αὐτὸν ἐκεῖ

And when they had crucified him,
they divided his garments among them by casting lots;
then they sat down and kept watch over him there

G REAT SOBRIETY CHARACTERIZES THIS PASSAGE describing the actual event of Jesus' crucifixion. Accustomed as we are in our time to sickeningly graphic displays of violence in both the written and the visual media, we moderns at this point will likely feel our appetite whetted for certain lurid details and even a touch of gore. Yet the evangelist practices admirable restraint. We must remember that everywhere the Gospel aims at moving hearts to permanent conversion and faith in Jesus Christ as redeeming Messiah and Son of the living God. A mere sentimental rattling of the emotions is a notoriously ineffective means of effecting such lasting transformation of the human heart. And so Matthew records a naked fact: Σταυρώσαντες δὲ αὐτὸν διεμερίσαντο τὰ ἱμάτια αὐτοῦ—"then, having crucified him, they divided his garments". The whole event of the crucifixion is contained in a single participle introducing the main verb "to divide".

In his *Confessions* (III, 2) St. Augustine analyzes for us the moral worth of the emotions felt by those who go to the theater in order to "experience" vicariously the suffering portrayed by tragic actors. He says that such merely æsthetic enjoyment is a counterfeit and, hence, morally dangerous because it can give us the illusion of having gained wisdom through participation in suffering, whereas in actual fact we have only had our superficial emotions titillated. In the end, we are worse off spiritually for having seen the play. Not only do we remain as ignorant as before concerning the real nature of human tragedy, but, in addition, we have grown in arrogance as a result, thinking ourselves wiser than before.

Matthew's sobriety of style, therefore, strives to present events, symbols, and attitudes very factually, as if provoking his reader to dig more deeply into the personal meaning he is going to derive from the text. What is more, without such intense participation by the reader or listener in the deeper meaning of the text, the narrative at this point remains somewhat lusterless, even anti-climactic. Without my active wrestling with its hidden depths, without my subjective appropriation of its explosive content and implications, the Gospel text remains barren, unappealing. Quite simply, it has no cheap entertainment value and strives only for lasting conversion of heart, something impossible without my plunging vigorously into its submerged ocean of dangerous grace.

We should not, then, be surprised if this passage is full of details that at first glance appear to have fallen into the narrative at random, disconnectedly, as if they were loose pieces of a puzzle that it is our task to assemble into a meaningful whole. Many objects, players, and actions we here encounter have the surrealist quality of quasi-incoherent symbols that puzzle and even alienate the reader by their strangeness. Among such enigmas are: Simon of Cyrene himself, the skull-like shape of Crucifixion Hill, the suspect brew, the divided garments and gambling soldiers, the tablet nailed over Jesus' head with its absurd inscription, the histrionic mocking of the passersby, the reviling robbers crucified alongside Jesus . . . What an odd mishmash of elements! Even a master playwright of the Theater of the Absurd, such as Samuel Beckett or Bertolt Brecht, handed such a list, would be hard put to create a coherent plot out of these widely scattered and disconnected components. Yet this is the canonical narrative that Matthew has fashioned, seeking to convert our hearts by the manner in which these strewn symbols allegedly manifest God's love for us in Christ.

A good beginning would be to say that the desolate landscape of Golgotha, covered with this litter of scattered dramatic elements, mirrors the present state of Jesus' human life and mission precisely in the *incoherence* that Jesus' earthly failure offers to human reason and ambition. George Eliot has spoken of Calvary as a place "where Reason mocks at Love".[2] When the Just Man par excellence is condemned to death, when God's goodness is defeated, when faithful disciples abandon their Master, when arrogance and hardheartedness and envy triumph over humility, compassion, and docility to God's Word, then we may say that chaos reigns in the world. And the chief feature of chaos is, precisely, the rule of incoherence, absurdity, randomness, arbitrariness, and brute force. The primordial question, then, is whether a power exists that abides outside this chaos and that rules at a higher level of existence? Or whether such chaos has finally come to reign supremely above all other forces, without the possibility of appeal to any other instance?

We will soon see how, at the moment of Jesus' death, a number of phenomena occur that raise the reign of chaos in the world from this immediate scene on Golgotha to truly cosmic proportions: we will see the "darkness over all the land" from noon until midafternoon and hear the shaking of the earth and the splitting of rocks (27:45, 51). The present happenings on Golgotha, with all their fragmentariness and barely controlled chaos, appear to be a prelude to the unleashing of a chaos of truly cosmic proportions when God expires on the Cross. Fragmentation, dispersal, incoherence, and the alienation and high anxiety they generate: none of it can be "synchronized" and made sense of from within the present moment in the narrative. These external details of the plot are but reflections of the interior collapse occurring in the consciousness and soul of Jesus himself as his human life and energy are being utterly disaggregated by torture and death. Any hope of reintegration and revitalization has to be looked for on the other side of death.

Against all Docetist tendencies in connection with Jesus' crucifixion, whether of the pious ("God couldn't *really* suffer") or the hostile ("the whole thing is an inflated illusion") variety, we must yet again emphatically affirm that the one and only incarnate Son of God—his

---

[2] See *Oxford English Dictionary* (Oxford: Clarendon Press, 1971), under "Calvary", 1878, p. 44.

whole person and not just his body—at a given historical moment underwent a real and mercilessly violent human death with everything this event implies, from the most crushing mental agony to the most literal wrenching apart of his human frame and the extinction of all its functions. This dispersion of narrative elements in Matthew's text is the objective correlative of the dissolution of Jesus' life, which thus takes body in the text.

The stony silence of the incarnate Word on Golgotha is like the withdrawal of a central lynchpin that causes the total falling apart of all the elements of harmony, meaning, continuity, and coherence that formerly held the narrative plot of the Gospel together. When the Logos himself becomes mute out of weakness, pain, and unimaginable sorrow, the creation itself, of which he is the sustaining principle (cf. Col 1:15–17), must totter and faint, and the narrative text is the facsimile of that Logos-sustained creation.

Until this moment on Golgotha, there has always been a logical succession of events, dialogues, causes, and effects both in the Gospel in general and even within the narrative of the Passion. This general coherence makes the task of the interpreter relatively easy since the connecting thread is normally identifiable. Now suddenly we are thrown by the text into a scene ruled by fragmentation and disaggregation, and the human mind must grapple with a disorienting incoherence. This is the effect on the landscape of the world when the incarnate God drinks the cup of human fragility and mortality to the dregs. Only Resurrection by the Father directly breathing the Holy Spirit again into his dead Son can restore to the inspired narrative of Jesus' life a center that holds, and only then can the Gospel text itself rise again along with Jesus. In the meantime, readers who take the text to heart must experience within themselves chaotic disorientation and the dismemberment of sense.

We must sit aghast, cowering in incoherent "darkness and in the shadow of death", in order to partake, albeit infinitesimally, in Jesus' own unfathomable experience of dissolution. We must learn to wait for the moment when "the tender mercy of our God" will bring about the rising of the Sun of justice (Lk 1:78–79). Our decision to abide with Jesus existentially in his death, invaded by vertiginous trembling and desolation, is our only possible claim to share eventually in his Resurrection, for "if we have died with Christ, we believe that we shall also live with him" (Rom 6:8).

However, the suffering Lord's poignant question also resounds in our ears: "Are you able to drink the chalice that I am to drink?" (20:22). We recall with some trepidation the remark of Thomas à Kempis: "There are many that follow Jesus as far as the breaking of bread, few as far as drinking the cup of suffering."[3]

"THEY DIVIDED HIS GARMENTS among them by casting lots": This factual allusion by Matthew to a casual deed by the soldiers at the foot of the Cross is an almost literal quotation from one of the psalms of darkest distress, as the unjustly persecuted one cries out to his God: "They divide my garments among them, and for my clothing they cast lots" (22[21]:18). We have already noted in v. 34 the probable allusion to another psalm ("They gave me gall for food, and for my thirst they gave me vinegar to drink", Ps 69[68]:21). Regardless of the specific meaning we may assign in each case to the presence of such scriptural references, subtly interwoven into the texture of Matthew's text, they obviously have the overall function of serving as major signifiers. They remind us, first, that all the macabre happenings of the Passion and, indeed, its whole downward spiraling toward Jesus' demise are nevertheless contained within God's providential plan of salvation. It is not so much that God "makes" the players in the drama do this or that, as if they were divinely programmed robots bereft of all personal choice and responsibility. Rather, what is suggested by these references is that the wise and efficacious work of God's omnipotence can and does fashion new life and new meaning even from man's most extreme attempts at overturning the sweet sway of love in creation.

Secondly, and following from this, the presence of those quotations from the Word of God, more or less literally cited, attests to the fact that the true and lasting meaning of this particular story and of all

[3] Thomas à Kempis, *The Imitation of Christ*, trans. Ronald Knox and Michael Oakley (New York: Sheed & Ward, 1959), II, 11, 1.

history is prophetic rather than political: ultimate significance is to be sought beneath the garish surface of world events. On the public stage of social transactions, it is human ambition and brutal power that normally carry the day. Therefore, it is not at that level that God's just ones can read the meaning of history or the thrust of the divine will.

Finally this network of recurring biblical allusions, by its quiet insistence, steadily proclaims Jesus to be the Suffering Servant and Messiah, the Redeemer of Israel and all mankind, the only truly Just One of all creation. He was appointed as such by his eternal Father, and in all of his deeds and teachings, he is nothing but obedient to the Father's design that he should redeem the world, not *despite* his suffering and human failure, but precisely *through* them.

At the same time, this scene of Jesus' denudation, and of his clothes being divided among the dice-throwing soldiery, is a prime illustration, on the microcosmic stage of Golgotha, of the overwhelming paradox that are Jesus' Passion and death on the metaphysical stage of being itself: I speak of the unthinkable, scandalous, world-overturning paradox that is the very backbone of Christian revelation. For who is this person, this common criminal Jesus, whom thugs now strip down to expose his bruised skin? Who is this One whose tattered garments are stolen off his back and who thus is made into the lowermost of all beings on the earth, "a worm and no man" (Ps 22[21]:6)? He is the Divine Logos, the eternal Principle of Being "for whom and by whom all things exist" (Heb 2:10), the One who can proclaim with truthful exultation:

> When [God] assigned to the sea its limit, so that the waters might not transgress his command, when he marked out the foundations of the earth, *then I was beside him*, like a master workman; and I was daily his delight, rejoicing before him always, rejoicing in his inhabited world and delighting in the sons of men. (Prov 8:29–31)

He whose garments are now being divided by lots is the very One who divided the sea before the Hebrews, "so that they went through the midst of the sea on dry land" (Neh 9:11), "and made the waters stand like a heap" (Ps 78[77]:13). He is the very One who commanded the leaders of the Hebrews "to divide the inheritance for the sons of Israel in the land of Canaan" (Num 34:29), the One who "scatters his lightning about him, and covers the roots of the sea"

(Job 36:30). This is, in short, the One whom a bright cloud over-shadowed on Tabor, "and a voice from the cloud said, 'This is my one dear Son, in whom I take great delight'" (17:5, NET).

א

WE HAVE ALREADY SEEN HOW in Pilate's courtyard, during a kind of vaudeville show, the soldiery stripped Jesus of his own clothes and dressed him in mock-royal garments even as they beat him and crowned him with thorns. After that bit of cruel fun, they put Jesus' tattered clothes back on him. But now on Golgotha, Jesus is totally stripped down before being crucified, no doubt as a supreme act of humiliation. We remember the curious verse in Genesis that comes right after the creation of Eve from Adam: "And the man and his wife were both naked, and were not ashamed" (Gen 2:25). But then we read the following as our first parents' instinctive reaction immediately after their shared sin: "Then the eyes of both were opened, and they knew that they were naked; and they sewed fig leaves together and made themselves aprons" (Gen 3:7).

In Scripture, nakedness, in the absence of sin, is a sign of a pure conscience and a harmonious relationship to God and to others; but a sinful conscience automatically instills a sense of shame at the sight of human nakedness. The Greeks appear to have been the great exception to this in the ancient world in their unabashed celebration of the beauty of the human body in its naked state, since to them the beautiful body was an epiphany of the beauty of a just soul. The Jews, along with most ancient peoples, saw nakedness as shameful and therefore looked upon "cover[ing] the naked with a garment" as a corporal work of mercy, an action typical of the righteous (Ezek 18:7). The virtue of the act of clothing the naked does not derive primarily from protecting a poor person from the cold but, above all, from delivering him from public shame.

When the drunk Noah lay naked on his bed, his sons "Shem and Japheth took a garment, laid it upon both their shoulders, and walked backward and covered the nakedness of their father; their faces were turned away, and they did not see their father's nakedness" (Gen 9:23). This clumsy "walking backward" with averted gaze shows the degree of humiliation and shame involved in being naked before God or others and in viewing another's nakedness, particularly in the case of a person to whom one owes respect.

Now the Scripture attributes the wearing of "clothing" to God himself. But, since God is utterly free of all shame, in God's case such "clothing" is the opposite of decorous concealment; rather, it is a dazzling *revelation* of his overwhelming inner being. This is expressed by Job in ecstatic language: "Out of the north comes golden splendor; God is clothed with awesome majesty" (Job 37:22). The "clothes" befitting God's nature originate in the magnificence of the cosmos he created, because only what God himself has made can best reveal God: "O Lord my God, you are very great! You are clothed with honor and majesty, who cover yourself with light as with a garment" (Ps 104[103]:1–2). No one covers God; God covers himself; and only the most sublime, spiritual, and everlasting element of his visible creation—light itself—is a worthy garment for the divine Being.

And so we return to the battered Jesus on the Cross on Golgotha, who has said: "I am the light of the world; he who follows me will not walk in darkness, but will have the light of life" (Jn 8:12). He has also said: "As long as I am in the world, I am the light of the world" (Jn 9:5). It was Roman practice to strip of his clothes a criminal about to be executed in order to heighten the punishment by public shaming at the basic level of the body. Stripping a person naked in public is the ultimate shattering of any residual bond he might still have with the accepted society of the "decent". Such nakedness isolates the accused frightfully in total ostracism. At the same time, the clothes of the criminal do not go to waste; they go to his executioners, who throw dice for them, partly out of greed but mostly to while away their boredom.

To the eyes of faith, which in the crucified Jesus see the incarnate Word, the Son of God in suffering human flesh, the whole traditional process of ritual shaming involved in an execution is utterly thwarted and reversed. Far from shaming Jesus, the stripping-off of his clothes becomes the occasion for the epiphany of his true glory, for the shining out of the resplendent glory of his love—to the eyes of faith, I say, because the dull eyes of cynicism and mockery that afternoon can only see a mangled, bloody, and gasping body dangling from nails on a plank. And, seeing it, no doubt some of the soldiers, long accustomed to the gore of executions, yawn at the tedium of it all.

Yet the famous painting *Cristo crucificado* of Diego Velázquez (1632) succeeds admirably in transforming such a body into a radiant source of pure light against a background of thickest night, with a soft mysterious glow emanating from the bent head. The greatest art can actually represent the vision of faith to the senses. In that painting, the crucified Christ ever so chastely imposes himself on our gaze as the only reality in the world worth our attention, as if Christ, even in death, were a more vital and enthralling presence than that of all the so-called living. Velázquez' masterpiece is a true æsthetic realization of the deep christological doctrine proclaimed by Jesus himself to his disciples long before his Passion: "Men [do not] light a lamp and put it under a bushel, but on a stand, and it gives light to all in the house" (5:15).

The *stand* here is the Cross, erected on Golgotha Hill. The *lamp* is Jesus himself, the Light of the World, out of the midst of whose suffering the full Passion of God's love for us radiates throughout the universe. The *house* is my heart, the world, the Church, the whole created cosmos, which thus becomes filled with the glory of the splendor of God's transfiguring love. And the *men* who, against their conscious purpose, actually do *light Jesus the Lamp* by nailing him to the wood and raising him on high are the Romans, the Jews, and all of us graceshirking creatures.

Our ironical attempt to do away with Jesus by our perverse rejection of God's love is transmuted by the alchemy of God's omnipotent wisdom into the obedient instrument of universal Redemption. Especially on Calvary, the divine principle of *parádosis* is at work: our handing-over of Jesus to death is reversed by the Father and becomes the Father's own handing-over to us of Jesus, the Light of Life. The stripping away of Jesus' tattered and bloodied human garments, far from exposing his shame, rather reveals all the more powerfully the glory, majesty, and goodness of the mystery his love contains. Jesus' denudation by the rough hands of brutal soldiers anticipates the event Matthew will shortly describe at the moment of Jesus' death: "And behold, the curtain of the temple was torn in two, from top to bottom" (27:51).

We recall that Jesus spoke of his body as the true temple of the Godhead (cf. Jn 2:20–21). The tearing-off of his clothes, then, corresponds precisely to the uncanny event of the rending of the veil of the temple. This stripping manifested all the power and beauty of the divine Presence dwelling within Jesus the Temple so that all, seeing it, can now come and adore God with awe and joy. The evangelist John goes even farther when he records how a soldier with his lance tore away even the second and ultimate veil, that of Jesus' flesh (cf. Heb 10:20), and thus opened the interior of his body, the Holy of Holies of his Heart, making its treasures flow forth upon the earth (cf. Jn 19:34). Let us not forget that there were, in fact, *two* curtains in the temple at Jerusalem (cf. 1 Mac 4:51): one of them (termed the *masákh*) was located at the entrance of the temple and separated the Holy Place from the outer court; the other (called the *parókheth*) divided the Holy of Holies from the Holy Place. In keeping with the imagery of Jesus' body as the true Temple of God, Jesus' garments are the *masákh* that the soldiers remove, giving access to the flesh of his breast, which is the *parókheth* pierced by the lance.

Such removal of tattered fabric and opening of fragile flesh preludes the mystery of *clothing with glory* contemplated by St. Paul: "When the perishable puts on the imperishable, and the mortal puts on immortality, then shall come to pass the saying that is written: 'Death is swallowed up in victory'" (1 Cor 15:54). Jesus allowed himself to be stripped ignominiously of his clothes on Golgotha only in order that we might, along with him, be clothed by the Father with immortal garments of light. God's Presence came down into his Temple on earth not only to be contained and adored there but above all in order to flow out upon the whole universe and fill it with divine life, as we read in Ezekiel:

> Behold, water was issuing from below the threshold of the temple toward the east . . . ; and the water was flowing down from below the [south end] of the threshold of the temple, south of the altar. . . . And it was a river that I could not pass through. . . . And wherever the river goes every living creature which swarms will live, and there will be very many fish; for this water goes there, that the waters of the sea may become fresh; so everything will live where the river goes. (Ezek 47:1, 5, 9)

This magnificent river of vivifying grace inundating the universe remains, in Ezekiel, but an Edenic promise,[4] a thrilling prophetic vision; but on Golgotha it becomes a physiological stream of life gushing quite literally from Jesus' all-too-vulnerable chest: "But one of the soldiers pierced his side with a spear, and at once there came out blood and water" (Jn 19:34). This event, seen by the Church Fathers as the wellspring of the sacraments of baptism and the Eucharist, may be said to be the completion of the Creator Father's work in the second chapter of Genesis, when "the LORD God planted a garden in Eden, in the east; and there he put the man whom he had formed. And out of the ground the LORD God made to grow every tree that is pleasant to the sight and good for food, the tree of life also in the midst of the garden" (Gen 2:8–9). In the new and definitive Eden that is Golgotha, all sins are washed away and Adam returns to his original state of innocence and friendship with God by virtue of the divine energy pouring out of the Man hanging like vital fruit from the Tree of Life. The Lord God, the cosmic Gardener, ploughs open the fertile earth of his Son's breast in order to make flow from his Heart a redeeming flood that drowns the world in grace.

When the event of Jesus' death tears the veil of the Temple from top to bottom, the Holy of Holies reveals for all to behold the mystery it has always contained: *a Crucified God.* Concerning this mystery, Joseph Ratzinger affirms in rather unusual language: "Christ is the infinite self-expenditure of God." And he goes on:

> Excess is God's trademark in his creation; as the Fathers put it, "God does not reckon his gifts by the measure." At the same time excess is also the real foundation and form of salvation history, which in the last analysis is nothing other than the truly breathtaking fact that God, in an incredible outpouring of himself, expends not only a universe but his own self in order to lead man, a speck of dust, to salvation. So excess or superfluity—let us repeat—is the real definition or mark of the history of salvation. The purely calculating

---

[4] "A river flowed out of Eden to water the garden, and there it divided and became four rivers" (Gen 2:10). The best iconographic representation of this river flowing from the foot of the Cross, the ultimate Tree of Life, and flooding the world with its vitality may be seen in the extraordinary twelfth-century mosaic filling the apse of the basilica of San Clemente in Rome.

mind will always find it absurd that for man God himself should be expended. Only the lover can understand the folly of a love to which prodigality is a law and excess alone is sufficient.[5]

א

27:37
Καὶ ἐπέθηκαν ἐπάνω τῆς κεφαλῆς αὐτοῦ
τὴν αἰτίαν αὐτοῦ γεγραμμένην·
Οὗτός ἐστιν Ἰησοῦς ὁ βασιλεὺς τῶν Ἰουδαίων

*And over his head they put
the charge against him, which read,
"This is Jesus the King of the Jews"*

TO BROADCAST A CLEAR WARNING to all potential evildoers, it was the Roman practice to inscribe the crime of a man condemned to death on a piece of wood and affix it to the cross just above his head. This question of Jesus' messianic kingship was already brought up by Pilate, to whose question concerning his royal identity Jesus gave a positive reply (27:11). What is highly ironical about the inscription proclaiming Jesus' crime is its tone of unequivocal affirmation: THIS IS JESUS THE KING OF THE JEWS, it reads. Note that the formula conveying the legal charge does not state that he *claims* to be such a king but positively affirms that he *is*.

Both rhetorically and theologically, moreover, the declaration is of a kind with Jesus' solemn statement at the Last Supper when distributing the bread and wine among his disciples: "THIS IS MY BODY. . . . THIS IS MY BLOOD OF THE COVENANT, WHICH IS POURED OUT FOR MANY

[5] Joseph Cardinal Ratzinger, *Introduction to Christianity*, trans. J. R. Foster, 2nd ed. (San Francisco: Ignatius Press, 2004), 261–62.

FOR THE FORGIVENESS OF SINS" (26:26, 28). In both cases, at the cenacle and on Golgotha, the most outlandish affirmations are made
that defy the credence of ordinary common sense. How can bread
and wine be this man's body and blood, as he claims?! And how can
this crucified wreck of a human being, all mangled and bloodied and
universally rejected, be the King of the Jews?! Bread and wine do
not *look* like flesh and blood, and this wretch certainly does not *look*
like any kind of king. The same structure of hidden, transcendental
identity underpins both proclamations and points to their mysterious
efficacy in God's plan of salvation.

At the eucharistic banquet, the Messiah's Body and Blood are borne
in concealment under the humble forms of bread and wine. At Golgotha, the one and only King of the Jews, the Messiah of Israel and
the Redeemer of the world, languishes in concealment under layers
of humiliation and abuse. The eucharistic sacrament of the divine
Logos' self-outpouring anticipates, prefigures, and permanently contains his actual historical death on the Cross. And the finality of each
is the very same: to atone for mankind's multitude of sins and, thus,
by virtue of this atonement ("at-one-ment"), to reunite man with
God and infuse into his moribund frame the very same eternal Life
circulating among the Divine Persons.

This Messiah, the King of the Jews, triumphs by dying out of love,
triumphs by allowing the forces of evil to defeat him physically, socially, and temporally in order that he might emerge from death with
a transfigured body and thus glorify, along with himself, all men,
granting them joyful communion in his own eternal life. Both at the
cenacle and on Golgotha we are witnessing A MYSTERY OF HIDDEN
GLORY—Glory trampled, Glory rejected, Glory beaten and defeated,
Glory pierced and murdered, but in the end *Glory triumphant*, whose
rays will beam out all the more resplendently precisely for having been
so smothered and extinguished for a season. This is the unfathomable
mystery we contemplate during the last two weeks of Lent, as we
pray: "Through the saving Passion of your Son the whole world has
received a heart to confess the infinite power of your majesty, since
by the wondrous power of the Cross your judgment on the world is
now revealed and the authority of Christ crucified."[6]

---

[6] Preface I of the Passion of the Lord.

This whole mystery is summed up with perfect simplicity by the inscription above Jesus' head, which implies that Jesus was not crucified because he *claimed* to be the King of the Jews but, rather, because he *was* the King of the Jews. Only true kingship and authentic goodness will be hated so consistently, so scornfully, and so thoroughly by the world as they were in the case of Jesus. In the end, only Jesus' boundless Divinity, concealed in a human form, can adequately account for the extraordinary lengths to which the powers that be went to banish him from the face of the earth. In a sense, we could say that only God merits such overwhelming contempt, because only God can bear it and not only survive but transform the hatred directed at him into a fruitful energy of love.

It is highly probable that the Roman lackey who inscribed the accusation against Jesus on that tablet was simply fulfilling one more tedious bureaucratic function that day, without giving much thought to the actual content and implications of the charge. We can practically hear one soldier quipping to another: "Will you look at that! The writ says, 'This is Jesus the King of the Jews . . . !' Oops! Perhaps the scribe made a mistake and forgot the correct wording, which should have been: 'This is Jesus *who claims to be* the King of the Jews.' Oh well, those are too many words anyway, which don't quite fit on that little board. Nail it up as it is. What difference does it make anyway? A dead Jew is just a dead Jew, after all. What matters is we got our job done like we were told. Let's get this whole bloody mess over, roll the dice for his rags and go home without fussing over details. . . ."

Yet the inscription, in fact, does terribly matter because it stands as a proclamation trumpeting essential truths of salvation to all ages in seven short Greek words: THIS IS JESUS THE KING OF THE JEWS. As with the bread and the wine at the Last Supper, so too here with Jesus' identity as King. Why was there any need at the Last Supper, and why is there any need now at Golgotha, for such disconcerting proclamations of identity to be made in the first place? *This is my body, This is my blood, This is Jesus the King.* . . . The reason is quite simple: the abyss is so vertiginous between the appearances of bread and wine and the Body and Blood of Jesus, on the one hand, and also between the traditional image of a majestic Messiah-King and this wretched body hanging from the Cross, that an authoritative voice has to bear witness to the mysterious reality around which the whole meaning of the Passion pivots and attest to the absurd-seeming mystery that natural reason recoils from accepting. "*This bread and wine* that you eat and drink, and *this bleeding body* that you see and shrink from, *this and no other*—believe it or not!—is the reality of the Son of God on earth."

This ordinary offering of bread and wine is, in fact, the Body and Blood of an incarnate Divine Person, who has assumed such a form in order to give away the substance of his being so that all may commune in his life. And this ravaged corpse hanging naked for all to see and mock—contradicting all common sense—really does belong to that very same Divine Person, God's only Son and Messiah, the King of Israel and all the universe. The reality underlying the human appearances has to be explicitly affirmed, against all probability of being believed, precisely because the truths involved are inherently the very least likely to occur to the prejudiced human mind, benighted as it is by greed and idolatry. But the wise work of redemption, wrought in this exact way by God himself, has to be proclaimed in all its naked truth with the same impartial serenity with which a man might scatter bread upon the waters. Will any seagulls come to feed in the nick of time?

The Spirit scans the horizon of the world yearning to see whether some spark of hungry faith is still roaming the earth, seeking some heart that miraculously treasures the satisfaction of love above the strictures of logic and gain. Once these extraordinary affirmations concerning the manner of Christ's presence and action in the world have been solemnly uttered by the Word of God for all to hear, then the question of their truthfulness has at the very least arisen for all time, and people will have to face them squarely and decide for themselves concerning their veracity. Before the actual events of the Incarnation, of the institution of the Eucharist, and of Jesus' Passion and death, not the merest flutter of a human thought could arise conceiving of the eternal God as truly present among us in deliberately embraced humiliation, defeat, and death. But this exact proposition, proffered to man by the Fire of Mercy, will from now on divide mankind into Christians and non-Christians.

The human mind instinctively proceeds on the basis of dichotomies. Black is the opposite of white, high is the opposite of low, exaltation is the opposite of humiliation, and, above all, *human is necessarily the opposite of divine.* Thus, when Christian faith affirms that the one eternal God appeared on earth in the form of a man, our automatic analytical response is that, therefore, God must somehow be *masquerading* as a human being, that the divine Spirit must somehow be "contained" and "hiding" within the mere *appearance* of a human body. Our intellect does not know what to make of the proposition that Jesus' body is not a mere temporary instrument that is used and then discarded but that *it truly and inalienably belongs to the Divine Person of the Logos*, without any possibility of "dis-incarnation", that is, of the Word reverting to his "more authentic" native condition as pure Spirit.

This is why faith is not content to affirm only that, in the Passion and on the Cross, Jesus of Nazareth did truly suffer. Beyond this, faith must and does affirm that *in Jesus, God, the Author of the universe, himself suffered.* Faith allows no room here for a comfortable dichotomy that would thankfully set the mind at ease. Faith does not declare that, while the man Jesus suffered, the divine Logos went on imperturbably enjoying eternal glory in a parallel dimension. With radical boldness, faith must affirm both that *God suffered on the Cross* and that, simultaneously, *Jesus reigned from the Cross as King of the Universe*, the latter BECAUSE OF and not despite the former.

Adoro te devote, latens Deitas, sings St. Thomas Aquinas before the Lord's real Eucharistic Presence. Our adoration of a "hidden" Godhead does not so much imply God's willingness to condescend to us—that is, that God loved us so much that there was no limit to his capacity to debase himself for our sake, to come down from his exalted divine heights to encounter us at our own very low level of existence. Such a thought is not false, but it is not the essence of the divine condescension. It would be closer to the truth to say that the depth of God's nature is most magnificently and faithfully revealed to us in Christ-God's humiliation and death because this event and this modality correspond exactly to what God is: *the eternal Lord and Creator of Life who lives only in order to pour himself out in one unceasing act of love.*

God never pretends at any level. On Golgotha, God is not pretending to lower himself to our level and suffer a little in order to cheer us up in our misery by dipping casually into the wretchedness of our condition. No! We must rather affirm that God truly *is* how he shows himself, that God does not show himself in a way he is not. If this were not so, how could we honestly speak of "unsurpassable revelation" in connection with Christ? Again and again, we must reawaken our wonted human perception to the fact that, against all our acquired standards of judgment, the failure and annihilation of Christ on the Cross on Golgotha is the supreme and most perfect form of the revelation of God's innermost nature.

The inscription on the Cross, THIS IS JESUS THE KING OF THE JEWS, affirms that the crucified Jesus now bleeding to death in our presence is the authentic Messiah sent by God to redeem Israel and all mankind. It proclaims that this heavenly Messiah sent by God from his majestic glory in eternity and this pathetic criminal Jesus with the horribly torn body are, in fact, one and the same person. And the inscription also declares that the redemption of the world could apparently occur most efficaciously precisely through the humiliation of the King of the universe, by his willingly subjecting his Glory to trampling under the feet of violent men. The incisive formula of accusation on the tablet (οὗτός ἐστιν Ἰησοῦς), proclaiming the identity between the crucified criminal and the Redeemer-Messiah of Israel, is echoed insistently (as τοῦτον τὸν Ἰησοῦν) three times by Peter in his address to the crowd on the first Pentecost:

> *This Jesus*, delivered up according to the definite plan and fore-knowledge of God, you crucified and killed by the hands of lawless men. But God raised him up, having loosed the pangs of death, because it was not possible for him to be held by it. . . . *This Jesus* God raised up, and of that we all are witnesses . . . Let all the house of Israel therefore know assuredly that God has made him both Lord and Christ, *this Jesus* whom you crucified. (Acts 2:23–24, 32, 36)

God does not masquerade as something he is not. On the contrary, being truth itself, God is therefore utter simplicity and, thus, always seeks the most truthful and efficacious means to communicate with his creatures so as to establish in them, too, the reign of his truth. God does not pretend to be what he is not or hide his true nature or masquerade under disguises alien to his being. In the Incarnation and at the Cross, the eternal God assumes the visible human form that most perfectly corresponds to his nature as Love and to his purpose to redeem the human race. *Jesus' Passion and death are not only the most extreme possible humiliation of God; they are by the same token the most exhaustive possible revelation of the depths of God's nature.*

Blind, rather, and self-deceptive is our own biased human perception, so obsessed with worldly success, power, and the cult of the ephemeral. It cannot understand why the omnipotent Creator of the universe would deliberately come among us as a social failure, why he would freely choose to take up permanently as his very own, from the woman Mary, the vulnerable flesh of the poorest and most generous of men. Our corrupt human vision is unable to see in Jesus' mangled countenance the most sublime embodiment of created beauty. This is why the Crucified Christ is at the same time the gateway to Paradise and God's judgment on our multiple idolatries.

"The truth, properly speaking, is unbelievable", Hans Urs von Balthasar loved to repeat often. And so what unloving human reason finds most unbelievable—that is, that the crucified Jesus of Nazareth is the all-conquering God in action—*this* is precisely what faith must believe and embrace as burning truth. Faith can behold this Fire of Mercy manifested in the three interlocking Christ-mysteries wrought by God's burgeoning imagination, as the deeds of his glorious right arm that are surely the apex of all his prodigious work as both Creator and Redeemer. These three mysteries are: the EUCHARIST, the CROSS, and the RESURRECTION—each of them a feat invented and enacted explicitly *pro nobis*, "for our sake". But will we accept God's invitation to enter Paradise strictly on this paradoxical path, which requires that we become as poor and as naked and vulnerable as he himself became on Golgotha? We glory, after all, in being his adopted sons and daughters, and our heavenly Father does not will for us anything he did not first will for his eternally beloved Son.

27:38   Τότε σταυροῦνται σὺν αὐτῷ δύο λῃσταί,
         εἷς ἐκ δεξιῶν καὶ εἷς ἐξ εὐωνύμων

*Then two robbers were crucified with him,
one on the right and one on the left*

W E ARE NOT TO THINK OF these two criminals, crucified along
         with Jesus to his right and his left, as petty "thieves". The
         ordinary Greek word for "thief" is *kléptês* (from which En-
glish derives "kleptomaniac"), and it refers quite simply to a person
who casually takes items here and there that do not rightfully belong
to him. It carries no nuance of violence or ulterior intent. But the
word used by Matthew here is not *kléptês* but *lêstés*, deriving from a
word for "booty" or "spoil" and translated correctly as "robber" or
"bandit". A *lêstés*, in other words, is a "plunderer", and the word thus
connotes aggression and violence.

In the context of the Roman occupation of Palestine, *lêstés* can refer
in particular to a "revolutionary" or "insurrectionist", that is, someone who not only plunders Roman goods like weapons or foodstuffs
but also violates the legitimate authority of Roman rule by inciting
the Jewish people to violence and revolt. This nuance is important
here because it calls our attention to one probable way in which the
Roman occupiers of Palestine view Jesus himself. Hence, the charge
could be a way for his executioners, proudly belonging to a nation
famous for the rule of law, to justify his execution. At the very least,
we can say that the Roman occupying forces, having arrived at a liv-
able compromise with the local Jewish authorities, distrust anyone,
Jesus included, who seems to be creating trouble within the ranks of
the Jews and can thus be accused of zealotry inciting to rebellion.
As a matter of fact, while the rawness of such a charge against Jesus
might at first shock us in its literal understanding, nevertheless, we
know that throughout the Gospel Jesus' words, attitudes, and actions
are often construed as potentially seditious by anyone, pagan or Jew,
clinging to the establishment for dear life and identity.

We have only to remember the panicky reaction of vainglorious
Herod at the beginning of the Gospel, when he heard about the

mere presence of the baby Jesus within the confines of his petty kingdom (2:1–8). A direct line may be traced from this first instance of a fearful rejection of Jesus by an established authority, through the endless conflicts he has to endure from the scribes and the Pharisees, and finally to his condemnation by the Sanhedrin and the approval of this death sentence by Pilate, whose soldiers actually carry out the deed of execution. No true insurrectionist would have been treated any differently from the way that Jesus was from his very birth. Indeed, the benevolent Word of God, always seeking to establish a reign of justice, peace, and love on earth, is always necessarily in violent conflict with the words, thoughts, and deeds of tightfisted man. The divine Word, whether prophetic or incarnate, must therefore be perceived by men as the ultimate threat to their cherished autonomy. Thus, although Jesus is not a threat to the powers that be in the literal, political sense they imagine, he does, nevertheless, pose a challenge to them at a much deeper level: he "threatens" them, along with all men, *by challenging them to conversion of heart.*

As described by Matthew, this scene of the three crucified criminals on Golgotha strangely evokes an audience in a royal throne room. The tablet above Jesus' thorn-crowned head has already identified him as King of the Jews. Then the carefully staged position of the two robbers at his right and left hands recalls the placement of court favorites during public ceremonies near the monarch. For instance, in the episode with the sons of Zebedee, their mother said to Jesus: "Command that these two sons of mine may sit, one at your right hand and one at your left, in your kingdom" (20:21). We find a similar disposition in the parable of the Last Judgment, but in this case the left hand indicates an adverse judgment: "When the Son of man comes in his glory, . . . then he will sit on his glorious throne, . . . and he will place the sheep at his right hand, but the goats at the left" (25:31, 33). And in the First Book of Kings, the prophet Micaiah has this vision of the heavenly court: "I saw the LORD sitting on his throne, and all the host of heaven standing beside him on his right hand and on his left" (1 Kings 22:19).

As is the case generally in the Gospel, and particularly in the narrative of the Passion, the symbolism used here is deliberately ambiguous and invites two radically opposed readings, depending on the reader's point of view. Let us call them "the worldly reading" and "the sympathetic reading". The more hard-nosed worldly reading would ask something along these lines: "Should we read the scene as both the senses and our common sense obviously dictate and simply shrug our shoulders at one more instance of a cruel Roman execution? The event might perhaps be regrettable for the families of the criminals involved, but otherwise this grim ordeal can probably serve effectively as a deterrent to bolster law and order in our society." But the sympathetic reading ponders more deeply: "There is too much gentleness and goodness on the face of that alleged felon in the middle. And the sign over his head does oddly declare him king: there *is*, after all, a crown on his head, albeit of thorns piercing his brow. I notice, too, a glaring contrast between his meekness and the attitude of the other two, who are seething with hatred and rage. And then there are other strange signs seeping all around, a sudden darkness at noon and growing tremors under my feet. I perceive a mystery I cannot understand but that entices me further. . . ."

This case-in-point of the scene on Golgotha is but an extension of the ambiguity that the mystery of the Incarnation itself continually provokes in anyone caring to ponder it. It is the mystery posed by the question of Jesus' deepest identity, beyond and beneath all the empirical evidence of the senses as conditioned by millennia of social convention and arbitrary definitions of good and evil, success and failure, beauty and ugliness, virtue and vice. The question "Who is this Jesus?" comes up in one way or another on almost every page of the Gospel: "When he entered Jerusalem, all the city was stirred, saying, 'Who is this?'" (21:10). "Where did this man get this wisdom and these mighty works? Is not this the carpenter's son? Is not his mother called Mary?" (13:54–55). "And they were filled with awe, and said to one another, 'Who then is this, that even wind and sea obey him?'" (Mk 4:41). In a moment the question of Jesus' true identity will return in this very place in mocking, ironical form: "If you are the Son of God, come down from the cross!" (27:40).

Society and the religious and political establishment have stood in judgment of Jesus and condemned him. But the judged and condemned Jesus himself now stands in judgment of us from his throne on the Cross. It is as if he were asking us: "Will you indeed see in my Cross nothing but an instrument of ignominy and death? Or can you not in some way intuit how contact with my flesh and the love overflowing from my Heart has transformed this wood into the Tree of Life and the Throne of my Glory? For God has no other Glory

495

to share but that which is identical with his everlasting Love and his capacity and desire to save you from every sort of death."

Christian art has often peopled the space above and around the Cross of Jesus with flitting angels in lamentation, some of them comforting him, some of them collecting in chalices the blood flowing from his wounds in order to proffer such a treasure to all who thirst for fullness of life.[7] And the bleak air of Golgotha is precisely where those bright angels belong in a strict theological sense, since they constitute the court of heaven, and loyal courtiers must always be in dutiful attendance wherever their king happens to be present, serving him with the work at hand.

THE ANGELS IN LOVING ATTENDANCE to their crucified King on Golgotha are present to him in a very different manner from that of either the soldiers or, above all, the two criminals crucified alongside Jesus. By giving Jesus these two companions, the authorities clearly intended to create a smokescreen of criminality that would encourage people to impute guilt to Jesus by association. "Of course he is guilty", people would hopefully say. "Just look at the company he keeps. Where there is smoke . . ." The incarnate Word himself, however, silently acquiesced not only to the trial, the condemnation, and the crucifixion, but very specifically to being crucified alongside these ruffians.

Now, Jesus' own reason for such acquiescence was, naturally, to proclaim unambiguously to the world the nature of his mission and of his deepest motivation: solidarity unto death with sinners. "God shows his love for us in that while we were yet sinners Christ died for us" (Rom 5:8). "For our sake [God] made [Christ] to be sin who knew no sin, so that in him we might become the righteousness of God" (2 Cor 5:21). How could such a vital truth, spring-

---

[7] I am thinking in particular of Giotto's *Crucifixion* (1305/1306) in the Arena Chapel at Padua.

ing from God's will into creative action on Golgotha, become more blatantly, more existentially proclaimed in the world other than by this painstakingly precise *identification of Jesus with human criminality* by his undergoing execution in the middle of two legitimately condemned men?

Again, Jesus is not *pretending* to be as guilty as they are; rather, Jesus has ontologically taken their guilt and the guilt of all mankind upon himself so as to remove it from their persons and turn terminal sinners into resplendent saints. We are not speaking here of moral exemplarity or even of condescending compassion. We are speaking of a fundamental change in the very being of persons, from death to life, wrought by the power of Jesus' transforming love, which is infinitely greater than the power of geological heat and pressure, persisting over millennia, to turn vile coal into coruscant diamonds.

This v. 38 uses an expression, in the literal sense, that in St. Paul becomes fundamental in the mystical sense: "two robbers were crucified with him (σταυροῦνται σὺν αὐτῷ)." Since Matthew intends the meaning in the physical sense, the preposition *with* still appears separated from the verb *to crucify* to stress the literal connotation. However, in St. Paul a Christian neologism unique to New Testament Greek emerges to refer to the believer's interior sharing in the Passion of Christ, in particular, to the believer's real sacramental and mystical partaking in Jesus' *crucifixion*. In Paul, the preposition becomes a prefix inseparable from the verb, as inseparable as the Christian's interior life is from Christ's death and Resurrection. Thus, referring to his own rebirth in Christ through faith in the mystery of the Cross, St. Paul pens the extraordinary statement that is emblematic for all Christian mysticism: "I have been crucified with Christ (Χριστῷ συνεσταύρωμαι—*Christô synestáurômai*); it is no longer I who live, but Christ who lives in me; and the life I now live in the flesh I live by faith in the Son of God, who loved me and gave himself for me" (Gal 2:20).

Lest anyone think, however, that by such a highly intimate witness Paul is referring only to his own person and subjective experience, we hear him repeat the expression objectively, always describing a fundamental event of the Paschal Mystery and, as such, of the life of *all* Christians, as for instance in this passage from Romans: "We know that our former man was crucified (συνεσταυρώθη—*synestaurôthê*) with [Christ] so that the sinful body might be destroyed, and we might no longer be enslaved to sin" (Rom 6:6). Quite simply, the believer must deepen his faith until he instinctively *counts Christ's death as his own*, for without such self-identification with his Savior's destiny, neither could he count Christ's Resurrection as his own. And the result of sharing in Christ's crucifixion mystically is this: "[Christ] was crucified in weakness, but lives by the power of God. For we are weak in him, but . . . we shall live with him (συζήσομεν αὐτῷ) by the power of God" (2 Cor 13:4). For "if we have died with Christ, we believe that we shall also live with him" (Rom 6:8). Crucifixion with Christ (Χριστῷ συνεσταύρωμαι—*Christô synestáurômai*) is the necessary prelude to fullness of eternal life with Christ (συζήσομεν αὐτῷ—*syzêsomen autô*). Whatever is his, at any stage of his Mystery, becomes ours, too, by mutual indwelling: "Abide in me, and I in you" (Jn 15:4).

Not even God, however, with all of his infinite might and desire to save, can coerce a human heart to embrace redemption. Iniquity does not annul and paralyze the freedom of the human will; if this were so, sin by that very token would cease to exist. The whole tragedy of man rests on the Satanic contradiction that is a free will turning against the Giver of free will. Proud rebellion and the possibility of conversion—of returning freely to friendship with our Creator—always coexist side by side in the human soul in this world. The wide range of attitudes and reactions to Jesus throughout the Gospel, and especially during the Passion, has shown this truth amply. This is why the physical presence of Jesus, crucified between these two robbers and thus in intimate solidarity with them and their fate, does not automatically guarantee their salvation. Salvation must be humbly embraced.

This exigency is illustrated beautifully in Luke's alternate version of the story, in which one of the robbers repents in the most famous conversion story of all time:

> One of the criminals who were hanged railed at him, saying, "Are you not the Christ? Save yourself and us!" But the other rebuked him, saying, "Do you not fear God, since you are under the same sentence of condemnation? And we indeed justly; for we are receiving the due reward of our deeds; but this man has done nothing wrong." And he said, "Jesus, remember me when you come [into your kingdom]." (Lk 23:39–42)

The violent, self-interested, and contemptuous attitude of the first criminal is eloquently juxtaposed by Luke to the nobility of soul, humility, and contrition of the other. Moreover, we could easily overlook the fact that the conversion of the one we call the "Good Thief" here appears triggered by a magnificent and liberating act of faith: faith that can discern between criminality and sanctity, and faith that recognizes Jesus' identity as Messiah-King under all his bruises and humbly begs for admittance to his company.

As always, differing versions of the same story among the four Gospels with regard to the details only serve to reinforce the solid meaning of the central narrative, which is the same in all the Gospels. The choice by a given evangelist of a slightly different tradition probably indicates an underlying theological nuance he wishes to underscore. For example, here Luke wants to stress the freedom of the human will until the moment of death, the fact that Jesus' sacrifice of himself on the Cross puts each of us in the position of having to make a choice for or against him and the continual availability of the grace flowing from the Heart of Jesus with its power to convert a willing human heart.

But Matthew portrays *both* robbers as obdurate in their iniquity and full of hatred to the bitter end. We may say that Matthew, by contrast to Luke on this point, wants to stress the fact that mere physical proximity to Jesus and an exclusively material sharing in his grim fate cannot on their own work salvation. There is no virtue in suffering per se, Matthew would say, but only in suffering that is embraced with love and humbly shared with the One who redeemed us by assuming all of our sorrow upon himself. These two versions of the robber subplot and its meaning do not contradict but rather complement each other.

After referring to the derision of the passersby and the mockery of the scribes and elders, Matthew concludes the passage with the sad affirmation: "And the robbers who were *crucified with him* (οἱ συσταυρωθέντες σὺν αὐτῷ—*hoi systaurôthéntes syn autô*) also reviled him in the same way" (v. 44). We have just reviewed some passages in which St. Paul coins the neologism *to-be-crucified-with-Christ* in order to proclaim a central experience of Christian faith. We are therefore now shocked to see the very same term used to refer to the condition of two persons who, while physically crucified alongside

Jesus, can in fact have no intimate relationship with the Savior. Far from wanting to be incorporated into the transforming power of Christ's love, the two robbers in Matthew have nothing but scorn and contempt for Jesus as they see their own sufferings and fate mirrored in those of the Son of God. As part of the chorus of scorners, they revile Jesus. They go to their death kicking and screaming, thereby affirming the very societal and worldly values that destroyed them in the first place. They are dying physically alongside the visibly crushed Jesus, but they are not dying interiorly with the Christ whose love exudes a radiant power to transform.

The obduracy of these two criminals in the face of their own death evokes the important question of the choices of attitude we have to make in the face of our own sufferings. When a lifetime of efforts, prompted indifferently by either good or bad zeal, in the end yields but a miserable crop of merits, at that crucial moment of decision—what will it be? Will I choose to die as a rebel in foolish autonomy, loudly proclaiming my vanity by contemptuous raging and last-gasp self-affirmation? Or will I bow my neck humbly to the pierced King dying with me and gratefully accept as my own the gift of the new life flowing from him?

27:39–40   Οἱ δὲ παραπορευόμενοι ἐβλασφήμουν αὐτὸν
κινοῦντες τὰς κεφαλὰς αὐτῶν καὶ λέγοντες
Ὁ καταλύων τὸν ναὸν καὶ ἐν τρισὶν ἡμέραις οἰκοδομῶν,
σῶσον σεαυτόν, εἰ υἱὸς εἶ τοῦ Θεοῦ,
καὶ κατάβηθι ἀπὸ τοῦ σταυροῦ

And those who passed by derided him,
wagging their heads and saying,
"You who would destroy the temple and build it in three days,
save yourself, if you are the Son of God,
and come down from the cross!"

I N THE GREEK, THE WORDS THAT the passersby hurl at Jesus in contempt form a five-verse chant whose jingle-jangle meter and rhymes imitate the derision they intend:

Ho katalŷon ton naón
Kai en trisín hêmérais oikodomón,
Sôson seautón
Ei hyiós eí tou Theoú,
Kai katábêthi apó tou stauroú.

Note that each verse ends with a stressed syllable, the first three with a rhyme in *-ón*, and the last two with a rhyme in *-oú*. As for the content, it constitutes a perfect miniature satire, oozing sarcasm and irony. The ditty first refers to the prophetic moment when Jesus, speaking of his body as the Temple of God, challenged the authorities to destroy it, promising he would restore it in three days: a clear allusion to his Resurrection (cf. 26:61; Jn 2:19). That is the first double irony, because the Jews thought he was speaking of razing their magnificent temple of stones and rebuilding it by himself in three days. They ridicule him with great hilarity because, having promised an immense and impossible feat that not even a Hercules could accomplish, Jesus cannot even bring his own puny body down from this miserable scaffold of wood! The mockers cannot conceive of resurrection even at an individual level, much less of resurrection as a cosmic event promised to all.[8]

The third verse, in the middle of the little "poem", presents an even greater irony because it calls on Jesus to "save himself". Such an injunction, *particularly* if fulfilled by Jesus, would precisely be the proof that he is *not* the Messiah, since "the Son of man came not to be served but to serve" (we might gloss: not to *be saved* and especially not *save himself*, but to *save others*), "and to give his life as a ransom for many" (20:28). This jeering challenge exactly repeats the temptation by Satan that Jesus withstood early in the Gospel: "If you are the Son of God, throw yourself down [from the parapet of the temple]" (4:6).

The mockers are here massively projecting a conception of God that envisions power as the supreme and almost exclusive divine attribute, or at least as the only divine attribute that interests *them*. And, indeed, they conceive of such power as a weapon wielded by a particularly self-serving scoundrel. In this, the crass passersby represent the general human inability even to imagine *inexhaustible self-giving* as being the very wellspring of the Godhead and, therefore, the keenest desire burning within Jesus on the Cross. Only the contemplation of such a divine desire can make any sense of the Incarnation in general and of the crucifixion in particular. Johannine language expresses the mystery with a powerful metaphor: "The thief comes only to steal and kill and destroy; I came that they [that is, my sheep, the dear human race] may have life, and have it abundantly" (Jn 10:10). The benighted jeerers, following a Satanic logic, are in fact demanding that Jesus put on the mind of a thief and renounce his Father's mission to save the world, and to do it *in order to prove his divine sonship!*

The Satanic principle cannot understand, and thus has no patience for, the divine principle that governs every last detail of Jesus' life, namely, that "God so loved the world that he gave his only-begotten Son" (Jn 3:16). The very essence of sin at every level is the endeavor to invert this divine law of self-giving embodied by Christ and substitute for it a law of self-serving autonomy and irresponsible "freedom"

---

[8] This is one of the central themes of the Letter to the Romans: The Savior was "designated Son of God in power according to the Spirit of holiness by his resurrection from the dead, Jesus Christ our Lord" (Rom 1:4). He "was put to death for our trespasses and raised for our justification" (Rom 4:25).

as fashioning a truly "sensible" human life. To this mind-set Jesus responds with the paradox of the Cross: "Whoever would save his life will lose it, and whoever loses his life for my sake will find it" (16:25).

The Satanic mind excels at corrosive irony and sarcasm, but it knows nothing of the liberating paradox of love: "Though he was in the form of God, [Christ Jesus] did not count equality with God a thing to be grasped, but emptied himself, taking the form of a servant. . . . He humbled himself and became obedient unto death, even death on a cross. Therefore God has highly exalted him" (Phil 2:6–9). In the face of that greatest of all paradoxes, St. Paul exclaims: "O the depth of the riches and wisdom and knowledge of God! How unsearchable are his judgments and how inscrutable his ways!" (Rom 11:33). This awe-filled exclamation of St. Paul's, which injects a moment of high doxology into his Letter to the Romans, applies most particularly to the Mystery of the Cross: namely, that it should have been in *this* scandalous manner and no other that God chose to redeem the world. Henceforth, the glory of the Son, the second Person of the blessed and eternal and consubstantial Trinity, would be inseparable from his intimate, inalienable identity as slaughtered Lamb who takes away the sins of the world, a reality most forcefully represented in the Book of Revelation:

> I heard around the throne and the living creatures and the elders the voice of many angels, numbering myriads of myriads and thousands of thousands, saying with a loud voice, "Worthy is the Lamb who was slain, to receive power and wealth and wisdom and might and honor and glory and blessing!" And I heard every creature in heaven and on earth and under the earth and in the sea, and all therein, saying, "To him who sits upon the throne and to the Lamb be blessing and honor and glory and might for ever and ever!" And the four living creatures said, "Amen!" and the elders fell down and worshiped. (Rev 5:11–14)

Jesus of Nazareth, crucified on Golgotha, is this Lamb, and there is no other.

The gruesome physiological details of the crucifixion—the wounds and the bleeding, the bruises and the suffocation—are there to remind us that this image of the slain Lamb is no mere metaphor but hard, painful, historical fact. At the same time, however, this "hour" of the Passion and crucifixion is for Jesus also the hour of his glorification, as he affirms during his great high-priestly prayer in John's Gospel: "Now, Father, glorify me in your own presence with the glory which I had with you before the world was made" (Jn 17:5). Exegetes agree on the crucial christological point that Jesus' eternal glory is not manifested only in the Resurrection but already *now* on Golgotha: "For Jesus of Nazareth, to glorify the Father means to manifest his extreme love for the world, and this is why the divine glory is present in the Son. . . . By his obedience unto death on the Cross, the Son finds again the glory he had in God 'before the world was made.' "[9]

How could Jesus, then, both gratify his mockers by "saving himself" and still remain the Son of God? How could Jesus suddenly turn to seek the glory of the world when his only glory came to him from his relationship with his Father and from obeying his Father's will? An unimaginable apostasy by Jesus would surely have merely confirmed his deriders in their worst prejudices and their corrupt conception of God. For Jesus to "come down from the cross" in order to "save himself" would have utterly destroyed the whole work of redemption, which was wholly oriented, not to his own benefit, but to that of others, not to a this-worldly affirmation of physical life and welfare, but to transcendental and everlasting life in the Kingdom of God. In a particularly insightful passage, Louis Evely once wrote that the root cause for Adam's sin was not pride but, rather, inventing an entirely false conception of God and of how divinity operates:

> [Adam] thought that God was an independent, autonomous being sufficient to himself; . . . and in order to become like him he rebelled and showed disobedience. But when God revealed himself, when God willed to show who he was, he appeared as love, tenderness, as outpouring of himself, infinite pleasure in another. Inclination, dependence. God showed himself obedient, obedient unto death.[10]

The passersby on Golgotha are not especially evil people: they are, rather, very ordinary children of Adam and heirs to his primordial

---

[9] Xavier Léon-Dufour, *Lecture de l'Évangile selon Jean*, vol. 3 (Paris: Éditions du Seuil, 1993), 286.

[10] This text, from Evely's book *We Dare to Say Our Father*, is quoted enthusiastically by Ratzinger in *Introduction to Christianity*, 267.

muddle concerning the true nature of their Creator. As such, they want Jesus to reinforce their sense of worldly security, to legitimize their mediocrity and their idea of God as a powerful talisman, a human possession that can magically waive away all difficulties. Pious Jews though they consider themselves, these people tread the broad path of sly equivocation. By contrast, long before Golgotha, Jesus has already laid down the blueprint of his own ethos and is now bringing it to its existential culmination on the Cross: "Enter by the narrow gate; for the gate is wide and the way is easy, that leads to destruction, and those who enter by it are many. For the gate is narrow and the way is hard, that leads to life, and those who find it are few" (7:13–14).

The true meaning and operation of divine omnipotence cannot be shackled to any Machiavellian scheme or self-seeking agenda. God's *only* power, we cannot repeat it too often, is outflowing love, bestowal of self. It was his divine omnipotence, inseparable from his wisdom and his nature as love, that impelled God both to create the world and to redeem fallen man. God never exercises any such thing as "raw power". For Jesus to "come down from the cross" would mean for him to forsake the sublime realm of his heavenly Father in order to blend in with the multitude of those who live only for self-gratification and self-justification in this world. Jesus cannot abandon the Cross any more than the Glory of God could abandon the tent of meeting:

A tent was prepared . . . in which were the lampstand and the table and the bread of offering; it is called the Holy Place. Behind the second curtain stood a tent called the Holy of Holies, having the golden altar of incense and the ark of the covenant covered on all sides with gold. . . . Above it were the cherubim of glory overshadowing the mercy seat. (Heb 9:2–5)

The Cross is the Throne of Jesus' life-giving Glory: "Then he showed me the river of the water of life, bright as crystal, flowing from the throne of God and of the Lamb through the middle of the street of the city" (Rev 22:1–2). The Cross is the ultimate Ark of the New and Eternal Covenant in his blood (26:28), the Tree of Life implanted at the center of the universe by God himself, the wise Gardener (Gen 2:9) who always toils to cultivate superabundant life (Jn 10:10). The Cross is the true Mercy Seat (ἱλαστήριον—*hilastêrion*) from which the power of Christ's forgiving and reconciling love radiates centrifugally, always flowing outward, away from self, to permeate all creation.

א

"AND THOSE WHO PASSED BY DERIDED HIM": The Greek word here translated "derided" is *eblasphêmoun*, with an obvious etymological link to our word *blasphemy*. This word has acquired a very specific religious connotation in the course of time, so that in modern languages we use it almost exclusively to refer to speaking impiously or irreverently of God. Normally, we do not apply the term "to blaspheme" to insults exchanged between human beings, and so there is good reason for contemporary translations of the Gospel to render the word in our passage as "to deride" (RSV), "to revile" (KJV, NAB), "to jeer" (NJB), and so on. However, the specific Greek word Matthew uses, *blasphêméô*, should be heard in all its density as containing both levels of signification. It is kerygmatic because it proclaims *both* an unjust offense against a fellow human being *and* a heinous offense against God. The contemptuous insults of the passersby are hurled at both a God and a man, nor am I speaking only of objective blasphemy.

The passersby may not be theologians, but simple virtuous humanity and especially Jewish piety should forewarn them against the savage barbarity of their insults, which do take on a specifically theological form. They taunt the crucified Jesus with the brazen challenge: "If you are the Son of God, come down from the cross." Does not such mockery presume to limit the mystery of the divine Nature by ruling out the possibility of God having sent his Son to earth? And would God have sent his Son if, in his wisdom, he had foreseen that there was no possibility that any human being would believe Jesus to be who he was? Did not all of Jesus' words, deeds, and even gestures manifest unambiguously that, in fact, he *was* the Son of God? Did not a few—true, very few—witnesses in fact confess their faith in his identity even before the Resurrection? The fact that the vast majority did not by no means excuses the deniers.

The jeering of the passersby, like that of the chief priests, scribes, and elders coming up in just a moment, does indeed constitute not only slanderous prejudice and insult but also *blasphemy* in the narrower, theological sense of the term, as portrayed by St. John: "He was in the world, and the world was made through him, yet the world knew him not. He came to his own home, and his own people received him not" (Jn 1:10–11). A human conscience that is truly seeking God, truly yearning to serve and adore God, would never venture to utter the insolent dare, "If you are the Son of God, come down from the cross!" even if it had no conceptual clarity concerning the victim's innermost identity. Such a righteous conscience, rather, would be implicitly aware of the Presence of God in every human being and, in particular, in a man suffering in Jesus' uniquely serene and luminous way, in a man whose very appearance portends the will to pacify and reconcile. No, at the foot of the Cross, in the face of such an unconditional outpouring of love by the Creator of the universe, and in the face of such a universal outpouring of contempt and rejection on the part of man, no one is forgivable although all will be forgiven.

Only Jesus himself can atone for the blasphemy incurred against him as the Son of God: "Is it nothing to you, all you who pass by? Look and see if there is any sorrow like my sorrow which was brought upon me, which the LORD inflicted on the day of his fierce anger" (Lam 1:12). In his prayer to his Father on the Cross, Jesus seeks to divert to himself the horrendous impact of God's righteous wrath, away from the guilty and onto himself, the innocent Lamb of God. The very last thoughts and concerns of Jesus' Heart as he hangs there gasping in his death throes are not sentiments of cursing, self-pity, and recrimination but, rather (and inconceivably to the worldly mind), pleas for absolution, healing, and liberation on behalf of the very ones who that same instant are seeking to exterminate his person. The ancient *Letter to Diognetus* is eloquent on this point and stresses God's long-suffering wisdom in the timing of the events of the Passion:

> When our wickedness had reached its height, and it had been clearly shown that its reward, punishment and death, was impending over us; and when the time had come which God had before appointed for manifesting His own kindness and power, how the one love of God,

through exceeding regard for men, did not regard us with hatred, nor thrust us away, nor remember our iniquity against us, but showed great long-suffering, and bore with us, He Himself took on Him the burden of our iniquities, He gave His own Son as a ransom for us, the holy One for transgressors, the blameless One for the wicked, the righteous One for the unrighteous, and incorruptible One for the corruptible, the immortal One for them that are mortal. . . . O Sweet exchange! O unsearchable operation! O benefits surpassing all expectation! That the wickedness of many should be hid in a single righteous One, and that the righteousness of One should justify many transgressors![11]

Forgiving—the most Christian of all actions—is enacted by the dying Jesus explicitly in Luke, when he pleads: "Father, forgive them; for they know not what they do" (Lk 23:34). But such an intense act of forgiving, which requires all the strength and faith of the human heart, is also implicit in Matthew's text, since the Crucified One here is none other than the Rabbi who solemnly commanded his disciples: "Love your enemies and pray for those who persecute you" (5:44). This bizarre and wildly counterintuitive commandment must nonetheless have had a certain sublime appeal coming from the mouth of this most enthralling of Masters in the context of the Sermon on the Mount, already so laden with outlandish doctrine. However, transposed to the context of the Cross, the imperative to love one's enemies and pray for those who persecute one becomes almost unbearable, and this is precisely why Jesus has to put his own commandment into practice first and in the most extreme of circumstances, which thus includes every other possible, less grievous instance.

At each step in these proceedings, the evangelist is giving us both the "view from below" and the "view from above" on what is happening to Jesus. Matthew gives us both the purely human point of view concerning the man on the cross and God's own vision of the meaning of Golgotha. And then we are left free to make our own decision: Shall we, yielding to the instincts of our own ungenerous passions and prejudices, join the jeering throng at least minimally, with our smiling and contemptuous indifference? Or shall our heart,

---

[11] *Epistle to Diognetus*, chap. 9, in *Ante-Nicene Fathers*, vol. 1, *The Apostolic Fathers, Justin Martyr, Irenaeus*, ed. Alexander Roberts and James Donaldson (Peabody, Mass.: Hendrickson Publishers, 1995), 28.

pierced by compassion, overwhelm Jesus and his Father with sentiments of sorrow, praise, and thanksgiving, by the power of the Holy Spirit? Shall we, along with the elders of the people on Golgotha, despise and insult the suffering Christ? Or shall we instead, with the twenty-four elders of the Apocalypse, "fall down and worship"?

To mock or to adore Christ Crucified: that is the question!

27:41-42   ὁμοίως καὶ οἱ ἀρχιερεῖς ἐμπαίζοντες
μετὰ τῶν γραμματέων καὶ πρεσβυτέρων ἔλεγον·
Ἄλλους ἔσωσεν, ἑαυτὸν οὐ δύναται σῶσαι·
βασιλεὺς Ἰσραήλ ἐστιν, καταβάτω νῦν ἀπὸ τοῦ σταυροῦ
καὶ πιστεύσομεν ἐπ᾽ αὐτόν

*So also the chief priests, mocking
with the scribes and elders, said,
"He saved others; he cannot save himself.
He is the King of Israel; let him come down now from the cross,
and we will believe in him"*

THIS IS YOUR HOUR, and the power of darkness", Jesus said to the amassed forces of the chief priests, scribes, and elders gathered at the moment of his arrest (Lk 22:53). The power of darkness will, for the rest of the Passion narrative, hollow out a zone of ugly desolation in the world. Here the forces of evil take the upper hand and are allowed to triumph for an interval. The Passion narrative invites us to taste the bitterness, disorientation, and despair of a world without God. This absence of God is not the result of God deliberately going away but, rather, of God being persecuted by man and banished from the earth. If we find such a world as bitter as the gall offered to Jesus, then perhaps we are on our way to salvation. But if we find ourselves in any way sympathizing with the crucifiers and the scorners, even if only through our indifference or our preference for pragmatic and "sensible" explanations, then we are fueling the power of darkness by contributing the substance of our heart.

Whenever the power of darkness gains the ascendancy, God must necessarily grow silent and the light of his Word is extinguished. At noon on this Good Friday, darkness will descend visibly over the whole world; but spiritual darkness, the stranglehold of evil over man, already began saturating the world the moment the Son of man, the Light of the world, was arrested and handed over into the clutches of men. The Word of God has been gagged and can no longer address to man any utterance of teaching, prophecy, healing, or consolation.

It is significant that we have not heard the suffering Jesus utter a single syllable since the moment in the prætorium when he replies to Pilate's query "Are you the King of the Jews?" Then he replies very simply, "You have said so" (27:11). Immediately the text twice stresses the deliberate silence of the incarnate Word (27:12, 14). After his brief answer to Pilate affirming his kingship, the only words Jesus will speak before his death are his prayer to the Father using the first words of Psalm 22[21]: "My God, my God, why have you forsaken me?" (27:46). After spending himself trying to reach man through human words, the incarnate Word now has only his death to offer by way of effective communication. And if someone's death for my sake cannot reach my heart and change it, then I am beyond hope.

However, where God's mighty silence creates a gaping vacuum, there man's noisy abuse and excited sarcasm will rush in to fill the world with venom. Part of the mystery of redemption is that God allows the forces of evil to exhaust themselves by enacting their worst impulses. The scene has been prophetically portrayed in great detail in certain psalms that stress the tendency of haughty human power to revolt against divine authority and the plans of God. Thus we read in Psalm 2: "The kings of the earth set themselves, and the rulers take counsel together, against the LORD and his anointed" (v. 2). And in Psalm 74[73]: "Arise, O God, plead your cause; remember how the impious scoff at you all the day! Do not forget the clamor of your foes, the uproar of your adversaries which goes up continually!" (vv. 22–23).

The perennial rebelliousness of the human spirit against God and

God's ways reaches its climax on Golgotha as mankind makes its best concerted effort to do away with God's goodness from the world once and for all by annihilating the human body of God's Anointed. The universality of man's guilt in the death of Jesus excludes no one, as we have seen stressed time and again in Matthew's narrative of the Passion, and as Peter and John affirm after the Resurrection in a prayer of thanksgiving after being released from prison: "Truly in this city [of Jerusalem] there were gathered together against your holy servant Jesus, whom you anointed, both Herod and Pontius Pilate, with the Gentiles and the peoples of Israel, to do whatever your hand and your plan had predestined to take place" (Acts 4:27–28). Crucial as well in this affirmation is the fact that the universal human collusion in the murder of Jesus does not escape God's providence but itself becomes an instrument of redemption.

The vacuum left behind by God's silence in the publicly condemned and humiliated Jesus is filled to the brim by the uproar of violent voices clamoring for vengeance. Matthew goes to great lengths to convey this cacophony of hatred by devoting verses 39 through 44 exclusively to the vituperation hurled at the Redeemer. No one seems excluded from having a part in this dissonant chorus of contempt. With the yelps of the mob at the prætorium still ringing in our ears, as well as the chortling of the soldiery as they crown Jesus "king", we now watch the parade of passersby with wagging heads and taunting tongues. Next comes the clique of pompous high priests, scribes, and elders, ostentatiously circling the Cross like self-appointed queens and frivolously screeching out sacred words like "salvation", "King of Israel", "faith", "trust", and "God's Son". And, last but not least, the two robbers crucified with Jesus find an absurd satisfaction in reviling, along with the rest of the scoffers, the Man in the Middle who is sharing their own fate. Perhaps, by joining the jeerers in their cowardly zone of safety, the robbers are attempting to create for themselves one final, momentary refuge from their own misery.

Indeed, in this passage Matthew seems to want to exhaust the Greek repertory of words for "mockery" and "contempt" in order thus to signify that all the hatred of the world is descending at once in concentrated form upon the head of Jesus. Three different verbs are used in this passage in a total of five occurrences. The verb *empaízō* appears three times, predicated twice of the soldiers (vv. 29, 31) and once of the high priests, scribes, and elders (v. 41). It connotes everything from "to ridicule, make fun of, and mock" to "deceive, trick, and make a fool of". Then the verb *blasphêméô* is attributed to the passersby, as we have seen (v. 39), and conveys rich nuances: "to revile, defame, slander, speak irreverently of, drop evil or profane words, speak lightly of sacred things, utter ominous words, and, finally, blaspheme". The third verb, *oneidízô*, is here predicated specifically of the two robbers (v. 44) and has the following connotations: "to reproach, upbraid, insult, blame". This last charge seems particularly apposite in the mouths of the two criminals crucified with Jesus. While the passersby and the religious authorities hurl pointedly theological mockery at Jesus, the robbers, in *blaming* Jesus, appear to think, in a wildly irrational way, that somehow Jesus is responsible for their common fate! The proud heart, indeed, must always find a scapegoat for its own inadmissible crimes.

"HE SAVED OTHERS; HE CANNOT SAVE HIMSELF." The mind reels before such an affirmation, hissed out with professional spite by the priests and not remotely intended by them as a simple expression of puzzlement before a mystery. Contemporaries of Jesus apparently conceive of "salvation" as a very precise and individual occurrence whereby one person heals another physically or otherwise delivers him from some dire situation such as imprisonment, demonic possession, or starvation. It does not occur to them that Jesus, whose very name means "Savior", aims at a far more all-encompassing and transcendental form of "salvation", namely, the liberation of sinners from their sin and its consequence, eternal death. Nor do they have the slightest inkling of the motivations that fuel the Heart of this Savior, who "did not please himself; but, as it is written, 'The reproaches of those who reproached you, [O God], fell on me'" (Rom 15:3). Jesus prefers his own death to the death of others, and he makes himself a shield to absorb the insults hurled at God by men. To put it very simply: the scoffers at the Cross are ignorant of the fact that the word "success" in its worldly sense does not exist in God's vocabulary.

In this scene, rather, it is as if the priests and scribes were saying:

"Look here what the great healer really amounts to when the chips are down! All those so-called healings of the leprous and the lame must have been either magic tricks or plain works of the devil. Now that we have him pinned down and disabled, he can no longer work his feats of illusion. We have unmasked his holy trickery for what it's worth! Any 'savior' of consequence could easily evade our restraints and save himself for all to see and be persuaded. And this weak fool would have us put our hopes in him! We have succeeded in exposing his elaborate pious act, and at the center of his person we find nothing but deceit and sanctimonious rhetoric. He is getting only what he deserves for trying to lead us and the people astray from our holy Tradition."

What all of the mocking charges against Jesus have in common— whether they proceed from the mouths of the rabble or from the priests, scribes, and elders—is this: they presuppose an agenda to *functionalize God*. The Divine, or anyone who claims to represent the Divine, is thought to be under obligation to demonstrate his authenticity by complying with the conditions of proof imposed by mere fallible creatures; and yet we know what Jesus himself, quoting Deuteronomy 6:16, has already declared himself on this point in a reply to the Father of Lies: "You shall not tempt [or 'test', οὐκ ἐκπειράσεις—*ouk ekpeiráseis*] the Lord your God!" (4:7).

The mockers' attitude and approach to the Mystery of God are, by definition, the height of impiety itself since it is creatures that ought to submit to God and not the other way around. Nor is it an acceptable excuse that those surrounding the Cross do not honestly believe that Jesus is the Son of God. While wandering in the desert after leaving Egypt, their ancestors behaved in the same way before the unmistakably one and only God of Israel: "And [Moses] called the name of the place Massah ['testing'] and Meribah ['contention'], because of the faultfinding of the sons of Israel, and because they put the LORD to the test by saying, 'Is the LORD among us or not?'" (Ex 17:7). Furthermore, this is no isolated instance, for the same pattern of revolt and disobedience against the Lord God is repeated countless times throughout Israel's history, particularly in its violent rejection of the prophets sent to them by God, of whom Jesus is the last and the greatest.

Both at Meribah and now on Golgotha, man arrogantly presumes to lay down conditions to God. This procedure of attempting to shackle the Divine to human standards is nothing less than the idolatrous endeavor to redefine Divinity in order to functionalize God, that is, to reduce God to a manageable power that man can store away and then manipulate in any way he wishes. The creature attempts to compel the Creator, in order to prove to man that he is God, to behave in the particular manner the creature dictates! Naturally, were this method to succeed, it would only prove that man had effectively routed the true God from the face of the earth and, instead, constructed for himself a pleasing and utterly false facsimile of Divinity, pliant to all human whims. Man is forever trying to tame the true God's insufferable unruliness.

But Jesus will not allow such a Promethean project to succeed. Jesus will not allow himself, even in the depths of his horrific suffering and weakness, to be interiorly reduced and functionalized, whether politically, religiously, or in any other way. Jesus chooses physical death rather than compromise by one iota the full revelation of his Father's nature as love, which was the mission he came to accomplish. Jesus has no attraction to pain or death for its own sake. But Jesus' death is the result of his refusal to allow man to functionalize God. We remember his scathing reply to those demanding that he give them "signs" by way of proof of his Messianic identity. It is an answer that refuses to point his hecklers, and us, in any direction other than the foot of the Cross: "An evil and adulterous generation seeks for a sign; but no sign shall be given to it except the sign of the prophet Jonah. For as Jonah was three days and three nights in the belly of the whale, so will the Son of man be three days and three nights in the heart of the earth" (12:39–40). Only the life-giving Cross can be the throne of the genuine Messiah, as we read in the Preface of the Solemnity of Our Lord Jesus Christ, King of the Universe:

> You anointed your Only Begotten Son . . . with the oil of gladness as eternal Priest and King of all creation, so that, by offering himself on the altar of the Cross as a spotless sacrifice to bring us peace, he might accomplish the mysteries of human redemption and, making all created things subject to his rule, he might present to the immensity of your majesty an eternal and universal kingdom, a kingdom of truth and life, a kingdom of holiness and grace, a kingdom of justice, love and peace.

א

"HE IS THE KING OF ISRAEL; let him come down now from the cross, and we will believe in him": As with a theological machine gun, the priests blast out in rapid succession three blasphemous charges against Jesus. *One*: He who allegedly saved others cannot save himself, which proves him to be a conniving deceiver and all his "good works" pitiful illusions. *Two*: The Romans wrote on the tablet above Jesus' head: THIS IS JESUS THE KING OF THE JEWS, a clearly socio-ethnic declaration of Jesus' kingship, formulated by non-Jews. But the Jewish authorities now verbally intensify the proclamation by stating HE IS THE KING OF ISRAEL, thereby refining the truth and referring to themselves and their nation by their official and proper name as the People of God. Nevertheless, they declare Jesus' precise royal title only in order to conclude that, although he claims to be the King of Israel, this claim is ridiculous. Its nullity is demonstrated by the fact that he hangs helplessly on a cross, a condition no king would tolerate, much less the Messiah sent by the one and only all-powerful God of heavenly armies (cf. 1 Sam 17:45; Is 44:6; Jer 46:10; Ps 2, and *passim*). His pathetic weakness proves him to be a sacrilegious impostor. And *three*: He is supposed to have always trusted in God unconditionally, claiming to be God's Son. "Well, then, if that is the case, *let God deliver him now* from the throes of death, for God always rescues his faithful ones. Yet see: nothing is happening. We don't see God coming down to deliver his alleged 'faithful one', and this proves Jesus is a fraud and his 'trust' in God mere rhetorical pretense."

Of the three charges, perhaps the third is the most heinous, since it hurls a challenge not only at Jesus but directly at Almighty God himself. What is astounding in the form of these sarcastic accusations against Jesus by the religious authorities is that each of them proclaims, albeit blasphemously, a fundamental truth of revelation about Jesus of Nazareth: his mission as Savior, his office as anointed King of Israel, and his innermost identity as eternal Son of the Father. Moreover, the text conveys these charges, not as ludicrous speculations ("they say he saved others", "he claims to be king", "he is supposed to trust God") but *as factual declarations of reality, in the indicative mood.* Thus far in each accusation we have nothing but pure Gospel truths, though mouthed by hostile unbelievers.

Each of the taunts follows a two-part formula, with a proposition and a conclusion: *Since* such-and-such is supposed to be true, *therefore* such-and-such should be the result. The great and unbridgeable dis-junction between humble faith and rebellious unbelief comes in the second part of the accusation, where the mockers draw the only con-ceivable conclusion given the truth of the first part. Because the re-sults they demand are not forthcoming, however, they must negate the truth that they themselves have affirmed in the opening propo-sition. This procedure puts the sanctity of the mind of God through the wringer of self-serving and idolatrous human logic. Elsewhere in the Gospel, we have already seen that the demons can objectively recognize Jesus' true nature without in the least being capable of an act of loving faith: "And immediately there was in their synagogue a man with an unclean spirit; and he cried out, 'What have you to do with us, Jesus of Nazareth? Have you come to destroy us? I know who you are, the Holy One of God'" (Mk 1:23–24).

Then, too, we remember the terrible pronouncement in the Letter of James: "You believe that God is one; you do well. Even the demons believe—and shudder" (Jas 2:19). In other words, when the heart is in revolt against God, shut against the coming of God's Presence to dwell subjectively within us, it is possible to mouth objectively cor-rect formulas of faith and cause this assent actually to *separate us even farther* from the living reality to which those formulas point.

Now, what might be the underlying reason for this revolt and shutting off of the human heart against the living and active Word of God? No doubt the fact that, quite spontaneously, we project our own narrow ideas and desires onto a big screen in our minds that we label "GOD", and then we proceed to call "divine and binding" all the petty prejudices of our own heart. In so operating, we blithely forget that, where the living God is concerned—the God who is consuming Fire (cf. Deut 4:24; Lam 2:3; Heb 12:29)—"'my thoughts are not your thoughts, neither are your ways my ways,' says the LORD. 'For as the heavens are higher than the earth, so are my ways higher than your ways and my thoughts than your thoughts'" (Is 55:8–9). In fact, the best indication of a well-formed and God-fearing conscience is the uneasy sensation of being almost permanently at odds with God's vision of the world. Whoever does not feel there is a gaping abyss between himself and God, between his ways and God's ways, is adoring a narcissistic idol of his own making.

This necessary and unfathomable abyss between the thoughts of

God and the thoughts of man poses its ultimate challenge to the human mind at the *kénôsis*, when

> Christ Jesus, . . . though he was in the form of God, did not count equality with God a thing to be grasped, but emptied himself, taking the form of a servant, being born in the likeness of men. And being found in human form he humbled himself and became obedient unto death, even death on a cross. (Phil 2:5–8)

The dazzling glory that here shines forth from the mystery of the Cross is, at the same time, the illumination of humble seekers after salvation and the blinding of proud minds closed to God's logic, which dictates his design for the redemption of the world: *"Because I am God, I will die out of love"*, is the essence of the divine thought as it motivates Jesus.

Those who are unable or unwilling to recognize the Presence of God in Jesus in his hidden form of humiliation on Golgotha shall be excluded from enjoying this Presence and Person in the form of manifest glory.

"HE TRUSTS IN GOD; let God deliver him now, if he desires (θέλει—thélei) him; for he said, 'I am the Son of God'" (27:43): This verse is not found in any of the other Gospels, and so it must have a special significance to Matthew's theology. Let us consider its precise wording, for it does in fact contain a piercing glance into the wondrous mystery of trinitarian love as well as a stunning intimation concerning the underlying power propelling Jesus' eventual Resurrection. It is before all else profoundly ironical that such choice revelations about the inner life of God should come from the mouth of unbelieving scoffers and at the precise moment when they are reveling over the Son's demise. However, this ironical fact is not without relevance to two essential elements of the Passion.

First, Jesus' betrayal into the hands of malicious men has indeed ushered in the triumph of darkness. It has turned the world of mortals into what the Fathers of the Church called a *regio dissimilitudinis*, that is, a "realm of incongruity" wholly at odds with God's intended creation, where the disfigurement of God's image in man has gained the ascendancy and reigns triumphant. In such a world, everything is equivocation, and pearls become the playthings of swine (cf. 7:6). Language, in particular, becomes the vehicle, not of truth, but of self-promotion and deceit, and fools enthrone themselves as authoritative sources of wisdom.

Simultaneously, however, we witness a second element at work here: namely, that God's will to save and enlighten prevails even in such a world because God's compassion is always greater and more powerful than the worst man can do to thwart the sovereignty of goodness and justice. Therefore, in such a climate, *fools and scoffers become, despite themselves, the instruments of revelation.* Even a true prophet never deserves being chosen as a prophet, and the omnipotence of God's Word is vindicated a fortiori when highest Truth burns its way through the throat and the mouth of the very ones who rage to squelch it.

But there is more, again in the order of language and what linguists call the "efficacy of speech-acts": Once the highly charged and truly transcendental statement "He trusts in God; let God deliver him now, if he desires him; for he said, 'I am the Son of God'" has been pronounced in the world—even in sarcastic scorn, even as a blasphemous taunt to the Crucified God—then the sheer potency of the words, their naked, breathtaking beauty and mystical perfection and rightness, makes really present in the world the extraordinary realities to which they refer. Divine beauty, always free to appear in what to us may seem the most unworthy of places and circumstances, will always ravish the soul of the spiritually starving. These will bravely risk the bite of the swine and bend down into the muck to wrest from it the precious pearls of God's Wisdom, recognizing in them an exquisite fare. They thus turn even a pigsty into a royal banquet hall. We are these starving beggars at the foot of the Cross on Golgotha, and to us who are fainting with despair the Father appeals through his humiliated Son, who has come to commune in our despair and is proclaimed Son and Savior by his very deriders. The Cross reveals both what God thinks of sin and what he is prepared to do about it, at a supreme cost to himself. No destructive power on earth can stifle the omnipotent yearning of God's love for his creatures.

This third conditional proposition, hurled at Jesus in mockery by the priests and their companions, is an almost verbatim quotation of Psalm 22[21]:8, which refers to the plight of the righteous man who is being persecuted by the impious: "He committed his cause to the Lord; let him deliver him, let him rescue him, for he delights (חָפֵץ— *chafétz*) in him!" In the psalm, the immediate context for this jeering challenge is set in the previous verse by a statement that feeds directly into Jesus' own experience on Golgotha: "All who see me mock at me, they make mouths at me, they wag their heads" (Ps 22[21]:7).

Now, in the place where the psalm verse in Hebrew has *for he delights* (*chafétz*) *in him* Matthew's allusive text has, literally, "if he wants (θέλει—*thélei*) him", a phrase that the RSV rightly renders "if he desires him". Even though the psalm verse literally says "if he wants him", with the persecuted man (that is, Jesus) as the object of the wanting, the phrase has sometimes been translated as if it referred to a mere act of *assent* by God's deliberative Will (for instance "Let God, if he wants to, deliver him now", NET) rather than to an act of intimate *desire* by God's loving Heart (that is, not *if he wants to [do it]* but rather *if he wants him*, which is what Matthew's text has). [12] The difference is important and not a mere nuance of language.

A detached *act of God's will* would merely evoke the image of a distant God concerned only with the successful realization of his master plan of salvation, whereas an *act of loving desire by God* would indicate an intimate involvement of the Father's Heart in the person of his Son and in this Son's fate. Our own heart, stupefied, misses a beat at this realization. It begins to dawn on us that, while frivolous human beings violently reject and mock the Son of God, inflicting on him every manner of injury, God himself tenderly recognizes his only Son in the pitifully mangled corpse hanging from the Cross *and desires him, longs for him, in this condition!* Purely human desire and goodwill grow cold and take to flight at the sight of a disfigured and defeated

---

[12] Thus we read: "Let him deliver him now, if he will have him" (KJV); "Que Dieu le délivre maintenant, s'il s'intéresse à lui!" (FBJ). Even the Latin Vulgate disappoints when it renders: "Liberet nunc eum si vult", although the Vulgata Nova corrects this to "Liberet nunc, si vult eum."

beloved. God, however, is steadily faithful, and his love endures for all ages regardless of the circumstances in which his Darling may find himself.

This divine characteristic now pierces through the ugliness and desolation of the scene on Golgotha and sears a deep imprint into our soul. We note, first, that in the original Hebrew the quoted psalm uses the word חָפֵץ (*chaféts*) to refer to the reason why God would rescue the persecuted man who trusts in him: "Let [God] rescue him, for he *delights* (*chaféts*) in him!" The Hebrew word *chaféts* could equally be rendered by the verbs "to take pleasure in" or "to desire". But if we look at the Septuagint translation of this Hebrew psalm verse, we discover that there it is translated as ἤλπισεν ἐπὶ κύριον, ῥυσάσθω αὐτόν, σωσάτω αὐτόν ὅτι θέλει αὐτόν (Ps 22[21]:8): "He hoped in the Lord, let him deliver him, let him save him because he *wants* him." How enlightening to see that the Septuagint translates חָפֵץ (*chaféts*) with θέλει (*thélei*), the very same term Matthew uses in his Gospel! This clarifies how, on the basis of the Septuagint and the Hebrew text that underlies it, Matthew understood the root cause of the Father's coming to Jesus' rescue to be *his longing desire for him*.

For Matthew, the Greek word θέλει, while literally meaning "he wants", in this case connotes the more passionate and intimate meaning of the Hebrew rather than the more detached and merely volitive sense of an act of rescue for the sake of fulfilling a plan. In other words, the Father *wants the beloved person of the Son for himself*, in the subjective sense of *desiring* his presence, of *delighting* in his existence, and eventually therefore in the ontological sense of *wanting to restore* the Son to fullness of life in the Resurrection. Similarly, the verb "to want" is used as an ordinary equivalent for "to love" in some languages.[13]

Nor is this moment on Golgotha an isolated instance of the manifestation of the Father's *loving desire* for his Son in the Gospel of Matthew. This radiant revelation of the Father's delight in his Son and his desire for union with him, broadcast on Golgotha through the most unlikely of messengers, is, in fact, the fourth instance of the

---

[13] For "to love" the Spanish verb *querer* (as in *Te quiero mucho*) is used far more frequently than *amar*, which is considered poetic and more specialized, while in Italian *Ti voglio bene* is the familiar way of saying "I love you." Both examples literally mean "I want you."

same proclamation in Matthew. The present circumstances obviously lend the declaration a uniquely turbulent character, like a geyser of scorching water that has to force its way outward to the land's surface against the stubborn resistance of the earth; and yet it is important to see this tempestuous epiphany within the context of previous, almost identical affirmations in very different Matthean contexts. Only then can we behold this revelation of the Father's steady fidelity to the Son in all its trinitarian and soteriological glory. We may say it is a leitmotif that permeates the Gospel of Matthew and rises to the surface explicitly at four strategic points.

The first instance of the series occurs at Jesus' baptism early in the Gospel. There, too, we witness a situation in which the glory of the Son is literally concealed by repentance and water, as he willingly humiliates himself by joining the rest of sinful humanity and seeks purification from the hands of John the Baptist. At the precise moment when Jesus emerges from the waters symbolizing death and steps up onto Jordan's bank, "a voice from heaven [is heard], saying, 'This is my beloved Son, with whom I am well pleased'" (3:17).[14] From the lowest point on earth, symbolized by Jordan's riverbed, and dripping with the waters of conversion that represent the drowning of sin, Jesus ascends to meet the voice of his Father descending from highest heaven. The relationship between Father and Son has expanded cosmically out of their eternity to encompass all of heaven and earth in their redeeming love. In this episode of the baptism, it is the Son's self-humiliation, and his willingness to take on the sin of all, that give the Father occasion to declare publicly the link between his love for his Son and the pleasure he takes in him, both intrinsically as a Divine Person and extrinsically as the perfect Executor of his design of salvation.

The second instance when the Father proclaims his pleasure in the Son is somewhat more muted than the scene at the Jordan, but it is just as powerful. It takes place in a synagogue on a Sabbath when Jesus heals the man with a withered hand. As on Golgotha, this occasion, too, is highly conflictive because "the Pharisees went out and took

---

[14] Other versions assign slightly different nuances to the verb εὐδόκησα, such as "in him I take great delight" (NET) and "my favor rests on him" (NJB). But they all stress the absolute centrality of Jesus the Son as primordial object of the Father's love. Whether we speak of pleasure, delight, or favor, *desire for the Son* is always implied as the Father's motivation.

counsel against him, how to destroy him." After the healing, Matthew concludes the episode by invoking the prophecy of Isaiah (42:1–4) at some length in order to justify Jesus' action of healing on a Sabbath: "This was to fulfil what was spoken by the prophet Isaiah: 'Behold, my servant whom I have chosen, *my beloved with whom my soul is well pleased*. I will put my Spirit upon him, and he shall proclaim justice to the Gentiles'" (12:14–18). In this case, the voice of God is not heard directly, out of the heavens, but only through the prophecy of Isaiah as applied to Jesus by Matthew.

In this manner, Matthew establishes an equivalence between "my Son" and "my Servant", a pairing that stresses the radically obedient nature of the eternal Son. If, in the first epiphany at the Jordan, the Father showed approval of the Son by expressing his paternal pleasure in his deed of self-humiliation, in this second epiphany in the synagogue, the Father is presented by Matthew as thoroughly endorsing with great satisfaction the Son's labor of healing mankind in body and soul.

The third epiphany is the visible and audible revelation of the Son's glory during his Transfiguration on Mount Tabor. At the climax of the episode, an astounding thing occurs: "Behold, a bright cloud overshadowed them, and a voice from the cloud said, *'This is my beloved Son, with whom I am well pleased; listen to him'*" (17:5). On this extraordinary occasion, when Jesus' "face shone like the sun, and his garments became white as light" (17:2), Jesus specifically intends to strengthen his chosen disciples inwardly by means of this experience so that they can endure the coming Passion as his companions. Both immediately before [15] and immediately after [16] the resplendent vision on Tabor, Jesus stresses to his followers the inevitability of his suffering and death, always with a view to his Resurrection. The Father's command to "listen to him" refers in such a context primarily to Jesus' insistence on the necessity of the whole Paschal Mystery in God's plan of salvation for the world. Here the Father's love for the Son is linked to the pleasure he takes in the Son's obedient acceptance of the imminent Cross. Together, Father and Son intend to create

---

[15] "From that time Jesus began to show his disciples that he must go to Jerusalem and suffer many things from the elders and chief priests and scribes, and be killed, and on the third day be raised" (16:21).

[16] "And as they were coming down the mountain, Jesus commanded them, 'Tell no one the vision, until the Son of man is raised from the dead'" (17:9).

the world anew as the earth is now irrigated, not by the rivers that flowed from Eden in the beginning (cf. Gen 2:10), but by the Son's blood as it flows from the Cross (cf. 26:28; Jn 19:34; 1 Jn 5:6; and *passim*).

And the fourth instance when the Father's pleasure in his Son is revealed is this present episode on Golgotha, during which, as we have seen, momentous trinitarian disclosures are made, with supreme irony and efficacy, through the very mouths of those who deny and insult Jesus' messianic identity. Despite themselves, Jesus' persecutors play a prophetic role. The tender place of delight Jesus occupies in his Father's Heart is manifested through the very mouths of those who all along have plotted his destruction. The plotters and their cohorts succeed literally, physically, and temporally in attaining their goals; yet they cannot keep the pleasure and the love of the Father for his Son from oozing powerfully through the very fabric of their hateful words. In this way, the Father establishes a very different sort of triumph.

This fourth occasion, however, for all its taking place at the very moment of the Savior's undoing, paradoxically reaches a higher peak of wondrous revelation than any of the other three. For now, in the final moments of Jesus' earthly life, the Father not only manifests total delight in the Son's obedience, wholehearted approval of his saving activity in the world, and full endorsement of every word that comes out of his mouth. Beyond all of this, as Jesus is about to give up his spirit in death, the Father reveals *his intense personal desire for this dying and annihilated One, his only Son*. How could it be otherwise? The revelation of the Father's desire for the Son is a profoundly moving and humble confession by the Father of what the redemption of the world has cost him: namely, in some real sense, a *separation from the Son*, because otherwise it would be absurd to say that the Father longs for the Son. The work of redemption, while being an enactment of the Father's love for the world, at the same time involves an unthinkable yet real separation of the Son from the Father. But what or who could ever quash this divine Mystery of Reciprocal Love and Desire that is the driving force at the center of the universe, at the center of Being itself, *the Love that moves the sun and the other stars*, as Dante has it? [17] To enact this Mystery and to draw sinful man within

---

[17] *L'Amor che move il sole e l'altre stelle* (Paradiso, XXXIII, 145).

it as a beneficiary, the Son first had to travel the infinite distance between holiness and iniquity, and for that mission, the Father had to let go of the Son and become temporarily bereft of him without whom God cannot be God. In the face of such an enormity, "the stone will cry out from the wall, and the beam from the woodwork respond" (Hab 2:11).

The persistence of that desiring love for his Son in the Father's Heart reaches out of eternity and bolts all the way to the slaughter on Golgotha, to enwrap the dying Son in wave upon wave of tender mercy, to rescue him from the cruel hands of his executioners and receive him back into his omnipotent embrace. He whose only glory has been to be the Son of such a Father is now desired more than ever by the Father whose will he has fulfilled to perfection. The Father cannot be fully Father without having the Son in his embrace; and so the Father yearns out of eternity with anticipated delight for the return of the Son to his home in the paternal Heart. This yearning, this desiring on the Father's part for the glorious presence of the Son: *this* is the divine energy that will work the miracle of the Resurrection. The Resurrection is an explosion of joy and reunion in the Heart of the Trinity. Nor is the Father's desire only for Jesus himself but is also for all who are now found in Christ, as we read in the Letter of James: "[The Lord] yearns jealously over the spirit which he has made to dwell in us" (Jas 4:5, NAB alt). This is none other than "the Spirit of his Son", which "God has sent . . . into our hearts" (Gal 4:6).

INTERLUDE IV:
MAKE ME
YOUR ATMOSPHERE

J ESUS SAYS TO EACH OF US: All your effort should go to applying to yourself the truths of my Passion, for that is the only way of truly knowing them. Knowledge is not at all a bad thing; it is a good thing, but on condition of making it the fruit and the seed of applied practice. Strive with full simplicity and total self-surrender to desire knowledge only in order to learn humility and increased detachment from your own thoughts, tastes, and ambitions. Have trust; I am like an atmosphere that is lacking only to those who isolate themselves voluntarily and asphyxiate. You have only to make a slight movement in order to move into me: just take a breath, and I will be yours. You are incessantly in need of my strength and my life; but by my Passion I have poured myself out for you: my blood is in the earth that nourishes you; my breath is in the air you breathe! If only you had faith and love . . . ![1]

[1] "Tu dois ne chercher qu'à t'appliquer à toi-même les vérités de ma Passion; on ne les connaît vraiment qu'ainsi. La connaissance n'est point mauvaise; elle est bonne, mais à la condition d'en faire le fruit et la semence de la pratique. Efforce-toi en toute simplicité et en tout abandon de ne désirer savoir que pour t'humilier et te détacher mieux de tes propres pensées, de tes goûts et de tes ambitions. Aie confiance; je suis comme l'atmosphère qui ne manque qu'à ceux qui s'isolent volontairement et s'asphyxient. Tu n'as qu'un mouvement à faire pour te mouvoir en moi, qu'une aspiration à produire pour que je sois à toi. Tu as sans cesse besoin de ma force et de ma vie; mais par ma Passion je me suis répandu pour toi: mon sang est dans la terre qui te nourrit; mon souffle est dans l'air que tu respires! Si tu avais la foi et l'amour!" (Maurice Blondel, *Carnets intimes*, I, 318; February 2, 1890.)

15. THE CRY THAT REFASHIONS THE WORLD

Jesus Sends Forth His Spirit (27:45–56)

27:45–46

Ἀπὸ δὲ ἕκτης ὥρας σκότος ἐγένετο
ἐπὶ πᾶσαν τὴν γῆν
ἕως ὥρας ἐνάτης, περὶ δὲ τὴν ἐνάτην ὥραν
ἀνεβόησεν ὁ Ἰησοῦς φωνῇ μεγάλῃ λέγων·
ΗΛΙ ΗΛΙ ΛΕΜΑ ΣΑΒΑΧΘΑΝΙ;
τοῦτ' ἔστιν· Θεέ μου Θεέ μου, ἱνατί με ἐγκατέλιπες;

Now from the sixth hour there was
darkness over all the land
until the ninth hour. And about the ninth hour
Jesus shouted with a loud voice, saying,
Eli, Eli, lema sabachthani?
that is, "My God, my God, why have you forsaken me?"

E WHO DID NOT SPARE HIS own Son but handed him over (παρέδωκεν—*parédôken*) for us all, will he not also graciously grant (χαρίσεται—*charísetai*) us all things along with him?" (Rom 8:32).[1] As we arrive at the threshold of Jesus' death, the supreme moment in St. Matthew's Gospel, these sober and luminous words of St. Paul to the Romans would appear to be the only worthy and sufficient commentary. Only Scripture itself is capable of granting us some access to the unspeakable Mystery. Any other human words would surely be brash, almost impertinent. What is

[1] My translation.

happening on this Cross on Golgotha *is* indeed literally unspeakable, in every sense of the word, both beyond the power of human language to convey it and heinous by its very nature. But Paul's serene and deeply consoling words give some relief to our dismay as they reveal what is in fact occurring at this moment in the depths of reality, that is, in the Heart of God and in the heart of man: what is truly occurring under the tragic phenomena of gloom, wanton cruelty, injustice, and the final defeat of God.

The apostle's sovereign affirmation concerning the Father's unfathomable generosity, leading to a potent question about our boundless reasons for hope, would seem to contain everything about the event that is simultaneously world-shattering and world-regenerating. Taken together, the two verbs παρέδωκεν (*parédôken*—"hand over") and χαρίσεται (*charísetai*—"graciously grant"), here used within the same sentence, appear to cover the full gamut of God's lavish love. The extravagant open-endedness of Paul's question ("Will he not also [graciously grant] us all things [along] with him?") seems to imply that *God exists only in order to give*, and to give not only created goods and benefits but what he himself holds most precious: the one and only Son of his Heart. In giving us Jesus, God is giving us nothing less than himself, the uncreated Lord, and the fullness of life of the Godhead.

The believer's first impulse before the mystery unfolding on the Cross, as I have said, is to abide in stunned silence. Nevertheless, the evangelist brings the person of our Lord, his crucified presence, and the mysteries of his life and death so close to us that their vivid presentation urgently prods some response from the distraught silence of our hearts. The crucifixion of God both shuts our mouth and shakes us out of our torpor. When the Word that made the universe cries out in torment, can we be mum? We want to run and hide, but there is no place left to hide. There is no safe place to weather out this particular storm, which seeps into the most secret interstices of creation. Superabundant grace has excluded every possibility of escape from the horror. Together with Jesus, we too must pass *through* the horror if we are ever to reach the far side of hope and light. Precisely because we cannot remain indifferent in the face of such an unimaginable event, *we must speak*, if only to stutter. Stuttering, or merely grunting or sighing, before the distressing Mystery may yet be the highest form of praise.

In contrast to the raging crowds, which take pleasure in hurling words like barbed arrows at the man on the Cross, all-encompassing Nature—the earth, the sky, the sun, and the enveloping air we take for granted—responds sympathetically, even reverentially, to the plight of its Creator and Savior. It is as if God, disowned by man, has to fall back on the support of elemental creation. In fact, more than one feature of the present narrative by Matthew easily transports us, no doubt surprisingly, back to the first page of Genesis and the beginning of the world. Let us survey the scene more closely against the background of the earth's first moments of existence.

We have already suggested that God's surrender of his omnipotent Word into the hands of violent mockers has transformed the created world into a "realm of incongruity" that amounts to a kind of *de-creation*: on Golgotha and to the ends of the earth, God-assigned values and identities are suspended and dark forces now hold sway. The protracted silence of the Martyr-Word has allowed the world to fill up with all manner of strident blasphemy. The shameless lie now triumphs. But during this interval—timed by Matthew between noon and three in the afternoon—literal *darkness* comes "over all the land", and this physical phenomenon becomes an epiphany of the reign of evil. The phrase ἐπὶ πᾶσαν τὴν γῆν (*epí pásan tên gên*) here translated "over all the land", can just as precisely be rendered "over all the earth", and this nuance would expand the commiseration of nature for her Savior infinitely beyond the confines of Palestine. At this point, only nature speaks transparently and says that, at least for the moment, darkness has won in the cosmic battle because hatred has defeated love and the great lie has swallowed up the truth. When Christ the Light dies, all creation dies with him.

Moreover, as I have hinted, this *darkness* (σκότος—*skótos*) that suddenly covers *all the earth* (πᾶσαν τὴν γῆν—*pásan tên gên*) strongly evokes the biblical context of the beginning (ἀρχή—*archê*) of time and all things, when "God created the heavens and the earth" (ἐν ἀρχῇ ἐποίησεν ὁ Θεὸς τὸν οὐρανὸν καὶ τὴν γῆν, Gen 1:1). At that moment, too, as on Golgotha now, "the earth [was] without form and void." This chaos of the very beginning of creation, however, consisted in the hopeful expectation of shapeless things as they innocently and eagerly awaited the fashioning hands of the Creator. It is, indeed, at another level, the ground-zero interior situation of the soul to which all Christian prayer yearns to return, the spiritual locus where the human heart again becomes malleable and full of divinely creative possibility.

But the terrible amorphousness of Golgotha, by extreme contrast, defines a gruesome condition of negative deformity that results from the murder and disfigurement of the Word that alone imparts both form and, with it, meaning. Creation necessarily falls apart when its in-forming and sustaining Principle perishes. The darkness that in Genesis hung "over the abyss" (Gen 1:2, NAB) was like a cosmic Paschal night, throbbing with hope, keenly awaiting the unfolding of the Creator's design to create the light-streaming sun and the rest of God's very beautiful conceptions. But this godless darkness that spreads to the whole earth from Golgotha is Satanic in that what it diffuses is the unthinkable extinction of the divine Light.

In Genesis, "the Spirit of God was moving over the face of the waters"; but here on Golgotha, Jesus, when he "cries out with a loud voice", sends forth his personal Spirit—his very Breath as creating Word—*to hover maternally over the blood from his divine Heart*. This blood flows in torrents upon the grim and battered earth in order to bestow new life on creation. The Spirit and the Blood work together in order to renew the universe. The Blood that Jesus emits from his arteries, the Breath and the cry that he sends forth from his throat at the moment of his death, are the sensory, bodily realities that bear the strongest witness possible to the fact that, in giving us Jesus, the Father has given us everything conceivable.

The darkness of Golgotha, in pushing to its outermost limits the worst that human hatred can accomplish, in a real sense *exhausts* that hatred and returns creation to the void of the beginning, a space "washed . . . in the blood of the Lamb" (Rev 7:14) where God's powerful Spirit may now engage in the work of re-creation. This work, however, is only now just beginning, in the midst of the darkness and the horror. Who can detect its activity? Jesus said to Philip, "He who has seen me has seen the Father" (Jn 14:9). Yet, here on Calvary, who has the eyes of faith that can pierce through the gore and see the Father by looking into the mangled face of the beloved Son?

Two fundamental events, one of darkness and one of light, occur simultaneously when Jesus dies on the Cross. First, his human nature is humiliated and crushed. Along with it there necessarily dies every shred of purely human hope. The humiliation and murder of the Son of God, the Messiah, at the hands of men makes "the day of the Lord" descend on the earth on this first Good Friday, a day of vindication and purification that fulfills the prophecy of Amos, when God will establish his justice definitively on earth. " 'And on that day,' says the Lord GOD, 'I will make the sun go down at noon, and darken the earth in broad daylight' " (Amos 8:9). This is the theological importance of Matthew's timing the great darkness of Good Friday between noon and mid-afternoon, precisely the time when the sun should be shining at full strength. The death of the Son of God convulses the course of nature. The material sun obediently allows the transcendental event to burst through normal temporal cycles and reveal God's awful judgment by means of a universal and unnatural gloom.

But the other event that occurs simultaneously with the crushing of Christ is the bursting through the darkness of the uncreated, divine Light. This advent of the Light does not, of course, happen in a manner perceptible to the senses, by means of some melodramatic *deus ex machina* procedure or some form of miraculous illumination such as we saw on Tabor. But the Light of God does, nonetheless, pierce through in a far more effective way in Matthew's kerygmatic reference to the breaking open of the tombs and the rising of many dead (vv. 52–53) as the explicit result of Jesus' own Resurrection, an event suddenly (and somewhat shockingly) anticipated in v. 53, in the midst of our sorrow within Golgotha's gloom. We shall return to this reference in due course.

In the meantime, we are utterly taken aback by the unpredictable manner in which God chooses to establish his justice definitively on earth, a divine intention proclaimed prophetically by the darkness at noon. Far from engaging in wholesale vengeance for the murder of his beloved Son, something that might have been logically expected and for which there is an unsettling image in the Parable of the Wicked Tenants (cf. Lk 20:13–16),[2] the Father instead *has mercy on all*. "As one man's trespass led to condemnation for all men," writes Paul,

---

[2] "Then the owner of the vineyard said, 'What shall I do? I will send my beloved son; it may be they will respect him.' But when the tenants saw him, they said to themselves, 'This is the heir; let us kill him, that the inheritance may be ours.' And they cast him out of the vineyard and killed him. What then will the owner of the vineyard do to them? He will come and destroy those tenants, and give the vineyard to others."

"so one man's act of righteousness leads to acquittal and life for all men" (Rom 5:18). Indeed, out of the heart of the chaotic darkness brought on by human iniquity, the Father makes to rise "the sun of righteousness . . . with healing in its wings", "to give light to those who sit in darkness and in the shadow of death" (Mal 4:2; Lk 1:79).

Before the sun of salvation can rise, however, and before divine Light can penetrate the being of fallen man, the full extent of the darkness of iniquity has to be revealed, and this is what happens when Jesus dies on the Cross crushed by man's rejection of him. Jesus' tormented face on the Cross and the immobility of his hands and feet nailed to wood proclaim loudly both the reach of the human capacity to inflict evil and God's infinite capacity to forgive and heal, after first bearing the wounds of sin in his flesh. The body of Jesus has to be repeatedly pierced in order for it to give forth the divine light and love it contains. If the spiritual dictum is true that, in our own experience of grace, "God enters through the wounds" of painful events and defeats, this truth is but the corollary of the fact that the life of God first went out with full force into the world through the wounds inflicted by mankind on Jesus' body. The simultaneity of the two events makes creation hold its breath: "He was crucified in weakness, but lives by the power of God" (2 Cor 13:4). Only where human nature has been voided of all delusions and extraneous contents can the life of God flood in unimpeded.

Christ makes himself deliberately vulnerable so that the power of his Father's love might shine into the world through his wounds. We have always been wonderfully comforted at reading in St. John's Prologue that "the light shines in the darkness, and the darkness has not overcome it" (Jn 1:5). We also find great consolation at hearing Jesus declare later in that Gospel: "I am the light of the world" (Jn 9:5). For, who would not want to be a disciple of that Light and feel utterly safe in him against the forces of darkness? But, though we are assured of God's ultimate victory, we never imagined what it would cost the Incarnate Light of Divinity, in terms of heartache, humiliation, and bodily harm, to engage in the battle unto death with evil. Only the atrocious Passion and death of the eternal Word could insure the triumph of the Light and, through it, the full revelation of God's nature as boundless Love. In the sublime hymn at the beginning of his Letter to the Colossians, St. Paul extols Christ as "the image (εἰκὼν—*eikôn*, visible representation) of the invisible God" (Col 1:15), an affirmation fraught with marvelous tension against the iconoclastic Jewish background. In our present context, we must underscore categorically that Christ is indeed the visible manifestation and revelation of the invisible God, not *except* during his humiliation and death on the Cross, but *especially then*, when the telltale signs of God's presence are holes in hands and feet, a fist-sized wound on the side, and a primal bellow of misery and trust emerging from the depths of God's created human soul. Christ's exhaustive downward *Kénôsis* (or "self-emptying") on the Cross is the painfully precise and utterly accurate manifestation of the upwardly soaring *Plêrôma* that is God's Being—the "Fullness" of the unfathomable Abyss of Divine Love. As von Balthasar remarks with his usual razor-sharp precision: "Through the suffering flesh of Christ the Father's light reaches us." [3]

This double event that takes place on Golgotha—the chaotic unleashing of the forces of darkness and the first glimmer of the Resurrection of Him Who Is Light—manifestly resets the stage of the world back to the *Archê*, the beginning of creation, the first Day of days when "God said, 'Let there be light'; and there was light" (Gen 1:3). In both cases—at the *Archê* and on Calvary—a creating and shaping word is spoken by God. In Genesis, this word was "Let there be light", uttered omnipotently yet with infinite serenity by the Lord of creation out of the depths of his eternal peace and benevolence. There was no theomachy at the origin of creation, no battle between contending deities, because the Lord who creates is only One. In the Judæo-Christian revelation, creation occurs out of sheer creative generosity. The one and only God wields an authority and a power capable of calling forth and forming something good and beautiful and useful out of nothingness. On Golgotha, on the other hand, the struggle is mighty because the love in Jesus' Heart has to overcome the opposition of contrary forces amassed against love's supremacy over all the millennia of human history, beginning at the Fall in Eden.

The King of Love will paradoxically win this battle only by allowing himself to be defeated and hurled into the jaws of death. This act of sacrificial self-surrender for the common good was prefigured by

---

[3] Hans Urs von Balthasar, *The Glory of the Lord: A Theological Aesthetics*, vol. 2, Studies in Theological Style: Clerical Styles, trans. Andrew Louth et al. (New York: Crossroad; San Francisco: Ignatius Press, 1984), 70.

Jonah's generosity, when he said to the mariners in the midst of the raging storm: "Take me up and throw me into the sea; then the sea will quiet down for you; for I know it is because of me that this great tempest has come upon you" (Jon 1:12). But Jesus' gift of self outdoes Jonah's immeasurably because, far from himself being responsible for the impending danger, Jesus rather takes on himself the guilt of all. In Jesus, love defeats hatred precisely by not responding in kind and by applying the courage necessary to allow itself to be assaulted and physically destroyed. But it is only then that the paradox can shine most magnificently, as the crushing of the fragile vessel of Jesus' body results in the outpouring of the elixir of immortality it contains: this is the antidote to death and the nourishment of life eternal. "You know that you were ransomed from the futile ways inherited from your fathers, not with perishable things such as silver or gold, but with the precious blood of Christ, like that of a lamb without blemish or spot" (1 Pet 1:18–19).

The King of Love rules only as the slain Lamb who has drowned the power of sin in his blood. "Worthy is the Lamb who was slain, to receive power and wealth and wisdom and might and honor and glory and blessing!" (Rev 5:12). Not only as risen and glorified Man, but already as God, Jesus Christ receives the doxology of all creation as the Paschal Lamb who has been sacrificed. The sacrifice of the second Person of the Blessed Trinity, the cosmic shedding of his redemptive blood, is a mystery of salvation and a mystery of the interior life of the Trinity that is never left behind as having been a merely instrumental event. Ever since the sacrifice on Golgotha, the creation of the world in Genesis and its recreation by the Word's willing death on the Cross are inseparable events. Together, the two moments constitute a single, divinely initiated and enacted Act of Creation whereby life, both natural and supernatural, is dispensed.

The opening sentence of Genesis affirms, "In the beginning (*Archê*) God created the heavens and the earth." Here the word *beginning* refers to far more than simply the setting in motion of things and events in time. More specifically, this crucial word *Archê* of the Greek Bible designates the principle and foundation from which all things flow. It is only this extensive flowing-forth of things from their Principle that secondarily gives the word its temporal meaning. In the opening of St. John's Gospel, we read: "In the beginning (*Archê*) was the Word" (Jn 1:1), and here it is difficult to doubt that the evangelist wanted explicitly to refer to the first page of Genesis when setting out to write his Gospel. The theological reason for this deliberate parallelism is clear. From the outset, St. John wants to proclaim the fact that through all of his words and deeds, and by virtue of the very presence of his person in the world, Jesus, the incarnate Logos sent by the Father, aimed at nothing less than creating the world anew through the power of God's love that inhabited him and determined his every move.

At the end of the sixth day of creation, God joyfully contemplated all the work of his hands: "God saw everything that he had made, and behold, it was very good" (Gen 1:31). The same joyful divine purpose may be heard from Jesus' lips as he declares: "I came that they may have life, and have it abundantly" (Jn 10:10). In both instances, we witness God's burning desire to bestow life and take joy in that life as constituting his exclusive intention in both the creation and the redemption. By glaring contrast, other creation accounts from various religious traditions typically represent the making of man by preternatural beings as a strategy to meet those deities' needs for sustenance, servitude, or flattery. Only the Judæo-Christian LORD bestows being expecting nothing but personal love in return, and even that expectation is for the sake of the creature and not the Creator!

Thus we must read Matthew's text relating Jesus' crucifixion and death on Golgotha as the central panel of a triptych of which the left leaf is the Creation Story in Genesis and the right leaf is the Prologue of St. John's Gospel. For, Jesus Christ is always and everywhere the eternal creating Word, whether in his appearance of dazzling glory or in his appearance of humiliated defeat. In either circumstance, the Word is always and only *bestowing life*: "All things were created through him and for him. He is before all things, and in him all things hold together. He is the head of the body, the Church; he is the beginning (*Archê*, the Principle, the Foundation), the first-born from the dead, that in everything he might be pre-eminent" (Col 1:16–18). Just as the Father *spoke the Word* over the abyss of darkness in the beginning "and there was light", so too on Golgotha, the Father *speaks his Word* into the world and floods it with Light and Life. But the form in which the Father speaks his all-powerful Word into the world on Golgotha is the cry that Jesus emitted "about the ninth hour . . . with a loud voice, . . . 'My God, my God, why have you forsaken me?'"

How, any reasonable person might ask, *how* can this cry possibly be full of powerful Light and Life, when it appears to be precisely the sign of defeated despair? How can it possibly be a *creating* word? And why does the uttering of this cry from Jesus' human and divine depths show him forth as truly being the *Archê*, the dynamic Principle, Foundation, and Source of a new creation? The short answer is: *Because that cry out of the depths of suffering and rejection proclaims the Word's abiding fidelity to the Father.*

Jesus went to the far end of the night of human dejection, abandonment, and distress in order there, and nowhere else, to manifest his indestructible love for the Father as sole Source of Life. As Jesus drowns in feelings of utter abandonment, universal rejection, and existential nullification, the Spirit of Love within Jesus hurls forth the deepest cry of his Heart, the strongest possible affirmation of the reality of God as sole source and support of all life, particularly when that divine Reality appears to be most distant and inaccessible.

Jesus' love for his Father at this moment triumphs over every form of separation, darkness, suffering, and seeming abandonment. Jesus' love conquers all obstacles to his union with God by the simple fact that in this, his final hour, as he flounders in the throes of death, the Lord does not appeal to any created consolation or source of power or support, nor does he yield to the temptation to despair. Rather, he confronts the dark void sucking him in and, instead of succumbing inertly to these destructive forces, into that void he mightily hurls his love's ultimate affirmation concerning the source of his own being. Into the gloom he shouts: *Eli! Eli!—My God! My God!* That almighty cry was no doubt what tore the veil of the temple, what made the earth shake and split the rocks, and what brought forth the bodies of the saints from their graves. This cry of Jesus as he dies is of a kind with the loud command that put life into Lazarus and made him emerge from his tomb: "[Jesus] cried with a loud voice, 'Lazarus, come out'" (Jn 11:43). Both texts use the expression φωνῇ μεγάλῃ (*phônê megálê*—"with a loud voice"), and in both cases the cry signifies the triumph of the power of God's creating love in Jesus over the forces of destruction and death.

The moment of Jesus' death is also the culmination of his prayer life on earth, "prayer" now having become sheer, brutally elemental clinging to the Source of all life, against all odds. By dying in this way, Jesus establishes a new foundation for human life, not only setting for all time to come an example of admirable, pious behavior in the face of death, but actually *infusing into human nature* the ability to transcend all temporal distress and decay and rise from death to new life in Christ, the ever-faithful Son. It is in this sense that the crucified Jesus becomes the definitive *Archê*, the living Principle and Source of a new creation. Henceforth, no one will ever have to lie alone, forsaken, and in despair, because Jesus transformed his own awful desolation and forsakenness into a place of vibrant appeal to the Father, and Jesus' desolation and forsakenness by definition contain all other desolation and forsakenness. The truth that *all death can henceforth become an occasion of new life* is no longer a mere poetic dream or religious wishful thinking or dogmatic speculation, but is hard historical and ontological *fact*, guaranteed by the spilt blood of Jesus and his world-convulsing cry from the Cross.

At the conclusion of his earthly life, Jesus reveals the innermost secret of the Holy Trinity, which is what he came to accomplish. He does it by pouring his life out as a sacrifice, and this as the only road he could take to complete his earthly mission and return—now rich with a harvest of humanity—to the Father's embrace. The trinitarian secret in question is that *the Three Persons cannot live and enjoy their divine intercommunion to the exclusion of their beloved creature, fallen man.* Even in its waywardness and loss, mankind still bears within itself the precious image of God that the Creator inscribed within it in the beginning when he blew into Adam's nostrils the Breath of Life. Jesus could return to the Father only by the road that led through human death as the shortest distance his love could find. This free act of self-surrender on his part both fulfills his mission as the Messiah sent by the Father and subsumes into itself all human darkness and suffering of all times and places, so as to redeem and glorify them. The *splendor* of this revelation is so intense that, on Golgotha on the first Good Friday, it can be perceived by human eyes only as the deepest and most disorienting *darkness*, what some mystics call the paradoxical "bright darkness of Divinity".

ELI, ELI, LEMA SABACHTHANI? The cry of Jesus from the Cross is recorded by Matthew in a mixed Aramaic-Hebrew form. These opening Semitic words of Psalm 22[21], in Greek transcription, stand out oddly from Matthew's text, floating on an ocean of authentic Greek words. Their very foreignness produces a powerful, mysterious effect on Gentile readers. The evangelist seems to strain to hear and record the very *sounds* of the words the Son of God uttered as he died, and not only their meaning. Jesus' divine nature never neutralizes his humanity. He is very much an individual Galilean from his time and place. As such, Jesus shows himself to be very much a devout Jew to the last breath. He embodies not only (from above) the eternal Word that inspired all the Scriptures but also (from below) the human Messiah who fulfills their every promise. At this moment, he assumes into his Heart and emits through his mouth the accumulated human sorrows of all eons. His infinite divine Being has on his humanity the effect of expanding his Heart endlessly until it breaks; and yet the cry that marks this shattering is not an act of rebellion and outrage but, rather, a visceral act in praise of the One by whom he feels abandoned.

Taken as a whole, Psalm 22[21] is a canticle of praise and thanksgiving and not a dirge of despair. The lament *My God, my God, why have you forsaken me?* is only the psalm's opening. For any pious Jew, and thus for Jesus also, the first words of this psalm or any psalm spontaneously evoke the thrust of the whole composition. As the prayer progresses, it eventually contains utterances that show the abandoned soul being slowly extricated from its woe and celebrating with great jubilation the effective succor that is already felt to be coming from God, as in these final verses: "The afflicted shall eat and be satisfied; those who seek him shall praise the LORD! May your hearts live for ever! All the ends of the earth shall remember and turn to the LORD; and all the families of the nations shall worship before him" (Ps 22[21]:26–27). Such is not the conclusion that unaided human reason would have predicted judging from the psalm's beginning!

Now, precisely because of who he is and what his death means, Jesus prays Psalm 22[21] as no one else ever had or ever would. We may say that the full power of the opening cry of dereliction reaches its climax only now that it comes forth from Jesus' mouth, and it does so as an affirmation of unwavering faith. The fact that Matthew quotes the words in a mixture of Aramaic and Hebrew grounds the Son's woeful lament in the depths of his human nature as an Israelite. In this cry of woe, we hear Jesus, the most believing of Jews, appeal with full heart to his God, and, simultaneously, we hear the eternal Son entreat his beloved Father with the undying love of a grateful, obedient child. Especially at this moment, the two natures cannot be separated because on their sustained unity depends the redemption of the world. In Jesus' one cry, we hear both God writhing in pain and man hoping for deliverance. *Communicatio idiomatum*, the ancient Fathers said: what is proper to the one nature also becomes the experience of the other within the unity of the single Person. The apparent abandonment by the Father, already beginning to flood Jesus' Heart in the terrible silence of Gethsemane, here reaches its peak of dread and becomes infinitely more painful than the physical cruelty of the soldiers or the raging contempt of the mob. These relatively secondary wounds were, after all, inflicted by mere humans. But the abandonment by the Father, which is the divine dagger that slays the Lamb, belongs to a properly trinitarian order of experience.

This is the first time Jesus has uttered any word since the night of Holy Thursday, when he briefly responded to Pilate concerning his identity as King of Israel. The gentle affirmation of his kingship is the last word that Jesus speaks to other human beings before his death. It is curious that the religious authorities seem not to grasp that Jesus is appealing to his Father with words from Ps 22[21]. When he says *Eli*, which means "My God", they think he is uttering the first two syllables of the name of the prophet Elijah. The scribes and Pharisees have nearly always gotten wrong everything Jesus has ever said, because they and Jesus exist on two different planes. For hours, now, they have been daring Jesus to appeal to his Father for salvation, and yet when Jesus does so, they do not realize what is happening despite Jesus' use of a well-known canonical text. While Jesus, with typical straightforward simplicity, limits himself to presenting his abandonment to the Father in the strongest possible terms, the authorities fantasize that Jesus is calling on Elijah to swoop down from heaven in a whirlwind and carry him off to salvation in a chariot of fire (cf. 2 Kings 2:11). This *deus ex machina* performance is the only kind of "proof" of Jesus' divine sonship they are prepared to accept. But Jesus himself seeks no escape from his plight. His last act on this earth before his death is to turn his whole being toward his beloved Father with an impassioned *Why?* His "salvation" consists in never breaking communion with his Source, even in the depths of abandonment and in the face of death.

27:48   καὶ εὐθέως δραμὼν εἷς ἐξ αὐτῶν καὶ λαβὼν σπόγγον
πλήσας τε ὄξους καὶ περιθεὶς καλάμῳ
ἐπότιζεν αὐτόν

one of them at once ran and took a sponge,
filled [it] with vinegar, and put [it] on a reed,
and gave it to him to drink

T HEY GAVE ME GALL FOR FOOD, and for my thirst they gave me vinegar to drink", we read in Psalm 69[68]:21, as the Just One complains to God about one of his tortures. Is the gesture of this man who brings Jesus vinegar to drink necessarily to be understood as a final insult added to the long list of those Jesus has already endured? In the parallel text in Mark 15:36, we note a significant difference. While in Mark it is the same person who both runs to fill a sponge with vinegar and also jeers at Jesus for allegedly invoking Elijah's help, in Matthew the man who gets the vinegar does only that while "the others" stop him from his deed in order to see whether Elijah will come. And in Luke "the soldiers also mocked him, coming up and offering him vinegar" (Lk 23:36), while in Matthew "the centurion and those who were with him" eventually recognize him, full of awe, as "the Son of God". Matthew then clearly sets the vinegar-bearing man and the soldiers apart from the scoffing majority. Why? I think it is because they show sympathy for, and perhaps even faith in, Jesus.

The French original (*vin aigre*) from which English derives the word "vinegar" means "sour wine", and this reminds us that in former times vinegar was simply wine that had turned sour. Vinegar preserved some of the qualities of wine, including the ability to have a sedative or numbing effect. Its greater acidity made it even superior to wine as a natural disinfectant for cleaning and healing wounds. Against this background, we remember that Matthew frequently introduces into his narrative starkly contrasting attitudes and actions in order to provoke in us, the readers, a crisis of conscience with regard to Jesus. It seems, therefore, in keeping with this technique for the evangelist at this point to single out one anonymous character who stands out from the bleak crowd of mockers and exhibits a glimmer of compassion to the man on the cross.

In this sense, the vinegar-bearer may be said to soften the unmitigated heartlessness of Golgotha, thereby anticipating the full act of faith of the centurion and his companions in v. 54. Why would vinegar have been at hand at all in this place and time? Only to add insult to injury? Or could it have been standard procedure to administer vinegar to the condemned as a humane detail and perhaps also to give the horrible penalty of crucifixion some aura of legality and civilized behavior? It is ironical, indeed, that Jesus the Messiah, who only a few hours before gave his own life to his disciples in the sweet wine of the Eucharist, should himself in his agony be offered nothing but sour vinegar. Nevertheless, the fact that the man runs "at once" for vinegar on hearing the howl from Jesus' chest and that others try to stop him persuades me that he means it as a spontaneous gesture of compassion to numb Jesus' pain and ease his passage into death.

27:50   ὁ δὲ Ἰησοῦς πάλιν κράξας φωνῇ μεγάλῃ
ἀφῆκεν τὸ πνεῦμα

*And Jesus cried out again with a loud voice
and yielded up [his] spirit*

THIS SECOND AND FINAL TIME that Jesus cries out from the Cross, he speaks no words of Scripture; in fact, he speaks no words at all. His feeling of abandonment by the Father, together with the quick onset of death, has pushed him into a dismal region beyond the reach of words. The whole being of the eternal *Logos*—in whom and by whom all things were created and from whom the universe receives its consistency and meaning (cf. Col 1:16–17)—has now become *alogical*, a single primal kenotic scream wedding agony to trust.

However, in an unexpected reversal analogous to the two inseparable meanings of *parádosis* we have explored at length, Jesus' howl out of abysmal pain and dereliction is at the same time the vehicle by which he sends forth his Spirit (*Pneuma*)—his very life's Breath (*Pneuma*)—into the world. Golgotha is the place where violent, diabolical hatred defeats the incarnate God; but simultaneously, it is the place where hatred's aggression is made instrumental in diffusing throughout the universe, and for all time to come, the incarnate Word's Blood and Breath, which contain the very Life of God. For, as the Psalmist exclaims to the Lord, "all things are your servants" (Ps 119[118]:91), and this includes all that we judge to be good and all that we judge to be evil. Nothing escapes the sway of God's providence.

This is why the great christological hymn from Colossians leads to a climax that harmonizes the two essential aspects of Christ's death (the destructive and the life-giving) that make it a true sacrifice: "For in him all the fulness (τὸ Πλήρωμα) of God was pleased to dwell, and through him to reconcile to himself all things, whether on earth or in heaven, making peace by the blood of his cross" (Col 1:19–20). In the blood flowing from the human body of Jesus, it is the omnipotent and all-transforming Fullness of Divinity, the inner Life of God itself, which streams out over the world. And the flowing of the blood goes hand in hand with the primal bellow from Jesus' breast, which sends his Creator Spirit bounding forth joyfully to refashion a new creation out of the old.

The particular meaning of Jesus' act of expelling his last breath in Matthew can best be seen by contrast to the same event as found in Mark (15:37). Here we read that Jesus ἐξέπνευσεν, that is, "breathed his last" or "expired", an English verb derived from the Latin *exspirare* and thus sharing the same root as "spirit". Poignant as this Marcan verb is in this context, nevertheless it pales next to the force of Matthew's more explicit phrase ἀφῆκεν τὸ πνεῦμα (*aphêken to pneúma*—"he surrendered" or "gave up the breath = spirit)". In comparison to this powerful wording, Mark's verb appears neutral, almost passive, as if Jesus suffered his moment of death merely as the necessary end of a natural physiological process of progressive weakening and organ deterioration.

The latter process is, of course, true as well, and the two senses are wholly compatible. But Matthew chooses, instead, to highlight the rich theological dimension of the physiological act of expiration. From this perspective, the power of death does not overcome Jesus as passive victim, but rather Jesus remains the active and forceful protagonist of his own life to the very end, sovereignly in control of the event of his own dying. The timing and power of two loud cries he emits just before dying imply that Jesus chooses the moment of his death.

These cries are full, not only of sorrow and pain, but also of determination and strength of will, and this is why Jesus' sorrow is itself redemptive: "No one takes [my life] from me, but I lay it down of my own accord. I have power to lay it down, and I have power to take it again; this charge I have received from my Father" (Jn 10:18). Simple suffering, simple bloodshed, do not on their own make for redemption; it is the identity of the divine and human Sufferer and his unswerving intentionality and fidelity to his Father that transform mere destruction into atoning sacrifice. Thus, Jesus in Matthew continues to show to the very end the control over his destiny he has exhibited throughout the Gospel, as expressed in his repeated prophecies concerning the necessity of his Passion and death (cf. 17:22–23; 20:18; 26:2). Moreover, this "control" never bears the character of a self-affirming act of autonomous and headstrong decision making.

We are, after all, speaking of the One for whom obedient, divine sonship is the very core of his being! Jesus choosing to give his life specifically on the Cross on Golgotha, and specifically at three o'clock in the afternoon on the first Good Friday, is synonymous with the most profound act possible of self-entrustment and obedience to God, as he himself states: "This charge I have received from my Father."

The active and deliberate surrender of his life to the Father via a sacrificial death is most dramatically expressed in his cry of abandonment. The Spirit he entrusts to God can arrive at its destination in the Father's Heart by no road other than that which leads through the desolate Heart of Man. In his one act of expiration, Jesus is simultaneously surrendering his whole being to the Father *and* bestowing his Life's Breath upon the world. In precisely this did the world's reconciliation with God consist, and in precisely this unthinkable manner was it accomplished.

Is it any wonder, then, that, when the Gospel of the Passion is proclaimed in the liturgical assembly, Christians around the world fall down on their knees or prostrate themselves fully on the ground at hearing the world-transforming words, "And Jesus cried out again with a loud voice and yielded up his Spirit"? This is no mere ritual act of devotion. By falling energetically to the ground in awe and gratitude, we choose humbly to place ourselves again in the dark and amorphous state of the beginning of creation, to allow the Creator Spirit to hover over us once more, and to beg for God's expertly shaping hands to refashion our whole being in the image of Christ, the first-born of the new creation: "For those whom he foreknew he also predestined to be conformed to the image of his Son, in order that he might be the first-born among many brethren" (Rom 8:29). If Christ does not rise from death within us, thereby investing us with our new identity as those who have risen with him, then his Passion and death have been for naught.

THE NET VERSION OF THE PRESENT VERSE is, "Then Jesus *cried out* (κράξας—*kráxas*) again with a loud voice and gave up his spirit", while its version of the first cry is, "At about three o'clock Jesus *shouted* (ἀνεβόησεν—*anebóêsen*) with a loud voice . . ." (27:46). This is the only contemporary English version I have found that distinguishes between the two verbs conveying Jesus' cry, as well it should, since the Greek original uses two very different verbs here: ἀναβοάω for the first cry and κράζω for the second. As reason for his choice of different words to evoke the same repeated action, Matthew must have had in mind more than superficial stylistic variation. Both verbs refer to loud sounds emitted from the throat, and as such they both imply great energy or passion as the force that impels the act. They signal the opposite of a weak whimper. However, each of them emphasizes a very different modality of making oneself heard.

The first verb, ἀναβοάω (*anaboáô*), means "to shout aloud, utter a loud cry". The specific five-syllable form it assumes in v. 46 (*anebóêsen*) has a prolonged, melodious sound that contrasts emphatically with the related verb in v. 50 (*kráxas*), with its abrupt, two-syllable shrillness. Normally the first of these verbs calls for some intelligible content, such as shouting out a declaration of war (in Xenophon) or some other meaningful communication, as is the case in v. 46, when Jesus utters his sense of abandonment by God by quoting a psalm. Such is the use of ἀναβοάω (*anaboáô*) in the tragedies of Æschylus and Euripides, where the verb signifies a wailing over specific misfortunes. We note, then, that in its pre-Christian history, the word *anaboáô* expressed passionate feelings of either aggression or mourning in belligerent or tragic circumstances.

The use of this verb by Jesus from the Cross in the final moments of his earthly life confers on his death a tragic splendor. It manifests the manner in which the human spirit can transcend physical obliteration and excruciating pain in order to assert its undimmed and energetic interior life. It must have cost the expiring Jesus a great physical and mental effort to emit that cry, which manifests the triumphant power of the spirit over the fading vitality of the flesh. By the same token, the spirit is reaching out to an end higher than death by affirming a purely spiritual relationship with God in dialogical fidelity (*My God, my God!*) and by seeking the deeper, hidden reasons for the present catastrophe (*Why have you forsaken me?*).

In the second cry in v. 50, the verb κράζω (*krázô*) implies a very different plane of expression, even though the context remains the same: Jesus is tragically entrapped in the throes of death. With this reprise, sorrow and agony are no longer being articulately expressed, nor is any cause rationally sought for the present state of things. This present cry of v. 50 may be properly called a *howl*, and its sole function is Jesus' surrender of his life's breath to the world and to the Father. In this terminal exhaling of the breath of life, Jesus is surrendering his whole being definitively to his divine Source and, at the same time, to those he came to vivify. Now these are not two acts but one single act with two aspects. In bestowing his life upon the world through the expiration of his breath, Jesus is fulfilling the precise will of the Father who had sent him into the world for this very purpose. It was *solely for this* that the whole history of salvation was designed, as Jesus affirms in John's Gospel: "I know my own [sheep] and my own know me, as the Father knows me and I know the Father; and I lay down my life for the sheep. . . . For this reason the Father loves me, because I lay down my life, that I may take it again" (Jn 10:14–15, 17).

In this extraordinarily dense statement, we witness the inseparability of Jesus' love for his Father from his love for his brethren, as well as the necessity for Jesus to hand over his life through a sacrificial death in order to communicate his life effectively. The result will be the indwelling in all the redeemed of Father and Son, who symphonically masterminded this plan of redemption: "In that day you will know that I am in my Father, and you in me, and I in you" (Jn 14:20). By virtue of Jesus' death, the indissoluble unity and mutual indwelling of the Persons of the Trinity become available through faith to all mankind. This is what it means to share the very life of God.

But the price for such a gift is that the eternal and omnipotent Word in whom all things were created had first to become word-less within time. The *Logos* had to become *a-logical*; such an internal contradiction implies that, humanly speaking, Jesus risked madness for our salvation. He who is Meaning itself had first to be reduced to muteness and meaninglessness, undergoing in his consciousness a total break in identity. He who is Fullness of Life had first to be emptied of all life and fall into the yawning abyss of nothingness. He who sings to the universe as his beloved Spouse (cf. Song 2:8) and whose mere voice enchants all the stars of the galaxies—"he called them, and they said, 'Here we are!' They shone with gladness for him who made them" (Bar 3:34)—this very One and no other is reduced, by human ferocity and the ardor of his own love, to elemental shrieking in a stifling desert of pain. It was to accomplish this moment of total self-emptying, total self-giving, that "the Word became flesh and dwelt among us" in the first place (Jn 1:14). He became human in order to redeem humanity.

Humanity, however, had fallen so low that its vices and evil desires had plunged the race of Adam to a subhuman level. (Pointedly, the primary meaning of *krázô*, the onomatopoeic verb here predicated of the dying Jesus, refers specifically to the croaking of *frogs*!) Here as in a dark cave, the human spirit, though created to contemplate beauty, generate love, and sing praise, instead was reduced to animalistic subjugation, like the two Gadarene demoniacs who dwelt in tombs, "so fierce that no one could pass that way" (8:28). They, too, are described by the verb *krázô* when they scream at Jesus (8:29). In his death, Jesus has to assume the wild madness of human sin in order to redeem it. He has to surround the beast with the tender love of his divine Heart in order to transform the wolf into a lamb like himself (cf. Is 11:6); but this action shatters his human nature because the embraced beast continues to rage in Jesus' interior.

The sign of this inward shattering is the animalistic howl of the grating verb *kráxas*, which with its frightful clarity and stridency reveals the depth of perdition to which Jesus has descended for our sake. On releasing that scream, both of desolation and of longing unto death, the eternal Word grows dumb and falls into the claws of death; but at once his emitted Breath inspirits the world with new life.

For the commentary on 27:51 (on the tearing of the veil of the Temple), please refer to the section on the stripping of Jesus at 27:35 (pp. 475–86).

א

27:52   καὶ τὰ μνημεῖα ἀνεῴχθησαν
καὶ πολλὰ σώματα τῶν κεκοιμημένων ἁγίων
ἠγέρθησαν

***the tombs also were opened,
and many bodies of the saints who had fallen asleep
were raised***

THE STATEMENT THAT MARKS the death of Jesus in our default RSV version, is: "And Jesus cried again with a loud voice and yielded up his spirit" (v. 50). However, the Greek does not have two parallel verbs in the past ("cried again" and "yielded up"), but rather a participle ("crying out") and a conjugated verb in the aorist ("yielded" or "gave up"). A more literal translation of the statement would therefore be: "And, crying out again with a loud voice, Jesus yielded up his spirit." This means that the two actions of bellowing and of emitting the last breath were simultaneous and not sequential: they practically constituted one single action. It is significant as well that Matthew, rather than use the ordinary verb for "to die" for this occasion, instead chooses the more descriptive circumlocution "yielded [his] spirit", obviously with a theological intent. The mighty scream, in other words, may be said to contain and be the vehicle for the communication of Jesus' Spirit.

By stressing the loudness of the cry, Matthew is underscoring its power, as of one laying claim to his act of dying and using it for his own purposes. Here, in seed form, we see the triumph of Jesus over the power death normally wields over defeated human nature.

Though Jesus' scream from the Cross is indeed a howl of infinite distress and pain, at the same time in its energy we hear "the voice of the LORD . . . upon the waters" as "the God of glory thunders, the LORD, upon many waters" (Ps 29[28]:3). At this point, the voice of Jesus explodes with both the boundless woe of a dying God and the imperious authority of the Creator God of Genesis.

It was necessary to stress in detail the particular character of Jesus' dying cry in order the better to understand what happens next in Matthew's text, and first of all in a strictly formal sense. In due course, we will focus on specific contents and their meaning. As happens frequently, it is the Greek original that alerts us in a forceful way to riches that might otherwise remain half-hidden.

Verse 50, then, signals the moment of death. There, somewhat ironically, we find two *active* verbs (in both the grammatical and the connotative sense) that convey a strong feeling of determination: "to cry out" and "to yield" (or "give up"). Applied to Jesus in this context, even the verb "to yield" suggests an energetic action, since yielding (or giving up) his spirit is portrayed here as a wholly self-motivated and free act. We have the impression of witnessing, not so much a regrettable loss of life, but rather the climactic action that crowns a long-standing and keenly desired mission.

After these verbs have been pronounced and Jesus has died, something quite unusual occurs in the text: namely, the affirmation κράξας ἀφῆκεν τὸ πνεῦμα (*crying out he yielded his spirit*) in v. 50 now unleashes a cascade of no less than nine highly descriptive verbs that tumble down in rapid succession and that structure the rest of the pericope (vv. 51–56). All these verbs are in the aorist tense, most of them in the passive voice, and all except one end with the typical aorist suffix -*thê(san)*, the rhythmic repetition of which gives the passage the sound of a poetic composition. The nine verbs in question are:

1. **ἐσχίσθη** (*eschísthê*, "the curtain of the temple *was torn*", v. 51a),

2. **ἐσείσθη** (*eseísthê*, "the earth *was shaken*", v. 51b),

3. **ἐσχίσθησαν** (*eschísthêsan*, "the rocks *were split*", v. 51c),

4. **ἀνεῴχθησαν** (*aneôchthêsan*, "the tombs *were opened*", v. 52a),

5. **ἠγέρθησαν** (*êgérthêsan*, "bodies of the saints *were raised*", v. 52b),

6. ἐξελθόντες εἰσῆλθον (*exelthóntes eisêlthon*, "*coming out* of the tombs they *went into* the holy city*", v. 53a),

7. ἐνεφανίσθησαν (*enephanísthêsan*, "they *appeared* or *manifested themselves*", v. 53b),

8. ἐφοβήθησαν (*ephobêthêsan*, "they *were afraid*, filled with awe*", 54b), and

9. ἠκολούθησαν (*êkoloúthêsan*, "women who *had followed* Jesus", 55b).

This ninth verb is qualified by two present participles that describe the actions and attitudes of the holy women: θεωροῦσαι (*theôroúsai*, "*looking on* from afar", 55a), and διακονοῦσαι (*diakonoúsai*, "*serving* or *ministering* to him", 55c).

The collective poetic effect of these nine emphatic and polysyllabic verbs, as the evangelist fires them rapidly from his pen, is that of a powerful explosion of words. The formal regularity of the grammatical inflection creates a symmetrical pattern of actions all of which seem to burst out simultaneously, radiating from a single center: Jesus' impassioned and imperious cry on expiring. An apprehension dawns that all of these verbs refer to effects directly generated by the howl of the dying Jesus as their direct cause. That impression, furthermore, is bolstered by the fact that the event of Jesus' death is described, as we have seen, with two very robust active verbs, while the nine verbs that follow the death are mostly in the passive or middle voice, as of things and persons being affected mightily by the action of another.

This is, in fact, the opposite of what one would expect, since we normally see dying as an event of weakness and the shaking of the earth and other such phenomena as mighty acts of nature. Here, instead, Jesus' act of dying is presented by Matthew as deliberate and forceful, while the tearing of the temple veil, the crashing of rocks, and the rising of the dead are all portrayed in the passive voice as actions performed upon things and persons by a mysterious force. Biblical rhetoric calls this grammatical form the "theological passive voice", denoting happenings that have God as their implicit agent. And so, since Jesus' shout and expiration are the immediately antecedent sign of divine intervention, we would have to read the narrative thus: "The curtain of the temple was torn *by Jesus' shout*"; "the earth was shaken *by Jesus' shout*"; "the rocks were split *by Jesus' shout*"; and so forth.

And, on reading that "many bodies of the saints who had fallen asleep were raised, and [came] out of the tombs", how can we not remember the raising of Lazarus? Foreseeing the death of another great man, Julius Cæsar, Shakespeare wrote:

> When beggars die there are no comets seen;
> *The heavens themselves blaze forth the death of princes.*[4]

On the occasion of Lazarus' death, Jesus wept and was deeply troubled in the face of his friend's demise. Then, too, he likewise *"cried with a loud voice, 'Lazarus, come out.' The dead man came out, his hands and feet bound with bandages"* (Jn 11:43–44). And in this very passage, we see Jesus' redemptive death as effecting the *raising* of some corpses from their graves (ἠγέρθησαν—*êgérthêsan*, v. 52), as an anticipation of his own mighty *Resurrection* (τὴν ἔγερσιν αὐτοῦ—*tên égersin autoú*, v. 53). Here the dead *are raised* (namely, by God's power) in the passive voice, while Jesus' *Resurrection* is an active noun that obviously names the dynamic power that worked the raising of those many others. This power, in fact, is so dynamic that it transcends time and can take effect by anticipation, that is, even before Jesus' own Rising has occurred. The same applies to the mystery of our Lady's Immaculate Conception: she was providentially freed from all taint of original sin from the first moment of her life in St. Anne's womb, years before her Son shed his blood in expiation for all sin.

The use of the noun ἔγερσις (*égersis*) by Matthew here, particularly as qualified by the definite article (*"the* rising"), is striking. This nominal form, unlike the verbal narrative form (ἠγέρθησαν—*êgérthêsan*, "they were raised") used to report the raising of the other dead, appears to sound a high kerygmatic note from out of the precise moment of Jesus' death. Its clarion call proclaims the centrality of Jesus' Resurrection for the whole Gospel, as if everything that has preceded in the narrative from the outset had been but a retrospective unfolding of this one mystery about Jesus, which is the great secret and foundation stone of Christian faith.

But unlike Lazarus (Jn 11:1–44) or the son of the widow of Nain (Lk 7:12–16) or Jairus' daughter (Mk 5:22–24), all of whom were raised by Jesus' personal intervention, Jesus himself has no one among mortals who can wrest him from the iron grip of death. In this sense,

---

[4] *Julius Cæsar*, Act 2, Scene 2.

the very Source of Life (Jn 6:51) and the Treasure-house of all riches conceivable (Eph 2:7) is the poorest beggar of all on earth (2 Cor 8:9), once he has emptied himself of all life (Phil 2:7). He knows that only his heavenly Father can raise his soul from Sheol and his body from the tomb, and this is why he bellows out to the vacant sky from the depths of death's abyss: "My God! My God! Why have you abandoned me?"

After such analysis, it is difficult to deny that Matthew presents all the subordinate events described in vv. 51–56 as somehow triggered by the one dominant event of Jesus' death, and specifically his earth-shaking scream together with the forceful exhalation of his Spirit. At this moment, Golgotha has become the center of the universe, the indispensable and inescapable reference point for all mankind and the source of a new creation. The gallows has become a font of future glory, and forevermore a New Humanity will begin to take shape around the sacrificial Cross whence radiates the transforming power of the Son's emitted Breath, thus recapitulating God's action at the dawn of creation:

> A mist went up from the earth and watered the whole face of the ground—then the Lord God formed man of dust from the ground, *and breathed into his nostrils the breath of life; and man became a living soul.* And the Lord God planted a garden in Eden, in the east; and there he put the man whom he had formed. (Gen 2:6–8)

On Good Friday, it is the water and blood from Jesus' Heart that irrigate "the whole face of the earth", and it is the very Breath of the Son, the Holy Spirit, that is infused into man by Christ, the New Adam. Thus Golgotha, formerly a place of misery, gloom, and desolation, has now become the New Eden and the Cross the New Tree of Life, because it was here that the Word, in whom all treasures of goodness and immortality reside, poured himself out, keeping nothing for himself.

Finally, we are struck by the simultaneously catastrophic and auspicious nature of many of these nine verbs depicting the immediate effects of Jesus' death. Like Jesus' death itself, the events described by these verbs instill both horror and promise, in the manner typical of all divine epiphanies. God's overwhelming power is terrifying, but in a way that reveals the intentions of an all-transforming love. The phenomenal events following Jesus' death are revelatory, symbolic of the way in which God is going to communicate new life. Nature (the earth, the rocks, the sky), the ancient covenant (embodied in the temple), and death itself (represented by the bursting tombs) cannot remain indifferent and unaffected at the moment the eternal Word, their Lord, expires. Verbs like "tear", "break open", and "quake" initially dismay us by their violent, destructive character. And yet each of them also introduces us to vast new horizons of existence that remain blocked until old walls and vices and prejudices come tumbling down. All these verbs signal the ending of the old dispensation of Law and the beginning of the new dispensation of grace, in which not only human souls and bodies but the whole created universe participates.

Other accompanying verbs, such as "open up", "arise", and "appear", are in themselves positive and offer a complement to the verbs of destruction. The phenomena of the earthquake, the splitting of rocks, and the resurrection of dead saints signal the arrival of the final age of the world, in which God's justice and grace will reign. Jesus himself had said: "Nation will rise against nation, and kingdom against kingdom, and there will be famines and earthquakes in various places: all this is but *the beginning of the* [*birth-pangs*]" (24:7–8). All these terrible signs nonetheless announce the fearsome purification of the world and the birth of God's Kingdom and its citizenry, fashioned in the image of the New Adam: "As in Adam all die, so also in Christ shall all be made alive" (1 Cor 15:22). In Christ on the Cross, corrupt human nature dies and glorified human nature is reborn— one nature, two radically different conditions. The old world has to dissolve and disappear before a new world can be created:

> And there shall be a time of trouble, such as never has been since there was a nation till that time; but at that time your people shall be delivered, every one whose name shall be found written in the book. And many of those who sleep in the dust of the earth shall awake, some to everlasting life, and some to shame and everlasting contempt. (Dan 12:1)

27:54

Ὁ δὲ ἑκατόνταρχος καὶ οἱ μετ᾽ αὐτοῦ
τηροῦντες τὸν Ἰησοῦν
ἰδόντες τὸν σεισμὸν καὶ τὰ γενόμενα
ἐφοβήθησαν σφόδρα, λέγοντες·
Ἀληθῶς Θεοῦ υἱὸς ἦν οὗτος

When the centurion and those who were with him,
keeping watch over Jesus,
saw the earthquake and the happenings,
they were filled with awe, and said,
"Truly this was the Son of God!"

THE CONFESSION OF FAITH in Jesus by the Roman centurion and his companions takes the specific form of the affirmation: "Truly this was the Son of God!" This is no casual formula. Indeed, it forms a huge inclusion that brackets the whole of the Gospel of Matthew and hearkens back to the first of Satan's temptations of Jesus in the desert of Judea: "If you are the Son of God, command these stones to become loaves of bread" (4:3). On that occasion, too, as now on Golgotha, Jesus was portrayed by Matthew in his vulnerability, weakened by intense hunger. That temptation scene, we recall, followed immediately on the heels of the great epiphany at the Jordan on the occasion of Jesus' baptism, when a voice from heaven was heard, saying, "This is my beloved Son, with whom I am well pleased" (3:17).

The question of Jesus' divine sonship is, thus, the pivot of Matthew's whole Gospel, the *sine qua non* on which all else depends. And between the lines, Matthew seems to be continually asking his reader: "But how can Jesus truly be the Son of God if he seems to be just as vulnerable, weak, and riddled with mortality as any other human being?" This is the quandary Matthew attempts to answer by his portrayal of Jesus' attitudes, deeds, and manner of death throughout his narrative. Yet again we see here that Matthew's deepest intention as evangelist is to put his reader before the critical issue of Jesus' identity as constituting the very essence of salvation. In Kierkegaard's manner, Matthew wants to provoke in his readers a crisis that will urge them to choose sides for or against Jesus, the Son of God—that is, EITHER to come to share the vision of the heavenly Father himself, as proclaimed at the Jordan, and of the Roman centurion and all those in whom the flame of faith is kindled, OR to take sides with Satan and all his cohorts, the nay-sayers and opponents of God's plan of salvation.

The dramatic proclamation of Jesus' divine sonship occurs, moreover, precisely at those moments when Jesus most glaringly manifests his human weakness (at the Jordan, in the wilderness, and on the Cross). This textual strategy shows Matthew's awareness of the great stumbling block Christian faith presents to unaided human reason: namely, that the true Messiah and Son of God in this world necessarily appears as a vulnerable and suffering Servant. He is the embodiment of a divine Omnipotence that most typically reveals itself through a condescending mercy (*misericordia*) that enacts love by making its own the misery (*miseria*) and wounds of suffering mankind. [5] Omnipotence that takes the form of infinite mercy and compassion is a proposition, revealed in the life and death of Christ, that undermines the very foundations of all the world's philosophies and religions as well as the root system of every self-serving instinct in the heart of man.

The verb ἐφοβήθησαν (*ephobêthêsan*, "they were afraid" or "filled with awe") is the eighth verb in the series of nine that, as we have seen, describe various effects triggered by Jesus' dying shout. In the radical conversion to Jesus of the centurion and his companions, we see the first direct fruit of his redemptive death. Their avowal of the truth of Jesus' identity, expressed in the vibrant confession of faith, also substantiates the fact that the catastrophic events that just took place (darkness at noon, quaking of the earth, splitting of the rocks, and Jesus' cosmic howl) all had a salutary finality, despite their initially terrifying shock. Deeply ironical as well is the fact that here, in the heart of Jerusalem and of the Jewish people, it should be a bunch of rough Roman soldiers, wholly ignorant of the revelation to Israel and of the messianic promises, who acknowledge Jesus as Son of God

---

[5] See the collect for the 26th Week in Ordinary Time: "O God, who manifest your almighty power above all by pardoning and showing mercy" (Deus, qui omnipotentiam tuam parcendo maxime et miserando manifestas).

and Source of universal salvation. They represent a classic instance of that biblical virtue of *fear of God* that is said by Sirach to be "the beginning [or foundation] of wisdom" (Sir 1:14).

Their total lack of either political or religious prejudice, coming from age-old ossified traditions, predisposes these simple military men to read with great openness of heart the phenomena that arise before them. Seeing the "earthquake and what took place, they were filled with awe", says the text. They allowed these (literally and figuratively) world-shaking events to invade their hearts and fill them with new light. Without being philosophers or theologians, they instinctively made the correlation between the extraordinary happenings surrounding Jesus' death and Jesus' hidden identity. They saw the world and all reality suddenly crystallize around the shout of the now dead prisoner on the Cross—the prisoner whom they themselves had cruelly mocked and the Cross to which they themselves had nailed him in the routine performance of their duty as Pilate's soldiery. They allowed the convulsive evidence before their eyes and at the gate of their ears to convert their wild and mean passions on the spot into a new energy of faith that must proclaim the Truth that is Christ without regard for any convicting consequences.

Some Fathers of the Church portray this conversion on the part of the centurion and his companions by giving their unexpected behavior a beautiful imaginative twist. They say that, having initially been hired as ruffians tasked by Pilate to carry out Jesus' crucifixion, these Romans were now suddenly transformed, by the sheer power of Jesus' death, into an elite bodyguard *watching over their King as he slept* (τηροῦντες τὸν Ἰησοῦν). In any event, it is a great irony that these first witnesses of Jesus' divine sonship and of the transforming power of his life and death should be pagans who make an explicit act of faith at the foot of the Cross in the presence of the dead Jesus. They express in human language what nature and its elements are saying in their own manner of speaking.

By their confession, suddenly the whole scene on Golgotha is transformed from within, even before Jesus' actual Resurrection, because all of nature and the very people appointed to execute the death sentence have joined in a communion of faith and praise, thus prophesying the conversion of the whole world to Christ. This collective conversion, too, is in a real sense the answer to Jesus' cry of anguish to the Father ("Why have you abandoned me?"), as if the Father were now replying to his beloved Son through the fact of the centurion's transformation: "I abandoned you to the necessary labor pangs, so that in your desolation you might give birth to these new children of light. Now our joy will be complete."

א

27:55–56 Ἦσαν δὲ ἐκεῖ γυναῖκες πολλαὶ
ἀπὸ μακρόθεν θεωροῦσαι,
αἵτινες ἠκολούθησαν τῷ Ἰησοῦ ἀπὸ τῆς Γαλιλαίας
διακονοῦσαι αὐτῷ

There were also many women there,
looking on from afar,
who had followed Jesus from Galilee,
ministering to him

FOUR MASTER STROKES IN MATTHEW'S NARRATIVE of the events on Golgotha shroud the scene in a refreshing mist of benevolence and faith. These subordinate aspects of the plot serve to counterbalance both the horrors heaped on Jesus and the frightful desolation and gloom of the place, which are the correlative symbols of the heartlessness of his aggressors. The first of these four mollifying instances is the action of the man who runs to put vinegar on a sponge so as to numb Jesus' sufferings at least minimally (v. 48). The second is the unashamed and explicit confession of faith in Jesus' divine sonship on the part of the centurion and his companions (v. 54). The fourth will soon be the incident involving the gentle Joseph of Arimathea, who piously took Jesus' corpse, "wrapped it in a clean linen shroud, and laid it in his own new tomb, which he had hewn in the rock" (27:59–60).

And so we look now at the third aspect of the narrative that introduces a soothing effect. It is conveyed by the ninth and final verb from the list of sudden affirmative happenings triggered by Jesus' death. This instance, however, does not really fit into the pattern of the other eight. In this case, we do not really witness any kind of "event", whether physical (like the splitting of rocks) or spiritual (like the confession of faith). Rather, we have to do with a deeply significant *manner of presence* at the Cross of Jesus. The verb in question is ἠκολούθησαν (*êkoloúthêsan*), and it refers to a group of devoted women who have faithfully followed Jesus down from Galilee, probably during the whole of his public ministry, *ministering to him* (διακονοῦσαι— *diakonoúsai*). The next verse names three of the women present (Mary Magdalene, Mary the mother of James and Joseph, and the mother of the sons of Zebedee), although it is clear that "many more" than just these three are in attendance, and they are all "looking on from afar". This third instance of active compassion at Golgotha, then, marked by the verb *êkoloúthêsan*, is not so much a specific *event* occurring along a plot line as it is a dynamic *presence* full of commiseration and love.

If anything, this quality of presence raises the significance of the women's fidelity above that of the other three instances of benevolent actions, because specific actions are confined to one moment, whereas a presence is something abiding and, therefore, manifests a mode of being. At the Cross, only these women bear witness to the fact that they enjoy a long-standing, deeply rooted relationship with Jesus. If they have lovingly ministered (διακονοῦσαι—*diakonoúsai*) to him in the past in any number of practical ways (such as providing money and meals to him and his disciples or welcoming them into their homes), on this occasion, they minister to him in what we may call a purely *contemplative* manner, that is, by the prayer of pure presence and the offering of their hearts' surrender as consolation in Jesus' hour of extreme abandonment. This wholly interior mode of ministry is in fact expressed well by the word θεωροῦσαι (*theôroúsai*, "looking on"). The word refers physically to the women's silent activity as they watch the events from the distance with great distress. Spiritually, however, the word refers to the attitude and quality of heart and soul that the women's insistent contemplation manifests.

The technical Greek word for "contemplation" in the philosophical tradition is in fact *theôría*, used here in its verbal form by Matthew.

These women, then, are not only *looking on* the unfolding of the distressing events; above all and at a deeper level, they are contemplating the scene of Jesus' death, and especially the person of Jesus himself, in all their significance, taking in through the eyes of their souls the torrents of mercy and grace pouring forth from their Savior and lavishing upon him in return all the love and devotion of their hearts. In a wondrous return of favors, these women are now, in his hour of need, ministering to him who is by nature the eternal Minister (*diákonos*) of all. By their manner of presence, by their relentlessly penetrating gaze, and by the unabating fidelity of their life, these women form, at the very end of the Passion narrative, a great inclusion with the virtuous woman with the jar of costly ointment who anointed Jesus at Bethany on the threshold of his Passion (26:6–13). This was the ordinary woman with the extraordinary imagination whose purely symbolic action of love and adoration Jesus praised in extravagant terms: "Truly, I say to you, wherever this gospel is preached in the whole world, what she has done will be told in memory of her" (26:13).

In the face of the aggressiveness and prejudices, with regard to Jesus, of a male-dominated Jewish society, in the face of the brutality and pragmatism of the Roman invaders, and in the face also of the cowardice and irresolution of Jesus' male disciples, the woman at Bethany and this large group of women on Golgotha together offer the world an unsurpassable paradigm of what the Christian identity is in the innermost sanctuary of the heart. This is what Jesus must have meant, at least in part, when he stated so trenchantly that the woman's deed of pure spiritual love and adoration, practiced on his person with a view to his death, would become an intrinsic part of the gospel kerygma. If we are going to be worthy of the name of CHRISTIAN, all of us Christians, whatever else we may do and believe, must in our heart of hearts incarnate the contemplative reality of these exemplary women who knew in their bones that the Father's gift of the Son to us and the Son's gift of himself urgently call for reciprocation on our part in the form of the surrender of our very selves in adoration, thanksgiving, and unconditional love.

At the most practical level of Christian living, we have to work out for ourselves, with the aid of grace, a form of life in which we follow Christ (ἠκολούθησαν—*êkoloúthêsan*) by embodying a foundational *contemplative stance* (*theôría*) that goes hand in hand with a *practice* (*diakonía*) that never tires of bearing fruit in concrete service to the whole Body of Christ incarnate in mankind. The indispensable complementarity of prayerful contemplation and active service in Christian living was captured by Luke in his icon of Martha and Mary (cf. Lk 10:38–42). This same complementarity is symbolized in this passage by Matthew's simultaneous use of the words *theôría* and *diakonía* to describe the two vital activities of the faithful women at the Cross. Such vibrant femininity, at once receptive and creative, is the very soul of creatureliness and of the Church herself and, consequently, also the interior pattern of each Christian's life, regardless of the individual's gender. This unity in Christian life of the contemplation of Christ crucified with ecclesial service is embodied in an exemplary way in the vocation of a great doctor of the Church, on whose feast day we pray as follows: "O God, who set Saint Catherine of Siena on fire with divine love in her contemplation of the Lord's Passion and her service of your Church: grant, through her intercession, that your people, participating in the mystery of Christ, may ever exult in the revelation of his glory."[6]

Matthew honors three of these women by inscribing their names for all time in the text of his Gospel: "Mary Magdalene, and Mary the mother of James and Joseph, and the mother of the sons of Zebedee" (v. 56). With the naming of these generous and relentlessly faithful feminine souls, the harrowing, and yet ultimately consoling, drama of Golgotha draws to an end. Even the mother of the sons of Zebedee seems to have had all her hypermasculine self-interest and opportunism (cf. 20:20–24) wiped clean from her soul by the fire of the Cross. Since her episode of greedy entreaty, her heart must have been torn in two like the veil of the temple by her contemplation of her sons' Lord, Jesus Crucified. Then, from deep within her, hidden streams of unselfinterested loving must have suddenly gushed forth. She has taken to heart, it seems, the teaching that Jesus imparted to her sons on that occasion as a correction to the family's spiritual am-

---

[6] "Deus, qui beatam Catharinam, in contemplatione dominicæ passionis et in Ecclesiæ tuæ servitio, divino amore flagrare fecisti, ipsius intercessione concede, ut populus tuus, Christi mysterio sociatus, in eius gloriæ revelatione semper exsultet" (Collect for April 29).

bitions: "The Son of man came not to be served but to serve, and to give his life as a ransom for many" (20:28). With her rapt presence at Golgotha, she has now replied, not with words, but with her life—by ardent contemplation and commiseration—to the piercing question Jesus asked of her and her sons: "Are you able to drink the chalice that I am to drink?" (20:22).

16. HANDLING GOD WITH TENDER HANDS

The Burial of Jesus (27:57–61)

27:57,
59–60

Ὀψίας δὲ γενομένης
ἦλθεν ἄνθρωπος πλούσιος ἀπὸ Ἀριμαθαίας,
τοὔνομα Ἰωσήφ, ὃς καὶ αὐτὸς ἐμαθητεύθη τῷ Ἰησοῦ . . .
καὶ λαβὼν τὸ σῶμα ὁ Ἰωσὴφ
ἐνετύλιξεν αὐτὸ ἐν σινδόνι καθαρᾷ
καὶ ἔθηκεν αὐτὸ ἐν τῷ καινῷ αὐτοῦ μνημείῳ

When it was evening,
there came a rich man from Arimathea,
named Joseph, who also was a disciple of Jesus . . .
And Joseph took the body,
and wrapped it in a clean linen shroud,
and laid it in his own new tomb

THE TERRIBLE GLOOM OF THAT AFTERNOON of the first Good Friday was, upon Jesus' death, followed by convulsions of the earth and other awe-inspiring phenomena. Matthew then introduces the scene of the many mourning women who have followed Jesus all the way to the Cross. Now they are quietly yet most ardently "watching from afar". Sorrowful as it is, this vivid tableau nevertheless arrives as a welcome mantle of peace descending on the horror of Golgotha. It dispenses the balm of human fidelity and compassion with which, through the ministry of their weeping eyes, the women anoint the wounds of the dead Jesus; and the soft bosom of their feminine devotion nestles his drooping head, riddled with the holes of driven thorns.

Every detail of the narrative relating the recovery and burial of Jesus' body develops our deepening sense of tranquility and relief, infused by the knowledge that the Lord's horrendous Passion has ended. Even the worst evil is always the product of creatures, and as such it is limited and must thankfully come to an end. Only God's "steadfast love endures for ever" (Ps 136[135], *passim*). The onset of evening, Joseph's tender initiative, Pilate's acquiescence, the silent wrapping of Jesus' corpse in a shroud and its swift entombment, the providential availability of a new grave, and the abiding presence of at least two of the women quietly sitting by the tomb: all of these events succeed one another seamlessly and in a profound hush, so that we can barely hear the final rolling-to of the great stone.

It seems that Matthew wants to communicate to his readers a palpable peace: not only the sudden cessation of dramatic suffering, but above all the experience of the harmony that the sacrificial death of Jesus has ushered into the world of sin's chaotic cacophony. We are persuaded by this sudden shift of mood in the narrative to look on all the circumstances surrounding Joseph of Arimathea, down to the shining whiteness of the linen shroud and the newness of the tomb, as a stirring depiction of God's everlasting Mercy coming down ever so gently upon his lifeless Son and, by association with him, upon the whole earth and its inhabitants. This vesperal Mercy, descending on Calvary with the blitheness of snowflakes, is the beginning of the great vivifying embrace that will raise Jesus from the realm of the dead on Easter morning.

And how can we fail to do homage to Joseph of Arimathea? In performing a very humane corporal work of mercy by seeking out and burying the corpse of his beloved Teacher, Joseph becomes for all time a living icon of the eternal Father himself, stooping with compassion to enfold within his throbbing breast the mangled body of his beloved Son, whom he himself handed over to sinners out of love for mankind. At long last, the Son of God on earth has fallen into the hands, not of sinners, but of a just and compassionate man! Joseph of Arimathea enacts the justice and love of God himself. Though the heavenly Father is by definition not directly representable in human form, and though ecumenical councils have repeatedly forbidden such iconographic attempts, nonetheless, Joseph of Arimathea, who in his humanity mirrors the eternal Mercy, may be seen as an adequate and desirable indirect representation of the loving Heart of the Father.

Our conventional pieties are likewise startled in this context by the Latin psalm verse *Expecta Dominum, viriliter age et confortetur cor tuum, et sustine Dominum!* (Ps 27[26]:14, Vulgate), of which a predictable rendering is: "Wait for the LORD; be strong, and let your heart take courage; yes, wait for the LORD!" (RSV). *Sustine Dominum!* Consider Joseph of Arimathea's vocation to take the body of his Lord down from the Cross, to handle it reverently while enshrouding it in dazzling white linen, and then to bury it in his own newly hewn tomb . . . These heartfelt actions on Joseph's part, expressing the deep personal devotion of the disciple for his dead Master, raise to a totally unexpected level of meaning the Psalmist's injunction, *Sustine Dominum!* in St. Jerome's Latin version, which has nourished the prayer of the West for sixteen hundred years.

Although the phrase is usually translated from the Hebrew as "wait for" (RSV), "rely on" (NET), or "put your hope on" the Lord, the Latin suggests a striking alternative, with *Sustine Dominum* meaning "support" or "sustain" the Lord, or even "put up with" (NJB) the Lord. This latter rendering points to a mystery deeper than the formulaic admonition "wait for the Lord" and links the psalm's conclusion directly to the Passion. For the thought that the ardent believer should "support" or "sustain" the Lord indicates precisely the paradoxical inversion that has taken place on Golgotha: here God has made himself weaker and needier than his human creatures and has now, astoundingly, become dependent on their ministry to his helpless, inert condition. Thus Joseph of Arimathea is said to bear tenderly in his mortal hands and dispose carefully of the sacred body of the One by whose mighty hands and outstretched arm the universe was created, "for his mercy endures forever" (Ps 136[135]:12, NAB). Indeed, at this critical juncture in the narrative of Jesus' life, the mercy has to be bestowed *by the creature on the Creator* and dumbfounded reason must, in faith, "put up" with the disconcerting designs of a Lord who chooses to defeat our death by his own dying. "Wait for the LORD; be strong, and let your heart take courage; yes," *sustain the Lord!*

Such is Matthew's *upward* horizon of vision, then: that we should perceive in human, mortal Joseph of Arimathea a faithful reflection of the heavenly Father's invisible mercy. But we see the evangelist equally intent on keeping his narrative grounded as well in a *downward* direction, within time and space and materiality. Early on in the history of Christianity, we can already identify two groups of dissenters from the perennial faith of the Church. One of these, the Gnostics, took an ultra-spiritualistic position that disbelieved the full reality both of Jesus' Incarnation and, consequently, of his death. At the opposite extreme, there were those skeptics, typical of all ages, who were prepared to admire the moral virtues and teachings of Jesus up to a certain point but could ultimately not confess him to be the eternal Son of God, especially not in his death; for what kind of a God could fail in such an egregious manner? Ironically, the two opposing viewpoints coincided in denying the reality of the death (and therefore of the Resurrection) of the Son of God. Within the sobriety of his account, Matthew, by implication, addresses both groups of dissenters as part of his proclamation of the total truth of the drama of Jesus Christ.

As a preparation for the wonder of the Resurrection, Matthew has first to establish the historicity and factuality of Jesus' death. He has already accomplished a large portion of his task by portraying in vivid detail both the humanity and the divine mystery indwelling Jesus inseparably. The trials before Caiaphas and Pilate, the flogging and crowning with thorns, the long way to Calvary in stumbling weakness, the nailing to the Cross and the abundant bleeding, the final cry of abandonment: all these details of the narrative have firmly grounded the true humanity of the incarnate Word in our earthly reality. It may seem surprising to us moderns, but in Jesus' time people could readily believe that a spirit was capable of possessing someone's body temporarily in order to feign death through it, for reasons of its own. Therefore, to banish any possibility of ghostly deception and underhanded preternatural monkey business, Matthew takes great care to "document" the literal veracity of Jesus' death through the use of significant details.

First of all, he reports a proper name and place of origin for the person who takes charge of Jesus' burial: Joseph of Arimathea is the man. The fact that Joseph is a *rich* man is of importance because only some measure of wealth could afford a perennial tomb hewn out of rock, probably originally meant for himself. Joseph going to Pilate and asking for Jesus' corpse both marks the passage of time since the death and gives official legitimation to the events of death and burial.

Then Joseph's taking the inert body of Jesus down from the Cross, wrapping it in the linen shroud, and laying it in the new tomb are actions that not only enact a work of piety but also bear witness to the extent to which the formerly alive person Jesus of Nazareth is now reduced to the status of a thing to be handled and disposed of at will.

Finally, the two Marys sitting "opposite the sepulcher" not only manifest their own abiding fidelity and commiseration at the mystical level, but they also constitute prime witnesses to the fact that the corpse of Jesus has been sealed in a tomb. All of these details jointly show beyond any doubt that the formerly dynamic Rabbi is no longer to be found in the realm of the living.

And yet Matthew's Christian faith very spontaneously contemplates a natural convergence of the realistic and mystical planes: yes, Jesus is dead; but this body in the tomb is Jesus' own body and has not become alien to the "spirit" that Jesus once was. The tender piety in the way Joseph handles the corpse together with the insistent presence of the women keeping watch by the grave bear eloquent witness to the fact that, even in death, those who knew and loved Jesus cannot for a moment dissociate his living Person and Presence from his dead body. There is more here than simple respect paid to a beloved dead person.

The sudden darkness and the seismic convulsion, the other phenomena already described, Jesus' loud cry on dying, and the explicit confession of faith made by the centurion and his men, proclaiming that the crucified and now dead Jesus "was the Son of God": all of these "mystical" data have also established in the narrative that this was no ordinary death because Jesus was no ordinary human being. In consequence, a very wide abyss of wonderment now gapes powerfully before Matthew's readers and holds them in tremendous suspense.

Such suspense, made palpable in the breath-holding hush pervading the burial scene, gives the strong impression that Jesus' story is far from over. Joseph's no-fuss efficiency and lack of emotionalism; his brisk departure from the scene, signaling the tidy conclusion of *his* role in the story; the surprising absence of any dirge or formal lamentation, rigorously called-for in ancient times;[1] the newness of

---

[1] Consider the typical reaction to a death in the family described by Mark in the case of the young girl whom Jesus then raised to life: "When they came to the house of the ruler of the synagogue, he saw a tumult, and people weeping and wailing loudly" (Mk 5:38).

the tomb and the purity of the linen shroud; above all, the *expectant* nature of the vigil kept by the two women sitting in front of the grave: all these details create a mighty mood of suspense where one would rather have anticipated only deepening gloom and mournful despondency. It seems a very odd thing not only for the women but for the narrative itself to give the impression of expecting so much to derive from the mystery of a *corpse*, which for the moment remains the sole point of access to a person whose words and deeds offered such abundance of *life*.

At this moment of the burial's completion, then, we perceive two distinct and contrasting levels at which the scene is playing out simultaneously: the inexorable fact that the beloved Jesus has now become a corpse *and* the equally palpable intimation that upcoming events can be strongly scented in the evening air. This promising tension in the plot of Jesus' life and death may be perceived in the fact that, in his description of Joseph of Arimathea's actions, Matthew uses two different nouns to refer to Jesus' final resting place. As in many other similar linguistic cases, we hardly think that the evangelist is solely aiming at stylistic variation by not repeating his lexical choices.

In v. 60, we read that Joseph "laid [the body of Jesus] in his own new *tomb*, which he had hewn in the rock; and he rolled a great stone to the door of the *tomb*, and departed." In this verse, for the word here translated *tomb* the Greek has μνημεῖον (*mnêmeíon*) both times. And then immediately we read in v. 61: "Mary Magdalene and the other Mary were there, sitting opposite the [*sepulcher*]". In this case, Matthew suddenly switches to the word τάφος (*táphos*), here rendered *sepulcher*, to refer to the same reality. Why this variation?

Let us take the second word first. *Táphos* is the more generic and literal term to refer to a burial place, with little figurative or emotional meaning attached. It shares the same root as the verb "to bury" (θάπτω—*tháptô*). *Táphos* can refer either to the act of burying or to the grave itself. Its relationship to the dead person and to death itself is purely objective and material. This does not imply, however, that, because this is the word used in v. 61, therefore the two devoted women sitting at the *táphos* are focusing only on the brutal fact of Jesus' death. But the usage does suggest that in this passage Matthew intends both to portray the physical reality of Jesus' death (by unequivocal reference to his corpse) and, at the same time, to open up for his readers the total vision of the meaning of Jesus' life through and beyond his death. The latter is what must, at that moment, motivate Joseph of Arimathea as well as the holy women, representing all believers, as they execute the concerted actions both of dutiful mourning and of thrilling, expectant hope.

As for Matthew's first lexical choice, *mnêmeíon* (in Latin *monimentum* or *monumentum*): the word comes from a root that conveys the idea of *memory;* indeed, the Latin *memoria* is its cognate. The word, therefore, immediately associates the dynamic concept of *remembering* with the place or "memorial" in which Joseph lays the body of Jesus. Now, one engages in actively remembering those dead who are worthy of the effort. Such remembering in a certain sense keeps the person alive by continuing to show his relevance to posterity. In the unique case of Jesus' *mnêmeíon*, however, the significance of the word goes much farther.

We remember Jesus' strong allusion to the power of memory in connection with faith at the conclusion of the episode with the woman who anointed him at Bethany just before the beginning of his Passion: "In pouring this ointment on my body she has done it to prepare me for burial (*entaphiásai*). Truly, I say to you, wherever this gospel is preached in the whole world, what she has done will be told in memory (*mnêmósynon*) of her" (26:12–13). Again in this passage, we see the two roots for "memory" (*mnêm-*) and "sepulcher" (*taph-*) associated. This insistence by Matthew in continually linking impending death with ardent remembering would persuade us that the death of Jesus contains a mystery and a power unlike that of any other man.

Only the disciple's memory, where all the events of Jesus' story converge into one act of faith, has the power to see beyond the relentless fact of death. If this suffering and death did not already throb with the promise and certainty of new life, why would there at all be a "gospel preached in the whole world" to begin with? And the anointing woman will be eternally memorialized as an essential part of that Gospel of New Life precisely because she was prophetically able to peer through the darkness of Jesus' impending death and see Resurrection happening out of that death.

In his account of the institution of the Eucharist, St. Paul likewise links the eating of the broken bread with the breaking of Jesus' body in the Passion and the drinking of the wine with the outpouring of Jesus' blood. The wonder of eternal life is thus communicated in the Eucharist as a result of Jesus' historical betrayal so that sacrament and history become inseparable: "For as often as you eat this bread and drink the chalice, you proclaim the Lord's death until he comes" (1 Cor 11:26). However, Eucharist does not just happen automatically; Eucharist is something Christ commands his disciples actively and frequently to do "in remembrance of me (ἀνάμνησιν— *anámnêsin*)" (1 Cor 11:24). And St. Paul, too, stresses the manner in which Christ's death out of a free and freeing love transforms the destructive nature of physical death into a source of new life. This is why the death of Jesus is to be *proclaimed* by his disciples through the eucharistic *celebration* as a source of a new and dynamic existence. Celebratory proclamation always has as content an event of great joy promising a new beginning.

Only the Christian *memory*, recalling the events of Jesus' life and never forgetting his command to celebrate his death, can behold ever-lasting hope springing from what the world dismisses cynically as mere defeat. The disciples' certitude that in Jesus God can make life come out of death is not the product of wishful thinking or of philosophical speculation or of the poetic imagination or, as Nietzsche would have it, the feverish attempt by weak souls to console themselves with a pitiful fairytale in the face of the harsh world's tragedy. Christian hope that can see through death is but the putting into practice of Jesus' own trustworthy teaching concerning his own destiny: "The Son of man is to be delivered into the hands of men, and they will kill him, and he will be raised on the third day" (17:22–23).

Jesus drilled that difficult and explicit teaching into the hearts and minds of his disciples at least four times during his ministry, in order to steel their faith against the approaching doom (cf. 12:40, 16:21, 20:18–19). It goes without saying, however, that in the end it is not mere words, even those of the Master, but only *the event itself of the Resurrection* and the flesh-and-blood encounters of the risen Jesus with his disciples that give rock-like substance to the words of his prophecies uttered when he was still mortal. As a fervent disciple who remembered all of Jesus' teachings, Joseph of Arimathea is very much performing an act of faith in Jesus' Resurrection when he so carefully and lovingly lays Jesus' body in his new tomb, which thus becomes a veritable *monument* to Joseph's own Christian faith in action. Joseph is thus a fellow disciple to the anointing woman at Bethany.

She anointed Jesus "to prepare me for burial" at the beginning of the Passion narrative (26:6–13), and now, at its conclusion (27:57–

61), Joseph of Arimathea forms with her the other wing of a triptych enclosing the whole story of the Passion. Nor should we forget the mysterious aid suddenly afforded Jesus in his exhaustion by Simon of Cyrene, who unexpectedly found himself drawn into the plot of the Passion as he carried the Cross of Jesus. All these acts of loving devotion, in blatant counterpoint to the hostility of the Jewish leaders and the rabble, tenderly enfold the person of the suffering Savior. Matthew clearly wants to bring to our attention these bright spots of consolation shining quietly against the unflinching darkness of the hour. Though Jesus felt almost universally forsaken in his agony, nevertheless, there were present around him in the world, though hidden under the tumult of the raging mob, courageous and compassionate souls who risked both loving him and showing this love in public by concrete acts of adoring devotion.

To remember Jesus and his great saving deed in such a committed fashion is to make oneself memorable as well, since one's act of remembrance is already a proclamation of the Gospel that makes the power of Jesus' redeeming grace come to dwell in many others and have its effect in their hearts. This is why the Eucharist, at once the greatest possible act of both adoration and evangelization, has its roots and whole reason for being in Jesus' express command: *Do this in remembrance of me* (Lk 22:19; 1 Cor 11:24–25). For all time, Matthew has memorialized in his Gospel not only what it cost Jesus to save us but, inseparably from that, also what the only worthy response to such superabundant love should be on our part—once we have contemplated with our own eyes "the mystery hidden for ages in God who created all things" (Eph 3:9).

CHRIST'S DEATH HAS a very strange effect not only on the *plot* of the Gospel narrative, as is to be expected, but also on its *form and style*. Up to his great cry in 27:50, every page of the Gospel has overflowed with Jesus' dynamic presence. His words, his actions, his teachings, and even his attitudes, gestures, and manner of glancing deeply into a person's eyes have all regularly elicited strong reactions from people, both of admiration and of contempt. Every line of the Gospel makes it very clear that Jesus himself is the Word of God and that his teachings, both in word and example, are but a manifestation of the living Person of the Word and, thus, of the very Being of God. Page after page, we have seen the world crystallize around Jesus and redefine itself by relation to his presence in it. Indeed, the whole world and all its creatures (and not only human beings) are continually portrayed by the evangelists as reacting in some way to Jesus' potent existence in its midst: think of the *star* of the Magi (2:9–10), the cast-out *demons* (8:16), the stilling of the *storm* (8:24–27), the drowned herd of *pigs* (8:30–32), or the withered *fig tree* (21:19–20). But now that Jesus is truly dead, a mighty void, a vast empty space, has been hollowed out in the center of the world and, consequently, also in the narrative. Such a chasm has now to be filled by the initiative of ordinary mortals, though still very much with reference to the person of Jesus and to his meaning in their lives. In other words, the void left behind by Jesus' death displaces our attention temporarily from Jesus himself to the other actors in the drama of his life and becomes a powerful stimulus for all sorts of emotions and actions on their part.

Throbbing with mystery at the center of this awe-inspiring void is the disquieting presence of Jesus' corpse. The dead body of the Messiah is a pledge of future hope for his disciples (since Jesus has assured them that "with God all things are possible", 19:26), and, at the same time, Jesus' corpse is an uneasy source of contention for the nay-sayers (because the deeply venerated and religiously entombed body abides as a sacred object extending the promise of immortality). Did not his disciples, on the eve of his death, hear enthralling words from their Master's lips? "Take, eat; this is my body. . . . This is my blood of the covenant, which is poured out for many for the forgiveness of sins. I tell you I shall not drink again of this fruit of the vine until that day when *I drink it new with you in my Father's kingdom*" (26:26, 28–29). This is no longer a mere teaching on Jesus' part but a most solemn promise and, in fact, a last will and testament that must have infused both awe and a mysterious, tentative joy into his followers' hearts. And this quiet joy can easily be construed by Jesus' opponents within the ruling class as a leaven of dissidence and subversion. We marvel at seeing the thoroughly effective way in which even the dead Jesus continues from the grave to align the world for or against himself.

Before concluding our meditation on the merciful deed of Joseph of Arimathea, who piously sought out and buried the body of Jesus, we must make explicit its obvious link to the crucial teaching of Jesus concerning the primacy of hands-on charity in the Parable of the Judgment of the Nations in 25:31–46.

It is highly relevant to the internal theological coherence of Matthew's Gospel narrative that the hard-hitting conclusion of this parable ("Truly, I say to you, as you did it not to one of the least of these, you did it not to me", 25:45) is followed immediately by this passage, introduced by a prophetic statement from Jesus' mouth: " 'You know that after two days the Passover is coming, and the Son of man will be delivered up to be crucified.' Then the chief priests and the elders of the people gathered in the palace of the high priest, who was called Caiaphas, and took counsel together in order to arrest Jesus by stealth and kill him" (26:2–4). The text thus establishes a deep kinship between the drama of the Last Judgment, with the central relevance to it of the suffering of the disenfranchised, and the drama of the Savior's own suffering. As he turns from the Judgment Parable to the narrative of the Passion, Matthew seems to be taking all the vivid suffering of mankind just catalogued by the Master and subsuming it under Jesus of Nazareth's personal experience of betrayal, ostracism, torture, and death at the hands of his fellow men.

Now the parable was very specific in portraying those *corporal* works of mercy that are called for by fundamental human needs: hunger, thirst, nakedness, homelessness, illness, imprisonment . . . By definition, these works are to be performed on the *body of mankind*. At the same time, Jesus there identifies himself unconditionally, indeed ruthlessly, with the least person on earth undergoing such suffering in any time or place. And the moment that he, the judging King, finishes the unambiguous proclamation of his royal criteria for either eternal punishment or eternal life (*as you did it [or did not do it] to one of the least of these, you did it [or did not do it] to me*, 25:40, 45), at once he turns to speak with equal solemnity about *his own personal body*, which shall soon be delivered up and put to death by crucifixion.

By this structural procedure, Matthew clearly wishes to establish a vital link between the physical sufferings of those Jesus fondly calls "the least of these my brethren" in the parable and Jesus' own suffering body in the Passion. In this Matthean context, we do not even have to refer to the writings of St. Paul in order to see the necessary correlation between the suffering body of man and the suffering body of the incarnate Word. St. Paul's doctrine that sees all human suffering subsumed in the Passion of the divine Son is no subjective, mystical "overlay". In the parable, it is Jesus himself who proclaims an identity between the two suffering bodies at the very moment he is entering his Passion and handing over his body to sinners. As he declares his crucial self-identification with all who suffer, Jesus strongly proclaims as well that all who call themselves Christian shall henceforth exercise the paramount ministry of *alleviators of suffering*. But it is St. Paul who expounds at length the Scriptures' explicit teaching on the Mystical Body of Christ (cf. Rom 7:4; 12:5; 1 Cor 12:12, 27; Eph 4:12; 5:23; Col 3:15),[2] which may be summed up in Paul's statement to the Corinthians: "You are the body of Christ and individually members of it" (1 Cor 12:27). Within the Gospel narrative, however, we remain more dynamically on the plane of Jesus' own drama as we pass from his teaching activity to his own existential baptism of fire (cf. Mk 10:38–39). In this transition, it is important to remember that, in the light of the Judgment Parable, we should see Jesus, not as only an individual sufferer going to his doom, but, indeed, as the New Man, the New Adam who bears in his breaking Heart all the suffering of the world (cf. 1 Cor 15:22, 45).

We see Joseph of Arimathea, moved by piety and compassion for his dead Teacher, seeking to obtain from Pilate the body of Jesus. And he enfolds it tenderly in a shroud, finally depositing it in a new tomb meant for himself. In acting thus, Joseph is lavishing mercy not only literally *on his beloved Jesus* but also mystically *on all with whom*

---

[2] Although St. Paul often identifies the Mystical Body of Christ with the Church, that is, the community of declared believers, in a seemingly exclusive manner, his doctrine has a universal application to all human beings. We do not minister to Christ any less in the body of a suffering unbeliever than in that of a suffering Christian. Christ's own example guarantees that (see, among many other instances, his ministry to the Roman centurion and his servant, 8:5–13, to the demoniacs of Gadara, 8:28–34, and to the Canaanite woman, 15:21–28, all of them ethnic and religious "outsiders"). Every person has been created to become a member of the Body of Christ and, therefore, in a real sense *already is such by God's intention*, whether the individual is aware of it or not. Along with the Jews, affirms St. Paul—thus proclaiming the universality of election in Christ—"the Gentiles are fellow heirs, *members of the same body*, and partakers of the promise in Christ Jesus through the gospel" (Eph 3:6).

Jesus has identified himself. Joseph manages to fill with his works of love the awful void left by his Teacher's death, in this way fulfilling Jesus' instruction: "If you love me, you will keep my commandments" (Jn 14:15). It should not surprise us, then, that Joseph of Arimathea is venerated as a great saint by the universal Church, for "grace [is] with all who love our Lord Jesus Christ with love undying" (Eph 6:24). His feast is celebrated on August 31st in the West and on July 31st in the East. Because of his brave, solitary deed to the person of the Savior, Joseph, became the icon of the total disciple: he not only *listens* to the Word, but he *practices* the Word, honoring every aspect of the Word's identity both in life and in death.

Joseph's devotion to the dead body of Jesus shows that "it is not the spiritual which is first but the physical, and then the spiritual" (1 Cor 15:46). In other words, first comes the disciple's intimate association with the person of the Master: his presence, his voice, his actions and teachings, all mediated by his physical *body*. Only later does faith expand to embrace Christ's whole Body—whether physical, sacramental, or mystical. We do not come to know the hidden mysteries of God except through the fleshly Body of Jesus, the Word incarnate of the Virgin Mary. Though the spirit is higher in itself, in our human experience, the body comes first as the basis of all higher ascensions.

Matthew is a very "corporal" evangelist. In the genealogy that opens his Gospel, he inscribes solemnly for all time, and in exhaustive detail, the fact that it took forty-two generations, and hence eighty-four human bodies (minus one), to generate the body of "Jesus Christ, the son of David, the son of Abraham" (1:1), whom Matthew also called, in almost crude clinical terms, τὸ ἐν αὐτῇ γεννηθέν (*to en autê gennêthén*), "that which is conceived in [Mary]" (1:20a). Only then, once his human carnality has been established, is Jesus said by Matthew to be ἐκ Πνεύματος Ἁγίου (*ek Pneúmatos Hagíou*), "of the Holy Spirit" (1:20b). The body comes first, both in the order of faith and in the order of charity. This is so because *fides ex auditu*, "faith comes from hearing" (Rom 10:17, ESV), a principle that requires the services of mouths and ears of flesh. One quenches the thirst of the parched before venturing to proclaim the Gospel to them, since "faith by itself, if it has no works, is dead" (Jas 2:17).

But then, at length, a further initiation into the Heart of the Redeemer communicates to the mature disciple the mystical knowledge concerning the deepest identity of Jesus of Nazareth as the *New Adam* who recapitulates all of mankind within himself. "If you love me," Jesus seems to say, "you must love everyone I love, everyone I *contain*. Otherwise, you are short-circuiting my love as it seeks to pass through you and reach all the needy." Here we see the deepest motivation for a life of consistently heroic charity, as deployed exemplarily by a Joseph of Arimathea, a Maximilian Kolbe, a Teresa of Calcutta, and countless other self-sacrificing, anonymous souls who step into the breach and bridge the gap between the Love that is God and the stony indifference that is unredeemed man. Only heroic charity, love so intense that it hurts, adequately spreads throughout creation the Fire of Mercy of the Word, who declares: "This is my commandment, that you love one another *as I have loved you*"—that is, *unto death, even death on a cross* (Jn 15:12; Phil 2:8).

Though such high declarations may initially evoke images of epic melodrama, the authentically lived, everyday, Christian reality of heroic charity is, in fact, much more quiet and unobtrusive and, therefore, all the more demanding, as suggested by the twentieth-century, inner-city mystic Madeleine Delbrêl (1904–1964), whose writings record her long-term experience: "It is not by organizing the world", she wisely observes, "that we are going to be grafted onto the wedding-feast of the Church. It will happen only if we carry within ourselves each person in this world and if we give them, not an organization of life, but *the right to live within our own life*."[3]

[3] "Ce n'est pas en organisant le monde que nous serons greffés sur les noces de l'Église; mais c'est en portant en nous chacun des hommes de ce monde, en leur donnant non une organisation de vie, mais le droit de vivre dans notre vie" (italics mine). Madeleine Delbrêl, *La joie de croire* (Paris: Éditions du Seuil, 1968), 148. Delbrêl lived and worked in a small community of laywomen in the working-class Paris suburb of Ivry-sur-Seine, a bastion of the French Communist Party. The titles of her books already tell us a great deal: *The Marxist City as Mission Territory* (1957), *The Contemporary Forms of Atheism* (1962), and two posthumous works, *We, the Ordinary People of the Streets* (1966) and *The Joy of Believing* (1968).

17. "IF YOU CAN GRASP IT, IT IS NOT GOD!"

The Tomb Is Secured (27:62–66)

27:62b–63 συνήχθησαν οἱ ἀρχιερεῖς καὶ οἱ Φαρισαῖοι
πρὸς Πιλᾶτον λέγοντες·
Κύριε, ἐμνήσθημεν
ὅτι ἐκεῖνος ὁ πλάνος εἶπεν ἔτι ζῶν·
Μετὰ τρεῖς ἡμέρας ἐγείρομαι

*The chief priests and the Pharisees
gathered before Pilate and said,
"Sir, we remember
how that impostor said, while he was still alive,
'After three days I will rise again'"*

OBSESSIVE FEAR STILL HAUNTS the religious leaders of the people, even after Jesus' corpse has been mangled to death, perforated with the holes of thorns, nails, and lance, taken down from the pitiless gallows, and very resolutely entombed. This fear that lingers in the powerful who have had their way is surely the sign of a bad conscience. One can kill a human body far more easily than one's own conscience! Of course, in order to justify their actions further, these leaders mask the deep disturbance in their minds and present it, perhaps even to themselves, as nothing but dutiful, common-sense, precautionary measures against all possible contingencies. It makes no difference to their subliminal anxiety that Jesus is now, beyond any doubt, dead and buried and that "a great stone" (v. 60) blocks the entrance to his tomb. The specters of paranoia haunt us from within.

This whole section on the securing of the tomb (27:62–66) is unique to Matthew. The evangelist must have seen a special symbolism in the authorities' attempt to subjugate even Jesus' dead body. Matthew stresses the stone's enormity no doubt with ironical intent. For, could even the greatest of all boulders or even mountains truly block the might of God, when the whole earth has just shaken convulsively at Jesus' cry and the stones of the countryside have been split and "the tombs also were opened" (27:51–52)? In any event, priests and Pharisees still feel the threat of Jesus in the very air they breathe. In fact the very inertness in death of their condemned criminal's body and the mysterious vacuum it has generated only seem to intensify the ubiquity of the Jesus danger. The resilient reality of Jesus has by now saturated the consciousness of the religious elite, and they cannot let go.

Their paranoia reminds us of Herod's after the death of John the Baptist, and, in both cases, the neurotic fear derives from the possibility that a dead man may rise from the dead and come to haunt his murderers (cf. 14:1–2). Unacknowledged guilt can generate whole infernos of anxiety, the more treacherous for being repressed. The pious Jewish conscience rested on the conviction that God's justice always triumphs in the end. In this light, we see why the nervous interior state of both Herod and the Jewish leaders reveals a profound insecurity, a high anxiety concerning the doubtful justice of their own actions regarding two men whom a right objective conscience must acknowledge to have been *tsaddikim*, "just and holy men" and, therefore, pleasing to and protected by the God of Israel.

On the occasion of their gathering with Pilate, the Jewish authorities have communally activated their power of *memory* (ἐμνήσθημεν, *emnêsthêmen* = "we remember"). The text points, however, to individuals who have lost their individuality and capitulated to thinking as a collective, with only expediency as their guiding light. Joseph of Arimathea acts as an individual in his initiative of mercy; the pious women at the tomb act as individuals when they brave public disgrace and recrimination by openly supporting a state-convicted "criminal". But, for the religious leaders, the text falls back on the hackneyed expression συνήχθησαν (*synêchthêsan* = "they gathered [together]", v. 62; cf. 22:41; 26:3, 57) to signal how these priests and scholars of the Law are colluding in their malice and taking refuge in each other's prejudices in order to continue constructing their own narrative about the status of the innocent man they have managed to get executed.

So when the leaders then say to Pilate, "we remember how that impostor said . . . ", this second verb, in the first person plural, marks an utterance of collective inauthenticity. Theirs is a remembering that has its roots in nothing deeper or richer than the political self-interest of a religious faction that adorns itself with an aura of piety and tradition, broad and all-encompassing as their fringes and phylacteries (cf. 23:5). Thus does the collective memory of cowardly schemers operate, finding strength in numbers and inspiration solely in the hunger for power and the compulsion to maintain the status quo. This act of the leaders' memory, nonetheless, brings forward in the Gospel the theme of *significant remembering* we have already encountered at the anointing in Bethany in connection with the anonymous woman (εἰς **μνημόσυνον** αὐτῆς—*eis mnêmósynon autês* = "in memory of her", 26:13), at the Last Supper in connection with the disciples (εἰς τὴν ἐμὴν **ἀνάμνησιν**—*eis tên emên anámnêsin* = "in remembrance of me", 1 Cor 11:24–25), and at Jesus' burial in connection with Joseph of Arimathea and his tomb's role as a place of active remembering (ἐν τῷ καινῷ αὐτοῦ **μνημείῳ**—*en tô kainô autoú mnêmeíô* = "in [the] new tomb ['monument' or 'memorial']", 27:60).

Moreover, by extending this crucial theme into the present episode, Matthew yet again puts his readers in the position of having to make a fundamental choice as to the end toward which they will engage their own power of memory. We can remember in order to rejoice and give thanks, or we can remember in order to give vent to fear and concoct strategies of self-defense. There is always something highly personal about the use of memory because what the storehouse of our deep memory chooses to lodge within itself for future retrieval becomes, in a real sense, an intimate part of the person remembering.

Now, our relationship to the world outside us assumes two basic modalities, determined by the choice either to *welcome* or to *reject* what comes at us from outside our person, depending on whether we judge it to be *life-enhancing* or *life-threatening* to our established selves. Consequently, I will use my memory in an open and embracing manner toward realities I consider hold the promise of greater life and happiness, or, conversely, I will behave in a closed and hostile manner toward realities I consider a threat and an endangerment to my self as I conceive it. In this context, we recall that what the religious leaders now remember in particular is the fact that Jesus, "while he was still alive", solemnly proclaimed to his disciples, with reference to his own death, that "after three days I will rise again."

We may ask ourselves why the chief priests and Pharisees should become so negatively fixated on a statement that promises new life springing out of death. Why do they now remember that specific affirmation of Jesus? And why must they follow up their memory of it so proactively, with such a passion for strategic detail? Why can they not simply impute Jesus' statement about rising again to the fantasies of a madman? Could it be that, contrary to both their human reason and their professed theology, they nonetheless harbor deep within themselves the uneasy apprehension that Jesus may have uttered a promise that he both intends to keep and is capable of keeping? And then the even more fundamental question arises: Why would anyone react so adversely, indeed, so spitefully, to a promise of new life, whatever its source? What kind of person feels threatened by the prospect of freshly enhanced and transformed life, particularly if such life should prove to be a victory over the power of death, sworn nemesis of the human yearning for immortality? In other words, what kind of soul and mind would seem to have *a vested interest in death*, to the detriment of every instinctive human desire for fullness of life?

The psychological mechanism now prompting the Jewish leaders has been evidenced before in the Gospel and is best exemplified by the treatment of many prophets in the Old Testament. Typically, an established power automatically sets out to quash any prophetic voice questioning its legitimacy by appeal to the transcendental power and incorruptible truth of God. Only human power that is at once unstable and greedy feels compelled to act as if it possessed omnipotence, an attitude sure to unleash violence on the world. Since they shun accountability like the plague, unjust rulers cannot abide the thought that there may somewhere exist an authority higher than themselves. Such was the case of Herod the Great in his savage slaughter of the Holy Innocents, who became victims of the petty king's fear that the legitimate King of Israel had at last arrived (cf. 2:2–3, 16). And such, too, was the case of his son, Herod Antipas, in his treatment of John the Baptist, an episode that prefigures the murder of Jesus.

Ruler paranoia seems to be an affliction communicated from father to son, especially among upstart kings. In both the Herods, we witness an unsurmountable rage that seeks to obliterate from the face of the earth any presence or voice that calls into question the entitlement of the authority holding power at the moment. And, while the ruler's only weapon is brute force, with its efficacy limited to the vulnerable body of flesh, the prophetic voice, by contrast, stands secure in its commitment to the unchanging truth, which must triumph in the end despite the temporary destruction of the prophet's body. However, despite their external grip on power, unjust rulers are afflicted by a troubled conscience insofar as they may still possess any glimmer of conscience. Thus the memory of John the Baptist is a phantom haunting Herod Antipas, who sees the prophet reincarnated in Jesus: "This is John the Baptist", Herod declares to his attendants, referring to Jesus. "'He has been raised from the dead; that is why these powers are at work in him.' For Herod had seized John and bound him and put him in prison . . . and had John beheaded in the prison" (14:2–4, 10).

This scenario of the two Herods frantically flailing to retain their hold on power will be repeated almost literally during the arrest, trials, and crucifixion of Jesus at the end of the Gospel, this time featuring the high priests, the elders, and the Pharisees as the empowered caste. All the verbs predicated of either Herod in their respective rampages and those describing the Jewish leaders during Christ's Passion manifest the same compulsion. In Jesus' infancy narrative, we hear: *search* and *destroy* (2:13) and *send* and *kill* [all the male children] (2:16). In the episode with John the Baptist, we read: *seize, bind, imprison, behead* (14:2–4, 10), while in the Passion narrative such verbs proliferate: *lay hands on* and *seize* [Jesus] (26:50); *put to death* (26:59); *spit on, strike, slap* (26:67); *bind, lead away, deliver* [like an object] (27:2); *crucify* (27:22); *scourge, deliver to be crucified* (27:26); *strike* [on the head] (27:30). All of these acts, seeking to squelch and banish the threatening force identified with the witness of a prophet (whether Jesus or John the Baptist), reach their ironical culmination (Jesus is already dead!) in the priests' present move to secure beyond all tampering the place containing the body of Jesus.

This initiative also demonstrates the petty-mindedness of the religious leaders as they project the shabbiest aspects of their own mentality onto the magnifying screen of Jesus' drama. If they now envisage the possibility of fraudulent theft and imposture on the part of Jesus and his disciples, it is precisely because this is their *own* habitual mode of operation, the paradigm ready at hand. Nor, despite their professed piety, do they in the slightest reckon with the possibility that the God of Israel has the power to raise the dead if he should so choose. In their case, every genuine religious conviction has long since been swallowed up in the swamp of partisan control and political gain.

Indeed, unjust holders of power are driven by a blind, irrepressible force to contain, silence, annihilate, and dispose of the Truth from the face of the earth. Quite simply, these persecutors intuit that the Truth, by its mere existence, is their competitor and that therefore they cannot coexist in the same world with the Truth. One or the other must perish. The priests and Pharisees cannot exist in a world in which Jesus is recognized as Messiah, Redeemer, and Dispenser of eternal life. Therefore, they must murder him again linguistically, after they have already murdered him physically, by calling him an *impostor* pretending to be the Son of God and declaring his *claim to a future rising* from the dead an even "worse fraud" than that earlier imposture.

This brief review of earlier strategies of repression in the New Testament is essential to grasp the symbolic import and implications of the religious leaders' present burning endeavor: the foolproof securing and sealing of Jesus' tomb.

27:64

κέλευσον ἀσφαλισθῆναι τὸν τάφον
ἕως τῆς τρίτης ἡμέρας,
μήποτε ἐλθόντες οἱ μαθηταὶ αὐτοῦ κλέψωσιν αὐτὸν
καὶ εἴπωσιν τῷ λαῷ· Ἠγέρθη ἀπὸ τῶν νεκρῶν,
καὶ ἔσται ἡ ἐσχάτη πλάνη χείρων τῆς πρώτης

Order the tomb to be made secure
until the third day,
lest his disciples go and steal him away,
and tell the people, "He has risen from the dead,"
and the last fraud will be worse than the first

THE TWO MARYS AND JOSEPH OF ARIMATHEA remembered Jesus' words concerning his Resurrection, "After three days I will rise again" (27:63), and the memory of those consoling words filled them, in the face of death, with a hopeful expectation of joy to come—the contemplative stance par excellence. They refused to accept that death had had the final word. The mysterious burning in their hearts urged them to persist in peering with infinite patience at that tomb. The thankful memory of Jesus, whether alive or dead, thus generates in soulful persons works of both *theôría* and *diakonía* (cf. 27:55)—ecstatic "gazing" and merciful "service"—the one vouching for the authenticity of the other. These must, indeed, always go hand in hand, and this is why Matthew wisely couples masculine and feminine talents as offering the total pattern of the disciple's love-driven life. Divorced from one another, the two aspects degenerate: the one into random activism and the other into spiritual hedonism. Yet the integrity of the Paschal Mystery demands that each of these two indispensable Christian stances and acts, which define the interior identity of every adherent of Jesus, be directed simultaneously *both* to the person of the Lord Jesus in himself as source of all love *and* to his whole Mystical Body subsisting in mankind.

The chief priests and Pharisees, on the other hand, remember those same prophetic words of Jesus, "After three days I will rise again" (27:63); yet the memory of them fills them, rather, with anxiety and discontent, prompting them to launch at once into a campaign of minute, preemptive strategizing with Pilate, the worldly power, with whom they seek an ungodly collusion. How we react to the advent of grace is a judgment and a revelation of who we are.

"Order the tomb to be made secure": Here we have the new form, fitting the changed circumstances, of the impetus behind all the verbs of enforced containment and repression we have surveyed above, predicated on the religious authorities. Some people cannot live and breathe at ease in the world without continually trying to "secure" themselves against anything they perceive as a contrary force or antagonistic presence. "Securing" can be a military euphemism hinting at *obliteration*. In the best of all worlds, I get to destroy what I do not like; and the increasing popularity of that tendency at a social level first legitimizes and then imposes the growing mental pathology. How much energy is collectively invested in a society to make sure that a dead arch-enemy *stays dead*? To what extent are our lives configured by our fear of what we conceive as ghosts and phantoms, even if the "ghost" involved is the Spirit of the living God?

This is now the second time that we hear an allusion to the Resurrection of Jesus since the moment of his death. The first time, we recall, was immediately after he breathed his last, when Matthew records that "many bodies of the saints who had fallen asleep were raised and [came] out of the tombs *after his resurrection*" (27:52–53). Now, in this speech to Pilate, the chief priests and Pharisees themselves first quote Jesus himself, who promised, "After three days I will rise again", and then they cite the disciples, who are imagined to be about to proclaim deceitfully, "He has risen from the dead."

As with the mocking salute by the soldiery at the prætorium ("Hail, King of the Jews!", 27:29), as with the sign posted over Jesus' head on the Cross ("This is Jesus the King of the Jews", 27:37) and as with the priests' jeering parody of his identity ("I am the Son of God", 27:43), so too now with these two statements by the religious authorities: Despite their malevolent intentions and despite the negative material evidence of the tomb hermetically holding its corpse, nevertheless, the very fears and elaborate strategies of the Jewish rulers in the end turn out, by a surprising reversal, to be instrumental in proclaiming the truth of the Gospel concerning Jesus' deepest identity and consequent triumph over death. Here, too, we do well to trace truth to its source through all the glimmers of light piercing the burlesque witness of Jesus' adversaries. The probing rays of faith's vision can contemplate the authentic Archetype of revelation even through its vulgar disfigurement, as Shakespeare suggests:

> . . . Yet sit and see;
> Minding true things by what their mockeries be.[1]

That is exactly what the holy women at the tomb do. They sit resolutely and they see clairvoyantly the true things of God contained within the outward defeat of Jesus (cf. 27:55–56, 61).

In order for grace to show its truly divine nature, the forces hostile to Jesus and responsible for his death must somehow be integrated positively into the narrative of his death and Resurrection. Matthew is here showing how divine grace can use even recalcitrant means to reveal God's power and plan to save: "As in Adam all die, so also in Christ shall all be made alive. But each in his own order: Christ the first fruits, then at his coming those who belong to Christ" (1 Cor 15:22–23). The two affirmations "After three days I will rise again" and "He has risen from the dead", coming from the very mouths of those who hate Jesus viscerally, act like bursts of blinding light out of the darkness, precisely because they are uttered in the context of a scheme to prevent any such eventuality. The evangelist here delights in juxtaposing ironically the sovereign design of God and the Lilliputian machinations of mortals.

The Jewish leaders are swimming in so constricted a religious pond that they truly believe they have been able to obliterate from the genuine world of vast reality and possibility the truth behind the incarnate Word's promise, "After three days I will rise again." They are confident that the hammer blows that drove in the nails and brought on exsanguination and asphyxia can truly squelch the upsurge of inconceivably irrepressible life welling up from within the depths of God's inert Son lying in his stony tomb. History and experience show us that the professionally religious are often, bafflingly, among the first to *disbelieve in practice though never in theory* that their Lord is a God of infinite possibilities. Our dogged subjective prejudice can often attempt to shackle the hands of God's freedom to act! And,

---

[1] *Henry V*, Act 4, Prologue.

paradoxically, such shackling can be unconsciously driven by highly devout argumentation.

Somehow, it is in the Jewish authorities' professional interest to "secure" God by concerting an assault upon God's visible and living form (or *icon*, cf. Col 1:15) on earth—Jesus, the Son he sent us. A God of surprises does not bode well for those passionately intent, above all, on the consistency of their official doctrines, the respectability of their reputation, and the stability of their hard-earned empowerment. Thus, there is deep irony as well in Pilate's reply to the priests: ἀσφαλίσασθε ὡς οἴδατε—*asphalísasthe hôs oídate*, "Make [the tomb] as secure as you can [*or*: as best you know how]" (v. 65). This unusual reply from the Roman governor seems to deliver to the petitioners a not so veiled challenge from God himself, as if the Lord were saying to them with an indulgent smile: "Try your worst, and we will see what prevails in the end, whether your power to squelch life or my power to bestow life as I wish—I who, remember, am the Creator of life."

But what human strategy, what ambition of the human heart, what tormented phobia of the human mind, what accumulation of brute strength, weaponry, or even mountain-sized boulders are capable of securing the world against the power of God's love or capable of securing the stony human heart against the assault of God's grace? For, make no mistake about it, this is precisely the drama being played out at Jesus' tomb under the guise of a mere political maneuver. Surely we are not ignorant of the fact that the devastating energy of God's love operates subversively *from within*—from within the walled-in fortress of our refusal, from within the hermetically sealed efficiency of our social and ancestral conventions, from within the tombs where we attempt to lock up forever our despair in the face of obliterating death?

On this occasion, the Jewish religious authorities are performing at the literal, historical level of the Gospel narrative an action that is highly symbolic of a universal human tendency. In this context, the corpse of the dead Jesus represents both our human despair in the face of death's certainty as well as our compulsion to contain that despair so that it will not vitiate the rest of our existence. First comes the persecution of Jesus as a threatening presence while he is alive, and then his body is "secured" in the tomb once the plot to do away with him has succeeded. Together, these two actions represent our phobia in the face of ultimate annihilation, a fear that must be managed and overpowered if it is not to wreak chaos in our lives.

This symbolic reading of the scene at the tomb opens up vaster horizons of religious phenomenology beyond the immediate story. In a famous sermon on the knowability of God, St. Augustine penned a five-word sentence that brilliantly lays down one of the defining axioms of Christian theology: "Si comprehendis, non est Deus!" (If you can grasp [it], it is not God).[2] One is tempted to translate Augustine's word *comprehendis* in this sentence with the English cognate "to comprehend", but this English verb is too abstract and primarily connotes discursive processes of thought and logic, while the Latin *comprehendere* has a far wider and more concrete range of meanings. Augustine likely intends something more dynamic and existential than mere mental "comprehension", something more literally *enclosing and containing* and, thus, more in keeping with the literal meaning of the Latin verb. Such a rendering makes Augustine's axiom highly relevant to the drama underway at Jesus' tomb. In more contemporary idiom, Augustine seems to suggest that we humans are always trying to "wrap our minds around" the idea of God so as to feel we have finally *mastered* God as one more concept among many. By that very token, the Bishop of Hippo is warning us that, the moment we think we have accomplished the foolhardy endeavor, our very self-satisfaction *proves* that it is not at all the living God that we have "grasped" because God is by definition ungraspable, uncontainable, and beyond manipulation.

The true God is always breaking out of the bonds of our attempted containment, out of the fortress of the concepts and expectations whereby we wall God in, in a titanic attempt at overpowering his mysterious and perpetually elusive Being. The Being of God, in fact, is just as fluid and free-flowing, just as unruly and irrepressible, as the Blood of Jesus pouring out prodigiously upon the soil of Golgotha and as swift and elusive as the Spirit of Jesus wafting forth in the mighty shout from the shuddering frame of the dying Word. "The wind [*Pneuma* (Spirit, Breath)] blows where it wills, and you hear the sound of it, but you do not know where it comes from or where it goes" (Jn 3:8). Who can catch it?

---

[2] Sermons 117.5 (*PL* 38:663).

Augustine's word *comprehendere* evokes the capturing, grasping, and subjugating action of human hands before they refer to the ambitions of the human mind. Has not this activity been precisely that of the priests, scribes, and Pharisees during Jesus' whole Passion, and especially now with regard to his body in the tomb? In our present text, Matthew repeats a form of the verb ἀσφαλίζω (*asphalízô*, "to secure, make safe") in three consecutive verses (64, 65, 66). He thus drives home the point that, on the occasion of Jesus' burial, the Roman and Jewish authorities, together representing all earthly logic, power, and ambition, are colluding to make sure the dead Rabbi *stays dead*. Thus, the world's cultural and political elites, embodiments of all self-serving human initiatives, are working hard to remove the threat that the world order, which they have constructed and now so profitably manage, might be overturned by One rising from the dead.

Normally connoting a positive endeavor, the verb *asphalízô* ("to make secure") is in this case stood on its head because what the powers that be are trying to make steadfast, firm, and immovable is death itself. The authorities of the world feel that in burying Jesus, in securing his tomb with a large stone, in sealing this stone and setting a guard of soldiers over it, they have succeeded in forever containing and neutralizing the energies of an all too unpredictable, untamable, and unmanageable God. We may even say that, in amassing such concerted efforts against Jesus, the leaders of this world are unintentionally bearing him a very potent negative testimony since, obviously, they have identified Jesus with a God-sized threat.

But God is the Lord of freedom and of endless possibilities and surprises, the Lord of Life, the extravagant Lover of Mankind (Δέσποτα Φιλόψυχε—*Déspota Philópsyche*, Wis 11:26). And the moniker of contempt that the Jewish leaders now hurl at Jesus—ἐκεῖνος ὁ Πλάνος—*ekeínos ho Plános*: THAT IMPOSTOR (v. 63)—stands in glaring contrast to the transcendental title the Roman centurion has already uttered with compelling faith at the moment of Jesus' death: Θεοῦ Υἱός—*Theoû Hyiós*: SON OF GOD (27:54). It is as if God himself, by such a juxtaposition in the text of his evangelist-prophet, were offering us, the readers of the Gospel, a critical option: "I have set before you life and death, blessing and curse; therefore choose life, that you and your descendants may live, loving the LORD your God, obeying his voice, and clinging to him" (Deut 30:19–20). "Choose life", that is, choose JESUS, cling to Jesus *even in his death* as did Joseph of Arimathea, as did the holy women at the tomb, for the human death of the Son of God contains a wellspring of divine energy bounding up to eternal Life. "And from his fulness (*plêrôma*) have we all received, grace upon grace" (Jn 1:16).

18. THE JOY OF ENCOUNTER

Meeting the Risen Lord (28:1–10)

28:1

Ὀψὲ δὲ σαββάτων,
τῇ ἐπιφωσκούσῃ εἰς μίαν σαββάτων
ἦλθεν Μαριὰμ ἡ Μαγδαληνὴ καὶ ἡ ἄλλη Μαρία
θεωρῆσαι τὸν τάφον

Now after the sabbath,
toward the dawn of the first day of the week,
Mary Magdalene and the other Mary went
to see the tomb

D AWN ON THE FIRST DAY OF THE WEEK. Urged by their fervor
and fidelity, the women anticipate the dawn and go again to
seek their Friend and Lord, even if that means only gazing
patiently at a mute and sealed tomb. Their love persists in preferring
the dead Jesus to any man alive. With a premonition of joy, their
actions are singing the psalm that declares: "Awake, my soul! Awake,
O harp and lyre! I will awake the dawn!" (Ps 57[56]:8).

The Greek phrasing here (ἐπιφωσκούσῃ εἰς—*epiphôskoúsê eis*) literally shows the dawn *"over-lightening into* the first [day] of the week".
These words make you see and feel the silent power of the light of
this particular dawn as it swiftly permeates the darkness, not only the
gloom of the preceding night of the historical Holy Saturday, but
the darkness of "the shadow of death" as such (4:16, Lk 1:79), in
an absolute and universally efficacious sense. Myriad points of burning light tenaciously pierce the gloom of millennial mockery, the
night of grimacing unbelief, the chaos of chronic despair. This new
majestic light ushers in the universal Day of forgiveness and fiery

mercy that, womb-like and unperceived, has from the beginning enfolded our world with an indestructible tenderness. "If you can encompass him with mercy, it must be man!" is God's reply to Augustine's dictum, "If you can encompass it, it is not God." "Before the world came to be," says God, "I am infinite maternal enfolding." For "in the brightness of the saints, from the womb before the day star I begot thee!" (Ps 110[109]:3, DRA).[1] The Resurrection of Jesus is the Father's definitive uttering and begetting of his eternal Word into our world. With it, God's eternity and God's own interior life have now entered our time and space to make their dwelling among us.

We have now arrived at the moment when the drama of Jesus' earthly life brings us face-to-face with the mysterious event of his Resurrection from the dead. At this point, we would naturally expect Matthew's text to dazzle us with the greatest of all theophanies. As a great relief from all the unremitting distress of the Passion, we would gladly now welcome some splendid show of unimaginable divine fireworks that would outdo all other visible and audible manifestations of God's glory. We think of the great Exodus from Egypt and the crossing of the Red Sea. We remember as well, from among many wondrous happenings, the thunder and lightning on Sinai at the giving of the Ten Commandments, the feeding of Israel with manna in the desert, the fire and brimstone raining on the Cities of the Plain, the falling of the walls of Jericho, and Elijah's rapturous ascent to heaven in a fiery chariot.

Even the New Testament is rich in epiphanies: Gabriel's annunciation to Mary, the singing of the angels on Christmas night, the Father's voice from heaven at the Lord's baptism, the changing of water into wine at Cana, and the dazzling radiance of Jesus' body at the Transfiguration, to say nothing of Pentecost. And in the narrative of the Passion itself, we have seen the darkness and the earthquake on Golgotha and the breaking open of the tombs.

Tremendous as all these memorable events were as landmarks of God's involvement in the story of man and in the history of his

---

[1] Both the Septuagint (Εν ταῖς λαμπρότησιν τῶν ἁγίων ἐκ γαστρὸς πρὸ ἑωσφόρου ἐξεγέννησά σε) and the Vulgate (In splendoribus sanctorum ex utero ante luciferum genui te) insist on this rendering from the Hebrew, and this version has also been canonized since ancient times by the liturgy (cf. communion antiphon for the Mass during the Night on the Lord's Nativity).

beloved Son on earth, nevertheless, in every case, they were limited by space and time. They were specific, transitory events along the continuum of elapsed time, although they live on in the grateful religious memory. Therefore, in the case of Jesus' Resurrection, too, we expect an extraordinary representation of this unheard-of, transcendental event by the evangelist. Above all in an age in which our sensibilities have been formed by cinematic special effects, our æsthetic instinct demands an explicit portrayal in living color of what precisely happened to the corpse of Jesus in that tomb. We yearn for some overwhelmingly moving depiction of the metamorphosis of his holy flesh as he shook death from himself and leapt up mightily into the plenitude of heavenly life.

What we get, instead, is something very different and, at least initially, something that disappoints by its ordinariness. While we long for an epic apotheosis of the risen Christ's triumph à la Cecil B. De-Mille, what Matthew gives us is a rather sober and very straightforward account of what happened. Above all, the narrative surrounds the actual event and moment of the Resurrection with total silence, a kind of visual blackout. Neither eye nor ear is privy to the mysterious happening; our imagination is given no image to cling to, and our reason receives no explanation. We experience only the aftermath, the results of the Resurrection. All our sense-bound, scientific curiosity about the when and the how feels frustrated, indeed. By means of his narrative details, the evangelist is inviting us to share the patient gazing and loving waiting of the holy women as they sit in rock-like silence and immobility before their Lord's tomb, the only obvious point of orientation given them. However, in the event, Jesus suddenly stands before them coming from an entirely different direction. Here, too, he is the God of surprises. His rising from the dead has anticipated even their own eager anticipation of the dawn. God is always present and active in wholly hidden ways within the background and underground of our visible lives. If you can pin down and comprehend his manner and reasons for acting, it is not God you are dealing with! The first condition for the reception of grace is silence in the soul, humility of mind at the service of a burning heart that rejoices at embracing the Beloved in the darkness of faith.

We last saw Jesus as a corpse when Joseph of Arimathea took him down from the Cross and laid him to rest in his own sepulcher (27:60). The actual Resurrection occurred sometime between the sealing of

Joseph's tomb (27:66) and the women's arrival at that tomb (28:1), for this is when the resplendent angel comes to them from heaven accompanied by "a great earthquake". Along with the women, however, we next encounter Jesus, very much alive and active, only at 28:9, as if Matthew were using a delaying technique to stress both the women's courageous persistence and the human need for grace-appointed mediators to bridge the abyss between our feeble capacities of understanding and the ineffable Mystery of God.

Moreover, when we and the women again encounter the living Jesus, we cannot even speak of an "apparition" in the supernatural sense of John's Gospel because this moment of sudden encounter between Jesus and the holy women in Matthew is beyond all manner of "special effects", such as the traversing of walls and the probing of gaping wounds (Jn 20:19, 26–27). What takes place, instead, is something quite simple: namely, a wholly unexpected meeting between old friends that affects *the heart* above else and not the senses, as always eager for the sensational. In both a theological and a literary sense, we would have to say that the strong persuasiveness of the passage as a witness to Jesus' Resurrection lies precisely in Matthew's *refusal* to introduce any "proofs" or argumentation based on extravagant preternatural or psychological phenomena.

The force of his text comes, rather, from the *manner of Jesus' presence*: though risen from the dead, the person whom the holy women encounter is still very much the Jesus they know and love from their previous personal experience. He seeks them out familiarly as he has always done and encounters them on their way to the disciples. The true marvel comes, not from sudden illuminations from above or the glowing of resurrected flesh or the heavenly harmonies of cosmic choirs, but precisely from the experienced reality that this man, Jesus, whom we have known and loved, but who then was killed and buried, is now inexplicably yet factually standing here before us alive and well, still seeking us out and addressing us familiarly as his own beloved friends.

It is the abiding sameness of this man Jesus, the utter continuity of his behavior and manner of presence and interaction with his own *before and after his death*, that provide the evidence for the truth that he has, indeed, triumphed over the dreadful abyss of death and carried his friends over with him into the Heart of the Father. When Jesus reassures the women with the fond greeting "Rejoice!", they instantly recognize him as their beloved Lord, so much so that they cannot refrain from falling down before him with excited gratitude and grasping his feet in passionate adoration.

The whole scene occurs at the horizontal level of a meeting between fond friends, where the emotions of the heart and the recognition of the Lord Jesus' identity blend flawlessly with the confession of an adoring faith in his person. For his part, Jesus enacts his long-familiar role of reassuring Friend ("rejoice", "do not be afraid", he says), loving Teacher ("go and tell my brethren . . .", he orders them), and ready Spouse who seeks out the beloved of his Heart—the Church, personified in these faithful women—along all the roads of life (Song 3:2) and allows her the bold intimacy of grasping, physical contact.

Ἐκράτησαν αὐτοῦ τοὺς πόδας—*ekrátēsan autoú tous pódas* = "they took hold of his feet": This verb for "grasping" (κρατέω—*kratéō*), referring to the impulsive action of the women seeking to secure Jesus' presence with them, is the very one used throughout the Passion to describe the authorities' unholy drive to apprehend and nullify Jesus by force (cf. 26:4, 48, 50, 55, 57). Ah, how this grasping of Jesus by these women with the passionate hands of faith serves at this moment to redeem infinitely all the past violence done to Jesus by the grasping and restraining hands of murderous men who hated him and grasped him only in order to destroy him! How different this grasping of his feet *for adoration* is from the authorities' grasping of his body *for containment and repression!* The powerful of the world wanted to keep the dead dead, but the women want to derive fullness of life from the living One. The leaders' relationship with Jesus was determined by fear, ambition, and hatred. The women's relationship with their Lord is determined by joy, desire, and adoration.

Truly the holy women are enacting here the part of the bride in the Canticle, who exclaims: "I found him whom my soul loves. *I held him* (ἐκράτησα αὐτόν—*ekrátēsa autón* = אֲחַזְתִּיו— *ʾᵃchazᵉtíw*), and would not let him go" (Song 3:4). Contrasting a vile grasping that intends to control, suppress, and asphyxiate, this is the passionate grasping of love and urgent desire, the only kind that can truly "comprehend" the passionate *God who is Love* (1 Jn 4:8). Only like can truly grasp like. The women's arms took hold of the Lord by his immortal ankles, seeking to retain him in their lives by the force of their love. They intuited the infinitely consoling truth proclaimed in the First Letter of John: "God gave us eternal life, and this life is in his Son. He who *has* the Son has life" (1 Jn 5:11b–12). How startling and intimate when applied to this context, the power of the simple verb "to have"! An inspired gloss on this ardent encounter with the Lord Jesus is found in the ancient Cistercian prayer at the end of this volume, in which we read: "I have found him whom my soul loves: I grasp him, and will not let him go. I embrace you, my Jesus, and experience the joy of my love. I encompass you, the treasure of my heart, from whom I have all that is mine."[2]

It goes without saying that strong theophanic elements are also present in our passage. First of all, there is the telltale earthquake that shatters the silence of this Easter morning and recalls two other *seismói*: the one that occurred at the moment of Jesus' death (27:51) and the previous one on the Lake of Gennesaret, when Jesus manifested his cosmic power by stilling the storm (8:24). Then there is the apparition of the angel clothed in lightning, who descends from above and effortlessly rolls back the huge stone. His very appearance makes the elite guards tremble with fear and fall down as though dead. The description of this messenger from heaven ("His appearance was like lightning, and his clothing white as snow") closely resembles the depiction of Jesus himself at his Transfiguration ("His face shone like the sun, and his garments became white as light", 17:2). This transfer of preternatural qualities from the transfigured Jesus to the angel on the occasion of the Resurrection strongly underscores Matthew's utterly austere and naturalistic portrayal of Jesus. Indeed, compared to the emphatically ordinary manner of the risen Jesus' presence here, these more stunning aspects play a clear secondary role, one of almost formulaic import. Since they are *theophanic* elements, these phenomena set the stage for an encounter with Jesus as a being endowed with divine qualities; and yet, when the encounter itself occurs, it is anticlimactic to our expectations since the evangelist seems to strip Jesus deliberately of all external marks of divinity and power. The tension between the ordinary and the extraordinary within the text, however, has the ultimate effect of making the deeper truth of Jesus' identity as the Loving and Living One emerge organically from within his unassuming person.

---

[2] Inveni quem diligit anima mea, tenui eum, nec dimittam. Te mi Jesu, amplector, et amoris mei gaudium obtineo. Te cordis mei thesaurum comprehendo, a quo omnia possideo.

The sudden descent of the angel from heaven, swift and dazzling as lightning, opens out the scene of death and mourning into an upward direction. If death is normally conceived in the Bible as a downward plunge into the somber regions of Hades (Num 16:32; Ps 49[48]:14), life is always associated with an upward soaring into the vast and luminous abode of God in the heavens (17:1; 2 Kings 2:11; Dan 7:13ff.). Before the angel explicitly announces Jesus' Resurrection, the scene has thus already been transformed from a place of death into a place of life by an irruption into the human sphere of cosmic realities and forces that reflect God's creative power. The familiar figure of Jesus will shortly emerge against this background of elements that proclaim the intimate Master to be also the Lord of the Universe.

The risen Jesus is for Matthew no *deus ex machina*, no literary invention artificially ushered in to solve the riddle of a dead Messiah. His appearance on the scene *does* exhibit theophanic qualities that reveal the active presence of God, yet not in an outburst of mythological inventiveness. The only "wonder" that Matthew wishes to record in connection with the risen Jesus is very simple and fundamental: the very fact itself that, having been killed, he is now alive. A violent death, having destroyed his body, was itself in turn destroyed by his Father's all-powerful love, relentlessly intent on raising his Son from the dead. For Matthew, this obvious and all-determining fact speaks for itself. Jesus has kept his promise to return to his friends after his suffering and death so that they, too, might accompany him into fullness of life. Any imaginative elaboration, any impressive symbolism, so useful elsewhere in the Gospel, would here cloud over rather than manifest openly the invisible light of transparent faith that evades the senses.

In this passage, we are witnessing the same mystery that the Book of Revelation proclaims in its apocalyptic style with solemn resonance. When the Risen One appears to him, the seer of Patmos echoes the experience of the holy women in Matthew: "When I saw him, I fell at his feet as though dead. But he laid his right hand upon me, saying, 'Fear not, I am the first and the last, and the living one; I died, and behold I am alive for evermore, and I have the keys of Death and Hades'" (Rev 1:17–18). The specific elements of a christological theophany have nothing to do with overwhelming external phenomena. Jesus is here revealing the presence and activity of his Divine Person solely by exhibiting traits that are specific and essential predicates of God's nature as Love: his fidelity to his friends, his desire to be with them, his keeping all the promises he has made, his determination to share his own life fully with them, and his design to knit them together beyond separation by his act of exhaustive self-giving on the Cross.

These wholly spiritual events, which have nothing in common with dazzling sensory fireworks, are the aspects that truly overwhelm us in Jesus' manner of appearing and interacting after his Resurrection. In other words, the Lord continues to be and to do all the things he was and did before his Passion and death, and this accounts for his clear recognizability by his own. But the Resurrection has now raised the Mystery of Christ in the lives of his followers and of the world immeasurably from the sphere of promise and inchoate realization to the dimension of divinely accomplished and irreversible fact. Insofar as the eternal Word possesses a full human nature, consisting not only of soul, mind, and spirit but also of all the mineral and vegetable compounds that constitute the flesh, we must say that Christ's Resurrection from the dead has changed the quality of creation itself. In him, the whole universe rises from decay and is flooded with divine light.

To sum up, then: The extraordinary external elements, typical of a theophany, which we see in Matthew's text merely create a general atmosphere of wonderment and suspense that make us hold our breath in expectation. Consequently, we are all the more struck by the absence of all unusual phenomena in direct connection with Jesus himself when he does appear. The divine Protagonist, the One who has just triumphed over death and thus opened for all mankind the path to life eternal, surprises the women (and us!) by slipping onto the scene casually, quietly, without any fanfare, almost anonymously. He expresses himself in the simple language of familiar love as he seeks out and finds his own. He radiates no conventional nimbus of extraterrestrial glory but, rather, a steady and discreet aura of reassuring joy and consolation, together with the intense desire to be reunited with his friends as soon as possible.

Indeed, what the risen Jesus embodies in this scene, brief as it is, is more the icon of a full and richly fleshed-out humanity than the inventive facsimile of an otherworldly deity. In this way, the Gospel text already contains, in austere dramatic form, the full reality of the cornerstone dogma of Chalcedon: *If you look at the Man you will see in him the God, and if you look at the God you will see in him the Man, beyond all separation or confusion.*

א

28:5–6   Μὴ φοβεῖσθε ὑμεῖς·
οἶδα γὰρ ὅτι Ἰησοῦν τὸν ἐσταυρωμένον ζητεῖτε·
οὐκ ἔστιν ὧδε· ἠγέρθη γὰρ καθὼς εἶπεν·
δεῦτε ἴδετε τὸν τόπον ὅπου ἔκειτο

Do not be afraid;
for I know that you seek Jesus who was crucified.
He is not here; for he has been raised, as he said.
Come, see the place where he lay

OUT OF THE THUNDER of the great earthquake and the lightning of the angel's form (ἡ εἰδέα αὐτοῦ ὡς ἀστραπή—*hē eidéa autoú hôs astrapê*), there now come vibrant words of reassurance and consolation. The angel's exact words to the women are, "Do not *you* be afraid!", with the use of the emphatic pronoun ὑμεῖς—*hymeís* (here meaning "as for you . . ."). The angel has obviously observed the trembling of the guards, expressing their fear at his descent on the scene; but it is not them he addresses reassuringly. The guards have good reason to be afraid since they have aligned themselves with the forces of death, those seeking to suppress even the possibility of resurrection. The women, on the other hand, approach the tomb with persevering love and hopeful expectation, and therefore in them the angel finds candidates apt to welcome the tidings of new life he brings. Heaven and earth may quake, but the barricaded heart committed only to self-serving endeavors will remain tragically impervious to the truly new things God wants to work for us all.

And the shining messenger's commanding greeting, "Do not be afraid!" is followed at once by his reason why they should not fear: "for I know that you seek Jesus who was crucified." How extraordinarily beautiful that the humble and hidden loyalty, through all hardship, of two very ordinary Jewish women's hearts should capture the interest of the Most High God and become the familiar knowledge of a resplendent angelic visitor! Indeed, these two faithful women are among the "little ones" of the Kingdom, whose "angels always behold the face of my Father who is in heaven", and these angels can therefore read in the Father's eyes his knowledge of men's hearts (18:10).

Those who persevere in seeking Jesus through thick and thin; those who seek Jesus, not in order to abuse and banish him from their lives or to suppress the life-principle that he bears within him, but, rather, seek Jesus motivated by nothing other than the steely simplicity of an unshakeable love that looks for no recompense other than the proximity of the Beloved, even in his death: *such* are the people who will find the risen Jesus as their Lord, Friend, and Dispenser of life eternal. Fidelity in love and nothing but fidelity in love is the vital link between a death out of obedience and a risen life beyond the clutches of death. No one will find the Risen One and be "united to the Lord" and "become one spirit with" Christ (1 Cor 6:17) who has not first sought the *Jesus who was crucified.* Hearts are saved and deified only by plunging into the total Paschal Mystery of the Word Incarnate.

Now, the comforting effect the angel has on the astonished women through his command "Do not be afraid!" mysteriously connects this angelic figure with the figure of Jesus himself, who appears before the women in v. 10, shortly after their encounter with the blazing messenger from above. Jesus repeats to the women the angel's exact words, "Do not be afraid!" The angel thus plays the role of forerunner to the Lord as he nimbly rolls back the great stone from the mouth of the tomb and fills the dark void within with his own splendor. The angel illuminates the absence of Jesus from the place of death in preparation for the women's personal encounter with Jesus in fullness of life. Against the accusations of the elders that the disciples would steal Jesus' body to deceive the gullible, the angel provides the definitive, divine point of view on what has transpired.

Joseph of Arimathea's previous action of *rolling forward* the stone to block the tomb's entrance (προσκυλίσας λίθον μέγαν—*proskylísas líthon mégan*, 27:60) served as an act of piety to the dead Teacher and confirmed the truth of Jesus' death. Conversely, the angel's present action of *rolling away* the stone from the entrance (ἀπεκύλισεν τὸν λίθον—*apekýlisen ton líthon*) so as to open up the tomb and reveal its empty interior serves to signal symbolically the nullification of the power of death's hold over Jesus. Thus the two correlative verbs προσκυλίω—*proskylíô* ("to roll up to", 27:60) and ἀποκυλίω—*apokylíô* ("to roll away", 28:2) together contain the whole Paschal Mystery: Christ, first swallowed up by death and then triumphantly escaping death's clutches, leaves behind him a radiant, silent space for faith's contemplation, to be filled with the faithful believer's wonderment, hope, and love. Our capacity to desire Jesus ardently and fully embrace him once we encounter him must be trained and intensified by the practice of persevering in silent expectation in the face of his absence.

Moreover, the angel's action of *sitting upon the stone* the moment he has rolled it back is the most specific and palpable sign of Christ's triumph over death; in this, too, the angel is an icon reflecting a mysterious event we cannot behold directly. The boulder that was a seal of death and an obstacle to life is suddenly transformed by a brilliant, imperious gesture into the cathedra from which the angel proclaims the Resurrection. The text's refusal to pry into the logical particulars concerning when and how the actual Resurrection occurs comes strongly to the fore here when we discover that, when the angel rolls back the stone, *the tomb is already empty!* The synchronicity of all these events is such that the text seems to suggest that the angel clothed in lightning came down from heaven *in response to* the women's desire to see Jesus' tomb. In other words, their fidelity to Jesus in death, their wanting at least to be in the vicinity of his corpse so as to pour their heart out with mourning, are virtues amply rewarded by a theophany that bears incontrovertible witness to the Resurrection.

The place left empty by the *vanishing of death* becomes the bright locus where loving human fidelity meets and is overwhelmed by omnipotent divine fidelity. And what a resplendent and superabundant "emptiness" it is! The "earthquake", the "lightning", and the "snow", as attributes of the angel, connect his figure with awe-inspiring cosmic realities of intense beauty and thus serve as warrants for the truth of his testimony to God's "[steadfast] love . . . established for ever" and his "faithfulness . . . firm as the heavens" (Ps 89[88]:2), both of which are manifested in the Resurrection. But this overwhelming manifestation of divine truth and power shown through the angel has diametrically opposed effects on the guards at the tomb and on the visiting women. At the angel's approach, the reactions by each group of observers at the tomb reveal crucial aspects of human interaction with God's grace at work in us.

Fear is normally at least one element of the human reaction in Scripture at the close approach of God's power. The weakness of man instinctively recoils from the power and holiness of God even when this God is believed to be intrinsically good and well-intentioned. The guards at Jesus' tomb were especially selected by the Jewish elders to thwart the massive fraud they suspected the disciples were about to commit: namely, steal the body of Jesus and thus claim he had come back to life. We surmise that those guards must have been robust and fearless soldiers from the military elite. And yet at the sight of the angel, we see them "tremble" (ἐσείσθησαν—*eseísthēsan*) and become "like dead men". This "trembling" of the guards corresponds in psychophysical terms to the quaking of the earth shortly before, which the text describes in the same terms (σεισμὸς ἐγένετο μέγας—*seismós egéneto mégas*, 28:2).

These strongmen, expressly engaged to serve the interests of the religious authorities, without any resistance are histrionically reduced to limp puppets who can only succumb before the authority from above. Without the least hesitation or show of force, ephemeral human strategy and power collapse like a house of cards, and the hearts and knees of tested heroes can now only shudder to the rhythms of divine ordinances conveyed by the convulsions of the earth and the effulgence of a majestic apparition. Nor should we miss the ironic dramatic reversal stressed by Matthew: while the Dead One rises to life, the living executors of power become like the dead (οἱ τηροῦντες ἐγενήθησαν ὡς νεκροί—*hoi têroúntes egenêthêsan hôs nekroí*). Those who were officially appointed to secure the tomb are in the end overwhelmed by the power emanating from the bright emptiness within!

"THE JESUS WHO WAS CRUCIFIED . . . is not here; for he has [been raised], as he said. Come, see the place where he lay": The angel explicitly invites the women to peer into the emptiness of the tomb. At its very center, the place of death is empty. The air vibrates with life where a corpse should be rotting. The empty tomb is the crucial symbol of the whole Paschal Mystery because it simultaneously looks back to death and forward to newness of life. In this emptiness, death and life are no longer struggling enemies, but, rather, death becomes the vehicle and occasion for new and immortal life. Christ is not visibly present here, but the place contains the whole history of Christ in summary form, and the believer needs to enter into this history and make it his own before he can encounter the Savior in his risen flesh.

The statement "The Jesus who was crucified . . . is not here" contains a double negative that, in the mouth of the angel, is transmuted into the only possible conclusion: *He has [been raised] as he said.* The total absence of death, the voiding of death, implies the fullness of life. The supine symbolism of *see the place where he lay* (ἔκειτο—*ékeito*) is supplanted by the erect symbolism of *he has [been raised]* (ἠγέρθη—*êgérthê*), and this affirmation by the angel is the most precise, though still veiled, form in which we witness the actual Resurrection. We insist that this crucial verb ἠγέρθη—*êgérthê* should be literally translated in its true passive form as "he has been raised" (NAB, NET, MNT)[3] rather than as the active verb "he has risen" (VUL,[4] RSV, NJB). A so-called "theological passive" verb is here involved that strongly connotes the action of the Father on his dead Son.[5] It is supremely important that, even and especially in his all-determining act of triumphing over death, Christ not be represented as an independent operator or a mythologically astounding titan powered from within himself. Both as Suffering Servant and as triumphant Lord, Jesus is always and forever the obedient Son of the eternal Father who begets him continually and ever bestows on him fullness of divine life and sovereignty over creation. Only the Father's faithful love for his Son constitutes the secret power that propels the Resurrection.

This is why Jesus can say without any contradiction both "I and the Father are one" (Jn 10:30) and "the Father is greater than I" (Jn

---

[3] Denn erweckt wurde er.

[4] Surrexit enim sicut dixit.

[5] See in this connection the following New Testament passages: Acts 2:24; 3:26; 4:10; 5:30; 10:40; 13:30; Rom 7:4; 10:9; Gal 1:1; Col 2:12; 1 Pet 1:21.

14:28), since "the Son can do nothing of his own accord" (Jn 5:19). The basic attribute of the divinity of the second Person is precisely to be Son and nothing but Son, which means he receives everything, beginning with his very Being, from the Father. Not just being a powerful *Creator* but also being a joyful and thankful *Receiver* is an essential modality of the Christian God. "The Father who dwells in me does his works" (Jn 14:10), proclaims Jesus, and the greatest of the Father's works is his beloved Son's Resurrection, his deliverance from the power of death.

Jesus' Resurrection from the dead, and not his conception from Mary, is, we may say, his temporal experience in his human nature of his eternal generation from the Father: "We bring you the good news", said Paul to the Jews in the synagogue at Antioch of Pisidia, "that what God promised to the fathers, this he has fulfilled to us their children by raising Jesus; as also it is written in the second psalm, 'You are my Son, today I have begotten you'" (Acts 13:32–33). Neither the Cross nor the Resurrection can ever be dissociated from the will and action of the Father in and through his beloved Son. It is precisely this that the theological passive verb ἠγέρθη—*êgérthê* here will not allow us to forget.

We have a tendency to reduce every great and admirable action to the level of merely worldly heroics, particularly in the case of bigger-than-life personages we identify as our "champions". And so we tend to project such self-generating, self-starting heroism onto the risen Jesus. But the direct experience of Jesus' empty tomb to which the angel invites us should inevitably bring us face to face with human mortality as such and with our own interior death in particular— our own emptiness, our own nothingness, our own terminal weakness and incapacity. All of these the Lord Jesus himself assumed in his humanity, and from them the Father had to deliver him so that, in so delivering him, he would simultaneously deliver us.

As it was with Jesus, so must it be with us: it is only from that locus of radically embraced humility and blessed abasement that we can raise our empty hands and longing hearts to the Father so as to be raised by him, together with Jesus, into the glory of his jubilant Heart: "If we have died with Christ, we believe that we shall also live with him. For we know that Christ being raised from the dead will never die again; death no longer has dominion over him. The death he died he died to sin, once for all, but the life he lives he lives to God. So you also must consider yourselves dead to sin and alive to God in Christ Jesus" (Rom 6:8–11).

28:7   καὶ ταχὺ πορευθεῖσαι εἴπατε τοῖς μαθηταῖς αὐτοῦ
ὅτι Ἠγέρθη ἀπὸ τῶν νεκρῶν,
καὶ ἰδοὺ προάγει ὑμᾶς εἰς τὴν Γαλιλαίαν,
ἐκεῖ αὐτὸν ὄψεσθε· ἰδοὺ εἶπον ὑμῖν

Then go quickly and tell his disciples
that he has been raised from the dead,
and behold, he is going before you to Galilee;
there you will see him. Lo, I have told you

THE ANGEL'S SUDDEN, BLAZING DESCENT from heaven, accompanied by the earthquake, shattered the stasis of the grave and ignited an impetus in the plot that is then communicated to the other players in the drama. In this strong driving energy, we perceive the *élan vital* of the Resurrection at work. The angel's two affirmations "He is not here, for he has [been raised]" and "See the place where he lay" bring absolute closure to the Passion narrative and act as springboards to propel the attention and action of the women elsewhere. When he then adds, referring to Galilee, "*there you will see him*", the angel is making a clear contrast with his previous statement, "he is not *here*". The *here* (ὧδε—*hôde*) of the place of death is negated in order to make way for the *there* (ἐκεῖ—*ekeí*) of the place of fullness of life, namely, the space of interaction between Jesus and his disciples.

Jesus himself will echo this emphasis on the eventual place of unitive encounter between Master and disciples when he says to the women, also referring to Galilee: *"And there* (κἀκεῖ—*kakeí*) [my brothers] will see me."* All hearts' desires, plans, and ambitions are unambiguously being oriented by an urgent grace, working through the angel and the risen Jesus, toward the place of meeting, unification, and mutual delight to be experienced as gift by the Lord and his followers, beyond any possibility of further separation. If the "empty tomb" symbolizes the locus of conquered death, "Galilee" symbolizes the ultimate trysting place. It represents the sphere of superabundant life where the Messiah will at last bring to fulfillment his purpose in coming to this world by forging out of those who share in his Resurrection a new redeemed humanity "of one heart and soul" (Acts 4:32). We speak of the Church his Bride.

Many specific words make the dynamics of grace of which we speak a palpable reality in the text, and the interior impetus of the faith that crafted the text greatly affects the reader. For instance, the word ταχύ—*tachý* ("quickly") appears twice, first when the angel tells the women to "go quickly" and then when the women obey him and "[depart] quickly from the tomb". This adverb then accelerates into action when the women do not walk but "[*run*] to tell his disciples". An urgency of joy and desire slowly comes to pervade the atmosphere, as if what has just happened to Jesus is the most unprecedented and momentous piece of news that ever was. In the wake of this verb *run*, there then follows a series of other verbs of swift movement: "an angel *descended* and *came* and *rolled back* the stone and *sat* upon it" (note the breathless polysyndeton, v. 2); "you *seek*" (v. 5); "he has [been *raised*]" (6a); "*come*, see" (v. 6b); "*go* quickly" (v. 7a); "he is *going* before you" (v. 7b); "they *departed* quickly and *ran*" (v. 8); "Jesus [*came upon*] them" (ὑπήντησεν—*hypêntêsen*, v. 9a); "they [*came up*] (προσ-ελθοῦσαι—*pros-elthoúsai*) and [*took hold of*] his feet and *worshiped* (προσ-εκύνησαν—*pros-ekýnêsan*) him" (the Greek here insists on the forward momentum by repeating the prefix προς—*pros-* ["toward"], even in the verb for "to worship" [literally, "to fall prostrate"], v. 9b); and, finally, "*go* and tell my brethren to *go* to Galilee" (v. 10). Indeed, this brief textual space bursts with movement! The clear goal of so much locomotion, both spiritual and physical, the desired end on which all these rushing lines of movement converge, is extraordinary in its utter simplicity: "There they will *see me*" (v. 10). If this were the Old Testament, I dare say that the text would in perpetuity have dubbed this privileged place of meeting *Kakeimeópsontai* ("there-they-will-see-me"), on the analogy of *Peniel* ("face-of-God")[6] or perhaps of *Hephzibah* ("my-delight-is-in-her"), God's pet name for Zion.[7]

It is startling that a passage that initially focuses on *emptiness and absence* nevertheless contains a significant number of verbs that surprisingly invite us to *see* the presence and the glory of God in the risen Christ. Jesus seeking out his loved ones to show himself to them and be with them in mutual delight corresponds precisely, like a glove perfectly fitting its owner's hand, to the disciples' distraught condition of confusion, dispersion, and longing for their Lord after his death. The momentary emptiness and absence left in his wake by the risen Jesus only serve to sharpen the edge of his disciples' yearning to see and interact with their lost Friend. The passage of ten verses contains no fewer than eight verbs of seeing, which alternate between the present viewing of the emptiness in the tomb and the projected future beholding of the Lord in person.[8] Thus, a text dealing ostensibly with mourning, emptiness, and absence is transformed into a kerygmatic proclamation urging the listeners to experience firsthand and with their whole being, simultaneously spiritual and sensual, the wonders of unimaginably new life in Christ.

A central aspect of this newness of life in Christ is the male disciples' experience of being forgiven for their collective betrayal of the Lord, which makes the women disciples' fidelity all the more impressive and precious. No doubt gnawing feelings of guilt such as Peter's troubled all Jesus' followers for abandoning him after Gethsemane, and this shame may well be one of the reasons, besides their unbelief, for why they have to be repeatedly persuaded to go encounter the risen Lord. In fact the angel's instruction to the women to tell the disciples "that he has risen from the dead, and behold, he is going before you to Galilee" (v. 7b), which is repeated to them by Jesus

---

[6] "So Jacob called the name of the place *Peniel*, saying, 'For I have seen God face to face, and yet my life is preserved' " (Gen 32:30).

[7] "You shall be called *Hephzibah*, and your land Married; for the Lord delights in you, and your land shall be married" (Is 62:4).

[8] V. 1 (ἦλθεν **θεωρῆσαι**), v. 2 (**ἰδοὺ** σεισμός), v. 6 (**ἴδετε** τὸν τόπον), v. 7 (**ἰδοὺ** προάγει, αὐτὸν **ὄψεσθε, ἰδοὺ** εἶπον), v. 9 (**ἰδοὺ** Ἰησοῦς ὑπήντησεν), v. 10 (με **ὄψονται**). Four of these verbs of "seeing" take the form of the interjection ἰδου, ("behold!" or "lo!"), which always points to a verifiable and significant event or truth. Thus the text invites us to both physical and spiritual vision.

himself moments later ("go and tell my brethren to go to Galilee, and there they will see me", v. 10b), is but the recurrence and fulfillment of Jesus' promise to his friends after the institution of the Eucharist at the Last Supper: "You will all fall away because of me this night; for it is written, 'I will strike the shepherd, and the sheep of the flock will be scattered.' But after I am raised up, I will go before you to Galilee" (26:31–32).

Galilee was the geographical location where Jesus initially sought out and called to himself the first apostles at the beginning of his public ministry. It is therefore fitting that the circle of the apostles' temporal acquaintance with their Lord should now be closed with the risen Jesus, at the end of his earthly sojourn, returning to Galilee to meet his chosen ones for the last time and send them on their world mission.[9] This promise of Jesus to meet his followers in Galilee, uttered during the Passion and about to be fulfilled in glory, fleshes out most concretely the modality of the risen Jesus' fidelity to those he loves. The disciples' shameful and cowardly abandonment of him in his moment of defeat shall not restrain Jesus from coming to be with his friends. He will unwaveringly keep the appointment he made before the crucifixion to meet them in Galilee, because "if we are faithless, he remains faithful—for he cannot deny himself" (2 Tim 2:13).

"So they departed quickly from the tomb with fear and great joy, and ran to tell his disciples": The women are so electrified by the angel's startling revelations and precise instructions to them that not only do they *depart quickly* in response to the command to *go quickly*, but they also intensify the generic verb *go* into the accelerated verb *run*. We must also note that, despite the extraordinary signs accompanying the angelic apparition and what must have been the enthralling beauty of that shining beatific face, the women, nevertheless, do not in the least hesitate to forsake this thoroughly concrete and inviting presence, these deeply reassuring words, in order to pursue hurriedly a still elusive and uncertain goal: Jesus in tangible form. While the disciples have forsaken Jesus out of fear, the women now forsake a splendid heavenly visitation for the sake of Jesus! One turns one's

---

[9] It is suggestive that the architectural term "Galilee" can also designate the outside covered porch of large Romanesque churches. Here penitents would come to be reconciled through confession before entering the nave of the church proper. Such a "Galilee" represented as well a place of joyous encounter between the Lord and forgiven sinners, as in the upcoming Gospel scene.

back reasonably on an angel only for the sake of the beloved of one's heart.

And these women are not in the least confused as to where their hearts lie. They love Jesus above all things, and they enviably proceed to pursue Jesus (even through shady death and elusive promise) over any other being in heaven or on earth, no matter how immediately palpable. Their hearts believe the angel's announcement of the Resurrection with a perfect faith, but they still do not have in their hands concrete proof of the event. Therefore, their merit is very great indeed in renouncing every other form of consolation and satisfaction, no matter how dazzling and divine. They will not dawdle, wasting precious time chatting with a mere dazzling angel, time that could, instead, be devoted to basking in the presence of the true Beloved. They have truly discerned the angel's exclusive role as forerunner. The certain promise of Jesus' presence and the dizzying prospect of sharing that promise with the male disciples fill the faithful women with the energy of transcendental joy. Unlike the guards at the tomb, who for fear of the angel "trembled and became like dead men", the women run to the disciples impelled by "fear and great joy".

The presence of both fear and joy in a religious experience is one of the signs of its probable authenticity as an occasion of life-giving contact with God. But the presence of fear alone belies a troubled relationship with the living God, who is thus being experienced negatively and only at a vast remove. In addition, the text does not say "with great fear and joy" but, rather, "with fear and great joy", which clearly shows the primacy of spirited exultation over soul-shriveling dread in this emotive blend. The simultaneity of awe and joy conveys a new and unique affective response to an unheard-of event. Everything here points to the energy of the Resurrection as communicated to the women. The grave could not contain Jesus the Life; neither can the women contain the Good News regarding him. Both the tomb and the women overflow with the life they contain and that bursts all boundaries in order to reach the whole world.

א

28:9 καὶ ἰδοὺ Ἰησοῦς ὑπήντησεν αὐταῖς λέγων, Χαίρετε.
αἱ δὲ προσελθοῦσαι ἐκράτησαν αὐτοῦ τοὺς πόδας
καὶ προσεκύνησαν αὐτῷ. . . .
Μὴ φοβεῖσθε· ὑπάγετε ἀπαγγείλατε τοῖς ἀδελφοῖς μου
ἵνα ἀπέλθωσιν εἰς τὴν Γαλιλαίαν, κἀκεῖ με ὄψονται

And behold, Jesus met them and said, "Rejoice!"
And they came up and took hold of his feet
and worshiped him. . . .
"Do not be afraid; go and exhort my brethren
to go forth to Galilee, and there they will see me"

T HE ANGEL SAID TO THE WOMEN that Jesus would "go before
[them] (προάγει ὑμᾶς—*proágei hymás*) to Galilee". At the literal level, this means of course that Jesus has already set off for
Galilee from Jerusalem, presumably from the tomb he has forsaken,
and is leading the way there for the women. However, in light of the
plot, we see that, at a deeper level, this angelic revelation refers to the
fact that God's grace is always "prevenient",[10] that is, that it anticipates and prepares the ground for a person's every graced decision and
move. We can never forestall or surprise God with either our good or
our evil actions. Grace is always ahead of us, easing the terrain before
us. In this case, Jesus, God's grace incarnate, is running in advance of
the women who are running toward him without knowing it, thinking
they are going to the disciples. Embodying the preemptive impulses
of true love, Jesus anticipates the women's desires and trajectory and
comes to them when they least expect it. They practically run into his

---

[10] The phrase *prevenient grace* is not only a technical term drawn from Scholastic
theology. It is also an extremely helpful and dynamic liturgical term. In connection
with the theme of *encounter*, see for instance the collect for Friday of the Third Week
of Advent, where the word *prevenient* is appropriately rendered in less Latinate language: "Præveniat nos, omnipotens Deus, tua gratia semper atque subsequatur, ut, qui
adventum Unigeniti tui summo cordis desiderio sustinemus, et præsentis vitæ subsidia
et futuræ pariter consequamur" (May your grace, almighty God, always *go before us*
and follow after, so that we, who await with heartfelt desire the coming of your Only
Begotten Son, may receive your help both now and in the life to come).

arms as they concentrate on reaching another goal. "The creature's every activity", writes von Balthasar, "rests on a still deeper passivity: in order to come into being [fully itself] it must place itself like clay in the shaping 'hands' of God and entrust itself to them."[11] Stated in geometrical language: human nature behaves like an asymptotic curve that can never on its own momentum reach God, the "plane" toward which it hurtles. The only way in which the creature can make contact with the goal it so ardently desires is if this goal, on its own initiative, advances to meet the straining creature in the midst of its effort.

Now, the angel did not lie to the women when he said to them that "he is going before you to Galilee; there you will see him." But, in fact, Jesus' own intention was to meet these faithful women he so loved *on their way to Galilee*. Perhaps he himself was too eager for the encounter and did not wish to wait! In any event, very soon after the women began running to bring the astounding news of the Resurrection to the disciples, "Jesus met them (ὑπήντησεν—*hypêntêsen*)" against all expectation, stopping them in their tracks.

This verb ὑπήντησεν—*hypêntêsen* ("he came to meet") in the aorist tense, indicating a punctuated action, clashes mightily *into* the previous verb ἔδραμον—*édramon* ("they were running") in the imperfect, connoting an ongoing action. In other words, Jesus' sudden arrival before them, as he moves in their direction, interrupts with sweet violence the path of the women's trajectory toward the disciples. The Lord has all along been closer than they thought! Matthew then stresses the great surprise of the moment by putting into Jesus' mouth almost verbatim the speech of the angel to the women: "Do not be afraid; go and tell my brethren to go to Galilee, and there they will see me." If Jesus' sudden arrival *anticipates* the women's expectations, it also *postpones* the goal on which they were focused. In this way, the evangelist wants to underscore the fact that Jesus came searching for the women in order to catch them deliberately off guard, before they reached the disciples, in order to thrill them with his long-awaited presence.

---

[11] Hans Urs von Balthasar, *The Glory of the Lord: A Theological Aesthetics*, vol. 2, *Studies in Theological Style: Clerical Styles*, trans. Andrew Louth et al. (New York: Crossroad; San Francisco: Ignatius Press, 1984), 64, with reference to Irenæus of Lyons, *Adversus Hæreses*, II, 299.

It seems as well that he himself could not wait to reenter their lives. What we have called a "clash" of verbs and intentions may equally be described as a joyously abrupt reunion, deriving unending pleasure precisely from its unforeseen character. Indeed, for the freedom of grace to operate unimpeded in our lives, we must be malleable. We must continually exercise an interior pliancy of will and expectation and be prepared for sudden changes of plans and direction. If we wish to be partakers of God's life, we must accept as a fundamental condition the fact that we must abide in glad submission to the unpredictable sway of a Heart that is always seeking to encounter us and delight us with his Presence.

Everything Jesus intends for his faithful friends is contained in his powerful word of greeting to the women: Χαίρετε—*Chaírete* ("Rejoice!"). Its dramatic impact is diluted when the verb, in the imperative, is rendered merely as a formulaic "Hail!" devoid of all affective content. Jesus' whole intention, after all, in revealing his Father's secrets to his friends and in seeking out their company, has always been "that my joy may be in you, and that your joy may be full" (Jn 15:11). He makes theirs his own joy in the Father by putting himself at the center of their lives. These women have already tasted, long before its composition, the experience described in the famous twelfth-century poem that begins thus:

> *Jesu dulcis memoria,*
> *Dans vera cordi gaudia:*
> *Sed super mel et omnia,*
> *Ejus dulcis præsentia.*[12]

> [Jesus' sweet memory
> Gives true joys to the heart:
> But more than honey and all things
> Is his sweet presence.]

The women have searched for Jesus and set out on their way to the disciples, obeying the angel's directions. But for the gift of joy to be truly a divine gift unequivocally deriving from the Heart of God, it is Jesus who must set out to find the women and, in this encounter, admit them personally to the experience of his love. His

---

[12] The hymn is often attributed to St. Bernard of Clairvaux. Its sentiments are in fact quite representative of Cistercian-Bernardine spirituality.

first word to them, as we have seen, is "Rejoice!" The objective joy he communicates to them by command (as if he were saying, "Now that I am with you, only joy is allowed!") is the joy of God himself at being God. Such joy authenticates and strengthens the subjective joy the women have already felt at hearing the news. Yet now their joy is perfect, fulfilled, complete (πληρωθῇ—*plêrôthê*, Jn 15:11) because it flows from the active and unsurpassably real presence of the desired Person. And the One urging them to rejoice is standing there big as life within their hands' reach, indeed, offering himself for the taking.

As the women run (ἔδραμον—*édramon*) toward the disciples, Jesus comes to encounter (ὑπήντησεν—*hypêntêsen*) them. In immediate response to his approach, the women "came up to (προσελθοῦσαι—*proselthoúsai*) Jesus and took hold of (ἐκράτησαν—*ekrátêsan*) his feet and worshiped (προσεκύνησαν—*prosekýnêsan*) him". It is difficult to imagine two short sentences more packed with physical action, reciprocity of feeling, swift movement, and intensity of expression than these. Even the final verb, προσκυνέω—*proskyneô*, here translated "to worship", is not a religious abstraction but describes the physical action of falling down before someone to show obeisance and self-surrender. The rendering "worship" appears in this context to be far too technical and ritualistic a term. The powerful beauty of this scene comes from the fact that every action by every player is simultaneously physical, psychological, and spiritual, all three inseparably. The joy, surprise, and delight of the spirit are poured out through the visible actions of the body, and in turn the body ardently seeks union with the risen Lord Jesus in the realm of luminous glory in which he dwells.

We are habitually so self-involved, and our mental world so orbits around ourselves, that we think we initiate and fuel every event worthy of note in our lives, above all the quest for God and ultimate meaning. We see ourselves as great pioneers of the divine and speak endlessly of "man's search for God". But then, too, Greek philosophy and every world religion do the same thing. However, when do we ever speak of "God's search for man", which should be the specifically Judæo-Christian formulation of the religious quest for meaning, the only focus worthy of a God who is faithful love? From the Lord searching for Adam and Eve in the garden (Gen 3:9) and alluring Israel "into the wilderness [to] speak tenderly to her" (Hos 2:14), to Jesus searching for his lost sheep (Lk 15:4) and the risen Christ knocking for admission at the door of our heart (Rev 3:20), the axis that traverses the whole of Sacred Scripture points to a God who is always on his way to us, always seeking us out in our need in order to give us . . . himself.

The present episode portrays a striking, dramatic reversal in the plot of the story, and it illustrates with stirring precision the whole Christian theology of grace. *Improviso invenitur quærens*: This phrase, Augustinian in flavor, sums up succinctly the principle of the antecedence of God's action that underlies the Catholic theology of grace. It also contains a paradox that is the source of all hope and consolation because it stresses the fact that no search for God is ever finally in vain since always *the one searching is unexpectedly found.*

JESUS IGNORED THE MOCKERS' TAUNT that if he was the true Son of God he should come down from the Cross and save himself (27:40–43). Compliance with the sarcastic challenge would have debased Jesus to the level of a cheap, crowd-pleasing wonderworker. In precisely the same way and for the same reasons, the Jesus risen from the dead now shuns every conventional mark of preternatural power, and it is this very restraint that demonstrates his divinity. The dazzle, rather, accompanies the apparition of the angelic messenger, a created being who, by definition, is infinitely lower in status than the risen Word. The unusual phenomena attendant upon the coming of the angel to the tomb serve to frame the scene as a theophany; and yet, ironically, when Jesus himself, God incarnate, appears to the women and the theophany actually occurs, the marks of divinity he exhibits are all spiritual, interior, relational, and perceptible only to the searching and loving heart, though of course manifested physically through his gestures and words.

The chief of these gestures moreover, at once so divine and so thoroughly human, is the act itself of Jesus' appearing before the women unforeseeably, his initiative in coming expressly to encounter them (ὑπήντησεν αὐταῖς—*hypêntêsen autaís*) along a trajectory and at a moment in time known only to himself.[13] Furthermore, it is this act of intentional encounter, this *hypántêsis*, that then makes it possible for the women to reciprocate Jesus' sudden coming to them with their own act of advancing vigorously toward him to grasp his feet in loving adoration. And yet, though the impassioned response is wholly the product of the women's love, its ultimate source lies in the Heart of Jesus because, in order to be grasped, one first has to make oneself *graspable*.

A valuable byproduct of the encounter is that it serves as well as an empirical demonstration of the veracity of Jesus' risen body, since a ghost's feet cannot be clasped. The women's swift and tumultuous actions of running toward, grasping, and adoring Jesus the moment they hear his voice show that they perceive his greeting of *Rejoice!* as an invitation to intimacy and that they can fulfill his command only through such unitive activity, since he himself is the only joy of their hearts.

The risen Jesus' very familiar and "egalitarian" manner of presence reveals that the authentic divine activity of grace affects above all the human *soul* as impacted by the invisible fire of God's undying fidelity and transformative presence. But what the women's eyes actually see, ears hear, and hands touch is *merely* the familiar Lord and Friend in his recognizable and comforting human form. All love, whether human or divine, operates subtly through steadfast, trustworthy affection, and reassuring presence. Jesus wants the power of his risen and

---

[13] The great theological importance of the biblical category of *encounter* is strongly reflected in the liturgy and spirituality of the Church of both East and West. Among the Greeks, the feast of Candlemas on February 2nd is called the *Hypapanté*, that is, the feast of the Encounter in the Temple between God and his people in the Baby Jesus. And among the Latins, the whole season of Advent, preparatory to both the Birth of Jesus and his final coming as glorious King at the Parousia, revolves around the concept of *encounter* with God in Christ. There is hardly an Advent collect that does not refer to the theme in some way, for instance that of the First Sunday: "*Da, quæsumus, omnipotens Deus, hanc tuis fidelibus voluntatem, ut Christo tuo venienti iustis operibus occurrentes, eius dexteræ sociati, regnum mereamur possidere, cæleste*" (Grant your faithful, we pray, almighty God, the resolve to run forth to meet your Christ with righteous deeds at his coming, so that, gathered at his right hand, they may be worthy to possess the heavenly Kingdom).

immortal Presence to penetrate into the core of our being. That can only happen in a manner that is not dependent on superficial sensory stimuli.

Only the awakened and passionate heart can perceive the full extent of God's eager love, communicated by the risen Jesus' approach in the most persuasively human and ordinary form. "The Word", after all, "became *flesh*" and not a dazzling angel! "For surely it is not with angels that [Jesus] is concerned but with the descendants of Abraham. Therefore he had to be made like his brethren in every respect, so that he might become a merciful and faithful high priest in the service of God, to make expiation for the sins of the people" (Heb 2:16–17).

28:10

τότε λέγει αὐταῖς ὁ Ἰησοῦς·
Μὴ φοβεῖσθε· ὑπάγετε ἀπαγγείλατε τοῖς ἀδελφοῖς μου
ἵνα ἀπέλθωσιν εἰς τὴν Γαλιλαίαν, κἀκεῖ με ὄψονται

Then Jesus said to them,
"Do not be afraid; go and exhort my brethren
to go forth to Galilee, and there they will see me"

AFTER THE FIRST STARTLING MOMENT of visible encounter, which is beyond all speech and commentary, Jesus then addresses three distinct commands to the two ecstatic women. First he commands them to *rejoice*. He wants to instill joy in his presence into his disciples' hearts as the wellspring of all their faith, prayer, and apostolate. Where Jesus is, there necessarily must joy also be: for the life of God is Joy. There only remains for the ardent disciple to "sell" all lesser joys in order to buy the whole field where God has hidden his treasure and so enter into the undiluted joy of his Master (cf. 13:44; 25:21, 23). As the twelfth-century Cistercian writer Guerric of Igny says marvelously in a sermon on the Resurrection: "Sufficit mihi si Jesus vivit. Si vivit vivo; cum de ipso pendeat anima mea; immo ipse sit vita mea, ipse sufficientia mea" (It is sufficient for me if Jesus lives. If he lives, I live, since my soul hangs on him, or rather, he is himself my life and my very sufficiency).[14] No better description of pure enduring joy, drunk from the source, can be imagined.

Next, after receiving with delight the women's response of overwhelming affection and devotion, Jesus commands them to banish all fear from their hearts. It may appear peculiar to speak of "commands" with reference to his urging them vehemently to rejoice and not to fear, since normally emotions cannot be prescribed even to oneself; and yet Jesus knows what he is doing. Grammatically the two plural verbs χαίρετε—*chaírete* (rejoice!) and μὴ φοβεῖσθε—*mê phobeísthe* (do not be afraid!) are in the imperative mood and so, objectively speaking, they are indeed commands. However, more than just grammar is involved here. Joy and fear are perhaps the strongest of the human emotions, and together they broadly cover the gamut of all emotions. We human beings are normally so subject to the complex circumstances always affecting us that it is very difficult for us to will ourselves either into a state of pure joy or into an act of the will that can banish all fear from our hearts. For this reason, the objective command-form of the two verbs in question serves to evoke a basic truth, namely, that the advent of perfect joy and the expulsion of all fear in our souls can only be the result of a divine intervention. Only an act of God's will can grant his chosen ones a share in the perfect bliss of his own internal life. Both unsullied joy and the absence of all fear, then, are correlative gifts of grace, and as such they can never be produced either by sheer brawny effort or artificial techniques and psychotropic agents. No one can wrest joy from God because the joy we speak of is one of the chief attributes of the divine nature itself, and we cannot by caprice steal aspects of God's Being.

Yet we note as well that these two first commands of Jesus correspond to the interior disposition that has already been present in the women since they heard the angel's words: they "departed quickly from the tomb *with fear and great joy*". This means that their faithful

---

[14] Guerric of Igny, *Sermon 1 on the Resurrection*, 5.

love for Jesus has already caused to be born in their souls an inchoate joy, although such joy still coexisted with a significant fear produced by uncertainty and anguish in the face of the unknown and the all-too-wonderful. Only the Person of Jesus himself, fully welcomed and embraced in the soul, can generate unalloyed joy in creatures.

The third command that Jesus directs to the women immediately after banishing their fear and bewilderment is ὑπάγετε ἀπαγγείλατε τοῖς ἀδελφοῖς μου—*hypágete apangeílate tois adelphoís mou*: "Go and [exhort] my brethren. . . ." We should note how the expulsion of fear and the gift of godlike joy are followed at once by a *mission*. The Lord's great deeds to our person cry out by their nature to be shared with others. "Go and tell my brethren . . ." is the typical rendering of this verse in most English versions; and yet we sense at once that the three short English syllables "go and tell" do not truly do full justice to the solemnity and import of the nine syllables of the Greek original.[15] Ὑπάγετε—*hypágete* more precisely means "go away" or "go forth", as spoken to one sent on a mission by the sender. In our context, this verb stresses the need for the women to detach themselves almost at once, after their joyous encounter, from their clear desire to cling to Jesus for the duration and abide with him in tranquil delight in the place where he encountered them. In other words, the Lord's command reminds them that intimate contact with him cannot be static or become an end in itself, especially in the light of Jesus' urgency to gather all his brethren together and found his Church.

The women's sudden mission to the disciples shows how their meeting with Jesus must bear fruits of universal charity. Jesus has risen from the grave for the sake of all and not only for these women's joy; yet blessed are they to be chosen as evangelists to the future apostles! The first verb "go forth" is at once completed by the second imperative ἀπαγγείλατε (*apangeílate*), closely yoked to "go forth" by the omission of a conjunction. Such asyndeton shows the inseparability of the two commanded actions. This third command of Jesus actually calls for two related but different actions. *Apangeílate*, at the heart of which we detect the root *angel-*, should be rendered "announce",

---

[15] More satisfactorily, some French versions have *Allez annoncer* (Go and announce, FBJ, TOB), and Luther's version has *Geht hin und verkündigt* (Go forth and proclaim, LUO).

"proclaim", or "exhort" rather than simply "tell" because it involves an unexpected and momentous declaration that constitutes the Good News to the disciples. These cannot later communicate to others what they have not first received and experienced in their own lives. In the end, Jesus' search for the women is quite organically extended, through their feminine kerygmatic mission, as Jesus' search for his male disciples.

We see here how the dynamic experience of the risen Jesus must by its very nature become amplified in ever-widening circles, like the ripples of a stone cast into tranquil waters. First the angel tells the women to go and find their Lord. Now Jesus himself tells the women to go tell his brethren to come to his encounter. And in due course, Jesus will tell the apostles to go tell the whole world, until the Good News eventually arrives to your ears and mine, still bursting with life and, in turn, requiring further transmission through our own willing service.

Ὑπάγετε ἀπαγγείλατε—*hypágete apangeílate*: *Go forth [and] proclaim to my brethren.* . . . Such a literal translation, catching the transcendental solemnity of the moment, by no means detracts from the utter simplicity, intimacy, and sheer humanity of the scene. Rather, it shows precisely the very ordinary, familiar, and accessible form that the Mystery of the Resurrection assumed in Jesus without the event losing any of its grandeur. While God may manifest himself within the ordinary, God himself is never ordinary! One aspect of the miracle that is the inspired text of the Gospel is precisely its ability to do justice to both these aspects and portray the transcendental revealed in the familiar. Reverence, gravity, and precision of language are often the best servants of an intimate and familiar love because they convey its sacred message with heartfelt devotion and an infinite attention to detail. Familiarity and solemnity are not incompatible. For a ready demonstration of this truth, one has only to think of the heightened language and bracing atmosphere experienced at the *seder* table of a Jewish family, where ease and awe go hand in hand and accomplish a single liturgical purpose: that of inserting this particular family, from the coziness of their own dining room, into the whole sweep of Israel's redemptive history across the centuries.

And there is more. These two tones of familiarity and solemnity, coexisting in creative tension within our passage, point to the two distinct levels at which Matthew's words should be simultaneously read: the temporal-historical and the kerygmatic-liturgical. On the one hand, the evangelist is recording the first meeting of the risen Jesus of Nazareth with his Jewish disciples on that first Easter morning just outside Jerusalem. The feel is local; the events are set in the immediate surroundings. This is the level of the foreground plot, and it enshrines for memory's sake the first stirrings of the historical Church after the Resurrection. On the other hand, and unmistakably, the text also means to communicate a kerygmatic thrust that, like a catching fire, sears through the limitations of that particular historical moment even as the Resurrection melted the barriers of mortal existence. Matthew's text longs to kindle new disciples in every succeeding generation of all human history. Indeed, as Paul exhorts, the Gospel must be preached not only to rational human beings but "to every creature under heaven" (Col 1:23), and this extravagantly categorical injunction requires that the language in which the Gospel is preached duly reflect the unbounded universality and breathtakingly transcendental quality of the mission.

TO SEARCH FOR THE RISEN Jesus afresh, after having sought him first as "the crucified one" among the dead, imposes the necessity of letting go of all previous comfortable notions of "God" in order to access a dimension of pure relational mystery, which is the only sphere where fullness of life can be found. True nourishing life will never come to me from mental notions, from moods and scenarios that I myself have manufactured and can therefore control. Such willful domestication ties the hands of God's seemingly reckless ways with me. I will enjoy vibrant life and be released into authentic freedom only to the degree that I can forsake every form of rigidity, prejudice, and desire to straitjacket the world and God within my own pitiful dimensions, fashioning it according to my own image and likeness. This transformative process can only be the fruit of Christ rising within me; the suspicion that things are subtly changing within me is in fact the sole warrant that I have allowed the Holy Spirit to internalize within my being the power of Jesus' Resurrection. Such a spiritual transformation in outlook and practice is implied in the angel's "catechesis" to the women, who originally came looking only for a corpse—the final earthly state of their crucified Lord, the only Jesus they knew, loved, and could humanly imagine.

However, the drastic change now required of faithful believers is even more explicitly enjoined by Jesus' sudden appearance before them. Those who came resigned to visit only the grim certainties of a grave are abruptly catapulted—much to their delight and dismay—into a disorienting yet liberating space of pure relation with Life Himself, where all static concepts and definitions and preconceived ideas have become obsolete in the face of the Resurrection. Here jubilant love and jubilant love alone is the stuff that is spoken, given, breathed.

INTERLUDE V:
GOD'S COSMIC NOTHINGNESS

ALL THROUGH THE BIBLE one can find again and again the notion of God's double mode of appearing in the world. God affirms his presence, first of all, of course, in the cosmic power. . . . But this is only one way in which God appears in the world. The other sign that he has adopted and that, by concealing him more, shows more truly his intrinsic nature, is the sign of the lowly, which, measured cosmically, quantitatively, is completely insignificant, actually a pure nothing. One could cite in this connection the series Earth—Israel—Nazareth—Cross—Church, in which God seems to keep disappearing more and more and, precisely in this way, becomes more and more manifest as himself. First there is the Earth, a mere nothing in the cosmos, which was to be the point of divine activity in the cosmos. Then comes Israel, a cipher among the powers, which was to be the point of his appearance in the world. Then comes Nazareth, again a cipher within Israel, which was to be the point of his definitive arrival. Then at the end there is the Cross, on which a man was to hang, a man whose life had been a failure; yet this was to be the point at which one can actually touch God. . . . Thus what is small be a cosmic or even wordly scale represents the real sign of God wherein the entirely Other shows itself, which even in relation to our expectations is once again the completely unrecognizable. The cosmic Nothing is the true All, because "for" is the really divine thing. [1]

---

[1] Joseph Cardinal Ratzinger, *Introduction to Christianity*, trans. J. R. Foster, 2nd ed. (San Francisco: Ignatius Press, 2004), 255–57.

19. PLATO'S CAVE IN THE TEMPLE

The Report of the Guard (28:11–15)

28:11
Πορευομένων δὲ αὐτῶν
ἰδού τινες τῆς κουστωδίας ἐλθόντες εἰς τὴν πόλιν
ἀπήγγειλαν τοῖς ἀρχιερεῦσιν ἅπαντα τὰ γενόμενα

*While they were going,
behold, some of the guard went into the city
and announced to the chief priests all that had taken place*

B Y A PROCEDURE OF GLARING CONTRAST typical of Matthew, we here see our evangelist offering the reader two diametrically opposed reactions to the fact of the Resurrection. Although they, too, initially experience some fear at the angelic apparition and the earthquake, the women swiftly move forward into a dimension of boundless joy as Jesus himself involves them in the drama of his triumphant life. But the guards at the tomb, after an overpowering fit of terror in the face of the mighty phenomena occurring around them, eventually return to their everyday normalcy. This means taking up again the slavish routine of accepting orders uncritically and carrying them out faithfully in return for monetary compensation. Unlike the women, who go *forward* into a brand-new dimension of giddy freedom conferred on them by partaking in the energy of the Resurrection, the guards go *backward* to their all too familiar routine, predetermined within the iron vice of a master-slave relationship with the local authorities.

Both the women and the guards are brought by destiny to the same extraordinary moment when the Old Age of Death is compelled by divine power to give way to the definitive Age of New Life. Both groups experience the very same preternatural phenomena of earthquake and blinding light, and yet these affect each in precisely opposite ways. No doubt this antagonistic outcome is the result of the fundamental orientation of each one's life. What are the women looking for? Clearly the beloved of their hearts, although they consider him nothing but dead and buried, which provides us with an extraordinary instance of fidelity, courage, and dogged perseverance. The women's ardent, remembering love impels them to break through the constraints of conventional logic and social behavior, first of all shattering the pattern of their own wonted mental habits. And what are the guards looking for? No doubt the security to be found in Plato's cave. Here physical warmth and nourishment, elementary subsistence and official protection are to be had, and a reputable and useful place in the social order, yet all of it at the cost of the soul renouncing all desire to see the light of the sun, all impulse to fly on the wings of Truth's wind. Temporal security and immediate comfort must be purchased by adopting the mentality, logic, and behavior of the slave.

Daily we all come into contact with the Body of Christ. Some handle him for selfless adoration and some for servile profit.

In order to enter fully into the sphere of perfect freedom opened to them by Jesus, the women first need to renounce all temporal attachments and securities. They demonstrate the fact that they have indeed accomplished such a clean break with mortal logic by preferring to abide by the barrenness of their Lord's tomb rather than join the school of a less tragic and more accommodating rabbi. The guards, for their part, manifest a fatal bent of soul by preferring steady employment at the service of unjust, power-wielding oppressors. They become eager and willing collaborators in the works of darkness (cf. Rom 13:12; Eph 5:11). In the antithetical reactions of the guards and the women to the event of the Resurrection, we see vividly illustrated the affirmation of St. John's Prologue: "[The Word] came to his own home, and his own people received him not. But to all who received him, who believed in his name, he gave power to become children of God" (Jn 1:11–12). We see as well a confirmation of Jesus' own words: "I have come as light into the world, that whoever believes in me may not remain in darkness" (Jn 12:46), "yet you refuse to come to me that you may have life" (Jn 5:40). In this sense, the experience of Jesus' Resurrection is also a trenchant judgment, because "the light has come into the world, and men loved darkness rather than light, because their deeds were evil" (Jn 3:19). A poem by Stephen Spender bluntly elucidates our contrarian knack for preferring the darkness to the light, much to our ruin:

> To break out of the chaos of my darkness
> Into a lucid day, is all my will.
> My words like eyes in night, stare to reach
> A centre for their light: and my acts thrown
> To distant places by impatient violence
> Yet lock together to mould a path
> Out of my darkness, into a lucid day.
>
> Yet, equally, to avoid that lucid day
> And to preserve my darkness, is all my will.
> My words like eyes that flinch from light, refuse
> And shut upon obscurity; my acts
> Cast to their opposites by impatient violence
> Break up the sequent path; they fly
> On a circumference to avoid the centre.[1]

Wholly avoiding this existential quandary of battling desires, the holy women take the difficult but brilliant risk of single-mindedly pursuing the path of freedom, which requires that they burn all their bridges behind them in order to go forth and meet the risen Jesus in the zone of unfettered divine freedom. They can therefore join Jesus in his new life because they, too, like Jesus, choose to leave their former selves, their former "darkness", behind. But the guards cling tooth and nail to the purely exploitive relationship between master and slave, dictated by reciprocal greed and the plundering of the innocent. While it is clear that Jesus, the women, and the disciples are all moving forward into a wholly new sphere of existence from what they have known until now, the guards—along with the chief priests and the elders—are still treading the same sempiternal mill, the same nauseous circle of gloom: the complex power-brokering, political strategizing, and avid currying of favors that are the telltale

---

[1] "Darkness and Light", from the collection *The Still Centre*, 1935, in *World within World* (New York: St. Martin's Press, 1994), epigraph.

marks of busy lives that are passingly prominent yet utterly meaning-less.

The guards at the tomb, just as much as the women disciples, experi-ence the phenomena of the dazzling angel and the earthquake as what the historians of religion term a *mysterium tremendum et fascinans*— an "enthralling mystery that makes one tremble". The guards, like the women, are suddenly confronted with the *fact* of a higher order of reality infinitely surpassing their own very limited and humdrum worldly existence. Such an experience instills into them awe and fear at the prospect of annihilation. Much so-called "spirituality" and metaphysical "questing" in our contemporary world resemble this experience of the guards. An unusual event shakes our psyche and even our body, often in an impressive natural setting, and the human sensibility is thrilled at the shock and stimulus of the transcendental. And yet the human *person* as such is by no means willing to forsake, as a result, previous self-indulgent attitudes and behaviors in order to allow his life to be morally and intellectually transformed by the invasion of God's sovereign grace.

There is a reason for readily welcoming the stimulating psycho-sensory experience while at the same time strongly shunning any change in attitude that would diminish self-centeredness. In our Gospel story, this reason may be traced to the two very different kinds of *fear* that hold the guards and the women in their grip. We read that "For fear of [the angel] the guards trembled and became like dead men" (28:4). The guards at the tomb are not merely sec-ondary players in the drama but crucial stand-ins for a whole sec-tion of mankind entrenched in a certain stance. In the face of the an-gel's stunning apparition, they respond exclusively with crippling fear. Their pragmatic function as law-enforcers in society affords them not only sustenance but even a pittance of renown as executors of the or-ders of the great. The result is that, unawares, they are so submerged in that function and have so become one with it that any disruption in their dull routine is perceived as a serious threat to their well-being and very identity. They enjoy the comforts of servility, and their crisis is consequently massive when the splendid messenger from the realm of light and freedom bursts into their little world. They can feel only fear in the face of the numinous event and immense anguish at what they can only view as the approaching destruction of the world as they know it.

The guards thus exhibit an utter incapacity to marvel, to wonder, or to hope that anything might be improved in their lives. They lapse into a state of interior shutdown against any manifestation of the unforeseen. Surprising grace has no place in their world view. This is why, after the angel has disappeared and they have recovered from their terrific fright, the guards' next action is to go back "into the city and [proclaim (ἀπήγγειλαν—*apêngeilan*) to] the chief priests all that had taken place". Ironically, Matthew here uses the same verb to refer to the guards' reporting the news to the priests as he used in the verse before (ἀπαγγείλατε—*apangeílate*, v. 10) to refer to the women's announcement to the disciples. He obviously means to underscore the sharp contrast in the two possible reactions to the Resurrection, resulting in two very different kinds of "proclamation". While the women bear to the male disciples the good tidings that Jesus lives and wants to be united with his friends, the guards bear grim tidings of threat and disruption to their own and their oppressors' lives.

These two "gospels" stand in stark contrast. The guards' is a message of fear and dismay, leading to strategies based on calculation, fraud, and the greed for lucre. The women's urgent announcement, on the contrary, proceeds from a personal experience of communion with the undying life of a faithful Lord. The joy that is the natural effect of every contact with Jesus must always continue to shape and quicken the Christian's words that offer Jesus to the world. To proclaim the Gospel joylessly, in a glum, uninspired, and tedious manner, is a *de facto* negation of what the proclaimer intends to communicate.

We are not speaking here of manufacturing gleeful emotions artificially, for the sake of public display and to promote the "success" of the mission. We speak, rather, of the *objective joy* that should always indwell a believing heart, joy flowing from the certainty of the active presence of the Beloved within us, a quiet energy of delight that can exist in our heart independently of all subjective states of relative gladness or sadness, generated by a host of variable causes beyond our control. This was the objective, inalienable joy experienced at the core of his being by Guerric of Igny when he exclaimed to his monks during the Easter season: "It is enough for me if Jesus lives. If he lives, I live, since my soul hangs on him."

Very poignantly, furthermore, the text says that the guards report to the chief priests τὰ γενόμενα—*ta genómena* ("the things that had happened"), which presumably means they give a full and accurate account of the facts: the earthquake, the advent of the resplendent heavenly being, the opening of the tomb, which revealed its emptiness, and the presence of the faithful women. Since the guards fell to the ground unconscious at the angel's apparition, they seem to have completely missed the angel's interaction with the women, including his affirmation of Jesus' Resurrection. Their souls are so sealed off against the realm of grace, so enchained by opportunism to the realm of shadows and darkness, that they do not have the spiritual organs needed to perceive truths from the realm of light or to interact with its messengers, either heavenly or earthly.

In the face of extraordinary events full of the promise of new life, but requiring radical personal and collective change, the guards can only cower and retreat, running back to the only form of authority and power they recognize even though it is tyrannical and chokes the life out of its subjects. The guards go back in servile fashion, seeking security from the chief priests and exercising a diabolical obedience, like dogs returning to feed on their own vomit (cf. Prov 26:11; 2 Pet 2:22). This is the only instinctive behavior available to fearful, dependent souls who have traded in freedom for security.

By diametrical contrast, the women offer a wholly different response although they are subjected initially to the very same numinous phenomena as were the guards. They, too, are afraid, just as the guards were, because they too are fragile human beings trembling in the face of the divine. But, in their case, the fear does not occupy the whole space of their soul, nor is it the chief emotion overpowering it. As we have seen, "they departed quickly from the tomb *with fear and great joy*" (28:8). Only faith is the portress that admits joy into the soul because only faith can dare to hope that it will eventually come into the possession of what it loves. Only faith can dare to be open to the truly and astoundingly new, to things that have never been heard or seen before but that nevertheless hold great promise of fulfilling every longing of the soul.

The women's fear is not servile as was the guards', who feared solely for their own safety and became frightened by a chaotic situation that would compromise their servitude to the powerful. In addition to the fear of being physically harmed by the earthquake or the evident might of the angel, the guards feared cruel punishment and probable dismissal for not having done their job. The women's experience of fear, by contrast, derives first of all from how close to them the divine has come and how unworthy they are to receive such a visitation. Such fear is a clear sign of a deep faith that knows the fundamental difference in status between God and man. Such fear is synonymous with awe, respect, reverence, adoration. This is why such healthy fear, based on the objective order of things, comes accompanied by *great joy* as by an elder sister, the one who holds decisive sway in the soul. Without fear, joy in the soul would become presumptuous and self-indulgent, and without joy fear would become a tyrannical, life-shriveling blight.

א

28:12–13 καὶ συναχθέντες μετὰ τῶν πρεσβυτέρων
συμβούλιόν τε λαβόντες
ἀργύρια ἱκανὰ ἔδωκαν τοῖς στρατιώταις
λέγοντες· Εἴπατε ὅτι οἱ μαθηταὶ αὐτοῦ νυκτὸς ἐλθόντες
ἔκλεψαν αὐτὸν ἡμῶν κοιμωμένων

*And when they had assembled with the elders
and taken counsel,
they gave a large sum of money to the soldiers
and said, "Tell [people], 'His disciples came by night
and stole him away while we were asleep'"*

THE AUTHORITIES, HOWEVER, do not punish the guards, no doubt because their further service is needed in hatching a plot to account for Jesus' absence from the tomb. The Gospel insists on the factuality of the tomb's material *emptiness*, as attested by every party at hand—the angel, the women, the guards, and even the chief priests. The only outstanding issue is the *reason* for that void. Any kind of hyperspiritual interpretation of the Resurrection, which would allow us simultaneously to believe in Jesus' rising from the dead and yet to continue to see his corpse materially occupying the tomb, would be the greatest fraud of all in the view of both Scripture and universal Christian tradition. St. Paul affirms: "If for this life only we have hoped in Christ, we are of all men most to be pitied. But in fact Christ has been raised from the dead, the first fruits of those who have fallen asleep" (1 Cor 15:19–20). In other words, if Christ did not rise from Joseph's tomb in his body, death has not been overthrown, and no one, believer or unbeliever, may aspire to fullness of life beyond the grave. An intrinsic part of the Christian Gospel would be sheer nonsense, and any believer in the Resurrection a pitiable fool.

The women's message to the disciples, and that of the disciples to the world, essentially derives from the palpable, first-hand, sensory experience of the Risen One such as the women enjoyed when they *saw* the risen Jesus approach, when they at once *grasped* his feet, and when they then *listened* to his words of comfort and command. Quite obviously the condition of the Lord Jesus' body following the Resurrection continued to include materiality, although in a manner that defies logical description or classification. Either Jesus' *body* rose from the dead and began a new life *as a risen body*, or there was no Resurrection, because surely neither his soul nor much less his divinity needed to rise from the dead! When thinking of the risen Jesus, we should keep foremost in mind the magnificent opening of the First Letter of John with its syntactically odd, stuttering, awestruck insistence that the risen Jesus, the Word of Life, was solidly *carnal*, sensorily *perceivable*, and manually *palpable*. Such adamant emphasis is all the more impressive given the sublimely mystical orientation of all Johannine literature:

> That which was from the beginning, which we have heard, which we have seen with our eyes, which we have looked upon and touched with our hands, concerning the word of life [τοῦ λόγου τῆς ζωῆς]— the life was made manifest, and we saw it, and testify to it, and proclaim to you the eternal life which was with the Father and was made manifest to us—that which we have seen and heard we proclaim also to you, so that you may have fellowship with us; and our fellowship is with the Father and with his Son Jesus Christ. (1 Jn 1:1–3)

It is deeply moving to see the author of this Letter compelled to fragment Greek grammar and fracture linear exposition by the daunting task of putting forward, as accurately as possible, the Mystery that could only be revealed as a personal truth by an incarnate and risen God, the Mystery that could never be invented by even the most prodigious human imagination. Such is the mystery of the Λόγος τῆς Ζωῆς—*Lógos tês Zôês*, the Word of Life who is eternal, universal, and all-encompassing and at the same time can be held by human hands as a baby in swaddling clothes, as a grown man whose head is anointed and whose feet are washed, as a condemned scoundrel whose brow is pierced by thorns and whose hands and feet are riven by nails, as a bloody corpse that Joseph of Arimathea takes down from the Cross and buries, and finally as the resplendent Lord whose pilgrim feet the women can grasp with their ardent hands. This and this alone is the *Verbum Vitæ*, the unique Savior of authentic Christian faith, the only one who, being fully human and fully divine, has the right to claim our whole prodigious human being for himself. For only such a Savior and Lord can bestow the fullness of love and joy that our souls and bodies require to enter the bliss for which they were created.

Now, it may seem that the present passage is nothing but a polemical attempt by Matthew to expose the deep fallacy and deception by unbelieving Jews as these try to explain away the absence of Jesus' corpse from the tomb, a place they have taken every measure to secure, seal, and guard against the disciples' tricks. The Jewish authorities are apparently counting on the social and religious prominence of their high office to sway popular opinion in their favor. This they endeavor to accomplish by creating a public your-word-against-ours situation, sure to smear the Resurrection claim by the believing Nazarenes,[2] whom they consider (and rightly so!) a rag-tag bunch of marginal fishermen and ne'er-do-wells.

---

[2] We must not forget that, in the Church's first generation, both those who accepted Jesus as Messiah and those who did not were all Jews, almost without exception. Those who did not believe in Jesus as Messiah and Savior called those who did *notzrim*, "Nazarenes", a toponym that avoids any recognition of "Christians" as followers of the true Messiah ("Christ"). *Notzri* is still the standard, although theologically controversial, Hebrew term for "Christian". But Jewish Christians call themselves in Hebrew מְשִׁיחִיִּים (*m⁰shichiyyím*, 'Messiahans'; see the Delitzsch Hebrew New Testament for Acts 11:26).

However, without denying the passage's *prima facie* apologetical intent, we must also look a bit more deeply at the incident's symbolic import. It seems that, in his juxtaposition of the activity of the holy women and that of the mercenary soldiers, Matthew is once again presenting us with a fundamental choice between the way of death and the way of life.

This may seem an odd moment in the Gospel to bring up the vocation of Abraham by God; and yet the angel's revelation to the women on this occasion is just as much an invitation and a call to obedience directed at Jesus' disciples as was God's call to Abraham. The situation of Jesus' empty tomb, and the going forth from it first of the women and then of the soldiers, begs the question concerning the deepest principle each group is obeying in so proceeding. In the case of Abraham and these women, what is essential is forsaking the familiar that lies behind and hastening into the unknown that lies ahead, solely on the strength of the divine call: "Now the LORD said to Abram, 'Go from your country and your kindred and your father's house to the land that I will show you. And I will make of you a great nation, and I will bless you, and make your name great, so that you will be a blessing'" (Gen 12:1–2). Entering into a new and ineffably fruitful sphere of existence for both Abraham and the women wholly depends on their willingness to trust, obey, and take the plunge into unimaginable promises relying exclusively on the witness of God's word. "Go quickly and tell his disciples that he has risen from the dead", the women hear from the angel. "So they departed quickly from the tomb" (28:7–8). By such an immediate and wholehearted response to God's invitation, the believer gives evidence of his capacity to love and be loved unconditionally and to experience transcendental joy.

The fullness of life promised the disciples if they will forsake the place of death and join the Lord Jesus in his state of Resurrection is symbolized in Abraham's call by God's reference to an abundance of land and descendants in the faithful one's future: "Lift up your eyes, and look from the place where you are, . . . for all the land which you see I will give to you and to your descendants for ever. I will make your descendants as the dust of the earth; so that if one can count the dust of the earth, your descendants also can be counted" (Gen 13:14–16). The broad panoramic perspective over the boundless land that Abraham enjoys at the Lord's invitation becomes, in our Gospel narrative, the Promised Land of Galilee, where Jesus will meet his disciples and from which the Church will spread out to fill the world.

The mercenary soldiers, however, are by definition motivated solely by material enticements, that is, security, employment, and monetary remuneration. The soldiers receive a large sum of money (specifically ἀργύρια—*argýria*, or "silver pieces") from the high priests as a bribe that will persuade them to sustain and disseminate the lie that Jesus' disciples "came by night and stole away" his corpse while they were asleep. Never mind that such a fabrication would expose them to inevitable ridicule for having proven to be utterly useless and indolent guards! So much for the elaborate preparation and care implied in Pilate's instructions to the chief priests and Pharisees: "'You have a guard of soldiers; go, make it *as secure as you can.*' So they went and made the tomb secure by sealing the stone and setting a guard" (27:65–66).

We can feel in this episode a certain undertow of comedy as we see these stalwart soldiers easily bested, not only by the silent ease with which God raises his Son from the dead and vacates the tomb, but especially by the steadfast fidelity and exultation of the two women. These admirably resilient and energetic female disciples not only, unlike the guards, withstand the terrors of the angelic apparition with marvelous alertness and imbibe his message with joy and understanding, but they go forward to meet Jesus and enter with him into a wholly new life. Throughout this drama of the women's encounter with the Divine and of the transformation of existence, the military macho men of legend are "asleep", or "like dead", or "trembling with fear". . .

A truly bewildering fact in the plot is how the guards behave after being exposed, right along with the women, to the extraordinary phenomena of the rumbling earth and the terrifying angel. What astounds in particular is not so much that "for fear of [the angel] the guards trembled and became like dead men" (28:4). Such a thing is only to be expected as an initial reaction, given human frailty in the face of overpowering numinous forces, and only rarely does one encounter as instantaneous and thorough a conversion as that exhibited by the centurion and his men at the foot of the Cross (27:54). Our astonishment, rather, comes from what happens then. Rather than engage in any reflection whatever concerning the meaning and implications of the awe-inspiring event they have just experienced, the guards instead revert at once to their usual manner of life and attitude, absolutely unaffected by the experience, as if nothing extraordinary had happened. Could it be that the skin of some people's souls is really so thick? The soldiers again take up their dreary calculations, worries, and strategies, without apparently missing one beat in their deadening routine. And, having confronted the Divine in the figure of the angel, they now return for enlightenment and vital support to the only source of light and hope they know: the scheming and arrogant priestly class, which can at least guarantee them their next meal along with steady employment.

In the end, their poverty of spirit, their total lack of either conviction or imagination, will allow them only to return like beaten dogs to their wonted servile existence, to seek consolation for their catastrophic performance by acquiring from their perennial exploiters a few silver shekels for committing fraud. It is a masterful touch of Matthew's irony that, even though the men assigned to the tomb have until now been referred to as either the κουστωδία—*koustôdía* (group of "guards", 27:65–66; 28:11) or οἱ τηροῦντες—*hoi têroúntes* ("those keeping watch", 28:4), they should only once be called what they most fundamentally are: στρατιῶται—*stratiôtai* ("soldiers", 28:12), and this at the very moment when they grovelingly accept the money of the bribe from the priests. Obviously, this is most indecorous behavior for persons trained in the virtues of martial fortitude and uprightness.

Our general impression of the sad servility of these soldiers' souls is confirmed when we last see them in vv. 14–15. Here we hear the priests reassuring their fawning accomplices by flaunting their power and influence: "If this comes to the governor's ears, we will satisfy him and keep you out of trouble [καὶ ὑμᾶς ἀμερίμνους ποιήσομεν— *kai hymás amerímnous poiêsomen*]." This last phrase, more literally rendered, would give us the sardonic "and we will make you carefree". It chillingly encapsulates both the priests' cunning penetration of the plebeian mind set and the highest aspirations of worldlings: namely, to be taken care of by their superiors. There then follow the evangelist's concluding words on the soldiers, which are damning in a most understated way: "So they took the money and did as they were directed."

Ἐποίησαν ὡς ἐδιδάχθησαν—*epoíêsan hôs edidáchthêsan*: literally, *they did as they had been taught*. These three words contain a succinct summary of the way religious or philosophical authority can corrupt the malleable human soul for its own nefarious ends by gradually substituting an ethos of protected pleasure and rewarded ambition for the soul's quest for God. This is the dogma, the *didachê*, of the world, which seeks to usurp the magisterium of the eternal Word in the hearts of men. On both the priestly "teachers" and their compliant disciples, St. Paul has pronounced this stark sentence: "Their end is destruction, their god is the belly, and they glory in their shame, with minds set on earthly things" (Phil 3:19).

In this passage Matthew has underscored textually the colossal irony involved when he makes ἀργύρια ἱκανά—*argýria hikaná* ("a large sum of money"), the reward in lucre that the guards receive from the high priests, correspond to the precious, life-giving *kérygma* (HE WAS RAISED FROM THE DEAD, 28:7) that the women received from the angel. Prompted by the angel, the women *proclaimed Jesus' gift of life* eternal to his disciples, together with his desire to see them and be with them. In strict parallel timing to this salvific proclamation, the guards, prompted by the high priests, pocket a few miserable shekels as incentive *to proclaim a lie* that strives absurdly to quash, through paltry machinations, the irrepressible upwelling of Life himself.

Matthew concludes the pericope on the guards' report to the chief priests with the polemical affirmation: "This story [i.e., that the disciples stole Jesus' corpse] has been spread among the Jews to this day" (v. 15). However, the striking irony involved in this statement does not become obvious until we realize that the Greek word Matthew uses here for "story" is *lógos*. Then we can see the glaring contrast he wants to establish between the *Lógos tês Zôés*, the "Word of Life" (1 Jn 1:1) proclaimed by the women—the risen Lord Jesus himself, who is from the beginning with God and is God (cf. Jn 1:1), whom they have personally encountered—and the lying Word of Death proclaimed out of self-interest by the high priests and their accomplices.

WE SHOULD NOT LEAVE this episode without stressing vigorously that such a passage, read intelligently, could never be used as a basis for Christian anti-Semitism, despite the very negative wording "this [lying] story has been spread among the Jews to this day." For one thing, "Jews" here is shorthand for *non-believing* Jews, for clearly all the apostles and the pious women are, by contrast, *believing* Jews. And, secondly, those who carry out the high priests' orders are Roman soldiers. Therefore, the lying strategy that seeks to expose Christ's followers as frauds is presented here—as was Jesus' crucifixion—as resulting from a *collusion of Jews and pagans*, that is, of all mankind, all those who reject the light of Christ and hence the joy of salvation. Is this not something that we all do in various ways and to different degrees? And what can more effectively slander both the holiness of God and the truths of the Christian faith than the attitudes, words, and behavior of many a self-proclaimed Christian?

Within the sweep of history, neither the death of Jesus nor the defamation of the Christian Church he founded can be attributed to the agency (and therefore the guilt) of any particular individual (Caiaphas, Pilate . . .) or ethnic group ("the Jews", "the Muslims"). The Law of the Gospel, in addition, absolutely forbids Christians condemning any ethnic or religious group as such, since only individuals sin and not collectivities. And are we not abundantly familiar with both the degenerate Christian and the virtuous pagan? Indeed, while we Christians have the obligation to condemn all sin in itself as an evil that separates from God, we may not convict any individual sinner without by the same token convicting ourselves as guilty of the same sin, either actually or potentially.

20. THE BRIDEGROOM ABIDES TILL THE END

The Great Commission (28:16–20)

28:16–17   Οἱ δὲ ἔνδεκα μαθηταὶ ἐπορεύθησαν
εἰς τὴν Γαλιλαίαν
εἰς τὸ ὄρος οὗ ἐτάξατο αὐτοῖς ὁ Ἰησοῦς,
καὶ ἰδόντες αὐτὸν προσεκύνησαν,
οἱ δὲ ἐδίστασαν

*Now the eleven disciples
went to Galilee,
to the mountain to which Jesus had directed them.
And when they saw him they worshiped him;
but some doubted*

AFTER A VERY LONG JOURNEY, we arrive at this final scene of Matthew's Gospel, which takes place on a mountain in Galilee. The evangelist subtly connects the occasion to an early moment in his narrative that also held great significance: the Sermon on the Mount. He does it in a very laconic and understated manner. In that earlier passage in the Gospel, we heard that, "seeing the crowds, [Jesus] went up on the mountain, and when he sat down his disciples came to him" (5:1). There, the elevation of the "mountain" served both as a symbol of Jesus' origin "from above", "from the Father of lights" (cf. Jn 3:31; 6:33; 8:23; Jas 1:17), and as a hierarchical marker that separated the chosen Twelve, by Jesus' call, from the vast crowds of the needy (cf. Jn 15:19; 1 Pet 2:9; Eph 5:9) and showed the special intimacy they enjoyed with their Teacher. Jesus' foremost intention in choosing these men, we recall, was *that they might be with him* permanently (ἐποίησεν δώδεκα ἵνα ὦσιν μετ᾽ αὐτοῦ—*epoíesen dôdeka hína ôsin met' autoú*, Mk 3:14).

This separation of the Twelve from all the rest, then, made possible their more intense association with the Lord, which in turn insured that their subsequent mission to mankind would be all the more authentic and effective for its having been received from the very mouth of the Master. Jesus, the incarnate Word, reveals or "explicates" (ἐξηγήσατο—*exêgêsato*) God unsurpassably to us as a result of his intimate, familiar, and eternal experience of God. For the Son's natural "habitat" is indeed the Father's "bosom" (τὸν κόλπον τοῦ Πατρός—*ton kólpon tou Patrós*, Jn 1:18). In a similar way, the apostles will be empowered as authoritative witnesses of the Heart and Being of the Savior as a result of their having been drawn apart time and again by Jesus into an exclusive relationship of familiarity and confidence.

Therefore, the scene of Jesus' election of the Twelve early in the Gospel and of their summons to sit at Jesus' feet to imbibe his teaching during the Sermon on the Mount (5:1ff.) forms a vast "inclusion" with this present convocation of the Eleven to the Galilean mountain, where they will receive their official commission from Jesus, likewise in an elevated desert solitude. These two major moments in the Gospel call out to one another and qualify all other intervening Gospel events as leading to Jesus' solemn bestowal of his mission on his chosen followers. The Christian vocation always produces a *mission*, that is, a *sending*, as its natural fruit, since the Christian vocation consists above all in communicating the life, the truth, and the commandments that have been received personally from Jesus.

Now, Jesus was never a populist leader of applauding multitudes. Even though occasionally Jesus performs certain works of compassion in the sight of all, such as the multiplication of loaves, normally the Lord prefers an intimate setting both to impart his teaching and to share his presence. His teaching, inseparable from his Heart, is a delicate and interior reality that may only be communicated within the protracted and shared silence of everyday coexistence with him and through the intense confidences that his Heart whispers to his followers' hearts. *Cor ad cor loquitur*. It is thus both fitting and necessary that this final encounter be solitary, intimate, exclusive. What the apostles are to hand on to the world is not a set of abstract and static ideas but, rather, something analogous to a vulnerable, newborn child. The Gospel is a still-growing and always living fruit of love—

love given us by God in Jesus and love received by others from us as those sent by Jesus. As we learn from this and many other scenes in the Gospel (call of the apostles, Sermon on the Mount, Transfiguration, Last Supper, Gethsemane, Pentecost), love always seeks the intimacy of solitude for its optimal communication.

In this mountain in Galilee, therefore, no crowds are present. We are invited to enter into the special atmosphere of poignant solitude surrounding Jesus and his chosen disciples, now termed "the Eleven" in the wake of Judas' defection from the group. At times, the Church grows, counter-intuitively, by first being reduced! The apostles' schooling in the paradoxical ways of God's Heart began with the Sermon on the Mount, when as yet they were barely emerging from the populace of the Jews as a group with a unique identity. Though no Ascension is recorded in Matthew, we strongly sense, nevertheless, that this moment of encounter between Jesus and his apostles on this mountain in Galilee is the occasion when his followers must bid farewell to the visible presence of Jesus among them. The mountain also points to heaven, as mountains always do, yet now to heaven not so much as the place of Jesus' *origin* but as the place of his imminent *destination* as he returns to the Father's bosom from where he had come to earth: "I go to the Father, and you will see me no more" (Jn 16:10).

This final encounter between Master and disciples by the same token signals the conclusion of their schooling, since now *they must become what they know him to be.* His many words to them, indeed, the Word that he is, must now become incarnate in their own persons and lives. Only the identification of Master and disciples will insure the Gospel's authenticity. This is why a good definition for an apostle would be "a Christian who is permanently undergoing conversion", so that the Lord's design might be fulfilled: "He who hears you hears me, and he who rejects you rejects me, and he who rejects me rejects him who sent me" (Lk 10:16). Such a transitive scale of mystical identification (Father > Son > disciples > humanity > Father) is the backbone of the Church's mission. What has primacy here are the ontological bonds among the members of the series, while the intellectual truth-content of Christian dogmas only serves to foster that communion in love. Without the interior mystical reality conveyed by Jesus in the above declaration of Luke 10:16, the Christian Gospel would be reduced to nothing but political and religious propaganda and activism, which at times might or might not be socially relevant but which is never efficacious as a work of eternal salvation.

The Kingdom of God that Jesus has ushered into the world can spread to the ends of the earth only by means of the living bonds of charity that descend from the heights of the Holy Trinity and are extended by Christ's ongoing redemptive labor in and through his Church. After Jesus' return to the Father at the Ascension, *the apostles must become the new visibility of Christ in the world.* This is one of the astoundingly revolutionary results of the energy of Christ's Resurrection. It has the power to transform very ordinary, sinful, and mediocre human beings into Jesus' ears and mouth, hands and feet, and, above all, his very Heart: "Truly, truly, I say to you, he who believes in me will also do the works that I do; and greater works than these will he do, because I go to the Father" (Jn 14:12).

If the Christians of the early Church were often called "atheists"[1] by the pagans, it was because they did not worship visible gods embodied in palpable statues or even in the magnificence of the Roman emperor himself. Instead, Christians had the subversive theological and social audacity to offer *themselves*—their persons, words, lives, and actions—as revealing the active presence in them of God's trinitarian life, as promised by Jesus: "If a man loves me, he will keep my word, and my Father will love him, and we will come to him and make our home with him" (Jn 14:23). And wherever God dwells, there, too, his divine energies accompany him and are necessarily at work.

This moment of encounter on the mountain is fraught with a tense solemnity that cuts deep into the flesh of the apostles' faith. Yes, they have responded to the summons that both the angel and Jesus himself sent them through the women. And yes, despite their misgivings, they have faithfully come to the precise place of their appointment with Jesus on this mountain. Nevertheless, it is all too evident that

---

[1] "[The proconsul] sought to persuade [the bishop Polycarp] to deny [Christ], saying, 'Have respect for thy old age,' and other similar things, according to their custom, [such as] 'Swear by the fortune of Cæsar; repent, and say, Away with the Atheists'. But Polycarp, gazing with a stern countenance on all the multitude of the wicked heathen then in the stadium, and waving his hand towards them, while with groans he looked up to heaven, said, 'Away with the Atheists.' " *Martyrdom of Polycarp of Smyrna*, 9, trans. by A. Roberts and J. Donaldson, in *The Apostolic Fathers, with Justin Martyr and Irenæus*, vol. 1 of *Ante-Nicene Fathers* (1885; Peabody, Mass.: Hendrickson, 1995), 41.

the apostles are not as unequivocally filled with joy as the two Marys were. The text tellingly makes no mention of rejoicing by the disciples in its description of their reaction on encountering their risen Lord. Instead we read: "When they saw him they worshiped him; but some doubted." There are different ways of interpreting this mixed response. I, for my part, read it as signifying a total shift of theological focus on the part of the evangelist as he portrays the meeting that is the climax of his whole Gospel.

It is true that all Eleven had one initial reaction that is identical to that of the women: namely, they *fell down in reverent adoration* before Jesus (with use of προσεκύνησαν—*prosekýnêsan*, the same verb attributed to the women in v. 9). Yet "some *doubted*" as well as *adored*. [2] This mention of a *doubt* that affects at least some of the group is a new element in the narrative, and by default it takes the place of the women's reaction of *fear and joy* and of their action of *grasping Jesus' feet*. The narrative balance is tipped emphatically away from impulsive affectivity toward awestruck uncertainty. What exactly are we to make, then, of the apostles' mixed reaction of profound reverence and wavering disbelief? [3]

At the same time, we cannot help but note that, compared to the

---

[2] Though most translations of 28:17 have "but some doubted", the Greek also admits the rendering of NAB: "When they saw him, they worshiped, but they doubted", which thus attributes both the worshipping and the doubting to all eleven apostles. I prefer avoiding so absolute a reading.

[3] Let us not forget that the verb used both at 28:9, referring to the women, and here at 28:17, referring to the men, is προσκυνέω (*proskynéô*), historically a complex act of religious and civic veneration akin to worship, originating in the Middle East, which the *Thayer Greek-English Lexicon of the New Testament* translates as "to fall upon the knees and touch the ground with the forehead as an expression of profound reverence". Its object was always the gods, the emperor, the king, or some representative thereof. Etymologically, it conveys the notion of simultaneously leaning-into and kissing. The act always has a physical component that expresses an interior attitude that, in the case of God, implies total submission and adoration. It is, thus, possible to perform the physical action of *proskýnêsis* while at the same time entertaining mental doubts concerning the full meaning of the act and the full identity of the person so honored. *Proskýnêsis* is still an essential ritual gesture in the Eastern Churches and may also be seen practiced in the Latin Rite in certain countries, particularly in Africa. I have seen many of the faithful in Nigeria, for instance, fall prostrate at the Elevation of the Mass and at Benediction, and this was indeed the practice until recently in certain monastic Orders in the West. The Carthusians still use their own version of *proskýnêsis* at prayer. Worship with the body has been progressively lost wherever Christianity has become

women's effusiveness at the sight of their Lord, the apostles here behave with an emotional restraint so stunning that it borders on the scandalous. Neither the two Marys nor these male followers of Jesus speak any recorded words in either scene; and yet the women's extravagant actions speak for themselves as revelatory of faithful obedience, thrilled delight, and steadfast desire. By comparison, the apostles strike us as impassive, almost apathetic listeners in Matthew's portrayal. The only emotion explicitly attributed to them is the *doubt* on the part of some—if indeed doubt can be termed an emotion, though it is at least a state of mind. The least we can say is that those who are supposed to love can sin egregiously by omission when a situation so forcefully calls for some expression of feeling. This reunion with the beloved Friend and Teacher they thought dead, and who in addition is about to be taken from their senses for the rest of their earthly lives, would appear to rate as such an occasion that cries out for some show of emotion.

It would not be very helpful at this point, by way of explanation, to opt for a conventional profiling of behavior according to gender, for instance, by stereotypically attributing greater emotionality to the women and greater pensiveness to the men as these more coolly ponder the meaning of what they are experiencing. Along such lines, I would, if anything, attribute to the women a greater openness to the transcendental (as shown, for example, by their courage on encountering the alarming angel, without fainting like the presumably braver soldiers!) and a greater obtuseness to the male apostles. These have to puzzle out laboriously the significance of events that a less flat-footed imagination would intuit in a flash. However, I now set such inconclusive considerations aside to propose a wholly different interpretation as accounting for the seeming indolence of the male disciples. My suggestion that follows tries to answer two questions: "Why do the female and male disciples of Jesus react so differently to his Resurrection?" and its corollary, "What implications, if any, do their contrasting reactions hold for our conception of the Church?"

In the story, the female disciples are assigned the role of ardent

---

a more purely conceptual religion and in cultures where the human being has suffered metaphysical fragmentation. Wherever God becomes more idea than concrete presence, so does man.

mediation, first between the angel and Jesus, and then between Jesus and the apostles. This mediating role of the women strongly contrasts with that of the male apostles, who receive a commission from the Lord that bestows on them the role of plenipotentiary *representation* of the person of the Redeemer. We will hopefully see in due course how this fundamental distinction between feminine *mediation* and masculine *representation* explains a great deal about the enigma of the apostles' silence, passivity, and apparent unfeelingness in this climactic scene of the Gospel. I am suggesting that the Gospel's narrative portrayal of these events offers in broad strokes *the archetypal pattern for the unity and variety of complementary charisms within the Church's ministries.*

28:18b–20a   Ἐδόθη μοι πᾶσα ἐξουσία
ἐν οὐρανῷ καὶ ἐπὶ τῆς γῆς.
πορευθέντες οὖν μαθητεύσατε πάντα τὰ ἔθνη, βαπτίζοντες αὐτοὺς
εἰς τὸ ὄνομα τοῦ Πατρὸς καὶ τοῦ Υἱοῦ καὶ τοῦ Ἁγίου Πνεύματος,
διδάσκοντες αὐτοὺς τηρεῖν πάντα ὅσα ἐνετειλάμην ὑμῖν

All authority in heaven
and on earth has been given to me.
Go therefore and make disciples of all nations, baptizing them
in the name of the Father and of the Son and of the Holy Spirit,
teaching them to observe all that I have commanded you

W HAT STRIKES US VERY FORCEFULLY at once in these solemn words of Jesus to the Eleven is their absolutist, all-encompassing character. He declares that he himself is the heir of *all* authority both in heaven *and* on earth; he commissions the apostles to go and baptize *all* nations; and he enjoins them to teach others to observe *all* that he has commanded them. To this we should add the immediately concluding promise that seals the Gospel of Matthew: "I [will be] with you [*all* the days until] the close of the age" (28:20b). This quadruple *all* in such a short speech underscores mightily the unassailable character of Jesus' own authority, which is the chief subject of his declaration. Such expansive absoluteness evidently leaves no room for dissent or even dialogue about either the content or the method of Jesus' commission, and it endows Jesus' magisterial speech-act with supremely revelatory and binding force.

Here we have the fully developed instance that confirms definitively a theological point stressed by Matthew early in his Gospel, when he wrote: "He taught them as one who had authority, and not as their scribes" (7:29). Indeed, the present occasion is almost a dress rehearsal for the Second Coming of Jesus at the end of time, as he himself described it when introducing the Parable of the Last Judgment: "When the Son of man comes in his glory, and all the angels with him, then he will sit on his glorious throne" (25:31). We remember that an angel has already been Jesus' forerunner in this scene, and Jesus has appeared exuding the glory of his Resurrection as he issues his dictates from the throne of his own authority. The NAB rightly notes that "this climactic scene has been called a 'proleptic [or anticipated] parousia', for it gives a foretaste" of Jesus' final Coming. "Then his triumph will be manifest to all; now it is revealed only to the disciples" precisely to strengthen their faith and impel them on their mission.[4]

We can see how this scene could easily be the basis for a theology of Christ as *Pantocrator*, the "all-powerful Lord of the Universe", as evinced in the impressive apse mosaics of so many Byzantine and Romanesque churches. The emphatically majestic certitude on Jesus' part—as expressed by this sovereign monologue high on a mountaintop—counterbalances dramatically both the worship and the doubt of the apostles, since by his attitude, Jesus regally accepts the adoration of the Eleven and expeditiously resolves their disbelief. In the face of Jesus' declaration and mandate, only one of two options is possible: on-the-spot defection or immediate obedient acquiescence.

No such either/or choice ever arises for the women. How typical of males to be torn by dichotomies! The women's dramatic profile is

---

[4] NAB, *ad locum.*

wholly different and more nuanced than the men's. The two Marys appear to enjoy a greater intimacy and familiarity with the Lord than the apostles, and yet, at the same time, their ministry seems wholly oriented toward these apostles. After helping and serving Jesus himself intensely during his public life,[5] they are now called to continue their ministry to Jesus *in the persons of his commissioned apostles*.

The women's role of *mediation* is dramatic, personal, subjective, that is, dependent for its execution upon their own personality and emotions. It is the women's presence and actions that give cohesion to the plot of the Resurrection story by interconnecting its disparate elements as the two Marys move from the experience of the soldiers and the empty tomb to the angel's coming and his speech, then on to the encounter with Jesus and his orders, and finally to their journey to the apostles, to whom they communicate Jesus' summons. Plotwise it is only because the women obey the angel and Jesus and run off at once to fulfill their mission that the apostles are motivated to go encounter the risen Jesus on that mountain in Galilee.

The phrase *apostola apostolorum*, in the feminine, is sometimes applied deservedly by the tradition to Mary Magdalen,[6] particularly in view of her own robust kerygmatic activity in John's Gospel (cf. Jn 20:1–3, 17–18); but the wonderfully precise epithet also applies to "the other Mary" here in Matthew's Gospel: they are both, indeed, the original *apostolæ* ("women apostles") to the subsequent *apostoli* ("men apostles"), in an inviolable order of precedence. In all the Gospels, it is the women who, significantly and perhaps even normatively, first hear of the Resurrection and experience the phenomena surrounding it, thus becoming the best authoritative eyewitnesses of Jesus' rising from the dead.

Furthermore, if the women had not in the first instance borne the message of Jesus to the men, these would not then have possessed the impetus to respond to the Lord's summons to the mountain, nor

---

[5] "There were also many women there [on Golgotha], looking on from afar, who had followed Jesus from Galilee, ministering to him" (27:55). Luke is more specific, speaking of many women "who provided for [Jesus and his disciples] out of their means" (Lk 8:3).

[6] The earliest witness is St. Hippolytus of Rome (ca. 170–235), who writes in his *Commentary on the Song of Songs:* "With a cry the synagogue expresses a good testimony for us through the women, those who were made apostles, having been sent by Christ."

therefore would they have explicitly received there from Jesus his personal *exousía*, or "fully empowered authority" (28:18–20), to evangelize the world. Thus the women not only communicate *information* to the male apostles but also act as conduits of the power of efficient *grace*. It is in this sense that the women's role may be said to be "interior to the household of the Church": that is, in the sense that their highly personal *ad intra* mission is the subjective source of the male apostles' objective *ad extra* mission to the outside world. It is undoubtedly the women's visceral fidelity, desire, joy, and obedience—their capacity to peer humbly yet without blinking into the overpowering Mystery of Jesus—that stirs the men to rise with courage to embrace their own specific vocation.

By contrast, the apostles' role of *representation* is sacramental, impersonal, and objective. It gives cohesion, not to the Gospel narrative itself—within which the male apostles remain hesitantly receptive and impassive to the end—but to the whole of ecclesial salvation history beginning at Pentecost, which is their moment of definitive empowerment by the gift of the Holy Spirit. By virtue of a prevenient grace that seems to give the holy women some share in Marian privileges, the *apostolæ apostolorum* may be observed to behave *before* Pentecost—starting at the discovery of the empty tomb and the Resurrection—with all the joyous impetus, audacity, and *parrhêsía* (or Spirit-induced "confidence") that the male apostles will not be able to display until *after* Pentecost and their reception of the Holy Spirit.

The women's role is to give interior unity to the household of the Church by their fervent witness and unwavering fidelity, such as they have manifested in the face of the void left by Jesus' death, and by their incessant prayer and fierce clinging to the Person of Jesus. All their behavior exhibits the burning in their hearts of a vigorous love that only Love Himself could have kindled by his sudden and wholly unexpected advent within the fertile horizon of their expectant faith. The apostles' role, on the other hand, is to imbibe teaching and receive authority and mission from Jesus directly so that they can visibly and effectively represent the Lord not only within the household of the Church but also *ad extra*, in the public square, in the face of all mankind and to the ends of the earth.

The women's particular vocation is to encounter the Divine face-to-face—an experience symbolized in their meeting with the dazzling angel—and then to mediate this angel's Gospel of Resurrection to the male apostles. In this respect, the two Marys have the privilege of participating in the salvific role of the great Mary, the Mother of Jesus, as *New Eve*. At the Annunciation, Our Lady was called upon to redress by her obedience the catastrophic sin of the first Eve, who had mediated between the serpent and her husband, Adam, but only to bring him a seductive message of death (cf. Gen 3:1ff.). Like Blessed Mary, however, for whom Gabriel changed EVA into AVE, the holy women, too, receive the visit of a glorious angel who entrusts them with the Gospel of Jesus' Resurrection and triumph over death. They then receive from Jesus in person the explicit command to communicate the Gospel of Life to the apostles, the first step that leads to these being regenerated as *other Christs*.

After encountering the risen Lord in person, the apostles are then to go into the world, not just as his second-rate "envoys" or "delegates", but as true *embodiments* of Jesus Christ, "the son of Adam, the son of God" (Lk 3:38): Christ Jesus who is the New Adam, the New Man. "For as in Adam all die, so also in Christ shall all be made alive. . . . 'The first man Adam became a living soul'; the last Adam became a life-giving spirit" (1 Cor 15:22, 45).

The apostles do indeed receive their own special privilege, which may be described in different ways. They are explicitly commissioned by Jesus to represent, embody, and impersonate the Gospel message so radically that they are called to become "vicars", "representatives", "deputies", "proxies", or "stand-ins" for the Word himself, in whom the message of the Gospel originates. None of these words, however, can do justice to the absolutely new reality that the Lord is *creating* in his apostles.[7] The words suggested above all derive from a secular vocabulary of administration that presupposes a necessary distancing and decline in quality as we descend from the integrity, excellence, and power of the original king or emperor to the far-removed reality of his lackluster lieutenants. But the kind of "representation" inseparable

---

[7] The Greek text of Mark 3:14 tells us, literally, that Jesus not only "appointed" his apostles but that he actually "made" them afresh, as a new creation (ἐποίησεν δώδεκα). This is an important reminder of the uniqueness of the apostolic mission, to which no other human task, office, or appointment is comparable. The apostle is one who by baptism, explicit vocation, sacrament, and mission has become one with the Christ he visibly and audibly represents. While St. Paul's declaration "If any one is in Christ, he is a new creation" (2 Cor 5:17) applies to all the baptized, it describes in a special way the transformation effected in the persons of his apostles by Christ.

from the new identity given by Jesus to his apostles is something wholly different. It should properly be termed a *sacramental* rather than a merely *symbolic* representation, since a symbol only reminds us at a distance of what is symbolized, while *a sacrament* literally makes present what it *represents*.

By its very nature, the Christian Gospel calls for such radical impersonation of Christ by his apostles precisely because it is not an ideology pointing to some remote reality outside itself. At bottom, *the Gospel is the Person of the Lord Jesus himself*, and this is why the Lord's apostles must not only *speak the words of Jesus* but must themselves become what they preach: they must *become Jesus, become other Christs*. This, too, is why the Christian proclamation of the Word is inseparable from the Christian celebration of the Eucharist, in which the Word becomes flesh and is consumed sacramentally. The Sacrament of the Holy Eucharist and the Sacrament of Holy Orders truly go hand in hand.

In this connection, it is highly significant that at this moment of solemn commissioning in Galilee, Jesus does not generically command those he is about to send forth simply to "preach the Gospel". Such a perfectly correct and comprehensible command would nevertheless interpose a third element—"the Gospel"—between Jesus and his apostles, as well as between the apostles themselves and those to whom they are sent. The Lord will not abide such distancing between persons by the intromission of a static third object, even if it be "the Gospel"! Instead, Jesus commands something more mysterious. He opens his discourse with all the solemnity of an imperial decree and the intensity of a new revelation: "All authority in heaven and on earth has been given to me", he rings out. Such a claim, extravagant to say the least in any human mouth, is the empowering premise then contained in the *therefore* of the command that follows: "Go therefore and make disciples of all nations." Jesus' declaration is unambiguous and uncompromising in its tenor and forms the basis for all that follows.

The Greek word here translated "authority" is *exousía*, which, first of all, refers to a person's freedom of choice and right to act or decide for himself, and then, in a second, specialized sense, connotes the absolute power exercised by a ruler by virtue of his office. Moreover, Jesus reveals the absolute cosmic expanse of his personal authority when he qualifies it as "all authority in heaven and on earth", which implies both temporal and spatial boundlessness. With these words, Jesus unambiguously declares himself to be the one eternal King of universal creation. An active, sacramental power may be said to be here at work insofar as the visible man Jesus of Nazareth, raised from the dead and no longer subject to death, is claiming for himself a prerogative that belongs by rights only to the invisible God. The risen Jesus is thus revealing himself to his apostles as embodying and representing the illimitable authority of God himself. The divine title *Kýrios* now belongs univocally both to the God of Israel and to the Lord Jesus.

Now, the verb used in this declaration, "all authority *has been given* (ἐδόθη—*edóthê*) to me", is a theological passive implying that God has freely bestowed plenipotentiary jurisdiction over all creation on his Son, the risen Lord. This bestowal *in time*, furthermore, is but a confirmation and an extension of the everlasting dominion that has by nature belonged to the Son *from all eternity*. "Truly, truly, I say to you, before Abraham was, I am" (Jn 8:58).[8] Such an understanding is crucial because it makes comprehensible the personal delegation of precisely that jurisdiction which Jesus immediately makes on his chosen band: *Go, therefore* . . . , as if he said: "My Father has freely given me universal authority, and I hereby choose with equal freedom to entrust that authority to you, my beloved friends, so that together we might accomplish *our* Father's design for the world's salvation." But such an extraordinary bestowal should properly leave us aghast at the realization that what is a divine prerogative that belongs only to Jesus by nature should by his Father's design now be communicated to his apostles as sheer gift of grace.

Jesus' declaration, both in language and content, has as background the famous vision of the prophet Daniel:

> I saw in the night visions, and behold, with the clouds of heaven there came one like a son of man, and he came to the Ancient of Days and was presented before him. And to him was given dominion and

---

[8] The truth of Jesus' divine origin and eternal authority is proclaimed not only by the Johannine and Pauline writings but also in Matthew, as in this polemical passage: " 'What do you think of the Christ? Whose son is he?' They said to him, 'The son of David.' He said to them, 'How is it then that David, inspired by the Spirit, calls him Lord, saying, "The Lord said to my Lord, Sit at my right hand, till I put thy enemies under thy feet"? If David thus calls him Lord, how is he his son?' " (22:42–45).

glory and kingdom, that all peoples, nations, and languages should serve him; his dominion is an everlasting dominion, which shall not pass away, and his kingdom one that shall not be destroyed. (Dan 7:13–14)

Jesus' speech to his apostles is thus clearly a fulfillment of Daniel's "night visions". But there is a crucial change as we go from the prophecy in the Book of Daniel to its fulfillment in the Gospel of Matthew. In the latter, the prophet's statement *To him was given authority* (ἐδόθη αὐτῷ ἐξουσία—*edóthê auto exousía*, LXX) becomes, in Jesus' mouth, *All authority . . . has been given to me* (ἐδόθη μοι πᾶσα ἐξουσία—*edóthê moi pása exousía*). By virtue of the change from the third to the first person singular, the prophetic vision has now become a historical reality by the personal, authoritative declaration of the One who cannot lie. Jesus here demonstrates that he is fulfilling in his personal human destiny the vision that he himself, as eternal Word, inspired in Daniel his prophet. And he offers the evidence of his Resurrection as first-hand warrant for this truth. By the same token, a more circumscribed *authority* is expanded boundlessly by Jesus' declaration into *all authority*.

Immediately after presenting his credentials as universal Lord by divine appointment, Jesus proceeds to bestow precisely the authority of which he speaks on the Eleven that he sees gathered around him, those who *worshipped but also doubted*. The whole passage is propelled by a strong dynamics of hierarchical transition: we are made privy to a mighty and unstoppable torrent of regenerative power and life descending from the heavenly Father as its divine source. The Father eternally bestows it on the Son, who then communicates it within time to his apostles together with the command that they are to impart such energy to "all nations". However, what I here call "a torrent of power and life" is not reduced in this text to a formulaic "preaching of the Gospel" or anything of the sort, as might have been expected. The parallel passage in Mark does enjoin exactly such a formula: κηρύξατε τὸ εὐαγγέλιον—*kêrýxate to euangélion* ("preach the gospel", Mk 16:15). But here in Matthew, Jesus' precise words about how the apostles are to carry out their mission are, Πορευθέντες οὖν μαθητεύσατε—*Poreuthéntes oun mathêteúsate*: "Go therefore and *make disciples* of all nations."

What Jesus is commanding here is so novel a reality that the verb μαθητεύω—*mathêteúô* is a New Testament neologism constructed from the noun *mathêtês*, "a disciple". A new word had to be invented to do justice to the Christian commission! In eccentric English, it would literally translate as "to discipulize"; more conventionally, it is rendered "to make a disciple of". The central point here is that Jesus did not bestow his *exousía* on his apostles intending them merely to communicate a message or a set of doctrines or an ideology, much less a book or ready-made, formulaic creed. Rather, they were to communicate a way of life, *discipleship itself*, and in a highly personal manner. This is why they are to *go forth*, that is, they must move to new places in order to make themselves wholly present to others wherever and however these others are to be found. Following the logic and pattern of the eternal Word's own Incarnation, the apostles are to enter the sphere of others' concrete lives and there offer all of themselves as exactly what Jesus' presence and action in them have made them to be.

If Jesus' own power and authority are being bestowed on these eleven ordinary men, it is to enable them *to do for others what Jesus has done for them*. They are to bestow the life, the experience, and the full reality of being a disciple of Jesus. They are to make others what they themselves have first been made to be by Jesus. This is why the commission is sacramental and "mysterial", in nature: that is, the apostles are not only or even primarily to *talk about* Jesus or *pass on the words and teachings* of Jesus. First and foremost, as *sine qua non* of their mission, they are to *attract others into the one living Mystery of Jesus* by the sheer force of their personal lives as transformed by the love of Christ dwelling within them. From the inexhaustible fountains of this Mystery, all disciples, both ancient and more recent, will then commune, drawing water "with joy from the wells of salvation", in keeping with the promise of Isaiah (Is 12:3).

Nothing could better illustrate the sacramental character of Jesus' mandate than the fact that, once he has bestowed his authority on the apostles and given them the command to make disciples of all mankind, Jesus immediately specifies the manner of doing so. The Lord's instruction has two parts: first, the apostles are to *baptize* in the Name of the Persons of the Holy Trinity and, second, they are to *teach* the observance of "all that I have commanded you". In other words, Jesus enjoins explicitly two things: *the sacrament of baptism* and *the Christian moral life*, as essential to the life of his disciples. As Raïssa Maritain has famously said, the whole Catholic tradition may be summed up in the tense duo of "mystery and law".

We should note as well that it is only after ordering his apostles to *make disciples* and to *dispense the sacrament of baptism* that Jesus, as a third command, enjoins on them the need to *teach*. Even in this case, however, what is to be taught is not a method to speculate brilliantly on the truth, as in the schools of philosophy of antiquity, or a rhetorical system for winning political and religious arguments. What the apostles are to teach is *the moral life*, that is, the concrete way of thinking, feeling, and acting that flows from Jesus' commandments, with the greatest of all at the summit: "This is my commandment, that you love one another as I have loved you" (Jn 15:12). Even the necessary expression "moral life" is already something of an abstraction in the Christian context, as if we were talking of self-evident universal principles of behavior, whereas Jesus' specific formulation is highly personalistic as he directs the apostles to teach potential new disciples "to observe all that I have commanded you".

Jesus' language remains intensely personal throughout this passage, portraying right human behavior as springing from the appropriation by new believers of the manner in which Jesus himself has lived and acted as witnessed, in turn, by the lives and teachings of his first apostles. Continually the indispensable context here is the Church founded by and gathered around Jesus as sole source of Truth and Life. In the concrete, we may say that, when a Christian acts in a God-pleasing manner, he does so, not by patterning his life according to an impersonal and universalistic philosophical doctrine, but rather *in personal obedience to what Jesus has commanded him through the apostles.* This nexus of relationships of Christians with Christ and one another in Christ, through the ministry of authentic apostles, is what we call "the Church". And it is most important not to reduce "the moral life", in Jesus' understanding, only to acts of social interaction. The Lord's instruction is quite broad, covering the whole of human experience and including anything that man *does* and *ought to do*. For instance, when he says, "teach them to observe all that I have commanded you", Jesus is referring not only to the "moral teaching" of the Ten Commandments and the Sermon on the Mount but also to specifically religious practices like prayer (above all the Our Father, 6:9–13) and the celebration of the Eucharist, as when he commanded: *Do this in remembrance of me!* (1 Cor 11:24–25).

WE NOW RETURN to our original question of why, in comparison to the holy women, the male apostles are portrayed by Matthew in this passage in such an impersonal and even passive way. The answer lies in the uncompromising centrality of the Person of the Lord Jesus at the heart of the Christian Mystery, something we have just examined. This exclusive centrality makes it both a mystical and an æsthetic requirement for the dramatic portrayal of the meeting in Galilee *that the apostles be shorn of all individual characteristics, emotions, and reactions* in order for them the better to be defined as vessels that *embody* the Word that is sending them out, the better, that is, for them to be able to *represent* the Word's own characteristics to the world with spotless transparency.

The principle operating here was first uttered by John the Baptist in his own preaching when he declared: "He must increase, but I must decrease" (Jn 3:30), and it is St. Paul who has captured most vividly (because autobiographically) the mystery of the apostle's subjective identification with his Lord: "I have been crucified with Christ; *it is no longer I who live, but Christ who lives in me;* and the life I now live in the flesh I live by faith in the Son of God, who loved me and gave himself for me" (Gal 2:20). In more modern idiom, the twentieth-century poet Gertrud von Le Fort has given striking graphic expression to this priestly and sacramental aspect of the apostles' mission:

> A priest at the altar has no face,
> and the arms that elevate the Lord
> are without ornament or dust.
> For God imposes silence
> on the one he commands to speak,

> and whomever His Spirit sets ablaze
> is himself extinguished.[9]

Such emblematic silence and "facelessness" in the apostle's persona are, of course, meant symbolically and not psychologically, but they are not for all that any less real. We are not speaking of a mutation, a neutralization, or indeed an annihilation of the apostle's individual personality as a result of "the word of Christ [dwelling] in you richly" (Col 3:16). If that were the case, the transforming power of Jesus' life in us would be something monstrous and vampiric! It does, however, mean that "unless a grain of wheat falls into the earth and dies, it remains alone; but if it dies, it bears much fruit" (Jn 12:24). The invasion by Jesus' love necessarily brings about a massive upheaval in my person, and the life I henceforth live can no longer have my own ideas, desires, and needs as ruling criteria. Inevitably, a true and painful death of the self-constructed social ego is indeed a requirement in the life of every disciple.

Nevertheless, the continuity of my unique, God-created personhood is at the same time assured since each one's individual identity reflects God's image irreplaceably from the beginning. And yet the new vital, organizing principle of my life can no longer come from me but must derive from Another, that is, from the will of the One whom, together with Jesus, I can address as "Our Father". By willingly entering such a process of transformation, I am only allowing full sway in my life and person to the supreme Force that rules Jesus himself, who reveals his interior dynamic to his apostles when he affirms: "Truly, truly, I say to you, the Son can do nothing of his own accord, but only what he sees the Father doing; for whatever he does, that the Son does likewise" (Jn 5:19).

Obedience is indeed not only a human virtue practiced by man with reference to God. No matter how surprising this may sound to those who can only conceive of an autocratic God, obedience is also a *divine* virtue, practiced among the Persons of the Trinity, and it is hence the binding paradigm for the life of faith. For obedience is one of the chief attributes of love, whether human or divine, because the

---

[9] "Ein Priester am Altar hat kein Antlitz, und die Arme, die den Herrn erheben, sind ohne Schmuck noch Staub, / Denn wen Gott reden heisst, den heisst er schweigen, und wen sein Geist entzündet, der erlischt." *Hymnen an die Kirche*, VIII (1924).

lover longs to please the beloved as the fundamental condition for his own happiness and reason-for-being. Jesus has revealed this principle in the simplest language: "I do as the Father has commanded me, so that the world may know that I love the Father" (Jn 14:31). In other words, Jesus commands his apostles nothing that he has not first himself received and obeyed as a commandment from the Father. Therefore, whatever commandment or mandate he gives his apostles is tantamount to his extending an invitation for them to join him, in strictest fellowship and joyful communion, to engage together with him in the work of the Father—with the Father working in Jesus and Jesus working in them.

The apostles' obedience to Jesus' commandments is thus nothing less than a mode of participating in the interior life of the Blessed Trinity, for the salvation of the world and the joy of their own hearts. And Jesus makes crystal clear both the hierarchical and the sacramental character of his divine obedience when he proceeds to say to his apostles: "The words that I say to you I do not speak on my own authority; but the Father who dwells in me does his works. . . . He who believes in me will also do the works that I do; and greater works than these will he do, because I go to the Father" (Jn 14:10, 12). Everything originates in the boundless love and creative will of the Father; but this "everything" is also communicated without stint to the beloved Son and, through him, to the Son's chosen apostles, so that what these do is truly and authentically *the Father's work through Jesus in them!*

Sacramental *representation*—the Son showing forth the Father and the apostles showing forth the Son who reveals the Father—is thus an essential structural component of Christian ecclesiology and of God's plan of salvation for the world. And the fundamental importance of this principle gains immense dramatic relevance from the fact that Jesus reveals it to the Church precisely at the moment when he is about to depart from this world corporeally, that is, when he will disappear from human eyes into the invisibility of the Father: his only visibility in the world will henceforth be his Church, under the *exousía*, or "authority", he has formally bestowed on his apostles. "He who hears you hears me, and he who rejects you rejects me, and he who rejects me rejects him who sent me" (Lk 10:16).

This is also why Jesus at this time enjoins the practice of the sacrament of baptism, with the explicit invocation of the names of the Persons of the Trinity, as essential to the life of discipleship. "Baptism" signifies the *immersion* into waters that drown the old life of sin, immediately followed by the *resurgence* to a new life that is none other than the divine and blessed life of the triune God now dwelling and acting within us. Christians are to live immersed in God's infinite circulation of love like fish swimming in water, from which they derive all their breath, nourishment, and well-being. The full trinitarian formula in the mouth of Jesus confers the highest authority on the sacramental practice of the primitive Church and reflects the central importance of the sacrament of baptism to Christian identity. One does not become a Christian as the result of a spontaneous mental act of individually discovering "truth" or of a decision coming only from within oneself. The Christian identity is something that has to be received from those who already possess it. It is a grace *mediated* from God, a grace given and shared through communion with others. And the effect of that grace, communicated through baptism, is to plunge the believer into the stream of full participation in divine and triune Life.

Only the existential embodiment by the apostles of the radical obedience of the Lord Jesus[10] can enable St. Paul to exclaim to the Thessalonians: "We . . . thank God constantly for this, that when you received the word of God which you heard from us, you accepted it not as the word of men but as what it really is, the word of God, which is at work (ἐνεργεῖται—*energeítai*) in you believers" (1 Thess 2:13). The Word of God, to be sure, is heard from Christians who are fallible, weak, and sinful human beings as well as disciples. But grace has made it possible for these fragile ministers, such as they are, so to hand over their entire being to God, so to identify with the divine Son in his mission, that the Father can effectively use them as vessels to communicate his Word totally and authentically, in such a way that the Word can "work its transforming energy" (ἐνεργεῖται—*energeítai*) in the hearers. In this specialized mystical sense, we can say that the apostle is called to *impersonate* Christ, without any of the negative connotations of "deceit" that this word has in other con-

---

[10] In both the objective and the subjective genitive: his obedience to the Father and the apostles' obedience to him, inseparably.

texts. It is Jesus himself, after all, who is commanding his apostles to assume such a role.

Yes, the apostle is to act and behave *in persona Christi*, in the fullest sense. He is not only to *act* in the person of Christ officially, with Christ's own authority and sacramental efficacy, but also, within his inmost heart, he is to *think* and then, externally, *behave* in the person of Christ, who twice commanded his followers with shocking rigor: "You . . . must be perfect, as your heavenly Father is perfect" (5:48), and "If you would be perfect, go, sell what you possess and give to the poor; and . . . come, follow me" (19:21). We should never allow such a phrase to lose any of its stark impact, for a logical and spiritual incongruity of the highest caliber is clearly involved in the proposition that mere men should act in the person of the incarnate Word of God. The magnitude of the dignity bestowed is matched only by the prodigious obligation it enjoins on its beneficiary, and no one has defined better than St. Paul the kenotic task of interior transformation required of the apostle: "Make your own the mind of Christ Jesus, who . . . emptied himself" (Phil 2:5, 7, NJB). In other words, the challenge to continual conversion imposed on an apostle by Jesus' call and mandate is, properly speaking, humanly impossible. And therefore the apostle must brave the quicksand of endemic *hypocrisy* as an occupational hazard, trusting with all his might that the same grace that made him an apostle will see him through relatively unscathed.

The phrase *in persona Christi* and its incandescent meaning, furthermore, should never degenerate in clerical mouths into a yawning lingo, a convenient bureaucratic tag that promotes self-justification and entitlement. Those of us who have been ordained into Christ's priesthood should never quite get over the sense of bewilderment and contradiction at the fact that *this* should have been what Jesus ordained both *for the Church's structure* and *for me* in particular. Indeed, when allowed their full impact, Jesus' intention and ordinance on this occasion on the mountain in Galilee ought to have, for the duration, exactly the effect they had on the Eleven: utter stupor, awestruck surrender, perfect silence, and hesitant doubt. No tiniest flicker of apostolic self-congratulation for such an unheard-of privilege is anywhere in sight in this passage. And, if the apostles are subsequently able to obey and enact Jesus' commands fruitfully, it is because their faith in Christ's power and judgment rests squarely on the foundation of their own self-doubt. Realistic self-doubt is purifying and empowering when the task at hand does not originate in my self.

Impersonation is, indeed, not too strong a term to refer to what Jesus is ordering his apostles to do in the world until his Second Coming. If Jesus has baptized the apostles with the Holy Spirit and with the Fire of his Mercy (cf. 3:11), so, too, does he now command precisely them to do the very same. If Jesus has made disciples of these Eleven, so too does he now command precisely them to "make disciples of all nations". And if Jesus has called his apostles "friends—for all that I have heard from my Father I have made known to you" (Jn 15:15)—so, too, does he now mandate precisely them to teach others to observe "all that I have commanded you". By virtue of his empowering authority and explicit, creative command, the apostles are to make both the Person and the illuminating activity of Christ Jesus visible and perceivable, in every sense, in this world. Only through the persons and activity of the apostles throughout the centuries can the redeeming Presence of the incarnate Word extend to the ends of the earth. Either this hierarchical and sacramental nature of the apostolic mission, which mysteriously *makes present* the Person of Jesus himself, is authentic and binding, or Christianity is but one more religious philosophy among many others and, therefore, one possessing a merely relative value.

AS HAS BEEN NOTED REPEATEDLY, the apostles' total silence and apparent impassivity during this episode of commissioning stands in glaring contrast to the attitude and actions of the two Marys, who positively sparkle with electric joy, passion, and movement. This contrast may be seen to derive from the entirely different and specific role Jesus is bestowing on his apostles. In their demeanor of dramatic silence and rapt stillness we should read a powerful metaphor for their attitude of total receptivity and communion with Christ. At this moment of encounter with Jesus, the apostles have become all porous presence, surrendered will, absorbing capacity, astounded expectation. They embody the impassibility of saints' figures in traditional icons, with eyes unnaturally dilated and mouths shut in the stanch silence of absolute, contemplative faith as they gaze in wonderment on the mystery of Christ. Both in these icons and in Matthew's text, lack of individual response and absence of unique identity are stylistic devices that make a central theological point: namely, that the Word comes whole and self-sufficient from the mouth of God and that the disciple's sole task at this moment of the drama is to assume an attitude of pure receptivity.

At this point in the Gospel, Jesus' solemn words, by their power and wisdom, may be said to be *re-creating* these simple men of Galilee into other Christs, envoys of Christ who embody him and whom he is sending forth so that they might, in turn, *re-create the world* through baptism and teaching, word and sacrament, and endless acts of love and mercy. The apostles' interior disposition as they are thus being remade by the hands of the Word may well be expressed in the classic image of Isaiah: "Does the clay say to him who fashions it, 'What are you making'? . . . 'O LORD, you are our Father; we are the clay, and you are our potter; we are all the work of your hand'" (Is 45:9; 64:8). And St. Paul takes up the image and applies it expressly to the person and mission of the apostles: "We do not preach ourselves, but Jesus Christ as Lord, and ourselves as your servants for Jesus' sake. . . . But we have this treasure *in jars of clay* to show that this all-surpassing power is from God and not from us" (2 Cor 4:5, 7, NIB).

At this stage of formation, it is the function of the clayey apostles to be as inert and malleable as possible in the hands of the divine Potter, offering no resistance or even a will of their own, providing only their earthen nature and substance, to be shaped exclusively according to the will, wisdom, and intention of the Master Artist. If the creature is to become an efficient agent of the Creator, it must first recognize its true nothingness in the face of the Creator's omnipotence and omniscience. This is the fundamental meaning of the apostles' immediate act of *proskynêsis* on meeting their Lord: "When they saw him they fell down before him [in worship]" (28:17, NJB), and this single act communicates the realization, the emotion, and the surrender that should at this moment occupy the whole horizon of the apostles' consciousness. Indeed, at this point, everything must come to the apostles from Jesus like a mighty transfusion of life, just as everything came to Jesus from the Father.

It is theological intent, then, and not faulty psychological penetration or deficient dramatic verve, that determines the apostles' characterization in Matthew's present scene. We remember clearly how, at other moments in the Gospel narrative, certain apostles have been portrayed vividly as fleshed-out and most passionate individuals, when the narrative focus fell on their personal initiative. How can we forget the impetuous reactions of Peter, for instance, as he cast himself with excitement into the water on seeing the Lord (14:28–29), or as he angrily refused to accept Jesus' prediction of the coming Passion (16:22–23), or as he shamefully betrayed his Lord and friend and then wept bitterly from the depths of his contrition (26:69–75)? And we recall the ambition and presumption of James and John, expecting the highest privileges at their mother's prompting (20:22). There comes to mind as well Matthew's own memorable readiness to follow Jesus, together with his splendid gift of hospitality to his new Lord (9:9–10). Seared in our memory, too, alas, we recall the indelible images of the scheming idealism, consuming greed, and final despair of Judas Iscariot (26:14–15, 47–49; 27:3–5).

We inevitably conclude, therefore, that the apostles' "inertia" in the present episode of their commissioning is an æsthetic feature of the narrative that dramatizes (by sheer *lack* of color!) the theological point we have described. No, the apostles have not now suddenly and permanently turned into robotic beings that need only to be divinely "programmed". We can see this is clearly not so from their lively, wide-ranging, and resourceful activities in the Book of Acts, once the power and inspiration of the Holy Spirit have energized them after the Ascension. In the present scene, rather, they are here being proposed to us as an abstractly drawn ecclesial unit, "captured" at one specific and crucial moment within the whole process of their becoming apostles. They are offered to us as the type of a receptive, ecclesial faith that can truly listen to, obey, internalize, and enact the Word of God they have intimately made their own within their flawless, undifferentiated communion with one another in the Lord Jesus. And types are by definition impersonal. This is the purely receptive, "Marian" phase of their vocation, if you will.

In view of all this, an important caveat is here in order. By no means should such literary stylization be interpreted with dull, dead-letter realism as evidence that obedience to the Word entails an obliteration of the human personality. Whether coming from persons hostile to an allegedly "dehumanizing" Christian mysticism or, indeed, from self-styled ultra-Catholic rigorists, such an interpretation of the present passage would constitute a gross aberration. It would obliviously violate every principle of both literary analysis and integral Christian humanism, which is based on the premise that union with Christ *restores* the whole of human nature to its full, vibrant potential as first envisioned by God at the creation. Christ is not only perfect God; he is also perfect Man, and union with him, therefore, promises participation in Christ's perfect humanness. In this connection, we remember Jesus' categorical saying, "I came that they may have *life*, and have it abundantly" (Jn 10:10), as well as St. Paul's exhortation, "For *freedom* Christ has set us free; stand fast therefore, and do not submit again to a yoke of slavery" (Gal 5:1). Life and freedom, then, are the two primary characteristics of transformation in Christ.

As evidence of this, we recall the concrete details from the final state of those fortunate individuals throughout the Gospel whose existences Jesus radically changes for the better by coming into contact with them: the healed lame leap up with joy; the tongue-tied speak correctly for the first time; the blind rejoice in newfound sight and insight; a dead child can again walk and eat; and demoniacs, who initially cower and growl like wounded animals among tombs, bruising themselves with stones, after the exorcism by Jesus are seen sitting down calmly, decorously clothed, and in their right mind. While in each of these cases, the visible miracle signals a spiritual transformation, nevertheless, the soul's reception of divine life from Jesus is inseparable from the body's restoration to lively, celebratory wholeness. Jesus, the New Adam, fashions us by his interaction with us into new, fully alive human beings and not into grotesque mutants who, in Pascal's phrase, are "neither angels nor beasts". William Blake has given splendid expression to a humanity vibrantly transformed by Christ in a painting like *The Dance of Albion* (ca. 1795), where we see the zenith of fulfilled and glorified human nature, both physical and spiritual. An art critic has analyzed this luminous image, so bursting with life, in a way that confirms our theological analysis of the impact on man of Jesus' work of re-creation:

This nude is delivered from all bondage and all untruth. It is beyond conflict, beyond [both exterior] and inner struggle, wholly realised. And yet this figure isn't stuck in final utopian lifelessness, as you might suspect. He holds an interplay between static pattern and dynamic tension. . . . His body is flung outward. His limbs unbend and reach out as far as they can, and each limb is free of others. He is absolute liberation.[11]

In my own interpretation, this resplendent figure called "Albion" represents simultaneously the qualities of life, joy, freedom, and intrinsic goodness that Christ possesses by nature *and* these same qualities as bestowed fully by him on those who commune with his person. Master and disciple coalesce mystically and beyond separation in a total communion of life and existence: a miraculous symbiosis.

28:20b

καὶ ἰδοὺ ἐγὼ μεθ᾽ ὑμῶν εἰμι
πάσας τὰς ἡμέρας
ἕως τῆς συντελείας τοῦ αἰῶνος

and behold, I am with you
all the days
until the close of the age

JESUS' FIRST DESIRE ON EMERGING from death's night of separation is to meet with his own, represented by the faithful women and the Eleven. This intense desire and its realization are not a mere aspect of Jesus' private emotional life; they constitute a messianic ful-

[11] Tom Lubbock, *The Independent*, Great Works Series, May 7, 2010. https://www.independent.co.uk/arts-entertainment/art/great-works/great-works-the-dance-of-albion-circa-1795-william-blake-1965101.html

fillment of God's role as shepherd of Israel, as portrayed by Ezekiel: "For thus says the Lord GOD: Behold, I, I myself will search for my sheep, and will seek them out. As a shepherd seeks out his flock when some of his sheep have been scattered abroad, so will I seek out my sheep; and I will rescue them from all places where they have been scattered on a day of clouds and thick darkness" (Ezek 34:11–12). All of Jesus' followers were literally scattered at the beginning of the Passion, after Jesus' arrest (26:31, 56). In the mission that he entrusts first to the women and then to the apostles, we witness the beginning of Jesus' foundation of the Church as a visible and enduring body on earth, continually gathered, strengthened, commissioned, and sustained by his own presence.

The Gospel of Matthew thus concludes with a vision of the future that is shot through with exultation, trust, and transformative energy, all deriving from the Lord's desire and promise never to forsake those he loves, always to abide in their midst and accompany them every step of their journey through earthly space and history. The risen Jesus belongs to this earth and to the Church on earth just as much as he belongs to the Father. As believers in the deeply unitive mysteries of the Incarnation and the Resurrection, we Christians can never indulge in the purely rational dichotomies that seek clarity by keeping apart heaven and earth, God and man. We should not lose from sight the great relevance, to this cosmic marriage between God and his creatures, of Jesus' dictum concerning ordinary nuptial union: "What therefore God has joined together, let not man put asunder" (19:6).

"I am with you always, to the close of the age": This is the RSV translation of Jesus' concluding statement in the Gospel of Matthew. However, the word "always" here is a rendering of πάσας τὰς ἡμέρας—*pásas tas hêméras*, which literally means "all the days", a phrase that conveys a different emphasis. While "always" certainly stresses Jesus' unflagging fidelity, it does so in a general and somewhat abstract way. The original "all the days", on the other hand, forcefully drives home the point that Jesus' presence with us is an enduring reality that renews itself each and every day of our lives, taking on every occasion the unique form of fidelity, consolation, and ready help required by the given circumstances. There is an important difference between a friend saying to you generically "I'll always love you" and that same friend saying "I love you today, and I will love you tomorrow and every single day after that, no matter what." The first expression is formulaic, the second more personal, concrete, and emphatic.

Now the sum total of "all the days" of Jesus' abiding presence with his disciples is contained in the last four words of the Gospel, *hê synteleía tou aiônos*, rendered by RSV as "the close of the age". Significantly, it is a phrase found only in Matthew (four times: 13:40, 49; 24:3; and here 28:20). This is an elegant way for our evangelist to conclude his Gospel, making the ending of the book a reference as well to the ending of time. Retrospectively, this reference transforms our experience of reading the text of the Gospel into a spiritual analogy to the Christian life itself, in which we encounter Jesus, convert our hearts to him as we listen to his teaching, imbibe his example, mystically die with him on Golgotha, rise with him on Easter, and finally spend the rest of our earthly lives sharing his vivifying presence, until our personal physical death or, for the Church, the end of historical time.

What the RSV terms *the close of the age* may be rendered in a variety of ways: "the end of the world" (KJV), "the consummation of the world" (DRA, following the Vulgate's *consummatio sæculi*), "the end of the age" (ESV), and "the end of time" (NJB). The expression always refers to the end of the *æon* or "age" of this world as we know it. It denotes the *synteleía*, or "completion" of the allotted period of this world's history, as decreed by God's will and executed by Christ the King at his Second Coming. At 24:3, for example, the disciples ask Jesus: "What will be the sign of your coming and of *the close of the age*?" And at 13:39, as Jesus interprets the Parable of the Wheat and the Weeds, he says: "The enemy who sowed [the weeds] is the devil; the harvest is *the close of the age*, and the reapers are angels."

A whole Judæo-Christian theology of time underpins this expression, revealing a firm belief that time is a creation of God and that the succeeding ages of creation are directly subject to the sway of God's saving providence. The end of this world—of time and history as man has always known them—shall not be the result of a cosmic accident or a random cataclysm but, rather, one part of God's benevolent and wise dispensation and, as such, an aspect of salvation history. Trust in the providence of God as good Creator and Father and faith in the abiding and sustaining Presence of Jesus with his disciples are the two unshakeable principles of the Christian view of history, both personal and collective. The word *synteleía*, after all, conveys a meaning that is precisely the opposite of an abrupt or accidental ending since it means "completion", "consummation", "perfection". Therefore, the end of the present age of the world shall be ushered in graciously, in strict harmony with the will of God, only when the Father sends his Son, Christ Jesus, the King of the Universe, in his Second Coming as Judge and Savior.

IN MATTHEW, there is no narrative of the Ascension. This absence has a surprisingly positive literary effect in that it lends to this concluding Gospel scene such great breadth, resonance, and open-endedness that it forever enthrones the icon of the Lord surrounded by his chosen apostles as the final happening of Jesus' earthly life. It thus keeps alive in our mind's eye the group's and the Lord's perpetual presence to one another in unclouded and limitless celebration on that mountain-top in Galilee. Whatever else may occur in the life of the Church throughout the coming centuries in a more exterior and empirical sense, *this joyful communion* between Christ and his followers is the underlying condition that permeates the Church's heart unceasingly and configures her interior reality.

The Incarnation of the Word as the true, historical enactment in the flesh of *God's desire to be with mankind* may easily be said to be the theological leitmotif of the Gospel of Matthew, what we could call the "Emmanuel theme". Already at the very beginning of the Gospel, the angel's announcement to the troubled Joseph in his dream ("Mary your wife . . . will bear a son, and you shall call his name Jesus, for he will save his people from their sins") gives Matthew the occasion to highlight the event as a manifestation of God's desire to dwell with his people. The evangelist summons Isaiah (7:14) as his witness: "All this took place to fulfil what the Lord had spoken by the prophet: 'Behold, a virgin shall conceive and bear a son, and his name shall be called *Emmanuel*' (which means, *God with us*)" (1:20–23).

After this emblematic declaration, writ large in incandescent letters

(EMMANUEL) over the threshold of the Gospel, the rest of Matthew's text is devoted to detailing *how* it is that Jesus, God-with-us, saves his people from their sins. The whole of Jesus' visible work as Savior is consistently shown to be the many-splendored fruit of *the one, central, ontological act of the incarnate Word already indwelling humanity*, living fully with and among men as a man. The inexhaustible specific means whereby Jesus communicates salvation are beyond counting because they are coextensive with every aspect and detail of his existence on earth: hours spent in silent prayer, personal encounters and conversations, miracles of healing and feeding, endless teaching tours, selection and training of disciples, debates with the Pharisees, shared meals and other social situations, denunciations of hypocrisy and sin, all the way to the events of the Passion and the Resurrection. GOD-BEING-WITH-MAN-IN-JESUS, in the strongest personal sense of the term *being*, is the nourishing ground out of which grows every particular operation of divine grace in the Christian dispensation. All the incalculably rich modalities through which the divine Life is communicated to man and to the cosmos spring out of this generative presence of EMMANUEL among us.

Matthew says that Jesus' conception by Mary and all the events surrounding it "took place to fulfil what the Lord had spoken by the prophet" (1:22). The quoted words from Isaiah are then inscribed in the Gospel text (1:23). Both this ancient quotation and Jesus' newly minted words of promise here at the other end of the Gospel (28:20) begin with the solemn term "Behold!", calling the listeners' attention to a transcendental proclamation that should never be forgotten because it communicates the unsurpassable thought of God's Heart. The prophecy itself then follows, full of future tenses, something natural for the prophetic mode: "A virgin *shall conceive* and *shall bear* a son, and his name *shall be called* Emmanuel." The Greek translation of "Emmanuel", Isaiah's name for the Messiah, is given by Matthew without a verb, in the Hebrew mode: μεθ' ἡμῶν ὁ Θεός—*meth' hêmôn ho Theós*, that is, in strict literal order, *With-us-God*, which can therefore be interpreted as an absolute affirmation of presence implying all tenses at once—'With us God *is*, *was* and *shall be*.'

"Behold, I am with you [all days] to the close of the age", declares Jesus to his disciples as a perpetual inheritance. When we read these last thirteen words of Jesus that close the Gospel of Matthew (28:20b), in juxtaposition with the prophecy of Isaiah in 1:23, something magnificent occurs before our very eyes. Now we are no longer listening to the voice of Isaiah, surely the greatest of Old Testament prophets, or even to the voice of Matthew the Evangelist interpreting Isaiah for us and shining the great prophet's light on the person of Jesus. Rather, Matthew chooses to close his Gospel neither with his own words, which merely point us *toward* Jesus, nor with the words of the prophet who delivered the chief messianic prophecy. No: Matthew concludes his Gospel by creating a great silence that allows the Messiah himself to speak to his beloved friends without intermediary, in the first person singular: "*Behold, I am with you [all days]!*" The same urgent *Behold!* Isaiah used now awakens us to the realization of a fulfillment that has no limits and that no longer has to be awaited because it is uttered by him who is himself the very Beginning, the Word made flesh and risen from the dead. In the person of Jesus, all of God and all of creation are recapitulated and enter into intimate relationship.

When the Master speaks to us in this way, declaring himself present to us beyond all possibility of future separation, we know that our search has been completed, that all our desires have been fulfilled, and that all fear has been banished. The *immovable* Source of Being has nonetheless *moved*, coming to embrace and overshadow us with his undying love and thus continue his work of creating and re-creating us endlessly. What else could I possibly seek after this? Indeed, how could I ever force myself to *turn away from* this most enthralling and nourishing Presence? Even the most wayward and stubborn eaglet knows when its mother has gathered it back safely into its nest of origin, there to be nourished and slowly trained in its new flying life.

The Lord Jesus affirms his presence to his apostles with the verb *I am!* in the present tense, followed by the phrase *with you all days*. This combination of the first-person singular present *I am!* with an unbounded length of days establishes once and for all the indefectible presence of Jesus at our side in the midst of history, and it does so in an extraordinarily reassuring and imperious way. For who would dare question the veracity of such a speaker? Who would dare call Jesus a liar or even a sly hoaxer, after all we have seen him do and suffer for our sake? Here we are no longer dealing with a prophecy or even with a promise. What we are receiving—directly from the Heart and mouth of the incarnate Word while his gaze bores its way into our soul—is a divinely guaranteed affirmation of a reliable fact that is *already* being lived here and now as a palpable reality, through a concrete experience that will never stop being such! Suddenly Jesus' true presence in the midst of the apostles, which implies the availability to them of everything that Jesus is and can provide, becomes a historical fact of experience as unshakable as the everlasting mountains and as blissfully overwhelming as ocean tides of joy.

The One now speaking is the very One Isaiah foretold, the Son whom the Virgin conceived and bore to the world, God incarnate. His presence is a promise realized and personified. We are no longer listening to others speak *about* him: he, Isaiah's Emmanuel, is himself addressing us *directly*, without intervening prophets, messengers, or witnesses. When he says *I am with you!* he means an ever-ongoing AM that is never left behind, and the YOU is each one of us. Therefore, in order to capture this glowingly new mode of presence of God with us, Jesus gives himself a correspondingly new and infinitely unsurpassable name. He no longer says, with Isaiah and Matthew, GOD IS WITH US, which would be pointing to a higher being beyond himself. Instead, he says I AM WITH YOU!, which is a revelation of such extravagant plenitude of Presence, such overabundant fullness of Being, that we are inundated by the gift of undying peace and joy that always flows from the union of lovers.

As long as we are willing to reciprocate presence for Presence, love for Love, we never need feel abandoned again, in life or in death. And our guarantee of the veracity of Jesus' declaration I AM WITH YOU ALL DAYS! is the fact that these are words that only a trustworthy, incarnate God can speak without folly or deceit. Clearly they are being addressed not only to the eleven disciples physically present on that mountain but to all people of all times and places with whom Jesus wants to share his life.[12]

But there is much more here because this all-determining and unconditional declaration on Jesus'part extravagantly outstrips the prom-

---

[12] A simple yet striking testimony to the power of Jesus' abiding presence with his disciples through the ages is Asia Bibi, a Pakistani Catholic who was sentenced to death in 2010 for alleged blasphemy against Islam. After more than eight years in prison, she was acquitted by the Supreme Court of Pakistan in 2018. After her release, she said in a Paris press conference in February, 2020: "I was accused because of the name of Jesus, and I knew I would be freed because of Jesus." And she added that, during her time on death row, her faith "was always strong because I knew that God was with me. God never leaves you alone; he always accompanies you. If you trust in God, your faith becomes stronger." *Catholic Herald* (catholicherald.co.uk), March 4, 2020.

ise of Isaiah concerning the historical conception of the Messiah from the Virgin. Because this Savior-Messiah whom God has sent is not only the greatest of all men but actually *the incarnate Word of God,* Jesus' assurance I AM WITH YOU ALL DAYS! in fact takes us back to Moses' experience of the Burning Bush, which may be said to be the beginning of Judæo-Christian salvation history, properly speaking. There, in the Egyptian desert, the Lord said to Moses: "I have seen the affliction of my people who are in Egypt, and have heard their cry because of their taskmasters; I know their sufferings, and I have come down to deliver them out of the hand of the Egyptians, and to bring them up out of that land to a good and broad land, a land flowing with milk and honey" (Ex 3:7–8). The stalwart compassion of the God of Israel, his constant vigilance over the fate of his people, and his determination to save them from affliction all provide the basis for the mystery of the Son's Incarnation, to be revealed in the fullness of time. God coming to the aid of his people personally, in his Son Jesus, is prefigured in this passage from Exodus in God's words "I have come down to deliver them." Historically, for that moment in Exodus, God comes down to earth and makes his mercy and love audible in the form of a physically burning bush and in his election of Moses as mediator between himself and Israel; but such an imperfect and mediated presence is but preparing the way for the Lord's ultimate coming as Himself, beyond all symbols, prophecies, or intermediaries. Christ is the supreme *Pontifex,* the true and efficient Bridger of ontological distances.

Moreover, the situation of oppression and affliction out of which the God of Israel intends to deliver his beloved people is geographically, historically, and ethnically circumscribed, and necessarily so. As such, this situation of the Jews in Egypt serves likewise as a prefigurement of the need for deliverance of the whole human race from the tyranny, no longer now of an earthly political ruler, but of Satan and of sin, which is the scourge this age-old adversary inflicts universally. No wonder the Fathers of the Church saw "in the Bush seen by Moses, as burning yet unconsumed" a figure of the Blessed Virgin Mary, who conceived and bore the divine Word while remaining a virgin—that is, without the benefit of a man's seed. [13] In the

---

[13] This ancient interpretation has been preserved for all time in an antiphon now used in the Roman Rite for Vespers on January 1, Solemnity of the Mother of God, and in many Cistercian monasteries at the end of daily Terce: "Rubum quem viderat Moyses

Incarnation, the fire of Divinity permeates the substance of Mary's and our humanity and, rather than destroying it, raises it to a new and unheard-of potency. The Son that Mary bore to the world is thus the Fire of Mercy that comes to transform, purify, and perfect human nature by uniting it with himself: "I came to cast fire upon the earth; and would that it were already kindled!" (Lk 12:49). "For our God is a consuming fire" (Heb 12:29 = Deut 4:24).[14]

The voice of God that spoke to Moses from the fire burning in the bush now speaks to the Eleven through the lungs, vocal cords, and mouth of Jesus of Nazareth risen from the dead. In a strict parallelism of scenes, the apostles succeed to Moses as hearers of the divine voice, and Jesus assumes his rightful position as enfleshed God. When Moses says to the invisible God, "Who am I that I should go to Pharaoh, and bring the sons of Israel out of Egypt?", God replies without hesitation: "I WILL BE WITH YOU!" (Ex 3:11–12), exactly as Jesus reassures the Eleven after he has entrusted his universal mission to them. The decisive difference from that communication to Moses, however, is that now the Word has become incarnate, speaks in a present tense of unsurpassable immediacy, and is not only audible but also fully visible and tangible to those he addresses. The Eleven intuited all this in a flash when, on first seeing Jesus, they fell down before him and "worshiped him" as true, present God (28:17), even though at the same time they recognized in Jesus one of their own human race: "For he who sanctifies and those who are sanctified have all one origin. That is why he is not ashamed to call them brethren" (Heb 2:11). God is present to them not only as Lord and Master but also as Brother and Friend.

Finally, when Moses asks God for his personal name so that he can identify for the Israelites the One entrusting him with the task of their liberation, God replies: "I AM WHO I AM. . . . Say this to the sons of Israel, 'I AM has sent me to you'" (Ex 3:14). We should be utterly astounded, and at the same time ecstatically overjoyed, as we witness the Lord Jesus here assuming in our presence his rightful

---

incombustum, conservatam agnovimus tuam laudabilem virginitatem: Dei Genetrix, intercede pro nobis." (In the bush seen by Moses, as burning yet unconsumed, we recognize the preservation of your glorious virginity. Mother of God, intercede for us.) Equivalent texts exist in the Oriental Rites.

[14] Cf. 3:11–12; 7:19; Mk 9:49; Jn 21:9; Acts 2:3; 7:30; 1 Cor 3:15; 2 Thess 1:7; Heb 1:7; Rev 1:14; 2:18; 19:12.

position as Lord of Glory in human form and abolishing by the power of his presence, actions, and words the gap of terror and alienation separating God from Man. *I AM* with you all days, he says.

Precisely as was the case with the Lord at the Burning Bush in Exodus, Jesus' *I AM* to his apostles has nothing abstract or other-worldly about it. In both instances, the context and the language make it clear that the divine *I AM*, far from being a philosophical revelation of essence, is inseparable from the prepositions *with* or *for*, indicating a necessary relationship of intense care and interest between God and his creatures. Jesus never merely "is", in a standoffish and static mode of existence. Rather Jesus always *is-with* and *is-for*.

We could in fact paraphrase the declaration *I AM WITH YOU!*, both by the Lord of Israel in Exodus and here by Jesus in Matthew as, "Everything that I am is for you" or "My place is always at your side." What could be a more irresistible declaration of unconditional love? All the reciprocal intimacy and boundless, heart-ravishing trust that this confidence—*I EXIST FOR YOU!*—established between God and Moses, Jesus now bestows on the group of the Eleven, that is to say, on the Church and, implicitly, on all mankind. Tirelessly he says to us: "Behold, I stand at the door and knock; if any one hears my voice and opens the door, I will come in to him and eat with him, and he with me" (Rev 3:20). And daily he awaits our response.

APPENDICES

LECTIO TIPS

1. *Inhabit the text*: Stick to the text itself always, because the text has been shaped by the Holy Spirit, working through human agents, to awaken our hearts and intelligence and communicate truths that we would probably want to evade unless grace prompted us. This means the text will at times necessarily present us with a struggle, at the levels of the intelligence, the heart, and the will, whenever our existing prejudices or ignorant blind spots are challenged.

2. Derive insight from *particular words and phrases*, and not from general impressions, which are bound to be distorted by our own sensibility. We want the life the text itself has to offer, and not just a re-hashing of our own old and outworn ideas and feelings. Allow the text to educate and shape your mentality, feelings, and points of view.

3. Especially in the Gospel narrative, *pay attention to context—what has gone before and what follows*. For example, in the episode of Peter's denial (26:57–75), note the importance of Christ's prophecy in Gethsemane, of Peter following Jesus in hiding, of the trial in Caiaphas' house occurring at the same time as Peter's encounters out in the courtyard. Why does Matthew interrupt the trial at some length in order to focus on Peter? Clearly, he wants each of us to find our place in the Passion narrative through the person of Peter, along with the many aspects his presence opens up. Matthew also wants the figure of the suffering and humiliated Jesus to "hover" behind other happenings as the background or horizon of everyone's personal story.

4. We believe Jesus Christ is the Son of God, *the eternal Word Incarnate*. How does the text of the Gospel manifest this truth in very concrete terms? How does the Gospel text attempt to express the humanly inexpressible, that is, the presence and activity of a Divine Person on earth? The Gospel text is a paradox of human language and divine revelation working together. We sense there is always a

further meaning that escapes us, so that we must become accustomed to living with the Mystery.

5. Note the *rhythm of Matthew's narrative*, how it moves out slowly to involve each and every person or category of person who was in Jerusalem during Jesus' Passion: the Jewish authorities, the Roman authorities, the soldiers, the disciples, the women, and individuals within these groups: each has a different motivation and point of view in reacting to Jesus as he does. What effect does this variety of involvement have on the reader?

6. Note Matthew's use of *symbolism*. The evangelist never speculates about what is occurring within a character's soul, but he uses speeches, actions, reactions, and animals or objects (solitude of Gethsemane, rooster, crown of thorns, cross . . .) to communicate the interior meaning of things. We can say that "two conflicting emotions of love and fear are battling in Peter's heart." But Matthew never states it explicitly! How do we know? Could it be that an essential part of the evangelist's intention is to involve us, the believing readers and would-be disciples, in the work of digging for meaning, because such work changes us in the process?

7. Matthew uses many *repetitions*, such as Peter's threefold denial. But repetition always has a function, which is to deepen the reader's exploration into the meaning of the narrative. Note how each apparent repetition really adds further evidence and nuances to what is being repeated, which thus comes to form the center of my awareness during *lectio*.

8. Allow yourself some *scriptural "free association"*, that is, allow other passages of Scripture to comment on the one you are reading at present. St. Paul very often provides key *theological* formulas that can unlock the deeper meaning of many *narrative* passages in the Gospel.

9. Do not forget that the whole of the New Testament at bottom has only one purpose: to foster an encounter with *the living person of Jesus Christ*. The writers of the New Testament offer Jesus to the contemplation of faith, so that believers will open up their inmost being to the transformative process Christ undertakes within them

by works of love and mercy. During *lectio*, our attention should never wander far from the person of Jesus.

10. All of Scripture is essentially an *ecclesial text*, given to us by the Church and having its full meaning only within the context of the community of the Church as Body of Christ. Scripture is not a vehicle for individual revelation and connection with God. It embodies the experience of God of the People of God, in both Testaments. Therefore the Scripture must be read with the mind of the Church.

11. No one translation can convey all the nuances of the *original Greek or Hebrew*. Especially with passages that interest you most, you should compare translations, perhaps even acquire an interlinear translation of the New Testament that provides the Greek original, a literal translation, and perhaps one or two other translations. In this connection, I recommend Alfred Marshall's *Interlinear NRSV-NIV Parallel New Testament in Greek and English*.

ON TRANSLITERATING GREEK

Greek vowels generally have the same sound as in Latin, Spanish, and Italian, and we here give the simplest approximation to the sound of the consonants:

Capital	Minuscule	Name	Roman Equivalent and Sound
A	α	alpha	a (as in *father*)
B	β	beta	b
Γ	γ	gamma	g; γγ is *ng*, γχ is *ngch*
Δ	δ	delta	d (like *th* in *though*)
E	ε	epsilon	e (short, as in *pet*)
Z	ζ	zeta	z
H	η	eta	ê, (long and sharp, like French *é*)
Θ	θ	theta	th (as in *thought*)
I	ι	iota	i (like vowel sound in *meet*)
K	κ	kappa	k
Λ	λ	lambda	l
M	μ	my	m
N	ν	ny	n
Ξ	ξ	xi	x (ks)
O	ο	omicron	o (short, without the trailing 'oo')
Π	π	pi	p
R	ρ	rho	r, rh
Σ	σ, ς	sigma	s (written ς in final position)
T	τ	tau	t
Υ	υ	ypsilon	y when single (pronounced like French u or German ü); u when in a diphthong (au, eu, ou, ui)
Φ	φ	phi	ph
X	χ	chi	ch (guttural, as in German)
Ψ	ψ	psi	ps
Ω	ω	omega	ô (long and deep, as in *ohm*)

The "rough breathing" (‘) over the initial vowel of a word (or the second vowel, in the case of a diphthong) indicates the sound of an English *h*: ὅτι = hoti, υἱός = huios. The "smooth breathing" (’) indicates the absence of an audible breathing: εὐαγγέλιον = euangelion.

The three accent marks (acute, ά, grave, ὰ, and circumflex, ᾶ) indicate where the chief stress of the word should fall. It would be too intricate to explain here the rules governing the use of these accents.

The iota subscript under certain vowels (ᾳ, ῳ) is not pronounced or transliterated in biblical Greek.

Greek uses the semicolon (;) as a question mark, and it uses a raised period (·) for a colon.

THE INVENI

I HAVE FOUND HIM WHOM MY SOUL LOVES: I grasp him and will not let him go. I embrace you, my Jesus, and experience the joy of my love. I encompass you, the treasure of my heart, from whom I have all that is mine. May my mind feel, I beg you, the power of your presence. May it taste how sweet you are, O Lord, so that, captivated by your love, it may seek nothing outside of you and love nothing if not because of you.

You are my *King*: do not forget my indigence and tribulation. You are my *Judge*: forgive my sins and have mercy on me. You are my *Physician*: heal all my infirmities. You are the *Bridegroom* of my soul: wed yourself to me for all eternity. You are my *Guide* and my *Defender*: keep me at your side and then any hand can fight against me. You became a *Victim* for my sake, and I will sacrifice to you an oblation of praise. You are my *Redeemer*: redeem my soul from the power of hell and save me. You are my *God* and my *All*.

What is there for me to seek in the heavens, and, apart from you, what do I desire on earth? The God of my heart and my lot are you, O God, for all eternity!

INVENI quem diligit anima mea, tenui eum, nec dimittam. Te mi Jesu, amplector, et amoris mei gaudium obtineo. Te cordis mei thesaurum comprehendo, a quo omnia possideo. Sentiat, obsecro, mens mea virtutem præsentiæ tuæ: gustet quam suavis sis, Domine, ut, amore tui capta, nil extra te quærat, nil diligat, nisi propter te.

Tu es REX meus, ne obliviscaris inopiæ et tribulationis meæ. Tu es JUDEX meus, parce peccatis meis et miserere mei. Tu es MEDICUS meus, sana omnes infirmitates meas. Tu es SPONSUS animæ meæ, sponsa te mihi in sempiternum. Tu es DUX ET DEFENSOR meus, pone me juxta te, et cujusvis manus pugnet contra me. Tu VICTIMA pro me factus es, et ego tibi sacrificabo hostiam laudis. Tu REDEMPTOR meus es, redime animam meam de manu inferi et salva me. Tu es DEUS MEUS ET OMNIA.

Quid enim mihi est in cœlo, et a te quid volui super terram? Deus cordis mei et pars mea, Deus, in æternum!